DRAWN SWORDS IN A DISTANT LAND

GEORGE J. VEITH

DRAWN SWORDS IN A DISTANT LAND

SOUTH VIETNAM'S SHATTERED DREAMS

Encounter
BOOKS
NEW YORK · LONDON

First American edition published in 2021 by Encounter Books,
an activity of Encounter for Culture and Education, Inc.,
a nonprofit, tax-exempt corporation.
Encounter Books website address: www.encounterbooks.com

Manufactured in the United States and printed on
acid-free paper. The paper used in this publication meets
the minimum requirements of ANSI/NISO Z39.48–1992
(R 1997) (*Permanence of Paper*).

FIRST AMERICAN EDITION

LIBRARY OF CONGRESS CATALOGING-IN-PUBLICATION DATA

Names: Veith, George J., 1957– author.
Title: Drawn swords in a distant land : South Vietnam's Shattered Dreams
by George J. Veith.
Description: First American edition. | New York : Encounter Books, 2021.
Includes bibliographical references and index. |
Identifiers: LCCN 2020039074 (print) | LCCN 2020039075 (ebook)
ISBN 9781641771726 (hardcover) | ISBN 9781641771733 (ebook)
Subjects: LCSH: Vietnam (Republic)—History. | Nguyên, Văn Thiêu,
1923-2001. | Vietnam War, 1961-1975.
Vietnam (Republic)—Politics and government.
Classification: LCC DS556.9 .V45 2021 (print)
LCC DS556.9 (ebook) DDC 959.7/7043—dc23
LC record available at https://lccn.loc.gov/2020039074
LC ebook record available at https://lccn.loc.gov/2020039075
LC record available at https://lccn.loc.gov/2020008204
LC ebook record available at https://lccn.loc.gov/2020008205

Interior page design and typesetting by Bruce Leckie

For my children:
Analiese, Austin, Allegra, and Adia,
the lights of my life

CONTENTS

ACKNOWLEDGMENTS

The African proverb "It takes a village to raise a child" applies metaphorically to writing a book, particularly one that seeks to portray a subject as vast and as historically remarkable as the rise and fall of a country. I was incredibly fortunate to receive the generosity of two groups of people: those who helped shape this volume, and those who contributed to it by graciously answering my questions, no matter how painful the memories.

The *primus inter pares* (first among equals) of those who assisted is Merle Pribbenow. Just as he diligently molded the manuscript that became *Black April*, he also profoundly influenced this one. Every Vietnam scholar knows him as a superb translator. I am fortunate that he also applied his other skills: correcting errors, pointing out new data, and providing rational alternatives for the actions of governments and individuals alike. No amount of gratitude can repay his generosity.

Two others provided great assistance. Dr. Chris Goscha's insightful commentary and relentless demands for clarity and deeper analysis brought light out of a dark bog of confusing details. I am deeply thankful for both his friendship and his teaching spirit. Dr. David Prentice also read numerous chapters and was instrumental in keeping me focused on the main themes. I am richer for their help. Lastly, my family and friends, particularly Sally Omani, sustained me on the long journey I took to complete this book. Their love and encouragement lightened my burden immensely.

Naturally, the many South Vietnamese who agreed to speak to me form the heart of this book. Many unfortunately passed on before its publication. My failure to complete this manuscript before they died is a wound I feel grievously. In no particular order they are Hoang Duc Nha, Nguyen Xuan Phong, Bui Diem, Pham Kim Ngoc, Cao Van Than, Nguyen Duc Cuong, Lan Cao, Mrs. Nguyen Van Thieu, Tran Quang Minh, Le Van Minh, Le Van Phuc, Doan Huu Dinh, Nguyen Xuan Tam, Mai Van Triet, and many others. Thank you all for your kind spirit. It is my fervent wish that I have told your unsung story well. You deserve nothing less.

George J. Veith

June 25, 2020

ABBREVIATIONS

AFC — Armed Forces Council
ADB — Agricultural Development Bank
ARVN — Army of the Republic of Vietnam
CIA — Central Intelligence Agency
CIDG — Civilian Irregular Defense Group
CIO — Central Intelligence Organization
CIP — Commodity Import Program
CORDS — Civil Operations and Revolutionary Development Support
COSVN — Central Office for South Vietnam
CVT — Vietnamese Labor Union
DMZ — Demilitarized Zone
DP — Democracy Party
DRV — Democratic Republic of Vietnam
FULRO — Montagnard Rebel Faction
GSF — Greater Solidarity Force
GVN — Government of (South) Vietnam
HES — Hamlet Evaluation System
HNC — High National Council
JGS — Joint General Staff
LTTT — Land to the Tiller Law
MACV — Military Assistance Command, Vietnam
MRC — Military Revolutionary Council
NLF — National Liberation Front
NCNRC — National Council of National Reconciliation and Concord
NSC — National Security Council
NSDF — National Social Democratic Front
PAVN — People's Army of Vietnam
PNM — Progressive National Movement
PRG — Provisional Revolutionary Government

PACM — People's Anti-Corruption Movement
PSDF — People's Self-Defense Force
RD — Rural Development
RDV — Revolutionary Dai Viets
RF/PF — Regional Forces/Popular Forces
RVNAF — Republic of Vietnam Armed Forces
SDA — Social Democratic Alliance
TDV — Tan Dai Viets
UBC — United Buddhist Church
USAID — United States Agency for International Development
VAT — Value Added Tax
VNA — Vietnamese National Army
VNAF — Vietnamese Air Force
VNN — Vietnamese Navy
VNQDD — Vietnam Quoc Dan Dang

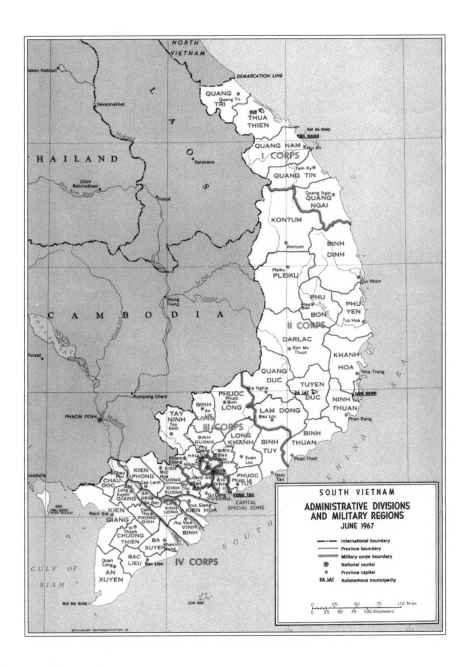

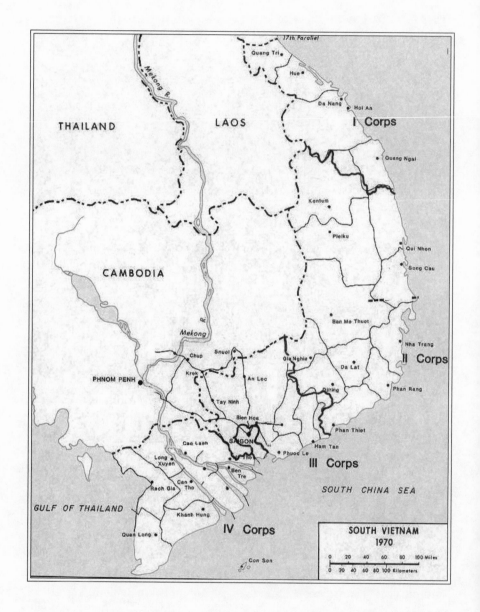

INTRODUCTION

Early on the morning of November 2, 1963, a frantic Colonel Nguyen Van Thieu jumped out of his jeep and rushed over to an armored personnel carrier parked outside the South Vietnamese military headquarters on Tan Son Nhut Air Base. For the last eighteen hours, he had led the military forces within Saigon that had overthrown the government of President Ngo Dinh Diem. Inside the vehicle were the mangled corpses of Diem and the president's brother, Ngo Dinh Nhu. Thieu had only joined the coup after being assured that Diem and his family would not be harmed. Now he needed to confirm the shocking news, to verify for himself that the promises that had been made to him and his fellow plotters had indeed been broken.

Colonel Thieu ordered the driver to open the back door. Years later, he recalled that seeing the bodies of the two brothers lying in pools of blood made him sick to his stomach.[1] He saluted them, then took off his helmet and bowed deeply in their direction. This terrible moment, while only a tiny drop in the vast river of modern Vietnamese history, marked the symbolic passing from Diem's First Republic to the Second Republic and President Thieu four years later. In that anguished instant, South Vietnam's political history was forever changed.

The saga of how the non-communist Vietnamese strove to build the sovereign nation called the Republic of Vietnam, more commonly known as South Vietnam, can be viewed as a four-act play: Bao Dai's State of Vietnam, Diem's First Republic, the subsequent four-year interregnum, and, finally, Thieu's Second Republic. Historian Brett Reilly has reviewed former emperor Bao Dai's often stilted endeavor to create a non-communist state.[2] Other historians such as Mark Moyar, Edward Miller, Geoffrey Shaw, and Jessica Chapman have explored Diem's reign in detail.[3] What remains mostly unexamined is the four-year interregnum that came after Diem's murder, the subsequent election of Nguyen Van Thieu, and the short life of the Second Republic.

My goal is to evaluate and append a deep appraisal of the last two periods to the already existing scholarship. Larger patterns, changes, and continuities emerge when avoiding the corseted narration of narrower histories. This book examines the South Vietnamese' tortured but failed effort to achieve an independent state. It focuses on the struggle to secure the countryside, the twists and plots of the political process, the attempt to forge national unity, and the evolution of South Vietnam's complex social, ethnic, and religious relationships. The economy is afforded equal treatment since it had far greater influence than is generally realized. Scholars have similarly overlooked Thieu's emphasis after 1969 to offer peace and win an electoral contest against the Communists.

By necessity, I concentrate on affairs in Saigon rather than in the provinces. Military aspects and political decisions made in Hanoi and Washington are only included where necessary to highlight salient points or to showcase how their assessments affected the evolution of the republic. Many of Hanoi's and Washington's moves were in reaction to events in Saigon, a causality that has surprisingly been forgotten. South Vietnam was always at the heart of the war, and this book explains why.

Although my purpose is to survey the South Vietnamese experience, I do not delve into questions like anti-colonialism, ecology, or the country's place in the Cold War geopolitical conflict. Other historians have reviewed or are in the process of examining these important subjects.[4] I have also set aside the question of whether or not the U.S. government should have joined battle in that distant land. Lastly, since there are no universally accepted labels for the two contending parties, and given that the South Vietnamese call themselves Nationalists (*nguoi quoc gia*), I will use that description for the anti-communists, and I will use Communist (*nguoi cong san*) to describe those following Ho Chi Minh.

While the confrontation between these foes was multilayered, chiefly it was a clash between two virulently opposed visions of how to modernize and build Vietnam. There was also a rancorous debate on this same topic within the Nationalist camp, which will prove to be a principal element in this story. The Nationalist quarrel was between those who wanted to rule via a centralized model of governance against those who sought a Vietnamese form of democracy that enabled more local control. The issue for the Nationalists was how to discard old ways and failed institutions and replace them with new ideas and modern establishments to develop an inclusive republican identity for an ethnically and religiously diverse country.[5] The war between the Communists and the Nationalists, and between the Nationalists themselves, was about how to achieve that political vision.

During the war, and for years afterward, South Vietnam was judged as a stereotypical kleptocracy. The narrative was simple: Hanoi was the anointed vessel of Vietnamese nationalism, and Saigon was destined to collapse. Given the dramatic fall of the country in April 1975, those judgments seemed proven and therefore unnecessary to revisit. The South Vietnamese, however, have their own narrative, one largely ignored outside the country. As one Vietnamese friend told me, "We had many dreams: the dream of freedom, the dream of independence, and the dream of lifting our people out of poverty. The Communists only had one dream: win the war no matter the cost."

The main argument presented here is that South Vietnam was not an artificial American creation, nor was the Second Republic a dictatorship like Diem's First Republic. As we shall see, Thieu and his government made significant efforts to build a modern democratic state that alleviated the endemic poverty of its people, a process for which they have never received credit. To accomplish this monumental task, they had to overcome the debilitating legacy of French colonial rule alongside the typical problems inherent in nation building: lack of national solidarity, military-civilian clashes, undeveloped political institutions, and so much more. Worse, they had to surmount these deficiencies with an implacable enemy at their throats. Since contested legitimacy is the rule, not the exception, in emerging states, the Nationalists faced an existential question: how can an emerging democracy and an open society defeat a totalitarian enemy, one skilled at infiltration, psychological and political manipulation, and intelligence penetration? Equally important, could South Vietnam survive the Communist threat on its own?

The answers require a deeper understanding of the Nationalists' attempt to create a viable state. As the eminent military historian Michael Howard contends, "to abstract the conduct of war from the environment in which it was fought—social, cultural, political, economic—was to ignore dimensions essential to its understanding."[6] This book covers those dimensions. That the South Vietnamese were defeated does not mean they failed to achieve political legitimacy. My contention is that they did, but South Vietnam suffered similar growing pains as other new countries, particularly those enduring long years of a deadly war. Ultimately, South Vietnam could not build and fight at the same time.

It is well to remember that democracy is always a work in progress, especially for a new country trying to find its footing during a difficult war. America has also legislated discrepancies between its stated values and reality during its own times of crisis. The Alien and Sedition Act of 1798 permitted the deportation, fine, or imprisonment of anyone deemed a threat or publishing "false, scandalous, or malicious writing" against the United States. During the Civil War, President Abraham Lincoln suspended much of the Bill of Rights, including free speech and habeas corpus. Moreover, post-9/11, full-fledged democracies have passed laws that concern many civil libertarians.

Since even mature countries have had to recalibrate in difficult times, South Vietnam was no exception. When the French refused to introduce democratic institutions into colonial Indochina, concepts like "free speech" and "loyal opposition" had only a small foothold in South Vietnam, a place whose historical experiences were so different from ours. Like other neophyte states emerging from colonial rule, republican Vietnamese first had to craft a constitution to express their political intent. The constitution defined the state apparatus—the legislature, the courts, and the national security system—and they had to create one amid violently competing social and religious interests.

Which brings us to the enigmatic man who will dominate these pages, former South Vietnamese president Nguyen Van Thieu. Since his career precisely matches his country's life span, he provides the perfect vehicle to examine the rise and fall of South Vietnam. This is not a biography of Thieu but an acknowledgement that he played the central role in the Second Republic. Yet despite this, Thieu is perhaps the least analyzed major American ally of the twentieth century. In most U.S. publications, he appears as a bit player within the larger American construct of the war or more commonly as a military dictator whose policies and repression of the South Vietnamese people led directly to the country's defeat. Further, this limited analysis of his tenure is often restricted to events such as the negotiations that led to the Paris Peace Accords. For the man who sat at the center of the Vietnam maelstrom from the inception of the U.S. combat role to his country's denouement, this neglect of his presidency has left a gaping hole in the war's historiography.

As we shall see, Thieu was the vital player in transitioning South Vietnam from a military regime into a constitutional republic. But how did Thieu react to internal groups, and how did he handle their challenges? How did he differ from President Diem? What was his governing style, how did he manage foreign policy issues, and what was his domestic agenda? Could he create and then manage a military and economic strategy to defeat a ruthless foe? For the most part, these questions were unanswered until now.

Why have historians not scrutinized Thieu's policies or appraised his reactions to internal and external events? The answer lies in the judgments made during the war. For over a decade, Vietnam was often the center of the global Cold War conflict. Western commentators usually painted Thieu in the same ideological hues that reflected their political outlook, and their heated rhetoric about him mirrored the absolutes of the era. Antiwar pundits typecast him as a corrupt, repressive dictator. The Communist Vietnamese simultaneously vilified him as a traitor and an American puppet. Internationally, his reputation was equally poor.

The South Vietnamese public, however, held more nuanced views. Like other presidents, Thieu's approval ratings rose and fell on the usual topics: security, economic prosperity, or the latest political scandal. Such verdicts often coalesced along traditional South Vietnamese fault lines: urban dwellers versus peasants, religious denomination, or regional bias. He had a base of supporters, a segment of fence-sitters, and a portion that viewed him with disdain. The percentage of each altered over time, dependent on the war's fortunes or the price of rice.

Even with the fall of Saigon, it is still necessary to provide a historical review of President Thieu. He was not the villainous and corrupt dictator portrayed by the antiwar left, nor an American "puppet." While he had the typical political-military ethos extant among senior anti-communist leaders in other Asian countries like Taiwan and South Korea, who viewed strong leadership as the best counterweight to Communism, Thieu was also determined to create a democratic, ownership-based society. These two conflicting attitudes relentlessly tugged at him, never to be reconciled. In particular, his democratic values were seemingly eviscerated when he was the only name on the ballot for the 1971 presidential election.

Basically, Thieu sought two overarching aims. First, he was absolutely determined to triumph over his adversaries. His view that any negotiated settlement with the Communists was a slippery path to defeat was based on firsthand experience, not any rigid and unrealistic ideology. Second, he wanted to build his country into a modern state, alleviate the abject poverty of his fellow citizens, and eventually lead them into something resembling democracy. Crafting a functioning state that raised the material standard of living while embedding into the nation's DNA the essence of democracy— not just the form—were his critical goals.

To achieve that, his policies were both evolutionary and revolutionary. He maintained long-standing Government of Vietnam (GVN) policies in certain areas such as peace negotiations. Conversely, he radically departed from the policies of his predecessors, particularly in land reform and restructuring the economy. Furthermore, he endeavored to remake South Vietnam in the American mode by strengthening local autonomy and revamping the stodgy bureaucracy. Equally important, he worked diligently to improve village security by arming the people to guard their dwellings, a radical risk in a country where peasant loyalty to the government was often in doubt. In sum, Thieu wanted to create prosperity among the rural peasants by providing the South Vietnamese people a capitalistic environment that gave them a stake in their own development via self-rule.

This is not to imply that Thieu was a liberal reformer. Some of his governing cues were taken from other autocratic, anti-communist Asian regimes. He had much in common with Chiang Kai-shek in Taiwan and Park Chung-hee in South Korea. Like them, he pursued his domestic goals while keeping a lid on political opposition, believing it only played into Communist hands. Although he accommodated other non-communist voices, and he recognized that the clamorous give and take of a democratic society was essential to its existence, he saw overt dissent as a cancer weakening the anti-communist body in its struggle against an unrelenting adversary. For him, national unity projected national strength, the key ingredient to convince Hanoi it could not win. Once Hanoi had accepted that, then true peace negotiations could begin. Conversely, public dissent equaled weakness, which only encouraged Hanoi to keep fighting.

Like other politicians, Thieu had personality foibles and managerial quirks that influenced his policies. Yet so many of Thieu's actions that appalled Western critics had an entirely different meaning in the Vietnamese context. For Thieu, the reaction of his domestic audience far outweighed those of his international detractors. Additionally, he approached his responsibilities with grim sobriety, infuriating those who sought political compromise with his equally resolute foe. Yet despite his flaws as a leader, many American officials believed no other Vietnamese statesman possessed the same combination of maturity, toughness, and intellect. He was, in their opinion, the best leader in South Vietnam.

Anyone who reaches the political pinnacle of their society is a fascinating amalgam of ambition, intelligence, and unrelenting drive.[7] Undertaking an analysis of a leader's policies alongside a forensic examination of their personality requires access to internal government documents and the willingness of confidantes to divulge details about private deliberations and their leader's motivations. In the case of Thieu, official U.S. military adviser records from the early years of U.S. involvement were destroyed, leaving a blank slate for his earliest interactions with Americans.[8] French reports on him are also extremely limited.[9] GVN documents are now held by the Communist regime, and access, while more open than in the past, remains more restricted than U.S. archival holdings. Scholars who have examined the archives report finding little on Thieu's thinking on various policies and programs.[10]

Despite these drawbacks, one can still analyze his agenda as president. The U.S. ambassadors meticulously reported his comments. However, other American embassy officials who found him difficult to fathom and cautious to a fault often based their opinions on information gathered from South Vietnamese political representatives or other elites. Much of this U.S. reporting, while often insightful, must be used carefully. Thieu was an extraordinarily closed man, rarely offering his opinion. He kept his internal decision-making circle extremely small, and the Vietnamese outside the government's upper echelon could only supply conjecture on the reasons for his decisions. Or worse, they assigned conspiratorial motives to his actions without any knowledge of how a policy was devised.

Thus, a combination of Thieu's speeches, GVN documents, U.S. records, and interviews with some of his confidantes provides an understanding of the dynamics of his foreign and domestic policies. South Vietnamese memoirs also offer insight, but much like solely relying on U.S. records, it is akin to dancing in a mine field. While an excellent source of material, caution must be exercised. Not only is memory fragile, many authors have a significant bias and are not afraid to display it.

Fortunately, I interviewed many senior South Vietnamese cabinet ministers and other officials who were responsible for designing and implementing government policies. These discussions revealed startling new historical information, including how the Diem coup was almost stopped, previously unknown details on the January 1964 countercoup, the Faustian pact that anointed Thieu over Nguyen Cao Ky for president, the true background on the Chennault Affair during the 1968 elections, and explosive details on perhaps the last, great secret of the Vietnam War that occurred in the final days.

While I believe a tremendous difference exists between President Ngo

Dinh Diem and President Thieu's visions for modernizing the republic, it is also important to concede that Thieu operated in a vastly different political milieu and era than Diem. In the four years after the coup, South Vietnam experienced enormous military, political, social, and economic upheavals marked by the intensification of the war and the escalation of U.S. involvement. Despite that chaos, largely thanks to the shepherding of Ky and Thieu, South Vietnam created a constitution and formed a Second Republic. Then major events like the Communist Tet 1968 attack, the implementation of land reform, and the arming of local citizens to improve security swung many previously neutral or antagonistic peasants to his side. Hanoi's offensive in 1972, however, damaged much of the economic and local government development that Thieu had achieved. The Paris Peace Accords and the subsequent U.S. withdrawal left behind a wounded South Vietnam, one that fell prey to North Vietnam's final attack in 1975.

Fortunately, the current scholarship on the conflict, much like our ever-changing culture, has evolved to embrace new perspectives on South Vietnam.[11] Hopefully, the ideological gulf that cleaved us then will not straitjacket readers now. All too often, extraordinary circumstances force imperfect men to make momentous decisions based on faulty information. Thieu was no different. As one reads this manuscript, try to see him, like most responsible heads of government, as a *politician* trying to do the best for his country rather than as a *dictator* only interested in maintaining power. With that concept in mind, quoting Shakespeare's Chorus in *Henry V*, it is now "your thoughts that must deck our kings" and what must judge Nguyen Van Thieu and South Vietnam.[12]

1

"THE BEST DAYS OF MY LIFE"

The Rise of the Republic of Vietnam

The origins of the country that became the southern-based, non-communist Republic of Vietnam began with Japan's collapse at the end of World War II, the return of the French to reclaim their colony, and the subsequent First Indochina War. When Ho Chi Minh declared the Democratic Republic of Vietnam in September 1945, no one could have imagined that two separate Vietnams would eventually emerge. Yet to comprehend the labored birth of a non-communist Republic, a quick history lesson is required. Our first section takes us swiftly through the events that led to the Republic's emergence, then a review of the early career of Nguyen Van Thieu, and finally a primer on the unwieldy factions that comprised this new country. Our main story will begin shortly, but background supports understanding, and South Vietnam's convoluted saga is no different.

IN THE BEGINNING

The Vietnamese pride themselves on a long and storied history, one that is notable for both internal strife and defense against numerous invaders, including the Chinese and the Cambodians. After years of civil war, in 1802, Gia Long declared himself emperor of a united Vietnam. It would not last. In 1858, the French, seeking colonial possessions, attacked Vietnam and captured the town of Danang in the central part of the country. Over the next two decades, the French conquered the rest of the country.

They divided Vietnam into three regions: two protectorates—Annam in the center and Tonkin in the north—and a colony in the south called Cochinchina. The French permitted the Nguyen Dynasty to continue to rule from the imperial capital of Hue, but only on French terms. In 1888, the French cobbled together Vietnam, Laos, and Cambodia into an Indochinese Union often called French Indochina.[1]

The Vietnamese soon challenged the French occupiers. Two men, Phan Dinh Phung and Phan Boi Chau, resisted colonial rule, the first on the inside until his death in 1897, the second in the surrounding Asian region until 1925, when the French arrested and returned him to Hue. The most well-known of these men, however, was Ho Chi Minh. After World War I, Ho traveled to France, Russia, China, and other countries, preaching his gospel of independence. After asking the French to help him build a colonial republic, he grew disenchanted by the French failure to keep their reformist and republican promises. He turned to Marxism, enthralled by Lenin's promise to help liberate colonies from their oppressors. Ho became an ardent Communist, and he slowly established a group of followers, but French security forces kept them at bay. An idea, however, does not recognize borders, and the notion of Vietnamese independence continued to grow.

At the start of World War II, the Japanese occupied Indochina, but they allowed the French to continue to rule, given the Vichy government's collaboration with Germany. On March 9, 1945, with Japan nearing defeat and fearing an Allied invasion of Vietnam, the Japanese overthrew the Vichy government in Vietnam. This action, as one scholar wrote, "dealt a blow to [French colonial] authority from which it would never fully recover."[2] Two days after the Japanese takeover, Vietnamese Emperor Bao Dai proclaimed the Empire of Vietnam, independent of France but a part of the Japanese empire. He asked a respected scholar, Tran Trong Kim, to form a government and to serve as his prime minister.

Two days after the Japanese in Vietnam surrendered to the Allies on August 15, 1945, a Vietnamese group called the *Viet Nam Doc Lap Dong Minh*, widely referred as the Viet Minh, launched a revolution across the country. Led by Ho Chi Minh, the Viet Minh were ostensibly a united front of resistance movements dedicated to fighting the return of the French colonialists. On August 19, the Viet Minh seized Hanoi, the capital of northern Vietnam. Bao Dai abdicated in favor of Ho, and Kim's government resigned on August 25. When Japan completely surrendered on September 2, 1945, Ho concurrently announced the Democratic Republic of Vietnam (DRV), the first fully independent Vietnamese state since the nineteenth century.

The U.S., the United Kingdom, and the Soviet Union had held a conference in late July to discuss postwar issues involving Germany and the future of Asia. Anticipating the Japanese capitulation, the British were assigned responsibility for occupying Vietnam below the sixteenth parallel, while Chiang Kai-shek's Nationalist Chinese would occupy the area above that line. France was excluded from the reoccupation because they were not among the Allies in Asia.

The French, however, had different plans. French leader Charles de Gaulle hustled his army to Indochina to reclaim the colonies, and on September 23, the British allowed French troops to disembark in Saigon. Fighting immediately broke out between the Vietnamese and the French. Although Saigon fell quickly, in the north, the Nationalist Chinese denied the French permission to reclaim their colony for fear that hostilities might erupt as they had in the south. This gave Ho's government a year to consolidate itself in the northern section of Vietnam. That yearlong respite proved crucial, giving the DRV time to organize itself and prepare for war. The Viet Minh grew stronger in the northern part of the country but remained weak in the southern part.

On March 6, 1946, the French and Ho signed an agreement to permit the stationing of French troops in northern Vietnam for five years to replace the Chinese, but Paris conceded to recognize the DRV as a free state within the French Union. In July, the French and the DRV opened new negotiations in Fontainebleau, France, to discuss Vietnam's independence and its role within the union, but the talks began under a cloud. Since the southern part of Vietnam was under French control, the French had created a separate Republic of Cochinchina (the start of South Vietnam) in June 1946. This rump government, with its capital in Saigon, was led by Dr. Nguyen Van Thinh, a prominent physician. Thinh agreed to cooperate with the French in exchange for self-rule within the French Union. Thinh envisioned a republic separate from a Communist-inspired DRV in Hanoi, although most of his compatriots favored a unified country. Paris, however, was not interested in autonomy, only in creating a Vietnamese government subservient to the French Union. Fearful that the French were using him, on November 10, 1946, Thinh committed suicide. He was replaced by Le Van Hoach, who continued to work with the French.

Despite the alliance between Ho's Communists and the non-communist political parties like the *Viet Nam Quoc Dan Dang* and the Dai Viets, the Communists soon tried to dominate the coalition. They began targeting the non-communist parties, who called themselves Nationalists and whom we shall meet later in more detail. These two parties had also originated in northern Vietnam, had launched an uprising in the 1930s and had been crushed by the French military. Hunted by the Communists, the Viet Minh alliance began to fracture.

Since Paris refused to give up its colonial hold on Indochina, the Fontainebleau negotiations failed. War erupted between France and the DRV in December 1946. To peel the Nationalists away from the Viet Minh, Paris attempted to offer the anti-communists limited authority over the country. Seeking a ruler with broad appeal, the French turned to former Vietnamese Emperor Bao Dai, who had broken with Ho Chi Minh. In September 1947, Bao Dai opened negotiations with the French to create a separate anti-communist Vietnamese government. Bao Dai hoped to force Paris to grant independence, but he only achieved a partial victory. On June 5, 1948, the French and the former emperor signed the Halong Bay Agreements, which granted Vietnam official status within the French Union and unified the three Vietnamese regions (Tonkin, Annam, and Cochinchina) under his rule. A Central Provisional Vietnamese Government was formed that was separate from Ho's DRV, and the Republic of Cochinchina was subsumed within it.

After further negotiations, on March 8, 1949, Bao Dai and French President Vincent Auriol concluded the Elysee Accords, which made Vietnam an "associated state" of Indochina along with Laos and Cambodia. All three countries, however, remained part of the French Union. On July 2, 1949, Bao Dai officially proclaimed the Associated State of Vietnam. The agreement fell short of granting independence but allowed Vietnam to conduct its own foreign policy, control its finances, and create an army. Ho and his followers immediately dismissed the former emperor and his cabinet as "race traitors."

The same day, the brand-new provisional government also established the Ministry of Defense, and in August it formed the Vietnamese National Army (*Quan Doi Quoc Gia Viet Nam*). For many Nationalists, fighting the Communist threat was more important than combating the French, and Bao Dai's embryonic administration and the French moved swiftly to build an indigenous military. They formed infantry battalions, and since Bao Dai needed Vietnamese officers to command these units, the French created the School for Regular Officers in Hue. The school became the forerunner of South Vietnam's National Military Academy. The first class began on December 1, 1948, and was called Phan Boi Chau after the famous pioneer of Vietnamese nationalism. One of the graduates of the first officer class at Hue was Nguyen Van Thieu, the future president of the Second Republic.

Meanwhile, events outside Vietnam exerted enormous influence over happenings inside the country. The Chinese Communist victory in 1949 forced the Americans to dramatically alter how they dealt with the French empire. As Chinese weapons began reaching Ho's soldiers in 1950, the French requested large-scale U.S. military assistance. America agreed, and the outbreak of the Korean War in June 1950 only reinforced Washington's commitment. Military and economic assistance began to pour in, and Washington diplomatically recognized the Associated State of Vietnam, followed by the British and the rest of the "Free World." The chief goal of Paris and Washington became forming an anti-communist government in Vietnam allied with France. The Associated State of Vietnam, however, had to protect itself and extend its rule, and Bao Dai needed the Vietnamese National Army (VNA) to accomplish that goal.

THE EARLY YEARS OF NGUYEN VAN THIEU

Since Thieu was one of the two most influential figures in South Vietnamese history—Ngo Dinh Diem being the other—let us review his early life. Since worldview is often an amalgamation of culture, upbringing, personality, and experience, it is necessary to examine how Thieu's rearing and early military career influenced his personality and future policies.

Unfortunately, our knowledge of his formative years is thin. Even basic biographic information about him is conflicting. For example, a senior news correspondent who spent years in Vietnam and who wrote Thieu's obituary for the *New York Times* repeated the popular misunderstanding of his actual birthday. Fox Butterfield wrote, "Thieu was born in November 1924, but in accordance with a frequently used Vietnamese custom took another date as his birthday—April 5, 1923—on grounds that it was better luck. He was the youngest of five children, born in a village on the central coast of Vietnam."[3] Others agreed that he had changed his birthday "on the advice of an astrologer."[4]

While true that rural Vietnamese occasionally changed their birthday to a more propitious date for astrological reasons, Thieu's wife claims that he did not. Although many believed that his true birthday was November 12, 1924, this was a youthful mistake made from his uncertainty over the correct date. According to Mrs. Thieu, when he was a young boy filling out an examination for school, the teacher asked him his birth date. Uncertain, he went home to query his mother. Not finding her, he returned to school and made up the date of November 12, 1924.[5] The teacher dutifully recorded it, and this wrong date became part of an official record. Although Thieu's mother later corrected her son, whether she had changed his birthday to something more astrologically significant is unknown.[6]

Thieu was born on April 5, 1923, in Tri Thuy, a picturesque village of fishermen and farmers nestled on an ocean inlet a few miles from the city of Phan Rang, the capital of Ninh Thuan. A coastal province about 150 miles northeast of Saigon, Ninh Thuan is roughly the dividing line between the central and southern sections of South Vietnam. His parents were not poor peasants tilling a rice field; they were a relatively prosperous middle-class family that owned land and several businesses. They instilled in him a strong work ethic and imprinted typical Vietnamese cultural values that remained with him into adulthood. His father, Nguyen Van Trung, and his paternal grandfather and great grandfather were sailors who traveled up and down the coast selling goods. After Thieu's birth, his father took "another occupation. He went to Qui Nhon and brought back animals and cows and so on, to sell in Phan Rang, and he went to Saigon and bought and sold merchandise."[7] Thieu's father had been orphaned at age ten, and he impressed the tough lessons from his difficult life onto his son. Thieu told a postwar interviewer that, "his father always taught him that he must be careful and cautious and should never be careless or reckless," a lesson that became Thieu's defining personality trait.[8]

Thieu was the youngest of seven children. He had four brothers and two sisters. As such, his nickname was "Tam" (Eight), as southerners use Two as the name of the first child, since the father was Number One (*Anh Hai*). Little is known about his sisters and two of his brothers, but his two oldest brothers, Hieu and Kieu, would become ambassadors for the Republic of Vietnam. However, his older brothers held little sway over him, an unusual occurrence in a traditional Vietnamese family. The oldest, Hieu, was born on April 4, 1906. The family sent him to France for a college education, an impressive achievement for a Vietnamese during the colonial period, as only several thousand Vietnamese attended French secondary (high) schools. Hieu received his undergraduate degree in law, a traditional entrance into the civil service, from the University of Paris in 1933. He returned to Vietnam and served as a magistrate in Hue until 1939.

Upon their father's death on January 12, 1969, as the eldest son, Hieu became the nominal leader of the family, but he had left Vietnam in 1956 for various diplomatic assignments. In 1966, he became South Vietnam's ambassador to Italy. When Hieu's wife died of cancer in 1966, Thieu generously adopted Hieu's daughter and raised her. It was a closely held family secret, known only to a few people. A Buddhist, Hieu was a quiet man with no political ambition, and after his appointment to Italy, he stayed out of Vietnamese politics and remained in Rome until the fall of Saigon.

Kieu on the other hand, was much more politically active. He was born in 1916, and at some point converted to Catholicism. Around 1940, Kieu became one of the founders of the South Vietnamese branch of the *Dai Viet Quoc Dan Dang* (Greater Vietnam Nationalist Party). The Dai Viets were a Vietnamese political party that competed with another political party, the *Viet Nam Quoc Dan Dang* (VNQDD, Vietnam Nationalist Party) for the allegiance of the Nationalists. Kieu eventually became the ambassador to Taiwan, but he also served as Thieu's chief messenger and intermediary with many of the South Vietnamese political and religious leaders.

Thieu's parents focused on educating their children, particularly Hieu and Kieu. To pay for their advanced schooling, a young Thieu helped his mother, Bui Thi Hanh, sell goods in the local market. He notes:

> While I was in school, I had to help my sisters sell rice cakes and sweet potatoes. Also, every day I went to the market for my mother and helped my sisters make money. My two brothers went to school and I stayed home and helped my sisters to bring goods back and forth. I worked very hard. My mother had a small grocery in the village, and I helped my mother in that store too. At that time, my father and my mother had to raise my two brothers and send them to school in Saigon. My father always tried to give us a good education. He worked very hard [as did] my mother and my two sisters to provide money to send my two brothers to primary school and then to high school, and then to send me to school.[9]

One Vietnamese who knew Thieu for many years agrees that Thieu came from a good family. He wrote: "Back then I particularly respected Thieu because Thieu's parents were good, moral elders who always made sure that their family followed the traditions of our Three Religions."[10] The three traditional Vietnamese religions are Buddhism, Taoism, and Confucianism. Ancestor veneration also plays a prominent role in Vietnamese worship. Thieu's values reflected his Confucian upbringing, a philosophy that guided one's life and place in society, but its precepts only partially explain his worldview. While he accepted Confucian concepts regarding social matters, his education exposed him to French culture, including concepts of liberty and democracy. His later visits to the United States convinced him that Vietnam needed to embrace American management and industrial techniques and reject centralized French-style management. This embrace of U.S. modernization was a key difference between Thieu and many other Vietnamese leaders. Military rituals reinforced his strong belief in tradition, particularly as seen through the prism of Vietnamese customs and mores. Later he would adopt the religious tenets of Catholicism, but it was always a layer upon his core Vietnamese values.

Since his parents emphasized learning as the path to success, Thieu acquired a good education by the standards of colonial Vietnam. Schooling honed his native intelligence, an advantage rarely granted to Vietnamese youth of his generation. He attended primary (elementary) school in his native village, but he went to elementary (middle) school in the city of Phan Rang. Twice a day he had to cross the lagoon between Tri Thuy and Phan Rang on a ferry. One of his teachers was the father of his second cousin, Hoang Duc Nha.[11]

This initiated the bond between the two, as Nha eventually became Thieu's closest advisor when he was president. Nha was born on August 21, 1942. His family were also landowners. In the late 1950s, he lived with Thieu in Dalat when he attended the prestigious Lycee Yersin school. After graduating, he passed his Baccalaureate II, the French exam required to attend college. In 1961, he was awarded a U.S. scholarship, a rare feat for Vietnamese youth of that era. He attended Oklahoma State University, where he became close friends with Tran Quang Minh, later head of the government's National Food Agency.[12]

Thieu attended secondary (high) school at the prestigious Pellerin School in Hue. Pellerin was one of only four French-run secondary schools for males in Vietnam, and entry would have required excellent grades and considerable pull from his older brother Hieu. When Hieu departed Hue in 1939, Thieu left Pellerin and moved to Saigon to live with Kieu, where he enrolled at a Vietnamese secondary school called Le Ba Cang. He graduated in 1942, earning his Baccalaureate I, a French final high school exam, but for some unknown reason, he did not take the Bac II exam. After high school graduation, Thieu returned to his village and worked on the family rice field and assisted on his father's boats.

The Japanese removal of the French in March 1945 unleashed Thieu's nationalistic sentiments. He told *Time* magazine that "[e]veryone at the time believed that the Japanese had given us our liberty from the French."[13] Naturally, he was infected with the same fervent nationalistic longings for independence that consumed his entire generation. Enthralled with the idea of kicking out the foreigners, in September 1945 a twenty-two-year-old Thieu joined the Viet Minh in his native province. He trained in the jungle, using bamboo poles in place of rifles. His efforts in the local youth organization earned him the position as chief of his village committee. Soon he was also made an advisor to the district committee.

Like many Nationalists of his generation, Thieu was anti-French, but he soon soured on the Viet Minh after discovering that the Communists secretly dominated it. Explaining years later why he quit the Viet Minh, Thieu remarked: "By August of 1946, I knew that the Viet Minh were Communists....They shot people. They overthrew the village committee. They seized the land."[14] He claims he fled his home when he learned that the Viet Minh had decided to assassinate him because he was an intellectual, i.e., someone with a French education.

Leaving the Viet Minh in August 1946—and to avoid reprisals on his family—Thieu returned to Saigon. He first attended electrical engineering school, but he quit and joined the School for Civil Navigation (École de navigation civile, often called the Merchant Marine Academy) from 1947 to 1948, where he won an officer's rating. He received an offer to work in a French shipping company, but he spurned the job when he discovered that the owners would pay him less than French officers holding the same position.

Piecing together Thieu's early military career was as difficult as divining his childhood. Despite prolonged interaction with American officials, the U.S. government created only a handful of biographical sketches of him. Worse, these accounts contain just a few bare facts that are often contradictory regarding his initial military duties. Astonishingly, even South Vietnamese profiles of Thieu are in error regarding his activities in the years preceding the coup of November 1, 1963.[15] For instance, several official summaries written during the war incorrectly claim he commanded the 21st

ARVN Division in 1954. That division was not formed until June 1, 1959.[16] Yet despite the scarcity of authoritative details about Thieu's childhood, by culling from various interviews and remarks from a wide range of South Vietnamese and American sources, a picture does emerge.

With few job prospects, Thieu volunteered for the initial VNA officer class in Hue. Among his classmates was Ton That Dinh, who would be Thieu's commanding officer during the coup against Diem, Nguyen Huu Co, Minister of Defense in the Nguyen Cao Ky government, and Dang Van Quang, who would later become Thieu's national security advisor. An instructional course designed to create infantry platoon leaders, Thieu completed the six-month class on June 1, 1949, and was promoted to second lieutenant.[17] According to a French record, Thieu graduated fourth out of fifty-three officers.[18]

After graduation, Thieu served as a platoon leader in the 1st Battalion, one of the first three VNA infantry battalions. Thieu's time as a platoon leader was short; he only served from June to September 1949. Soon after the first military class graduated, Bao Dai handpicked ten officers from the ranks of Vietnamese lieutenants to attend the Advanced Infantry Course at Coetquiden, France.[19] Thieu, Tran Thien Khiem, and Dang Van Quang were three of the ten. The course ran from December 1949 to June 1950.

Many accounts claim that Thieu and Khiem met at the Merchant Marine school, but that is incorrect. Their first meeting was on this voyage. The pair would eventually dominant the South Vietnamese political scene, as Khiem became South Vietnam's prime minister under the future president. The U.S. embassy in Saigon wrote that "Khiem has been considered the closest thing to a confidant that Thieu has had throughout his armed forces career."[20] The embassy's assessment, one accepted by historians, is also incorrect. According to Khiem, they "were not friends but working colleagues for most of their lives...[and] never socialized outside of work....[H]e met Thieu in an official work capacity and in that capacity, he was higher ranking and as such, would not have socialized with him."[21]

The group traveled to France on the French ocean liner SS *Pasteur*. On board, a Vietnamese officer showed Thieu a picture of four sisters from My Tho, a provincial capital in the Mekong Delta in the southernmost part of Vietnam. The officer told Thieu that three of the girls were engaged, but one, Nguyen Thi Mai Anh, was still single. Thieu extracted a promise from the officer to make an introduction. Upon his return from France, Thieu was introduced to Mai Anh, and he soon asked to marry her. According to

Mrs. Thieu, her only condition was that he convert to the Catholic faith, as it was against church policy for a Catholic to marry a non-Catholic. This apparently caused some family issues, and the two fathers spent a year working out the details.

Nguyen Thi Mai Anh came from a prominent Delta family. Born on June 20, 1930, in My Tho, both of her parents were Oriental medicine doctors. Her father treated adults, while her mother specialized in children. Her mother was a devout Catholic and donated much of her practice to charity. According to a Vietnamese biography, "The family lived simply, and the children were raised in the strictest of old Vietnamese traditions. The girls attended the local Catholic convent in My Tho."[22] Eventually, Thieu's father agreed to let him convert to Catholicism. Although Thieu delayed baptism for years, he married Mai Anh on July 18, 1951.

Unlike the wives of other senior leaders, Mrs. Thieu did not engage in politics. She was shy and not close to the spouses of the other generals. According to Thieu, she "had never played a political role, had always remained in [the] background."[23] She confirmed this to a journalist, stating that she did not "advise my husband on affairs of state or how to run the government." Instead, she focused on social welfare, raising money to build a hospital for handicapped children or visiting wounded soldiers.[24] Thieu sought to protect her from political intrigue, particularly the vile dealmaking engaged in by other officers' wives that tainted their husbands. He also knew that if she did partake in such activities, it would spark jealousy among these wives, who would then incite their husbands and thereby create enemies for him.

Upon graduation from the French infantry school, Thieu served from August 1950 to June 1951 as a company commander with the VNA 5th Battalion, a unit that operated in the Soc Trang area in the lower Mekong Delta. After company command, at the personal request of Bao Dai, Thieu was tasked with training cadets at the military school in Dalat, which had moved from Hue to the beautiful resort city north of Saigon where the former emperor had a vacation home. While on paper the French had allowed Bao Dai to create an army, it was not until 1951 that Paris, pushed by the French High Commissioner and Commander in Chief Jean de Lattre, truly took the VNA seriously. De Lattre imposed a draft on Vietnamese males, instituted a general mobilization law in 1951, and ordered the creation of better training programs to develop an officer corps capable of running a modern army. Thieu was an integral part of that. Promoted to first lieutenant on June 1, 1951, Thieu taught at Dalat for almost a year. The last group he instructed was the famous 5th Class, which produced more general officers than any other. Included in this class were future corps commanders Nguyen Van Toan, Nguyen Vinh Nghi, and Pham Quoc Thuan, men who would become pillars of his military apparatus.

As the fighting grew fiercer, especially in the north, French commanders sought to utilize the growing ranks of the VNA to win the war. In late May 1952, Thieu moved to Hanoi to attend a three-month staff course. Also attending this program was the future head of the South Vietnamese military, Cao Van Vien, and future chief of state Nguyen Khanh. The class was designed to teach tactics and higher-level command and staff methods. This was the most intense period of the war. De Lattre had just beaten back three major attacks in the Red River Delta in northern Vietnam by division-size elements of the People's Army of Vietnam (PAVN). General Vo Nguyen Giap, leader of the PAVN, believed he could overwhelm the French fortifications with massed infantry assaults. When the French deployed napalm against Giap's exposed troops, they died by the thousands. The French, however, desperately needed Vietnamese troops to help them defend the local villages, a job that Americans would call pacification. The conflict had morphed into two separate wars, just as it would with the Americans. The first was conventional, including artillery, large units, and set-piece battles. The second was a war in the villages, as the Communists attempted to slowly strangle French-held cities like Hanoi by cutting them off from the countryside.

Thieu graduated on September 27, 1952. The head of the French school, Colonel (later *General de Division*) Paul Vanuxem, who would develop a long friendship with Thieu and will reappear at the very end of this book, rated the future president as "very intellectual and energetic. His high moral quality, his intellectual value, his character, and his strong personality should enable him in all employments. Ranked: Very good, and he will rise up in the near future."[25]

After graduation, Thieu was assigned as the operations officer, the staff position responsible for planning military activities, of the Hung Yen sector, which stretched south from Hanoi to Hai Duong Province. In July 1952, the French turned Hung Yen, an area of strong DRV influence, over to the VNA, the first sector given completely to the Nationalists. Hung Yen was part of the Red River Delta, and Thieu and his fellow officers engaged in the first all-Vietnamese effort at controlling the villages. Here he learned pacification, French-style. Long before he took command of

South Vietnam, he got a close-up view of how the PAVN worked conventionally and unconventionally. Cao Van Vien also served on the sector staff as the intelligence officer. The Thieu and Vien families lived together, but according to Mrs. Thieu, "The relationship was normal, but we did not socialize."[26] Reminiscing with an American reporter, Thieu "recalled those days as among the best of his life."[27] Another reporter noted that Thieu also called his pacification duties "the most valuable experience of his military career."[28]

After serving a year in Hung Yen, Thieu left in late October 1953 and was assigned to the staff of the army's newly formed 2nd Military Region, then comprising the coastal provinces of central South Vietnam. Once more serving as operations officer, he held that position until March 1954, when the 2nd Military Region shifted from central to northern South Vietnam, covering what later became I Corps. This timeframe corresponds with Operation Atlante, the last major French effort of the war. A multi-battalion effort, Atlante lasted from January to July 1954. Using a combination of French and VNA units, the attack sought to clear the Viet Minh from the coastal provinces of central South Vietnam. Atlante had three phases. The first phase landed troops in Tuy Hoa, the capital of Phu Yen Province, directly north of Ninh Thuan, Thieu's home province. Following the recapture of Tuy Hoa, the French in mid-March opened Phase II, which assaulted the city of Qui Nhon, the capital of Binh Dinh Province. However, at the same time, the Viet Minh launched an attack on Dien Bien Phu, resulting in the famous French defeat that ended the war. The conquest of Dien Bien Phu forced the French to abandon Atlante's third phase.

Overall, the VNA performed poorly in Atlante, as many units declined to fight. The new French commander in Vietnam, General Henri-Eugene Navarre, sneered at the VNA, telling correspondents that "Vietnamese troops used in Operation Atlante had not stood up well." Navarre further stated the VNA's "national spirit was still lacking."[29] Rather than accept that many rank-and-file Vietnamese did not want to fight for the French, Navarre's comments reflected the belief of many French that the Nationalists were a sordid lot at best. This opinion would lead senior French government officials to conclude that the Nationalists could not win and that the only recourse to the war was neutrality for South Vietnam, a judgment that would drive French policy for years.

Thieu participated in Atlante from March to July 1954. Promoted to major on March 1, 1954, he apparently assumed command of a newly formed Ninh Thuan regional regiment and concurrently became sector commander in March 1954, although this is not confirmed. He related to *Time* magazine that during Atlante, he had led VNA forces to clear his own village. "The Communists retreated into Thieu's old home, confident that he would not fire on his own house. Says Thieu with grim satisfaction: 'I shot in my own house.'"[30] He also claimed to have participated in Phase II of Atlante, stating, "I was the first man to embark and recapture the Cau River, south of Qui Nhon, because that zone was under control of the Viet Cong."[31]

Afterward, Thieu returned to the 2nd Military Region, now headquartered in Hue, as the Operations Officer. By September 1954, he had risen to deputy commander, 2nd Military Region.[32] Why he never commanded a VNA battalion remains a huge question, especially since he was given high marks by his French commanders. Do Mau, who served with Thieu in Hung Yen, states that Thieu was "serious, wise, and his talent for staff work was rated very highly by French General De Linares [who] had evaluated Thieu as follows: 'Keen intelligence, hard-working, methodical, and meticulous. A good officer with a remarkable understanding of organizational matters and the need for secrecy.'"[33]

The French defeat at Dien Bien Phu hastened the signing of the Geneva Accords on July 20, 1954, which split the country into two parts at the seventeenth parallel. Until then, North or South Vietnam did not exist, but the accords forced the two competing states that had claimed dominion over all of Vietnam to accept the division of the country. While the Nationalists would soon be swept up in the massive changes coming with the arrival of Ngo Dinh Diem, to complete our overview, let us first discuss who precisely they are.

THE NATIONALISTS

Readers are frequently baffled by the complexity and chaos of Vietnamese politics and the irrationality of its actors. Americans at that time trying to understand the inner workings of Vietnamese personalities and politics personified the biblical phrase "For now we see through a glass, darkly."[34] American reporters and embassy officials usually learned Vietnamese politics through the filter of Saigon-based elites, whose main pastimes were gossiping and maneuvering for power, usually to the detriment of other Nationalists. The Vietnamese journalist and covert Communist spy Pham

Xuan An is a perfect example, as he was often the main conduit for inside information for American reporters.

Although Confucianism still influenced the villagers in Vietnam, its sway was felt the least in the southern part of the country. Yet hard-working peasants tilling rice fields generally accepted the traditional principles outlining the roles of the ruler and the ruled. Hence their reaction to a ruler's stern response to dissent was often indifference. This apathy, combined with the centrifugal tendency of Vietnamese society, the clandestine roots of its political parties, and the authoritarian mindset of its leaders explains why most Vietnamese rulers adopted a strongman governing style. Unfortunately, a repressive regime, regardless of circumstances, did not match the Western view of governance, and it formed the basis for much of America's divisions over South Vietnam.

There were four bases of socio-political conflict among the Nationalists: political, religion, region, and ethnicity. In the political arena, the two largest and oldest Nationalist parties were the Dai Viets and the VNQDD. Both originated in North Vietnam as revolutionary, anti-French organizations. They were not comparable, in American terms, to the Democrats and Republicans. They were really competing strains of the same philosophy.

The failure of the Nationalists to achieve political dominance in Vietnam was twofold. The first problem was leadership. Both the Communists and the French targeted and often killed the main Nationalist political leaders. The second was the Nationalist's inability, shared with the Communists, to function openly during the colonial period and afterward. The Dai Viet's, for instance, were banned by the French colonial administration and again by the Communist's when Ho seized power in Hanoi in 1945. The Communists claimed the Dai Viets were plotting "to carry out actions harmful to Vietnam's economy and its national independence." If the Dai Viets continued "to assemble and hold party meetings the violators will be prosecuted severely under our laws," meaning they would be exterminated.[35] Ngo Dinh Diem would also bar Dai Viet operations, seeing the Dai Viets as competitors for power rather than as anti-communist partners. This repression badly weakened any impulses toward a democratic, republican form of government like the Indian Congress under the British.

Forbidden from open political life, the Nationalists went underground to organize, grow, and above all, protect themselves. Party cells, mainly among urban dwellers, used covert techniques to communicate. Leading Dai Viet leader Nguyen Ngoc Huy noted that these secret operations "hindered the propagation of their platforms and prevented them from enlarging their political base."[36] Under these difficult circumstances, instead of building from the bottom up, Nationalist parties sought to rule from the top down. Each pursued the creation of "a party of loyal comrades, large enough and pervasive enough to control local administration throughout the nation, as well as the external forms and processes of democracy (the legislature and elections)."[37]

A charismatic leader and intellectual named Truong Tu Anh formed the Dai Viets on December 10, 1939, in Hanoi. The Dai Viets were probably the largest Nationalist party in South Vietnam, even though they were outnumbered by their archrivals, the VNQDD, in the northern provinces of South Vietnam. When Anh disappeared sometime in late 1946, the Dai Viets believed that the Viet Minh had assassinated him, forcing many Nationalists to side with the French against their murderous rivals.

Anh's death also eliminated the man who had held the party together, and it eventually splintered into three groups. The first was a small northern faction, which was often sneeringly called the Mandarin (*quan lai*) group, because it mainly consisted of educated northerners. Men such as Bui Diem, Phan Huy Quat, Tran Van Do, Dang Van Sung, were part of this circle, and all of them at some point worked for Bao Dai's government. As northerners, they had little grassroots appeal in South Vietnam, but their education made them attractive candidates for his administration. Although they sought a constitutional government that would legalize fundamental freedoms, their limited numbers forced them to rely upon persuasion, a disadvantage in a society ruled by men with guns.

The second Dai Viet faction was the Revolutionary Dai Viets (*Dai Viet Cach Mang*). This group was mainly based in Quang Tri and Thua Thien provinces in Central Vietnam. Ha Thuc Ky ruled this chapter, but it would not formally become the RDV until 1965. Ky was born on January 1, 1919, in Hue and attended the University of Hanoi. He became a Dai Viet member in 1939, and later joined the Viet Minh to fight against the French. He fled the resistance in mid-1946 when he discovered that the Communists had marked him for assassination. In late 1950, he was chosen to head the Dai Viet's Central Vietnam branch, where he soon became another polarizing figure in the highly charged political atmosphere of central South Vietnam. After Diem's ascension, Ky's group fomented a rebellion in Quang Tri Province among a small group of Vietnamese National Army units. Called the Ba Long Incident, the mutiny was put down on March

15, 1955, by loyal VNA troops. Ky went into hiding in Saigon and set up a clandestine radio station that broadcast pro–Dai Viet and anti-Diem messages. In mid-October 1958, he was arrested and sentenced to life in prison. He was released after the coup against Diem.

The last faction, and the largest and the most powerful Dai Viet group, was the southern chapter. Led by Dr. Nguyen Ton Hoan and Nguyen Ngoc Huy, it included many southern gentry in its ranks. Diem exiled Hoan and Huy to France, but both returned after the coup.[38] Despite the party's authoritarian roots, Hoan and Huy eventually concluded, like the northern Dai Viets, that representative democracy was the better political system. Huy was one of the Nationalists' top intellectuals, and he would be a driving force in transforming the southern Dai Viet's political thinking from a revolutionary group attempting to overthrow the regime, to a political party seeking power through the ballot box.

Ha Thuc Ky, however, disagreed. His faction continued working surreptitiously to influence the senior officials running the government rather than winning power via voter appeal. His formation of the Revolutionary Dai Viets was an attempt to stay true to the party's roots. Faced with irreducible party factionalism, Huy and Hoan formed the New Dai Viets (*Tan Dai Viet*) in late 1964. In 1969, the Tan Dai Viets developed into the Progressive Nationalist Movement (PNM), the most important political party in South Vietnam's Second Republic after Thieu's Democracy Party (*Dang Dan Chu*) and labor leader Tran Quoc Buu's Farmer-Worker Party (*Dang Cong Nong*).

Vietnam's oldest Nationalist political party was the *Vietnam Quoc Dan Dang* (VNQDD). Formed on December 25, 1927, its first leader was Nguyen Thai Hoc. The VNQDD launched a famous revolt against the French on February 10, 1930, at Yen Bai in North Vietnam. Using a combination of rebellious Vietnamese troops and VNQDD followers, Hoc's men killed some colonial soldiers, but the French quickly crushed the mutiny. Hoc was captured and executed, but his famous deathbed slogan inspired thousands of Vietnamese to join the Nationalist cause: "Even if we shall not succeed, we shall have done our duty."[39]

Like all Vietnamese party organizations—except the Communists, who eliminated any internal deviants like Trotskyites—the VNQDD also split into factions after its founder's death. A northerner named Vu Hong Khanh eventually took control of the major faction. Autocratic in character, Khanh was a northerner and a founding member of the party who had fought in the ill-fated Yen Bai uprising. He then fled to China, where he joined Chiang

Kai Shek's Nationalist army. While he initially joined the Viet Minh, after seeing Ho's Communist designs, he broke with him. Khanh went south in 1954, and he also led his group into opposition against Diem. By 1955, he was leading a small guerrilla band in Quang Nam Province, but like Ha Thuc Ky's failed revolt, his rebellion was quickly put down. Arrested in 1958, Khanh was released shortly after the Diem coup. His group was strongest in northern South Vietnam and held the largest membership of any political party in that area.

THE MILITARY AND SECULAR GROUPS

Within the country, the party that held the most power was the military. Often called the Khaki Party (*Dang Ka Ki*), the military remained the most organized Nationalist element in South Vietnam, but it was also riven by factionalism. Southern-born officers often disliked northerners, while many officers distrusted those who had defected from the Viet Minh. Buddhist-Catholic enmity also simmered beneath the surface. Seniority straitjacketed promotions: an officer who had graduated from an earlier class often hated working for someone who had graduated after him. The regular army looked down upon the provincial forces, and the elite units like the Vietnamese Marines, Airborne, and the Rangers often refused to take orders from other branches or commanders. Lastly, "business interests," otherwise known as illegal commercial activities, strained relations. Over time, additional tensions emerged between those who followed Nguyen Cao Ky versus those who supported Thieu. Collectively, these divisions exacerbated military inefficiencies, adding to the normal stressors of combat operations, casualties, poor pay, low morale, and family displacement.

Another major pressure group were the students, predominately those in Saigon and Hue. Normally quiet, they erupted in protest against Diem. The president in turn dispatched the police against them, which gave birth to their political consciousness. The combination of activist students and militant Buddhists was a volatile political mix, one that lasted for years. In 1970, the students became the principal vehicle of unrest in the cities.

Other non-government Vietnamese groups, such as labor, also welded political power. The Vietnamese Confederation of Labor was the country's preeminent union. Known by its French initials, CVT, the union was based mainly in Saigon, but had important affiliates in Danang and the Delta. Its membership varied, but at its peak the CVT claimed three hundred thousand participants. Tran Quoc Buu led the union. Born in Binh Dinh Province, Buu moved to Saigon in the late 1930s. He was arrested in February 1941 for anti-French activities and sent to Con Son Island, the main French prison. One of his cellmates was Phan Khac Suu, future chief of state. Buu was released in 1945, and after a brief sojourn with the Viet Minh, he formed the union in November 1949.

Ngo Dinh Nhu, the brother of President Diem and his chief advisor, was an early union supporter. He helped Buu build the CVT, both as an anti-French bulwark and to foil the usual Communist playbook of subverting industrial workers. Although the relationship was initially fruitful, by 1961 the two began to battle over union control. By October 1963, Buu was fed up with the brothers. His relationship with the military before and immediately after the coup is murky, but he apparently pledged his support for the coup, which consequently allowed him to remain in charge of his beloved labor movement. Over time, Buu developed three overarching philosophies: strengthening the union, devotion to Nationalism, and political pragmatism, a viewpoint he saw as remaining outside the government but refraining from inflammatory political opposition. Buu's ability to work with the government yet remain aloof made him one of the few outsiders able to influence policy.[40]

Another secular pressure group influencing Vietnamese society were the exiles in France. In typical fashion, they were not a cohesive group. Some were former Bao Dai officials, while others were disillusioned ministers who had served under Diem. Most proposed a neutralist solution or a willingness to compromise politically with the Communists. They had little support in South Vietnam, but from time to time the names of certain figures were bandied about as representatives to fill the gap between the Communists and the Nationalists if a neutral solution to the war became possible.

The last secular pressure group was of course, the Communists. Whether one agreed or not with their methods or philosophy, the Communists had articulated a collective social and political program that appealed to segments of a disenfranchised people. They offered a singular, communal contract to reorder society, whereas the Nationalists' political thinking floundered among competing ideas from China, Japan, and France. As social upheavals in the 1960s swept the globe, the southern Communist organization called the National Liberation Front (NLF) became appealing both as a movement and an ideology to left-wing sentiments, regardless of whether its interpretation of freedom held the same meaning as in the West. They grew in strength until the 1968 Tet Offensive, when heavy losses and the retreat of Communist main force units in 1969 enabled Thieu's government to considerably reduce their numbers.

RELIGIOUS GROUPS

The political parties and secular organizations, fragmented and badly weakened by years of Communist assassinations and Diem's repression, were nowhere near as important as religious and regional identification. The Three Teachings (Buddhism, Confucianism, and Taoism) and ancestor worship formed the bedrock of Vietnamese social and cultural values. Buddhism, Confucianism, and Catholicism, and to a lesser extent the Hoa Hao and Cao Dai sects, were the principal religions. Buddhism, another in a lengthy line of cultural imports from China, was the largest of South Vietnam's religions. Of South Vietnam's population of roughly twelve million people in this period, about three to four million were Buddhists, of which approximately half were active practitioners. Another three to four million followed Confucian precepts. Some of these had a loose connection to Buddhism but also to Taoism and ancestor worship. About one and a half million were Catholic, and another two million belonged to the Hoa Hao or Cao Dai sects.

The Buddhists in South Vietnam had numerous sects but were essentially divided into three political factions. Not surprisingly, they were split along regional fault lines. One faction was from the northern provinces of South Vietnam, the other were refugees from North Vietnam who had settled around Saigon, and the last were based in the Mekong Delta region. The more militant Buddhists were located primarily in northern South Vietnam, the area encompassing I Corps. Thich Tri Quang, who would become the most prominent Buddhist activist in the country, commanded this group. While technically holding only a spiritual title, he was an effective mobilizer. To rally South Vietnam's often politically indifferent clergy and galvanize public opinion, he cast political issues in graphic religious terms such as "defense of the faith" or "freedom of worship." While often accused of harboring Communist sympathies, Tri Quang's rhetoric instead revealed a highly nationalistic, anti-capitalist agenda combined with a "peace at any price" manifesto. He was not pro-communist, but his platform was politically naïve, and some of his rhetoric was ideologically too close to Hanoi for Saigon or Washington's comfort.[41]

Thich Tam Chau led the group around the capital.[42] Many were transplanted northerners and thus more pro-government. Chau was chairman of the General Buddhist Association, a weak governing structure for Vietnam's various Buddhist organizations. Like Quang, his main goal was to unify the numerous factions, and he supported a government charter to create a Unified Buddhist Church (UBC) in South Vietnam to give the church legal status. Chau successfully convinced fourteen of the sixteen Buddhist factions to join the unified church. After the Diem coup, he initially teamed with Tri Quang, but he eventually broke with him and threw his support behind the Saigon government. The third group, mostly Cambodians in the lower Delta and other southerners, were politically inert.

The Catholic Church represented the most highly structured organization in South Vietnam next to the military and the Communist Party. It dwarfed the Buddhists in financial investments, enabling the church to fund a massive network of schools and publications that formed an impressive countrywide infrastructure. It was also tied into a global network of Catholic lay organizations that helped staff various welfare institutions. Unfortunately, since priests were French-trained and educated, and the church had prospered under colonial benevolence, it was often identified with French interests. Many ardent Buddhists saw the Catholics as quislings and surrogates for French domination. One folk saying epitomized this attitude: "Vietnamese Catholics are the claws by which the French crab has crawled across our land." While the militant Buddhists and the Communists attempted to paint the Catholics as French stooges, both the local church and its lay people were ardent Nationalists and hence virulently anti-communist.

Catholics in South Vietnam were led by Archbishop Nguyen Van Binh. Moderate in tone, he was widely respected, even by most Buddhists. Binh was quietly critical of Diem but a staunch supporter of future governments. The Catholics, while ostensibly more unified than the Buddhists, also had regional fissures. Father Hoang Quynh was the best-known representative of the roughly eight hundred thousand northern Catholics who had fled to the south. In North Vietnam, Quynh had commanded the famous Phat Diem district self-defense militia that had held off Communist forces for years. After the Geneva Accords, Quynh had led his people south, eventually settling his parish in Saigon, where he grew close to Diem. The threat posed by the militant Buddhists in 1965 prodded Quynh to form the "Greater Solidarity Force" (GSF), which eventually transmuted into a Catholic political party called the *Nhan Xa*. Quynh became an outspoken political leader, and the

GSF gave him a platform from which he demanded military victory over the Communists. Lastly, there was a small but vocal group of antiwar, left-wing Catholic priests, whose ranks grew as the war progressed.

The other significant religions in South Vietnam were the Cao Dai and the Hoa Hao. The Cao Dai faith was formally established in the city of Tay Ninh in 1926. Despite an unusual polytheism of beliefs, the religion quickly gained adherents and dominated the area along the Cambodian-Vietnamese border west of Saigon. The Cao Dai formed a large militia, but Diem was able to co-opt the church leadership into joining his government.

The Hoa Hao was a Buddhist revival movement formed by Huynh Phu So in 1939 in the western provinces of Chau Doc and An Giang in the Mekong Delta. Considered a prophet by his followers, he was both anti-French and anti–Viet Minh. After the momentous events of September 2, 1945, in Hanoi, and given the growing Communist political influence, on September 9, Huynh Phu So attempted to drive the Viet Minh out of Can Tho, the capital of the Mekong Delta. Without adequate weapons or military training, the Viet Minh slaughtered them. Realizing that the Hoa Hao would not cooperate, the Viet Minh captured and executed Huynh Phu So on April 16, 1947.[43]

The killing of their leader put the sect permanently at odds with the Communists. Like other Vietnamese groups, the death of its leader divided the Hoa Hao. Two branches formed, but the differences were never about religion but the usual culprits of personality and politics. Although fiercely anti-communist, the Hoa Hao refused to integrate with a Saigon-based government. The French had formed a Hoa Hao militia, but to extend his control over the country, Diem sent his troops in 1956 to destroy the Hoa Hao irregulars. With no recourse, the church reluctantly paid fealty to Saigon, and soon the main Hoa Hao provinces of Chau Doc and An Giang were almost completely free of Communist influence. As the war dragged on, however, the old Hoa Hao desire for autonomy resurrected itself, and in 1974, the church and Thieu's government spared over a desire for its own self-defense force. For the most part, though, the Hoa Hao saw the GVN as a bulwark protecting their lands against the Communists.

ETHNIC DIVISIONS

Ethnicity also played an important national role. The most significant minorities in South Vietnam were the Khmer (Cambodians), concentrated in the Delta; the Chinese, of which about seven hundred thousand of the approximately one million were entrenched in the Saigon and Cholon areas; and the mountain people in the Central Highlands called Montagnards. A million Montagnards—some linguistically Malayo-Polynesian, some Mon Khmer—were divided into roughly thirty-five different tribes and tribal sub-groups. They lived a semi-nomadic existence in the forests, mountains, and plateaus of Central Vietnam.

The Vietnamese discriminated against all three, aggravating the ethnic hatred between the groups. The Khmer, descendants of a Cambodian empire that once covered the Delta, were often denied promotions in the military and the civil service. The Montagnards were generally considered little more than savages whose lands and timber were there for the taking.

Given the long dominance of China over Vietnam, the most intense ethnic animus was between these two. Part of the Chinese empire for a millennium, often there was violent opposition to Chinese rule yet a great deal of cultural sharing. Of all the minorities in South Vietnam, the Chinese held the greatest sway. Commerce was the reason, and like other overseas Chinese communities who dominated the markets of Southeast Asian counties, Vietnam was no different. The French brought in Chinese laborers and allowed the Chinese to maintain their preexisting commercial networks, especially in the rice trade in South Vietnam.

The eventual withdrawal of most French mercantile interests left commercial activities largely in Chinese hands. Most Vietnamese businesspersons and government officials resented this Chinese supremacy, and the desire to curb Chinese economic influence through legislation grew over time. So enormous was the Chinese business presence and their influence over the Vietnamese economy that Diem passed several anti-Chinese business laws. For example, new rice mills could only have Vietnamese owners. The GVN had to be careful, though, as it could not risk its ties with Taiwan and Singapore over undue repression of Chinese business dealings. While most Chinese eked out a subsistence living as laborers or small shopkeepers, about two dozen families dominated local industry. Seven to ten families controlled the bulk of the rice trade, while others ruled the textile industry, export and imports, and non–bank lending. These families often served as the major corrupting influences on Vietnamese government and police officials, one of the seamy untold stories of venality in South Vietnam. In turn, they were often strong-armed by Vietnamese politicians for financial donations, ranging from funding for political parties to civic projects.

REGIONAL RIVALRY

The most pernicious factionalism was regionalism. As the Vietnamese engaged in the "March to the South" (*nam tien*), many internal Vietnamese conflicts were region-based, particularly between the Trinh lords of the north and the Nguyen Dynasty based in Hue. *Nam tien* was essentially Vietnam's colonial expansion southward, and it sparked civil wars in the seventeenth and eighteenth centuries, and one might argue, again in 1945. The rugged geography spawned dialect and cultural differences between the areas, as did judgments about personality traits. Northerners (*Bac Ky*) looked down on southerners (*Nam Ky*) as easygoing and somewhat lazy, while the southerners considered the northerners aggressive and pushy. Central Vietnamese, particularly from the imperial capital in Hue, saw themselves as Vietnam's rightful leaders and resented either region's efforts to rule them. The French exploited these bitter rivalries and aggravated them by creating the three regional divisions of Vietnam. Thus, when almost a million northerners fled south after the Geneva Accords, many of the southern elite, particularly those schooled in a French-run *lycee*, resented the dominance of northern and Central Vietnamese within the South Vietnamese military and the government.

In reviewing the score card of political factions, religious schisms, regional hatred, and ethnic bigotry, many rightfully saw the Nationalists' fragmentation, compared to the monolithic Communists, as South Vietnam's greatest weakness, one that might well lead to its destruction. After the great powers, Hanoi, and Paris concluded the Geneva Accords that split the country into two halves, the one in the north controlled by Ho Chi Minh built a stable governing structure. They developed an impressive army and won the allegiance of most of the population. Bao Dai's government in the south barely extended beyond Saigon, had a weak and dispirited army, and still had to deal with the remaining French. The former emperor needed someone to help him rule, and he found a new leader in Ngo Dinh Diem. Here then begins our main story.

2

"IF THE ARMY WAS WEAK, THE REGIME WOULD BECOME WEAK"

The Struggle for Supremacy

S hortly before the signing of the Geneva Accords, on July 7, 1954, Bao Dai appointed Ngo Dinh Diem as his new prime minister. Born on January 3, 1901, Diem was in many ways a Shakespearean hero: a man whose faults—over-reliance on his divisive brothers for one—eventually overshadowed his laudable qualities and led to his demise. Early in his tenure, Diem exhibited impressive leadership. A fervent Catholic, a strong anti-colonialist and anti-communist, he was incorruptible, hardworking, and devoted to Vietnam. During the First Republic of Vietnam's developmental period, by sheer will, courage, and a monastic lifestyle that endeared him to his people, Diem stitched a cacophonous mess into a viable country.

His political and economic visions for South Vietnam, however, was a hoary combination of new development models grafted onto old Vietnamese cultural traditions. Diem's exposure to the West provided a veneer of democratic idealism, but his "background and behavior were heavily imbued with the character of Confucian education."[1] Diem scholar Edward Miller writes that "Diem's thinking about politics and society was defined above all by his determination to fashion a new vision of how Vietnam might become a modern nation. This vision was an ambitious attempt to synthesize certain contemporary ideas and discourses about Catholic Christianity, Confucianism, and Vietnamese national identity."[2]

On the other hand, the major Communist rallying cries were unification and demands for land reform. They appealed to Vietnamese xenophobia to cast out all foreigners, painted South Vietnamese officials as "puppets" of the Americans, and played up grievances against Saigon's policies and actions. To win the people's allegiance against the Communists, Diem sought to articulate a political philosophy that was distinct from Communism. Yet he never completely endorsed the concepts of democracy, personal freedom, and capitalism, thereby undermining the foundational ideas that Americans believed were fundamental to defeating Marxism. Diem thought they were inappropriate to Vietnam at this stage in its development, especially while facing a ruthless foe. Instead, Diem tendered his obtuse canon of Personalism, but few Vietnamese understood the doctrine. His critics charged that he had simply implemented a family-run dictatorship, one that was leading South Vietnam to defeat. Eventually, the struggle to define South Vietnam's political philosophy would end in bloodshed.

KICKING OUT THE FRENCH

Once he was appointed prime minister, Diem immediately sought to remove French interference in South Vietnam's affairs. First, he needed to gain control of the army, which remained under French command, an effort that instantly proved problematic. In 1954, Lieutenant General Nguyen Van Hinh led the VNA. While ethnically Vietnamese, Hinh was a French citizen and a French military officer. On March 8, 1952, Hinh was named the first chief of staff of the VNA, and in June 1953, he was promoted to lieutenant general. Since its inception in 1948, the VNA had grown considerably. Reaching a peak strength in June 1954 of 219,000 troops, it included 175 infantry battalions and nine Mobile Groups (basically a regiment). While the army was poorly trained and motivated, it was the principal functioning authority for an emerging South Vietnam.

As a French officer, Hinh resisted Diem's moves to gain control of the military. Many Vietnamese saw his defiance as a last desperate French attempt to maintain control over the southern part of the country, a label that would haunt people and events for years. Yet Hinh was not simply a French tool; he judged that South Vietnam could not survive without strong leadership. Hinh saw Diem as a civilian outsider who did not possess the necessary skills to lead the country. Only the military, Hinh believed, could properly lead South Vietnam in its struggle against the Communists.

According to Ton That Dinh, "In Hinh's opinion, the current government headed by Prime Minister Diem could not respond to the demands of the times...for that reason, he believed that the time had come for the army to take control of the government."[3] Many VNA officers shared Hinh's attitude that only the military could effectively steer the government and win the war against the Communists.

At the same time, Nguyen Van Chau, a VNA officer in Hue and a fervent supporter of Diem and his brother, Ngo Dinh Nhu, was organizing the first cells of the clandestine Can Lao Party, a covert political organization within the military that was loyal only to Diem. According to Chau, "During the last two years of the Franco-Vietnamese war, many sub-cells of the Can Lao Party were established in units of the newly formed Vietnamese Army and in the governmental apparatus in Central Vietnam, especially in Hue and Nha Trang. In 1954, Ngo Dinh Nhu formed the Can Lao Party in Hue to unify all the old and new comrades and supporters of Diem."[4]

Another part of Hinh's rationale for deposing Diem was that these Can Lao cells posed a direct challenge to his authority and the chain of command. Hinh was correct, and when he defied Diem, many VNA commanders from Central Vietnam, subverted by the Can Lao, backed Diem. The CIA reported that only 20 percent of VNA officers supported Hinh, 20 percent were anti-Hinh, and the rest were neutral.[5] With Hinh refusing to obey Diem's orders, on September 11, 1954, Diem relieved him and ordered him to take a six-month leave in France. Hinh refused and formed his own political party within the military called the Eagle Party. Believing he had French support, along with that of the Cao Dai and Hoa Hao religious sects, he threatened Diem with a coup. When the U.S. backed Diem, and the French refused to aid him, Hinh capitulated and left Vietnam in November for France.[6] Diem had survived his first crisis with his military. He too believed that Hinh was a French stalking horse to retain power, and he had risked the overthrow of his government rather than accept that outcome.

Throughout the Hinh crisis, Nguyen Van Thieu had remained in Hue on the 2nd Military Region staff. Tran Ngoc Chau, an officer also assigned to the 2nd Military Region and a close family friend of Thieu's who became a cause célèbre in 1970, confirms that Thieu and Tran Thien Khiem "were firmly in Hinh's camp."[7] One VNA officer who worked on the 2nd Military Region staff at this time and later became an ARVN lieutenant general, corroborates that Thieu and Khiem "wore [Hinh's] eagle emblem on their shirts."[8] When Hinh's coup attempt collapsed, Thieu found himself in deep political trouble: "After General Hinh was forced out of Vietnam, Major Thieu and his group were brought down to Saigon for investigation and questioning. To escape from the suspicious gaze of the Diem regime, Thieu took advantage of the Catholic connections of his wife's family."[9] This was Thieu's first significant brush with Vietnamese politics, one in which he chose the wrong side. A summons to Saigon and an investigation of his political leanings was career-threatening, and it probably accounts for some of his later caution in political matters.

Adding to Diem's suspicion, Thieu and his older brother Kieu belonged to the Dai Viet Party, a rival Nationalist party that both Diem and Nhu feared as a competitor to their Can Lao organization. During their time together on the 2nd Military Region staff, Thieu and Khiem had dabbled in Dai Viet politics. Although Ha Thuc Ky, a senior leader of the Dai Viets, would later claim that both men were initiated into the party in a ceremony in early February 1964, Khiem denies it.[10] He says "Ha Thuc Ky did take me to some Dai Viet activities in 1964, but he did not induct me. Thieu and I joined the Dai Viets around 1952." Khiem states, "Although I was in the French army, it was just a job. I was not joining the Viet Minh, and there was only the French-controlled army. So I secretly worked with the Dai Viets as the only plausible organization that was Nationalist and anti-French but non-communist."[11]

Thieu survived his clash with the Ngos but he was assigned to an unimportant position. In March 1955, he was sent to command the National Military Academy at Dalat. In October, he was promoted to lieutenant colonel. Putting him in Dalat kept Thieu out of Saigon politics and without troops to command. He remained at the academy for the next four years, building the school into a major institution.

With the failure of the Hinh coup, the French turned power over to Diem. After the French departed, to create a new identity and revoke its French roots, on October 16, 1955, the VNA changed its name to the Army of the Republic of Vietnam, or ARVN (*Quan Luc Viet Nam Cong Hoa*). After Diem organized a national referendum that elected him head of state and deposed Bao Dai, Diem quickly declared the first Republic of Vietnam on October 26. Now in complete control, Diem needed competent officers he could trust to command the military, and he began testing ones who had uncertain loyalties. Joining the Can Lao Party was a key hurdle for men like Thieu and Khiem to gain Diem's trust.

Khiem had also been a member of Hinh's clique. After Hinh's departure for France, Khiem, like Thieu, was summoned to Saigon for investigation by a military court. He escaped penalty when Huynh Van Lang, a senior Can Lao organizer, and a close associate of Nhu, interceded. Lang needed Khiem's help building the Can Lao Party among southern-born officers.[12] Khiem agreed, and he later admitted to U.S. officials that "he had been one of those charged by Diem with organizing Can Lao Party branches within the military."[13] While many believed Khiem had converted to Catholicism, he did not, but he "had been drawn to Catholicism since childhood."[14] This ability to straddle the religious fence enabled Khiem to draw close to the president.

Born in Saigon on December 15, 1925, Khiem's parents were land-owners from Long An, a province immediately south of Saigon. While his family were Buddhists, he attended and graduated from the respected Lycee Petrus Ky (a Catholic Vietnamese high school patterned on the French curriculum) at the end of World War II. Sometime in 1946, Khiem joined the French Colonial Army and participated in the first and only officer training class at the *Ecole Militaire d'Extrême Orient* in Dalat.[15] Khiem graduated on July 1, 1947, after which he and three other students promptly deserted and joined the Viet Minh in the northern section of the Mekong Delta. Like Thieu, Khiem did not last long with the maquis. After four months, he returned to Saigon and rejoined the colonial army.

Khiem's short sojourn with the Viet Minh, however, created long lasting consequences. According to one South Vietnamese source, the Viet Minh cadres who welcomed Khiem's group was Pham Ngoc Thao.[16] Thao was then chief of the DRV's Cochinchina Secret Intelligence Office. Although Thao later rallied to the Nationalist cause in 1954, he secretly remained committed to the DRV. Politburo member Vo Van Kiet states that the future leader of North Vietnam, Le Duan, had personally ordered Thao "to stay behind in South Vietnam as a strategic intelligence agent, not to supply information but instead to worm his way deeply into the senior ranks of the Saigon government to manipulate events in order to prepare for the reunification of our nation."[17] He accomplished this assignment by befriending important Nationalists such as Khiem, Nguyen Khanh, and Archbishop Ngo Dinh Thuc, Diem's older brother.

Thieu, though, had rejected the Can Lao. Thieu's wife claims that her husband had told her that he "wanted to succeed and be recognized for my ability, not because I had joined a party."[18] Yet as Thieu sat in Dalat, his career stalled, far from the upper tier of the army's leadership, he could only watch as Khiem surpassed him. For example, Khiem was promoted to colonel in August 1957 and served on the Joint General Staff. On March 17, 1958, he was given command of the 4th Field Division, the predecessor to the 7th ARVN Division.

This may have been the triggering event for Thieu. According to one journalist, Thieu had "postponed his baptism as a Catholic for years after his wife had converted him because he had not wished to seem to be currying favor with the president."[19] Yet with Diem entrenched in power, and with Thieu watching others being promoted, he finally relented. On November 11, 1958, in Dalat, Thieu was baptized into the Catholic Church and concurrently joined the Can Lao. The person who baptized him and welcomed him into the party was Father Nguyen Phuc Buu Duong, a well-known priest and perhaps more importantly, one of the chief theoreticians of the Can Lao Party. Not coincidentally, within four months Thieu turned command of the academy over to another competent but anti-Diem officer, Major General Le Van Kim.[20] Thieu had succumbed to the realization that to advance in the army, he needed to prove his loyalty, and the best way to accomplish that was to join Diem's party and religion.

Meanwhile, Diem continued to consolidate his power. After the Hinh escapade, he convinced the Cao Dai sect to join his government. Afterward, Diem sent several Airborne battalions to oust the Binh Xuyen, a semi-criminal outfit that controlled parts of Saigon. The Binh Xuyen were quickly routed. Diem next turned his attention to the Hoa Hao in the Delta. Brigadier General Duong Van Minh led the campaign that easily defeated the sect's militia.

By defeating the Hoa Hao, Duong Van Minh became Diem's favorite officer. Known as "Big Minh" because he stood much taller than most Vietnamese, Minh would become one of the most important figures in South Vietnamese history. He was born on February 19, 1916, in what became Long An Province. He graduated in 1936 from a French school in Saigon and joined the French colonial army in January 1940 as an enlisted man. He then attended a military school and was commissioned as a second lieutenant in October 1942. After the Japanese coup of March 1945, Minh fought with the French colonial forces against the Japanese. He was captured, probably in July, and he and Diem's future prime minister, Nguyen Ngoc Tho, were imprisoned together in Saigon for a month. The Japanese beat Minh severely, knocking out all but one of his front teeth.[21] The two men bonded over their shared prison ordeal, and their close relationship would be important after the Diem coup. Promotions soon followed, and by 1957, Minh was a major general. However, he resisted Diem's entreaties to convert to Catholicism or join the Can Lao, and he slowly began to fall out of favor. In 1959, he was placed in charge of the Army Field Command, a newly created position that existed in name only. Shunted aside, Minh's career was now in a holding pattern,

Thieu's assignment after Dalat was chief of staff to Major General Minh. He was promoted to colonel on October 26, 1959. According to one of Minh's U.S. advisers, "Thieu had great loyalty to the general, and Minh thought very highly of [Thieu's] capabilities as a soldier."[22] This close relationship would be crucial in Minh's recruitment of Thieu for the coup against Diem. While Thieu's career was still mired, the outbreak of war would provide him the opportunity for rapid career advancement.

A NEW WAR

With most of his challengers either co-opted or defeated, Diem turned his attention to both building the country and defeating the remaining Communist infrastructure in South Vietnam. His forces scoured the countryside, killing thousands of Communist cadres. This period of the late 1950s became one of the most difficult times for the Communists, and they decided to fight back. In January 1960, Communist forces in South Vietnam resumed the armed struggle.

They struck their first blow by sparking a rebellion in Ben Tre Province (called Kien Hoa by the government) that overran a few police posts and shot some government officials. The Ben Tre uprising is often considered the opening of the war in South Vietnam. Later that month, Communist forces mounted their first major assault by attacking the base camp of the 32nd Regiment, 21st ARVN Division in Tay Ninh Province.[23] On January 26, 1960, Communist forces took advantage of the Tet holiday when many ARVN soldiers were celebrating. Striking hard, they killed forty soldiers and absconded with six hundred weapons, a major haul. The debacle caused some senior commanders, such as Brigadier General Tran Van Don, to question Diem's policy of sowing Can Lao officers within the military. Don explains:

after reviewing the incident, we decided that this defeat had been caused by weak commanders and the fact that the Can Lao Party had placed

officers who were party members in important command positions
for which they were not qualified. These problems would continue to
weaken the army, and if the army were weak, the regime would become
weak, and the entire nation would become weak. We began to monitor
the activities of the Ngo brothers from that moment on.[24]

Don's assessment was correct. Officers with real war records who were
passed over for command became infuriated as they watched the spectacular
ascent of men like Lieutenant Colonel Tran Thanh Chieu, who commanded
the 21st Division during the defeat. A Diem loyalist with limited combat
experience, Chieu was handed this plum assignment because he had known
Diem from an early age, was from Central Vietnam, and had converted to
Catholicism. Do Mau, while a known anti-Catholic, claims that this overt
promotion of Catholic officers alongside the disillusionment from Can Lao
meddling, played a key role in the military's discontent. Mau says that when
Diem first assumed power in 1954, "The number of field-grade Catholic officers was small, as few as leaves on a tree in autumn. Diem and his brothers
had to rapidly promote Catholic officers and place them in important positions.... The policy of 'Catholicizing' the army caused great dissatisfaction
within the officer corps, and that was one reason for the series of mutinies
and attempted coups that took place between 1960 and 1963."[25]

Diem, though, was not blind to the defects of a promotion policy based
solely upon such limited criteria. He did boost the careers of several officers
who had not joined the Can Lao or converted religions. Tran Van Don is
one example. Don was a French citizen who had served in the French army.
He was Hinh's chief of staff at the Joint General Staff, where he remained
until he became commander of the 2nd Military Region on October 15,
1957.[26] Nor did Diem ignore military failures. Despite the internal grumbling over his promotion policies, one of Diem's first moves was sending
Khiem to replace Chieu as commander of the 21st Division. It would prove
judicious.

THE NOVEMBER 1960 COUP

The military's dissatisfaction with Diem erupted in Saigon at 3:00 A.M.,
November 11, 1960. More a poorly planned mutiny than an army-wide
insurrection, several army units revolted against him. That some of South
Vietnam's most elite units led the rebellion was a serious indicator of

military frustration. These included the Airborne Brigade, part of the 3rd Marine Battalion, and the newly formed Ranger Group. Just how much the enlisted troops or even the junior officers understood their actions or even supported a coup remains open to question, but the commanders of these units certainly did.

Most authors report that Colonel Nguyen Chanh Thi, the Airborne Brigade commander, led the takeover, but that is incorrect.[27] The main plotter was Lieutenant Colonel Vuong Van Dong, then director of the War College's Staff Training Faculty. Another was Major Pham Van Lieu, a close friend of Thi. According to an officer involved in the coup planning, "It was organized at the War College by mostly northerner officers, a few of whom like me were Dai Viet. Because we had refused to join the Can Lao, we had been moved out of troop commands. South Vietnam had become a family dictatorship, and we were against the Can Lao interfering in the army. We used the Airborne to conduct the coup, but Thi was not involved in the planning."[28]

The Airborne attacked the palace that morning, but the Presidential Guard unit repulsed the first assault. Some heavy firing continued, and then both sides began to negotiate. After failing to capture the palace, Dong and Lieu brought Thi into the coup attempt. Convincing him was not difficult. Thi, although born near Hue, was another senior officer who had grown disillusioned with Diem. While he was initially close to the president, he detested Nhu and hated Can Lao interference in the military. More important, Thi came from a poor, intensely Buddhist family and hence had little in common with the rigidly Catholic Ngos. A paratrooper most of his career, he was known as a brave, tough, soldier, but one given to emotional eruptions and political naïve. Now faced with condemning his beloved paratroopers or joining the rebellion, Thi sided with his troops. His appearance later that day heartened his men, but it was too late. Stalling tactics by the brothers enabled them to rally loyal forces.

When the attack first began, Brigadier General Nguyen Khanh was in Saigon after having recently relinquished command of the Mekong Delta military region to Colonel Tran Thien Khiem. Khanh, the future prime minister, was born on November 8, 1927, in Vinh Binh Province in the Mekong Delta. He joined the Viet Minh at the close of World War II and worked for them for about one year. He left them and joined the French army, graduating from the same French-run military school in Dalat in July 1947 with Khiem. He then attended the staff school in Hanoi in 1952 with Thieu. A superb troop commander, in December 1953 he was given command of the 11th Mobile Group, a prestigious assignment. Khanh and his unit saw heavy fighting until the signing of the Geneva Accords. Diem liked the combative southerner, especially after Khanh joined the Can Lao in 1955. Diem promoted Khanh to colonel and assigned him to lead the 1st Field Division. In March 1960, he assumed command of the Delta and was promoted to brigadier general in May.[29]

Khanh climbed a palace fence and joined Diem inside. Khanh worked the phones, contacting several commanders, including Khiem, who brought his troops to Saigon and "established a Capital Liberation Corps which effectively thwarted the coup attempt and relieved the siege of Independence Palace."[30] Dong, Thi, Lieu, and a dozen other coup officers commandeered an Air Force C-47 and flew off into exile in Phnom Penh, Cambodia's capital. Khiem and Khanh were hailed as national heroes.

Much like the Hinh affair, the failed 1960 military insurrection left profound scars both on Diem and South Vietnam's military. An enraged Diem arrested the wives of the officers who had escaped to Cambodia and threatened to execute them if their husbands did not return and face justice. The men refused. The wife of the Marine battalion commander said, "We were held incommunicado for six months at the intelligence headquarters. They kept us all day in the hot sun in a shed with a tin roof, sweating terribly. Several women, including Mrs. Nguyen Chanh Thi, divorced their husbands to escape the punishment."[31]

U.S. Embassy Rural Affairs chief Rufus Phillips confirmed that the rebellion "further isolated Diem from a number of key Vietnamese civilians and military officers who had been his supporters. Nhu, with his paranoid cast of mind, concluded that many of them had secretly supported the coup."[32] Loyalty now became paramount. Uncertain as to whom he could trust, Diem marginalized some senior officers and arrested several opposition figures. One key miscalculation was the handling of Major General Le Van Kim. During the mutiny, Dong had issued a proclamation listing Kim as the new prime minister. Dong and Kim knew each other from their joint attendance at the U.S. Command and General Staff College in 1958, but Kim was not involved. Regardless, Diem sent Brigadier General Ton That Dinh to Dalat to arrest Kim. Asking permission to collect a few personal belongings, Kim returned home and called Nhu, setting in motion a series of events that eventually led to the brother's deaths.

Family and school ties were always critical in Vietnam, especially among military officers. Kim had married Tran Van Don's younger sister, and her parents owned a house in Dalat near Bao Dai's home. Don's parents were friends with the parents of Tran Le Xuan, the woman who in 1943 had married Ngo Dinh Nhu. Madame Nhu's mother was a cousin of Bao Dai, and in the spring of 1947 the Nhu's moved to Dalat and stayed with the Kim's, where the families became close companions. Madame Nhu spent considerable time with Bao Dai, a relationship that helped the former emperor choose Diem as his prime minister.

Fearing that the volatile Dinh might kill him, Kim phoned Nhu and asked to come to Saigon to deny his involvement. Nhu relented and sent a plane to Dalat to pick him up. Although cleared, Kim's treatment solidified his anti-Diem stand. Kim was then assigned to Saigon as a special assistant to Major General Duong Van Minh, who remained idle as head of the Army Field Command. The two men and their families became close, and both often took the opportunity to visit Kim's brother-in-law Tran Van Don, then commander of I Corps. When Don was cashiered as commander of I Corps and returned to Saigon, the three men and their families became even more tightknit. Thus, Nhu's old family friendship with Kim inadvertently brought together the men who would lead the coup that would kill the brothers.

Don, another critical figure in South Vietnamese history, was born on August 17, 1917, in France, where his father served as a medical doctor with the French army. His family was closely tied to French interests, and Don attended the prestigious Lycee Chasseloup-Laubat in Saigon, the best secondary school in South Vietnam. Don was studying in Paris when World War II broke out, and he joined the French army. After release from German captivity, he went to Indochina and served with the Vichy French government until it was overthrown by the Japanese. Afterward, he served in a variety of roles, and by August 1953, he was a colonel in the VNA and the chief of staff for Lieutenant General Hinh. Don remained neutral in the fight between Hinh and Diem, and he survived that conflict. Don also directed some of the forces that drove the Binh Xuyen out of Saigon, and Diem promoted him to brigadier general for his loyalty and devotion to duty.[33]

Besides linking Kim, Minh, and Don, another effect of the coup was the souring of Diem's relationship with the Americans. The coup was driven by growing military discontent with Diem, but the presence of American officers near the conspirators and the U.S. ambassador's obvious reluctance to support Diem generated the typical suspicions that the Americans were involved. Diem and Nhu became even more resistant to U.S. advice, a situation that clouded relations and helped generate the terrible events of 1963.

The November coup also directly influenced Communist plans. North Vietnam held its Third Party Congress in Hanoi in September 1960. At this major conference, the Politburo had created a new front organization that would bind together all the anti-Diem forces into the *Mat Tran Giai Phong Mien Nam Viet Nam* (South Vietnam National Liberation Front, or NLF). Organizing the Front would hide Hanoi's hand in the war. The coup attempt convinced the Politburo to speed up the formation of the NLF:

> We must present the Liberation Front to the public immediately, without waiting to determine the personalities who will make it up....The weakness of our movement in South Vietnam over the past several years has been that we have not been able to attract widespread support of the anti-Diem elements among the upper classes, that we have not been able to form a united Front with elements opposed to the U.S. and Diem, and that we have not had a name to use in public to appeal to the population and to use in our strategy to sow division and isolate Diem. This is a favorable opportunity for us to correct that weakness in our movement by forming the Liberation Front for South Vietnam.[34]

The 1960 coup attempt also created deep divisions among South Vietnamese officers that rebounded in the tumultuous events of 1963 and 1964. For example, the treatment of Nguyen Chanh Thi and Pham Van Lieu in Cambodia would echo years later. Shortly after Thi and Lieu arrived in Phnom Penh, Cambodian intelligence asked them to provide information on ARVN troop dispositions. Both men refused. They were tossed in jail, where they languished for over a year. After their release, they lived in poverty. Vuong Van Dong, however, enjoyed greater freedom, and after two years in Cambodia he went to France. According to Thi, "After going to France, Dong worked for the gang of pro-French politicians like Tran Dinh Lan and Nguyen Van Vy."[35] An angry Thi nursed a grudge that would erupt in January 1964. Years later, Dong denied any French involvement in the coup or that he was pro-French, but he did eventually join other Vietnamese exiles in Paris who advocated neutralizing South Vietnam.[36]

Dong was not the only enemy the 1960 coup created for Thi. Suppressing the coup created hatred between Thi and Khiem. Yet the 1960 upheaval also reinforced connections that deeply affected later events. The relationship between Khanh and Khiem, first formed in 1947 when they attended officer school at Dalat, grew stronger and would bear fruit in the coup of January 30, 1964. Khanh's reward for his actions during the November 1960 coup attempt was a new role as chief of staff of the Joint General Staff (JGS), the South Vietnamese military command. Khiem also continued his meteoric rise in the army. On December 20, 1962, he was promoted to major general, replacing Khanh as chief of staff when Khanh was assigned to command of II Corps. With Khanh and Khiem in the Diem camp in 1960 was Ton That Dinh. After the 1960 coup, Dinh became the commander of III Corps, the military area encompassing the provinces surrounding Saigon.

Thieu had also remained loyal to the president. This support finally earned Diem's trust, and on October 1, 1961, Thieu was given command of the 1st Division in Hue. Thieu replaced the energetic Colonel Nguyen Duc Thang, who moved to take command of the 5th Division, then stationed at Bien Hoa, a town just northeast of Saigon. While far from Saigon, the 1st Division was an important command. Long considered the best of the regular ARVN units, the division defended the Demilitarized Zone (DMZ) between North and South Vietnam and the two northernmost provinces in South Vietnam, Quang Tri and Thua Thien. This area abutted Laos and the main infiltration routes into South Vietnam. Apparently, Thieu's time as 1st Division commander was successful, for on December 20, 1962, he assumed command of the 5th Division.

If the 1st Division was an important military command, the 5th was a critical post with political overtones. As the closest major unit to the capital, only one of Diem's most trusted officers would have been given control of the 5th Division. Yet during this time, there was a growing chorus of dissent in the army about the Ngo brothers. Those who had been firmly in Diem's camp during the 1960 coup effort—Khanh, Khiem, and Ton That Dinh—had now merged with Don, Minh, and Kim in their anti-Diem attitudes.

Given simmering military frustration with the Ngo brothers, another effort was predictable. Consequently, on February 27, 1962, two Vietnamese Air Force (VNAF) pilots, Nguyen Van Cu and Pham Phu Quoc, took off at 7:00 a.m. from Bien Hoa Air Base outside Saigon. Cu was the son of a prominent political leader whom Diem had briefly imprisoned for "anti-government activities," while Quoc believed that the president was a dictator. Taking off, they immediately flew their airplanes toward Diem's Gia Long Palace, intending to kill the brothers. The first bomb smashed into a room where Diem was reading but did not explode, enabling him to escape. After dropping more ordnance and severely damaging one wing of the palace, the planes turned away. Cu flew to Cambodia and was granted asylum, but Quoc was hit by antiaircraft fire from Vietnamese Navy ships and crashed into the Saigon River, where he was rescued. Diem's response was predictable; he blamed the U.S. media for the incident, promptly tightened restrictions on his own press, and cracked down further on political dissidents.[37] However, while discontent within the military over the brothers' authoritarianism continued to increase, given a combination of new U.S. military technology, expansion of American advisers to ARVN units, and the new strategic hamlet program, dissension would remain muted, for now.

CRISIS AFTER CRISIS: THE BATTLE OF AP BAC AND THE BUDDHISTS

1963 began with a surge in optimism about the war. Deliveries of new U.S. equipment in 1962, including armored personnel carriers, enabled the ARVN to form two mechanized infantry companies. One company was assigned to the 7th Division, which patrolled the area south of Saigon. The division's 7th Mechanized Company quickly proved its mettle in battle. Commanded by Captain Ly Tong Ba, this new unit inflicted several major defeats on NLF forces.[38] Additionally, the U.S. began supplying helicopters for use in rapidly ferrying troops across the Mekong Delta's marshy terrain. These two technological advantages gave ARVN forces superior mobility and firepower over enemy units.

Given these setbacks, NLF commanders sought to counter the new weapons by changing tactics. Instead of their normal pattern of fleeing at first contact, they decided to prepare strong defensive positions and lure ARVN forces into a trap to inflict heavy casualties, which they could then turn into a propaganda victory. An NLF force totaling approximately 350 men was assembled at Ap Bac, a hamlet adjacent to the Plain of Reeds in the upper Delta. The NLF troops built solid fortifications and prepared kill zones in likely helicopter landing spots. When U.S. intelligence picked up NLF radio chatter from the area, the ARVN was ordered to destroy the enemy.

Brigadier General Huynh Van Cao, who had replaced Khiem as commander of IV Corps in late December 1962, mustered a multi-battalion task force.[39] A Catholic born in Hue, Cao joined the Can Lao Party and had supported Diem over Hinh in 1954. He became commander of Diem's personal bodyguard unit and was close to the brothers. In January 1959, he was named commander of the 7th Division. He did well, and hence was given command of IV Corps. However, like many ARVN officers, he did not have the training to handle the difficulties of corps command.

Despite possessing numerical superiority, harsh weather and poor command prevented Cao from coordinating his attack prongs. Surprised by the unexpected defensive stand, the South Vietnamese lost eighty men at Ap Bac. Three U.S. soldiers were also killed, and several helicopters were shot down. Enemy losses were unknown. Unfortunately, the American press, which had grown highly critical of Diem's regime, transformed a tactical setback into a major defeat by proclaiming that the battle had exposed gross ARVN incompetency.[40] The Communists also used the victory to proclaim they were winning, and to improve the morale of their own forces.

Soon after the well-publicized Ap Bac defeat, long-simmering religious tensions in South Vietnam suddenly erupted in Hue. Strains had first begun in the city when Diem's older brother, Ngo Dinh Thuc, was appointed in 1960 as archbishop of the old imperial capital. A strict Catholic, Thuc's ill-concealed derogatory attitude toward Buddhism in the religion's stronghold of Central Vietnam was a field of dry grass waiting for something incendiary. The match was lit in early May 1963, when Catholic organizations in Hue flew flags and banners commemorating Thuc's twenty-fifth anniversary as a bishop. Attempting to prevent religious strife, on May 6, Diem enforced a long-standing regulation banning outdoor flag flying by non government entities. Unfortunately, his effort backfired when Buddhist activists, who had planned a celebration of Vesak Day, a commemoration of the Buddha's birth and life, defied the injunction. On May 7, thousands of Buddhist flags sprang up in Hue, only to be torn down by the police at Thuc's urging. Hundreds of protesters gathered at the Hue radio station the next day. Egged on by a fiery speech from a bonze named Thich Tri Quang, who claimed Diem's prohibition was an example of religious persecution, they demanded that the government permit Quang to air his grievances over the radio.[41] The station director refused, and the crowd grew restless. Local authorities attempted unsuccessfully to disperse the throng using fire hoses. Soldiers soon arrived. Suddenly an explosion occurred in the crowd, killing several. Reacting to the tumult, the troops opened fire. Nine civilians died, and another fourteen were wounded.

The radio station massacre marked a watershed for Diem. Most scholars cite Catholic repression as the rationale for the Buddhist revolt, but the Buddhists themselves point to an earlier revival movement as the chief driver. Begun in the 1930s to counter colonialism and Western culture, the Vietnamese *Sangha* (community) "launched a campaign to reform the religion…into an engaged Buddhism" that used social activism and concern for injustice to fight the French colonialists.[42] The Buddhists sought a "middle way" between the alien philosophies of Marxist totalitarianism and democratic capitalism. Buddhist temples soon became a clandestine rendezvous for anti colonial forces, leading the French to craft Ordinance 10, which classified the Buddhist church as an "association." Only the Catholic Church was an officially recognized religion, giving the Buddhists a huge rallying cry of discrimination.

Others attribute the discord to NLF proxies, suspecting that Tri Quang was a Communist *agent provocateur*. No evidence, however, has emerged to confirm that allegation, and Quang was placed under house arrest after the fall of South Vietnam. That, however, was not absolution; many undercover cadres were forced to spend time in reeducation camps to stamp out any corrosive Western attributes they may have acquired. Still, while not an agitation agent like Pham Ngoc Thao, Quang's actions would accomplish the same goal: his on-again, off-again protest movements over the next four years would rock a succession of South Vietnamese governments.

After the Hue radio station debacle, Diem offered to ameliorate the Buddhist demands, and by early June, a tentative agreement appeared close. Then disaster struck when Nhu's wife publicly condemned the Buddhists as agitators. The Buddhist leadership felt betrayed and turned to an elderly monk named Thich Quang Duc, who had offered to immolate himself to protest the Diem government. On the morning of June 11, Duc sat down on a street in downtown Saigon. Someone poured gasoline on him, and he then lit a match. As the fire engulfed the eerily still monk, an American reporter named Malcolm Browne snapped a photo. The picture soon circled the globe, a symbol of protest against a repressive regime. Any hope of conciliation between Diem and the militant Buddhists died with Quang Duc.

Throughout the summer of 1963, the Buddhist demonstrations intensified. They were soon joined by student protestors after the Buddhist Youth Wing, led by an intense monk named Thich Thien Minh, egged them on. If Tri Quang was the Buddhist's intellectual wizard, Thien Minh was Quang's canny tactician. When the Buddhist demonstrations began in May 1963,

Thien Minh immediately used his Youth Wing to incite student passions. University and high school students, who had traditionally been apolitical, were stirred into action. Protest groups were formed in each of the country's four main universities.

When the army also raided temples in Hue, Tri Quang left the city for the Xa Loi pagoda in Saigon to coordinate the demonstrations, making Xa Loi the center of Buddhist activity. One Buddhist activist wrote that the reason Tri Quang moved was because that's "where all the reporters and diplomats were gathered...It was a clever tactic because thanks to mass communication, the plight of the Buddhists was heralded beyond Vietnam."[43] It worked, and by August, after several other monks had self-immolated, the U.S. exerted pressure on Diem and his brother to make concessions to the Buddhists. While Diem had initially hoped to strike a deal with the monks, Nhu took a much harder line. He began to speak publicly about strong government action to repress the protesters. Given that Nhu was head of the Can Lao Military Committee, which was a parallel army chain of command, the threat was serious. Although the military wanted to focus solely on fighting the Communists, following a massive demonstration of twenty thousand people at Xa Loi on August 18, Tran Van Don and Ton That Dinh asked to confer with Diem and Nhu. On August 20, they met to discuss their concern about the rapidly deteriorating situation.

Don was now back in favor with the Ngo brothers. Precisely why is difficult to determine, but it appears that Nhu sought to use him. Don recommended to Diem that he declare martial law to quell the demonstrations, but he emphasized that internal disturbances should be handled by the police and not the army. Don insisted that the military's focus was on combatting external Communist aggression, not their own people. Diem agreed with the proposal to declare martial law, and he also appointed Don as Acting Chief of the JGS.

Nhu decided to use the martial law decree to arrest Thich Tri Quang and destroy the protest movement. He ordered the Special Forces and police to clear Xa Loi and the other pagodas. Nhu has been accused of using the Special Forces to make the attack, but that is false. According to then Captain Pham Duy Tat, leader of Special Forces Group 31, his commander, Colonel Le Quang Tung, ordered him to keep his troops out of the temples. Tung met with the director of the National Police, Colonel Nguyen Van Y. They agreed that Tung's soldiers would secure the perimeters while Y's Combat Police (like SWAT) would clear the buildings. Tung ordered Tat "not to go inside, or touch anyone or anything. Consequently, I only secured the perimeter of Xa Loi, while Major Pham Van Phu, who commanded Group 77, secured the perimeter at the other pagodas. None of our soldiers entered the temples."[44]

Shortly after midnight on August 21, the police assaulted the pagodas and arrested over fourteen hundred people. Although Don admits that the operation was "successful from a military point of view," his rage at "Nhu's decision to attack the pagodas and implicate the army with myself as its temporary head turned out to be his and his brother's ultimate downfall."[45]

While the police raids had smashed the Buddhist protest, they failed to seize Tri Quang. As Tat sat in his jeep outside Xa Loi, monitoring radio traffic, an ARVN officer approached him and requested that Tat authorize a movement order allowing the officer to transport an unknown person from the pagoda to the American embassy. Although Tat refused, after the police left, he watched a sedan carrying Tri Quang depart the temple. Captain Tat let him pass. "I could have easily arrested Quang," Tat said, "but Tung's orders were not to touch anyone." The Buddhist monk had slipped through Nhu's fingers.

Although the raid accomplished Nhu's goal, his strategy simultaneously pushed the generals and the U.S. into each other's arms. The U.S. government responded forcefully to what it viewed as a looming disaster. The State Department sent a message to the new American ambassador to South Vietnam, Henry Cabot Lodge, that read:

> It is now clear that whether military proposed martial law or whether Nhu tricked them into it, Nhu took advantage of its imposition to smash pagodas...thus placing onus on military in eyes of world and Vietnamese people. Also, clear that Nhu has maneuvered himself into commanding position. U.S. Government cannot tolerate situation in which power lies in Nhu's hands. Diem must be given chance to rid himself of Nhu and his coterie and replace them with best military and political personalities available. If, in spite of all your efforts, Diem remains obdurate and refuses, then we must face the possibility that Diem himself cannot be preserved.[46]

The proverbial die had been cast.

3

"EITHER DIEM CHANGED HIS POLICIES, OR WE WOULD CHANGE DIEM"

Death of Diem

Diem sought to strengthen the state against Communist aggression and overcome the Nationalists' chronic infighting by creating an authoritarian regime. Sadly, his messianic attitude and paternalistic certainty, the very characteristics that had helped him succeed in the early years, eventually blinded him and alienated his supporters. Like all public leaders, he had a shelf life, and the personal attributes that had enabled him to succeed during a time of great turmoil had grown old in a period of relative stability. His long-winded monologues and refusal to accept criticism, as well as his belief that democracy was untenable for an emergent and fragile Vietnamese state engaged in a fratricidal war, in time estranged most Americans. By 1963, many Vietnamese political and military leaders also feared he was steering the country to defeat. Faced with mounting internal hostility, he became more repressive, forcing a desperate Vietnamese elite to use violence to overcome oppression.

While many blame the U.S. for instigating the coup, the generals had Vietnamese-centric reasons for their revolt. One of them was a great fear that Diem and Nhu were secretly meeting with the Communists to neutralize the country. Aware of Diem's outreach, and in a near panic that the president might attempt to neutralize the country, the generals decided to remove him. But first, they needed reassurance that their main ally would not desert them.

Although there is no doubt that American approval bolstered their resolve, it was a Vietnamese affair, not a U.S. initiative. Still, the Americans' tacit approval created tragic long-term consequences for U.S.-Vietnamese political relations. It reinforced South Vietnamese beliefs that the CIA controlled or was behind every event and that no coup could succeed without American support. U.S. endorsement for Diem's overthrow became a double-edged sword. While the generals were grateful, their instinctive suspicions about hidden U.S. motives had been exacerbated, never to be soothed.

In reviewing the totality of the generals' rationales for the November 1963 coup, one might argue that the generals had misjudged their own people regarding Diem and his policies or that their actions contained a strong whiff of self-advancement. Although the belief that the U.S. supported the coup was critical in their calculations, and the pagoda raids was the tipping point, the generals' decision to depose Diem stemmed from many dynamics. These numerous concerns had coalesced into a sense that the only way to reverse the situation was for the military to act and save the country, just as the military had done in other nations. Ultimately, while the U.S. shoulders some responsibility, the coup was a Nationalist affair conducted by the South Vietnamese military for specific Vietnamese reasons.

THE PLOT THICKENS

For many of the president's supporters, the pagoda raids were the final straw. Diem's foreign minister, a devout Buddhist named Vu Van Mau, immediately resigned and shaved his head to show solidarity with the monks. Some of Diem's strongest backers, including the III Corps commander, Ton That Dinh, covertly joined a group of coup plotters centered on the three senior generals in the army, Tran Van Don, Le Van Kim, and Duong Van Minh. Another officer who had been recently recruited was Brigadier General Mai Huu Xuan, commandant of the Quang Trung training center outside Saigon.

One officer the conspirators desperately needed to win over was Major General Tran Thien Khiem, Don's main assistant and chief of staff of the JGS. The plotters could not make troop movements or issue orders without Khiem's knowledge, but his previous close association with Diem made them wary. After deliberating, in mid-September 1963 Minh was entrusted with sounding him out. Minh was stunned when Khiem informed him that both he and his old friend Nguyen Khanh were also scheming to overthrow

Diem. Khiem agreed to join Minh's group, and he was conscripted into the coup committee. Khanh, however, was held at arm's length, as Don believed he was an opportunist who would betray them if Diem discovered the plot.

Alongside the usual reasons given for the coup, there was another significant fear that played a key role, but one that has rarely been examined. Many senior officers accepted stories beginning to swirl in the summer of 1963 that the Ngos were secretly conducting negotiations with Hanoi. Although most U.S. scholars have rejected the notion that a dread of neutralization helped spark the coup, believing that any Diem-Nhu effort in that regard was a minor sideshow, that analysis does not account for Vietnamese sensibilities. Vietnamese pre- and postcoup accounts often mention this significant concern, and in Saigon's politically charged atmosphere, the accusation added to the generals decision to act. These efforts, which have been described as everything from feelers designed to reopen trade relations with North Vietnam to peace offers, were transformed into a plot to "neutralize" South Vietnam.[1] Ton That Dinh called it the "deepest reason" for the coup.[2] Colonel Do Mau, the leader of the military's counterintelligence unit, separately agreed, claiming the "first important result of the coup's success was that it prevented Diem and his brothers from carrying out their stupid, insane plot of selling out South Vietnam and handing it over to Ho Chi Minh."[3] Nguyen Khanh was also aware of Diem's clandestine efforts, and shortly after the pagoda raids, he told a CIA contact that he was alarmed that "the regime might cut a deal with North Vietnam rather than accept U.S. pressure to accommodate the Buddhists. Khanh said that he and his friends would then rebel."[4]

In an interview in late 1969, Diem's former vice president, Nguyen Ngoc Tho, confirmed that Diem was trying to reach an accommodation with Hanoi. According to Tho, "In order to free himself from the crushing and contradictory demands of the Americans that he win the war and at the same time turn South Vietnam into an American-style democracy, Diem conceived the idea of negotiating an end to the fighting with Hanoi, proposing some sort of federation with the North, and eventually holding the postposed 1956 elections to unify the country. This plan triggered the 1963 coup."[5] Tran Van Dinh, then GVN Ambassador to the U.S., agrees with Tho's assessment. Dinh recalled that Diem ordered him to "negotiate a ceasefire with Hanoi and to agree to the departure of all U.S. forces and the acceptance of the NLF representatives in the government, as well as an election... in which the NLF could participate."[6] CIA officer Lou Conein, who was the main liaison between the generals and the embassy, agrees that Diem "figured he...had to make a deal with the...north. His brother Ngo Dinh Nhu in early 1963 told...me personally that he was dealing with...North Vietnam."[7]

This threat, a negotiated coalition with the Communists that would make South Vietnam a neutral country, was a key factor in the general's decision. Why were they so disturbed by the possibility of neutralization? Many other Third World countries were attempting to steer an independent course between the free world and the Communists, so why not South Vietnam? The answer to that question lies in Vietnam's bloody past. Vietnamese Nationalists and Americans, reflecting their own historical experiences, saw neutralism quite differently. While Americans generally viewed neutralism as a person or country that was nonaligned in the power struggle between the two world blocs, most Nationalists defined a Vietnamese neutralist as a crypto-communist. Nationalist canon fervently held that the Communists saw neutralization followed by a coalition as a political stepping-stone to victory. Any such union was a death trap. This was not partisan anxiety following an election loss; these fears had genuine roots. The Nationalists had suffered through a Communist-led purge after they had collaborated in a coalition government with Ho Chi Minh in 1945–46. Many Nationalist and religious figures either disappeared or were murdered by the Communists. The mock trials and subsequent executions during the 1950s Land Reform pogroms in North Vietnam extinguished any lingering doubts regarding their fate if the Communists achieved power.

At the end of the First Indochina War, France became the leading proponent of neutralization to end the strife. Paris believed that U.S. efforts to build an anti-communist South were doomed. At its base, the French saw Ho Chi Minh as the only legitimate Vietnamese leader and believed that Hanoi would eventually control the entire country. The Nationalists naturally distrusted French intentions, and their skepticism had its origins in the past. Many Nationalists alleged that the French had secretly employed the Communists during the 1930s and 1940s, to decimate their ranks. They suspected that French commercial interests were behind the policy, hoping that helping Hanoi neutralize South Vietnam would ensure a future special economic relationship between the two countries. Diem thus rejected all French neutralization proposals, believing that they were simply disguised coalitions.

The U.S. also rebuffed the French proposals for a neutral South

Vietnam. Confronted by American intransigence, Paris sought to mollify Washington's concerns. The French opined that the war was unwinnable because the Nationalists did not have popular support, while a unified Vietnam under Hanoi's rule would not pose a threat to Western interests. Moreover, the historical animosity between China and Vietnam would keep the country free of Beijing's gravitational pull. While these claims are debatable, the French thesis would shape the thinking of many Americans who opposed the U.S. effort to support Saigon.

Neutralization, however, was not solely a French plan, nor was it confined strictly to Vietnam. When fighting erupted in 1960 in neighboring Laos between government forces, neutralists, and the Hanoi-supported Communist insurgents called the Pathet Lao, both the Americans and the Russians quickly intervened. To end the Laotian civil war and prevent a superpower confrontation between the U.S. and the Soviet Union, the Cambodian head of state, Prince Norodom Sihanouk, proposed in late 1960 to end the fighting via a conference like the 1954 Geneva Accords. The plan gained traction when the U.S. agreed to attend, and a fourteen-nation conference opened in Geneva in May 1961. All understood that for the accords to succeed, a neutral coalition government would have to be formed that would require Hanoi to withdraw from Laos and halt infiltration into South Vietnam.

Diem insisted, however, that a Laotian coalition government would inevitably lead to the "communization of Laos by legal means."[8] He was not alone in his fears. According to historian Mark Moyar, the neutralization of Laos "caused great alarm among American hawks and the leaders of Asia's non-Communist nations."[9] While a neutral Laos survived until 1975, everyone's assessment of Hanoi's intentions was correct. Both neutrality and a coalition were a Communist subterfuge, a means to achieve victory without spilling blood. In February 1962, the Politburo informed its cadres that with respect to South Vietnam, "We are currently both fighting and demanding the formation of a coalition government, demanding general elections, and demanding peace and neutrality. These things are intended to create transitional steps that will enable our movement to advance more easily, that will further isolate the warmongers, and that will win over those who want to sue for peace inside the enemy's ranks."[10]

This sudden shift in U.S. policy from fighting the Communists in Laos to accepting the principle of neutralizing the country sent shockwaves through Diem's government. The Geneva conference generated a new fear among South Vietnamese elites, particularly among the northerners who had fled to the South: a U.S. deal with Hanoi at Saigon's expense. Mistrustful of foreign and Communist intentions, the anxieties of GVN officials were heightened when DRV representatives at the Laos conference requested including the topic of neutralizing South Vietnam. Fortunately for Diem, the other delegates ignored this trial balloon when the North Vietnamese Politburo arrogantly proposed an onerous condition: Diem must resign before Hanoi would agree to talk about neutralizing South Vietnam. Many years later, Hanoi would also demand that Thieu resign before peace talks could begin. It was a clever diplomatic stroke: eliminate your rival while concurrently creating suspicion and tension among your adversaries, not to mention scoring propaganda points that Hanoi alone was seeking peace.

Following the Politburo's strategy, the NLF announced that it favored neutralization to halt the fighting. This was probably the Communists' first overt diplomatic effort to drive a wedge between Saigon and Washington. Capitalizing on the eighth anniversary of the 1954 Geneva Accords, on July 20, 1962, the Liberation Front's Central Committee released a four-point proclamation. They calculated that a public offer to stop the war might spur war-weary South Vietnamese to demand the Americans leave and thus destroy the Diem administration. The NLF proposed a variation of the Lao formula. This entailed a coalition in exchange for the elimination of Diem's government and a ceasefire if all American forces withdrew from the country. Further, the Front asked to be granted legal status as a political entity, followed by an election for a National Assembly. After the vote, a new government would combine with Cambodia and Laos to create a "neutral area."[11]

The South Vietnamese soon captured secret NLF instructions to its cadres that described the true purpose behind the July 20 declaration. The proclamation was not a peace offer but instead a "big political attack" to "isolate the American imperialists...disunify enemy ranks" and "gather more forces to our revolutionary side."[12] Highly classified documents created at that time by COSVN, the Communist command for the southern half of South Vietnam, and published after the war confirm that the neutralization proposal was a ploy: "We had to make everyone clearly understand that we were not changing our policy, and that this was strictly a stratagem on our part."[13] Further, Le Duan, the Communist First Secretary in Hanoi, sent a letter to COSVN stating that he viewed neutralization as a disguised surrender by Saigon. Since an NLF military victory seemed unobtainable in the short run, a negotiated settlement offered the best option for over-throwing Diem. Le Duan wrote, "Based on the balance of forces between our side and the enemy...the goal of the revolution in South Vietnam [is] one of gradually, step by step, driving back the American imperialists and...overthrowing the puppet government and forming in its place an independent and neutral government."[14] Given Diem's animosity to a co-alition government, plus the exposure of Communist aims in the captured documents, he rejected the NLF proposals.

Diem also did not believe the DRV would honor the Laotian accord. His fears soon proved justified. As historian Pierre Asselin points out, Hanoi "wanted not actual or permanent neutrality of Laos, but neutral-ity on its terms and for as long as those terms served the purposes of the Vietnamese revolution..."[15] Despite the conference ban on infiltration and a mandate to withdraw its troops from Laos, Hanoi continued to infiltrate men and weapons into South Vietnam and failed to withdraw its forces in Laos as it had promised. Nationalists soon sarcastically rechristened the Ho Chi Minh Trail the "Harriman Memorial Highway" after Averell Har-riman, the chief U.S. negotiator for the accords. The French would retort that these failures were due to the ongoing war in South Vietnam and that the accords had eliminated an American-Russian confrontation over that small, impoverished country. French opinion convinced no one. Hanoi had agreed to the accords' stipulations regardless of ongoing events and then promptly defaulted on its signed guarantee. Worse, Hanoi's broken promises did not auger well for any future assurances that it would abide by international agreements.

Diem was convinced that the accords had also weakened his country by convincing other Southeast Asian countries to seek neutrality or exchange diplomatic ties with Hanoi. In August 1962, Sihanouk had requested that the Geneva conference also discuss neutralizing Cambodia, but it went nowhere. In late September 1962, Diem demanded Laos repudiate its rec-ognition of Hanoi, but when it refused, citing its neutrality based on the Geneva agreement, Diem recalled his ambassador to Laos and broke off relations. South Vietnamese policy was clear: if a country recognized either the DRV or the NLF, Saigon would sever diplomatic relations.

Regrettably, despite significant U.S. efforts over the next decade to reassure Saigon of the constancy of American support, the Nationalists' dread of U.S. abandonment would never disappear. It would relentlessly color South Vietnamese analysis of American motives. Yet the U.S. viewed the situation in Laos and South Vietnam as profoundly different. For the U.S., the signing of the Geneva Accords on July 23, 1962 was "based on fundamental assumption that [the Lao army] was totally incompetent to prevent complete Communist over-running of Laos so long as Viet Minh units remained actively engaged. We have therefore concentrated our effort on international agreement which would provide for withdrawal [of] Viet Minh and establishment provisional coalition government."[16] The Americans frankly thought that the South Vietnamese would fight and that the Lao would not, but convincing the perpetually apprehensive Vietnamese of that policy distinction was challenging.

While dormant for a period, the French neutralization scheme suddenly reemerged at the end of August 1963. French President Charles de Gaulle, in reaction to the pagoda raids, remarked that France would happily "cooperate with the Vietnamese people in an effort to unify the country and throw off foreign influence."[17] The timing of De Gaulle's statement surprised and angered Washington, as it seemed a calculated attempt to interfere with American efforts to pressure the Ngo brothers into changing their policies in a variety of areas. Moreover, the U.S. administration became deeply concerned that De Gaulle's proposal might strengthen Nhu's growing anti-Americanism or that Diem would use the French proposal as a counterweight against American pressure for reforms.[18] When U.S. officials expressed displeasure with De Gaulle's statement to French representatives, they dismissed American protests, claiming that De Gaulle was simply restating his long-held beliefs. That was patently false. For De Gaulle, the neutralization proposal was part of his effort to create a global role for France that was independent of the U.S. He believed the old East-West power blocs were breaking apart and that France could develop new alignments. If it caused American discomfort over Vietnam, where French pride still smarted after its replacement by the U.S., so much the better.

Given Diem's deep-seated opposition to neutralization or a coalition government, one can only imagine his mindset when he suddenly reversed course and opened secret talks with Hanoi. Yet Nhu did exactly what Washington dreaded: he began exploratory contacts for potential talks with the Communists. The Ngos' precise goals remain unknown, but Roger Lalouette, the French ambassador to the Republic of Vietnam, had already begun working covertly with Nhu sometime in the summer of 1963 to convey messages between Hanoi and Saigon. Mieczyslaw Maneli, the Polish representative to the International Control Commission, the body designed by the 1954 Geneva accords to monitor the ceasefire, also began secret contacts with Nhu. Maneli reported to Hanoi that in his first conversation with Nhu on September 4, 1963, Nhu's purpose for inviting him "was to establish contact which would not bind [anyone] to anything for now. In his defense against the U.S., [Nhu] turns to us while presenting himself as a statesman able to negotiate with the North."[19]

While the Manelli talks had been inconclusive, rumors began to circulate in Saigon that Nhu was secretly meeting with Communist representatives and that Ho Chi Minh was considering De Gaulle's proposal. The generals became alarmed at the convergence of the renewed French neutralization scheme and the reports of Nhu's overtures. As noted earlier, Ton That Dinh and Do Mau specifically cited Nhu's efforts as one reason they joined the coup. This sentiment was also shared by Tran Thien Khiem, who told a CIA officer that "the Generals would under no condition go along with Nhu should he make any step toward the North or even toward neutralization a la Laos."[20] Le Van Kim echoed similar sentiments shortly after the coup, telling a journalist that "We know that Nhu had contact with the North— that is one of the reasons we fought."[21]

Besides this deep fear of a coalition with Hanoi, there had also emerged among the coup participants a belief that Diem had badly strayed from Nationalist ideals. Duong Van Minh and the others termed the coup a revolution, an effort to rid South Vietnam of what they called a "family government" (*gia dinh tri*). The secret police, the Can Lao informers, and the absence of political freedoms rankled those who were fighting a war against similar repressions in North Vietnam. Perhaps terming it a revolution was simply a cloak to cover a heinous act. They had initially welcomed Diem's forceful actions to build the country, but over time, the very characteristics that had made Diem so appealing—his strength of will and uncompromising vision, his overriding sense of Vietnamese nationalism—had morphed into an inflexible attitude. Rightly or wrongly, the coup plotters judged Diem and his brothers as not having betrayed Western democratic principles but instead their own standards of Vietnamese nationalism and political freedom. By developing into a dictator, Diem was losing the people and hence losing the war. Removing Diem and his brothers became as much a political desire to reorient South Vietnam back to its Nationalist roots, as it was to prevent a Communist takeover. In their minds, the military was the country's guardian, and they not only had a duty but also a sacred right to safeguard South Vietnam. For Tran Van Don, "Either Diem changed his policies, or we would change Diem."[22]

Another key player in the coup, one that also has had little examination, was the covert maneuvering of the Dai Viet Party. The two older Nationalist political parties, the Dai Viets and the VNQDD, remained bitter adversaries of Diem. After the president banned them, they sought to overthrow him. After being outlawed, they went underground and continued to recruit, mainly among military officers and civil servants. They were moderately successful, and some battalion commanders, like Major Duong Huu Nghia, who led a Saigon-based armor unit, were secret Dai Viet members. The Dai Viets targeted Big Minh, and the party member who established Minh's confidence in the Dai Viets was Major Huynh Van Ton. He later helped convince Minh that Khiem could be trusted. The Dai Viet planning paid off, and when Minh began plotting against Diem, senior Dai Viet leader Nguyen Ngoc Huy claimed that Minh "was supported immediately by the Dai Viet Party network in the army."[23] Unfortunately for Minh, allowing the Dai Viets to assist him would lead to his undoing. The Dai Viet intrigues became a plot within the plot, and their constant machinations would roil South Vietnamese politics for over a year.

The spark for Nghia and the other Dai Viets to begin secretly plotting against the Diem regime was the suicide on July 7, 1963, of a highly respected Nationalist writer named Nguyen Tuong Tam. Although a member of the rival VNQDD party, Tam, a northerner and Diem opponent, was a famous literary figure (his pen name was Nhat Linh) whose works had inspired many people to join the Nationalist cause. Along with twenty others, Tam was charged with involvement in the abortive coup of November 1960. Shortly before his appearance at a military tribunal, he killed himself. His suicide, coming soon after Quang Duc's self-immolation, and published death note aroused many students to join the growing Buddhist opposition. "History," Tam wrote, "only can judge my life. . . . The arrest and sentencing of all national opposition elements is an abominable crime that will push the country into the hands of the Communists. I oppose these acts and kill myself as the Venerable Quang Duc burned himself to warn those who would crush every kind of freedom."[24]

When his hearse was driven to the Xa Loi pagoda for funeral rites, police blocked students from placing banners on the coffin. A struggle ensued between the police and the students. Suppressing the commemoration of Tam's death aroused student activists to join Buddhist demonstrators on

Saigon's streets. After the subsequent pagoda raids, resentment among university and high school students spread like a plague and resulted in large protests. Diem's police responded by arresting hundreds of students, but the crackdown only enflamed the students, leading to further social disruption. It was one more reason to act against Diem.

ZERO HOUR

Bringing in Tran Thien Khiem provided the final piece Minh needed to overthrow Diem. Now that the various groups were aligned, the coup plotters parceled out responsibilities. Minh was in overall command, and his job was to convince selected officers to join. Kim would handle creating the future government, while Dinh planned the military maneuvers. Don's role was to liaise with the Americans and to work on the four corps commanders and other important military leaders. Huynh Van Cao in IV Corps was a staunch Diem loyalist, so they decided against contacting him. Khanh at II Corps in the Central Highlands was kept out of the main loop. Don, though, waited to contact Do Cao Tri, the commander of I Corps, the area adjacent to the DMZ.

While Don was close to Tri, he was uncertain how he would react. Tri was considered loyal to Diem, and the two had a long history together. In April 1955, Tri had commanded the VNA's Airborne units that had cleared the Binh Xuyen gangsters out of Saigon. However, in late April, Diem became furious with the hard-fighting officer after a dustup over choosing the new chief of the military. Diem replaced him as Airborne commander with Nguyen Chanh Thi. Eventually, Tri worked himself back into Diem's good graces, and in December 1962, Do Cao Tri replaced Thieu as 1st Division Commander. When the Buddhist protests erupted in Hue, Tri initially stayed on the sidelines, but within a month he adopted a much tougher line. In early June 1963, he sent his troops to smash the protests in the city. Eighty Buddhists were injured in the melees that followed, and Buddhist leader Tri Quang left for Saigon because of Tri's attack. Diem promoted Tri to brigadier general on July 1. In a further effort, in coordination with the Saigon pagoda raids on August 20, Tri's troops assaulted and cleared several temples in both Hue and Danang. That exploit earned him a promotion to I Corps commander. Tri's actions against the Buddhists and the resultant promotions made Don cautious, and he did not contact Tri until October 29. Given their old connections, Tri agreed to join the plot. Don later remarked that he was thankful that Tri had not arrested him since Tri was carrying hand-written orders from Diem to seize anyone who asked Tri to join a coup.

Another key officer was Nguyen Van Thieu, who commanded the 5th Division, the largest unit closest to Saigon. While Thieu respected Diem's uncompromising anti-communism, he also was disenchanted with the pres-ident's mounting repression. Fearing that Diem's autocracy was destroying South Vietnam and ruining relations with its most important ally, he joined the coup. Oddly, neither South Vietnamese memoirs nor U.S. reports pro-vide any details on how or why Thieu joined the coup. The only insight comes from Thieu and his wife. Mrs. Thieu states that Duong Van Minh conscripted her husband and that his main condition for joining the coup was that no harm come to Diem.[25] Thieu provided similar information to an interviewer after the war. Minh, Thieu said, had summoned him "to Saigon and asked him to participate in the coup. The reason Minh gave to him for the coup was that if Diem continued to serve as president, the U.S. would reduce its assistance to our army."[26] In Thieu's only public discus-sion of the coup, he said that Minh contacted him in early October 1963. Before joining, Thieu named four conditions: that the new government should more energetically "pursue the anti-communist war," that it must have U.S. support, that "a strong military government be set up after the coup to correct the deteriorating position of the Saigon regime against the Communists," and that Diem's life be spared.[27] According to Thieu, Minh agreed to all conditions except for a heavy military presence in the new government, as he intended to quickly restore civilian control. Yet another key element in Thieu's conditions, which only one reporter noticed, was that the new government "not move toward a policy of neutralism."[28]

Much of the discussion of events leading up to and during the coup has focused on the U.S. knowledge and approval for the regime change. The actual military actions on the ground are not widely known, mainly because Ton That Dinh kept the operational details of his plan secret. Since the death of Diem cast a pall over the event, no one wanted to discuss his role in the coup. Consequently, few officers publicly described their roles until years later.

Dinh's plan called for Thieu to be the main leader of the ground forces. Dinh also insisted on showing mercy to Diem, and he instructed Thieu to surround the palace but to refrain from a direct attack. This would allow Diem an opportunity to arrange political asylum with the Americans or, failing that, a guarantee of safe passage from the generals. Because Thieu was the insurgents' ground commander, many—who were unaware of Dinh's instructions—have claimed that Thieu deliberately held back his troops to see how the coup would turn out before committing himself. They assumed his only target was Gia Long Palace, and since he did not mount a vigorous attack against the palace until early the next morning, the charge seemed proven. Both assertions are completely wrong. His initial mission was to capture the Cong Hoa barracks, which housed the Presidential Guard unit. He was not given the palace as a target until the night of October 31.

In a surprising twist, Nhu inadvertently helped the coup plotters. Mindful of the enormous discontent among the senior officers, he instructed Dinh to organize a "fake" coup that would expose the conspirators. To facilitate his counter coup, Nhu transferred the 7th Division, normally assigned to Huynh Van Cao's IV Corps, to Dinh's III Corps. He also assigned two battalions of Marines to Dinh and, more importantly, the two Special Forces groups in the capital that had previously been directly subordinate to Nhu. In making these changes, Nhu had unwittingly provided Dinh command of virtually every unit he needed to launch the rebellion.

Mindful of the mistakes during the 1960 coup attempt, Dinh planned a rapid attack into the city but hoped to refrain from a major firefight. His forces would surround the palace and the Presidential Guard barracks, occupy key positions in the city, and block any loyal commanders from coming to Diem's rescue. He would send the Marines to seize the Saigon radio station and the National Police headquarters. Afterward, an Airborne battalion and several armor units, one of them led by Major Ly Tong Ba, would capture the Presidential Guard barracks. After securing those locations, the Marines, the armor, and Thieu's troops would capture the palace. Diem and Nhu would leave the country. Casualties were to be kept to a minimum.

The coup was to commence at 1:30 p.m. on Friday, November 1. Most civil servants would be out of their offices for the standard Vietnamese two-hour lunch break, which would limit civilian deaths. To ensure that no local commanders loyal to Diem could interfere, Khiem invited many senior officers to a lunch at the JGS headquarters. During the meal, guards would occupy the area and each officer would be forced to declare their support for the coup leaders or would be arrested as Diem loyalists. Tri and Khanh would cut off communications with Saigon and ban all troop movements in their respective corps. Colonel Nguyen Huu Co was dispatched to the 7th Division to replace a Diem supporter as the division commander. Co's job was to prevent Huynh Van Cao in IV Corps from sending troops to rescue Diem. At the same time, two Air Force officers, Majors Nguyen Cao Ky and Do Khac Mai, would arrest the Vietnamese Air Force commander and take control of the Air Force.

There is an old military adage that no plan survives first contact with the enemy, and the carefully crafted plot to overthrow President Ngo Dinh Diem was no exception. The first mix-up on November 1 occurred when the deputy Navy commander, trying to keep the Navy commander occupied, panicked and unexpectedly killed him shortly before noon. Fearful that Nhu had been alerted, Minh immediately ordered the coup forces to move. Departing Bien Hoa, the 1st and 4th Marine Battalions sped along the Saigon-Bien Hoa highway. The 1st Battalion quickly occupied the Saigon radio station at 1:00 p.m., while the 4th Marines seized the National Police headquarters. Generals Tri and Khanh cut off communications between the capital and their corps headquarters. Colonel Co's 7th Division tied up the ferries at the key My Tho river crossing on his side of the Mekong River to prevent any troops still loyal to Diem from advancing on Saigon. Ky and Mai arrested the Air Force commander and secured Tan Son Nhut Air Base. All these moves went off without incident.

At the same time, three columns of armor began to converge on Saigon. Captain Phan Hoa Hiep, deputy commander of the Armor School then located near Vung Tau on the coast, led one mechanized force. Lieutenant Colonel Vinh Loc commanded a second taskforce comprising the 6th Airborne Battalion and additional armor from Phuoc Tuy, the province next to Vung Tau. These two columns were to link up with an infantry battalion from Thieu's 5th Division. A third armored column led by Ly Tong Ba from the 7th Division would move up from the Delta.

Minh's decision to launch early upset Dinh's timetable, which called for the Marines, the armor columns, and Thieu's troops to enter the city at the same time.[29] The armor columns coming from Vung Tau had to travel over sixty miles, so timing was critical. The revolt hinged on the two columns, which consisted of the bulk of the coup forces, getting into Saigon to capture the barracks and the palace. The Marines sudden move, however, tipped off Diem's Presidential Guard, who quickly erected a blockade on a major bridge on the Saigon–Bien Hoa highway into the city. Guard tanks now blocked Thieu's group. Since he was unwilling to fight his way into the South Vietnamese capital, Thieu sat there until Vinh Loc tricked the Guard commander into letting the column pass by convincing him they were coming to support Diem. Loc's quick thinking prevented heavy fighting and probably saved the coup, something Thieu never forgot.

After passing the roadblock, Vinh Loc's armor and the 6th Airborne surrounded the Cong Hoa barracks around 3:00 p.m. Thieu's 2nd Battalion, 9th Regiment took up positions around the palace to prevent any Guard elements from reinforcing the barracks. Listening to the radio broadcast and learning about the troop movements, Diem now realized that this was not a fake coup but a real one. At 3:30 p.m., he called Tran Van Don at the JGS headquarters and protested the military's actions. Don stated that they had warned Diem many times that he needed to reform his government. Don asked the president to surrender and offered him safe passage out of Vietnam. Minh also spoke to Diem and made the same request. When Diem refused to capitulate, Minh threatened to destroy the palace with air strikes and artillery. Diem hung up on him.

After speaking with the two renegade generals, Diem attempted to contact loyal officers such as Huynh Van Cao, who was then far to the south on the Ca Mau Peninsula monitoring the effort to rescue three American advisors recently captured by enemy guerrillas. Due to a poor telephone connection, Cao was unable to hear Diem. He then flew back to his headquarters in Can Tho to reconnect with the embattled president, but Cao could not reach him. Soon thereafter, Cao received a phone call from Do Mau and Khiem at JGS headquarters. Mau told Cao that while he had supported the president for more than a decade, he now opposed Diem "because the President had joined with the Communists."[30] After speaking with the two men, Cao reluctantly said he would join the coup, but only if Diem and Nhu were not harmed. Khiem agreed, and Diem's ability to halt the coup was rapidly fading.

Loyal forces defending the Cong Hoa barracks were relatively weak since most of the Presidential Guard troops had moved to the Saigon radio station and the bridge. Cong Hoa was an old two-story wooden building less than a mile from the palace. A determined attacker could easily capture it, but Thieu held back, hoping to avoid bloodshed. He called upon the Guard troops to surrender, but they refused. Around 4:00 p.m. that afternoon, Don ordered Nguyen Cao Ky to send two planes to make a short strafing run to convince them to surrender. Don was undoubtedly trying to persuade Diem and Nhu that Minh had meant his earlier warning, but the generals still hoped that Diem and Nhu would surrender peacefully and leave the country. The two planes made a quick firing pass on the barracks and then departed. Enlisting Ky, however, had unintended consequences. By making Ky an active plotter, Don and the others had set events in motion that would prove impossible to undo.

Nhu's most loyal officer was Colonel Le Quang Tung, commander of the Special Forces. Tung was arrested at the luncheon at JGS headquarters to prevent him from interfering with the coup. Although Dinh had earlier sent Major Pham Van Phu's Group 77 out of the city, he had kept Captain Pham Duy Tat's Group 31 in town so as not to raise Nhu's suspicion.

Dinh's decision, though, came perilously close to destroying the revolt. After learning that a coup had occurred, around 4:00 p.m., on his own initiative, Tat took four tanks and his men to the JGS compound. Only a handful of guards were present. According to Tat, "There was nothing between me and the coup generals but a few guards. I could have easily swept in and arrested them."[31] Without orders and uncertain what was transpiring at JGS headquarters, Tat could not assault the base, so he left his men at the compound and traveled to the Special Forces headquarters. There, the deputy SF commander ordered Tat not to attack. Tat returned to his men and retreated from the JGS, unaware that he was five hundred meters from changing the course of history. Afterward, he learned that his unit's appearance had caused Minh to panic. Minh ordered a pistol put to Tung's head, and at 4:30 p.m., Tung ordered his Special Forces units to capitulate.[32] At 6:00 p.m., Minh's bodyguard, Captain Nguyen Van Nhung, executed Tung. Minh's action should have warned Don and the others that he was unlikely to keep his promise not to harm Diem or Nhu.

Astonishingly, the Ngo brothers still refused to surrender, and by late afternoon, Dinh was under pressure from Minh to occupy the palace. Dinh relates:

> JGS Headquarters was urging me to act quickly to overrun and take Gia Long Palace, saying that if I did not then the Air Force and our artillery would level the Palace...At that time, I was preparing to contact Colonel Thieu by radio to discuss with him the progress of the operation. Everything was going smoothly. No major problems had arisen. However, the attack on Gia Long Palace continued to drag on. I felt that Thieu was still cautious in dealing with the defenders. If this situation continued to drag on, there might well be unforeseen consequences.[33]

The cause of the delay was the refusal of the Guard unit at Cong Hoa barracks to surrender. The Marines had launched a perfunctory assault but had retreated after being fired upon. While Thieu could have overrun the barracks, doing so would have created heavy casualties on both sides, which he wanted to avoid. "Thieu and I held the same position, which was that we did not want to push our opponent totally into a corner," Dinh later acknowledged. "Therefore, seeing that I was still keeping silent [had not yet issued an order], Thieu continued to stay his hand in order to allow [Minh] and the U.S. embassy to continue to negotiate with [Diem] in the hope of being able to give them a way out that would preserve their honor as well as their lives!"[34]

To convince Diem to surrender, Dinh sent Thieu to the palace and dispatched another officer, Lieutenant Colonel Lam Van Phat, to command the assault on the barracks. Around 7:00 p.m., Thieu called the president. One of Diem's aides answered the phone, and Thieu queried him on Diem's health and location and encouraged them to surrender. Diem and Nhu still refused, but their inability to contact any loyal units convinced them that they needed to leave. Around 8:00 p.m., Diem, Nhu, and several aides walked out of the palace, climbed into a car, and headed off to their fate.

Unaware that Diem had left the palace and frustrated by Diem's refusal to surrender, at 8:20 p.m. Minh ordered Thieu to assault Gia Long. Thieu's troops moved forward after another short artillery barrage, but Thieu halted the attack when the Presidential Guard continued to resist. This decision was what later caused Minh to declare that Thieu had allowed the brothers to escape. With few troops, Thieu did not press hard against the defenders, as he still hoped to resolve the coup with limited bloodshed. Dinh then sent the 4th Marines to the palace to reinforce Thieu's 2nd Battalion, leaving Vinh Loc's armor and the 6th Airborne to deal with the Cong Hoa barracks. To keep casualties low, Phat launched his assault at night. Around 9:30 p.m., Vinh Loc's armor broke through the main gate. The 6th Airborne entered the barracks area and slowly began to clear the facility. By midnight, the Guard at Cong Hoa finally surrendered.

Thieu then began shifting troops from Cong Hoa to positions around Gia Long Palace. Just as important, Ly Tong Ba and his armor had finally arrived in the city around 11:00 p.m. According to one of Diem's military aides, as the palace defenders saw the rebel forces growing in number and firepower, at 2:00 a.m. he called and "informed General Khiem that President Diem had left the palace. . . . [The aide] asked Khiem to issue an order not to attack the palace to avoid killing any of our soldiers, saying that the President had already fled from Gia Long. Khiem asked him what time the President had left the palace. [He] said that the President had left at about 8:00 p.m. Khiem hastily said, 'OK' and said he would take care of it."[35]

Soon after the call to Khiem, white flags appeared in several palace windows. Thinking the Guard was surrendering, coup forces moved forward. Suddenly Guard soldiers opened fire and killed one of Ly Tong Ba's armor officers. The trickery left Thieu no choice. At 3:00 a.m., he opened fire. Mortar rounds crashed down, and tanks and machine guns blasted away. Ba's troops made one assault, but Guard units fought back, knocking out several personnel carriers. Around 6:00 a.m., the Marines blew a hole in the palace wall and entered the grounds. According to Ba, "I and a squad of Marines were the first people to jump through the hole into the Palace grounds. By being first in I hoped to prevent any unnecessary clashes and bloodshed....I moved forward and occupied the stairwell leading up to the upper floor of the Palace in the hope that we would find the President."[36] Finding Diem and Nhu gone, rebel troops began looting the palace.

Shortly thereafter, Diem called Khiem from his hiding place in a Catholic church in the Cholon section of Saigon and offered to surrender in exchange for safe passage out of Vietnam. Khiem told an American journalist that the president had asked that he come get them, but "Minh would not let me go."[37] Thieu, upon learning that Diem had conceded, called Minh and asked permission to retrieve the brothers so that he could protect them. Thieu wanted to put them in an open jeep and personally drive them to the JGS, believing no one would dare attempt to kill them in public. Minh declined, telling Thieu that he had already sent other officers. The deliberately slow pace of the assault, which was to avoid casualties and allow Diem to leave, had worked. According to Dinh, only four Guard soldiers were killed and forty-four wounded, while Dinh lost nine dead and had forty-six wounded.[38]

All accounts agree that after Diem's call, Minh gathered the generals onto a balcony at JGS headquarters to mull the surrender offer. Don claims he recommended they allow the brothers to depart, but then he conveniently left to oversee preparations for the brothers' arrival. Do Mau states there was some discussion about putting Nhu on trial, but one general recommended killing the brothers.[39] Mau claims he protested, but no one backed him. Eventually, the generals decided to send Brigadier General Mai Huu Xuan, Major Duong Hieu Nghia, and Captain Pham Hoa Hiep in a convoy consisting of a platoon of Hiep's armored personnel carriers and some jeeps to escort Diem and Nhu to the JGS. At the last minute, Minh assigned his bodyguard, Captain Nguyen Van Nhung, the aide who had killed Colonel Tung, to escort Diem and Nhu.

Most believe that Minh alone gave the order to kill Diem and Nhu on a spur of the moment decision. The more likely scenario is that it was a consensus judgment among select officers who agreed not to publicly assign responsibility. Both Nguyen Khanh and Lou Conein confirm that it was a group decision but acknowledge that an oath was taken among the Vietnamese officers to not reveal who gave the order. However, many in Saigon, from journalists to U.S. embassy officers, attempted to uncover who ordered their deaths and how they died. Some participants eventually published their own version of events, and other details were included in confidential embassy reports, but what transpired remains a partial mystery fogged by Vietnamese finger-pointing and denials. The death of Diem immediately created deep divisions among the generals, it was a leading cause for Khanh's "reorganization" three months later, and it reverberated in South Vietnam's presidential election in 1971. Understanding the circumstances for the actual murders provides context for these later problems.

While Don's memoir provides testimony from various accomplices as to what transpired after the balcony meeting, as well as from those involved in Diem's death, few accounts agree with Don on virtually any element. Don claims that Brigadier General Mai Huu Xuan and another key aide of Minh's informed him that Nghia and Nhung fired into the armored personnel carrier, killing the brothers. The U.S. was given a similar account by Pham Ngoc Thao, who told an embassy officer that Nghia had killed them with a submachine gun and that Xuan "gave the order and pushed [Nghia] into doing it."[40] Most have accepted this version of the killings, but that is implausible. No professional soldier sitting inside an armored personnel carrier would open fire with an automatic weapon. To what degree Xuan was involved remains unknown, but Don relates that when Xuan returned from the church, he walked into Minh's office and said in French, "Mission accomplished," indicating that he had carried out Minh's orders.[41]

Shortly after the coup, Nghia was interviewed by American journalist Stanley Karnow. Nghia claimed that Nhung, who hated Nhu and was upset over the death of the armor officer at the palace, began arguing with Nhu inside the M-113. The quarrel grew heated, and Nhung pulled a knife and stabbed Nhu. He then drew his pistol and shot Diem in the head before turning and firing a bullet into Nhu's head as well. Karnow's account indicates Nghia was also inside the vehicle

In Nghia's postwar account, he again claims that Nhung killed the brothers. He states that Minh's chief aide, Colonel Duong Ngoc Lam, told him that Minh had recommended they kill Nhu but let Diem live. Naturally, Lam denied that he ordered the killings.[42] Nghia states that Nhung was assigned the task of killing Nhu. Upon Nghia's arrival at the church, Diem and Nhu were led out to a waiting armored personnel carrier that Nhung had ordered driven into the courtyard. Nhung told the brothers to get in. The brothers' hands were tied behind their backs, and Nhung sat with them as a guard. Shortly thereafter, the convoy left for the JGS. Nghia claims that he and Hiep were riding in a jeep in front of the convoy. When it stopped at a railroad crossing, Nhung killed Diem and Nhu. According to Nghia, Nhung said that he had first stabbed Nhu to death, and when Diem resisted, Nhung stabbed Diem as well. He then shot both brothers once in the head.[43]

An NBC News investigation in 1971 that included interviews with several participants, including Khanh and Nghia, confirms that Nhung was the lone assassin, although some details of the actual murder are contradictory. The program claims that Minh radioed Lam while at the rail crossing and ordered the murders, although Lam again denied it.[44] A Vietnamese officer, who was Kim's military aide during the coup, spoke to Nhung and Nghia after the incident.[45] He states that Nhung told him that Minh had decided to kill both Diem and Nhu. According to Nhung, Colonel Lam ordered Nghia and him to place the brothers in separate vehicles. Nhung would kill Diem, and Nghia would kill Nhu. When they arrived at the church, Nhu refused to be separated from Diem. According to Kim's aide, Nghia said he did not want to kill Nhu, so he got into Hiep's jeep, leaving Nhung to accomplish the mission. At the train crossing, Nhung took advantage of the train clatter to kill them. The convoy then proceeded to the JGS. The Minh government proclaimed that the brothers had committed suicide, then reversed itself and said they had died trying to escape, a position that subsequent regimes never altered.

Dinh, Thieu, Khiem, and other generals were horrified to learn of the brother's death, but the issue of culpability for Diem's killing faded after the Khanh coup on January 30, 1964. However, the question of who ordered Diem's killing arose again during the run-up to the 1971 presidential election. The first hint occurred in 1970, when Dr. Tran Kim Tuyen, Diem's former internal intelligence chief, published a book with the shocking title *How to Kill a President.*[46] In response, Thieu addressed the issue in an interview to a small Canadian newspaper, in which he blamed the brother's deaths on the "military junta," which observers took to mean Minh and Don.[47]

With the matter now reopened and combined with a recent nostalgic rekindling of South Vietnamese interest in Diem's government, Tran Van Don, Do Mau, and Ton That Dinh serialized their respective memoirs in the late spring and early summer of 1971. Shortly thereafter, a series of articles discussing the coup and Diem's death appeared in the newspaper *Lap Truong,* which was owned by Nguyen Cao Ky. The articles, eventually sourced to several of Don's aides, resurrected Diem's ghost when they included fictionalized dialogue that claimed Thieu had talked Minh into killing the president.[48] Since Don's men were supporting Ky in the election, they had concocted this exchange to smear Thieu. Whether Don approved of his aide's actions is unknown, but his English language book and his Vietnamese language memoir solely blamed Minh for their deaths.

Minh remained silent on Diem's murder until the release in mid-June 1971 of the highly classified U.S. study of the war known as the Pentagon Papers. The study's detailed review of American involvement in the 1963 coup forced Minh to explain his role during those fateful days. During an interview with several reporters in mid-July, Minh blamed Thieu for Diem's death by claiming that Thieu had delayed taking the palace, allowing the brothers to escape, which had led to their deaths. Minh's charge was an outrageous smear. Thieu had only joined the coup after Minh had promised not to kill Diem, had delayed assaulting the palace under direct orders, and had requested that he be allowed to transport the brothers so that he could keep them safe. When the South Vietnamese press heavily reported Minh's comments, Thieu called a press conference to refute Minh's false claim. Thieu told the assembled journalists that Minh was a "coward and a liar," that his initial target was not the palace, and that he had been "shocked to learn" that Diem had been killed.[49] For a culture that shunned public confrontations, it was a major uproar. A day later, Minh backed down, stating that, as the coup leader, he accepted full responsibility for their deaths. The issue never arose again.

4

"REPRESENTING ALL NATIONALIST TENDENCIES"

Duong Van Minh Charts a New Course

Diem's strongman rule had bound the country together, but the demise of the First Republic unleashed previously suppressed political and religious groups in South Vietnam. The new military government suddenly faced resurgent factionalism, a development that would tear South Vietnam's delicate social fabric. At best, the South Vietnamese body politic was a patchwork of competing interests, personality clashes, and regional bias, all previously stitched together by Diem's iron will and heavy hand. With the tight lid that Diem had clamped on South Vietnamese political activity now lifted, the old power blocs reemerged and began to maneuver. The Nationalist political parties (Dai Viet, VNQDD, etc.), religious rifts, ethnic divisions, and long-simmering regional bias resurfaced, each group seeking to gain power at the expense of the others.

After Diem's death, Nationalist politics became essentially two worlds. The first was the real world of increasingly political generals and their power games, and the second was a tragicomic opera of factional infighting, a phantasmagoria of alliances, fronts, and parties, combining like amoeba and then splitting into new organisms. The centrifugal instincts of South Vietnamese Nationalist elites would prove difficult to heal and nearly handed South Vietnam to its Communist enemy.

The four-year interregnum between Diem's First Republic and Thieu's Second Republic was marked by serious civil discord, failed experimentation in civilian rule, worsening economic conditions, and a rapidly expanding war. Given its short life—from November 1963 to January 1964—Minh's government has received little scholarly examination. Most have written that the generals seemed poorly prepared to govern and that the country drifted aimlessly while the Communists gained strength in the countryside.[1] This analysis stems both from the apparent lack of achievements during the junta's brief reign and later accusations made by Nguyen Khanh, who was attempting to justify his counter-coup of January 30, 1964.

A deeper analysis of Minh's regime, however, reveals that it did initiate important programs. Minh sought to reconfigure Diem's pacification and foreign policies to construct a new, more inclusive South Vietnamese political identity. Through outreach to various constituencies that Diem had either suppressed or ignored, Minh started a seismic change in South Vietnamese governance: an effort to forge a Vietnamese version of democracy that sought the population's willing acceptance of Saigon's authority, one that would endure until full reunification. All these efforts would influence future efforts by successor administrations.

MINH SETS A NEW COURSE

As the man who had rid South Vietnam of a despised dictator, General Duong Van Minh was the hero of the moment. He quickly formed a Military Revolutionary Council (MRC) to rule the country, but the senior general's governing style soon exacerbated tensions in the MRC. On November 9, Colonel Do Mau informed the CIA's William Colby that the council was rapidly dividing into two groups.[2] It was a message the U.S. would hear often in November. The split was both procedural and generational. The senior group of Minh, Don, and Le Van Kim, along with newly installed Prime Minister Nguyen Ngoc Tho, were oriented toward the highly legalistic French bureaucratic methodology. The second group of Khiem, Khanh, and Thieu wanted the new government to use its decree powers to make quick decisions backed by strong action to solve the nation's problems. Swift rulings by the leader followed by action, a military trait, was not characteristic of democratic institutions, which require debate and then compromise to achieve policy decisions. The tension between the two mindsets in a nation fighting for its survival would mar Saigon politics until the very end.

Critically, Minh did not seek a military dictatorship. He envisioned a transition to a civilian government, and he assigned Le Van Kim to plan the postcoup political entity. During the summer of 1963, Kim secretly met with Bui Diem and Phan Huy Quat to design a postcoup civilian government. Kim knew both men from their previous time together in Bao Dai's government. Quat was a northerner and a medical doctor who had served as minister of defense for the former emperor, and Kim and Bui Diem had worked together under Quat. After the Geneva Accords, the Dai Viets had pushed Bao Dai to select Quat as prime minister instead of Diem. It was a slight Diem never forgot. The antagonism between Diem and Quat was further enflamed on April 29, 1960, when Quat and seventeen other senior civilian leaders published a manifesto demanding Diem reform his government. Collectively called the Caravelle Group, Diem initially ignored this group of intellectuals and former ministers, but the day after the failed November 1960 coup, he jailed many of the signatories.

Part of the Dai Viet's northern faction, Quat and Bui Diem did not seek a Dai Viet monopoly of power but instead hoped for a constitutionally based unity government comprising all non-communist elements. Dodging Diem's secret police, they conferred with another Dai Viet, Dang Van Sung, who outlined for an American official the group's effort to combine the various constituencies. These blocs included "the Dai Viet Party, the VNQDD...and the Hoa Hao sect. Sung stated that in spite of the historic inability of Vietnamese groups to form a united front, he has made definite progress in bringing these groups together since the present atmosphere is so favorable." Given Diem's sagging fortunes, Sung's purpose was "to make political recommendations to the senior officers in case there is a change of regime." Sung felt that the military's "reaction to the general nature of these recommendations has been assuredly favorable although a final decision as to details of the form and structure of a new government has not been made."[3] The group proposed to Kim that Quat lead the country as prime minister.

Despite all the pre-coup maneuverings to patch together a unity government, Minh made a major error and disregarded their work. Instead of choosing Quat, he selected his old friend and Diem's vice president, Nguyen Ngoc Tho.[4] Unknown to Kim, Tho had colluded with Big Minh before the coup to fashion the cabinet. According to Kim's son, his father returned home visibly upset after Big Minh's announcement, grumbling that appointing Diem's vice president "was not a revolution" but a revival of regionalism. "Minh in his heart of hearts did not want to appoint a northerner [Quat] as the new prime minister of South Vietnam," notes Kim's son. "Nor did he particularly like the northern Dai Viet members like Quat, preferring instead the southern Dai Viets. My dad thought picking Tho was a huge mistake."[5]

Most Vietnamese shared Kim's reaction, who believed the choice reeked of cronyism. The declaration immediately created doubt in the minds of many Vietnamese; was this a revolution, as the general's claimed, or simply a power grab by Minh and the armed forces? Worse, Minh failed to clarify his rational for choosing Tho. Not until a 1968 interview did Minh explain that he had chosen Tho to manage the economy and administrative functions that Minh knew he was incapable of handling. "We, the military, were not versed in technical matters, and we thought it necessary to maintain the continuity of the administration. Tho accepted responsibility for one year only."[6]

Tho then compounded Minh's mistake by not revealing his own role in the coup. "Had Tho's role been disclosed the day of Diem's fall, his appointment as prime minister would have been welcomed by the Vietnamese people," claims Nguyen Ngoc Huy, "but because it was not revealed, the Vietnamese people were disappointed to see Diem's highest civil servant becoming chief of the new government."[7] Upon his return to Saigon from France in mid-November, Huy convinced Minh to rectify his mistake and reveal Tho's pre-coup involvement, but it was too late. Within a month, the U.S. embassy reported that Tho was "resented by many Vietnamese who claim he is weak, without firm principles, and regional in his outlook. Civilian members of Tho's cabinet, who are predominantly native southerners, are technically competent but lack the political and administrative skills to shape policies or influence the military."[8] Equally bad, as a French-trained bureaucrat, Tho was inflexible and unwilling to make quick decisions. When combined with Minh's *laissez-faire* attitude to work, it was a deadly mixture.

Having overthrown Diem, Minh now needed help in reshaping GVN policy. Minh wanted to work closely with the Americans, and he immediately requested CIA advice in forming a new government. Lodge, however, "moved equally promptly to ensure that no such guidance would be given."[9] The ambassador wanted the new regime to appear independent of overt U.S. influence, so he seized total control over American input to the MRC. Previous ambassadors had allowed the CIA station chief wide latitude with senior officials, but Lodge limited the agency's role to matters pertaining to intelligence and pacification.

It was a huge mistake; Minh and the MRC desperately needed U.S. counsel in building a new government. Moreover, Lodge's stricture set a precedent for both America and South Vietnam; while the CIA, the military, and the U.S. Agency for International Development (USAID) all possessed critical expertise in their respective areas, the current (and future) American ambassador became the sole spokesman for the U.S. administration, the U.S. president's direct conduit to South Vietnam's leader. It was a lesson the generals took to heart: no political program or coup could occur without consulting or gaining approval from the U.S. ambassador. Yet Lodge did not have the in-country experience to provide the cogent political advice Minh wanted. Worse, his imperious temperament prevented him from developing the personal connections necessary to shape the policies of Saigon's leaders. Lodge's imperfections, of course, do not absolve the South Vietnamese from responsibility for their own missteps, but his decision to limit access cost the U.S. a precious opportunity to help guide the post-Diem regime and contributed directly to the junta's outward lethargy. It also blinded him to Khanh's counter-coup scheme until it was too late.

Despite the discord over the brothers' killing and his governing style, Minh began a series of policy shifts to reverse Diem's despotic rule. Minh sought to build wide support for his regime, not just among the South Vietnamese military and civilian population but with the U.S. as well. On November 5, he announced the formation of a new government. The MRC, comprised of twelve generals, would remain in place. Minh was appointed chief of state and concurrently chairman of the MRC, and Don was chosen minister of defense. The MRC dissolved the cabinet, tossed out the recently elected National Assembly, and shelved the October 1956 constitution.

While the new government had a heavy military presence, Minh proclaimed himself in charge of a provisional regime, not a permanent military regime. The MRC announced that, if possible, it would restore civilian control within six months. To back that pledge, on November 6, Prime Minister Tho's second decree formed a Council of Notables, an advisory body that would draft a new constitution and hold elections for a new National Assembly. Seeking to rally every faction in the South Vietnamese body politic, the Council comprised people "representing all Nationalist tendencies and walks of life."[10] Looking for regional balance, Minh chose

Tran Van Van, a wealthy southern landowner, as general secretary, and Bui Diem, a northerner, as Van's deputy. Formally introduced on November 23, the Council held no power, but it was an embryonic effort to infuse democracy into Vietnam. President Diem had created a similar committee to draft the First Republic's constitution, but he stymied its efforts when he overruled several clauses the committee had inserted that limited the president's powers.[11] Diem, like Ho Chi Minh, mainly ruled by decree, as the constitution enacted in 1956 had invested almost all power in the executive branch. Unfortunately, the generals decided to personally evaluate each prospective member, thereby delaying the Council's implementation until late December.

Minh had also released hundreds of students and Buddhists arrested in the police roundups after the August pagoda raids. Others discharged included more long-term political prisoners, like Dai Viet Party leader Ha Thuc Ky and VNQDD head Vu Hong Khanh. Minh's intentions were admirable, but they had unintended consequences. In his eagerness, Minh unwittingly freed dozens of Communist espionage agents, spies who had been caught but who had not confessed. Included in this mix were Vu Ngoc Nha, a northerner who had come south and ingratiated himself with the Diem family. Nha would eventually gain close access to President Thieu, and the cracking of Nha's spy ring at Independence Palace in 1969 was the worst public espionage scandal of the war.

Minh further sought to eliminate Diem's loyalists at all government levels. He began purging province and district chiefs, a housecleaning that devastated local administration from the province down to the hamlets. Like the dismissal of Baath Party members in Iraq after the overthrow of Saddam Hussein in 2003, Minh swept out numerous civilian and military administrators associated with the Can Lao or Diem. He justified his actions by informing U.S. officials that many local officials were corrupt. Whether true or not, like an accusation of being a Communist, it was a surefire way to eliminate a rival. Since Diem and Nhu's governing philosophy was neo-mandarin—a centralized, top-down approach that Americans would call micromanagement—Minh's wholesale replacement of officials, both competent and inept, along with a sudden lack of direction from Saigon, paralyzed rural administration.

Nothing, however, created more turmoil among the MRC than the return of certain ex-officers, many from France. Their homecoming reopened old schisms. The first rumbling occurred when Nguyen Chanh Thi and

Pham Van Lieu, the officers involved in the 1960 coup attempt who were still living in Cambodian exile, asked to return to Saigon. On November 8, Minh granted their request. On November 16, the army reinstated the pair to their former ranks, irking Khiem, who had staunchly opposed the 1960 coup attempt. Minh subsequently assigned Thi as Khanh's deputy commander in I Corps.

One of the first émigrés to return from Paris was Vuong Van Dong, the leader of the November 1960 coup. Thi and Lieu were outraged, as they believed he was working for French intelligence, a still highly charged allegation. Another example was Duong Van Duc, Khiem's classmate at the school in Dalat. Duc was volatile, but he had helped Minh defeat the Hoa Hao militia in 1956.[12] Diem had rewarded Duc by making him one of his first generals, but he and the president had a falling out in the aftermath of the 1960 mutiny. Like other Vietnamese who had soured on Diem, Duc retired and went to Paris. On November 8, he returned to Saigon and was restored to his old rank of major general.

Another contentious application submitted to the MRC was Tran Van Don's request that his old friend, Major General Nguyen Van Vy, be allowed to rejoin the army at a senior position. Vy had also served in the French army with Don and Kim. Diem had kicked Vy out of the country when Vy backed Lieutenant General Hinh in 1954–55. Don states that in early December 1963, Duc visited him to protest Vy's return, claiming that Vy continued to work for the French. Duc told Don that "Vy was a counter-revolutionary and that if Vy was allowed to return to the army, Duc would refuse to serve in our army."[13]

The MRC disregarded Duc's claim and granted approval, but when Vy asked that Tran Dinh Lan, another key participant who had worked for Hinh against Diem, also come home, uproar ensued. Everyone believed that Lan was a traitor who still worked for French intelligence. Vy, however, personally vouched for Lan, and after investigating, Don cabled Lan on December 29 that he could return. Infuriated, Duc immediately began agitating among the other generals that allowing Vy, Dong, and Lan to return indicated that Don and Kim were conspiring with the French to neutralize South Vietnam. Disgust at the return of the former officers and newly aroused suspicions regarding Don and Kim's true allegiance generated more opposition in the military to the senior generals. Yet while infighting among the military simmered in the background, the most pressing issue remained the war in the countryside.

PACIFICATION—THE KIEN HOA AND LONG AN PROGRAMS

Developing the proper war-fighting strategy was always in the forefront of allied thinking, but the grand conundrum was in pinpointing, via Carl Von Clausewitz's famous phrase, the Communist's "center of gravity." By identifying and destroying the focal point of the enemy's strength, they hoped to defeat the Communist "war of national liberation" strategy. The war, however, was multi-dimensional, a model not easily understood by conventionally trained officers in either the South Vietnamese or American militaries. The Vietnam conflict posed a unique challenge in that the Communists had multiple centers of gravity, ones that shifted in priority as the war progressed. Many proved difficult to defeat, including enemy sanctuaries in Laos and Cambodia and the supply corridor known as the Ho Chi Minh Trail. In this environment, some unconventional U.S. officials saw building South Vietnam's political and economic institutions as the best means to inoculate the citizenry against Marxism rather than trying to defeat the guerrillas with military force. They asserted that the Communists had no center of gravity that reasonable military means could defeat, but the entrenched bureaucracies in Washington and Saigon ignored these voices. This debate, often called a "political" versus a "military" strategy to win the war, would rage for years. Eventually the allies realized that success required integrating both military and political components, but this process, known as pacification of the countryside, would undergo numerous fits and starts before achieving this holistic approach in late 1968.

Diem's pacification effort involved shifting people as much as redistributing property. His goals were to resettle the massive influx of northern refugees plus relocate people from overpopulated regions to fallow sections in the countryside. His first attempt, called the Land Development Program, transferred people to new territories. The idea was to provide a security belt against Communist infiltration and subdue former rebel areas with an influx of (assumed) pro-government settlers. He targeted the Central Highlands along the Laos border, the Hoa Hao territory in the western Mekong River area adjacent to Cambodia, and unoccupied sections of the southern Delta. By opening lightly populated lands, the new hamlets would drive economic growth by increasing exports of rice and other goods such as lumber, seafood, and rubber.

With the uptick in Communist attacks in 1960, Diem switched his pacification priorities to security, especially in the Delta, where the population was diffuse compared to the more tightly centered hamlets in the center and the northern parts of South Vietnam. He decided to group Delta residents closer together into newly constructed settlements called agrovilles. These small new towns would contain schools, clinics, and other amenities, and with the population banded together, defense would correspondingly be easier. The agroville program also failed, hindered by GVN mismanagement, lack of funds, and Communist terror attacks. By the fall of 1960, Diem cancelled the program, and he and his brother began the search for a new pacification strategy.

By early 1961, Diem and Nhu had settled on a different scheme. Based upon an amalgamation of British counterinsurgency concepts successfully tested in Malaysia, Israeli kibbutz theory, and French pacification ideas, they decided to build "Strategic Hamlets." Rural communities would be converted into fortified hamlets to defend against NLF guerrillas. Nhu was both the architect and overseer. According to Colonel Hoang Van Lac, Nhu's main aide for Strategic Hamlets, the program was to "reverse the [military] situation with a new revolutionary concept instead of reorganizing the army according to an outmoded conventional concept. Strategically, to separate the communists from the people, physically and morally," thus denying the enemy the support mechanisms that it needed to survive.[14]

For the Ngos, however, the strategic hamlet program was more than just security; pacification was the primary vehicle to implement their political revolution, to establish, according to Lac, "social justice and democracy...to revive the village traditions...and to modernize rural life."[15] Grouping people into secured hamlets was the perfect opportunity to reshape personal belief systems while concurrently denying the guerrillas a support system. Diem and Nhu wanted to move rapidly and complete the strategic hamlet program by the end of 1963. To achieve this aggressive timetable, forced labor was used, which aroused peasant ire. Many outside observers roundly condemned the strategic hamlet's involuntary relocation program, particularly for hamlets in districts around Saigon and in the Delta. Despite the discontent, the plan achieved some success, especially in the central provinces south of Danang, but headway in the Delta was spotty.[16]

Despite the imperfections of the allied approach to pacification, Communist efforts were also not faultless. They also used compulsory labor to develop bases in areas under their control. Moreover, Communist taxation policy, involuntary drafting of youths, forced marriages, and terror tactics often drove villagers toward the government. What differentiated the NLF

approach and made it more effective, though, was its coordination of both
military attacks and political struggle. At the most basic level, they sought
to defeat Diem's army and at the same time win the people's allegiance. The
Communists always viewed the war as one that was fought in three main
arenas: political, military, and military proselytizing (convincing South Vietnamese soldiers to switch sides or remain passive). In later years, diplomacy
became an additional factor, but this strategic combination, this collective
policy, facilitated Communist success.

After the coup, the Politburo saw a tremendous opportunity to win the
war. It exhorted the NLF to increase its attacks on what it considered the
GVN's greatest weakness, its structure at the village and hamlet level. The
Politburo ordered the NLF to annihilate "the enemy's entire network of
Strategic Hamlets, to liberate key areas...so that we can change the balance
of power between ourselves and the enemy."[17] While the Ap Bac victory the
previous January was used to convince NLF troops that they could defeat
helicopters and armored personnel carriers, the Politburo needed to destroy
the other arm of Diem's control, the Strategic Hamlets. After the coup, the
Communists swiftly took advantage and overran many of the Strategic Hamlets that had not already collapsed during the summer. This was especially
true in Long An province, the key Delta province directly to the south and
west of Saigon. As a result, Long An would become a proving ground for
Minh's revision of Diem's pacification program.

Developing the proper template for pacifying the countryside remained
a work in progress. The CIA, for example, had tested several counterinsurgency programs. One achieved modest success with the hill tribes in the
Central Highlands. Known as the Civilian Irregular Defense Group (CIDG),
the CIA had trained and armed teams to defend the local villages. Another
incubator for using local teams to roll back NLF gains was attempted in Kien
Hoa Province, called Ben Tre by the Communists, in the upper Delta. Its
location as the NLF birthplace and its entrenched Communist infrastructure
had earned that province the nickname "Cradle of the Revolution." Diem
assigned a former Viet Minh officer named Tran Ngoc Chau in early 1962
as the new chief of this difficult province. Like many Vietnamese, Chau had
fled the Viet Minh in disgust at Communist control. He joined the VNA,
serving in a variety of posts, including at the Military Academy in Dalat,
where he and Thieu became good friends.

Upon arrival, Chau quickly realized that the villagers were unresponsive
to the government. Chau decided to form small "Census Grievance" teams

that would canvass the villages for information on both NLF activity and poor government performance. Using this model, Chau's teams soon began reversing Communist gains in this long-time NLF stronghold. The Communist postwar provincial history for Ben Tre notes that "From March 1962 through the first months of 1963, a difficult and ferocious struggle raged throughout the province to resist enemy sweep operations and to counter enemy efforts to concentrate the population and build Strategic Hamlets." Even after receiving weapon shipments in 1963 from North Vietnam, NLF forces saw no relief. "A ferocious back-and-forth battle raged between the enemy and our forces. The enemy had been able to establish 129 Strategic Hamlets throughout the province. The size of our liberated zone had shrunk. We were fighting an extremely difficult struggle to secure control of the population, to counter enemy sweeps, to destroy Strategic Hamlets, and to gain control of villages and hamlets."[18]

Nevertheless, Chau's efforts were a nonstarter for Minh. The new South Vietnamese leader had long considered the French "oil spot" method the best pacification technique. Like an oil stain, the military first made one spot totally secure and then slowly spread out from there. In the spring of 1960, Minh responded to an American "request for a pacification plan with a proposal to adapt the 'oil spot' strategy of gradually expanding territorial control that the French had employed in Morocco. But his American adviser . . . had dismissed the idea out of hand, asserting that Minh simply did not understand the need for mobile operations that carried the war to the enemy."[19] Although the Americans saw destroying enemy combat units as the main pacification task, Minh, Tho, and Kim viewed the war as more political than military in nature. That meant a South Vietnamese shift in both theory and tactics.

Shortly after the coup, Minh publicly outlined his new pacification plan. He told assembled journalists that the Strategic Hamlets were "good in theory," but he specifically rejected the Ngos policy of using the Strategic Hamlets for social engineering. According to Minh, "Nhu used Strategic Hamlets for political rather than pacification purposes," and "that is why the people in the villages suffered very much."[20] Minh believed this caused the people to turn away from the government, and without rural support the war could not be won.

Ten days later, Minh met Rufus Phillips, the U.S. embassy chief for rural affairs, to outline his pacification thinking. While Minh "favored the basic concept" of the Strategic Hamlets, he thought it was "important to fit the strategic hamlet into an overall concept of pacification, and to understand that pacification, not spectacular combat missions...was the main mission of the military forces." Minh then outlined a fundamental change in South Vietnamese policy; he would break the ARVN into small units, assign them to a specific territory, decentralize authority to empower local unit commanders and civilian officials, and deal harshly with local corruption.[21] Moreover, the MRC declined a U.S. offer to assign advisers down to the district level, as it did not want Americans entering the villages and providing fodder for the Communist propaganda mill.

The depth of Minh's redesign of South Vietnam's pacification program is striking. Minh adopted the "oil spot" theory to expand control by building on rather than eliminating the existing strategic hamlet program. He would defend those hamlets that were still operational, but discard forced relocation and labor schemes, scale back the stress on rapid growth, and abandon large-scale military maneuvers. In early December, the MRC issued a decree to the province chiefs to cease pressing peasants to move into the fortified hamlets and to refrain from enforcing compulsory labor and financial contributions to the program.

Aware of the rapid Communist gains in Long An Province, Minh chose to test his new pacification program in that beleaguered area. The province, a major rice-growing region, was formed in 1957 and initially stretched south and west of Saigon. Two main roads ran through the province: Route 4, the main artery south from Saigon into the Delta, and Route 5, which ran east to the sea. Long An remained relatively peaceful until the beginning of 1960 when, in a coordinated attack during Tet 1960, the Communists assassinated numerous local government officials. After rearming a provincial main force battalion and several district-level companies, within eighteen months, Communist forces had conquered large tracts of Long An.

In response, Diem replaced the civilian province chief in October 1961 with ARVN Major Nguyen Viet Thanh. A native of Long An, Thanh would rise to major general and command of IV Corps before dying in a helicopter crash in 1970, one of South Vietnam's greatest wartime losses. Upon assuming command of Long An, Thanh launched a counterattack using his own province units and regulars from the 7th Division, which pushed the NLF units away from many villages. Thanh's approach worked for a time, but by early 1963 the military situation had deteriorated again. Communist cadres had reorganized and revitalized units with new weapons from covert sea-borne shipments from North Vietnam. Events moved rapidly downhill when in June 1963, Diem fired Thanh for refusing to fix the upcoming National Assembly elections.[22]

Diem, however, was cognizant of the deteriorating security situation in Long An. In September 1963, he transferred the recently raised 9th ARVN Division from its original home in Binh Dinh to the northern part of the Delta. Unfortunately, the transfer of the 9th left a partial vacuum in that critically important coastal province, and the Communists soon seized the initiative there. Yet the shift permitted Diem to permanently assign the 21st Division to the southernmost part of the Delta and to use the 7th Division in a more mobile role in the Delta. With more combat units, Diem attempted to arrest the security decline in Long An. On October 15, 1963, he formed Hau Nghia Province (west of Saigon) by annexing two districts on the Cambodian side of Long An as well as a district from Tay Ninh and another from Binh Duong Province. By combining insecure zones of adjoining provinces into one administrative unit, Diem hoped to concentrate resources to secure a problem area. Unfortunately, both moves failed. Hau Nghia remained a hotbed of enemy activity, while by November fewer than forty of the 219 Strategic Hamlets in Long An were still functioning. Without Thanh's vigorous leadership, the provincial Civil Guard units refused to respond when a hamlet was attacked, fearing the Communist tactic of ambushing the relief column. By late November, the NLF controlled virtually everything in Long An except the provincial and district towns.

Such was the situation facing Minh in late November when disaster suddenly struck. On the night of November 22, Communist forces overran a major CIDG camp near the Hiep Hoa sugar mill in Hau Nghia Province. The NLF captured four American advisers, along with a considerable number of weapons. Given the losses at Hiep Hoa and an alarming report from Earl Young, a USAID officer serving in Long An, the U.S. embassy pressed Minh to speed up his plan. Minh immediately assigned Major Le Minh Dao as the new Long An Province chief. Dao was an excellent choice. His grandparents were from Long An, he had spent part of his youth there, and he was a driven, highly effective officer. Shortly after the coup, Minh had dispatched Dao to inspect the province. Dao's report had impressed the general, and Minh appointed him as province chief on November 24.[23]

To help Minh, Lodge created an embassy task force to focus on Long An. Lodge ordered a survey of the hamlets in the area designated for the first "oil spot" operation near the Long An provincial capital. USIS (United States Information Service) field operations officer Frank Scotton organized and led three mixed Vietnamese American teams. This survey, conducted in mid-December 1963, was the first to examine the political situation in the hamlets, assess current security, and determine peasant attitudes toward the government.[24] The teams canvassed fifteen hamlets, and what they found was shocking. Communist elements moved almost at will among and within the hamlets, and most people were either neutral or moderately pro-NLF, a result as much from government ineptitude as Communist proselytizing. Minh needed to move now, before the entire province was lost. Pacification, however, was just one facet of Minh's plan to win the war. While Minh was moving to retake Long An, he was also reversing many of Diem's political and foreign policies.

POLICY CHANGES

Minh and Prime Minister Nguyen Ngoc Tho were determined to win back the various disaffected segments of South Vietnamese society through energetic political and economic reforms. The two men sought to form a majority coalition among the various Nationalist factions that would attract and then include the non-communist segments of the NLF. They believed this united front could politically and militarily compete against the Communists and therefore speed negotiations to end the war. Prime Minister Tho told historian George Kahin that the "strategy of the new government was first to consolidate itself with the Cao Dai, Hoa Hao, Cambodian minority, etc., and then to try to bring over the NLF out of opposition into support of what would be termed a government of reconciliation."[25] Tho did not mean a coalition with the NLF but an opening of the political process so that all South Vietnamese factions could peacefully compete for power. Whether this view was naïve or whether Tho was another in a lengthy line of commentators who believed a compromise between the NLF and Saigon could freeze out Hanoi is difficult to judge.

Minh's first move was to immediately release any imprisoned monks. He then overturned Diem's ban on Buddhist political organizing. Consequently, the bonzes politically supported the MRC. With this critical backing secured, Minh next reversed Diem's policy of suppressing the Hoa Hao and Cao Dai religious groups. He sought to enlist both as allies against the NLF, believing that if he gained their cooperation, the anti-communist sects would eliminate the NLF in their territories, thus freeing ARVN forces to concentrate elsewhere. Despite having led the ARVN forces that had conquered the Hoa Hao, Minh first targeted the sect. Visiting the Hoa Hao territory on November 27, a large crowd gathered to hear him speak. He pledged that the "disastrous policy of the former regime who tried to crush you has ended."[26] Minh next moved to sway the Cao Dai, and on December 27 he attended an elaborate public ceremony at the main Cao Dai temple near Mount Ba Den on the border with Cambodia.

While Minh was working internal relations, Le Van Kim oversaw foreign affairs. Long considered the brains behind Minh, Kim's first policy move was a restoration of diplomatic contacts with Cambodia. Kim's outreach to Cambodia had the secondary effect of pleasing the large and often oppressed Cambodian minority in the Delta, but restoring relations was not a simple assignment. Cambodian head of state Norodom Sihanouk had suspended contacts with Saigon in August 1963 over the pagoda raids. Although Diem and Nhu had attempted early in their reign to develop a close alliance with Sihanouk, relations floundered when fighting in South Vietnam resumed. For Saigon, an unfriendly Cambodia made defeating Communist aggression nearly impossible. Cambodia sits on South Vietnam's western flank, and the two countries had a long, unmarked, jungle-covered border. Since geography directly correlates to military defense, a hostile Cambodia meant stretching Saigon's limited resources along a lengthy and challenging boundary.

When the war resumed in 1960, relations with Cambodia became increasingly tense over border demarcation issues, control of offshore islands, and South Vietnamese harboring and arming of Cambodian anti-Sihanouk dissidents. When Sihanouk rejected Diem and Nhu's overtures and instead stated that a Communist triumph in Vietnam was inevitable, the brothers viewed Sihanouk as deliberately undermining their efforts to build a viable anti-communist country. Consequently, Nhu secretly arranged a coup to overthrow the prince, hoping a new ruler would change Cambodian policy from hostility to open support. When the plot failed, Nhu attempted to assassinate Sihanouk. That effort also failed, and when it was exposed, relations thereafter became understandably cold.

While the MRC remained upset at Sihanouk's pronouncements on neutralization, Kim hoped to "end the bitterness that had divided the two Indochinese neighbors" during Diem's rule.[27] Saigon needed to reestablish good relations with its neighbor, hoping it could convince Cambodia to seal its border. The MRC sent a goodwill mission led by Kim to Cambodia in mid-December. He proposed to demarcate the poorly defined border and offered to drop the Diem-era claims on offshore islands between the two countries. The trip opened the door for a reciprocal visit by the Cambodian foreign minister at the end of the month. Yet despite these hopeful signs, relations remained problematic given Sihanouk's repeated calls for neutralization.

While Kim was leading this mission, Minh continued his efforts to build a future civilian government. Minh decided to reaffirm his desire to form a civilian government when the appointed Council of Notables held its inauguration ceremony on January 2, 1964. Displaying a political maturity few knew he possessed, Minh stated that "the time will very soon come when the essential democratic institutions are established on solid foundations, so that we may turn power over to a civilian government elected by the people." Further, he wanted the council to draft a constitution that had "a clear-cut separation of powers, an effective protection of individual liberties, and the promotion of a legal and constructive opposition." He also eloquently remarked that "we will keep fighting so long as the obstacles on our road to democracy have not all been removed, and so long as there is doubt that we and our children may not live a life worthy of free men."[28]

These noteworthy political, military, and diplomatic moves were occurring, however, alongside growing internal dissatisfaction with Prime Minister Tho. On December 9, Minh held a hastily arranged press conference to defend Tho. The press, previously heavily controlled and now suddenly free to publish anything, had begun printing commentary ranging from insightful discourse to inflammatory rumors. Senior Vietnamese government officials were unused to press criticism, and they reacted poorly to journalistic scrutiny. At the conference, rather than reassure the public about Tho, the prime minister promptly got into an intense argument with the newly assertive Vietnamese press. Tho had to defend himself against charges that he had failed to protect the Buddhists while he was working for Diem and that his cabinet was too southern-oriented.

It was the first but no means the last time that charges were leveled over a perceived regional bias in the government. A week later, Kim denied during another press conference that Tho was about to be replaced or that the prime minister was promoting only southerners within the government. Despite his denial, rumors soon circulated that Kim wanted to replace Tho and take over the government and neutralize the country. After the showdown with Tho, in mid-December 1963, press restrictions were reinstated and three newspapers were shut down.

THE FEAR OF NEUTRALIZATION RETURNS

South Vietnamese fears of neutralization, exacerbated by the return of allegedly pro-French officers, were stirred further in late November 1963 when Sihanouk revived his prior appeal for a Geneva-style conference to formalize his country's neutrality. His latest plan proposed a semi-federated neutrality zone with South Vietnam if Saigon halted military action against the NLF. Sihanouk's proposal generated much publicity, but the South Vietnamese generals did not become seriously concerned until a *New York Times* editorial on December 8 recommended the U.S. government consider Sihanouk's plan. The generals saw the *Times* as a bellwether of official U.S. attitudes. At Minh's press conference to support Tho, he also announced that the MRC "rejected any possibility of neutralizing South Vietnam while North Vietnam is still Communist-dominated, and he opposed calling an international conference to guarantee the neutrality of Cambodia." Kim, attempting to dampen rumbling about the exiled military officers, also stated that the MRC would not allow Vietnamese to return from France if they "are with the Communists and the neutralists."[29] When the U.S. did not immediately reject Sihanouk's plan, Minh, Kim, Don, and Prime Minister Tho summoned Lodge on December 11 to discuss American policy. According to Lodge, the Vietnamese leaders "pointed out that apparent acceptance of proposal on neutrality conference on Cambodia and of Vietnam negotiation prior to victory by such influential journal as the *New York Times* was having serious effect on morale Vietnamese engaged in anti-Communist struggle."[30]

Lodge strongly denied any American plans for neutralization by reading directly from a State Department telegram that provided details on the U.S. government's stand against it. His explanation had no effect. A senior American official visiting Saigon in December found that

> talk of neutralism has spread like wildfire through the Vietnamese community. The [*Times*] editorial and [other] columns on the subject were a body blow to morale in Saigon. The equivocal U.S. stand regarding a conference on Cambodian neutrality took on ominous meaning for many Vietnamese. Even high officials asked: are we next? Rumors of French recognition of the Peiping regime added fuel to the flames.... It is impossible to determine how many Vietnamese are thinking of neutralism as a possible solution to their problems. What is most depressing

is the growing feeling among them that this may be U.S. policy and that they better be prepared for it. Recent assurances from us have doubtless helped ease the situation but much more needs to be done to counter this line.[31]

Realizing he needed to denounce neutralization in stronger terms, Minh agreed to a rare interview with the English language *Saigon Post*, a paper owned by Bui Diem. Minh emphasized that his government did not "accept among us anyone who wants to push...a solution of neutrality which, we are convinced, would open the floodgates for Communism...[W]e estimate that the Communists are resorting to these neutralist maneuvers only as a war ruse." He then summed up South Vietnamese opinion of the 1962 Laos Accords: "[T]he example of Laos is perfectly eloquent for us: neutralization of that country has essentially served the Communist...aim of taking over the country." Minh then dismissed the French efforts as "unacceptable."[32]

Despite Minh's rebuff, the French were not giving up. The rumors about France and China were confirmed when De Gaulle announced in early January 1964 that France would officially recognize China. Enflaming the situation even more, on January 18, 1964, the official French news organ Agence France Presse (AFP) published an expansive article titled "The Asian Policy of France." The commentary suggested that France's recognition of Beijing was part of its plan to neutralize Indochina. The next day, the *New York Times* published a similar analysis. Drawing heavily from the AFP piece, the *Times* reported that "from the standpoint of the De Gaulle government, the great merit of recognition is the assistance it is supposed to give to a negotiated settlement in Southeast Asia. This...has now become the chief reason for recognition."[33] Furious, on January 23, the Council of Notables demanded that Saigon sever diplomatic relations with Paris. The MRC also rejected France's proposed new ambassador, withdrew its own candidate, and quietly backed student protests at the French embassy. The escalating fears over neutrality would soon have tremendous repercussions.

MILITARY MOVES

Faced with these internal and external difficulties, as 1964 began, Minh struggled to formalize his new pacification and military strategies to defeat the Communist insurgency. Minh initially wanted to reveal his new pacification plan, called "New Rural Life Hamlet" (*Ap Tan Sinh*), in early January, but the MRC was unable to finalize the details. When he postponed the announcement, it convinced most South Vietnamese that Minh and his coterie were dithering. He was not; the enormity of the tasks the regime faced was one reason it had moved so slowly to implement a new strategy. For example, while the regime was developing the National Pacification strategy to integrate military and civilian energies to revitalize the contest in the countryside, it was also revamping its psychological operations (psyops). To improve Saigon's image, the ARVN held a conference on January 9 for all psyops officers. The MRC intended to launch an "informational effort...to tell the people what the government is doing." Enhanced civic action would be a key component of the new psyops campaign, which meant providing "economic benefits for rural people...as proof that their government is concerned with their welfare."[34]

Yet while this emphasis on rural construction was a critical component of pacification, Prime Minister Tho had to find a way to pay for it. On January 9, he publicly stated the government's dilemma: "We have to balance a scanty budget without overtaxing the population, stabilize an easily perturbed market while boosting production in every sector, intensify the anti–Viet Cong war effort while seeing to it that more schools, hospitals and houses are built, and more jobs are available to the working class."[35]

His announcement highlights one of the most vital but overlooked factors of the conflict: Saigon's antiquated tax structure could not provide the revenue to pay for the war effort, let alone build the countryside. Second only to dedicated cadres at the grassroots level, money was the key to revamping pacification and implementing land reform, long considered the cornerstones to winning peasant loyalty. The MRC had designed major programs to enhance village infrastructure, yet they faced an economic paradox. While these were popular economic decisions, how would the regime pay for all those new schools and health clinics? Only American aid money could bolster the government's treasury. Not surprisingly, on the same day as Tho's statement, the U.S. and South Vietnam signed a $31 million dollar "Food for Peace" contract, the largest at that point in U.S. history. Ninety percent of the revenue from the sale of food to Vietnamese commercial importers would go to Saigon's budget. Saigon's need for U.S. aid money to build out the countryside would be never be resolved.

Despite the MRC emphasis on revising the government's social, economic, and foreign affairs, the chief concern remained the military conflict. By early January, Major General Khiem had finalized the pacification plan, called *Dien Hong*. His design was a two-phase scheme to win the war by the end of 1965. Employing the oil spot technique, the army, using a combination of military force and civilian ministries operating under the army's command, would concentrate first on pacifying the most "densely populated and prosperous areas...to destroy the enemy infrastructure, and to push the [enemy] forces into their secret bases or combat zones."[36] The concept was to defeat the insurgency by January 1, 1965, in the most populous provinces around Saigon. The ARVN would then clear the remaining provinces by July 1, 1965, after which Phase II would destroy the last NLF units in South Vietnam by the end of the 1965.

The plan was largely theoretical. A practical scheme for "destroying the enemy infrastructure" had not been developed, nor had it been determined who would fill the cleared areas vacated by ARVN as they moved forward to expand the oil spot. Khiem's plan also contained dubious estimates about both South Vietnamese forces and their enemy. At the end of December 1963, Khiem had publicly announced that ARVN morale after the coup was "very high" and that the army could "win the war by 1965."[37] His new plan, however, was based on two specious assumptions: NLF attacks had peaked, and the NLF's strength would soon wither away. Such assumptions were not surprising given that Minh and Tho believed that the NLF included many non-communists. They thought that since the opposition's *raison d'être* had died with the president, soon only hard-core Communists would populate the NLF. Several NLF pronouncements after the coup stating that its forces were prepared to halt the fighting and enter a coalition government had further lured Minh into imagining that he could eventually hold elections to form a unity government.

Minh and Tho were not the only people to succumb to the siren song of compromise and a "political solution" with the NLF. Many others would as well, including the French and the American left. Even some within South Vietnam shared this view, but the most powerful and organized segments of South Vietnamese society—such as the military, the educated elite, the Catholics, and the sects—were adamantly opposed to any accommodation with the NLF. "Even at the time of the NLF's formation," wrote Vietnam expert Douglas Pike, "the professional politicians, government officials, and religious leaders throughout the country correctly assessed the NLF as a Communist-dominated front group seeking exclusive power for the Communists."[38] This rejection of a political compromise by the governing strata of South Vietnamese society was the defining characteristic of Saigon politics, and it would constrict the actions of any Nationalist government tempted to offer such a settlement.

If a political compromise with the NLF was anathema to the military, why did Minh hold a differing view? Evidently, the Dai Viets were not the only political party to view Minh as a malleable commodity. Minh's belief had received encouragement from his younger brother, an officer in the People's Army. The other generals were unaware that during January 1964, Minh's brother, Senior Captain Duong Van Nhut, was secretly visiting him. In 1960, the Communist Enemy Proselytizing Department, the agency responsible for subverting ARVN officers, "decided to target Minh. A number of our senior leaders recognized that, although he was a general officer serving the Saigon government, he had some personal characteristics that would allow us to contact him and win his sympathies so that we could induce him to take actions that benefited the people and the nation."[39] Minh's falling out with Diem provided Hanoi an opening, and Nhut was dispatched to try to manipulate him. The hope was that if Minh ever achieved power, Nhut's influence could sway Minh's policies.

Nhut spent ten days in January 1964 in Saigon secretly visiting Minh. His purpose was to "appeal to the spirit of patriotism and love of the people so that Duong Van Minh would limit the brutal actions of the Saigon Army, and when the opportunity arose, that he would help the revolution drive out the American aggressor army and their lackeys." Nhut focused on two themes: the "American imperialists" were the aggressors in South Vietnam, and the NLF "was comprised of patriotic Vietnamese, including people who were not Communists, who had gathered together to struggle against the American imperialist aggressors to liberate South Vietnam and unify our nation." While he was unsuccessful in convincing Minh of Hanoi's righteousness, another high-ranking Communist proselytizing officer claims that Nhut convinced Minh to eliminate the Strategic Hamlet program. Minh supposedly agreed, but only if the "revolution did not destroy their hospitals, schools, and barbed wire fences."[40] Khanh has claimed in various postwar interviews that Minh did decide to eliminate the Strategic Hamlet program, but what Minh really intended is open to interpretation.

Given the Nationalist fears over neutralism, one can only imagine the other generals' and the Dai Viets' reaction if Minh's dalliance had been revealed. While other issues had created tension among the ruling generals, they still paled in comparison to the threat of neutralization, South Vietnam's version of the "third rail" of politics. Despite Minh's denunciations of neutralization, rumors had appeared that Le Van Kim and the other French-trained generals were strongly considering it. If Nhu's efforts to open talks with Hanoi had helped spark the November coup, any hint that Minh's junta might do the same was all the justification other generals needed to move against them. The old saying that the "revolution eats its children" would never prove truer than in South Vietnam.

5

"THE EARTH IS ROUND. WE WILL MEET AGAIN ONE DAY"

Nguyen Khanh's Countercoup

There were four compelling factors that drove Brigadier General Nguyen Khanh's countercoup against Minh on January 30, 1964. The first was Diem's murder. While many had celebrated the coup, few rejoiced over his death. His killing instantly created tension in the MRC, as most generals had joined the rebellion only after receiving Minh's explicit assurances that no harm would come to the president. The second was the resentment felt by Khanh and Khiem over their postcoup sidelining by the senior generals. The third was the regime's inability to move quickly. Most important, though, was an uproar over an alleged neutralization scheme of South Vietnam by Le Van Kim and Tran Van Don. Using these rationales, the southern branch of the Dai Viet Party secretly maneuvered to achieve power. This "reorganization," as Khanh called it, would unleash a devastating internal struggle among the Nationalists.

ANIMOSITY BUILDS

Tran Van Don's attitude toward Khanh and Khiem is clear. Writing after the war, Don denigrates both men while concurrently claiming he was close to them. While the events of 1964 no doubt colored hiss postwar accounts, Don claims that the senior generals did not trust either man. Don writes that "we were correct in approaching [Khiem] cautiously and probably should not have given him a high position in the government."[1] Khiem immediately sensed this coolness from the clique of senior generals. He told one friend that after Minh and the others had murdered Diem, "the success of the [Diem coup] resulted in trouble for me. As soon as it ended, Minh, Don, Kim, wanted to get rid of me right away."[2]

As for Khanh, Don and Minh suspected that he was playing both sides. Don remarked that Khanh was a "complete opportunist," so they "informed him [only] a day in advance and did not give him any details of the plot," a wariness that proved correct.[3] Despite his earlier plotting against Diem, Khanh admitted in several postwar interviews that he considered supporting the president when the coup occurred. Huynh Van Cao claims that on the afternoon of November 1, Khanh called and urged him to send troops to rescue Diem. When Cao asked Khanh if he was also sending forces, Khanh said he was too far away.[4] Khanh states that Diem had called him, asking that he rescue the brothers. Khanh dissembled again, saying Pleiku was too distant from Saigon, but if Diem could survive for four days, he would switch sides.[5] After seeing the coup's success, early on the morning of November 2, Khanh issued a statement supporting the MRC.

While Diem's murder deeply troubled Khanh, his arms-length treatment and lack of postcoup elevation added resentment to his growing list of imagined grievances. Sensing Khanh's unrest, on December 12, Minh sent the overly ambitious officer to Hue to command I Corps, switching commands with Do Cao Tri. By sending Khanh as far from Saigon as possible, Minh hoped to eliminate a major source of discontent while solving another issue: Buddhist leaders were agitating for Tri's removal given his vigorous suppression of them during Diem's last months.

American desire for a stronger prosecution of the war also inadvertently started the second coup. Ton That Dinh was currently holding two roles: III Corps commander and minister of the interior. The U.S. believed Dinh was overwhelmed, and it pressured Minh to nominate a new III Corps commander. Minh demurred, but after he received a letter from President Lyndon Johnson that included this recommendation, he agreed. On January 5, Minh shifted Khiem from chief of the Joint General Staff to replace Dinh as III Corps commander, and he replaced Khiem with Le Van Kim. Like many well-intentioned American ideas, the move immediately backfired. Khiem saw the change as a demotion, and given his current bitterness, his resentment hardened into a desire for revenge.

Although Minh's prime concern was reversing NLF gains in the countryside, after he delayed the announcement of his new pacification plan, the

U.S. pressed him to finalize his policy. Prime Minister Tho finally signed the pacification degree on January 23. The law stipulated that the government would provide material to assist the peasants, local elections would be held, and farmers would no longer be forced into compulsory labor. The result, Minh believed, would be prosperous hamlets that would fight the NLF. Yet while Minh was disdainful of Nhu's social engineering designs for the villagers, his own program began with an appeal for the people to develop a "spiritual characteristic," essentially a dressed-up version of anti-communism.[6]

Oddly, the delay in launching the new pacification program, symbolic of the regime's apparent lassitude, was blamed on Tho rather than Minh. Don claims that he and Ton That Dinh were so exasperated by Tho's bureaucratic mentality that in December they both decided to resign. Minh persuaded them to stay, but Don relates that by late January, "the majority of the generals were against keeping Tho on as Prime Minister, but because they knew of the personal relationship between Minh and Tho no one dared to say so openly. On January 23, the generals brought up the problem of Tho for discussion in the Council. When I raised the question of replacing Tho, Thieu said, 'the army carried out the coup, so the army should be given this job.'"[7] Minh declined Thieu's suggestion, but his request clearly displays the mindset, one that hearkened back to 1954 and Lieutenant General Nguyen Van Hinh, that the military should run the government to improve efficiency.

Replacing Tho provided another justification for the Khanh coup. One contender reportedly being considered was Nguyen Ton Hoan, the Dai Viet chieftain living in exile in Paris. However, in the swirling Saigon rumor mill, Hoan was not the main conspirator against Tho—it was Le Van Kim.[8] Nguyen Ngoc Huy claims that Kim "sought to replace Tho as prime minister. He contacted politicians and encouraged them to criticize Tho's government."[9] Pham Van Lieu, a long-time Dai Viet member and keen reporter of the Saigon scene, also alleges that Kim was conspiring with the Dai Viet's northern faction "to elevate Kim to the post of prime minister."[10]

The rumor that Kim was seeking the prime minister's position was the final straw for many officers. The perception of Kim is that while he was the brains behind Minh, his prior service in the French army and his former French citizenship meant that Kim was pro-French and favored De Gaulle's plan for neutralization of South Vietnam.[11] Thus, many generals and lower-ranking officers readily believed allegations that Kim and the other Francophile generals like Don were plotting to neutralize the country.

The accusation, in effect one of treason, was so grave that after the coup, Khanh ordered some intelligence officers to search the files for documentary evidence against Kim. They found nothing because the charge was ludicrous.

Minh flatly denied the accusation. In a conversation with an American military officer, "Minh said he is absolutely positive that the charges of neutralist and plotting with the French are completely false.... Kim was always the most adamant in denouncing De Gaulle's views to the point where Minh had to remonstrate with Kim about his violent reaction."[12] Kim's close friend and Dai Viet member Bui Diem also denied that Kim wanted to become prime minister, as did Kim's sons and Kim's postcoup military aide.[13] Bui Diem notes that while Kim "was in a perpetual state of angry frustration over the incompetence and lethargy of the junta [but] some interpreted Kim's move to the new job as Chief of the JGS as an attempt to consolidate his own power."[14]

Most concluded that Khanh's coup was conducted purely for personal ambition, cloaked by the excuse that the French-trained officers would neutralize the country, or believed it was simply infighting among the senior generals. Numerous South Vietnamese sources instead describe the coup as a plot within a plot. Although Khanh became the face of the coup, the true conspirators were the resurgent Dai Viets and Khanh's old friend, Tran Thien Khiem. Hints about Dai Viet involvement in the coup have surfaced over the years, but like most Saigon gossip, nothing coalesced to provide a clear picture for U.S. investigators. The Dai Viet involvement was deliberately kept hidden by the plotters. A postwar Dai Viet history, written by the younger brother of Dai Viet founder Truong Tu Anh, states that "the generals who were not involved in the reorganization operation knew nothing about what was going on, and this also applied to the American advisors, both military and political."[15]

According to this postwar Dai Viet history, "Kim and Tho were leaning toward following the neutralist policy advocated by De Gaulle, and they harbored and supported the [Vuong Van] Dong clique. Faced with this situation, the Dai Viet Party's Central [National] Chapter decided to direct the Party Military Commission to carry out a reorganization to reverse this situation. Lieutenant Colonel Huynh Van Ton was assigned responsibility for carrying out this important task."[16] Ton was a critical player. He was the officer who had introduced the Dai Viet philosophy to Minh, and he was Khanh's cousin. After the Diem coup, Minh had appointed Ton as chief of Gia Dinh Province, the area surrounding Saigon.

The Dai Viets' scheming, however, was not merely a power grab. Much like the generals' motivation for toppling Diem, the Dai Viet leadership termed the countercoup *cuoc chinh ly*. While translated as "reorganization," in truth it meant a correction, a return to the path envisioned in 1939 by Dai Viet founder Truong Tu Anh. His political philosophy—*Dan Toc Sinh Ton*, or "People's (or National) Survival"—was militantly anti-colonialist and anti-communist. Anh envisioned a meritocratic stewardship of political and economic opportunity that contained large measures of social engineering and restrictions on capitalism. Calling it a "guided economy," he sought a centralized "regime with extended powers as strong as the presidential system of the U.S.," which was a misreading of the American political system but a reflection of Anh's true philosophy.[17] As noted earlier, a philosophical split existed between the two main Dai Viet leaders, Ha Thuc Ky and Nguyen Ton Hoan. Ky wanted to establish an authoritarian regime along Anh's original design, but Nguyen Ton Hoan and Nguyen Ngoc Huy were "determined to build up a democratic system of government and to collaborate frankly with the other political forces."[18] The tension between the two competing political visions would eventually tear the Dai Viets apart.

Like the Dai Viets, Khiem's true role in the coup has also been minimized. Khanh's deputy in I Corps, Nguyen Chanh Thi, was shocked when he learned the identity of the real principal behind the shakeup. According to Thi, "Only after sunrise [on January 30], when I met with the coup leaders, did I finally realize that the primary mover behind this plot was not Nguyen Khanh—it was Khiem who had actually played the key role. Khanh had only been put forward as a shield, and it appeared that Khanh enjoyed performing that role. In addition, alongside Khiem were several military men who were members of a political party."[19] The political party was the Dai Viets, and the French embassy in Saigon reported the same facts. They quickly informed Paris on January 31 that the coup "was in fact led by General Khiem, assisted by [Thieu and Ton]. The Dai Viet Party...put the weight of all of its political force behind General Khanh."[20]

If Khiem was the organizer, how did Khanh become involved? Pham Van Lieu states that when Hoan and Ky learned that Kim was seeking to replace Tho, they "sought to oppose this move and contacted Khiem and Khanh to get rid of the Don-Kim faction. Both the central and southern [Dai Viet] factions did not like Kim, and they sought to head off Kim's move."[21] Both men had long-standing and good relations with Khanh, Khiem, and Thieu. According to Huy, "Khiem and Thieu were then convinced that Kim was working for the neutralization of South Vietnam according to the French policy."[22] Hoan later informed an embassy source that "Khiem and Thieu were real leaders of, and had Dai Viet support for, the January coup and at the last moment decided to push Khanh forward as leader."[23]

Khanh was not even involved in the original planning. Tran Van Don writes that while in Dalat under house arrest, on May 17, 1964, Khiem and Khanh met with him to discuss Don's potential release. During the conversation, Khiem outlined the background to the coup. When Khanh claimed ignorance of the real reasons behind the coup, Khiem agreed, stating that Khanh only "joined the reorganization at the last minute." Khiem then explained how the plot unfolded. The mission of the Dai Viet officers such as Majors Huynh Van Ton and Duong Hieu Nghia did not "change after the 1 November 1963 coup. They used their positions to expand the power of their party...Their goal was...to make Hoan the Prime Minister, and that is why we conducted the reorganization. We did not want Hoan to be Prime Minister so instead we installed Khanh."[24]

In sum, the central and southern Dai Viet factions sought to defeat Kim's alleged power play to replace Tho as prime minister and convert South Vietnam to neutralism. The Dai Viets used the highly emotional anti-French and anti-neutralism atmosphere to persuade Khiem to act first and replace Tho with Hoan. Their plan backfired when Khiem maneuvered Khanh into place instead because the generals wanted the military, not a civilian, to lead the government.

When did Khiem mastermind this move? While most Vietnamese sources indicate that Khiem began active plotting in early January, these same sources are silent as to who had instigated Khiem and Thieu. The French embassy in Saigon claims the troublemaker was Duong Van Duc, Khiem's classmate. In a cable detailing the coup's origins, the French embassy informed Paris that Duc was angry at Don for allowing the pro-French Vietnamese officers back into the country. Duc and another unnamed group of "senior officers" plotted "on the very first days of January, to get rid of Kim and Don." This timeframe corresponds precisely to the return of Vuong Van Duong and Tran Dinh Lan to Saigon. Since Khiem "resents the widening influence of Kim and Don," Duc persuaded Khiem to remove the pro-French generals from power before they could neutralize South Vietnam.[25] This group later convinced Thieu and Khiem that Kim would arrest the four corps commanders on January 31, the same day that De Gaulle was holding a press conference. While true that De Gaulle was making a major announcement that day, its purpose was to discuss the recent announcement of the opening of diplomatic relations between China and France.

Thi corroborates Duc's heavy involvement in the coup. At Khanh's behest, Thi flew to Saigon to meet Duc on January 20. Duc raged to Thi about the MRC's alleged failures. After gaining Thi's concurrence with the coup, Duc told Thi that he "will fly up to Danang when everything is ready" to inform Khanh.[26] Duc was true to his word. Having finalized preparations, on January 28, Khiem sent Duc to Danang to inform Khanh that preparations were complete. Khanh decided first to check with the Americans. He dispatched his adviser, Colonel Jasper Wilson, to Saigon to determine if both the embassy and General Harkins, commander of the Military Assistance Command, Vietnam (MACV), supported the coup.

What transpired next is a perfect example of cultural disconnect. Khanh claims the U.S. posed no objections to the coup, which is only partially correct. After General Paul Harkins was briefed by Wilson on Khanh's main question—would the U.S. back a countercoup to oppose neutralism?—Harkins replied that he found the neutralism charge "difficult to believe" given "all the public statements of the MRC" against it.[27] Wilson conveyed that Khanh was resurrecting the specters of 1954 by claiming that Don and Kim were conspiring with former General Hinh to neutralize South Vietnam. However, after receiving Wilson's report that neither Harkins nor Lodge had denounced the coup, Khanh took the lack of direct American opposition as a yes, which it was not. Since Harkins and Lodge became partially aware of the impending coup roughly thirty-six hours beforehand, and since neither informed Minh, their lack of action opened the door to conspiracy theories that the coup had American backing. Most Vietnamese, who assumed American connivance in political maneuvers, soon called it the "the Pentagon's coup," a nickname later publicized by George Kahin. A senior aide to Minh told Georges Perruche, the French deputy ambassador in Saigon, that the coup "was organized by a faction of the CIA in contact with General Harkins" and that Hoan was an "American import."[28]

While Harkins and Lodge believed Khanh would provide better leadership than either Minh or Don, no American initiated the coup.[29] Despite unhappiness over the MRC's slow efforts to launch its programs, both men were reluctant to become involved in another South Vietnamese political spasm. Unfortunately, neither knew precisely what was transpiring. Lodge's petty power struggle to restrict MACV and CIA access to the South Vietnamese senior leadership had finally tripped him up. Both the CIA and the embassy only reported Khanh's political rumblings after Harkins alerted them to Wilson's report. The Pentagon Papers confirmed that "the Khanh coup of 30 January 1964 came as a complete surprise to the mission and to Washington."[30]

After Wilson returned to Danang and briefed Khanh, the three generals—Duc, Khanh, and Thi—then flew to Saigon. Thi immediately began canvassing the elite units to determine their support. He discovered that most officers were upset over the rumors of neutralization. He states, "One thing was clearer than anything else—everyone had been affected by the stories about neutralism that the press had been printing for the last several weeks."[31] Just as rumors about Nhu's dalliance with the Communists had helped to spark that coup, playing on long-standing Nationalist fears over neutralization was the perfect excuse to launch a second rebellion.

In more hidden fallout from the Diem coup, Khiem was aided by Colonel Cao Van Vien, commander of the Airborne Brigade.[32] Vien had been arrested on November 1, 1963, and marched into Minh's office. Minh offered Vien the opportunity to join the coup forces. Vien refused. He was close to Diem, and he did not believe the military should be involved in politics. Vien thought Minh would execute him, but he was spared after Khiem persuaded Minh to pardon Vien. He was released but put under house arrest. Vien's wife then contacted Khiem's wife (the two were close) and convinced her to have her husband reinstate Vien as brigade commander. Khiem quietly issued the order without checking with Minh. Thus, Vien was greatly indebted to Khiem, and when Khiem secretly contacted Vien a few days before the January coup, Vien states, "It was a given that I would help Khiem to repay him for the favor...I did not concern myself with whether or not Minh, Don, Dinh, and Kim were really in favor of neutrality."[33]

Moving quickly, at 4:00 a.m., January 30, Vien's Airborne troops plus local Gia Dinh provincial units under Lieutenant Colonel Ton occupied the JGS headquarters and surrounded the homes of the various generals. Given his powerful position, Ton That Dinh was also arrested. To prevent any backlash, Khanh censured Dinh for "unbecoming conduct," which was an easy accusation since he was a well-known nightclub devotee. The other generals suspected of collaborating with the French, Mai Huu Xuan and Nguyen Van Vy, were also detained.

The coup was accomplished quietly and without bloodshed, except for one casualty. Captain Nhung, Minh's aide who had killed Diem and Nhu, was arrested and imprisoned at the Airborne Brigade headquarters. He was forced to write a confession. The next day, he was found hanging by his bootlaces, an apparent suicide. According to journalist Arthur Dommen, it was staged. Khanh, still upset about Diem's death, ordered "the arrest and execution of Nhung. The story was put out that Nhung had committed suicide in his jail cell."[34]

Generals Xuan, Kim, Don, Vy, and Dinh were detained and brought to the JGS. Vy was held in Saigon, but Don, Xuan, Kim, and Dinh were taken to Tan Son Nhut airport, where Thi would escort the four generals to Danang. Just before boarding the plane, Dinh turned to Thi and snarled, "The earth is round. We will meet again one day."[35] The four generals were eventually moved to the resort city of Dalat and placed under house arrest. The fear of neutralization was so pronounced among the military that not one single unit reacted against the removal of the senior generals. Prime Minister Tho was also held but released shortly thereafter. Vuong Van Dong managed to hide in Saigon for three months before the NLF smuggled him out of the country. Tran Dinh Lan was arrested and quickly exiled to France.

There are two other telling indicators for Dai Viet involvement. First, while Captain Nhung died from "suicide," the other alleged Diem/Nhu triggerman, prominent Dai Viet member Duong Hieu Nghia, was untouched. Second, given the anger among certain generals at Minh for murdering Diem and the supposed drift of the country under his leadership, why was Minh not deposed? The answer is simple: the Dai Viets still held Minh in great regard, Diem's death was inconsequential to them, and they wanted Minh to remain as chief of state so they could influence him. Nguyen Ngoc Huy confirms that "Khiem and Thieu did not plan to remove Minh from his role as Chairman. They only wanted to replace Tho by General Nguyen Khanh. This latter was a close friend of Khiem and Thieu."[36]

Khanh immediately asked Minh to remain in the government. He agreed, mainly to prevent the military from fracturing. In a 1968 interview, he said that "Khanh's real strength was insignificant. It could have been crushed at any time." However, "a number of generals were detained as hostages. Fearing for their safety, I had to restrain myself from acting." Plus there were "other political and personal considerations," which he left unnamed.[37]

If Khiem had masterminded the coup, why did he place Khanh in control? Khiem believed his previous allegiance to Diem made him anathema to Thich Tri Quang and the Buddhists. Khanh's past association with

Diem also tainted him, but he was a Buddhist, and his wife and brother-in-law were reportedly close to Tri Quang. While the Buddhist reaction was important, just as critical was the American response. In a rare interview, Khiem insisted that the

> reason Khanh was brought in was because there were Vietnamese newspaper articles claiming Khiem was the adopted son of Diem [meaning that Diem had participated in a ceremony in which Khiem had converted to Catholicism]...Given the fact that [Vien] was also involved, and since Vien had not participated in the Diem coup, combined with the stories about Khiem, they did not want the Vietnamese people to see the coup as bringing back Diem. Plus, since the Americans had opposed Diem, connections to Diem could not be allowed to surface in a way that made the U.S. think this was a return to Diem's policy, so we brought in Khanh as a front.[38]

Like Thi, the Americans also learned further details on the morning of January 30. At Khanh's request, Colonel Wilson stayed with him at coup headquarters. However, when the other Vietnamese officers saw Wilson, memories resurfaced of Americans hovering near the November 1960 coup leadership and of CIA officer Lou Conein staying close to Minh during the 1963 coup. Wilson's presence generated Vietnamese paranoia that the "hairy hands" (*ban tay long la*, a Vietnamese epithet for Americans) were again interfering in their affairs. Wilson's attendance, though, enabled him to learn from Khanh that "planning for an operation began five days ago. Was brought to head by belief that corps commanders would be arrested at a meeting scheduled for today...Khanh indicates that much of the intelligence upon which the group based its actions came from Vietnamese in France who wanted to come home after the November coup but was advised by the French that subsequent actions would lead to a neutralist Vietnam."[39] Undoubtedly, the Vietnamese in France was Nguyen Ton Hoan.

With the coup accomplished, Hoan was invited to return to Saigon. Khanh welcomed him home from France on February 5, but Hoan did not receive the reward he was expecting. Hoan thought he would become prime minister, but in a meeting to discuss his role in the new government, Hoan's wife claims that Khanh began to backtrack given Buddhist sensitivities. "Since Hoan was a Catholic, if Hoan was appointed as the Prime Minister the Buddhists would rise in opposition, creating a situation that would be just like when Diem was President. For that reason, Khanh suggested that Hoan take the position of Deputy Prime Minister and promised that anything involving political matters would be discussed with Hoan and done only with his approval."[40]

The Dai Viet history confirms Mrs. Hoan's recollection. The Buddhists would not welcome another Catholic as the nation's leader, so "Hoan would be given the post of First Deputy Prime Minister for Pacification, with seven cabinet ministries under his authority, while Khanh, who was not a Catholic, would take over the post of Prime Minister." In exchange, Khanh "solemnly promised that he would not interfere in the political leadership of the nation and only asked for military authority to fight the Communists."[41] Hoan reluctantly agreed, and Khanh was appointed head of the MRC and prime minister. Khiem became first deputy chairman of the MRC, minister of defense, and commander of the military. Thieu was made chief of staff of the JGS under Khiem. Minh was kept as a figurehead.

The Dai Viets had struck the equivalent of a back room deal, one that would roil the country for a year and bring it virtually to its knees. If the Diem coup had been received with some joy, alongside sadness at his death, the Khanh coup was greeted with apathy. The Dai Viets, however, were not finished with their political maneuvering.

HANOI REACTS

For the Politburo in Hanoi, the Diem coup presented a major opportunity. To address the situation in the south and a host of other issues, in December 1963, the DRV's Central Committee held the Ninth Plenum, one of its most critical conferences of the war. Two paths—peace or war—were available to the Politburo. Yet despite considerable opposition from some senior North Vietnamese leaders, the hardline faction led by Le Duan carried the day. While the new orders contained in the now famous Resolution 9 to accelerate the armed struggle in the south were the result of a complex internal debate, the Diem coup gave the hardliners the opening they needed. Encapsulating its message in Resolution 9, the Politburo ordered the nation onto a total war footing.

The Politburo also gleefully greeted the Khanh putsch as an American-inspired opening for the revolution to score "many important new victories on all fronts." The Politburo accurately predicted that the coup would deepen the divisions within South Vietnam and would cause South Vietnamese morale to "deteriorate and become even more frightened and uncertain."[42] Hanoi immediately cabled instructions to COSVN, stating that "The Politburo's assessment...is that the U.S. pulled the strings from behind the scenes in Khanh's coup...in order to try to end the crisis and confusion within the puppet government." COSVN was then instructed to "intensify the armed struggle to annihilate enemy personnel and destroy large enemy regular army units." Lastly, while the NLF would expand the fighting, it would also continue to dangle a diplomatic solution that was little more than a disguised surrender: "Broaden our front...and conduct struggles to demand peace and neutrality to isolate the American imperialists and their reactionary lackeys."[43]

Following orders, the NLF immediately appealed for negotiations and offered a ceasefire during the annual Tet New Year holiday. Consumed with the formation of a new government, Khanh ignored them. Since Khanh had given Hoan authority in political matters, the Dai Viet leader chose most of the cabinet. Consistent with his belief in cooperating with the other parties, Hoan did not seek a Dai Viet monopoly of power. Unlike Diem, who had chosen to suppress his rivals, Hoan's main goal was to coalesce the various parties into a "United Nationalist Front" against the Communists. His first step was to form the most balanced cabinet in South Vietnamese history, with representatives from each major political party, religion, and region of the country.

Announced on February 8, three deputy premiers, one from each region, controlled the bulk of the ministries. Hoan, a southerner, oversaw pacification and the critical posts of Defense, Interior, and Rural Affairs, formerly the focal point for the Strategic Hamlet program. A northerner ran Economy and Finance while a native of Central Vietnam ran Social Affairs. Hoan also appointed Thieu's older brother Kieu, a long time Dai Viet, as Commissar for Youth and Sports. Only Justice and Foreign Affairs reported directly to Khanh. Three Dai Viets held significant roles in the government, and each one represented a major faction of the party: the southern-born Hoan was in charge of pacification, central native Ha Thuc Ky was minister of interior, and northerner Phan Huy Quat was foreign minister. The bulk of the cabinet were Buddhists, and two belonged to Tri Quang's militant Buddhist faction.

Hoan moved equally quickly to enact new policies. Pursuing his goal of creating a united front, he announced on February 19 that the government would accept the formation of an opposition party and encouraged the various smaller parties to merge and create such an entity. Hoan hoped that the Dai Viets would become the government party, while the others coalesced into a loyal opposition. Accordingly, he began rapidly seeding the government with Dai Viet followers in the hopes of expanding his party among the unorganized rural masses. This theme of creating a "government party" alongside a smaller opposition party would remain a constant refrain in South Vietnamese politics, with unfortunately limited results.

Well aware that many villagers were not siding with Saigon, Hoan planned to send teams of cadres from the various parties to convince the peasantry to oppose Communism. By choosing people from each party, Hoan hoped that the resulting partnership and shared sacrifices in the hamlets would help forge his united front. To promote his new government, Khanh also began touring the countryside. He visited the sects, inspected military units, and explored some of the remaining strategic hamlets. His frequent travels and blunt, aggressive manner made some Americans see a mirror image of themselves in this squat Vietnamese officer.

Despite the outreach efforts, Vietnamese public reaction to Khanh remained guarded. The goateed general was considered an ambitious opportunist who had ousted a man who was arguably the nation's most popular military figure. To help solidify Khanh's shaky standing, in late February, Harkins used a forthcoming trip to Saigon by Secretary of Defense Robert McNamara to prod Khanh to produce a viable plan to win the war. Harkins' ploy worked. After receiving Harkins's recommendation, Khanh introduced his pacification plan on February 22 by simply renaming Minh's military and pacification policy from *Dien Hong* to *Chien Thang* (Victory). His announcement also mimicked Minh by declaring he would accomplish his programs' objectives within one year so that elections could be held to form a civilian government.

With respect to pacification, he also intended to emphasize psyops, increase local forces to help defend the hamlets, and decentralize government power. Khanh also kept Minh's oil spot strategy, which would be renamed "clear and hold" by the Americans. Like Minh, he also demanded "quality rather than quantity."[44] In reality, except for the decision to dispatch political cadres into the villages, former Diem confidante Dr. Wesley Fishel observed that "the initial acts of the new [government] included several which had been planned... by [Minh], but for which General Khanh's government now took credit."[45]

Meeting McNamara, Khanh outlined his *Chien Thang* program. Given the dire state of the eight provinces surrounding Saigon, Khanh's pacification plan was to first concentrate in that area. Consequently, he ordered the 25th Division to transfer from its original home in Quang Ngai in I Corps to Cu Chi west of Saigon in III Corps. With the removal of the 9th Division and now the 25th Division, only two ARVN divisions remained to cover the vast middle portion of South Vietnam. Moving these two units crippled government control in II Corps and would eventually require the introduction of Korean and American forces to replace them.

For the Americans, Vietnamese political stability remained paramount. Under orders from the White House, McNamara sought to display unconditional U.S. support for Khanh, which led to McNamara publicly raising his hand together with Khanh's and shouting a mangled Vietnamese phrase. Despite his gaffe, most Vietnamese understood that America was unequivocally backing the general, but McNamara's effort to show U.S. support rebounded. Instead of using it to reassure the nation, Khanh exploited McNamara's display of support to eliminate his Dai Viet sponsors. Khanh signed a decree establishing a new Central Pacification Committee to oversee the pacification effort, but he appointed himself as chairman instead of Hoan. Hoan felt completely betrayed by the general who had promised to leave pacification matters to him.

Hoan's anger, however, was simply the latest manifestation of a growing friction between Khanh and the Dai Viets. Like his fellow senior officers, Khanh had an ill-concealed contempt for civilian officials, often calling them "boudoir politicians."[46] Relations had deteriorated between Khanh and the civilian politicians in his cabinet when Ha Thuc Ky took several unilateral actions without consulting Khanh. When Ky then released some important prisoners, reputedly for large bribes, Khanh harshly criticized him at a cabinet meeting. A resentful Ky began to solicit other Dai Viets to oust Khanh. Hoan and Huy, while increasingly wary of Khanh, rejected this effort because they knew Khanh was right about Ky, and they feared the effect another coup would have on South Vietnam.

By late February, the CIA had uncovered indications of Ky's machinations, as did Khanh, who finally had enough. While Huy rightly notes that "American officials working in Vietnam at that time knew little of the Dai Viet Party," the U.S. did not care who was trying to unseat Khanh, it only wanted the machinations to stop.[47] Khanh took steps to cement military backing, including raising pay and promoting certain colonels to general in exchange for their support. His efforts paid off, and on March 22, the MRC gave him a unanimous vote of confidence. On firmer political ground, in early April, Khanh "called a private meeting with his three deputy prime ministers and told them about Ky's plans. Khanh told Hoan directly that "Ky accepted my invitation to become the Minister of Interior. He has been involved in many scandals and incidents involving money. He is plotting to overthrow me. If I did not have such respect for you and for the Dai Viet Party, I would have already arrested Ky."[48]

On April 4, Ky was forced to resign. On April 12, signaling a formal break between himself and the Dai Viets, Khanh publicly assailed Saigon's "teahouse intellectuals" sitting in the capital and criticizing the government but who did nothing to fight the Communists. Khanh then dissolved Minh's Council of Notables shortly thereafter but promised elections within six months for a National Assembly that would draft a new constitution.

With Hoan sidelined, Khanh took control of the pacification effort. First, he relieved Le Minh Dao of command in Long An since Dao was viewed as a Minh crony. This move devastated one of the most important allied initiatives just as gains were being made. Khanh also returned Tran Ngoc Chau to his former post in Kien Hoa Province. Chau found that the situation had sharply deteriorated in the eight months since he had left. Although he reconstituted his Census Grievance teams, rolling back NLF gains this time proved much more difficult. The war, and the NLF, had dramatically expanded during Chau's absence from Kien Hoa.

Khiem's military planning had assumed that NLF attacks had peaked and that small guerrilla units would flee once ARVN troops entered an area. However, by the end of 1963, the NLF had grown from small guerrilla bands into sizable and well-armed main force units. Minh and Tho's belief that NLF strength would melt away with Diem's removal had proven horribly wrong. While NLF units during 1963 had generally remained unable to defend against ARVN regulars, the NLF was quietly undergoing a dramatic change. Recruiting in 1963 had markedly increased, with over twenty-four thousand new conscripts added to its ranks. By the end of 1963, Front strength stood at seventy thousand.[49] More important, heavy weapons and well-trained officers—mostly southern-born cadres returning from North Vietnam—were converting these small, lightly armed NLF units into formidable, battalion-size formations. Lastly, while the allies were vaguely aware of improved Communist firepower, many Western correspondents mistakenly thought that most NLF weapons were captured

South Vietnamese stocks, but that was incorrect. From mid-1963 on, captured arms were only a small fraction of the NLF inventory.

These cadres and new weapons were being clandestinely ferried to the south by North Vietnamese ships designed to resemble South Vietnamese fishing vessels. The Ho Chi Minh Trail, still in its infancy, barely reached the northern end of the Central Highlands. Seaborne shipments were the only solution to supply the southern half of South Vietnam, and the first of these new ships arrived at a secret dock in the Mekong Delta in March 1963. By the end of 1963, more than twenty voyages had covertly delivered 1,300 tons of military supplies.[50] Armed with these new weapons, bolstered by thousands of new recruits, and stiffened by well-trained officers, the NLF was ready to switch tactics when the new instructions in Resolution 9 arrived from Hanoi. COSVN immediately disseminated orders to step up military attacks and "create a fundamental change in the balance of forces in South Vietnam between our side and the enemy. . . . Massed combat operations by main force units would play the decisive role on the battlefield."[51]

Thus, just as Khanh was ready to implement *Chien Thang*, fierce clashes erupted between ARVN and NLF forces. One of the first major engagements greeted Tran Ngoc Chau. In mid-March, the newly formed NLF 263rd Battalion in Kien Hoa ambushed and mauled an ARVN battalion from the 7th Division. By late April, the NLF had formed another battalion in Kien Hoa—one with 1,500 men, roughly the size of a small regiment. Chau was no longer facing small guerrilla units. He was now fighting main force troops that could hold their own against ARVN regulars.

From late March to mid-April, five bitterly contested, battalion-size engagements occurred in South Vietnam. Losses on both sides soared, including a surge in American casualties. The ARVN, however, was not cowering in its barracks. Prodded by Khanh to increase its operational tempo and take the war to the enemy, army units in early April destroyed two enemy base camps and inflicted heavy casualties. Yet while the allies were trying to determine the reason for the sharp increase in fighting, the biggest confrontation of the war to date erupted in Chuong Thien Province, located in the center of the Delta. At 2:00 A.M., on April 12, an NLF battalion overran the district seat of Kien Long, publicly disemboweled the district chief, and then shot his wife and son along with other government supporters.[52] After the ARVN flew in reinforcements and retook the town, the NLF deployed a second battalion to counterattack, but the ARVN dropped an Airborne battalion on top of them. The elite Red Berets scattered the enemy, but the NLF brought in a third battalion and prepared to attack again. The ARVN, in turn, reinforced with a regiment from the 21st Division. The battle raged for four days and represented the first regimental-size engagement of the war. When it was over, both sides had suffered losses totaling more than four hundred dead and wounded. NLF casualties for April were 4,687, including 2,310 dead, the highest monthly figure to date. ARVN losses were 610 dead, while six Americans were also killed in the fighting. *Chien Thang* was finished before it had started.

Given the change in Communist strategy and the major increase in firepower and unit size, whether the ARVN would have performed better under Diem rather than Minh or Khanh is difficult to gauge. Hanoi's decision to expand its infiltration efforts facilitated the creation of battalion-size units just as the two coups badly shook South Vietnamese morale and organizational stability. In these circumstances, the Politburo and the southern NLF leadership saw the death of Diem as an opportunity to achieve total victory, not as a chance to obtain peace.

LAOS AND CAMBODIA

While quietly maneuvering behind the scenes to usurp political power from Hoan and the Dai Viets, Khanh remained committed to Minh's policy of improving external relations. His top foreign policy priority was securing a united front with Cambodia and Laos to eliminate the NLF sanctuaries in Cambodia and obstruct infiltration from the DRV through Laos. He believed that the key to victory was for anti-communist forces to occupy southern Laos and block the enemy supply routes. Khanh's first foreign policy move, like Minh before him, was to try to eliminate the Communist logistical bases in Cambodia.

Several days after Khanh's coup, Sihanouk resumed his demands for a Geneva-style conference for Cambodia. Fully backed by De Gaulle, the impulsive prince requested that the U.S. discuss border issues, neutrality, and other pressing matters. Khanh instructed Foreign Minister Phan Huy Quat to inform the U.S. that Saigon could not accept Cambodian neutrality. The Laotian disaster still loomed large in the South Vietnamese worldview. Given Khanh's intransigence and the American opposition to French efforts to neutralize Indochina, the U.S. declined Sihanouk's demand. Washington's believed its hands were tied. Secretary of State Dean Rusk informed the U.S. ambassador to Cambodia that our commitment in Viet-Nam is so great that we must regard our other actions in [Southeast Asia] in light of their possible effect on achieving our objectives in Viet-Nam.... A conference to internationalize Cambodia's neutrality will in Vietnamese eyes be step two [step one was Laos] in eventual neutralization of all Indochina. If the U.S. supports this, then the [Vietnamese] will to continue their struggle will diminish. We might be faced in SVN with the alternative of pulling out, putting in massive US force, or ourselves agreeing to some sort of neutralization.[53]

When the allies rejected Sihanouk's terms for the conference, the prince reacted with his typical scorched-earth tactics. On March 9, he went public and blamed them for the impasse. To his credit, Khanh did not respond negatively but instead announced he remained willing to send a delegation to Phnom Penh. Sihanouk agreed to accept the South Vietnamese team. On March 18, a GVN delegation headed by Brigadier General Huynh Van Cao landed in Phnom Penh to open talks on the various issues between the two countries.

As luck would have it, the next day a South Vietnamese unit in hot pursuit of NLF guerrillas crossed the Cambodian border and entered a village. It withdrew shortly thereafter, but South Vietnamese airplanes later appeared and bombed the village, killing seventeen people. Khanh expressed regret for the mistake, and Cao visited the village and offered compensation, but the damage had been done. Cao's delegation spent five days calming impassioned nerves instead of settling the contentious border issues. Sihanouk, as usual, tossed gasoline on the fire by once again calling for France to host another Geneva-style conference. His request was designed to force both Washington and Saigon to act. Khanh remained calm and responded by offering to welcome a Cambodian delegation to Saigon. He then proposed on April 6 that the two countries hold a conference to discuss all issues. Sihanouk declined the repeated overtures.

Meanwhile, Khanh was also secretly courting the right-wing Lao generals, and here he was making progress. Laotian politics were a delicate balancing act between the Communist Pathet Lao, the neutralists, and the right wing led by General Phoumi Nosavan. On March 14, Khanh secretly met with Phoumi in Dalat. According to the CIA, Phoumi agreed to allow Vietnamese Air Force (VNAF) planes to bomb Communist bases along the Ho Chi Minh Trail and to allow ARVN forces to engage in hot pursuit across the border. In exchange, Khanh would reinstate diplomatic relations with Laos and appoint a new ambassador.

On March 18, shortly after his delegation had departed to Phnom Penh, Khanh announced his three-country initiative. Since Diem had broken relations over Laotian recognition of the DRV, Khanh offered to reestablish diplomatic ties. This was a major departure from long-standing GVN policy; Saigon had previously declined diplomatic relations with any country that recognized the DRV. Laos, though, was too important, and Khanh made an exception based on his desire to halt the flow of men and material along the Trail.

Laos accepted Khanh's olive branch, and by late March diplomatic relations between the two countries were restored. Soon, ARVN officers were secretly coordinating with Laotian units to begin attacking Communist elements moving supplies into South Vietnam. However, when the press in early April reported the covert arrangement, Phoumi had to deny Khanh's offer of a military alliance due to his government's neutrality as codified by the 1962 Geneva agreement. Phoumi had acted on his own and had not received permission from his government.

Yet despite his public denials, on April 8, Phoumi's aides were in Saigon asking for increased ARVN assistance. The true reason was more ominous than eliminating the Ho Chi Minh Trail. Phoumi wanted to emulate Khanh's coup. The Lao general sought to unify the anti-communist Lao against the Pathet Lao much in the same manner that Khanh had supposedly united the Vietnamese Nationalists. Khanh admits in a postwar interview to have privately backed Phoumi's coup plans, an act suspected at the time but never confirmed. He states that "we were able to overthrow [Lao leaders] Souvanna Phouma and Kong Le and replace them with...General Phoumi....When Phoumi came down to visit Saigon, he signed an agreement with me—at that time, I was the Prime Minister—a diplomatic treaty with us granting permission and requesting that the ARVN help them to defend the Bolovens Plateau. This was a diplomatic act. It was not just us sending troops in. This was a request from the Lao."[54]

On April 20, Phoumi's troops staged the coup. The U.S. immediately denounced the act and demanded that Souvanna Phouma be reinstated. Within two days, the coup crumbled, Phoumi was disgraced, and Laos remained neutral. When Sihanouk also turned his back on Saigon, Khanh's master plan to create an anti-communist front that would deny sanctuaries to the Communists lay in ruins. Unable to eliminate the NLF's external support, and with the escalation of battalion-size attacks, Khanh desperately proposed attacking the north as the only means to defeat the growing insurgency. He also sought to unite the Buddhists to help stem the Communist tide. When those efforts failed, and with his political world disintegrating, Khanh did exactly what he had accused Kim and the others of attempting: he sought peace with NLF.

6

"A REAL MILITARY
GOVERNMENT NEEDED"

Reaping What They Sowed

The heightened NLF attacks, the heavy ARVN casualties, and the foreign policy failures in Laos and Cambodia weighed heavily on Khanh. For the first time, he began questioning the conflict's cost in blood, and by extension, the struggle's raison d'être. As Khanh reviewed the rising tide of internal discontent and a rapidly expanding war, he was handed a gift: direct U.S. military intervention against North Vietnam after an attack against a U.S. destroyer on August 2, 1964. Known as the Gulf of Tonkin incident, this seminal episode led to the massive escalation of the war and provided Khanh the opportunity to act against his internal foes. His subsequent deeds set in motion profound events that transformed the Saigon political landscape, sapped the country's morale, destroyed virtually all of Diem's accomplishments, and lead inexorably to the involvement of American combat forces.

INTERNAL CHALLENGES

On May 4, Khanh summoned Ambassador Henry Cabot Lodge to his residence to discuss his declining fortunes. Khanh ruminated over the hard choices he now faced. Should he dissolve his cabinet, mostly civilian political appointees whom he despised, and place the country on a war footing? Would the U.S. bomb the north if Hanoi continued to interfere in South Vietnam? More important, the South Vietnamese were becoming war weary, and Khanh thought it "illogical, wasteful, [and] wrong to go on incurring casualties 'just in order to make the agony endure.'"[1]

Khanh's musings set off alarms in Washington, particularly about not continuing to endure agony, which many assumed meant seeking a negotiated settlement. Although Lodge excused Khanh's remarks as that of a man deliberating difficult choices, Secretary of State Dean Rusk replied that Lodge's message "raises extremely grave issues and we feel that our reactions must be developed with care."[2] President Johnson again dispatched McNamara to Saigon to meet with Khanh to discuss options and reassure him of the constancy of American support. Khanh told McNamara during his visit that he "had to cope with serious religious problems. It happened that almost any political question [also] included a religious question... The importance of the religious problem could not be exaggerated."[3] Khanh's insight was not hyperbole. For the next two years, only the war was a greater issue than religious tension.

Khanh's spiritual anxieties had been raised in early April when the Buddhists, who had remained quiet since Minh's ouster, suddenly resumed their agitation. Buddhist unrest again centered on Thich Tri Quang, the leader of the militant Buddhists from northern South Vietnam. Quang's oratorical skills stirred youthful Vietnamese, and the greater his acclaim grew, the more his ambition to dominate the political scene expanded. He sought an undefined "peaceful settlement" to the war, convinced that his popular appeal could stymie Communist designs for a dictatorship of the proletariat. Yet Quang refused to accept a government role, preferring to remain a power behind the throne, ready to topple regimes that did not conform to his concept of Vietnamese nationality. He was a nightmare for a socially fragile nation, a mesmerizing demagogue with the ability to destroy but no compulsion to build.

Despite Khanh's attempts to placate Quang, the militant bonze published a letter on May 8 in a Saigon newspaper criticizing the government for allowing local officials to continue "despotic" actions and demanding new laws to protect "religious rights." Worried about the monk, the next day Khanh declined to halt the execution of Ngo Dinh Can, Diem's younger brother. Khanh also declared that the Catholic officer whose troops had opened fire on the Buddhist protestors in Hue in May 1963 would stand trial. Further attempting to appease the Buddhists, Khanh then signed a decree that legalized the earlier formation of the UBC. He hoped his action would create a Buddhist front that could "stop the red tide of aggression through the use of a yellow barrier line [yellow was the color of the monks' robes in the provinces south and west of Saigon]. This was a line of Theravada Buddhism, not the Northern form of Buddhism [Quang belonged to the northern Mahayana branch], a line that stretched across to Phnom Penh and on to Thailand and Burma."[4]

Far from mollified, on May 26, the Buddhists held a massive demonstration in Saigon to celebrate Buddha's birthday. With an estimated total of two hundred thousand participants, it was the largest rally held in Saigon in a decade. Not to be outdone, on June 8 the Catholic community in Saigon organized a counterdemonstration. A crowd assessed at thirty-five thousand marched peacefully through the capitol's streets waving pro-government and anti-communist banners. Caught in the middle, Khanh did not attend either assembly. Instead, the next day he sought to dampen any potential religious strife by telling journalists that "this is a free country. The people are free to express themselves as they see fit...I do not think we will have another religious crisis."[5] For a man accused by his Vietnamese detractors of political incompetence, it was a remarkably well-timed statement that temporarily assuaged the concerns of both sides.

Five days later, on June 13, he convened a conference of all the political parties and religious groups to discuss a proposed new law that would encourage a two-party system, basically Nguyen Toan Hoan's idea of a government party and an opposition party. Khanh opened the conference by pleading for all strata of South Vietnamese society to close ranks for the sake of the "survival of the nation in this decisive period."[6] He warned the emissaries that the Nationalist's unending bickering was weakening the nation. The delegates ignored Khanh's pleas, and the conference dissolved into squabbling that accomplished nothing.

The conference failure convinced Khanh that the civilians would never work together for the good of the country. Echoing Diem's sentiments, Khanh told Robert Shaplen, the legendary Far Eastern correspondent for the *New Yorker* magazine, "We can only provide the formula for democracy now. We can create a foundation, the institutions for a state, but we cannot achieve full democracy for some time, perhaps for another generation."[7] Khanh's frustrations, like those of other South Vietnamese rulers, centered as much on the insoluble qualities of Vietnamese society as they did on how to win the war.

Infuriated by sustained criticism from opposition politicians and members of his own cabinet, Khanh finally retaliated. He publicly lambasted

Saigon's intelligentsia for disparaging his government while failing to assist the war effort. He then engaged his next foil, Saigon's resurgent press. The newly freed journalistic scene bordered on bedlam, with wild rumors often printed as fact to sell papers. To rein in journalistic malfeasance, he instituted new press rules. He set up a council to review articles, decreed that publishers could not have a police record or have Communist or neutralist tendencies, and required each paper to deposit money with the Information Ministry before a publishing license was granted. The new censorship rules also permitted the government to confiscate any paper deemed to have violated "national security," a catchall that gave Khanh enormous discretionary power. To demonstrate his resolve, in late May, the Interior Ministry suddenly closed nine papers for allegedly printing seditious materials.

Like Minh, Khanh had initially hoped to turn the reins of government back to civilian control, but faced with this factional disarray, he reverted to authoritarianism to impose cohesion. Many in the military shared Khanh's belief. There were three reasons for this conviction. First was an impulse toward strong leadership, a mentality reinforced by typical military hierarchical thinking. Essentially, this instinct saw society as governed from the top down, not from the bottom up. Second was the grim realization that the bickering civilians usually thought only of themselves rather than for the good of the country. Third was a refusal to open the political process to allow Communist participation. The Nationalists believed that permitting the NLF even the smallest electoral foothold was a slippery slope to defeat. While these beliefs strongly influenced Khanh's and other Vietnamese leaders' actions, the left castigated the result as a "right-wing military dictatorship," which it was in form but not in substance.

Pressure was also building on Khanh to decide the fate of the four imprisoned generals arrested on January 30, 1964. Tran Van Don, Ton That Dinh, Le Van Kim, and Mai Huu Xuan remained in Dalat, awaiting Khanh's final verdict. Both Khanh and Khiem had visited them in late April to discuss the general's future, whereupon Khiem had counseled Khanh to delay releasing the quartet until late May. Khiem believed that the Dai Viets, who were adamantly against releasing the four generals, were still too powerful to risk such a move. But the longer Khanh left the generals uncharged, the more it appeared that the true goal of his January coup had been to seize power rather than to block a French neutralist conspiracy. After failing to find any hard evidence, on May 30, Khanh announced the MRC's verdict.[8] He released his fellow generals without punishment for the alleged plot but censured them for their extravagant lifestyles. He also denied them any command functions within the army but allowed them to retain their ranks.

Their newfound liberty, however, was short-lived. Within a day, Don received a message from Khanh that the four generals had to remain in Dalat. Don feared Dai Viet involvement, and his suspicions were confirmed when "a friend told me that Hoan did not want us to return to Saigon because he was afraid that we would take action and speak out about the January 30, 1964 reorganization."[9] Don's friend was correct. On June 3, the CIA reported that Dai Viet leader Dang Van Sung had criticized Khanh for not deporting the generals and that Hoan was considering demonstrations against releasing them.[10]

SHAKE-UP IN SAIGON

Religion, the press, and foreign policy failures, however, were not Khanh's only pressing issues. Consumed with internal political maneuverings, Khanh had devoted little time to pacification, yet his refusal to cede pacification authority to Hoan plus rapidly increasing NLF strength and government instability were sapping the program's vitality. South Vietnamese reversals were forcing the Americans to again search for a successful strategy to buttress its faltering ally, one that was losing control in the countryside to an externally supported and metastasizing insurgency. To correct the worsening situation, in June, Lieutenant General William Westmoreland, Harkins's deputy commander at MACV, lobbied Khanh to replace *Chien Thang* with an American-designed pacification program named *Hop Tac* (Cooperate). Westmoreland's concept involved pacifying the eight provinces surrounding Saigon first, then pushing out from there. Since this plan was a version of the oil spot technique, Khanh acquiesced, happy to let the U.S. take a larger role in the war so that he could deal with the internal bickering.

At the same time, the U.S. leadership in Saigon was reorganized. In mid-June, Westmoreland supplanted Harkins as commander of U.S. forces in South Vietnam. Concurrently, for personal reasons related to the 1964 presidential elections, Lodge resigned as ambassador. President Johnson chose Chairman of the Joint Chiefs of Staff General Maxwell Taylor to replace him. The transfer of America's top military commander to become the new ambassador, the replacement of Harkins, and the increasing number of U.S. military advisors convinced many Vietnamese that the Americans were preparing to take over the war. The Communists read it the same way. According to an NLF official, they assessed that Westmoreland's and Taylor's roles were to "provide the leadership and organizational competence for stepped-up American involvement."[11] This Vietnamese misjudgment on both sides that America would soon take over the war would cause serious strategy modifications that would lead to a full-scale war.

Since his talk with Lodge on May 4, where he had requested U.S. bombing of North Vietnam, Khanh had continued to urge America to act. U.S. officials had agreed to joint planning with the Vietnamese for increased air strikes and other options, but they asked Khanh to refrain from publicly discussing this possibility. U.S. generals, however, had secretly advocated limited attacks against the DRV to force Hanoi to cease support for the NLF. Johnson had dismissed this option for fear of widening the war, but he had authorized small and highly classified military strikes against North Vietnam. With the conflict in the countryside worsening, elements of the South Vietnamese press began openly clamoring for the U.S. to attack the north. While recognizing the growing necessity for overt American military support, Johnson remained determined to avoid direct involvement, especially given the upcoming U.S. presidential campaign.

With Taylor's arrival, however, Khanh began to forcefully press this option. When he met continued U.S. resistance, the upcoming tenth anniversary of the 1954 Geneva Accords provided him an opportunity. The government had scheduled a huge rally on July 19 to denounce the signing of the accord that had divided Vietnam. After two hundred thousand people had assembled in downtown Saigon, Khanh addressed the crowd. Desperately seeking to rally South Vietnamese society, he called upon the Buddhists, the Catholics, and the students to work together to save the nation. Khanh then asked the crowd to unite so they could *Bac Tien* (march north) to liberate North Vietnam from its Communist oppressors and unify the country.

For Khanh, *Bac Tien* was more a rallying cry for his besieged people than a realistic call for action. However, officials in Washington, overly sensitive during a presidential race to any statements about widening the war, read it literally and reacted. Rusk immediately cabled Taylor to warn Khanh against further public outbursts about expanding the war. Taylor responded that while Khanh had "launched deliberate campaign to associate U.S. with policy of increased military pressure on North Viet-Nam," his speech had been shaped more by Vietnamese domestic pressures than a real desire to invade the north. According to Taylor, Khanh believed he needed to overcome a combination of war weariness, religious strife, constant sniping from his cabinet, ongoing press criticism, and foreign policy failures. Taylor observed that Khanh "seems to have reached conclusion that frustrating and ineffective instruments of government at his command are not adequate to master Viet Cong by counterinsurgency means alone. He and his colleagues seem to have decided that they can bring about cessation of Viet Cong harassment only by bringing direct pressure to bear on North."[12]

His assessment of Khanh's outlook was correct, but Taylor's rebuff sent the diminutive general into another crisis of confidence just as the war dramatically turned against him. In July, the NLF had made twelve battalion-size attacks, more than the combined total for the first five months of 1964. Khanh had now become convinced that the current allied strategy offered little hope of victory and that it was time for a different approach. Rumors soon began swirling that Khanh, while publicly talking *Bac Tien*, was furtively seeking negotiations to end the war. Earlier, on July 8, United Nations Secretary-General U Thant had advocated reopening the 1954 Geneva conference to halt the fighting. More important, two weeks later the CIA learned that Khanh was sending a secret emissary to the French to ask the French to open talks with the NLF. Several days later French President Charles De Gaulle publicly reiterated his call for a conference to end the war. Significantly, the GVN Foreign Ministry on July 21 rebuffed U Thant's proposal but said nothing about De Gaulle's.

At the same time, Le Van Hoach—one of Khanh's cabinet ministers, a senior Cao Dai religious leader, and the former leader of the Republic of Cochinchina—launched a covert effort to open discussions with the NLF. On July 7, the British informed the State Department that in late June, Hoach had told the UK ambassador that he "had established contact with Viet Cong with the 'tacit consent' of General Khanh. Hoach indicated contact could provide channel through which negotiations could be conducted by GVN with VC to settle struggle in Vietnam."[13] In late July, Hoach in turn informed Taylor that he was seeking a ceasefire and negotiations with the NLF leadership. Hoach, however, denied to Taylor that Khanh was aware of his efforts. When confronted by Taylor, Khanh also disavowed any knowledge. Both men were lying. In an interview years later, Khanh described his thinking. Like Tho and Minh before him, "We had to get the NLF to rally to us. Then, after we had an agreement with the NLF for peace in South Vietnam, if North Vietnam continued to commit aggression, I would attack

North Vietnam, I would 'advance north.' I was the first to advocate it. Why did I advocate that? It was because we could not fight in South Vietnam and at the same time also attack the North. We were not strong enough to do that... So, I asked my Minister of State, Dr. Hoach—and Dr. Hoach was a person with great prestige in the South—I asked him to contact the NLF for me to reach an honorable solution."[14]

Such was Khanh's state of mind when the Gulf of Tonkin incident occurred. On August 2, North Vietnamese torpedo boats attacked the U.S. destroyer *Maddox*. After an alleged second attack two nights later, President Johnson ordered retaliatory airstrikes against the boat base and support facilities. Several days later, Congress authorized Johnson to take any measures to maintain security in the area.

With the U.S. now directly engaged, Khanh believed that the ever-squabbling Vietnamese needed a strongman to provide the political stability to win the war. He planned to replace the civilian politicians with a military-based government, remove Big Minh, reenergize his people's morale, and create new legal measures to fight Communist terrorism. According to official GVN statistics, since the beginning of the year, NLF assassination squads had killed or abducted over nine hundred local officials.[15] These losses, combined with the constant propaganda and military attacks, were eroding the government's already weak presence in the villages.

When the South Vietnamese press lauded the U.S. attacks on North Vietnam, Khanh decided to take advantage. On August 7, he imposed press censorship, banned strikes and demonstrations, and proclaimed a state of emergency. The law also gave military courts the authority to arbitrate any "violation of public order or national security" and sentenced to death any terrorist or economic speculator.[16] This venue change, designed to deal with the NLF's growing terrorism, eventually became one of the government's most vilified measures.

Khanh also promptly ordered the drafting of a new constitution to replace Minh's provisional structure. While he claimed he desired a "loyal opposition," any aspiration to return the government to civilian control was now gone. Like his cohorts, Khanh believed that only the military could lead the country. A new constitution was quickly drafted and presented to a meeting of the MRC in the resort town of Vung Tau on August 16. A vote was held, and the constitution was immediately ratified. Known as the Vung Tau Charter, Khanh was proclaimed president and head of the MRC, thereby removing Minh from his post.

The key figure pressing Khanh to revamp South Vietnam's government was Brigadier General Nguyen Van Thieu. Tran Van Don had promoted him to brigadier general on the morning of November 2 for his successful leading of the coup forces. Thieu revealed to a senior U.S. army officer on August 27 that "the August 16 charter had been his brain child; that he had convinced Khanh that real military government needed."[17] Much like what he had stated in January 1964 to Tran Van Don, he was convinced that only the military could effectively run the country. Given the weakness of the bickering civilian leaders, Thieu believed that South Vietnam needed a strong leader like Diem but without the deposed ruler's totalitarian streak and family baggage.

Khanh, though, had badly underestimated his domestic support. Buddhist leader Tri Quang immediately denounced the August 7 decree and the August 16 charter as imposing another dictatorship. Taking advantage of the one-year anniversary of the 1963 pagoda raids, on August 21, Quang launched public demonstrations to demand the government return control to civilian leaders. Spurred by his condemnation, within three days, the ranks of the student protesters had swollen to thousands. On August 23, the protests in Saigon, Hue, and Danang turned violent. Khanh, fearing a repeat of Hue in May 1963, ordered the police not to fire on the protesters.

Attempting to settle matters, the next day Khanh met with Quang and several other Buddhist leaders. The conspiratorial-minded Quang claimed that a secret plot by a cabal of Can Lao, Catholics, and Dai Viets lurked at the heart of the government and that Khiem and Thieu were the chief culprits. He demanded that the Vung Tau charter be revoked and replaced by a new constitution, that the MRC elect a president and then disband itself, that all press censorship be lifted, and that any Can Lao or Dai Viet elements be removed from the government. If Khanh agreed to their demands, Quang and the Buddhists would support him.

Confronted with Quang's ultimatums, Khanh capitulated. He believed he could not win the war without Buddhist backing, nor did he want to create martyrs by shooting protesters. On August 25, Khanh called together the MRC. They voted to rescind the Vung Tau charter. Another MRC gathering would be held the next day to elect a new leader. Although Quang sent Khanh a letter pledging his support, that evening Khiem and Thieu began contacting the other MRC members, seeking to oust Khanh at the election and replace him with General Minh. While neither were blind to Minh's laziness, Khiem believed that Quang was "maneuvering aggressively for a neutralist solution for South Vietnam," confirming that the old dread of neutralism remained an overriding concern for many Nationalists.[18]

One hidden reason for Khanh so readily agreeing to Quang's demand for revamping the government was Khanh's desire to rid himself of the Dai Viets in his government. The Dai Viets, however, were not going away quietly. Upset that Khanh had bowed to Buddhist stipulations and aware of Khanh's plan to purge them, the Dai Viet leadership decided to mount a coup. The party leadership held an emergency meeting and formed a plan to seize power. The party history states, "In accordance with Khanh's demands, Hoan and Huy would leave the country to go into exile. This would set Khanh's mind at ease and make him overconfident and careless. Then, on September 1, 1964, a coup would be organized to overthrow Khanh. The Dai Viet Party Military Commission gave the responsibility for organizing this coup to Colonel Huynh Van Ton," who now commanded the 7th ARVN Division.[19]

Catching wind of the plotting, on the morning of August 26, Taylor visited Minh to inform him that the U.S. was adamantly against a coup. Just as critical, Taylor also sent envoys to both Khiem and Thieu to warn them against it. The effort worked. Thieu told his U.S. counterpart that while he believed that Khanh had become "power mad," he now "felt obliged to support Khanh because of U.S. threats to withdraw support if more coups were to take place."[20] The Dai Viet history succinctly states that "In the face of this unexpected strong reaction, the Party Military Commission was forced to back down and seek some other solution."[21]

At the MRC meeting on August 26, Khanh launched a "scathing attack [on] the Dai Viets, accusing them, and Vice Premier Hoan specifically, of being merely interested in advancing their party ... Khiem took exception to Khanh's remarks on the Dai Viets; claimed that he was responsible for the November 63 and January 64 coups, and he said that Khanh had to be replaced."[22] Despite the hostile exchange, many MRC members asked Khanh to resume his former position as prime minister, but he refused unless he had every generals' full support. Although sensitive to Taylor's threats, both Khiem and Thieu asked that Minh assume the presidency, but Minh also declined. With no clear leader, after two days of acrimonious exchanges, the MRC voted to dissolve itself and install a triumvirate of Khanh, Minh, and Khiem to lead the nation.

Minh was tasked to create a High National Council (HNC), an ad hoc body of prominent civilians that would form a new government and write a constitution. The triumvirate would temporarily govern the nation until the constitution was written. Once completed, they would resign and return political control back to civilian authorities. A deadline was set for October 27. Khanh told Taylor that, given the enormous backlash from the Buddhists, he wanted to remove the military from politics. However, he said that the armed forces would remain vigilant in case any civilian government sought a coalition or a neutral solution, a covering statement given his secret efforts along those very lines.

After the MRC meeting, Khanh held a press conference during which he publicly accused Hoan and the Dai Viets of planning a coup. Then, claiming ill health, he announced his resignation as president and retreated to Dalat. Yet despite the efforts to appease Quang, the Buddhist leader had so broadly stoked the fires of religious tensions that even he could no longer contain the street protests. Bloody sectarian violence erupted between Catholic and Buddhist gangs, with more than a dozen people killed. With no other options available, the military sent an Airborne battalion into Saigon to clear the streets. Order was soon restored with rifle butts and bayonets.

After Khanh's press conference, on September 1, Hoan, openly citing his numerous difficulties with Khanh, resigned. On the same day, Khanh asked for and received signed oaths of allegiance from all four corps commanders and from Khiem and Thieu. Even though Khanh and the government had acquiesced to Tri Quang's demands, the bonze instead issued yet another ultimatum. He now demanded the resignation of seven key officers, including Khiem and Thieu. Considering this new requirement, Khiem offered to leave the country for a few months to "pacify the Buddhists . . . Khiem said he [had spoken] to Quang late on September 1. Quang had told Khiem directly that he did not trust him and that he was convinced that Khiem would try to displace Khanh and create a Catholic government endangering the Buddhist movement."[23]

While Khanh accepted Khiem's proposal, Khanh was now fully convinced of Thieu's loyalty, claiming Thieu was a soldier first and a Dai Viet second.[24] On September 4, Khiem and Thieu pledged their support for Khanh as head of the government and said they had severed ties with the Dai Viet Party. Khanh, now backed by the military and Buddhists, returned to Saigon from Dalat and resumed control. He immediately ordered Hoan and Huy to leave the country. Although Khanh thought he had turned aside the Dai Viets, once again, he was mistaken.

THE LAST DAI VIET SPASM

Believing he had eliminated the Dai Viet threat, Khanh moved to garner additional support within the army. He released the four generals in Dalat and offered them positions in his new government. Khanh now viewed the senior generals not as French lackeys but as a bulwark against the Catholic generals who strongly disapproved of his pro-Buddhist tendencies. The men agreed, and their return to Saigon was set for September 13.

Khanh, however, had not counted on the impulsive Major General Duong Van Duc, commander of IV Corps, and the inspiration for removing the four generals in the January 30 coup. Upset at Khanh's capitulation to the Buddhists and angry over the release of the four generals, Duc and Colonel Huynh Van Ton struck. At 4:00 a.m. on September 13, units of Ton's 7th Division began rolling toward Saigon. By 10:00 a.m., they had occupied positions in the capital. More farcical theater than actual rebellion, no shots were fired, and the Saigon populace ignored them.

Duc and Ton were soon joined by Brigadier General Lam Van Phat, who had recently been fired as interior minister. Ton was married to Phat's younger sister, and he had agreed to let Phat draft and announce the political agenda for the coup forces. It proved his undoing. Phat's rabid announcement over Saigon Radio that he wanted to restore Diem's philosophy of governance alienated the other commanders. Many rallied to an embattled Khanh, ignoring the entreaties of Duc and Phat. They despised officers like Duc, whom they saw as irredeemably tainted by their French training and self-aggrandizement.

These political intrigues over the last month had infuriated a group of younger, recently promoted generals. They had coalesced into a dominant new faction known as the Young Turks. The group was initially comprised of about ten officers who held strategic commands. Thirty-four-year-old Air Force commander Nguyen Cao Ky had slowly emerged as the clique's spokesman, and he would soon become the most powerful man in South Vietnam.

Ky was born on September 8, 1930, in Son Tay, North Vietnam. Drafted by the French, he had graduated from the French-run Nam Dinh military academy in Hanoi in May 1952. Ky became a second lieutenant and was assigned as an infantry platoon leader, and he saw heavy fighting. Accepted into flight school, he graduated in September 1954 and by mid-1955, he was named commander of the VNAF 1st Transport Squadron. Ky did not hide his dislike of Diem and had contemplated joining the November 1960 coup, but he had refrained. Despite Diem's suspicions, Ky avoided punishment and retained command of his squadron. He had been eager to join the 1963 coup.[25] His colorful personality and position as head of the Air Force had enabled him to rise quickly, and this new spasm gave Ky the opportunity to take center stage.

The Young Turks included Cao Van Vien, commander of the Airborne Brigade, and Le Nguyen Khang, leader of the Marine Brigade. Ky and Khang were old friends. Both men had been born in Son Tay, and they had attended the Nam Dinh military school together. After hearing Phat's broadcast, and tired of the endless plotting, the Young Turks backed Khanh, not because of his leadership but to halt the country's dangerous drift toward anarchy in the face of a strengthening NLF.

With the population largely ignoring the spectacle, and no other Vietnamese commanders backing Duc, Khanh asked the Young Turks to suppress the coup. Ky threatened Duc with air strikes if he advanced any farther. Another member, Nguyen Chanh Thi, now commanding the 1st ARVN Division, flew to Saigon and bluntly told Duc to withdraw his forces or face attack. Thieu, who was at JGS headquarters, established radio contact with Khanh in Dalat and pledged his fidelity. He and Khiem then publicly denounced the coup, and Khanh ordered Thieu to join him in Dalat, crushing any Dai Viet hopes to rally the military to their side. With no internal support, by the afternoon of the 14th, the coup collapsed.

It is difficult to call this absurd episode the nadir of South Vietnamese politics, as events would continue to bounce along in a trough of futility for months. Khanh had survived another political challenge, mainly by building an alliance between the Buddhists, the Young Turks, and the Americans. This alliance was a marriage of convenience, with the latter two aligning only because of their common desire for governmental stability and the continuation of the war.

Khanh arrested the coup perpetrators, and in October more than twenty officers were tried in a military court. Duc's defense was that this was not a coup but rather a "display of forces," a demonstration to convince Khanh to mend his ways. On October 23, the tribunal agreed and found them not guilty, but as soon as the trial ended, the perpetrators were brought before a Military Disciplinary Council headed by Khanh. The Young Turks wanted the officers severely punished, and they were outraged when Khanh handed out light verdicts. Duc and Phat were sentenced to sixty day's confinement and discharged from the military. Ton was given thirty days' confinement and discharged. The other officers were jailed for a brief time and then returned to active duty.

AFTERSHOCKS

If anyone came out of this strengthened, it was Nguyen Van Thieu. His demonstrated loyalty to his commander rather than to a political party, a trait that stretched back to General Hinh in 1954, earned him Khanh's gratitude and the respect of the Young Turks. Khanh rewarded Thieu by appointing him the new IV Corps commander. In the following months, the quiet officer from Ninh Thuan Province would move even closer to the pinnacle of power. Thieu's choice to remain loyal to Khanh during the September 13 coup, much like his career-changing decision to join the Can Lao Party, would dramatically alter his life as well as the fate of South Vietnam.

Khiem, however, was not so lucky. On September 21, he informed a senior U.S. official that Khanh had kept him in Dalat for a week investigating him for involvement in the coup. According to Khiem, Khanh had become "suspicious" of his colleagues, doubted "the 'sincerity of American statements,'" and had "become critical of the American embassy."[26] Khanh finally absolved him on September 20, but even after Khiem was cleared, relations remained strained between the two old friends. Worse, Khiem's enemies were joining forces, and now his time in the sun was over. In return for their continued support of Khanh, Ky and the others insisted that Khiem and several other older generals either leave the country or be cashiered out of the military.[27]

Nguyen Chanh Thi was also instrumental in convincing Khanh to remove Khiem. Thi still harbored a deep animus for Khiem over the failed November 1960 coup. Khiem was everything Thi despised: a French-educated, landowning southerner, an alleged convert to Catholicism for personal gain, a Can Lao Party hack, and a coup plotter. Yet Khiem had emerged with power and promotions. All these attributes had merged into a singular hatred for Khiem. Now it was payback time for Thi's own exile to Cambodia. With Tri Quang also demanding that Khanh banish Khiem, at the beginning of October, Khanh sent Khiem to the United States to become the GVN ambassador. Khanh also sent that inveterate instigator, Pham Ngoc Thao, to Washington to serve in the embassy.

Khiem, of course, resented his deportation. In a meeting with a CIA official in Washington on December 14, Khiem "railed about Khanh's indulgence of Buddhist dissidence, and said that only the lack of hard proof of Buddhist neutralism and anti-Americanism prevented him from mounting a coup against Khanh."[28] Khiem's anger at his former close friend was profound, for shortly afterward, Thao disappeared from the embassy. Leaving his wife and child in America, he returned to Vietnam in early January 1965 to mount more coups at Khiem's behest.

Despite Khanh's victory, South Vietnam appeared almost rudderless, and the rest of September provided no succor. On September 20, long-festering disputes between the Montagnards and the Vietnamese over autonomy erupted. Members from the Rhade tribe serving under U.S. Special Forces advisers partnered with a separatist Montagnard organization called FUL-RO (*Front Unifie de Lutte des Races Opprimees*). They occupied Ban Me Thuot, the largest city in the southern Central Highlands, took numerous Vietnamese prisoners, and killed over seventy Vietnamese during several firefights. The Rhade irregulars held out for over a week despite repeated entreaties to stand down. Their demands included an autonomous region for the tribespeople and a halt to Vietnamese settlers occupying their lands. GVN policy under Diem had encouraged this land rush, and U.S. statistics showed that since 1953, almost 150,000 Vietnamese had moved into the highlands, aggravating the already existing ethnic tensions. Only after extensive negotiations conducted by local U.S. commanders and threats by Khanh to send in the Airborne to quell the uprising did the Rhade and FULRO end their revolt.

Problems with Cambodia also returned to bedevil Khanh. On September 4, Cambodian military units fired artillery into a Vietnamese village, and a Cambodian MiG fighter chased and shot at two Vietnamese aircraft. Vietnamese public anger over these incidents forced Khanh to respond. On September 20, he held a press conference and threatened to blockade the Mekong River if Sihanouk did not halt the border violations. Yet despite labeling Sihanouk "hostile" to Vietnam, Khanh offered once more to settle the border disputes, but only if the Cambodian president displayed "good will."

Aware of Saigon's turbulence, on September 1, the Politburo sent a cable to COSVN, its command for the southern part of South Vietnam, ordering it to dramatically step up political warfare in the cities, particularly among the "laboring classes." After noting that the GVN was enmeshed in a "deep political crisis," COSVN was instructed to incite new unrest by recruiting "a number of intellectuals and notables who have great prestige and insert them as representatives of the people's livelihood and democracy movements in order to attract a large mass following"[29] Known as the Intellectual Proselytizing Section, these efforts would pay off, and within a year a vocal peace movement would emerge among a small band of left-wing Saigon intellectuals.

Hanoi was often accused, or at least suspected, of having whipped up the student and Buddhist protests of late August, but the party has not taken credit for these disturbances. But the aborted coups and the rising tide of NLF battlefield victories had convinced Hanoi that the GVN was near political collapse. In late September, the Politburo made a critical decision: "We had to mobilize the entire Party, the entire army, and the entire population and concentrate all resources and forces to secure a decisive victory during the next few years."[30] The Politburo ordered the 325th Division, which had been preparing for months to go to South Vietnam, to begin its movement to the south. Just as important, they dispatched General Nguyen Chi Thanh to South Vietnam to take direct command of the war effort. Thanh's instructions were simple: organize major combat formations, initiate large-scale fighting, and conquer South Vietnam. There would be no negotiations to end the war unless the U.S. agreed to Hanoi's terms to withdraw, remove the current government, and replace it with a coalition government or neutralize the country. Neutralization or a coalition government would be quickly followed by reunification under Hanoi's control. This policy, in various forms and permutations, would remain essentially intact until October 1972.

7

"WE ARE FED UP WITH COUPS"

The Return to Civilian Rule

A hoary combination of protestors and military in-fighting forced Khanh to restore civilian rule to South Vietnam. For the next eight months, Saigon's civilian political elite governed the country. Yet by instinct and experience, the generals remained deeply suspicious of these bickering politicians. They were right. A succession of civilian governments would prove unable to govern the country effectively due to the country's catastrophic inability to unite its many clamorous blocs, and they were forced to return power to the military.

Nguyen Van Thieu's proximity to the leadership allowed him to witness firsthand the tumultuous political infighting that occurred. While determined to prevent another dictatorial ruler like Ngo Dinh Diem, this tormented time confirmed his deep disdain for Vietnamese civilian politicians. He was not alone in this belief; most military commanders insisted that, as the men fighting the war, they had the right to intercede if the government was failing or was implementing policies they viewed as inimical to the national interest, particularly neutralism or a coalition. Intensely determined to save his country from the Communist peril, he had initially supported military rule to protect and build the country. However, after witnessing Minh's efforts and then the Khanh disaster, Thieu was beginning to modify his opinion, a profound change that would eventually set South Vietnam on the path to a constitutional government.

STARTING OVER

As Saigon lurched toward political collapse in September 1964, the lone encouraging note was Duong Van Minh's successful efforts to establish the High National Council. He chose prominent civilian leaders to represent the major religious and regional groups. Thich Tri Quang gave his blessing to the HRC, which promptly calmed the situation. On September 26, Minh, Khanh, and Tran Thien Khiem finalized the membership, and the HNC began drafting a new provisional constitution. In late October, the council promulgated a charter and chose a respected non aligned politician named Phan Khac Suu to lead them.

Suu was born on January 9, 1905, near Can Tho, the capital of the Delta. While he had earned a French college degree, as a staunch Nationalist he fought the colonialists, earning him four years in prison on Con Son Island for his patriotism. A leading Cao Dai and a man esteemed by the southern elite, Suu served in Diem's first cabinet as minister of agriculture, but he quickly fell out of favor. On April 26, 1960, he led a collection of intellectuals who published a manifesto at the Caravelle Hotel in Saigon. Called the Caravelle Group, they demanded Diem grant democratic freedoms. Shortly after the abortive November 1960 coup, Suu was arrested and tried for supporting the uprising (he had not) and was in prison when Diem was overthrown. As the first Caravellist to achieve power, Suu would have the opportunity to bring forth the ideals described in the manifesto he had helped draft in 1960.

Ambassador Maxwell Taylor, who had been maneuvering behind the scenes to appoint Minh as chief of state, was upset "over the choice of Suu who was slipped in ahead of Minh at the last minute by pressure on the HNC by a delegation composed of Buddhist, Catholic, Hoa Hao, and Cao Dai leaders. Suu is a respected man of high principles, but old beyond his years and clearly lacking in physical stamina." Taylor was correct; Suu's prison sojourn had indeed exacted a heavy toll, but Taylor could only vent from the sidelines. He concluded: "Our hopes for the future rest heavily upon the new government which is being formed. In reviewing the disappointments of recent months, we should not forget that there has never been a stable government...since Diem was overthrown last November."[1]

Keeping his earlier promise, on October 27, Khanh handed authority over to Suu. The new head of state chose another Caravellist as prime minister, a highly respected southerner named Tran Van Huong. A former teacher, Huong was born on December 1, 1903, in the Delta province of Vinh Long. Although he came from a poor family, he graduated from the French-run Lycée Chasseloup-Laubat school in Saigon. Huong taught in the Delta for twenty years, where his pupils were drawn largely from the South Vietnamese gentry. Like Suu, though, Huong had serious health problems. He had suffered an adverse reaction to a rabies shot in 1937 that damaged his heart, and he had chronic malaria and poor eyesight. He joined the Viet Minh for a brief time but quit over Communist dominance. He refused, however, to work with the French, choosing instead to eke out a modest living in Saigon as a private tutor. In October 1954, Diem appointed him mayor of Saigon, but in April 1955, Huong resigned over Diem's autocratic style. Like Suu, Huong was arrested and imprisoned for signing the Caravelle document. In early September 1964, Khanh reappointed him Mayor of Saigon.[2]

Huong entered office determined to create a stable, civilian-led government, one that removed the military and religious leaders from politics. On November 7, he presented his cabinet. He chose competent civil service technocrats, many who had served under Diem, rather than the usual assortment of career politicians, religious figures, and military officers. Worse, Huong had a well-known bias against northern and Central Vietnamese, and thus his ministers were mainly southerners.[3] In typical fashion, his failure to include these groups subjected him to heavy criticism. The Buddhist's "immediately launched an all-out campaign to dislodge him because [they] regarded him as another American puppet."[4] Thich Tam Chau, Tri Quang's rival for leadership of the Buddhist church, bitterly complained that none of the cabinet were Buddhist supporters. Huong dismissed Chau's complaint, but then he made a grave tactical error: instead of working quietly to assuage Chau, he publicly asserted his republican view of governance. Church and state should be separate. This was the real reason for the Buddhist response; they believed they controlled the nation's destiny, and relegating them to a secondary political role was anathema. Huong's refusal to placate Tam Chau's demands would prove costly.

The Buddhists were not the only irate group. Northerners resented the cabinet's southern tilt, while student leaders believed that Huong had betrayed the Diem revolution by appointing ex-Diemists. They quickly formed two mass organizations: a General Students Association for college students and a similar one for high school students. Acting in tandem, the two student groups launched demonstrations to protest Huong's cabinet. Unlike

Khanh, though, Huong was determined to control Saigon's streets. Huong banned demonstrations, ordered the police to clear the thoroughfares, and threatened to conscript any arrested student protestors into the army. Although the protests initially dissipated, egged on by Buddhist activists, the students regrouped and launched a massive rally on November 22. Huong dispatched the police, who used teargas and water hoses to break it up. Hundreds were detained, and when further rallies turned violent, Huong extended curfew and carried out his threat; he inducted thirty-four arrested students into the army.

Huong also publicly blamed the demonstrations on Communist activists and stated eleven NLF agents were among those arrested. Since he offered little proof, his claim was met with skepticism given that the GVN habitually charged anti-government disturbances on Communist agitation. Yet Huong's accusation was correct. Hanoi's numerous agents in the student movement were deeply involved, they were reading the pulse of political dissent in the south, and they counted on using it to their advantage. According to Communist accounts, their political cadres had infiltrated the student leadership bodies. One history notes that "after the 1 November 1963 coup...we decided that our agents needed to secure positions in the overt, public high school and university student organizations, such as class president and school representatives, while at the same time we pushed forward and intensified the high school and university student struggle movement by demanding better living conditions for the people, democracy, and reduction of school fees and costs."[5]

By late 1964, the "Saigon-Gia Dinh City Youth Group had recruited many agents. Of the fourteen schools and faculties at that time, we had been able to insert our people into the representative committees of the Faculties of Science, Pedagogy, Literature, Forestry and Agriculture, Medicine, etc. In addition, by organizing press, entertainment, and social welfare groups, we had been able to attract many supporters and had incited many different movements in a number of the schools and faculties."[6]

The Buddhist's reacted swiftly to Huong's crackdown. On November 24, Tam Chau and Tri Quang released a statement denouncing Huong's actions, demanded that Suu and the HNC free the arrested students, and that the army and police take no additional reprisals against the protestors. Huong responded by invoking martial law. His tough response, however, came with a price. He needed military support to back him against the Buddhists and students. To gain the military's blessing, on November

24, he appointed Khanh as commander in chief and promoted him to lieutenant general.

More important, Huong gained the endorsement of the Young Turks, the commanders who controlled the military. They agreed with his determination to halt the demonstrations. Despite his promotion and his new assignment, however, Khanh only gave Huong a lukewarm endorsement. He was too beholden to the Buddhist leadership to openly declare against them. The Young Turks became infuriated at Khanh's tepid backing of Huong, suspecting him of secretly collaborating with Tri Quang to again become prime minister. Ky's group had become increasingly critical of Khanh's embrace of Quang, and the new disturbances only widened the rift. Clashes erupted between Khanh and some Young Turks at an MRC meeting in early December. Although nothing was settled, after the discussion, the Young Turks quietly decided among themselves to let Khanh remain as head of the military, but they were adamant that he not be allowed to regain political power. If he tried, they would depose him.

It was the beginning of the end for Khanh, and the Young Turks began to reduce his support base within the army. Ky and those coalescing around him decided to purge some of the old guard. On December 18, four officers—Thieu, Ky, Nguyen Chanh Thi, and Navy Admiral Chung Tan Cang—formed a small governing body within the military. Calling themselves the Armed Forces Council (the latter two were part of Ky's informal clique, while Thieu was not), they asked Khanh to petition Suu to retire eight senior officers, including Duong Van Minh and the four generals who had been held in Dalat. Khanh dutifully brought the request before the HNC, but since Minh had appointed the members, the HNC balked at the demand. Suu also refused to sign. Knowing that the Young Turks wanted Minh gone, Khanh exploited Suu's obstinacy. He lied to the Young Turks, telling Ky that "Minh and four members on the HNC were planning to depose Suu and Huong and take power."[7]

The lie worked, and events rapidly deteriorated. Acting impetuously on this information, late on December 20, Ky ordered the military police to arrest Minh, several of the student protest leaders, and most of the HNC. Suu and Huong remained in power, but Minh was exiled to Thailand, while the civilian government was imprisoned in far away Pleiku, the capital of the Central Highlands. A furious Taylor summoned Khanh to the embassy, but Khanh declined. Instead he sent the four officers from the Armed Forces Council (AFC). In a now-famous episode, Taylor heatedly admonished them over the military's renewed interference in the government. Taylor then invoked the U.S. trump card: he threatened to cut U.S. aid if the military continued to meddle in politics. Taylor's vehement denunciation enraged the proud Vietnamese and forced them to renew their support for Khanh. Within two weeks, however, cooler heads prevailed, and Khanh, Taylor, and Huong began seeking a solution to the impasse. Talks were held between all three parties to find a means to restore the Huong government.

Thieu had now joined the inner political sanctum. On January 1, 1965, Khanh promoted him to the rank of major general. Thieu was happy to accept, but he held no illusions about Khanh's motivations. Angered that he had been dispatched to bear Taylor's acrimonious diatribe and suspicious of Khanh's motives, Thieu sought to enlist supporters in case Khanh attempted to fire him as IV Corps commander. Thieu's long friendship with Brigadier General Dang Van Quang, one of the Young Turks and now the 21st ARVN Division commander in IV Corps, provided vital backing, but he also wanted other patrons. Thieu found an ally in Tran Quoc Buu, the well-known civilian labor chief. It was the first joint meeting between the two, but "not the last time Thieu [sought] to have Buu on his side during a test of strength."[8]

On January 18, a political compromise was reached with Huong, and the military regained a strong voice in a recrafted government. Four officers joined the new cabinet, including Thieu and Ky. Thieu became second deputy prime minister in charge of pacification, while Ky became minister of youth. Two days later, Thieu turned over command of IV Corps to Brigadier General Quang. Ky, still angered at Khanh's alliance with the Buddhists, contemplated arresting Khanh while he was attending Thieu's change of command ceremony, but other generals dissuaded him.

The new cabinet did not appease the Buddhists, but since the population had not enthusiastically responded to the Buddhist or student protests, on January 21, Tam Chau and Tri Quang began a "fast to the death" to force Huong's resignation. Given this new turmoil, on January 24, Khanh gathered the AFC, now expanded to include several other Young Turks. With Suu and Huong present, Khanh pressed the AFC to mollify the Buddhists and force out Huong but leave Suu as chief of state. Khanh wanted Suu to remain since he was apprehensive that the Americans would cut aid if the military removed another government. Although Suu offered to resign, Huong refused, fearing the Buddhists would become a shadow government. The AFC decided to support Huong but warned him that if he could not

restore stability, the military would step in. Thieu and Ky then further recommended that if the military supplanted Huong, his replacement should
come from their own ranks. Shortly thereafter, a vote was taken to determine
which military officer, if necessary, would replace Huong. Thieu garnered
the most votes, followed by Nguyen Chanh Thi, but Thieu declined. He
realized he was an inflammatory choice. "A practicing Catholic...he was
under strong attack from the Buddhists. It was unthinkable that he could
do the job under these circumstances."[9]

The next day, Khanh sent Thieu to tour Hue and report back on conditions in the city. Thieu's assessment was grim; the situation had badly
deteriorated. Many businesses had shut down, banners demanded Taylor
leave the country, and students were boycotting classes.[10] Thieu's report
shocked the AFC, and over the next two days, they mulled the worsening
circumstances. Khanh again pressed to remove Huong. He claimed that,
much like in late August 1964, he had struck a deal with the Buddhist leadership. This time, in exchange for Huong's removal, the Buddhists would
refrain from politics, and Tri Quang and Tam Chau would leave the country. On January 27, the council grudgingly approved, perhaps swayed by
the preposterous notion that the two most active and prominent Buddhist
leaders would depart Vietnam. Huong's stormy tenure was over. His civilian
government had fallen, undermined by continuous military and religious
interference in South Vietnamese politics. Suu and the new cabinet would
remain as caretakers. In early February, Huong was sent to Vung Tau, where
he would remain in virtual seclusion until late 1966.

1964 had been the most tumultuous year in South Vietnam's history
since the ascent of Diem ten years earlier. Marred by religious, regional, and
social crosscurrents, South Vietnam's fluid political scene impeded efforts
to form a stable government. Taylor summed it up perfectly:

> Until the fall of Diem and the experience gained from the events of the
> following months, I doubt that anyone appreciated the magnitude of
> the centrifugal political forces which had been kept under control by his
> iron rule...At least we know now what are the basic factors responsible
> for this turmoil—chronic factionalism, civilian-military suspicion and
> distrust, absence of national spirit and motivation, lack of cohesion in
> the social structure, lack of experience in the conduct of government.
> These are historical factors growing out of national characteristics
> and traditions, susceptible to change only over the long run. Perhaps

other Americans might marginally influence them more effectively but generally speaking we Americans are not going to change them in any fundamental way in any measurable time.[11]

Despite this turmoil, South Vietnam's political tremors were far from over.

KHANH COVERTLY SEEKS NEUTRALISM

At a press conference on January 28, 1965, Khanh attempted to justify the AFC's actions, claiming that it had acted because the current political difficulties and the anti-U.S. protests in Hue were harming the war effort. He further declared that while the military had no ambition for power, it was essential that it play a mediating role in the country's political life. Despite Taylor's previous demands to be informed in advance, Khanh told the embassy only an hour before he replaced Huong. Consequently, Khanh bristled in anger when asked by Vietnamese journalists if this move had been cleared with the U.S., piqued at having his independence questioned.[12]

Shortly after this muddled coup, the Buddhist leadership called off their hunger strike. Rumors continued to float that Tri Quang and Tam Chau would leave the country, but Thieu was highly skeptical that either would depart Vietnam or refrain from future political intrigue. He informed General Westmoreland that given Khanh's "gentlemen's agreement" with the Buddhists, the AFC must now take "strong measures to allay suspicion" over any "alliance between the Armed Forces and the Buddhists" or that the army was "under the influence of the bonzes." Thieu further clarified that "no [civil] disorders of any type would be allowed. Since Khanh had based his takeover on the excuse that Huong could not control the situation, it was mandatory that Khanh exercise firm control." When Westmoreland pointed out that this had not been done in August 1964 after the Vung Tau fiasco, Thieu replied that "lessons had been learned during that period and the same mistakes would not be repeated."[13]

Khanh had survived another ordeal, but few trusted him, and many believed he was conspiring with the Buddhists to neutralize the country. While Tran Thien Khiem had voiced suspicions in mid-December 1964 that Khanh was seeking a neutralist solution, he had no proof. Two weeks later, however, the CIA reported that Khanh had again contacted the French to discuss neutralization with the NLF. The CIA noted that while "alleged approaches to the French by Khanh are by no means uncommon," unfortunately, there was "little fact and much speculation."[14] Le Van Hoach's efforts in July 1964 apparently had proven futile, as the CIA learned in December that Khanh had now sent three separate representatives to Paris to contact the Communists and the French. The CIA believed, though, that there was "no chance" Khanh could start negotiations with the French, as he would be "opposed by almost all of the military leadership."[15]

Luckily for Khanh, several key generals dismissed the rumors. Marine commander Le Nguyen Khang denied to the CIA that Khanh was attempting to contact the French or was conspiring with the Buddhists for a neutralist solution. Khang did clarify that if they discovered that "Khanh was engaged in such political shenanigans he would quickly be removed from his position as commander in chief."[16] Ky had heard similar allegations, but like Khang, he "flatly denied rumors which he alleged were being disseminated by the Viet Cong to the effect that Khanh and the Buddhists had joined to propel the country toward a neutralist settlement."[17]

Although Ky and Khang rejected the stories, other generals did not. On February 2, Brigadier General Huynh Van Cao told the U.S. embassy that he "is now convinced that if Khanh is successful [in obtaining power] he plans to lead country toward negotiation with Liberation Front and a neutralist solution, Khanh envisaging himself as the 'Sihanouk' of SVN."[18] Even Taylor was leery of Khanh's true intentions. Taylor remarked that the "most sinister aspect of this affair [Huong's removal] is the obvious danger that the Buddhist victory may be an important step toward the formation of a government which will eventually lead the country into negotiations with Hanoi and the NLF."[19]

Everyone's fears were correct. Khanh had secretly contacted Huynh Tan Phat, then secretary-general of the NLF Central Committee. According to Khanh, in late 1964 he wrote a letter to Phat seeking talks because he was opposed to the "Americanization of the war and felt a political deal was possible only among the Vietnamese themselves."[20] Khanh claimed that the NLF was ready to settle, that he had established an "atmosphere of trust," and that he wanted to begin "negotiations for a return of peace to South Vietnam."[21] After the war, Khanh asserted that he could have achieved his aims because "we in the South had special connections with one other."[22]

How did Khanh contact Phat? According to Tran Van Don, after Taylor's eruption in December, Khanh secretly released Phat's wife from a Saigon jail. Don wrote, "Khanh ordered that she be released, and he gave her a personal letter to deliver to Phat."[23] Don claimed that Khanh feared that Taylor wanted to replace him, not out of any grand design to halt the war.

Years later, Khanh publicly disclosed Phat's reply. The letter was dated January 28, 1965, and was probably written after Khanh's press conference that same day. It states that Phat approved Khanh's "determined declaration against American intervention," and that as "you pursue this goal, you may rest assured that you also have our support."[24] How far Phat was really prepared to go is unknown, nor is there any indication that Hanoi would have backed peace talks through the Front. On February 10, Hanoi publicly reiterated its prior demands that all foreign troops must leave South Vietnam before any negotiations could occur.

Given the extremely sensitive charge of neutralization, why did Khanh's fellow generals not depose him if there was even a hint that he was seeking a coalition with the NLF? Undoubtedly a combination of factors gave them pause: no evidence of Khanh's perfidy, uncertainty over the American reaction to removing Khanh, and the fear of a split in the military if they arrested him. However, there is another possibility: Ky and Thieu, as the two most powerful military officers in South Vietnam next to Khanh, may have quietly decided among themselves that Khanh had to go, especially after journalist Robert Shaplen published an article on December 20 outlining that Khanh's brother-in-law had traveled to Paris to discuss neutralization with the French.[25] In perhaps the most ironic episode in GVN politics, the man who had achieved power through the false charge of neutralization was now furtively seeking the very thing that he had so viciously denounced.

NEXT IN LINE: PHAN HUY QUAT

The challenge now was to find a consensus nominee to replace Huong. Khanh tried several candidates, including Thieu. Khanh asked the Buddhist leadership if Thieu would be acceptable as prime minister, but Tri Quang and Tam Chau were lukewarm. Khanh dropped it, but this was the second time that Thieu had been proposed to head the country. While Thieu still feared that his personal background would only fuel the political disarray, the notion that Thieu was a viable leader was growing.

Khanh then turned to his uncle and a current cabinet minister, Nguyen Luu Vien, another older, respected southern politician.[26] In a harbinger of future events, the Buddhists wanted Nguyen Chanh Thi to serve as interior minister, an appointment that Vien adamantly opposed due to the general's close ties to Tri Quang. Between fears about what the Vien-Khanh family connection might spawn and Vien's refusal to budge on Thi, on the evening of February 14, the AFC instead selected Phan Huy Quat, the man whom Bao Dai had passed over in favor of Diem. Quat took control on February 16.

Although former Rural Affairs Chief Rufus Phillips considered Quat the most "able and experienced of the available civilians," he recognized that Quat had a serious liability: he "lacked a firm power base" among the various South Vietnamese blocs.[27] Born on July 1, 1909, Quat was the first northerner to run South Vietnam. A medical doctor and a Buddhist, Quat had held various cabinet positions in both Bao Dai's and Diem's governments. Although often described as a quiet and reasonable man, Quat had fought with Diem over the president's despotic tendencies. Consequently, he had also joined the famed Caravelle Group. Quat was arrested, but oddly he was not jailed. Quat's last government position was as Khanh's foreign minister, but he left with the advent of the Huong government.

Unlike Huong, Quat carefully choose his ministers to appease Buddhist sensitivities, seeking to create a "climate of unity" that was "essential to stability." Without it, Quat said, "We cannot win the war."[28] Several generals were included in the cabinet, and Thieu remained as deputy prime minister and defense minister. Quat's cabinet included a healthy mix of Buddhists and Catholics, but it was dominated by a small group of well-known civilian politicians who were an unusual blend in South Vietnamese politics. While most were northerners, they were moderates who belonged to either the Dai Viet or the VNQDD political parties. For example, his vice premier was Tran Van Tuyen, a northerner, a Buddhist, and a high-ranking member of the VNQDD. Tuyen was another well-known politician. He was highly educated, a distinguished intellectual, and a member of the Caravelle Group. After the group's pronouncement in April 1960, Tuyen was arrested and sent to jail for three years at Con Son.

Bui Diem was another important civilian. As Quat's closest associate, the new prime minister appointed him as his chief of staff. According to Bui Diem, Quat's first goal was to calm Saigon's turbulent waters. As he notes,

> the social atmosphere at the time was very tense. The Catholics resented the Buddhists, and there was great animosity between the southerners and the northerners. Quat delegated me to visit Tam Chau and Tri Quang to smooth relations with the Buddhists. He suspected that the

NLF had infiltrated them, but we had no proof. Although Quat was not a practicing Buddhist, when the Catholics learned of my visits, they became suspicious that he was pro-Buddhist.[29]

Quat's desperately sought goal of stability was immediately shaken when Communist mole Pham Ngoc Thao again stirred up trouble. Thao had journeyed back to Saigon in early January 1965 to foment a coup. He took advantage of the simmering anger of some Catholic, Dai Viet junior officers in local units over Khanh's appeasement of the Buddhists. He also coopted several of the officers who had supported the September 1964 coup attempt, men such as Huynh Van Ton and Lam Van Phat. Thus, like the September spasm, this plot took on a Catholic, Dai Viet, faintly Can Lao aura, which doomed it from the start. Yet while both Ton and Phat played key roles in the conspiracy, they were deeply skeptical of Thao's true loyalties. Ton feared that Thao would invite NLF units into Saigon if he gained control of the city. To counter any potential scheme, Ton surreptitiously placed Dai Viet officers loyal only to him in the coup headquarters.

At noon, February 19, Thao launched his mutiny. Coup forces seized Tan Son Nhut Air Base and JGS headquarters. They attempted to arrest Khanh by surrounding the diminutive leader's home near the Navy docks, but Khanh narrowly escaped. Thao then broadcast that Tran Thien Khiem would return to Saigon and replace Khanh as commander in chief. Hearing the news, Khiem announced that the mutiny was directed solely against Khanh and was not anti-Buddhist.

Like September's farce, the coup swiftly went awry. No shots were fired, the plotters failed to arrest Khanh, and no other military units supported Thao, nor did the Saigon populace rise up. Instead, the Young Turks quickly crushed it. Ky flew Khanh out of the city, and Nguyen Chanh Thi was again brought in from Danang and ordered to suppress it. Thi rallied loyal troops and broadcast that the coup forces should return to their bases or be fired upon. Hearing the announcement, the attempt crumbled, and Thao once more slipped away into the night.

The attempt gave Ky the perfect excuse to dethrone Nguyen Khanh. Most histories, including Ky's, claim that Thao's coup convinced his fellow generals that Khanh had to go. The reality, however, is that Ky and a few others had been contemplating removing Khanh since late November 1964. According to General Westmoreland, Ky had visited him at that time to discuss removing Khanh. Westmoreland had emphatically told

Ky that the U.S. would only support Khanh's dismissal by "legal" means. Ky agreed, and Westmoreland remarked that "Ky had given me a blueprint of things to come [but] its significance remained undetected."[30] Ky and the others were ready to remove Khanh in December 1964, but the blowup with Taylor forced the AFC to rally around their commander. Ky again contemplated removing Khanh in late January at Thieu's change of command ceremony but was talked out of it.

This new debacle, however, finally persuaded Khanh's remaining supporters that it was time to depose their commander. Thieu, Ky, Thi, and a few other generals met and drafted a decree to dismiss Khanh. It was taken to the palace, where Suu and Quat signed it. Although Khanh fought his removal, he soon caved. On February 22, he was asked to leave Vietnam, which he did on February 24. In a dramatic gesture at the airport, he scooped up a handful of dirt and placed it in a plastic bag, claiming he wanted a piece of Vietnam's sacred soil with him wherever he went. The short, tumultuous reign of Nguyen Khanh was over. He would never return.

Before the coup, Tran Thien Khiem had written a letter to Thieu and had asked an American journalist traveling to Saigon to deliver it. Once the journalist realized what he had, he published parts of it. Khiem was circumspect in his letter, but he asked Thieu for his advice on when he should return to Vietnam. Although he had not backed the mutineers, in the hyper-suspicious world of Vietnamese politics, the letter and other factors—Thieu's relationship with Khiem, his religion and his Dai Viet affiliation—placed him under a cloud of suspicion. Quat harbored misgivings that Thieu had secretly supported Thao's effort, while others had concluded the opposite, that Thieu had set up Thao. Shortly after Khanh departed, Ky reminded Westmoreland that their action against Khanh had been "legal," leading Westmoreland to believe the coup attempt was a "staged farce with Thieu and Ky directing the action to demonstrate that Khanh was no longer capable of controlling the armed forces... Thieu and Ky enlisted Phat and Ton as fronts with a promise of amnesty for their September action."[31]

Did Ky and Thieu secretly collude to use Thao's coup attempt as their excuse to rid the country of Khanh? It is certainly possible, and given their later joint government, perhaps even plausible but unfortunately unsubstantiated. Thieu could have easily used Ton and Phat to monitor Thao, whom he called "the evilest influence in Vietnam today and [who was] collaborating with the VC."[32] Ky certainly knew that Thao was plotting a coup. According to Truong Nhu Tang, a secret Front cadres living openly in Saigon and who would eventually become the NLF's minister of justice, he was present when Thao called Ky and informed him that he intended to remove Khanh.[33] Lam Van Phat would claim to U.S. embassy officials in March 1971 that "he had received full support for the coup from Thieu...and a promise of support from Ky." Yet, with no evidence to back Phat's claim, the embassy officer stated the consensus: "most sources agree that Thieu did not involve himself [in the coup]."[34]

Despite Quat's suspicions, Thieu's military colleagues saw him different-ly. Since Thieu had not joined the coup despite his obvious links to Khiem, Thieu's action reinforced his reputation among the generals as a man who was loyal to his country and not to his own advancement. The AFC voted for Thieu to replace Khanh as secretary-general, making him head of the military's leadership body. The CIA started to investigate him, stating that Thieu had "a number of strong qualities, including ability and integrity."[35] When the agency attempted to dig deeper, however, they found few Viet-namese who knew him well. Unlike many generals, including most of the northerners, Thieu was not a CIA source. The CIA found his reserved personality "difficult to judge," and a brief canvass of some fellow officers found a man described as "cautious, perhaps to a fault; some thought him xenophobic and suspicious to the point of paranoia."[36]

The U.S. military had a different opinion of the future president. West-moreland considered Thieu to be "bright, popular with his colleagues and nimble enough to keep himself in an uncommitted position so that he is not swept away in changes of regime. He had done an effective job on previous assignments and could be voted into office by his colleagues." Westmoreland confirmed that, while recently mentioned as a candidate to run the govern-ment, the savvy Thieu "rejected such suggestions on the grounds that his religious and political affiliations would make him a divisive factor."[37] He was correct; Tri Quang was "nearly paranoid about Thieu's alleged Catholic and Diemist sympathies."[38] Thieu, though, was a man on the rise.

FINDING STABILITY

No sooner had the furor over Thao, Khiem, and Khanh settled down than a new uproar ensued: nongovernmental groups openly discussing a diplomatic solution to the war instead of a military triumph. For the Nationalists, anything other than advocating total victory or a complete withdrawal of Communist forces was blasphemy. Scholars have unfortunately paid little attention to the origins and evolution of Saigon's policies, but the GVN did offer a means to resolve the war. Surprisingly, those policies began with Quat.

In mid-February, a few Buddhist monks and student protestors began making vague demands for talks with the NLF, but no one noticed. That changed on February 28, when a high-ranking monk in Saigon named Thich Quang Lien announced the birth of a Buddhist group dedicated to finding peace in Vietnam. Whimsically named the Movement for Peace and National Happiness, Lien's program demanded the simultaneous withdrawal of both Communist and American troops, followed by negotiations solely between the Vietnamese. Lien failed to gain the formal endorsement of either Tri Quang or Tam Chau, but he went forward regardless. He launched his program from the An Quang Pagoda in Saigon. This temple was now the center of Tri Quang's opposition to the GVN, while the Xa Loi Pagoda would remain the headquarters of the Southern Buddhists, who were not followers of Tri Quang.

Quat's initial cabinet meeting focused on Quang Lien's proposal. The ministers agreed on a set of conditions that became the first official post-Diem response to an internal South Vietnamese demand for negotiations with the Communists. Bui Diem remarked that "Quat was against neutralism or a coalition government. The consensus in the cabinet was that since Quang Lien appeared to favor the Communists, Quat needed to take a tough stand. Thieu said little at this meeting and did not contribute to the discussion."[39] Thus, Saigon's initial peace provisions were first defined by civilians, not the military, but these conditions would survive until the end.

At this first cabinet meeting, Quat had essentially ignored Thieu since he still harbored suspicions that the general had secretly helped Thao with the February coup. According to Bui Diem, Thieu was offended by Quat's attitude. Thieu "left very upset, almost growling about how Quat had not shown him any respect." Thieu complained bitterly to Bui Diem that "Quat does not consider me." Quat then sent Bui Diem "to see Thieu and to tell him that he had no intention of not showing Thieu the proper respect."[40] It was the first time that Bui Diem was dispatched as an emissary to smooth relations between someone and Thieu, but it would be far from the last.

Quat's initial news conference as prime minister was devoted to responding to Quang Lien. Quat agreed that "the question of negotiation is entirely an internal Vietnamese matter" but "one the South Vietnamese government has never tackled." He then laid out Saigon's policies for negotiations.

Regarding peace, Saigon would not settle for a "mere truce" that the Communists would exploit. South Vietnam was defending itself against external aggression from the north, and if Hanoi genuinely wanted peace, Saigon's requirements were simple. The Communists must "end the war, infiltration, subversion, and sabotage" and must "guarantee the safety of South Vietnam." Quat said that that Saigon wanted peace despite the Communist's "fallacious propaganda maneuvers" that deceived "public opinion." Lastly, he rejected any "international solution that has not received the agreement of the Government and people of Vietnam," a clear rebuke of those calling for a resumption of the Geneva Accords or involving the French.[41]

Quat's forthright responses were completely overlooked when American and Vietnamese air strikes escalated against North Vietnam. On March 2, the first of an expanded bombing campaign called Rolling Thunder was carried out by over one hundred U.S. Air Force planes and nineteen South Vietnamese Skyraiders against targets just north of the DMZ. Given the rapidly escalating military situation, General Westmoreland had earlier requested and received permission to bring in American troops to protect the vital air base at Danang. On March 8, two battalions of Marines came ashore at Danang, the first commitment of U.S. ground troops to the conflict.

While the U.S. bombing of the DRV stiffened South Vietnamese resolve, both Quat and Bui Diem were loath to allow regular U.S. combat forces into Vietnam, fearing it would enable the Communist's potent propaganda machine to drive a "wedge...between the government and the people."[42] They were right that the Communists would take advantage of the American presence to vigorously exploit Saigon's glaring internal weakness. Truong Nhu Tang notes that the NLF wanted to either militarily defeat Saigon or intensify the "political struggle" to cause a government collapse. Tang helped form the National Self-Determination Movement, whose leader was a lawyer named Nguyen Long. A second group, called the Committee for Peace, was also spawned by this effort. The idea was to "galvanize popular pressure in the cities for talks," thereby creating "a political crisis which the Americans would be powerless to affect. Our first step in this direction was to establish an open and legal movement to mobilize opinion and agitate for negotiations and an end to hostilities—a movement with no visible ties to the NLF."[43]

The landing provided the opportunity this small posse of secret agents and left-wing anti-GVN Vietnamese in Saigon needed. Hours after the Marines came ashore, the Committee for Peace held a press conference. They demanded the removal of U.S. troops and negotiations between the GVN and the NLF. The leader of the group was Pham Van Huyen, a northerner and a French-trained veterinarian who had come south in 1955 and served for a time as Diem's minister for refugees. Huyen's daughter, a lawyer named Pham Thi Thanh Van, also participated in the press conference. In 1948, she married another northerner named Ngo Ba Thanh, and Mrs. Ngo Ba Thanh would eventually become, next to student activist Huynh Tan Mam, the most well-known radical dissident in South Vietnam. While never influential in Vietnamese politics, she acquired a flair for handling the Western press and obtained worldwide notoriety, in part due to her excellent English that she had learned while studying law at Columbia University. As her embassy biographer stated, over the next ten years, she "devoted her energies relentlessly to vocal, fiery protest against the 'corrupt, war-mongering clique' governing SVN at the 'behest of American imperialism.'"[44]

On March 12, Quat again publicly denounced the peace movement, although he was extremely careful in his statements not to conflate the Buddhists with Huyen's group. He claimed that his government was committed to a "total struggle" against the Communists to win the war. Quat succeeded, and with Quang Lien receiving no internal support from the Buddhist leadership, on March 17, he resigned his church position and departed for a conference in Japan.

Ky backed Quat's remarks, and he told an American journalist that the AFC was "fed up with coups and countercoups."[45] If Quat's first goal was to stabilize the political scene, his second was to remove the military from politics. He used Ky's remark to convince the military to confine itself strictly to the war. After six weeks of discussions, Quat was successful, and on May 5, the Armed Forces Council disbanded. All officers serving in Quat's government resigned, including Thieu, although Quat quickly retained him. Thieu issued a proclamation stating that the AFC had been formed to protect the country's interests, and now that stability had been achieved, the military was returning to its main mission of fighting the Communists.

Quat appointed Colonel Pham Van Lieu as his director of police, and he promptly ordered Lieu to arrest the leaders of the Committee for Peace and the National Self-Determination groups, including Mrs. Ngo Ba Thanh and Truong Nhu Tang. On March 19, Huyen and two other leaders were marched across the bridge on the Ben Hai River in Quang Tri Province and handed over to North Vietnamese guards. The remainder of the group's membership were tried in a military court under the provisions of the

August 7, 1964, decree instituted by Khanh. In early August 1965, the trial was held. Some were acquitted, but Nguyen Long and three others were sent to prison. Mrs. Thanh and Tang received suspended sentences.

Although this confrontation between the government and leftist dissidents did not achieve the NLF's aims of starting negotiations or halting the inflow of U.S. troops, it did accomplish one goal. It generated widespread international denunciation over GVN "repression." This censure would intensify dramatically over the years as critics claimed that the GVN was painting anyone a Communist who sought a peaceful solution to the war and then harassing or imprisoning them. This condemnation—that America was propping up a dictatorship—became one of the chief arguments of the global antiwar movement. Vilifying Saigon's opposition to negotiations while ignoring the Communist Party's role in using peace demands to advance its control over the country served the antiwar movement's purpose of delegitimizing the GVN.

The government claims were correct. As would be true with most of its internal malcontents, many of the new peace leadership were secret Communist cadres. According to a postwar Vietnamese official publication, Nguyen Long had been a Communist agent since 1948, when "he was assigned to conduct covert operations in Hue. From 1953 until 1972, he was a member of the Lawyers Association in Saigon, serving as legal advisor and in other positions. This provided him cover to carry out operations for the revolution within the enemy's ranks."[46] While Quang Lien was not Communist, one of the NLF's most influential covert operatives was his deputy for the peace committee, a lawyer named Trinh Dinh Thao. According to his memoirs, Thao had also been an underground operative since the late 1940s. Thao had insinuated himself into the Buddhist movement during the anti-Diem protests and allowed them to use his small farm as a safe house. Thao, who was instrumental in launching Long and Huyen's peace committees, was also arrested, tried, and given a suspended sentence.[47]

Although Quat had provided the first South Vietnamese peace proposal, the Nationalists had never defined what peace meant, as anything short of absolute victory over the Communists was considered defeatist. The Americans, however, were constantly searching for a means to end the war, which always raised Nationalist suspicions of a sell-out. On April 7, President Lyndon Johnson gave a major foreign policy speech in which he announced that he was open to "unconditional negotiations" to find a peaceful solution to the conflict. In his address he offered a daring program to underwrite the economic development of Southeast Asia, but he reaffirmed his determination to continue fighting to achieve his goal of an independent South Vietnam.

DRV Prime Minister Pham Van Dong responded by proposing that the U.S. withdraw from Vietnam, that both sides refrain from joining military alliances or allowing foreign military bases on their soil, and that the situation in South Vietnam be resolved between the NLF and the GVN without outside interference. Basically, Hanoi wanted the Americans out before negotiations could begin, while Saigon wanted the Communists removed from South Vietnam before talks could commence. It was a perfect stalemate.

GVN Foreign Minister Tran Van Do had a long history of involvement in South Vietnam's foreign policy. Born on November 15, 1903, in North Vietnam, he was a medical doctor and a respected Nationalist. President Diem had appointed him to head South Vietnam's delegation to the Geneva conference. With Diem's approval, in a dramatic denouement, Do rejected the negotiated division of the country. He proclaimed that "the Vietnamese government [protests] the provisions of the agreement that do not respect the deepest aspirations of the Vietnamese people. The Vietnamese government…reserves for itself complete freedom of action…in the implementation of unification, independence, and freedom for the nation."[48] South Vietnam refused to sign the accords and was not legally bound to observe them, a point conveniently overlooked by the vociferous antiwar crowds who later claimed that Saigon had violated the treaty by rebuffing countrywide elections.

Soon after Quat made his public statements about the GVN's peace policy, and with the Americans secretly engaged in multiple peace initiatives with the British, the U.N., the Soviets, and the Canadians, Deputy U.S. Ambassador Alexis Johnson met with Foreign Minister Do on May 1 to seek an explanation of the GVN's policy. Do told Johnson that Saigon disagreed with the DRV, the U.N., the U.S., and the French that convening another Geneva conference was necessary. For South Vietnam, the 1954 accords had proven futile. Moreover, the Nationalists were certain that Hanoi would consider a new Geneva conference to be simply a pause in their war to unite Vietnam on their terms. Do pointed out that the International Control Commission, which had been appointed by the accords to monitor military violations, had been useless in halting infiltration. Without an "effective force which could be rapidly called to meet future aggression," the DRV had openly flouted both the 1954 and

1962 Laos accords.[49] Given Hanoi's track record, he remarked, why did anyone believe it would respect another pact?

Instead, the Quat government believed it was more important to achieve sway over the population since "an agreement with the VC would be useless unless the GVN could control the villages." That required two critical items: a ceasefire and a Communist withdrawal. If the NLF did not withdraw its forces from South Vietnam, "all that would have been accomplished was the division of the country, and then the GVN would have to negotiate with the NLF. This is why the GVN had asked for the withdrawal of the VC....[Do] reiterated that a ceasefire without a withdrawal would be very dangerous and that neither the government nor the military could accept such an arrangement."[50]

These were precisely the issues over which the Nixon administration and Thieu would so vehemently disagree during the period right before the signing of the Paris Peace Accords. They went to the very heart of what constituted an independent South Vietnam. While Thieu would very reluctantly agree to allow Communist troops to remain in country, mainly in exchange for Nixon's promise of more aid and to militarily respond to a major violation of the ceasefire, he had not dreamed up these rationales for refusing to accept the U.S. peace plan. The GVN had laid down these conditions long before the tumultuous events from October 1972 to January 1973.

Suspicious that the Americans were maneuvering behind their backs to arrange a negotiated settlement, the GVN asked for a meeting on May 26 between Quat and Taylor to flesh out their respective positions. The GVN side was represented by Quat, Do, and Bui Diem, and the American side by Ambassador Taylor and two senior embassy officials. The Vietnamese objectives "stated in broad terms are restoration of peace with liberty and full sovereignty and independence of SVN." Reunification was desired but was recognized as currently impractical. Regarding the NLF, the GVN's position was "absolutely firm." For Saigon, the NLF was a "creature of Hanoi," and Quat and Do would not accept it as an "element in the GVN administration, either as a bloc or a political force or organization."[51]

Speaking for the U.S., Taylor repeated what President Johnson had outlined in his April 7 speech. While the U.S. shared the South Vietnamese demand for a "securely guaranteed" independence, the U.S. favored restarting the Geneva Accords. Quat disagreed and reiterated the Nationalist's main point. The 1954 agreement was an "armistice between the French and the VC but not a political document governing the future of SVN." However, if the two sides did return to a Geneva conference, he wanted an American assurance that the U.S. would militarily respond if the Communists violated any new treaty, another harbinger of the difficulties in resolving the future Paris accords.

Then the South Vietnamese revealed their true anxiety: the challenging political climate inside the country to peace overtures. Because of the bombing halt and other U.S. peace proposals, the "Vietnamese press and opposition groups [are claiming] that basic decisions concerning SVN are being made without GVN's being a party." For that reason, they said, the GVN had "made no attempt to initiate direct or indirect talks with the DRV" because of the "obvious political difficulties of appearing to deal with the enemy."[52] Quat could not offer negotiations without further inflaming those who loudly proclaimed he was being soft on the Communists. Saigon's sensitivities to its internal divisions would continue to dictate the GVN's peace policy for years.

ENDGAME

Oddly, it was a slip of the tongue that began Quat's undoing. In early April, he dispatched Tran Van Tuyen to Paris to spike French efforts to neutralize South Vietnam. Shortly before Tuyen's trip, Quat again publicly reiterated his pledge that he would not accept a ceasefire, nor would he negotiate with Hanoi, unless all Communist troops were withdrawn. However, while he refused to recognize the NLF as an independent political entity, he would allow NLF representatives to join the North Vietnamese side during talks. For die-hard Nationalists, this was a dangerous concession, one that would reappear in October 1968. Given these instructions, while in Paris, Tuyen made some vague comments that were misrepresented in the Saigon press as advocating neutralization. Combined with rumors that several of Quat's ministers were seeking peace with the NLF, the Catholics immediately protested.

Previously, Father Hoang Quynh, erstwhile leader of the northern Catholics, had begun carping in late March over Quat's supposed "softness" on Quang Lien and the Buddhist peace proposal. In early May, Father Quynh announced the formation of a lay Catholic political organization called the Greater Solidarity Force. This group combined five different Catholic organizations into one body and for a time became the most important Catholic political force. With the northern Catholics demanding Quat take a harder line with the Buddhist peaceniks, many southerners began to lament their loss of influence after the fall of Huong. A message was passed to Big Minh, living in exile in Bangkok, to return home.

Minh was now an isolated and forlorn figure, having fallen precipitously from his position as the most esteemed military leader in the country. His rather obvious desire for a prestigious post, combined with his unresolvable enmity with Khanh, had cost him the goodwill and admiration of most of the officer corps. Yet he still commanded respect from southerners and Buddhists for overthrowing Diem. On May 12, Minh boarded an airplane and headed to Saigon. As the plane circled Tan Son Nhut, Quat denied the plane permission to land.

Quat's refusal to allow Minh's return, along with a recent court-ordered death penalty for Le Van Phat and Pham Ngoc Thao for their roles in the February coup escapade, confirmed for many southerners that Quat was aligned against them. Then Thao created chaos once more. Acting on a tip, on May 20, police arrested over thirty officers for alleged involvement in another Thao-led coup. Although Thao was in hiding, the South Vietnamese Military Security Services (MSS) captured and tortured him to death on July 17, 1965.[53]

In typical conspiratorial fashion, many southerners and Catholics believed that Quat had concocted the coup as an excuse to arrest these mostly Catholic officers. Several groups that normally did not work together suddenly coalesced into a southern bloc aligned against the northern-born Quat. Elements of the Cao Dai, the Hoa Hao, and many southerners now joined Father Quynh's Catholics to protest against Quat's government. To appease the protesters, Quat decided to replace a couple of his northern ministers and with southerners. He submitted his list of changes to Suu, expecting the aged chief of state to automatically sign the decree.

Quat, though, had not discussed his cabinet changes with Suu in advance. Moreover, the prime minister had often ignored Suu, and the prickly octogenarian resented what he viewed as Quat's dismissive attitude toward him. Suu refused to sign off on two of the five cabinet changes. Smelling blood, on May 27, Father Quynh quietly met with Suu and presented a petition of "no-confidence" in Quat. Other groups soon followed. Given that the October 1964 provisional constitution was too vague for Quat to force Suu to sign off on the changes, he called on Thieu to request that the military intervene to fix the problem with Suu.

For Quat to request Thieu's help amply displays his desperation, for the two men remained at loggerheads. When the CIA's George Carver visited with Thieu on April 29, Thieu told him that if some political element challenged Quat, "the armed forces might not consider it in the national interest to back Quat in a crisis situation. Thieu made it obvious that the armed forces feel they are...the principal custodians of the national interest, and the Armed Forces Council is the 'supreme umpire' in contemporary Vietnamese political life."[54] Yet despite their personal enmity and the earlier dissolution of the Armed Forces Council, Thieu agreed to help Quat during this "cabinet re-organization" crisis, but he warned him that "the generals want to avoid the impression of intervention and to retain their newly acquired non-political status." Thieu met with Suu and "made a forceful presentation of the military view that political crisis must be avoided, and current impasse ended."[55] If not, Thieu said, the military would have to intervene in the country's political life once more. Suu refused to budge.

Thieu then tried to convince Quynh "to avoid demonstrations and acts that would be injurious to the country at this critical time. He explained to him that he was a soldier, a Catholic, and a native of Central Vietnam and therefore not allied with any regional group. He was against religious involvement in politics. Thieu told Quynh that he viewed the army's role as supporting the aspirations of the people rather [than] supporting personalities. The army backed Quat because he was legally the Prime Minister."[56] Quynh also disregarded Thieu's plea, and in early June, his followers returned to the streets. Waving banners, they blockaded the palace. This exposed Quat's major weakness: he had no power base other than goodwill, which was in short supply. Only the military could keep Quat in power, but he received no succor from that quarter. After calling together the military leaders and Suu to resolve the impasse, Suu still refused to cooperate. On the night of June 9, a frustrated Quat abruptly resigned. Suu also quit shortly thereafter.

Quat blamed Thieu for his fall. Talking several months later with a U.S. embassy official, Quat said that "the person who really betrayed him was General Thieu, and he added that Thieu was maneuvering 'poor little Ky,' who, Quat suggested, probably did not realize how he was being used."[57] Thieu had warned Quat that the military would only support him if it was in the national interest and not simply to keep Quat in power. When Quat and Suu proved unable to bridge their differences, the military decided both must go.

The two significant problems identified by Bui Diem at the start of Quat's tenure—regional animosity and religious battles—had destroyed Quat's government, just as it had collapsed Huong's. This time, however, it was the Catholics who had brought down the government, not the Buddhists. Civilian rule would not be restored until the last days of the war. For the three men who had attempted to reestablish civilian government in their beleaguered country, fate had different destinies for each. Quat, though, would never again serve in the government despite being, as one U.S. embassy wag proclaimed, "Mr. Always Available." Regardless, the civilians had failed. Now it was up to the military.

8

"I WANT TO TRULY CHANGE THE LIVES OF THE PEOPLE"

New Leadership

I n June 1965, South Vietnam was near collapse. In the year and a half since the overthrow of Diem, the country had almost torn itself apart. To stabilize the government and win over the populace, newly installed leader Nguyen Cao Ky needed to quickly articulate his vision for saving the country. He was acutely aware that to ensure Saigon's survival, it was vital to provide political stability, defeat the Communist insurgency, and solve endemic rural poverty. To address these issues and many others, he planned to launch a social revolution, but his design was stillborn by the rapidly worsening economic and military situation. With South Vietnam's fate hanging in the balance, Ky and Thieu were forced to make a series of momentous policy decisions. All their choices would have long-term repercussions, but nothing would have more lasting consequences than his request for U.S. ground forces to defeat the Communist offensive.

NEXT UP: KY AND THIEU

With the resignation of Quat and Suu, the choice of who would lead the country fell back on the military. The Armed Forces Council was reconstituted and expanded to include all the major commanders. To govern the country, on June 14, the AFC elected a ten-man committee called the Directorate to choose South Vietnam's new leaders. After a quick poll, the new council voted to make Thieu the new head of state, replacing Suu, while

Ky supplanted Quat. Like the previous two prime ministers, Ky would wield all the power, while Thieu's role was mainly ceremonial. Details, however, are sparse on how Thieu and Ky were selected to lead the new government. According to Ky, he first proposed Thieu for prime minister, but Thieu refused because he believed his Catholic background made him a lightning rod for the Buddhists. Other accounts state that Nguyen Chanh Thi was initially offered the position, but he declined after his old friend Pham Van Lieu advised him to not to take the job given Thi's political inexperience. After demurring, Thi recommended Ky, who then accepted. Since Thi had offered the position to Ky, he believed he had leverage over the young pilot. Ky immediately rejected Thi's effort to control him, setting up their future conflict. The new government was announced on June 19 (which later was celebrated as Armed Forces Day) and formally installed on June 21, 1965.

Were Ky and Thieu the men to lead South Vietnam out of the proverbial wilderness and provide the leadership the country so desperately needed? Outsiders knew little about Thieu, but among his fellow Nationalists, he was respected for his managerial talent and careful avoidance of overt grand aspirations. They admired his adroit handling of the Americans, a Vietnamese priority with foreigners in general and the U.S. in particular. Ky's meteoric ascent, however, stunned most outside observers, and they judged him harshly. His youth, gaudy dress, wild off-the-cuff remarks, and playboy reputation made South Vietnam appear to be nothing more than a cheesy, two-bit military dictatorship.

One typical imbroglio resulted from Ky's interview in early July with the London *Daily Mirror*. In the interview, he implied that Hitler was his hero. In fact, Ky had only meant that he admired Hitler's success in quickly rebuilding Germany from a defeated state, something Ky also hoped to achieve, but the journalist was more interested in an inflammatory quote than nuanced debate. Ky's remark instantly tarnished his international image, and this negative worldwide view of Saigon rulers came at precisely the wrong moment for his country. South Vietnam had just endured international criticism for its arrests of the peace activists in early March, and his remark only magnified the impression that Saigon was a dysfunctional regime.

Personality-wise, the two men were opposites. They had differences they would eventually be unable to overcome. For now, they were united by necessity rather than mutuality, but their stark contrasts were obvious even in the beginning. While Thieu enjoyed tennis and fishing, Ky preferred

gambling, a peccadillo for which Thieu had no appetite. Ky's two passions
were cockfighting and mah-jongg, a popular Chinese game played with tiles.
While Thieu was self-effacing but quick with a dirty joke, Ky was a braggart,
a point that even his closest associates would not disagree with. Thieu was
cautious to the point of paralysis, while Ky often spoke without thinking, a
mannerism that frequently landed him in political trouble. Thieu appeared
unflappable, while Ky was moody. Ky believed his destiny had already been
written and claimed that "every major fortune teller in Vietnam agreed."
Thieu was stodgy and reserved, while Ky's most well-known trait was his
flamboyance. He paid "great attention to his appearance" and was "very
conscious of impressions and images." His black flying suit, ivory-handled
pistol, lavender scarf, and stunningly beautiful wife gave rise to the nickname
"Captain Midnight," after the film series about a daring aviator.[1]

With Thieu now the nominal head of state, American journalists began
probing his character. For example, the *New York Times* reported that Thieu
"survived the jungle of Vietnamese politics often by acting more as a phil-
osophic elder statesman than an ambitious soldier. . . . Away from politics
and the army, [he] behaves more like a university professor than a government leader. He is an inveterate pipe-smoker and likes reading, movies and
gardening. He plays an indifferent game of tennis."[2] While these surface
judgments appeared damning when matched against the ostentatious Ky,
Pham Van Lieu, a bitter critic of the future president, disagrees. He states
that "Thieu prepared himself for this role ahead of time [and] in comparison with the other generals whose stars were on the rise during Nguyen
Khanh's time in power, one must admit that Thieu was the smartest, the
wisest, and the most solid."[3]

Ky, though, was also far more than some feckless dandy. What truly
separated him from the other generals was youthful energy, and he was
determined to exploit it. To Ky, "all around us the decisions seemed to be
taken by old men. . . . But now I was able to do something about it at last
. . .We had no political ambitions. . . . [but] this was no time for doddering
old civilians with one foot in the grave to direct the destiny of a country
like ours."[4] Thus his cabinet emphasized young technocrats, equally balanced between northerners and southerners. The youngest, a twenty-nine-
year-old southerner named Nguyen Xuan Phong, was an Oxford-educated
businessman. Phong was chosen as minister of labor mainly because he
had hammered out the first Vietnamese collective bargaining agreement
between a company (Esso, his employer) and a local union. Phong was

told to appear the night of June 18 to meet Ky and join the new cabinet. If he declined, his recently received draft notice would be enforced by a visit from the military police. An erudite, highly intelligent man, Phong would eventually rise to become minister-in-state in charge of negotiations for South Vietnam at the Paris peace talks. Phong described Ky as "very much a man of action—a complex mixture of impulsiveness, intuition, and decisiveness in times of crisis."[5]

On June 19, the leadership council approved a hastily cobbled together charter to replace the one from Minh's HNC and to provide the legal framework for the new government. The Directorate, comprising the key military commanders, ran the country. As head of state, Thieu would have certain powers, such as signing decrees, but his duties were limited. As prime minister, Ky could draft laws, make policy, direct governmental bodies, and appoint the cabinet. To protect himself against any general with ambitions, Ky assigned his close friend, Marine Commander Le Nguyen Khang, as commander of the Capital Military Region (Saigon and surrounding Gia Dinh Province). To keep a careful watch on coup plotters, he appointed another ally, Colonel Nguyen Ngoc Loan, to head counterintelligence. Since both men were northerners, to placate the capital's mostly southern civil servants, Ky tapped a southerner as mayor of Saigon, the Airborne Brigade's former chief medical officer, Major Van Van Cua. Ky was clever; Cua was Loan's brother-in-law.[6]

BUILDING SOCIAL JUSTICE

Despite his outward ostentation, Ky entered office determined to "restore peace and build an advanced and prosperous nation." Although the "November 1 revolution broke out because then the government was dictatorial and unable to ensure victory over the Communists," democracy was not an option for him.[7] He would rule as a strongman, believing that his ability to make quick decisions unrestrained by a legislature was crucial to avoid the mistakes of his predecessors. They had moved too slowly, too encumbered by Saigon's stifling bureaucracy and the inhibitions of their French training.

The thirty-four-year-old air marshal was resolved to set South Vietnam on a new course by launching a social revolution that profoundly changed the lives of the people. In a toughly worded speech on June 19, Ky laid out a massive twenty-six-point agenda promoting radical social change. He acknowledged that the military situation was grave, but he pledged to reverse the situation while cracking down on corruption and profiteers. Despite Ky's best intentions, his program was a pipe dream. Ambassador Maxwell Taylor summed up Ky's formidable internal challenges:

> basic religious and regional antagonisms and divisions remain unchanged and constitute facts of life for this GVN as for any other. At present...this government starts with Catholics predisposed against, [Buddhists] in favor (though opposed to Thieu); [Southerners] probably against anything but pure [southern] government, Centrists (following Tri Quang) in favor; Saigon politicians against (as they are against any government that excludes them from power).[8]

Although religion remained one of South Vietnam's yawning fissures and Father Hoang Quynh and Thich Tri Quang were hostile to a military government, for the moment, both held their fire. The Vatican had sent word to Quynh to reduce the street demonstrations, a remonstration that throttled Quynh's more ardent supporters. Although Ky was on relatively good terms with the Buddhists, Tri Quang had only grudgingly accepted the Catholic, Dai Viet, Can Lao–tainted Thieu. Tri Quang told the U.S. embassy that the "Buddhists would reluctantly accept him as Chief of State because to oppose him would have caused too much trouble."[9] Tri Quang later told another embassy officer that if Thieu "refrained from anti-Buddhist activities, Buddhists would not openly oppose him." However, "Quang reiterated that Buddhists would never forgive Thieu for his role in anti-Buddhist actions last year and would watch his actions closely."[10] Oddly, Thieu found no comfort from his coreligionists, as Quynh's more zealous followers also attacked him. According to Lieu, "Some people accused Thieu of being a 'traitor to the religion' because he did not adequately defend the Can Lao Party or give the Catholics special privileges."[11]

Realizing the importance of calming Tri Quang's volatile followers, Thieu and Ky traveled to Hue to reassure a group of local civil and religious leaders. Trying to dampen accusations that they were simply another military dictatorship, Thieu asserted that the army's role was "to serve the nation rather than any special groups and that it has assumed power" due to circumstances, not because it was "power hungry." However, 1,500 students gathered outside the building, demanding to speak to them. The two went out to face the crowd, where they answered numerous questions about their roles in the recent political upheavals. Reflecting the militant

Buddhist dislike for Thieu, leaflets were circulated calling him "Diem's pet" and accusing him of participating in the failed coups of September 1964 and February 1965.[12] Ky would later remark that he was "surprised by Thieu's unpopularity there," a handicap that Thieu would never overcome.[13]

At a press conference on June 24, Thieu and Ky provided further details on their plans. To address the country's precarious condition, Thieu outlined a new decree for a state of war. It allowed the government to impose a curfew, prohibited the hoarding of goods for speculation, outlawed strikes and demonstrations, increased censorship, and banned the printing of materials considered seditious. In addition, those accused of violating "national security," an umbrella term covering a multitude of offenses, would be tried before a newly established and soon to be highly controversial military court. The leaders had resurrected Khanh's idea from last August, one that would prove a blunt and often misused instrument to defeat subversion during a civil war.

DEALING WITH PEACE

Ky's immediate concern was a peaceful resolution to the widening war, but the political convulsions that had forced Quat's resignation had halted any further progress in refining Saigon's peace policies. While Ky planned sweeping domestic changes, he entered office woefully unprepared for the intricacies of foreign policy, something he initially gave "little importance."[14] Believing he would act as his own interlocutor with the Americans, Ky retained Tran Van Do as his foreign minister. Unaware of the expansive U.S. efforts to find a peaceful solution and under pressure from the embassy to state Saigon's peace terms, on June 22, Ky allowed Do to publicize the program presented to the Americans on May 26. Do announced the government's four major conditions for a settlement. First, an end to Communist military and political subversion, the disbanding of the NLF, and the withdrawal of all infiltrators back to the DRV. Second, the right of South Vietnam to settle its own affairs. Third, the eventual withdrawal of friendly foreign troops. Fourth, effective guarantees of South Vietnam's independence and freedom. Ending with a strongly worded declaration, Do proclaimed that if "Hanoi sincerely wants peace, if it puts the interests of the nation above those of an ideology or a party, if it wants the Vietnamese people and the other peoples of Southeast Asia to live in peace instead of war, prosperity instead of poverty, freedom instead of slavery, it only has to put an end to aggression."[15] Both sides had now proclaimed their demands for peace by demanding that the other side withdraw. Whomever did so first would undoubtedly be seen as the loser.

Unfortunately, the world ignored Do's eloquence. While breathing new life into the 1954 Geneva Accords seemed like a logical beginning, it remained a nonstarter for Saigon. In late July, Thieu and Ky put the final dagger into that idea,

> with Thieu making spirited exposition to effect that their 'honor and political situation' did not permit them to recognize binding effect of document which French sought to impose upon them by signature of French General...Thieu said they could accept the 'factual situation' created in 1954 by the Geneva Accords but GVN could not change what had been consistent and basic position of all South Vietnamese since 1954. However, Ky said that GVN could take position that, while GVN had not signed accords, they had always and would continue to respect their principles.[16]

Thieu spent considerable effort that summer articulating the GVN's policy. The path to reconciliation, he said, was for the Communists to "withdraw their troops and cadres to the North. As far as we are concerned, the above preconditions have to be met if the VC want to talk about negotiations and peace."[17] Ambassador Lodge remarked that "no other member of the Directorate has spoken so often or so consistently on the subject. Thieu, who is probably the most sophisticated politician among the generals...seems determined to put his ideas on record to make certain that no negotiation or negotiating position is decided without GVN participation. There is no doubt he is reflecting opinions widely held within and outside GVN circles."[18] Lodge was painfully aware that Thieu's proclamations reflected the Nationalist's not-so-secret fear of "foreigners" making a peace deal that "sold them out" to the Communists.

The GVN's refusal to negotiate with the NLF did not stop the overly optimistic Le Van Hoach, Khanh's former cabinet minister who had attempted a year earlier to arrange contacts with the NLF to discuss peace. On June 3, Hoach informed an embassy officer that after extensive discussions with Front representatives, the NLF was now prepared to agree to a six-month ceasefire and negotiations to form a coalition government. The Front would also compromise by allowing U.S. troops to remain during the negotiations. Hoach felt that the Front was "tired of war, that they did not have enough rice, and that they were most anxious to terminate hostilities in an honorable way."[19]

Given Hoach's information and the strong U.S. desires to find a negotiating channel, Assistant Secretary of State for East Asian and Pacific Affairs William Bundy asked the CIA whether it could indirectly contact the NLF using third-party "cutouts." The CIA responded affirmatively but warned that if Saigon found out, "the reaction of the GVN's new leadership would almost certainly be adverse and our very suggestions would raise grave doubts in their minds about United States constancy and reliability."[20] The new Hoach effort was ignored, and peace had no chance for now. All sides were locked into a rigid position by ideology, experience, and internal political demands.

DEALING WITH THE WAR

Abruptly, the military situation became even more critical than the chaotic political scene. On May 11, 1965, the NLF launched the largest offensive of the war. Until the 1975 debacle, May–June 1965 was the nadir of the Republic of Vietnam's Armed Forces (RVNAF) military fortunes. Desertion and casualty rates had skyrocketed, and RVNAF military concepts had not been updated in over eighteen months due to the political turmoil.

South Vietnamese war operations in 1965 were guided by Plan AB 139.[21] Last published in December 1964, the plan basically rehashed Khanh's *Chien Thang* design, which in turn was essentially a rewrite of Tran Thien Khiem's *Dien Hong* strategy finalized in January 1964. Between the increased NLF military pressure and the lack of a current strategy, ARVN commanders were increasingly in a defensive posture. Given these problems, the Pentagon Papers claimed that "Westmoreland had reached the conclusion by early March [1965] that the RVNAF simply did not have the capability to overcome the VC by itself. Outside forces were going to be required to take up the slack until the GVN forces could be revamped and built up."[22]

At the end of May, Communist forces inflicted heavy casualties on South Vietnamese forces at the battle of Ba Gia in Quang Ngai Province in southern I Corps. The setback reinforced Westmoreland's certainty that a demoralized ARVN was in danger of splintering. He judged that Hanoi had moved into the third and final phase of revolutionary warfare, that of large-scale military operations. Hanoi, he suspected, sensed victory and was preparing to attack.

Faced with what he considered a dire situation, on June 7, Westmoreland sent one of the most important cables of the war to Washington, one that began the Americanization of the conflict. Declaring that Communist forces could now operate in regimental strength across the country, and with manpower declining dangerously in ARVN combat units, he informed the Joint Chiefs that "the force ratios continue to change in favor of the VC." Moreover, he said that "I believe that the DRV will commit whatever forces it deems necessary to tip the balance and that the GVN cannot stand up successfully to this kind of pressure without reinforcement." Therefore, "I see no course of action open to us except to reinforce our efforts in SVN with additional U.S. or third country forces as rapidly as is practical during the critical weeks ahead."[23]

As if on cue, between June 9–13, the ARVN suffered one of its worst defeats of the war at Dong Xoai, a district town in remote Phuoc Long Province. Two NLF regiments attacked and overran much of the town and then decimated three ARVN battalions sent in to retake it. The first relief column was the 52nd Ranger Battalion. They survived an initial ambush, then fought their way into the district headquarters. When a battalion from the 5th ARVN Division was sent in to relieve them, it was also ambushed and virtually wiped out. Then the elite 7th Airborne Battalion was dispatched to rescue the survivors. One Airborne soldier, the famous writer Phan Nhat Nam, described finding a horrific sight: "Corpses were strewn over a mile radius, sprawled out in all kinds of positions...we had to stay [overnight] and sleep on the ground next to the dead. The monsoon poured down on the rotting bodies and a suffocating stench hung in the air. All officers and men had to work together to [move the bodies]." Soon they, too, were attacked, and within a day, the Airborne had suffered several hundred dead and wounded. That night, Nam listened as the Communist troops "with pistols and machetes in hand, begin to finish off the wounded Airborne soldiers, those moaning for help. Amidst the sound of rain, I hear handguns and machete chops. They curse and shoot the wounded Airborne soldiers."[24]

Between Dong Xoai and other battles, the ARVN had been badly bloodied; casualties in mid-June were twice as high as any previous week of the war. By late June, two regiments and nine separate battalions had been rendered combat ineffective by battlefield losses. Westmoreland believed the

Dong Xoai losses vindicated his analysis. While the NLF had also suffered heavy casualties, most of their main force units had yet to be committed. He believed if these other units attacked, the ARVN would be unable to stop them.

On June 13, Westmoreland sent another decisive cable that rejected an "enclave strategy" proposed by some senior U.S. officials that restricted American troops to guarding the major population centers and installations. Westmoreland opined that without the rapid injection of American units into action to blunt the NLF offensive, the country might fall. "It is MACV's considered opinion that RVNAF cannot stand up to this pressure without substantial US combat support on the ground."[25] To justify his request for reinforcements, he laid out a new strategy in which the Americans would fight the war while the ARVN would handle security and pacification with the civilian population. It seemed like a logical decision, but in practice would flounder badly.

Acknowledging the need for the South Vietnamese to conduct pacification, he wrote,

> There is no doubt whatsoever that the insurgency in South Vietnam must eventually be defeated among the people in the hamlets and towns. [The people] must be provided security of two kinds: Security of the country as a whole from large well organized and equipped forces including those which may come from outside their country. Security from the guerrilla, the assassin, the terrorist and the informer. MACV is convinced that US troops can contribute heavily in the first category of security...but that only the Vietnamese can make real progress and succeed in respect to the problem above. Unfortunately, the ARVN is being drawn away from the people and their security in order to meet the challenge of the main force offensive....We should generally concentrate US forces away from major population centers and whenever possible do the bulk of our fighting in more remote areas.[26]

Then, in a telling comment, he added: "The RVNAF commanders do not believe that they can survive without the active commitment of US ground combat forces." Many would later decry that his plan, often referred to as the "big-unit war," was unsuited to what was chiefly a political conflict or that the Vietnamese should have played the main combat role instead of U.S. troops. While valid arguments, Westmoreland had correctly deduced Hanoi's intent: the Politburo was going for the kill. After the U.S. bombed the north and landed Marines at Danang, Hanoi believed it had to move rapidly before the Americans could tip the balance of power back to Saigon. In late March 1965, Hanoi held the 11th Plenum of the Central Committee. The plenum's report clearly stated its intentions: "In this new situation, our basic responsibility is to...seek an opportunity to concentrate the forces of our entire nation to secure a decisive victory in South Vietnam within a relatively brief period of time."[27]

The area chosen to make the main effort was the Communist B-1 Front, more commonly known as Military Region 5. This zone, which stretched from the Central Highlands to the coastal provinces of Binh Dinh and Quang Ngai, had been a hardcore Communist area since 1945. This territory was probably the true cradle of the southern Vietnamese revolution rather than the Party's anointed claimant, Ben Tre (Kien Hoa) Province in the Mekong Delta. While shifting the 9th and 25th Divisions out of Binh Dinh and Quang Ngai provinces to the upper Mekong Delta and west of Saigon had partially stabilized local security in those areas, it opened Central Vietnam's coastal area to Communist encroachment. Thus, it was no accident that Hanoi had dispatched the 325A Division into this area instead of the much closer I Corps. Acting on the 11th Plenum decision, in late April 1965 the Central Military Party Committee instructed Military Region 5 "to conduct a wave of operations lasting from May 15 through August 30, 1965. The goals of operations were to continue the destruction of significant elements of the puppet army, to destroy strategic hamlets, to capture most of the rural lowlands, and to expand our liberated zones in the Central Highlands."[28]

While the Politburo's goal was to conquer South Vietnam, both Westmoreland and Hanoi had misjudged the NLF's capabilities. The Front, even after being reinforced by the 325A Division, did not possess the combat power to defeat the Saigon government, nor could Hanoi quickly reinforce the southern battlefield. The fabled Ho Chi Minh Trail at that time was simply a primitive maze of foot trials, and the principal means of transportation were human porters. Logistically, the Trail could not handle the massive numbers of troops and equipment or sustain the operational tempo needed to win the war. The entire 325A Division planned to be present in the Central Highlands by the end of March 1965, but its trip south was so arduous that the division's combat readiness was seriously affected. According to the division history,

The paths were slippery, swampy, and dangerous. There were many sheer cliffs and steep slopes that had not yet been developed into an actual path. These took great strength to overcome. Along many stages of the route our way stations and supply caches had been attacked and destroyed by the enemy, food stocks were almost gone, and the units had to search for jungle roots and vegetables to eat instead of rice for weeks at a time.... many times, there was only enough to make gruel to feed our sick, while the soldiers had to go hungry.... The jungles were wild, some showing evidence that they had never been touched by human hands and were filled with disease-bearing germs.... In many units marching down the trail the percentage of sick rose to two-thirds of the unit. There were not enough able-bodied men left to carry the litters of the sick and support one another as they marched forward. More than a few soldiers died of acute attacks of fever.[29]

Despite its grueling four-month journey, when the 325A finally launched attacks in the Kontum/Pleiku area, the well-trained regulars quickly overpowered local militia units. When ARVN forces were drawn to the Central Highlands in response, NLF regiments attacked the coast. With Saigon's units in II Corps stretched to the breaking point, Westmoreland's options seemed clear: do nothing and hope the RVNAF could hang on, or take the offensive with U.S. troops. The MACV commander chose to take the war to the enemy.

Based on Westmoreland's dire analysis, and with the Thieu-Ky government having just assumed power in Saigon, on June 26, President Lyndon Johnson granted him the authority to commit U.S. forces to battle. Consequently, the MACV commander Westmoreland requested a massive increase in U.S. troops, including an initial tranche of forty-four maneuver battalions for 1965 and perhaps many more in 1966. In one of Saigon's most critical wartime decisions, Thieu and Ky agreed. On June 28, Ambassador Maxwell Taylor visited the two leaders. According to Taylor, Ky quickly came

to his principal point—the need for additional U.S. ground combat forces. [Ky] is impressed with need for injection of additional U.S. (or other third country) forces to tide over monsoon offensive period and to take off VC pressure while mobilization measures are being taken and, to use his expression, 'while rear is being cleaned up.' By latter term, he appears to mean actions needed to stimulate pacification, to energize public opinion, and to establish better security measures against VC terrorists.[30]

Ky, dreaming of an Asian anti-communist front, also asked for a South Korean combat unit. On June 24, he requested that Seoul dispatch an infantry division, which he wanted to insert into the hotly contested II Corps coastal area. The Koreans had anticipated the request. In exchange for sending troops, Seoul demanded more U.S. aid to "simultaneously bring economic growth and greater security [and it] hoped to use its troop contribution as leverage in the Status of Forces Agreement (SOFA) negotiations, which had been fraught with difficulties since their start in 1962."[31] The Koreans won and were rewarded with aid and more modern arms.

Aware of Westmoreland's sobering evaluation and his requests for heavy reinforcements, Johnson once more sent McNamara to Saigon to discuss the situation with the Vietnamese. In one of the key summits of the war, Thieu and Ky met with the secretary of defense on July 16 to discuss allied military strategy. The Vietnamese concurred with Westmoreland's request for more battalions, and in fact they wanted an additional division. Thieu, however, was cognizant of the political repercussions of bringing in U.S. troops. He recommended that U.S. units occupy the Central Highlands and areas north and west of Saigon. He said, "GVN should commit ARVN primarily to [protecting the people] and to deploy Vietnamese units along the coastal lowlands and in the Delta. Under this concept...the primary mission of the US/allied forces would be search and destroy operations and the protection of important bases. The primary mission of ARVN would be to engage in pacification programs and to protect the population."[32]

McNamara then asked whether the Vietnamese people would accept such a large influx of Americans. Although Quat and Taylor had argued against introducing U.S. troops,

> Ky said he anticipated no real problems and Thieu added that it would be necessary to explain carefully to the Vietnamese people that U.S. personnel were in South Vietnam only to help fight the war. Thieu believed that most Vietnamese did not consider the U.S. as having any colonialist aspirations but he thought the GVN should embark on an extensive propaganda program to explain U.S. presence....[I]f U.S. forces were concentrated in separate military zones away from the major population centers and areas of dense population the impact of American presence

can be minimized. He said that this consideration was fundamental in suggesting [how] U.S. forces operate in the Highlands and against Zone C and D [the areas north and west of Saigon]. If ARVN troops could work actively on a pacification program, the current government could demonstrate to the people that it is capable and qualified to govern. [Ky said] [t]he GVN desired more U.S. troops not because the Vietnamese were unwilling to continue the fight but that it would relieve ARVN for important pacification tasks.

Thieu feared that giving U.S. troops the main combat role would make the GVN vulnerable to both Communist propaganda and to the understandably anti-colonialist feelings of the Vietnamese people. To counteract that, Thieu publicly insisted in a press interview in early August that "direct combat with the Viet Cong is the duty of Vietnamese forces. Accordingly, the major duty of all friendly forces, including the Korean troops, is to guard the rear so that Vietnamese forces can engage in combat to the maximum extent possible."[33] Despite his efforts to justify asking for American troops, many Vietnamese officers remained uncomfortable. Thieu attempted to calm them in a speech to an armed forces convention held at Vung Tau in late September. He said that "if timely assistance had not been given to us...we would have lost military equilibrium and we could have lost the highlands; even the capital city would have been threatened."[34]

Although Westmoreland has been accused of "Americanizing" the war, he was not alone. Thieu and Ky had requested the U.S. intervention because they believed the disaster at Dong Xoai and the looming divisional thrust out of the Central Highlands had foreshadowed the possible military collapse of South Vietnam. Westmoreland's mistake, and to a lesser extent McNamara's, was their rejection of Thieu's strategic concept. To be fair, although Westmoreland had initially supported the dual role, he changed his mind for two critical tactical reasons. He wrote, "South Vietnamese leaders asked at first that I restrict American presence to remote areas, I declined, unwilling to see my flexibility fettered." Second, the enemy was so strong "in some populated regions, such as the coastal sectors of the northern provinces, that American troops would have to stage major operations there" to clean out these Communist units.[35]

However, like the NLF's military strength, had Westmoreland also misjudged RVNAF capabilities? While II Corps and III Corps were in bad shape, I Corps and the Delta remained stable. Fueled by a gung-ho mentality, Westmoreland refused to wait and see, and by the end of August, he had formalized his plans. The U.S. would assume the burden of the fighting while the ARVN would rebuild its forces. With troops from Hanoi and Washington soon engaged in direct combat, both sides would escalate the war while the South Vietnamese would be shunted aside. A reluctant Johnson had wanted to avoid direct intervention, but faced with a looming collapse of South Vietnam, his advisors had convinced him he had to act. The war was on.

FAILURE TO LAUNCH

Despite his desire to address rural poverty, during the summer of 1965, Ky faced enormous challenges that none of his predecessors had contemplated. Concurrent with the calamitous military situation loomed an economic crisis that overwhelmed his planned social revolution. There had been a steady inflationary uptick since January 1964, as the money supply had risen 70 percent to meet growing budget deficits caused by increasing war costs. Worse, NLF troops had placed an economic noose around the capital by interdicting the roads, canals, and power lines leading to the city. Suddenly, Vietnam's most essential food staple, rice, was in short supply in Saigon. Speculators took advantage of the crisis to dramatically raise prices, causing massive inflation in this vital commodity. Ky threatened to arrest any speculator, a warning aimed directly at the Chinese businessmen who dominated the rice trade. He carried out his threat on July 6 when police detained almost a hundred shopkeepers for black marketeering.

When the price did not come down, on July 25, Ky reacted. Thieu signed another decree that anyone caught hoarding rice or speculating in rice prices would be executed, and he threatened "death or seizure of property [if] found guilty of spreading false rumors to create confusion about the country's economic or financial situation."[36] Moreover, young men of Chinese-Vietnamese origin, who had been exempt from the draft due to Vietnamese concerns over their loyalty, were now eligible for conscription. Thieu and Ky, desperately needing new manpower to replace battlefield losses, were intent on signaling to the Chinese community that their children would not be permitted to lounge in Saigon while the sons of Vietnamese peasants were dying by the hundreds every month. Although the issue of "Saigon cowboys"—those bell-bottomed, long-haired youths hanging out in the capital who avoided the draft due to well-placed bribes—was never fixed, Ky was trying to placate a source of social resentment felt by the Vietnamese against the Chinese.

Trying to implement social justice and economic development at the same time proved impossible. Ky needed to address the rice shortfall, and he worked with the U.S. to import thousands of tons of American rice under a program known as "Food for Peace," or Public Law (PL) 480. Conducted under the auspices of USAID, America provided food assistance to millions of people around the world. Although importing American rice stabilized the price, South Vietnam's inability to feed itself remained a major unresolved crisis. The widening war had curtailed the ability of peasants to plant, harvest, and ship rice to Saigon, where merchants would then resell it to the central and northern sections of South Vietnam that had a rice deficit. Food was becoming another weapon of war.

Besides rice, racial turmoil in the Central Highlands also setback Ky's plans. Like Khanh before him, Ky had to deal with ethnic minority grievances, but fortunately for him, Quat had made progress in this area. In May 1965, Quat had formed an Office of Ethnic Minority Affairs to deal with Montagnard complaints. Despite these efforts, the FULRO organization was not appeased. In mid-July, it struck again and raided a CIDG camp, tied up the Vietnamese officers, and raised the FULRO flag. Only after lengthy negotiations between Saigon and FULRO did the tribesman withdraw, and on September 15, Ky flew to Ban Me Thuot to welcome back into the ranks almost five hundred dissident tribesmen. He then called for "ethnic unity" between the Highlanders and the Vietnamese and said that "the task of preserving the unity of the South Vietnamese people requires [no] discrimination as to social position and race. To that end, the principle of ethnic union [between the two races] should be promoted above all else."[37] Ky's remarks astonished many Vietnamese, who generally considered the tribal people as savages.

In August, Henry Cabot Lodge returned to Saigon to replace Taylor as ambassador. Ky presented his social justice program to Lodge on August 20. Ky vowed to wipe out corruption, improve local government, institute a land-reform program, and mobilize youth. Land reform was at the heart of social justice, and Ky wanted to restart the long-moribund program. He hoped to ameliorate the NLF's most powerful economic appeal: providing free land to tenant farmers who were paying exorbitant rents. While the NLF had redistributed land to local peasants, the Front had also caused discontent by imposing high taxes on them. Ky sensed an opportunity to win back the peasants, but like growing and shipping rice, he quickly faced major roadblocks. Since the large landholdings had already been broken up under Diem, the major issue was disentangling landownership among thousands of tenant farmers. Many records were nonexistent, and the NLF had erased previous tenure by moving farmers onto lands once occupied by others. Worse, Ky's plan was stymied because much of the land was now under NLF control. Land reform, like many other local initiatives, would have to wait until the government could take back the countryside.

RESTORING CIVILIAN RULE

One hopeful sign in the otherwise bleak political scene was the successful holding of municipal and provincial elections at the end of May. Approximately 73 percent of registered voters participated, an amazing electoral event considering the tumultuous circumstances of May 1965. These elections created provincial councils that would "advise" the appointed province chiefs, but more important, they formed the basis for reasserting civilian control of the government. Like prior military leaders, Ky and Thieu stated that their goal was to eventually return power to civilian control. In fact, the new charter promulgated on June 19 stated that governmental authority was only temporarily vested in the military.

Ky deferred to Thieu on the subject of elections. At the June 24 news conference, Thieu stated that national elections were impracticable with the NLF controlling half the country. Like improving rice production and instituting land reform, nothing could begin until the GVN had restored its control in the countryside. But by mid-September, with U.S. troops pouring into the country and pushing back the Communist units, Thieu began to explore the formation of a National Council, similar to the provincial councils that had just been elected. This National Council would serve as a consultative body to the Directorate and would be tasked with drafting a constitution.

Thieu, who had earlier lobbied both Tran Van Don and Nguyen Khanh for the military to rule, apparently had had a change of heart, especially since actions speak louder than words. Thieu spent several months planning, and by late November, the ruling generals approved the council's formation.[38] Once the council members were appointed, they would begin work in early 1966. They would travel around the country and canvass local people regarding what they wanted in a new constitution. Afterward, the National Council would draft a constitution and then the military government would hold national elections.

Next, they turned to the arduous task of regaining control of the countryside. The pair first moved to jump-start pacification. On July 30, Ky abolished the Central Rural Reconstruction Council established in April under Quat and created a new one called Rural Construction that reported directly to him. When the first minister of the new council died in September in a plane crash, Ky tapped his fellow northerner, Brigadier General Nguyen Duc Thang, as the new minister.[39] To explain Ky's plans for pacification, a meeting for province chiefs and representatives from the provincial councils was held on October 11–12, 1965. This important conference, one of the first of its kind, was designed to reenergize the pacification effort, but oddly it also helped shape South Vietnam's constitutional future.

Thieu's efforts to begin the process of restoring civilian rule had not gone unnoticed. At the end of the conference, the newly elected provincial council members signed a declaration encouraging the junta to "prepare for the election of a constituent assembly."[40] The chief voice behind the request was Dr. Phan Quang Dan, a well-known physician. Dan had been a long time critic of Diem who had been jailed for his alleged participation in the aborted November 1960 coup. After his release in November 1963, he revived his medical practice and became a popular figure by treating the poor, often for free. In May 1965, Dan had been elected to the Gia Dinh (the province surrounding Saigon) provincial council, where he was chosen as chairman. Working tirelessly to solve local issues, he became one of the Nationalists' few independent politicians with genuine grassroots appeal, although it was localized to Saigon.

The council's request encouraged Thieu. He gave a speech on November 1, 1965, which the military had redesignated as "National Day" to commemorate the overthrow of Diem.[41] Although Thieu admitted that his government had barely achieved stability, he again promised that the military would reestablish democratic institutions in 1966, beginning with elections for a National Assembly. Ky, however, was less sanguine. While he supported elections for civilian rule, Brigadier General Thang had informed Ky that it would take two years before at least half the population was secure. Fearing Communist intimidation at the polls, Ky was adamant that elections could not be held until the army could protect the population. Thieu and the military class were caught in a predicament. They wanted to enshrine civilian rule but feared that the Communists would take advantage by forcing people to vote for them. Thus, Ky foresaw democratization as a gradual process predicated on first achieving population security rather than the quick elections advocated by some political and Buddhist leaders.

Fortunately, the earlier public demand by the admired Dan helped Thieu push a reluctant Ky toward civilian government. In early December 1965, Bui Diem informed the U.S. embassy that he, Ky, Thieu, and another senior officer, Lieutenant General Pham Xuan Chieu, had finalized a plan to democratize the country. Thieu had tapped Chieu to manage the shift to civilian rule. When the embassy contacted him to confirm that the Directorate was committed to "democratizing" the country, Chieu corroborated that the generals had approved Thieu's plan to form an advisory committee that would visit the provinces and gather local input. The council would then write a statute governing the operation of political parties, draft a constitution, and design an electoral law.[42]

On February 7, 1966, Thieu signed the decree "Establishing the Consultative Council for the Building of Democracy." The council's statutes were similar to the Council of Notables that had been organized shortly after the Diem coup. The Buddhists, however, had no appetite for Thieu's plans. They had designs of their own.

9

"ONLY ONE SHOT FOR MADNESS TO FOLLOW"

The Long First Year of Nguyen Cao Ky

I n fits and starts since the death of Ngo Dinh Diem, the South Vietnamese had tried to forge a new and arguably more inclusive national identity, but rather than achieving unity, the fissures of Vietnamese society seemed unbridgeable. Thieu and Ky had to juggle the aspirations, jealousies, and entrenched passions of southerners, centrists, northerners, Buddhists, Catholics, and Hoa Hao alongside ethnic divisions and political disagreements. Even in the face of the Communist onslaught, appeals for unity floundered given that the Nationalists had no history of political compromise.

The war also exacerbated other issues that shredded the two leaders' attempts to create a stable and durable government. Economic problems had become burdensome as food shortages and raging inflation in the cities generated vociferous complaints. Ongoing U.S. diplomatic efforts to find a peaceful solution to the conflict alarmed the always suspicious Nationalists. During their first year in power, Thieu and Ky endured a perfect storm of political, economic, and social unrest. This toxic cauldron culminated in a particularly bitter confrontation with Thich Tri Quang and the Buddhists that almost ignited a civil war. Yet despite these seemingly insurmountable problems, the Thieu-Ky government survived, marking the beginning of stability and growth for South Vietnam.

STILL SEARCHING FOR PEACE

For the Americans, the military's desire to restore civilian rule was welcome news, but Lyndon Johnson was searching for a proposal that would persuade Hanoi to discuss peace. After Westmoreland had informed Washington that 1966 would be a long, brutal fight, and with Johnson pressured by growing domestic and international antiwar sentiment, the president began contemplating a bombing halt to entice Hanoi to negotiate. The administration had been heartened by various signals that the Politburo might now be amenable to discussions. Consequently, on December 24, 1965, Johnson announced a halt to the bombing of North Vietnam in conjunction with a worldwide "peace offensive" to prod the Politburo to negotiate.

Concurrently, Henry Cabot Lodge in Saigon received a more direct offer from the NLF via Archbishop Angelo Palmas, the Vatican apostolic delegate to Vietnam and Cambodia. Palmas had informed Lodge several times that a source had told him that the NLF wanted a ceasefire. On January 6, 1966, Lodge was suddenly summoned to a meeting with Palmas's source, Le Van Hoach, who had been attempting since the summer of 1964 to arrange a ceasefire. Hoach claimed he had been "sent as an emissary" by both Nguyen Huu Tho and Huynh Tan Phat, the two top men in the NLF. He stated that they wanted to "stop the slaughter...independent of Hanoi." They offered a ceasefire but slyly sought U.S. recognition for "a new government in South Vietnam," a crafty effort to ascertain American enthusiasm to depose Ky and Thieu. Lodge would have none of it. While he expressed his willingness to discuss a ceasefire, Lodge stated it was impossible to talk peace without GVN involvement.[1] Despite the NLF overtures, it remained difficult to discern a path to peace, and the effort died when NLF spokesmen, parroting Hanoi's denunciations, publicly censured the U.S. request for talks.

Hoach represented an emerging trend among some Nationalists. A few South Vietnamese were contemplating whether to attempt to negotiate peace with the enemy rather than pursue a military victory. While the army, the Catholics, and many others remained adamantly against negotiations, after the coup, Duong Van Minh and Nguyen Ngoc Tho believed a secret outreach might convince the non-communist NLF elements to switch sides, followed by a political compromise. Although they had been unable to follow through, since then, the militant Buddhists and a few others had made the first public demand for peace talks. While Thieu and Ky remained firmly against negotiations, it would prove impossible to put the genie back into the proverbial bottle. Moreover, despite repeated South Vietnamese government statements rejecting negotiations with the Communists until they halted their attacks and withdrew, Johnson continued covert U.S. diplomatic activities. South Vietnam had accepted a devil's bargain when it asked the U.S. to save it from the encroaching enemy. An external protector comes with a price: the junior partner cannot control the dominant power's actions, particularly since its interests will always trump its ally's. Such would be the fate of South Vietnam.

For example, in a discussion with Ambassador Lodge in mid-October 1965, Thieu opined that he believed the enemy would only agree to negotiate when "they were convinced they could not achieve a military victory with main force units...The purpose of accepting an offer to negotiate would be to end or suspend the U.S. military activities [so that] it would be difficult, if not impossible for us to continue operations."[2] Thieu believed that peace talks with the Communists was simply another tactic to wear down the U.S. Worse, any agreement like Geneva that permitted Communist participation in elections threatened the very survival of the republic.

Thus, Saigon was shocked when the U.S. administration admitted publicly on January 10, 1966, that Hanoi had accepted a letter from Washington proposing peace talks. The South Vietnamese reacted harshly. Tran Van Do immediately declared that the GVN's four points for peace, first articulated the previous June, remained unchanged. Saigon was opposed to both peace negotiations and a formal ceasefire, nor would it countenance the NLF's ongoing presence within its borders. Do viewed the NLF as puppets on Hanoi's string. Peace, he reiterated, would only come after the Communists halted their aggression and left South Vietnam.

Secretary of State Dean Rusk, currently visiting Asia, was immediately dispatched to Saigon to mend fences, but the meeting was contentious. Thieu rebuked Rusk over what he considered high-handed U.S. policy. Although Rusk claimed that the bombing halt and Johnson's call for unconditional talks had put Hanoi on the diplomatic defensive, Thieu countered that the bombing pause had only provided enemy forces an opportunity to rebuild. Worse, Johnson's peace offensive had put his government

> in difficulty with public opinion on peace moves or meetings with the communists. The Army and the public have the feeling the GVN has not been kept informed of all measures the USG has taken in the peace offensive. This has made it difficult for the Government....[A]ny time

there are proposals for a truce or negotiations or decisions on bombing, the Vietnamese should be consulted.... to maintain morale, the Government would not offer a soft position. When anyone talks about the four points of Hanoi or about the National Liberation Front, this has an effect on morale, and helps those who wish to weaken the Government or those who wish to offer an easier [meaning neutrality] solution. The Vietnamese Government does not doubt the U.S. commitment, but it is concerned with the psychological impact of what is going on.... The Government is seeking to develop a democratic viewpoint and promote constitutional development in the future. But the basis of unity is a strong national policy.[3]

This statement was a clear insight into Thieu's future policy. For Thieu, ensuring South Vietnam's survival meant no concessions to Hanoi that would let the Communists undermine them from within. Withdrawing all Communist forces was the key step in guaranteeing the republic's existence.

Rusk's visit coincided with the opening on January 14, 1966, of the Second Congress of the Armed Forces. Thieu gave the inaugural address. He informed the assembled officers that the government's priorities for the new year were a military offensive to retake the countryside and stabilization of the economy. Equally important were a renewed emphasis on pacification via the new Rural Construction program and political development to "gradually" build democratic institutions from the "hamlet to a solid national structure." The new year would see "a period of nation-building," but Thieu declared that the "war can be ended only by a complete victory, both military and political, and that peace for Vietnam can only be that of a country fully independent in terms of its territory and sovereignty."[4]

Ky concluded the congress with a state-of-the-nation speech in which he repeated the three major objectives for 1966. He also announced that a National Council would be appointed shortly to draft a constitution that would then be submitted in October 1966 to a national referendum. He pledged that the new constitution would serve as the basis for a democratic government and promised national elections in 1967. Ky, however, was more direct in condemning American peace feelers. "No other nation," he stated, "is qualified and able to decide on our destiny...[W]e can never tolerate any interference harmful to our national sovereignty...There is no other alternative...than to defeat the Communists and rout them from their strongholds."[5] Both men had now warned the U.S. not to make peace without considering GVN desires.

Historians have questioned if the allies had any chance at achieving peace with the Communists in these early years. With Le Duan in charge, the answer was no. In December 1965, the first secretary gave a bellicose speech at the 12th Plenum of the Central Committee outlining his now-famous "talk-fight" negotiating policy:

> We advocate fighting until the puppet army has essentially disintegrated and until we have destroyed an important portion of the American army so that the will of American imperialists to commit aggression will be shattered and they are forced to recognize our conditions [for peace]! That means the question of fighting and then talking—fighting until we win and then talking—or of fighting and talking at the same time, is a matter involving the correct stratagem, and it is linked to our political and military policies mentioned above....Currently, the American imperialists...are eager for us to sit down with them at the negotiating table so that they can force us to make concessions. As for our side, we believe we cannot sit down at the table until we have caused the puppet army to disintegrate and until we have crushed the American imperialist will to commit aggression. [This was] very secret, and we have not yet advised any of the fraternal [Communist] parties of our position on this matter.[6]

Like Thieu and Ky, Le Duan was not interested in peace; he wanted victory.

CONTINUING DOMESTIC STRIFE

Ky came to power intent on creating a social revolution that changed the lives of the people, but too many intractable issues prevented him from accomplishing that goal. Refugees were another severe problem, particularly in Central Vietnam. The total had grown swiftly due to heavy fighting in that area during the summer of 1965. Massive temporary refugee camps had sprung up, and the conditions were abysmal, including poor sanitation, no schools, and limited medical facilities. GVN policy was to return fleeing families to their original village, but this proved impractical given the ongoing fighting. The GVN decided instead to resettle many refugees on nearby abandoned land. Families were provided money to rebuild and buy a six-month supply of rice.

Responsibility for refugee administration was split between the Ministry of Social Welfare and the new pacification program called Rural Construction, which in late 1965 had taken over resettlement duties. Recognizing that refugee assistance needed a single manager, on February 22, 1966, Ky removed refugee responsibilities from both agencies and formed a Special Commissariat for Refugees. In mid-April, Ky appointed Dr. Nguyen Phuc Que as commissioner and backed him with a budget of 1.3 billion piasters. Que also received substantial USAID funds to help construct new housing, build classrooms, and improve health conditions. Managing the hundreds of thousands of refugees became an ongoing struggle for the GVN, one that it handled with varying degrees of success.

Adding to Ky's woes was resurgent ethnic strife. Despite Ky's efforts in September 1965 to placate the Montagnards, negotiations had stalled when FULRO leaders continued to demand a semi-autonomous state for their people. The GVN refused, fearing that FULRO was a Trojan horse for either the Cambodians, the French, or the Communists. At loggerheads, FULRO struck for a third time. On December 17, 1965, FULRO raided a district capital, killing thirty-five Vietnamese officers and soldiers and wounding numerous civilians. While ARVN troops quickly put down the uprising, Saigon and Washington desperately needed the tribesmen if they hoped to prevent Communist inroads in the lightly populated Central Highlands.

Ky again promised to implement better land policies, and on February 22, 1966, he replaced Quat's Office of Ethnic Affairs with another special ministry that reported directly to him. Ky tapped Paul Nur, a French-educated administrator of Montagnard descent, to lead the Special Commission for Montagnard Affairs. Nur launched programs to increase health and education benefits to the tribesmen and stepped up efforts to replace Vietnamese civil servants with Montagnards. Although the twin issues of autonomy and Vietnamese land grabbing remained unresolved, Nur's endeavors paid off and calm was restored.

Given the ongoing strife between the Montagnards and Saigon, it is surprising that the Communists never succeeded in exploiting the ethnic divisions in South Vietnam. Although they invested significant efforts to attract the Montagnards, the Cambodians in the Delta, and the Chinese in Saigon to their cause, it was a noteworthy flop. While COSVN achieved some limited recruiting success among the ethnic groups, they failed for three reasons. First, Communist propaganda proclaimed the war was about uniting the country, and the minorities had a long history of opposing Vietnamese sovereignty. Second, COSVN, blinded by ideology, was as ham-handed as Saigon and viewed FULRO as "a reactionary political organization set up by the imperialists in a plot to sow divisions within our nation and to attack and sabotage the revolution."[7] Third, many Vietnamese treated the minorities with undisguised contempt, resulting in a deep mistrust of Vietnamese on either side. Thus, the Khmer and the Montagnards joined the U.S.-led Mike Force or CIDG in droves, hoping that the Americans would support their efforts to keep their lands from becoming completely "Vietnamized."

Urban social unrest also continued to simmer, but unlike in the countryside, it was normally fueled by political turmoil, not ethnic animus. Yet in 1966 a new issue arose: mounting economic turbulence. Housing, food, and other prices in Saigon skyrocketed due to the rapidly expanding American presence. By early 1966, inflation had driven up the standard twenty-five-pound bag of rice over 68 percent in less than a year. Everyone was deeply affected by the rapidly increasing cost of living, especially civil servants on fixed salaries, which naturally led to corruption to earn money.

Several triggers affected food prices. First, Communist units often blockaded the roads leading to the capital. Second, the fighting had driven away many peasants who tilled the land. Rice plantings had dropped so significantly that Vietnam went from a rice exporter to a heavy rice importer in roughly a year. To compensate, in March 1966 Washington and Saigon signed a new aid deal, and the U.S. brought in another two hundred thousand tons of rice to help ease the food shortage.

What most Vietnamese focused on, though, were widely believed accusations (which were true but also ethnically motivated) of price gouging by prominent Chinese merchants in Cholon, the mainly Chinese suburb of Saigon. These families controlled the rice trade, from purchasing unhusked rice and transportation to—most important—milling the grain. Sensing a profit, they hoarded rice, hoping to buy low and sell high. Ky had publicly threatened on several occasions to shoot profiteers, and in early March 1966 he kept his promise. Two Chinese importers in Saigon were arrested and charged with hoarding, black marketeering, and bribery of government officials. One man, Ta Vinh, was sentenced to death and publicly shot on March 18, 1966. Although the Chinese community did not protest his execution, Ta Vinh's death did have one important consequence: the Cholon business leaders began making quiet overtures to Thieu, and they would provide him with financial backing during the 1967 elections.[8]

Since COSVN had earlier created a Chinese Proselytizing Section to influence the normally apolitical Chinese in Saigon, they attempted to use Ta Vinh's execution to woo the community to its cause. They recruited some people and fomented a few minor strikes among the numerous Chinese manual laborers, but generally they failed again due to their own missteps.[9] In December 1965, COSVN had sent letters to the ethnically Chinese editor of *Chinh Luan*, South Vietnam's top newspaper, warning him to cease his "pro-American" editorials. The editor, Dr. Tu Chung, answered their threats with a fiery frontpage denunciation. The Communists responded by assassinating him in front of his house on the morning of December 30, 1965. Ta Vinh's execution was about business, but killing Chung was political, and it swung the Chinese to the GVN.

Another key inflationary driver was vastly increased GVN spending to finance the war. Since Vietnam had no personal income tax, roughly 90 percent of government revenue came from custom duties or via favorable currency exchange rates. With the expansion of the conflict, Saigon was now confronting an onerous budgetary gap. The number of piasters in circulation had mushroomed, and the deficit had likewise swelled. In 1964, the GVN budget was roughly twenty-five billion piasters with a deficit of five billion piasters. By the end of 1965, the budget had increased to almost 46 billion, with a shortfall of roughly twenty billion. To pay for pacification and increased troop strength, the 1966 budget was expected to rise to fifty-five billion. This combination of deficit spending, commodity shortages, and U.S. purchases had created a massive spike in prices, and inflation was projected to rise almost 30 percent in 1966.

Seeking to boost revenue and dampen inflation, on October 15, 1965, the GVN launched an anti-inflationary program, which included a significant rise in import taxes. To dam the flood of American money, Westmoreland switched the pay of U.S. servicemen from dollars to military scrip. He also attempted to crack down on the burgeoning black market in U.S. goods from military stores and the brisk trade in illegal currency exchanges, but it proved impossible to contain. In early February 1966, the U.S. agreed to enlarge its economic aid under the Commodity Import Program (CIP) and PL 480 Food Program to $400 million. The GVN decided to use the additional aid to double its import program, which, in conjunction with the increase in import taxes, would account for another 11 billion piasters.

While Saigon was attempting to address its ethnic, social, and economic woes after several years of turmoil, the Johnson administration faced hardening congressional opposition to U.S. involvement. Congressional resistance had coalesced over the sharp increase in American casualties coupled with the subsequent resumption of bombing at the end of January 1966 and the vast sums of money earmarked for Vietnam. In early February 1966, Senator Robert Kennedy (D-Mass.) suddenly called for a coalition government between the GVN and the Communists. Shortly thereafter, Senator William Fulbright (D-Ark.) announced that he would hold hearings to examine the president's Vietnam policies.

To quell the growing criticism, Johnson abruptly scheduled a meeting with Thieu and Ky in Honolulu. Johnson wanted to address the pacification and political issues confronting Saigon, and he wanted Ky to speed up the elections that had been announced for 1967. The meetings, held on February 6–8, were a major success. Johnson promised to support pacification by providing considerable sums to improve health, education, agriculture, and even the construction of a television broadcasting system to help the government inform the people. For their part, Thieu and Ky agreed to pursue any forum for peace, which was an easy concession since they did not believe the Communists would talk. Moreover, they consented to quickly appoint Thieu's proposed National Council, then publicly declared in a joint statement that a constitution would be ratified via secret ballot.

Despite productive discussions and a vast increase in U.S. assistance programs, some South Vietnamese perceptions of the meeting were diametrically opposite. Few Vietnamese understood that Johnson was essentially "doubling down" on Saigon despite growing antiwar sentiment. Most Vietnamese saw the conference as evidence that Thieu and Ky had the backing of the all-powerful Americans, while other Nationalists resented the appearance of their leaders being summoned. When a picture was published showing Johnson embracing Ky, as had happened with the photo of McNamara holding Khanh's hand aloft, it exacerbated Vietnamese xenophobia. Many Vietnamese simultaneously accepted that Ky was the American choice but loathed the impression of U.S. control. It was an emotional chord that the ever-restless Thich Tri Quang would shortly use to his advantage.

IDENTITY POLITICS

To forge national unity, Ky and Thieu had embarked on an effort to bring the country's powerful forces into some form of a political coalition. Overcoming religion and regional difference was critical to success, since without a national political consensus other than anti-communism and anti-neutralism, religious and regional identity remained the focal point for dissent. The two leaders, though, had learned from Diem's failure that the carrot was better than the stick.

Regionalism was also resurfacing as a contentious issue. In the spring of 1965, Tran Van Don had been elected head of a new southern-centric organization called The Southern Old Students' Association (*Hoi Lien Truong Mien Nam*), which the embassy called Lien Truong. Organized partially in response to Quat's supposed bias against southerners, the association's membership was limited to those born in the south and who had graduated from one of the four French schools established in Cochinchina during the colonial period. Although ostensibly apolitical, Lien Truong had been formed to provide southerners a bulwark against domination since 1954 by either central or northern-born Vietnamese. Many southerners believed the war was really between two factions of northerners, and they often invoked the phrase "We cannot let one million northerners stand on the necks of fourteen million southerners." While only a thousand strong, the group represented a high percentage of the southern professional class. Given their wealth and prestige, the Lien Truong could threaten Ky's government if it began making political demands for increased southern representation or allied itself with either the Buddhists or Catholics. The rise of the Lien Truong would spark the second most damaging political storm of 1966—the cabinet revolt.

Upon returning from Hawaii, Ky reorganized his cabinet to implement Johnson's promised aid programs, and he used the opportunity to placate two key groups. Ky replaced his minister of economy, allegedly the recipient of massive Chinese bribes, with Au Truong Thanh, a French-trained, thirty-year-old southerner from Saigon whose parents were lower-middle-class Chinese immigrants. Ky also hired another French-trained southerner, thirty-one-year-old Vo Long Trieu, as minister of youth. While the pair reflected Ky's desire to attract youthful voices into the government and highlighted his claims that he was rooting out corruption, the appointments were a disguised attempt to appease the Lien Truong. Thanh also placated Chinese business leaders by elevating one of their own to oversee the economy. Thanh, though, came with baggage. While he had been jailed twice for political opposition to Diem, he had also been accused of Communist sympathies due to a long history of involvement with left-leaning organizations. Thanh was not pro-communist, but he was a neutralist with socialist economic leanings.

Trieu also provided crucial political benefits. Prior to his appointment, he had been working as a statistician in the Ministry of Agriculture, but he was also one of the most important Catholic lay leaders in the country, an ardent southerner, and a key member of the Lien Truong. Born in the Delta, he was a delegate of the Archdiocese Liaison Bureau, which directed Catholic political activities, and he often acted as an intermediary between the church and the Buddhists. Unfortunately for the energetic but politically inexperienced Ky, his choices of Thanh and Trieu would backfire when the pair would lead the cabinet uprising of late 1966.

Government relations with the main religious groups from July 1965 to March 1966 had been relatively calm. Like Minh and Khanh before them, Thieu and Ky had sought to build a majority coalition to govern the country, particularly the religious and ethnic minorities in the Delta. On July 12, 1965, Thieu signed a decree granting the first official recognition of the Cao Dai and Hoa Hao religious faiths. Similarly, on February 15, 1966, the GVN donated 5.5 million piasters to the Cambodian Theravada Buddhist Congregation to appease Cambodian Buddhists in the Delta. The funds were allocated to help build a school. It worked, and the Cambodian Buddhists never joined Quang's revolts.

The relationship between the Buddhists and the GVN, the most critical in the country, remained stable. Ky and Thich Tri Quang had a decent rapport, but as noted, Quang did not speak for all of Vietnam's Buddhists. Thich Tam Chau, chairman of the Institute for the Propagation of the Faith, commanded the allegiance of the northern-born Buddhists and those around Saigon. To keep relations cordial, the government engaged in a serious outreach effort to the monks. In November 1965, army engineers began constructing the Vinh Nghiem temple, one of the largest in Saigon. The number of Buddhist chaplains in the military, a program that began under Khanh, was expanded. Moreover, the United Buddhist Church began building the first Buddhist college in Saigon, Van Hanh University. Land had been donated by one of the wealthiest men in South Vietnam, Nguyen Cao Thang, who had just returned in November 1965 from a year abroad. Thang's wealth derived from his ownership of the "Office Pharmaceutique du Vietnam" (OPV), Vietnam's main pharmaceutical company. Originally a French firm founded in Hue in 1950, Thang had purchased it in 1956.

Since he was a Catholic from the Hue area and his wife was a distant relative of Diem, Thang quietly became a financial backer of the Ngos in exchange for one of the few licenses to import Western medicines. Under Thang's leadership, OPV grew into the largest and most modern company in South Vietnam.

Thang made the land donation when the Catholic leadership had requested his help in establishing closer relations with the Buddhists. He also provided funds to erect a home pagoda for Thich Thien Minh, head of the UBC's Youth Wing. Thang's decision to assist Minh was not charity. Minh was Tri Quang's closest lieutenant, he had been instrumental in organizing the Buddhist rebellion against Diem, and he was a leading militant. After making these contributions, Thang became Thieu's main financial benefactor, and he would play an instrumental postelection role for the new president with both the Buddhists and the National Assembly.

THE BUDDHIST CRISIS ERUPTS

After the Honolulu conference, an emboldened Ky moved to strengthen his rule, but many forces were opposed to the creation of a strong, central government. His first effort was to reduce the power of the four corps commanders. These generals were virtual warlords within their regions, where their writ was often greater than Saigon's. Nowhere was this more evident than with the ambitious and temperamental Lieutenant General Nguyen Chanh Thi, commander of I Corps. Thi often rejected directives from Saigon and had begun badmouthing Thieu and Ky after the Honolulu meeting, accusing them of being American lackeys. Considering Thi's refusal to obey instructions and his overt contempt, when Ky discovered that "Thi had recently approached the [Lien Truong] group led by Don in an attempt to arrange a political alliance," he decided to investigate.[10]

On March 3, 1966, Ky traveled to Danang to meet Thi, hoping to mend political fences. It did not go well. When Ky chastised Thi for his disobedience and warned him against any involvement with Don, the hot-tempered Thi reacted to Ky with disdain. Ky then attended a dinner with local government officials, including the mayor of Danang, who openly confronted him on the regime's lack of progress on social reform despite Ky's lofty words. Believing he had been challenged, Ky returned to Saigon determined to sack Thi, setting up the worst internal crisis since the Diem coup. Two concepts were about to be tested. The first was national versus regional authority. The second was the role and power of nongovernmental groups versus the South Vietnamese administration. Whoever won the showdown would rule South Vietnam.

Summoning the Directorate, on March 9, Ky demanded that Thi be removed from command. The group agreed, and Thi was ordered to appear in Saigon the next day. Arriving at JGS headquarters, Thi was relieved for disobeying orders. To save face, the Directorate would announce he was resigning for health reasons and was being sent to the U.S. for medical treatment. The next morning, when Thi went to the airport to fly to Danang to gather his belongings and children, he was arrested. Who gave the order is unknown, but when the news broke that Thi had been relieved of command and detained, the mayor of Danang organized a "Struggle Committee" to demand Thi's immediate release.

Ky expected some limited protests, but he had hoped for Buddhist acquiescence. To placate Thich Tri Quang, after the Directorate meeting on March 9, Ky dispatched an old friend of the Buddhist leader to brief him on the decision. He "brought back assurances [from Quang] of no serious trouble."[11] Within days, Quang claimed that it was "absolutely false...that the Buddhists would not oppose the ouster of Thi."[12] Many thought that Thi and Quang were close (a claim that Thi does not make in his memoirs), but the two men kept each other at arm's length. Whether Quang had double-crossed Ky or used Thi's ouster as the pretext to launch a protest movement, he had clearly deceived Ky.

Why had the enigmatic monk chosen to launch another major wave of unrest? Given his history of agitation and his total disdain for Thieu, many feared it was only a matter of time before another crisis erupted. Historian James McAllister believes that Quang "desired a 'revolutionary' regime that he largely defined in practice as one free of all Catholic, Diemist or Can Lao influences. The main problem...was that Tri Quang often implied that he alone had the authority to determine the legitimacy of South Vietnamese regimes, as well as the right to remove these regimes from office."[13] Undoubtedly, a "power behind the throne" mentality was prevalent in Quang. His supporters, on the other hand, claim that Tri Quang's true motivations were "a popularly elected government which could claim its legitimacy as well negotiate with the NLF to end the war."[14]

There are elements of truth in both analyses, but many Buddhist lay leaders did not share Quang's fervor, nor was he the sole arbiter of Buddhist political demands. The Buddhist movement did not even have universal support in Central Vietnam. The Dai Viets, the VNQDD, and the Catholics opposed him.[15] Ha Thuc Ky's Revolutionary Dai Viets controlled the local government in the districts surrounding Hue.[16] The VNQDD held administrative posts as appointees by the GVN in much of Quang Nam Province, long known as the party's "sanctuary." Tri Quang, though, remained a formidable opponent. His inflammatory oratory could, like flipping a switch, instantly rally a powerful combination of youth, university students, and Buddhist clergy fervently assisted by a leftist faction in the faculty of Hue University.

On March 12, Thich Tam Chau joined Quang in denouncing the government. Chau held a press conference in Saigon where he laid out four demands, including quick elections, reinstatement of the generals who had overthrown Diem, and that the junta resign and turn power over to civilians. Ky was outraged, seeing the ultimatum as grandstanding since he had already announced plans to return the country to civilian rule. Nor in Ky's mind was there any "viable democratic civilian alternative," let alone a mechanism in place to hold a national election.[17] Just as disconcerting was the request to reinstate the former generals, as Ky sensed Don maneuvering in the shadows with his old Buddhist allies.

With the Buddhists engaged, students in Hue also began demonstrating after Quang cleverly used the firing of Thi to stoke Central Vietnamese resentment over Saigon's dominance of local political affairs. Over the next several days, Quang used Thi's dismissal as a rallying cry, and the protests gathered strength, culminating in the seizure of the radio station in Danang on March 15. The next day, Tam Chau held a ten-thousand-strong rally in Saigon to demand the restoration of a civilian government. In a surprising turn, two days later, Father Hoang Quynh agreed with Chau's call for the restoration of civilian government. After Quat's fall, Quynh had focused on building an interfaith committee called the Front of all Religions that would unite the Catholics, the Buddhists, and the sects on a common political agenda. Quynh, though, renounced general elections, fearing the Communists would win, preferring instead that a combination of the military and senior civilians to choose a new civilian government.

Most of the Directorate wanted to take a hard line, but just like Khanh in August 1964, Thieu and Ky were fearful of repeating the killing of Buddhist protestors. They convinced their fellow generals not to deal forcefully with the crowds. As one senior general exclaimed, "It would only take one shot for madness to follow."[18] At the same time, Lieu, who had traveled to

Hue and Danang to appease the students, ordered the police in both cities not to interfere.

Instead, the Directorate asked Thi to return to I Corps and calm the protestors. After Thi promised to act as a moderating influence, he went back to Danang on March 16. His efforts proved futile—so over the next two weeks, Ky and Thieu held meetings with the Buddhist leadership to discuss their demands. They agreed to toss out Thieu's original election plan and instead appoint a committee to write a constitution within two months. The committee would consist of one representative from each of the provincial councils elected in May 1965, along with an equal number selected from religious organizations. Elections would be held by the end of 1966. On March 25, Ky announced a "National Political Congress" would be formed to draft a constitution.

Despite the agreement, Tri Quang sensed Ky's willingness to acquiesce, and he decided to press the advantage. The Buddhists backtracked and began clamoring for elections within two months. On April 1, Thieu publicly ridiculed the Buddhist timetable: "Democracy cannot be built in a day. We need time to draft a constitution, to educate the people, to draft a referendum, and to prepare a general election for the national assembly to set up a civilian government."[19] Quang brushed aside Thieu's concerns, noting that Quat had held successful provincial elections when security was far worse. Since the GVN claimed that security was much better now, why could they not hold national elections? The men were at an impasse.

Ky, though, was enraged at what he saw as another Quang swindle. Although he previously had not believed that Quang was a Communist, he had flipped. The appearance of anti-American banners made the Nationalists suspect that the Communists had infiltrated the ranks of the protesters, and GVN leaders accused the senior Buddhist leadership of being covert NLF agents. In typical conspiratorial tones, Ky told Lodge that "he now thought [Quang] was a Communist and that undoubtedly, we face a great Communist conspiracy to take over the government, ask the Americans to leave, and turn the country over to Hanoi. Ky said he realized now that he had had too much faith in the value of making concessions to the Buddhists."[20]

To the world, this knee-jerk labeling of any opposition as Communist-driven had become a staple of GVN politics. Outsiders rejected government claims that a protest or opposition was inspired by covert Communist cadres because the South Vietnamese smeared everyone with that charge, often without proof or by offering what seemed like trumped-up evidence.

While postwar Communist histories agree that they did not instigate the 1966 Buddhist uprisings, once the uprisings began, they ordered their people (some Hue University professors and student organizers were underground cadres) to redirect the protests to sow further divisions between the U.S. and Saigon and within the regime itself. The Communist provincial history for Quang Nam states that "our Party organizations and agents entered the fray to shift the direction of the struggle and turn it into a patriotic mass movement directed against the Americans and their lackeys...We worked to widen the internal conflict within their opposition groups and to gradually transform the movement into a movement opposing the U.S. and Thieu."[21]

Writing in Hanoi a year later, Le Duan noted that

> the uprising by the people of Danang against the Thieu-Ky government between March and May 1966 has provided us a useful lesson in exploiting contradictions within the enemy ranks. While this uprising was not something that we initiated, by exploiting the opportunity provided by internal conflicts within the enemy's ranks, we were able to draw together and incite the masses to rise up and take control of the city....We should not simply sit and wait for the fruits of such contradictions to fall into our laps. The ability to seize the opportunity by exploiting such internal contradictions is an active, aggressive task exactly in line with the strategic principles of the revolution.[22]

Le Duan believed that South Vietnam was a tinderbox and that by exploiting the "internal conflicts," he could hasten victory. This conviction added to his rationale for the 1968 Tet Offensive: the urban population would immediately rally to the Communists if given a chance.

Given the new Buddhist demands, an angry and frustrated Ky sent several battalions of Vietnamese Marines to Danang to retake the city. Ky flew in to lead the attack, but local military units that had joined the Struggle Movement blockaded the air base. With I Corps on the verge of civil war, Ky retreated. To reestablish calm, Ky caved to another key Buddhist request to restore the generals who had overthrown Diem. Although Ky refused to reinstate Big Minh or Tran Van Don, on April 9, he made a politically astute move and appointed Lieutenant General Ton That Dinh, a native of Hue, as the new commander of I Corps.[23]

In preparation for the National Political Congress, Thieu realized he needed to build a coalition of forces opposed to Tri Quang. Thieu quietly worked to gain the backing of the Catholics and southern Buddhists, along with the sects, minorities, and the remnants of the political parties, to side with the government against the Quang faction. Westmoreland thought Thieu was the perfect choice to build an anti-Quang coalition. Thieu, he said, is "exceedingly shrewd and uncommonly cunning. His great strength appears to reside in behind the scenes manipulation," an exceptionally prescient appraisal.[24]

On April 6, Thieu held an organizational meeting with twenty-four representatives from these various groups. He reiterated his oft-repeated position:

> [T]he Army was just the caretaker of the national interest because others had not been strong enough for this role...Did other Vietnamese think that they could do what the present GVN had done—get a Rural Construction program started, fight the VC so hard...and take action against corruption, such as shooting Ta Vinh? He and Ky were criticized for the economy... [but] Vietnamese had to understand these problems and not just criticize. The army would step out of the government the moment that a good leader was ready to stand up before all the people and say, 'I take full responsibility'...Thieu added that such a leader would have to be an anti-communist, pledge to serve the best interests of the country [and] perform social welfare for the people.[25]

Seeking a counterweight against Tri Quang, Thieu asked Dr. Phan Quang Dan to lead the congress. Dan had been demanding elections since the provincial council meeting in October 1965, and given Dan's popularity and his sterling politician reputation—plus he was on good terms with the Buddhists—it was a smart choice. The congress was fruitful, and the leaders decided to hold elections for a constitutional assembly in three to five months. The Buddhists accepted this formula and agreed to halt calls for the government to resign. On April 14, Thieu signed the decree formalizing the elections. Thieu's efforts had paid off brilliantly. His diligence shaped the opposition into a cohesive majority that prevented Quang from calling the shots. While Thieu and the Directorate had wanted a two-year program to educate the populace and ensure security so that "the country could move towards democracy in an orderly and harmonious way," they had appeased the people by bending to popular demands for a constitutional government.[26]

Quang then flew back to Hue. Speaking extemporaneously in front of a large crowd, he requested that the protests stop and that they cease demanding that Thieu and Ky resign. Retaining the leaders, he said, would "make them keep their promises" since each new regime "betrays us." In the words of one American official, Quang's speech was a "brilliant political performance."[27] A superficial calm quickly descended on I Corps.

Ky and Thieu, though, still faced solid internal opposition to their concessions. The pair's refusal to use force had created significant tension among the Directorate. Now they needed to restore unity not only among the ruling generals but in the entire armed forces, as some military elements in I Corps, including a considerable group of 1st Division soldiers, had joined the Struggle Movement. Worse, a new power bloc had emerged within the military that could not be ignored. On April 21, Ky had appointed his close friend Nguyen Ngoc Loan as director general of the National Police to replace Pham Van Lieu, a Thi supporter. Loan had become the leader of a group of senior field grade officers known as the Baby Turks. This small group consisted of the commanders of the military's elite units (Airborne, Marines, Rangers), and hence they possessed an inordinate amount of armed muscle. The Baby Turks insisted the military remain in power until it could transfer authority to a civilian government, and they would not allow a neutralist like Tri Quang to seize power. They were prepared to act with force to prevent either scenario. Keeping them from overreacting to the Buddhist demands became a delicate balancing act for Ky.

Other power blocs also gave the two leaders fits. The pair had sought support from other groups, but they were disappointed. The southerners in the Lien Truong had remained aloof. They had not encouraged the demonstrations, but they had also declined to participate in the congress. The usually more disciplined Catholics had also succumbed to the curse of factionalism, and they had split. Father Quynh's efforts to seek limited co-operation with the Buddhists had come under heavy pressure from hardline Catholics who wanted to counterprotest the Buddhist demonstrators in Sai-gon. When Quynh instead called for cooperation, some Catholics criticized him as "old and soft."[28] His leadership among the hardliners now irrevocably damaged, new leaders opposed to cooperation with the Buddhists such as Vo Long Trieu began to emerge and replace Quynh.

Although Trieu had been working with the Catholic hierarchy to support the government, like many, he expected to be rewarded for his efforts. Thieu, however, refused to openly side with his coreligionists. Trieu lambasted him, claiming the general "found his religion a source of embarrassment and consequently bent over backwards to avoid any possible criticism."[29] Despite Tri Quang's accusations, Thieu never promoted any group or party while in government. He was all too aware that his religion was used against him on the national scene. Thieu told Lodge that he recognized "I am a problem because I am Catholic" and that Quang was trying to "get me to kill a Buddhist rioter" to justify a revolt.[30] Determined not to fall into that trap, Thieu had instead reduced Quang to one voice among many. It was a lesson that Thieu would use for the rest of his career. Rather than "divide and conquer" as the French had done, he would instead build a majority coalition to trump the divisive voices in South Vietnam.

Like the Buddhists, Ky soon backtracked. The electoral law drafting committee held meetings, but the process stalled when Ky argued that any election law they wrote needed to be approved by the cabinet. Why Ky suddenly insisted on tortured legalities is unknown, but there is evidence that his Directorate colleagues forced him. The CIA reported that on April 18, the Directorate decided that the "country's survival and the military effort...requires that a military-backed government continue in power until a new civilian government is duly formed under a new constitution to which the military can safely transfer power." Colonel Loan, speaking for the Baby Turks, supported this agreement and stated that if Quang or anyone forced Ky's resignation, they would "either take preventive action or [mount] a coup to restore the interim military government."[31] In late April, Ky told Lodge of the Directorate's refusal to relinquish authority to the elected assembly. Ky had tried to rule by consensus among the military commanders, and it proved a double-edged sword. Fearing the military might fracture if hotheads like Loan staged a coup, on May 7, Ky publicly reneged on his promises. He announced that elections would be held in the fall but only for a new assembly to draft a constitution. Once completed, national elections would occur in late 1967, but until then, the military would remain in power.

Although the Buddhists threatened to resume demonstrating, they refrained from any overt reaction. Yet government control continued to deteriorate as students in Hue began arming themselves with stolen weapons, and radio broadcasts from Danang spewed an increasingly anti-American tone. Ky believed that if he waited much longer, the situation might become irreversible. Faced with a near-insurrection and under considerable pressure from the Baby Turks, the Catholics, and the Directorate, he decided to forcibly smash the Buddhist revolt. On May 6, he told Tran Quoc Buu that "he now realized that the Buddhists were the 'dirtiest of all' and that their actions 'lead to Communist takeover' and he intends to crush them."[32] Picking a time when Lodge, Westmoreland, and Thich Tam Chau were out of the country, Ky launched an assault. Acting unilaterally, early in the morning of May 15, he ordered two Marine battalions and one Airborne battalion to Danang. Led by Lieutenant General Vien and Colonel Loan, they swiftly moved into the city and captured the I Corps headquarters and city radio station. The Buddhists and some dissident soldiers fought back, but over the next week, Loan slowly expanded control over Danang. In response to Ky's move, Tri Quang asked Don to mount a coup, but he declined.[33] Numerous dangerous confrontations between dissidents and U.S. Marines and government troops were averted only by the narrowest of margins. Finally, on May 23, Ky had regained control of South Vietnam's second-largest city. Rough estimates put casualties at 150 dead and 700 wounded.

Washington vehemently protested Ky's *fait accompli* and withdrew U.S. military advisers from local units. When Lodge returned, he counseled Ky to act with caution, so Ky decided to let Hue wither on the vine rather than conduct a second full-scale assault. Despite Ky's restraint, city streets exploded over the Danang attack. Students burnt down the USIS library and later sacked the U.S. consulate. In Saigon on May 26, Vietnamese Marines broke up a demonstration of four thousand Buddhists chanting "down with Ky." Perhaps in response, Quang's close friend Thich Thien Minh was returning from an unproductive meeting with Thieu and Ky when he stepped from a cab and was greeted by a grenade blast. Badly injured, he was rushed to a hospital and survived.[34] The assailant was unknown, and since no Communist postwar history has taken credit for the attack, it was probably either local Catholic hardliners or one of Loan's henchmen.[35] In protest, four monks self-immolated, forcing Thich Tam Chau to issue a plea to halt such political suicides.

Deeply concerned over the escalating situation, a group of leading religious figures, including Tam Chau and Father Quynh, signed a letter demanding the government step down. Ky invited them to meet, and shortly thereafter, Ky agreed to expand the Directorate's ranks to include ten civilians. The representatives would come from the religious groups and political parties. With a bargain in place to add civilians to the leadership, by mid-June the newly expanded Directorate and electoral commission had hammered out a process to hold elections for an assembly in September. Thieu signed two election decrees on June 19 that laid out the powers of the new assembly and election campaign.[36] At the same time, to celebrate the government's one-year anniversary, the military declared June 19 to be Armed Forces Day.

With Danang under control, and after striking a deal for elections with the other groups, Ky moved to end the Struggle Movement. On June 10, he sent several hundred specially trained Field Police to Hue under Colonel Loan's command. Loan took control of the local police force and boxed in the remaining dissidents. Between June 15–17, two Airborne and two Marine battalions commanded by Lieutenant Colonel Ngo Quang Truong joined the police, and by June 19, resistance from the Buddhists and military dissidents had collapsed. The struggle was over.

Despite various missteps, public gaffes, and occasional miscalculations, Ky and Thieu had successfully walked the proverbial tightrope. They had faced down the Buddhists' tremendous external pressure while also navigating significant internal tensions. Determined to avoid creating martyrs, Thieu and Ky had first maneuvered politically rather than resort to force. Summarizing their approach, Thieu told Lodge that the last three months were "unquestionably the most serious political crisis which South Viet-Nam had had in three years. Their opponents had tried everything. In particular, they had tried to stir American emotions by the self-immolations [and] the demonstrations…[I]f the GVN had operated against Danang early, the consequences might have been dangerous. The GVN, he said, wanted to allow time for the people to understand so that when they finally did move, they had public support and people thought they were reasonable."[37] Naturally, Ky took full credit in his memoirs, writing that by "crushing the revolt, I established our Second Republic and prolonged our national existence for many years."[38]

While the Second Republic would not be established for another year, Thieu and Ky had asserted Saigon's primacy. No general would ever again challenge the government. Nguyen Chanh Thi was exiled to the U.S., never to return. More important, the pair had crushed the religious opposition in South Vietnam. Tri Quang, who had launched a hunger strike to protest Ky's attacks, was flown to Saigon and put under detention. While he remained a major figure in South Vietnamese politics, Quang would never again command the national stage like he did in 1966. While the Buddhists remained a force in South Vietnamese politics, they now had to choose a different path, one of political participation rather than barricades. Having survived the worst internal crisis since the Diem coup, Ky and Thieu could now turn to their main job: building the nation.

10

"RICE IS AS IMPORTANT AS BULLETS"

Building the Country

Having weathered international scrutiny, demonstrators chanting "down with Ky" and "Thieu must go," the near mutiny of some I Corps military units, and strong internal demands for action, South Vietnam's leaders now had to engage in the delicate business of reconciliation and rebuilding. Although Ky had emerged from the Buddhist crisis politically stronger, he knew his promised social revolution had failed to materialize. Worse, the internal storms had only temporarily abated, and the second half of 1966 would again test their leadership. These included the election of a Constituent Assembly, jumpstarting pacification, continued economic woes, and the challenge to Ky's reign by a resurgent southern political movement led by several cabinet ministers. Despite the headlines, though, not all was gloomy. U.S. troops had reversed the dreadful battlefield situation, and President Lyndon Johnson was pumping money into the country to get pacification moving. In the second half of 1966, gains in rural security from U.S. aid and troops plus a GVN focus on the countryside laid the groundwork for South Vietnam's growth in 1967, a foundation that would enable the country to withstand the massive 1968 Tet Offensive.

KEEPING HIS PROMISE

Despite mounting concerns about pacification and the economy, Thieu and

Ky were forced to remain focused on the political situation. They now had to work closely with the man chosen to lead the committee drafting the election law, Tran Van Van. While a strong anti-communist, Van had a pronounced southern regional bias and wanted the military out of politics. Both traits immediately triggered friction with the northern-born Air Marshal Ky.

Van was born on January 2, 1908, to a prominent landowning family in An Giang Province in the Delta. He earned a degree in agricultural engineering in Paris. An ardent Nationalist, he had participated in anti-French activities, but in July 1949 he joined Bao Dai's cabinet, where he became close friends with Phan Khac Suu. After Ngo Dinh Diem's election in 1955, Van followed Suu's lead and became a vocal critic of Diem. In April 1960, Van signed the Caravelle Manifesto, and in response, his family's acreage was seized under Diem's land-reform program. After the 1963 coup, his opposition credentials and southern roots led Big Minh to choose Van to head the Council of Notables. Nguyen Khanh later tapped him to serve under Phan Khac Suu as secretary-general of the High National Council, but Van was arrested in December 1964 during the council purge. He was detained until he was released by Quat in February 1965.

Van's appointment to head the election law committee quickly sparked contentious negotiations between the committee and the Directorate. Seeking to remove the military from politics, Van demanded that the military cede power to the new legislature after the election for the assembly. The Directorate refused, fearing the militant Buddhists might achieve an electoral majority in the upcoming election, but they offered a compromise. They proposed that a majority vote of the elected assembly could approve a draft of the new constitution. The Directorate and the assembly would then jointly approve the constitution, but only a two-thirds majority of the deputies could override the military's veto of any specific article. Once the constitution was approved, an election for a new government would be held in the fall of 1967. The two sides agreed, and Thieu signed the decree on June 19.

Unable to influence the drafting of the election law, Tri Quang's faction instead demanded that Thieu and Ky resign before the voting for the assembly, fearing the military would tamper with the results. The Buddhists threatened to boycott the election if their ultimatum was not met. Bui Diem, who knew Tri Quang well, claimed that the intense monk saw "plots and conspiracies behind everything," calling him a "Buddhist Ngo Dinh Nhu."[1] Revealing the growing dispute within the United Buddhist Church

(UBC), Thich Tam Chau proposed a different deal. On July 3, he offered to suspend further protests and to participate in the balloting if Ky agreed to remove the police from the temples, repair any damage, and not press charges against those arrested. Ky acquiesced, and in a goodwill gesture, he released several hundred jailed demonstrators.

Chau's concession had enormous ramifications: it split the Buddhist ranks. One activist lamented that "Tam Chau's defection to Ky was the biggest loss ever for the UBC."[2] When Quang's followers on the Institute for the Propagation of the Faith council censured Chau's compromise, a furious Chau on July 13 announced that he would depart the country until after the elections. He refused, however, to resign as chairman. In response, ten days later, the militants appointed a Quang follower as acting chairman to replace the absent Chau. Having the institute under his control provided Quang the opening he needed to reassert himself. Despite his ongoing fast and house arrest, he agreed on July 15 to join Father Quynh's fledgling union of anti-government religious factions, now called the "Front of All Religions." With Quang on board, Quynh's group issued a communiqué also demanding that Ky resign, or they too would boycott the election. In a clear sign of Quynh's waning prominence, Archbishop Nguyen Van Binh, head of Vietnam's Catholic Church, denounced Quynh's petition. Binh's censure destroyed Father Quynh's efforts to forge an interfaith committee, and he faded in significance.

Vietnam's two main religions were as divided as the country. The moderates, led by Thich Tam Chau and Archbishop Binh, were frantically battling the militants for control, a clash that had grave consequences for each church and consequently national unity. Removing military rule had fostered one common goal between the two churches, but it was not enough to overcome their core differences. These internal clashes highlighted the incredible difficulties that South Vietnam's leaders had in creating a state where most people shared the same vision.

Under Van's leadership, the election law, while reflecting Vietnamese realities, was surprisingly liberal. Voting requirements, for example, were straightforward. Eligibility consisted of three rules: one must be at least eighteen years old on December 31, 1965, have a valid ID card, and be in "good civil standing," meaning no criminal record or military service issues. Candidates had somewhat stiffer qualifications. One had to be at least twenty-five years old, have no "civil standing" issues, and had to have been born in Vietnam or to have held Vietnamese citizenship for at least five years, thus permitting the Chinese, whom Diem had forced to acquire Vietnamese nationality, the right to participate. The key litmus test, however, was that candidates could not have worked "directly or indirectly for Communism or neutralism."[3] The committee took its cue from their own experience and from other Asian countries like South Korea, Malaysia, and the Philippines, which had also outlawed the Communist Party.

The new law also provided for the direct apportionment of seats for the various minorities, including eight for the Montagnards. Ky shrewdly asked FULRO to supply four candidates, seeking to appease the rebels since negotiations had stalemated again over FULRO demands for greater autonomy. With Quang and Quynh threatening a boycott, FULRO pressed its advantage and refused to participate in the vote unless its requests were met. Ky caved, and on August 12, he agreed in principle to grant the Montagnard's greater legal rights.

After the application deadline for candidates had passed, a panel convened in late July to review their qualifications. Of the hundreds of candidates who filed, the panel rejected forty-two. The election law council met on August 12 to review candidate protests. About half were reinstated, but the rest were disallowed for either having avoided the draft or for being suspected Communist sympathizers. A final total of 542 candidates would compete for 117 seats.

Communist Liberation Radio also began broadcasting appeals demanding that the people reject the election and warned of dire consequences if someone voted. When Ky announced that FULRO had agreed to participate, the NLF turned up its rhetoric. On August 21, it threatened to kill any candidate or government personnel assisting the election. Ky appealed to the nation on August 25 for a large turnout, lifted press censorship, and provided public funds for candidates to use to campaign. Ky then tapped newly promoted Major General Nguyen Duc Thang, head of Rural Construction, to run the election. Ky gave him strict orders to prevent cheating. The GVN, marshaling an efficiency no one thought it possessed, launched a large "get out the vote" campaign and created detailed plans to protect the Vietnamese people's freedom to choose.

Many Vietnamese saw Tri Quang's opposition to the vote as ludicrous, especially since the Buddhists had nearly incited a civil war demanding an election. On September 11, they overwhelmingly rejected his appeal to boycott. Almost 81 percent of eligible voters went to the polls. In a stunning rebuke to Quang, 86 percent of eligible voters in the militant stronghold of Hue cast ballots, although to be fair, 11 percent of those ballots were defaced and deemed invalid. Lodge crowed that the astonishingly high voter turnout repudiated both the NLF's intimidation tactics and the Buddhist extremists. He was right, and the election was a resounding triumph for the GVN. The tally of winners reflected the country's mosaic. Catholics won thirty-three seats, the Hoa Hao fifteen, and the rest were Buddhist. Southerners won forty-four seats, while northerners won twenty-seven. Dai Viet and VNQDD candidates also won seats, as did many well-known politicians like Phan Quang Dan, Tran Van Van, Phan Khac Suu, and Dang Van Sung. Most of the delegates were young; half were under forty-five.

The election was a successful first step in South Vietnam's evolution toward representative government. The Communists and the militants had lost considerable face, and the vote was a clear sign that the people desired a voice in their future. Moreover, while the military still monopolized power, their future removal from power seemed assured. But creating a constitution to enshrine the appropriate government model—authoritarian, government party, or democratic—remained a raging debate among the Nationalists. It was a conflict that went to the heart of how the South Vietnamese articulated and constructed internal legitimacy. The Nationalists desired independence and freedom, but these lofty ambitions required finalizing a concept of governance that gained mass appeal and offered a stark contrast to Communism. Achieving consensus, though, remained a dream. There was only one point they could agree on: no compromise with their implacable foe.

"RICE IS AS IMPORTANT AS BULLETS"

With American troops pouring into South Vietnam, the U.S. placed heavy pressure on Saigon to begin the arduous process of winning back the countryside. In December 1965, Thieu signed a series of decrees laying out the policies, guidelines, and budget for Ky's new Rural Construction program.[4] After returning from the Honolulu conference in February, a meeting was held in early March 1966 in Saigon to explain to provincial officials how newly formed Rural Development (RD) teams would go into the villages and improve government services. The first three thousand RD volunteers had just begun training at a school in Vung Tau under Colonel Tran Ngoc Chau, the former Kien Hoa Province chief. To coordinate the U.S. side, on

March 28, 1966, President Johnson appointed Robert Komer as a special assistant to the president for pacification in Vietnam. Komer's job was to report on the disparate U.S. programs supporting pacification.

For the Americans, the doctrinal basis for pacification was first achieving security for the population against Communist depravations. Afterward, they would convince the people to actively support the Nationalist cause by distributing goods and services like education and health care. Improved local government would then conclude the effort. Thieu and Ky, anxious to modernize the country, agreed to this process. However, there was an opposing South Vietnamese view of pacification, one that embraced traditional values centered on the ancient responsibilities for leaders and the governed. Vietnam was still influenced by Confucian values and ancestor veneration, and a growing chorus of conservative Vietnamese viewed the American presence as debasing their culture and creating a materialistic society, one far removed from the Confucian ideal. Pacification, they believed, should remain strictly a Vietnamese affair, one conducted at the grassroots level.

The most outspoken proponent of this approach was Tran Ngoc Chau. His father was a stern Confucian moralist, and he imprinted these values deeply into his son. For Chau, the best pacification tactic was not lavish material goods but a value-based approach highlighting "the idea of winning others over by persuasion and presenting an exemplary example." Diem, for instance, had "based his leadership on a Confucian concept that when men of high morality govern, their moral qualities are reflected by the actions of their government."[5]

In the Vietnamese Confucian worldview, there are four functions or roles. In order of importance and supposed moral character, they are intellectuals, peasants, workers, and merchants (*si, nong, cong, thuong*).[6] Military officers were viewed as deficient in social stature and breeding, which were vital leadership qualifications in an Asian society. Chau claimed that Ky was a perfect example of why South Vietnam's leaders had failed. Ky "lacked a strong background in Vietnamese culture and traditional moral training [and] had little education outside the military." In his view, the generals were corrupt oligarchs kowtowing to the Americans, men who had "adopted foreign ways so thoroughly they had little understanding of their own people." Without cultural prestige and exemplary morals, they would fail to convince the peasantry to identify their fortunes with the Nationalist cause.

Chau's rose-colored view obscured the fact that only a small elite ever practiced the strict Confucian moral code. Thus, basing pacification on moral inducement was a particularly difficult challenge. The Communists had also tried a similar program, demanding their cadres in the south model virtue and inspire by example. Ideologically, the cadres rarely discussed Marxism but instead highlighted local grievances and exacerbated latent xenophobia. Economically, their main appeal was land reform, but that success was quickly subsumed by peasant anger at high taxes and the conscription of young males. When the limits of persuasion were reached, the cadres turned to mass organizations, public humiliation, and eventually terror to sway people.

Chau believed that generals like Nguyen Duc Thang had mistakenly adopted the impatient American desire for quick progress. According to Chau, Thang "viewed the program only in concrete, material terms...[T] heir concept of pacification was simple: add more weapons, more commodities in and around hamlets and villages, which would then be 'pacified.'"[7] Chau viewed this over reliance on data and material goods as missing the more essential task of converting a person's attitude. Yet for Americans of the 1960s, steeped in the merits of industrialization and management theory, inserting moral agency into the pacification equation was culturally incomprehensible. Statistics offering U.S. government financiers measurable insights were a necessary evil since American government funds and manpower came with demands for accountability, which required quantification to calculate progress. Although Vietnam-era figures were often allegedly manipulated to provide indications of success, it was impossible for U.S. planners to gauge the current situation and draft plans without verifiable information. This rift was not simply a divergent cultural outlook but a situation where both sides had competing truths.

Given Chau's success in Kien Hoa Province, how valid are his arguments? Unfortunately, Chau's frustrations with the allied design for pacification soon led him to resign from the RD training camp at Vung Tau. With his departure, Chau missed the evolution in Thang's thinking. In the 1967 RD plan, Thang articulated a new concept that sought a middle ground between Chau's emphasis on moral suasion and the U.S. material efforts to improve peasant livelihood. Thang emphasized that local communities should design their own projects and then request RD assistance, which would supply materials while encouraging peasant political involvement and loyalty to Saigon. Chau further overlooked the seismic changes in Vietnamese society as it entered the modern world. While conservative attitudes often alter glacially, many urban Vietnamese were rapidly shedding old ways and incorporating new ones. The introduction of Western culture and vast quantities of commercial goods was transforming the outlook for city dwellers. Previously, societal rank was achieved by following proper Confucian behavior, but status was now increasingly calculated by wealth, the very materialism decried by the remnants of conservatism.

The countryside, though, adopted Westernization more slowly. Government appeals for national unity bumped up against the peasant's instinctual first loyalty to their extended family rather than allegiance to a nebulous republic. The motto of *ai lo phan nay* (everyone for themselves) perfectly expressed the peasant mind-set, making it a monumental task for Saigon to change villager attitudes about participation in civic affairs, regardless of how efficient or persuasive GVN bureaucrats might become.

Aside from the debate over how to win peasant loyalty, and given Johnson's strong emphasis in Honolulu on improving rural economic and social conditions, pacification was now as important as beating the enemy's main force units. Similar to efforts with Diem, the Americans were pushing Saigon hard to build a viable state. One-quarter of USAID's total budget for 1966 was designated for South Vietnam. It was the "largest sum dispersed [to any country] in any year since the U.S. began giving foreign aid in 1948."[8] With security slowly improving, American advisers pressed their GVN counterparts to take advantage and implement new pacification plans or speed up existing ones. Several programs for rural electricity and education were already in progress, while others like land reform and improved agriculture methods needed better security before they could be fully implemented. The American organizations providing help included the military, the CIA, and USAID, but their programs were not coordinated, a drawback that worsened as the U.S. footprint in the countryside expanded. The GVN solved its own coordination dilemma in mid-July 1966 by merging all pacification duties under Major General Thang. His RD ministry absorbed the pacification functions performed by Interior, Agriculture, and Public Works.

While shifting all pacification duties under Thang streamlined the notoriously inept Vietnamese bureaucracy, Ky had a hidden agenda for the move. It was his opening gambit to fire the southern born but scandalously corrupt Minister of Defense Nguyen Huu Co and IV Corps commander Dang Van Quang without stirring southern resentment.[9] Ky had vowed to tackle corruption, and both Co and Quang were easy targets. Since Thieu and the two men were longtime friends and had attended various schools together, both appealed to him for protection. Thieu refused but did caution Ky that after the Buddhist crisis, this was an inopportune time to "rock the boat" and fire the two officers.

Thieu, though, had mastered the black arts of Vietnamese politics. He secretly advised Ky to wait until after the September elections and to patiently build "a fence around these people, so that when [Quang and Co] are removed there will be no repercussions. If they were removed now," Thieu warned, "it would solve one problem but create two others," meaning it would incite southern discontent and possibly fracture the Directorate.[10] Despite U.S. pressure to clean up corruption, the two leaders needed to move slowly, as Saigon did not need another eruption. They were juggling their benefactor's demands against the danger of internal discord, a struggle that would never dissipate. It was an extraordinarily narrow line to walk in a time of peace let alone during war.

While Saigon's leaders were regularly and sometimes accurately accused of being out of touch with the countryside, that was not always true. In conjunction with the U.S., plans were being developed to dramatically improve rural life. Clearly, for pacification to work, security needed to improve, as RF/PF units were ill-trained and poorly armed, and they often retreated into their fortifications at night, leaving the villagers defenseless. Besides improving security, the main impediment to implementing pacification at the hamlet and village level was the lack of competent local GVN cadres. However, even if Saigon could train and assign qualified cadres to the countryside, Communist kidnapping and assassination squads made survival chancy. The GVN reported that in the first six months of 1966, 420 local officials were either captured or killed. While a substantial decline from the 991 officials lost or killed during the first half of 1965, the CIA described the terror campaign as designed to "demonstrate to the people...that the government is unable to provide simple physical security for its representatives [and] to intimidate those inclined to cooperation with the government."[11] Moreover, it was not just local bureaucrats who were besieged. Communist units began attacking refugee centers and resettled villagers as well if they refused inducements to return to Communist control. In just one example among many, on May 13, Communist troops attacked the An Than refugee camp in Quang Tin Province, killing 11 refugees, wounding another 13, and burning 249 family dwellings to the ground.

With the military tackling security, the RD teams were intended to help local officials implement GVN programs. The first RD class of some 4,500 students graduated on May 21, 1966, but the performance of these first teams varied. Some graduates demonstrated excellence while others were mediocre stewards. Despite the March conference, local GVN officials often misused the RD team's for security duties or pressured them into corrupt activities by coercing the team leaders to divert U.S. construction materials for black market resale. To rectify the situation, Thang held seminars from August–October in each military region to impress upon the province chiefs that for Saigon, the "RD program is now more important than military operations, and the Vietnamese must take charge of these programs for themselves."[12] Thang also took corrective action to weed out poor performing RD cadres and instructed provincial leaders regarding the team's proper role. He also ordered the Vung Tau training school to apply "lessons learned" for the second class, which graduated in September. While Chau emphasized moral rectitude to earn loyalty, Thang thought creating an effective government apparatus would gain peasant fidelity.

One of the vital RD programs for 1966 was improving education. Successive GVN regimes realized that for South Vietnam to modernize, it needed thousands of educated workers. Schools are an essential tool for state building, and the high illiteracy rate severely hampered Saigon's ability to develop the country. Educating the millions of unschooled peasants, however, was a massive task. According to a USAID study, in 1955, only 20 percent of eligible students attended school. The number dropped to 3 percent for high school and even less for college. The French lycee system was geared toward producing a governing elite, not educating the citizenry. Plus, the French schools were in the cities, limiting attendance to only a handful who either achieved a superb test score or whose family could afford the tuition.

Saigon planned to offer free countrywide schooling at the hamlet level, but despite valiant efforts, the attendance numbers had only marginally improved due to a lack of schools, teachers, and money. USAID funds filled the gap. In 1966 alone, over 2,200 new hamlet classrooms were built using American-supplied materials under Thang's Self-Help Program. Alongside this massive increase in public schools, the GVN also encouraged the expansion of trade and private schools to build an educated population and workforce.[13]

Obviously, more teachers were needed, and in 1966, over three thousand were trained to serve in the hamlets. Many were women, highlighting an emerging gender role change that also annoyed Vietnamese conservatives.

With most men inducted into the military, women were rapidly joining career fields formerly viewed as male professions. While popular media often portrayed the pernicious social effects such as prostitution on Vietnamese society from the massive American presence, Vietnamese women were succeeding in business and other enterprises. It was one of several communal transformations South Vietnam was undergoing due to wartime pressures and changing economic and living conditions.

Yet like any country at war undergoing major societal renovation, nothing was straightforward. The soaring enrollment had forced schools in Saigon to run three shifts, but overall attendance remained spotty in the countryside. Fighting often closed rural schools, resulting in students having to repeat classwork. Teacher pay was extremely low, and teachers faced Communist intimidation and propaganda, which lead to a shortage of qualified instructors. Still, while educational improvement was uneven, overall it was an unsung success for Saigon.

Refugee care remained another crucial but often makeshift program. In the two-year period from June 1964 to June 1966, the fighting had created one million refugees. About half remained in temporary shelters, while the other half had either returned to their native villages or had been resettled elsewhere.[14] The statistics, unfortunately, only reflected those who had officially registered for assistance, leaving uncounted thousands who had fled to the cities or who had moved in with relatives. On April 12, 1966, now armed with both U.S. and GVN funding, Ky's energetic Commissioner for Refugees Dr. Nguyen Phuc Que ordered the formation of new relief centers in each province. Recognizing that few men were available to staff his new offices, Dr. Que mandated another social change: preferential hiring for discharged veterans and widows.

By late summer, although I Corps experienced difficulties in refugee assistance due to the Buddhist uproar, Que's agency had opened forty-five new refugee centers. With abundant USAID money, on August 1, Dr. Que raised the daily refugee payment rate from seven to ten piasters. Given the shortage of land in central South Vietnam, and often unable to return families to their homes, the GVN decided to move volunteer refugees to locations farther south. The first such interprovincial move occurred on May 17, when the U.S. Navy shipped 852 refugees from Phu Yen Province on the coast to Cam Ranh Bay, where numerous construction jobs were available.

Even with Que's efforts, by the end of August, another one hundred thousand new refugees had swelled GVN rolls. Most were assigned to Que's temporary shelters, but the sheer numbers were overwhelming the poor health system in the new camps. Dr. Que moved to expand medical services. In an agreement signed in late October between Que and the Ministry of Health, facilities and personnel were added to each site. Depending on camp size and location, new dispensaries were built and staffed with a rural midwife, a hamlet health worker, and a laborer. In keeping with Que's sense of social justice, he ordered that hiring preferences for the laborer position be given to "widows and orphans of soldiers who died for the country."[15] Moreover, in mid-December, he also added female supervisors and female camp workers to "enlarge the domain of Social Welfare activity for bettering the livelihood of children, youth and women at temporary refugee camps."[16]

For 1967, Que planned to significantly reduce the refugee numbers by restructuring provincial programs. In a late November 1966 message to province chiefs, Que again highlighted the importance of refugee care: "[O]f particular concern to the GVN is the ever-growing influx of [refugees] from Communism...A triumphant emergence of GVN from this struggle will have a strong influence on pacification, on economic development, and on democratization in the countryside."[17] Regrettably, despite substantial U.S. financial assistance, the refugee problem often overwhelmed GVN resources, and the GVN's mixed record overseeing hundreds of thousands of refugees became a crusade for U.S. congressional leaders like Senator Edward Kennedy (D-Mass.). From May to October 1967, Kennedy held a series of congressional hearings that heavily criticized refugee care, a proxy to censure both South Vietnam and the war.

Besides improving education and refugee treatment, two other major programs for 1966 were launched to add electricity and improve health care. Surveys conducted by the GVN and the USAID indicated that the improvement villagers wanted most was electricity, and in response, Saigon acted. Bringing electricity to the villages would be a key step in improving South Vietnam's rural economy. In early March 1965, Prime Minister Quat requested that USAID formulate a plan for rural electrification. On October 15, 1965, the GVN signed an agreement with USAID to begin the project. The Vietnamese created a National Union of Electric Cooperatives to serve as a liaison between USAID and newly formed local electric cooperatives, most of which were in the Delta. Despite numerous obstacles obtaining materials, on May 25, 1966, Thang signed a decree for thirty sites to house electrical generators that would begin a new Rural Electrification Program. The Communists soon targeted the program by sabotaging the power lines.

Health care was also chosen for upgrading. South Vietnam had inherited an abysmal health system that was, like its education system, designed primarily for the French or urban residents. Extremely limited rural care led to high infant mortality. Diseases like malaria and tuberculous were rampant. Most villagers relied on traditional healers who used ineffectual herbal remedies. With a grave shortage of Vietnamese doctors, most of whom had been drafted into the RVNAF, the U.S. military and visiting health teams from other countries began providing health care to villagers. In the first half of 1966, American military medical personnel administered over two million treatments to civilians.[18] Gradually, a belief in the curative powers of Western medicine became ingrained in the peasantry, and they demanded improvements in their clinics.

In early June 1966, Major General Thang and the Ministry of Health signed agreements to launch the Rural Health Development Program. The U.S. trained local medical workers in simple medical procedures and built infirmaries at the village and district level. Provincial hospitals were expanded to include surgical wards. One focus was on women's health. On July 26, Thang authorized the construction of thirty new maternity wards in fourteen provinces. Dr. Nguyen Le Hieu, a South Vietnamese doctor who worked for the Ministry of Health, outlines the total effort. "Specific health problems were targeted," he notes, "and appropriate programs were set up to fight or control them, i.e., anti-malaria (shots and spraying), Hansen (anti-leprosy)…Mobile teams were set-up to travel to villages to help train and provide care." Unfortunately, the Communists also targeted health care. According to Dr. Hieu, "Several health activities were labeled by enemy propaganda as [having a] military purpose, i.e., DDT spray by anti-malaria workers and notations of houses already treated were claimed by the enemy as 'mapping and indexing for military information collection.'"[19]

Advances in education, refugees, rural electricity, and health care were only part of a vast undertaking in the countryside. Other significant RD efforts included Public Works, which built or repaired almost three hundred miles of roads, around 150 bridges, and dredged or dug almost one hundred miles of canals. A hamlet Self-Help Program completed over 2,300 projects constructed by local inhabitants. Police departments were expanded, as were defector programs (*Chieu Hoi*) and psyops campaigns to convince peasants to pledge allegiance to Saigon. Overall, while his ministry had fallen well short of the 1966 goals set in Honolulu for increasing the number of secure hamlets, Thang believed the foundation had been set in 1966 that would eventually provide significant improvement for the peasants. His main impediment remained the stranglehold that the NLF still had on large tracts of the countryside, but allied forces were slowly retaking it.

While pacification programs were improving, the economy continued to severely hamper national growth. The GVN had acquiesced to several key U.S. economic recommendations but had failed to follow through, and commercial conditions remained dreary. The U.S. government was dismayed, and at a meeting in late May 1966, Robert Komer, President Johnson's special adviser for pacification, blasted Ky's aide, Bui Diem. Komer demanded that "draconian measures must now be taken to control inflation," or the economic consequences could threaten Vietnam's future. Bui Diem agreed that the GVN had fallen short and granted that "economic reconstruction was as important as military or political gains." He confessed that "Ky was...not very interested in these problems [but] he was willing to back any measures that had a chance of success even if they were politically risky."[20]

To handle the demanding situation, on June 10, Thieu signed a decree giving Ky sole power to arbitrarily decide economic and financial legislation for three months. Given that inflation had sapped the earnings of civil servants and servicemen on fixed incomes, with his new decree powers, Ky instantly approved a pay hike for them. More important, after a strong recommendation by Nguyen Huu Hanh, one of his economic advisers, on June 18, Ky signed off on a politically hazardous but necessary economic shock: devaluing the piaster. The plan raised the official rate to 118 piasters to the dollar, increased import taxes again, subsidized rice prices, and sold gold on the open market to soak up piasters. The devaluation hit many people hard by creating a short-term spike in prices, but by mid-October, the Saigon Retail Price Index, a basket of over twenty commodities used to gauge the cost of living, had fallen below the June mark.

Unfortunately, the relief was only temporary. By mid-November, rice was again in short supply in the capital. Massive flooding had significantly impeded deliveries from the Delta, with two provinces losing 80 percent of their crop. The U.S. embassy estimated that rice deliveries to Saigon, whose population had jumped, were 40 percent lower than 1965, which were already lower than 1964. The dire situation had forced the U.S. to ship about three hundred thousand tons of rice to make up the shortage. Even with the U.S. largesse, the shortfalls combined with increased urban consumption had resulted in major cost spikes. Rice prices were now 30 percent higher than before the June devaluation. The rise devastated Saigon's poor, whose diet consisted mainly of rice and *nuoc mam*, the pungent Vietnamese fish sauce. Even the price for the cheapest bag—the hundred-kilogram bag with 25 percent broken rice—had substantially increased. Solving the food problem was crucial. "Rice," Komer emphasized to Bui Diem, "is as important as bullets."

Regarding the multitude of economic issues, ranging from Saigon port congestion and taxes to foreign currency reserves, the financial fixes provided only momentary relief. Saigon was starved for revenue and desperate to reduce the excess money that its own deficit spending had created. Yet the government was unable to collect enough taxes to ease either issue. Nor would any widely expanded consumer goods import program absorb the vastly enlarged money supply or generate enough import duties to dent the deficit. Avoiding taxes was a long-standing tradition in Vietnam, and there was little enforcement machinery available to apply the existing laws. Rice subsidies, while keeping the price in Saigon reasonable, had in turn discouraged Delta farmers from selling it to the GVN or to the ubiquitous Chinese merchants. The farmers could get better prices smuggling it to Cambodia or selling it to the Communists. Tax reform, though, was nowhere near the top of Ky's agenda. He had other pressing issues.

FACTIONALISM CONTINUES

With the election over, the elderly leader of the Vietnamese Buddhist church appealed to Tri Quang in mid-September to halt his hunger strike. Quang agreed, but he refused to fade away. He feared that the South Vietnamese military intended to codify in the new constitution a continuing role for the armed forces in the country's political life. In a fiery letter to the press, he denounced Ky and Thieu, claiming they wanted to form a "regime based on the one in South Korea—a Diem regime without Diem."[21] For once, the normally conspiratorial-minded Quang was at least partially right.

South Korea did provide a potential blueprint for building South Vietnam. After the 1950–53 war, the Koreans, like the South Vietnamese now, were desperately poor, painfully lacking in trained leaders, and facing an ruthless enemy. In May 1961, the Korean generals seized power from their own faltering civilian rulers. Like Thieu and Ky, they also proclaimed a desire for elections, and several of the leading generals took off their uniforms and became politicians. General Park Chung-hee won an honest election in December 1963. He then began a large-scale and successful effort to modernize South Korea. Although Park would eventually become a military dictator and was assassinated in 1979, in the early years he led his country in a vigorous strongman style that produced rapid economic growth, a governing style the Saigon generals appreciated but were reluctant to outright copy.

Thieu had attended Park's inauguration in December 1963, and he recommended to Ky that South Vietnam seek close relations with the South Koreans. Thieu told a U.S. visitor that Park's party was essentially a "party of the army," which he admired since Thieu wanted the military to "participate officially and constitutionally" in the new government. While Thieu had changed his opinion from prior years and now insisted that the army was not seeking power, the Diem years had instilled in him a deep desire to avoid complete civilian control over the military. The army, Thieu proclaimed, must be able to prevent any president from "becoming a dictator." However, while the Korean system "was applicable in many ways," Thieu recognized that "the Vietnamese situation is really more difficult," meaning his country was at war and South Korea was not.[22] Hence, despite Quang's charge, while both Thieu and Ky admired Park's economic achievements, South Korea did not provide a governing model for South Vietnam.

With the new assembly beginning to work on the constitution, Johnson asked to meet Ky and Thieu in Manila in late October to review the progress in pacification since Honolulu. In typical fashion, two Saigon political storms immediately erupted. Earlier in the summer, Ky sought to curry favor with the southern elite—and thus counterbalance the current hatred of Central Vietnamese toward him—by bringing more southern politicians into the government. In mid-July, he shuffled his cabinet and appointed a distinguished southerner, Nguyen Luu Vien, to serve as deputy prime minister. Vien had earlier declined an invitation to join Ky's cabinet since he was against military rule. Now persuaded that Thieu and Ky were sincere about reestablishing civilian governance, on July 13, 1966, Vien accepted Ky's offer and became the deputy prime minister.[23]

Festering north-south animosities, however, could not be soothed by a few cabinet appointments. In late September, the minister of health, a northerner and a close friend of Ky's, departed for an official overseas trip, leaving his deputy, an avowed southerner, in charge. The deputy promptly replaced some northern-born doctors within the ministry with southerners. Upon his return, the minister grumbled to police chief Brigadier General Loan about his deputy's actions. Loan, never known for subtly, arrested the deputy minister on September 29 for the nonexistent crime of "inciting divisions between northerners and southerners."[24]

Cabinet minister and southern firebrand Vo Long Trieu learned of the arrest and berated Ky, fuming that Loan's arbitrary actions were "turning us into a police state" and "caused the government to lose prestige and lose face in the eyes of both our own public and the world community as well." Trieu demanded that Ky fire Loan and denounce his behavior. Ky, beholden to Loan for cleaning up the Buddhist mess and leery of offending the Baby Turks in the military, refused. A rebuffed Trieu immediately began agitating among other southern cabinet members, including Nguyen Luu Vien and Economic Minister Au Truong Thanh. To calm the situation, on October 4, Ky forced the minister of health to leave the government. However, two days later, an editorial appeared in a northern-owned newspaper calling the southern ministers "a bunch of base cowards who are hungry for power" and "bastards only worthy of cleaning the spittoons of their masters."[25]

Infuriated, Trieu convinced Vien, Thanh, and four other ministers to resign in protest over Loan's actions and the article. Scrambling to avert a cabinet crisis, Ky suspended the offending newspaper, forbade all newspapers from printing articles about the dispute or highlighting north-south differences, and appointed a southerner as the health minister. Ky understood that a public eruption over these two contentious issues—the north-south divide and the civilian-military dispute—might tarnish the positive atmosphere gained by the September elections or generate unfavorable foreign press on the eve of the Manila conference. Moreover, it might provide a rallying point for the large southern bloc in the assembly, who in turn might insert constitutional clauses (like an age restriction for the presidency) that directly affected Ky.

Naturally, shortly after Ky's actions, the irascible and often intoxicated Loan made threatening phone calls to both Nguyen Luu Vien and Trieu, reopening the wounds that Ky was desperately trying to close. Worse, the two southern generals, including Nguyen Huu Co and IV Corps commander Dang Van Quang, began secretly advising Trieu to take a hard line with Ky. Their action did not go unnoticed. Ky and Thieu held a Directorate meeting and upbraided both men for encouraging dissent. Tran Van Van then became another southern thorn in Ky's side when he denounced Ky in the assembly over Loan's actions. The swelling north-south turmoil irritated the Americans. Secretary of State Dean Rusk became "gravely concerned" about another Saigon political storm before the upcoming

Manila conference. Rusk told Lodge that the situation "was very close to the worse days" of Tri Quang, and he ordered him to make "a maximum effort" to induce the GVN to "produce an international impression of solidarity in Saigon," including if necessary a tough talk with Loan to curtail his "Gestapo tactics."[26]

Aware of U.S. discontent, Ky pleaded with the unruly ministers to not embarrass the government shortly before his meeting with Johnson. After a charm offensive that included appeals to their patriotism and several posh dinners, Ky convinced them to postpone any resignation until after the summit. He was inadvertently helped when former Prime Minister Tran Van Huong sent a handwritten note to both Vien and Trieu urging them not to resign. Huong's letter convinced Vien to rescind his resignation, while Trieu only agreed to delay his departure. After the conference, Ky met repeatedly with Trieu and the others to convince them to stay, but to no avail. Secretly nursing his own political ambitions, Thanh was particularly recalcitrant. Eventually, of the initial seven, Vien and two others remained, while Trieu, Thanh, and two others choose to leave. While the cabinet crisis had dissipated, the specter of a future internecine battle between the Nationalists simmered below the surface.

Concurrent with the cabinet crisis, the dispute within the Buddhist church finally broke open. With the assembly election over, Tam Chau had returned to Saigon on September 15 and vowed to retake the institute from his militant opponents. The head of the Buddhist church called for a conference to settle the dispute between Tri Quang and Tam Chau. Seeking to gain power before the conference, on October 2, Tam Chau seized the institute's Quoc Tu Pagoda and forced the council to resign. Chau intended to elect a new council and rid himself of Quang's followers. Given Chau's actions, the conference, held on October 21–22, immediately degenerated into shouting matches, with militants claiming the U.S. had bribed Chau with "one million dollars" to become "pro-government."[27] It was a charge both false and ironic, considering that the CIA had been paying Quang for several years.[28]

With the conference in shambles, Quang's supporters returned to the An Quang Pagoda and elected their own council. Chau denounced this alternate council and proclaimed plans to form a revamped Unified Buddhist Church. With quiet support from Ky, by the end of 1966, Chau had succeeded in building a coalition from the various factions that comprised the Vietnamese Buddhist church, leaving Quang isolated in the An Quang

Pagoda. One journalist wrote, "[H]ounded by police, torn by factionalism and politically humiliated by the failure of the [election boycott], Tri Quang and his disciples seem to have lost virtually all of their leverage."[29] Quang's sway over national politics was diminished, but the reports of his political demise were premature.

With the cabinet crisis temporarily averted, the Buddhists' self-destructing, and the new assembly organizing, Ky and Thieu flew to Manila to meet Johnson to assess pacification. Major General Thang admitted that pacification had fallen short of the program goals the allies had set in Honolulu, but there had been significant improvements. The U.S. agreed to expand the pacification program in 1967, but it wanted one major change: switch ARVN operations from a "search and destroy" strategy to "clear and hold." Since security was the first step, the ARVN would become the screen behind which the RD teams could operate.

Since that idea was close to the one that Thieu and Ky had recommended to Westmoreland in July 1965, they agreed in the Manila joint communiqué to "train and assign a substantial share of the armed forces to 'clear and hold' actions in order to provide a shield behind which a new society can be built."[30] ARVN would still have the primary responsibility for clearing enemy forces in heavily populated areas, but they would then hold the reclaimed ground until RF/PF forces could assume that duty. While an intelligent division of tasks—Vietnamese troops handling the villages while U.S. forces fought PAVN main force regulars away from populated areas—there was one worrisome catch: ARVN's dismal record of treating civilians. Plus, the army was reluctant to be assigned to what it viewed as a mission for police or militia units.[31] How well the regular army would perform this new task remained an open question.

The underlying reason for shifting from destroying enemy units to securing the population was the belief by the allies that they were now winning the war. In March 1965, Le Duan had ordered Communist forces to defeat South Vietnam before U.S. troops could enter and tip the balance. That decision kicked off the "big-unit war." From the spring of 1965 till late summer 1966, more battalion and regimental-size battles occurred than any other period of the war, including the Tet and Easter Offensives.[32] After taking severe casualties, by fall 1966 the Communists had retreated, and large battles had sharply declined. The Pentagon Papers confirmed that "the key assumption underlying the new emphasis on population control was the growing belief, in late 1966, that the main force war was coming to a gradual end. No other single factor played as great a role in the decision to commit troops to pacification."[33]

In fact, the U.S. had badly misjudged Hanoi. The drop in major offensive actions was due to slow resupply along the Ho Chi Minh Trail and the replacement of casualties from the earlier battles. After rebuilding, the People's Army planned to launch two waves of operations from October 1966 to April 1967. Hanoi believed the U.S. strategy was to defeat its forces and compel the Politburo to negotiate, which was precisely its own strategy for allied forces. Based on this assessment, the Politburo decided to attack first. Their plan was to inflict huge losses, forestall U.S. offensive operations, and gain a decisive victory in the two-year span between 1967–1968.

Upon returning from Manila, and with the cabinet crisis behind him, Ky set his sights on confronting corruption. First, Ky announced on November 18 that he had appointed four new ministers, all southerners, to replace the ones who had resigned. It was an obvious concession to southern regional interests, but it achieved acquiescence for his next move: firing the corrupt Major General Dang Van Quang. On November 19, Ky removed the IV Corps commander and replaced him with Brigadier General Nguyen Van Manh. Thieu's plan to first set the groundwork had worked perfectly, and there was little dissension. Thieu picked Manh as Quang's replacement, as he had worked for Thieu in the 1950s when Thieu was chief of staff for the old 2nd Military Region based in Hue. Thieu, in a bit of sophistry, explained to Westmoreland that while rumors were rampant that Quang and Co were corrupt, "they did not have the evidence to support charges," which was ludicrous, but since the "rumors were so prevalent, they had no choice" but to replace Quang.[34] Thieu, however, valued Quang as a staff officer, so he assigned him to head a new Ministry of Planning and Development.

Meanwhile, the assembly had completed organizing. Led by Phan Quang Dan and Tran Van Van, they immediately sought to upend the earlier electoral compromise with the Directorate. They were positioning themselves to challenge the military's monopoly on power in a future election, and they had begun to rival Thieu and Ky in prominence. On November 9, the assembly voted unanimously to amend Article 20, the clause that permitted the military to override any part of the constitution. Van castigated Article 20, proclaiming that the Directorate "does not consist of elected officials and they should not be permitted to exert greater power in shaping the constitution."[35] Van submitted the request to change Article 20 to Thieu on November 18. Several weeks later, the Directorate gave its answer on Article 20: an emphatic no.

While preparing for a renewed offensive, Hanoi also looked for other means to aggravate Saigon's internal disfunction. The Politburo chose to stoke civil-military tensions and ordered "the [Saigon-Gia Dinh] Region Party Committee and the [T4] Security Section to direct the Saigon City armed reconnaissance forces to kill one of three targets: Thieu, Ky, or [Tran Van] Van."[36] Since Thieu and Ky were heavily guarded, the Saigon security team decided to target Van. After studying his movements, a plan was set in motion. On the morning of December 7, Van got into his car and began driving to the assembly. As he slowed to make a turn, two Communist assassins on a motorcycle fired three rounds into the car, killing him. Van's police escort chased the killers and caught one. The other escaped. Liberation Radio immediately "broadcast a commentary stating that this was the result of an internal dispute in which the enemy factions were killing one another. Our cadres and our overt organizations operating in Saigon influenced both the Vietnamese and the foreign press to create the impression that Van had been assassinated because he was planning to run for President in the upcoming elections."[37]

In the conspiratorial world of Vietnamese politics, the charge found fertile soil. Thieu vehemently denied that the GVN had any role in Van's death. When that did not suffice, the GVN put the shooter on television, where he confessed that the killing was a Communist plot. It still was not enough. One assembly member, Ly Qui Chung, a southerner, spoke at Van's funeral and refused to blame the Communists. To maintain uncertainty over Van's death, a Communist agent slipped his widow a note at the funeral that said, "You must tell Thieu that the VC did not kill your husband. If you do not do this, you will suffer the same fate as your husband."[38] Terrified, Van's widow asked Thieu not to execute the assassin, and Thieu reduced the sentence to life in prison on Con Son Island. He was freed on May 1, 1975.

Shortly after Van's death, there was another assassination attempt. As Dr. Dan got into his car to drive to the assembly, an explosion ripped a hole in the seat next to him. Amazingly, he was only slightly wounded. Who tried to kill Dan remains a mystery. The various postwar Communist Public Security publications provide detailed descriptions of virtually every attempted or successful assassination of senior GVN officials. The Communists are proud of "striking a blow" against the "puppet regime figures" and are not shy about discussing these actions. Yet like the grenade attempt against

Thich Thien Minh in late May that wounded the Buddhist bonze, there is no mention of the attempt against Dan. While absence does not absolve the Communists, the lack of comment on these two attempts is telling and points to a Nationalist culprit. Dan had been pushing hard to enshrine land reform rights in the constitution, a program strenuously objected to by many southern landlords. Regardless, it was the last attempt on an assembly member's life.

Despite the economic upheavals and political turmoil, Ky and Thieu remained committed to forging a better life for their people. The transformation of South Vietnam had begun, and the combination of U.S. and GVN efforts to improve South Vietnamese living standards would achieve meaningful results. Whether it could attain its goals of converting peasants to Saigon's side, however, remained an open question.

11

"THIS CONSTITUTION IS OFFICIALLY ADOPTED"

Showdown with the Directorate

The U.S. commitment to South Vietnam hinged on Saigon transforming itself into a democracy. Under pressure from the U.S. and internal voices like the Buddhists to form an elected, constitutional government to earn legitimacy among its own people and in the world, the Directorate agreed to speed up the democratization process. Yet in one of the least known but most critical success stories of Saigon's evolution, the GVN made the difficult leap from a military junta to a constitutional republic relatively smoothly only because Ky and Thieu convinced the Directorate to back down. Had Ky and Thieu failed, South Vietnam's political future would have been very dark, but their success came at a price. Few cabals give up power willingly, and the Directorate was no different. Ky and Thieu were obliged to accept a Faustian bargain to survive, one that would haunt Thieu for a year.

While all eyes were focused on this critical electoral transformation, another equally important change was occurring that few recognized: the nascent expansion of the South Vietnamese state back into the countryside. After building an organization to reclaim the rural areas, Ky and Thieu decided to hold hamlet and village elections to restore local authority. Steering the country toward representative government also compelled the chronically unstable Nationalists to begin working together. This philosophical decision to decentralize governmental power, on top of the RD efforts begun in 1966, would prove crucial.

PICKING A CANDIDATE

Now that the military had agreed to turn over power, who would stand for president became a hot topic. Beginning in July 1966, journalists began peppering Ky over his intentions. Several times that summer, Ky told reporters that he would not run, often wistfully mentioning his desire to return to flying. Instead, he promoted Thieu as a candidate, even proclaiming once that "I do not see anyone better than General Thieu."[1] When asked why Ky kept endorsing him, Thieu replied, "because Ky likes me."[2] Apparently, despite the later falling out between the two men, during this time they remained allies. Even in late November 1966, Thieu told Westmoreland that he had heard rumors of "friction" between Ky and him but that they "had no basis." Thieu stated that Ky "needed his advice" since if "Ky had gone his own way the Danang crisis would have been a disaster. He had restrained Ky until the ground had been prepared."[3] Ky agreed, saying that Thieu was "really wise" and that Thieu "has thought a lot about what Vietnam needs." Thieu, Ky admitted, "would make a good first president."[4]

Ky, however, hedged his bets. While publicly promoting Thieu, he also told a visiting Dr. Henry Kissinger that in an election, although the military would unite around Thieu, he was unpopular. "Even the Catholics do not like him," exclaimed Ky. He asserted that most candidates "could beat Thieu," including the elderly Phan Khac Suu. That a civilian might win worried Ky, but it was a risk worth taking "if the Vietnamese were to ever have a government which was respected and supported by the people, and which would therefore be able to win the war."[5] While Ky entertained returning to the cockpit, that a civilian might triumph who would not prosecute the war with the appropriate vigor began to gnaw at him, setting the seeds for his later change of mind.

Presidential politics soon began shadowing the military. With the ARVN scheduled to switch its mission to village protection, in late 1966 Thieu began visiting units and stressing the vital importance for the army to assist in pacification. Thieu's barnstorming, however, set off speculation that he was really engaged in electioneering for the upcoming presidential race, which forced Ky to reevaluate his candidacy. By late 1966, Ky was leaning toward running, but given his earlier promotion of Thieu, he needed to know Thieu's intentions. They held a private discussion in early January 1967. Thieu informed Ky that he was undecided, and he asked that they postpone a decision until after the constitution was approved. Ky agreed and replied that he would defer to him if Thieu choose to run. Neither wanted a joint ticket, believing they needed a civilian to balance the slate. Thieu told Lodge in early February 1967 that an all-military ticket "would make the whole constitutional effort look like a trumped-up affair."[6] The U.S. also desired a civilian-military alliance, preferably with a prominent civilian as president and either Ky or Thieu as prime minister.

Although many thought Thieu was testing the presidential waters, while discussing the situation in early February 1967, Thieu instead broached the idea of him commanding the South Vietnamese military rather than running for office. He opined that if a civilian was elected, "it would take real unity among the military to give loyal support to the new constitutional government, so that there would not be a coup six months later, as well as to provide national stability if Hanoi negotiates a peace."[7] While Ky concurred that Thieu was a good choice to head the RVNAF to keep the military under control, he cynically saw it as Thieu's fallback position. Ky sneered that Thieu was "very clever and maneuvering carefully to become president [while] keeping way open to return to army as its commander."[8]

Both men were subtly trying to uncover whom the U.S. preferred for president. Thieu was trying to determine the American position on his candidacy, while Ky's denigration of Thieu as unpopular was him obliquely advising the U.S. against supporting Thieu. Ky claimed that the leading commanders had already quietly urged him to run, but the Directorate was loath to formally choose. They wanted Ky and Thieu to decide privately on the military nominee. Subordinate officers, given the standard hierarchical military structure, do not want to vote against a superior. Since Thieu was senior to Ky in rank, age, and technically by position, the generals believed Thieu had the right of first refusal. Ky's only option was to use indirect persuasion to convince Thieu not to run. Both leaders, however, had delayed a formal decision, and by late February 1967, with the assembly nearing completion of the draft constitution, the senior generals were becoming impatient. The jockeying had begun.

CHANGING OF THE GUARD

After the Manila conference, Thieu and Ky were determined to build on the previous year's achievements. Both believed 1967 would be a critical period. Putting their ambitions aside, they realized that new strategies and new personnel were needed, and the first order of business was inaugurating a new government seat. Opening ceremonies for the recently completed Independence Palace were held on October 31, 1966. For both leaders, the new structure signified Saigon's resilience and their growing confidence that the worst was behind them.

Personnel changes were required as well. Bui Diem, a close Ky adviser and one of the few civilians in the government, had been promoted to deputy foreign minister in July 1966, a move which increased southern bitterness over northern carpetbaggers. Believing he had become a lightning rod for regional animosities, Bui Diem broached his resignation with Ky after the Manila meeting. Shortly thereafter, Ky informed him that "the brothers in the army think you would be most useful as an ambassador."[9] Bui Diem agreed, and in early December 1966, Ky assigned him as the new GVN ambassador to the U.S., where he would serve until June 1972.

Born on October 1, 1923 near Hanoi, Bui Diem was the rarest of Vietnamese. A college graduate, widely traveled, and liberal in social outlook, he came from a family of mandarins. He attended a private secondary school founded by his father, where one of his classmates was Tran Van Tuyen, Quat's former cabinet minister and a respected VNQDD leader. His history teacher was Vo Nguyen Giap, currently the commander of the People's Army. His uncle, Tran Trong Kim, was Bao Dai's first prime minister, and Bui Diem and the former emperor became close friends. Over time, he knew or worked for many of the leading Vietnamese Nationalists. After graduating secondary school, he enrolled at the University of Hanoi, where he earned a mathematics degree. Strongly anti-colonialist, when the French war erupted, he had a short dalliance with the Viet Minh, but he soon soured on them and fled to Phat Diem, the Catholic stronghold in North Vietnam. In the fervor of Vietnamese politics, he chose democracy, finding Marxism "cold and unconvincing."[10] His friend Dang Van Sung recruited him into the Dai Viet Party. He called himself a non-communist rather than an anti-communist for a distinct reason. "As a philosophy," he said, "South Vietnam needed more than anti-communism. It was not enough to motivate the people. We needed something more constructive, and that was social reform." He repeatedly weaved concepts like "helping the poor" into Ky's speeches. Although "Ky was not an idea man," Bui Diem recalled, "he was open-minded and reacted candidly to my proposals."[11]

On January 19, 1967, he presented his credentials to President Johnson. In his opening remarks, he repeated Thieu and Ky's assessment that they were winning the war. "The road ahead of us is long and difficult," he declared, "but we have left behind us the days of despair."[12] As the representative of a controversial government, he arrived in Washington determined to improve U.S. perceptions of South Vietnam and to expand congressional contacts. As a former journalist (he still owned the *Saigon Post*), he resolved to have lunch every day with different correspondents, valiantly attempting, as he told the author, "to get them to understand the war."

He soon developed excellent relations with several senior senators, particularly Senate Minority Leader Everett Dirksen (R-Ill.). He decided against meeting the antiwar senators like McGovern or Fulbright. He was not hesitant about "confronting their ideas," but "instead of informed arguments I heard the facile language of demagogues who reduced the situation to a matter of aiding corrupt generals."[13] Although dismissive of these congressional doves, he was shocked to discover the degree of antiwar unrest in America. He returned to Saigon in early March 1967 and informed Ky that if the GVN failed to stabilize, the peace movement might force Johnson to abandon the war. Ky understood, but Bui Diem would repeatedly inform Saigon's leaders over the burgeoning American antiwar movement and its potential impact on South Vietnam.

Having promised to fix corruption, Ky had followed Thieu's advice to lay the groundwork before ridding himself of the scandalously dishonest Lieutenant General Nguyen Huu Co, the last southern-born general in the Directorate. In mid-January 1967, Ky dispatched Co on a trip to various Asian capitals. As soon as Co departed, Ky called an emergency Directorate meeting and demanded that Co be relieved as minister of defense. The vote was unanimous. Co was informed by cable of his demotion on the afternoon of January 22 and told to fly to Hong Kong. Upon arriving, the GVN chargé handed Co a letter from Thieu telling him to remain there. If he returned to Saigon, he would be arrested and tried for corruption. Lieutenant General Cao Van Vien replaced Co as minister of defense and was promoted to a four-star general, making him the highest-ranking officer on active duty. Like Quang's firing, there was no southern outrage. In early March, Co was discharged from the army. He would not return to Saigon until January 1970.

In another key move, on March 18, Ky appointed Nguyen Huu Hanh as the new economic minister.[14] Hanh, an able administrator and the originator of the piaster devaluation the previous year, was currently the head of Vietnam's National Bank. He made Hanh a "super minister" over four separate ministries (Commerce, Finance, Industry, and Communications).

Ky, who took little interest in fiscal matters until pressed, gave Hanh carte blanche to solve South Vietnam's perennial economic woes, especially the seemingly intractable inflation issue.

Mirroring Saigon, the U.S. also underwent personnel changes. Ambassador Lodge resigned on February 19, 1967, citing personal and professional reasons. Johnson picked a veteran diplomat, Ellsworth Bunker, to replace him. Bunker arrived on April 25, 1967, beginning a six-year stint. Westmoreland got a new deputy, General Creighton Abrams, who focused on improving the RVNAF. Lastly, Robert Komer, Johnson's assistant for pacification, was sent to Vietnam to head a new pacification organization under Westmoreland.

Ky's moves—dispatching Bui Diem to Washington, exiling Co and replacing him with the apolitical Vien, and ensconcing the well-respected Hanh as economic czar—would pay dividends for South Vietnam. But for now, Ky once again had to navigate turbulent political waters.

FINALIZING THE CONSTITUTION

Since November 1966, the assembly had been busily designing a new constitution that would create a governmental structure to ensure stability and provide administrative strength under wartime conditions. Although several touchy issues arose between the Directorate and the drafters, for the most part the assembly conducted its business with little military interference. However, the two issues that had confounded relations from the beginning, the military's veto power and the assembly's continued existence post-constitution, remained contentious. Members of the assembly believed that as elected officials they had a popular mandate to draft the constitution without military meddling. Given the Directorate's refusal in December 1966 to delete its veto power under Article 20, the assembly instead requested to override a veto with a simple majority vote rather than the required two-thirds. In mid-January 1967, Thieu told the assembly that the Directorate had again refused, but he assured them that the junta would not enforce the censure unless provoked.

While Ky and Thieu kept the Directorate from interfering with the assembly's deliberations, they did seek to cajole the assembly members to revise several draft articles. Their means of persuasion, however, spoke volumes about their personalities and, by extension, their methods of governing. Assembly member Dang Van Sung opined that each had separately held dinners with assembly members, but Thieu "kept such occasions strictly official. He made formal speeches giving the government's views and had no personal contact with his guests." Ky, however, "gave no speeches, was completely informal, and engaged in friendly conversations with his guests, who were greatly impressed."[15] Ky, according to Sung, had built up much goodwill with the assembly, support that would soon prove decisive.

A key architect of the new constitution was southern Dai Viet leader Nguyen Ngoc Huy. Given Huy's background in constitutional law, he had "some influence in drafting" the new constitution.[16] Sung and Phan Quang Dan then handled much of the internal assembly negotiations. One of the most vital issues was the delineation of power between the executive and the legislature. Both the deputies and the Directorate agreed that checks and balances were needed to prevent complete presidential domination, but the key question was, how much? Some members, still scarred by Diem's monopoly of authority, wanted to endow the congress with most of the political muscle. Others like Huy, Sung, and Dan preferred a strong presidency. With South Vietnamese society still fragmented and under Communist assault, they favored a robust executive who could easily direct the country, so they brokered a compromise with the deputies who favored a dominant legislature. While most clout was imbued in the presidency, Dan and Sung designed the prime minister's role to encourage "division of powers to lay to rest the ghosts of the Diem era and to lighten the load of the president."[17] They inserted a serious brake on the presidency by giving the assembly control in areas like the budget and drafting laws, and they could remove the prime minister with a two-thirds vote. Given these concessions, the assembly rapidly achieved consensus on other issues, a testimony to the awareness that crafting a constitution that provided political legitimacy for South Vietnam was central to defeating the Communists.

The deadline to submit the draft was March 27, but the committee completed its work on March 10. Clearly ignoring the Directorate, the assembly added an article to the constitution granting itself full legislative powers until a new elected congress was in place. The republican-minded civilians had directly threatened the Directorate's hold on power. Thieu took a hard line. He was a man who believed in following regulations, and the decree he had earlier promulgated spelled out the law. He sent a stern letter to the assembly demanding that it abandon the article or face a veto. Worse, he warned the deputies that even if they succeeded in overriding it,

Thieu feared the generals might take drastic action to prevent the civilians from assuming power.

To diffuse the standoff, Ky held several late-night meetings with the senior assembly members, and using the rapport he had built, forged a deal. A formula was accepted on March 16 whereby the assembly would remain but limit its jurisdiction to drafting the laws for the presidential and legislature election. The Directorate would continue to handle the normal executive functions but would turn over power after the inauguration.

Although Thieu wanted a strict interpretation of the decree, he and Ky met on the morning of March 18 to discuss Ky's compromise. He convinced Thieu to accept the bargain, and the revised draft was presented to the full assembly later that day. As the deputy's names were called, the vote was unanimous to accept the constitution. At 7:32 p.m. on March 18, 1967, Phan Khac Suu, the elected assembly speaker, rose and proclaimed, "I declare that... this constitution is officially and legally adopted."[18] South Vietnam was firmly on the road to democracy.

Except that it was not. Ky gathered the Directorate the next day to obtain its acceptance, but suddenly he was faced with dissension. Several generals protested both the concession and Ky's sole effort in crafting it. III Corps Commander Lieutenant General Le Nguyen Khang led the opposition. He declared that Ky had reopened the door to chaos after two years of hard-fought gains to save the country. Ky, however, refused to back down, and he demanded that they accept his compromise so he could provide a ratified constitution to President Johnson at a just announced conference in Guam. It was essential, Ky stated, to present the U.S. with tangible proof that Saigon was achieving political stability. Thieu also urged the Directorate to accept Ky's decision. Faced with the two leader's pleas, they grudgingly agreed. Ky denies in his memoirs that his lone-wolf approach with the assembly had created animosities within the Directorate, but that is a ridiculous assertation. Khang was determined to protect the military's interests, and he was not going away. Not wishing to upset its U.S. patrons, Khang would wait until Ky returned.

THE GUAM MEETING

Thieu and Ky flew to Guam the following day to meet Johnson. Their opening speeches highlighted the progress South Vietnam had made since the Honolulu conference in February 1966. Thieu discussed how the military tide had turned in their favor, assembly elections had been held, a constitution had been drafted, and village and hamlet voting would soon follow. By the fall of 1967, Thieu proclaimed, South Vietnam would join the world's democracies. As Ky began to speak, he handed Johnson a copy of the new constitution. Overall, Bui Diem recalled, "it was a proud moment for them and for the South Vietnamese government."[19] Johnson emphasized to the Vietnamese leaders that political cohesion was vital. America could not afford more turmoil in Saigon. Ky and Thieu promised they would take no action that would split military unity.

In Guam, while the topic of how the South Vietnamese were slowly transitioning an autocratic regime into something resembling a functioning democracy was high on the agenda, the war remained the chief focus. Believing the main war was winding down, Ky stated that pacification was his government's primary concern. He admitted that the GVN's Rural Development program was still moving too slowly, although it was making progress. The foundation has been laid in 1966, and his plan for 1967 was to consolidate and improve the secure hamlets. For the Americans, that was unacceptable; the U.S. wanted Saigon to rapidly expand into the insecure areas. Ky planned baby steps, while the Americans needed the Vietnam undertaking to quicken. Rising sentiment against the war plus increasing U.S. casualties and financial costs had sparked protests ranging from college campuses to city streets. The conflict was not just exacerbating a widening cultural chasm in American society. Congressional, academic, and cultural elites were questioning the previously sacrosanct foundations of U.S. foreign policy. Under these strains, American public support for the war was wavering. The ultimate question was whether it would crack before the GVN could build a viable country that could win the war, or at least handle the Communist threat without full-scale U.S. support. Hanoi was betting it would.

For Johnson, who had championed American social progress via his own Great Society program, Vietnamese social reform was an instinctive response to the National Liberation Front's political challenge. After the Manila conference in October 1966, he had begun warming to the concept of combining all U.S. pacification agencies—the military, the State Department, the CIA, and USAID—into one organization under the command of a civilian who reported directly to General Westmoreland. The idea was the brainchild of Robert Komer, who had advised Johnson that only the military had the personnel and resources to carry out the ambitious pacification programs the U.S. envisioned. Civilian agencies detested uniting in a shotgun marriage under military control, but Johnson, anxious for quick progress, accepted Komer's proposal. It would lead to the birth of a key component of the U.S. mission in Vietnam, the office of Civil Operations and Revolutionary Development Support, or CORDS. On May 9, Johnson appointed Komer as head of CORDS with the rank of ambassador reporting directly to Westmoreland.

Although Ky desired to improve the secure hamlets first, he knew he needed to build an effective government at the local level to retake the countryside from the NLF. Thus, on December 24, 1966, he signed two decrees that began the necessary process of building a democratic state in the countryside. These little-known but decisive rulings restored power to its traditional locale, the village. While villages under Vietnamese kings were never fully autonomous, for centuries they had elected their own leaders and enacted local rules. Every Vietnamese knew the ancient phrase "The Emperor's law stops at the village gate" (*phep vua thua le lang*). Diem, however, had banned village council elections and had appointed village chiefs. This had caused resentment, and while Khanh had reconstituted village elections in May 1964, further efforts to invigorate village administration had stalled until Ky reestablished the village as the basic government unit.

The principal edict was Decree 198, which mandated a popular vote for two village councils. A Village People's Council would create a deliberative body to adjudicate local disputes, while a Village Administrative Council would coordinate the various RD tasks.[20] The decree urged local governments to encourage the peasantry to join local civic groups such as the Women's Association or the Farmer's Association. Participation in these new organizations was not repeating Diem's forced labor program to build Strategic Hamlets. They were designed to push the villagers to engage with the RD teams and develop an identification with the GVN. Thang stressed this concept by emphasizing that "the people must play the active role while [RD] cadres assume the campaign task and the government provides support only."[21] After pouring money into pacification in 1966 to build new schools and roads, the GVN now sought to increase peasant bonding with Saigon by restoring some semblance of local autonomy.

In late February 1967, Thang further outlined Saigon's two main development goals for 1967: build local democracy and increase RD efforts in the already secure hamlets. Building democracy meant first holding local elections for hamlet and village officials and then training them to hold general elections later that year for the presidency. Having set the base in 1966, the GVN would consolidate it in 1967 and then gradually expand into contested territory.

On March 2, 1967, Thang signed a series of memoranda summarizing the new program. Like Decree 198, the main concept was decentralization. All material improvements would be "decided by the population under the guidance of the hamlet managing boards and with the assistance of provincial technical cadres."[22] Basically, all construction projects in education, roadwork, irrigation, health, and agriculture would be chosen by local authorities in conjunction with the RD teams. The underlying idea was that if the people selected the projects and the GVN paid for it and helped them build it, the population would become progovernment, or the projects would lure peasants from insecure locations to these areas.

After Thieu's countrywide tour to overcome ARVN distaste about its reassignment to support RD, by the end of April 1967, one third of army maneuver battalions had been permanently assigned to pacification. There was no doubt that the ARVN needed to provide a security screen for the RD teams, as the first two classes had suffered a 20 percent attrition rate in 1966. Statistics showed that "593 RD cadres were killed and 75 captured, 86 were discharged, 696 resigned, and 603 deserted."[23] Communist forces had continued to target the cadres, and from January through the end of April 1967, RD losses totaled 557 dead, wounded, and missing.

DECISION TIME

Upon returning from Guam, Ky now had to submit the constitution to the larger Armed Forces Council for final approval. Fearful because the assembly had threatened military control of the government, on the morning of March 27, the AFC met and voted against accepting the constitution. Not surprisingly, the main sticking point was converting the assembly into a legislative body before the election of a permanent congress. According to Thieu, after recessing for lunch plus "some music and drink" after a "great deal of very hard reasoning by Thieu and Ky," the AFC took the two leaders' "word that the national and international considerations were such as to justify overlooking that defect."[24] Ky deserves much credit for successfully concluding South Vietnam's constitution. He had artfully navigated strong internal resistance by recalcitrant generals while convincing Thieu, who had initially fought any compromises, to support him. By any measure, it was an impressive political performance. On April 1, Thieu formally promulgated the constitution in a moving ceremony attended by numerous dignitaries. The pair had again stuck together and won.

The new constitution called for separate branches of government, including a legislature, an executive, and a judiciary. The legislature had two bodies: a Lower House, with 137 deputies serving four-year terms, and a Senate with 60 senators who would serve six-year terms. Every three years there would be an election for half of the Senate, every four years for the full House. The president had considerable power, but bills, budgets, ambassadors, etc., had to be submitted to the legislature for approval. While the assembly had rejected federalism, meaning Saigon's power was not limited or shared with the provinces, the constitution did enshrine republicanism. It guaranteed citizens' rights, freedom of speech, and permitted opposition forces to conduct political activities without government interference. A newly established Supreme Court would consist of judges elected by the Vietnamese Bar Association. Unlike the U.S. Supreme Court, however, the Vietnamese justices were not permanent but were reelected every six years. Huy believed the constitution's "greatest failure" was not assuring "the real independence of the justices."[25] Still, despite its critics, South Vietnam had achieved a remarkable milestone.

With the constitution completed, Assembly Speaker and elderly Cao Dai leader Phan Khac Suu immediately announced his intention to run for president. He chose Phan Quang Dan as his vice president. Dan, a northerner and a Buddhist, provided the ticket regional and religious balance. Suu was reelected assembly speaker on April 14 by a wide margin, giving him an early edge in the race. Tran Van Huong also indicated he would run, but he did not make a formal proclamation, a tactic to provide some wiggle room since both Thieu and Ky were offering inducements to join them. Other civilians, including Ha Thuc Ky from the Revolutionary Dai Viets, also declared their entry.

The most tantalizingly political question remained the eventual military nominee. The military candidate was strongly favored to win, having the usual benefits of incumbency plus formidable advantages in organization and funding. While each civilian entrant had pockets of strength, none had national appeal. Only Suu and Huong posed a threat, but since they would split the southerners, the military candidate automatically became the front-runner. The Directorate, though, remained averse to breaking the Thieu-Ky impasse, and since both men had promised Johnson in Guam that neither would disrupt military cohesion, each had avoided a direct confrontation. In late March, Ky explained to Lodge that the "armed forces [council] will not choose a candidate. The situation is very simple. If Thieu decides to run, I will support him. He is senior, and it is up to him to have the first chance at it."[26]

But with Thieu still waffling, on March 31 several leading generals cornered Thieu and Ky at a small party, beginning three months of maneuvering until the climactic final decision was made on June 30. The ever-cautious Thieu informed them he remained undecided, but he would "volunteer" if they asked him. Thieu's "humble patriot" offer was an unspoken desire to be drafted rather than openly declaring his political ambitions. The generals responded by encouraging him to discuss with Ky which one was the more popular candidate, a quiet surfacing of the canard that Thieu was not well liked. Their recommendation was an indirect means of telling Thieu they supported Ky, and naturally it backfired. According to Bui Diem, Thieu mistakenly interpreted the advice as "support for his candidacy," but it was all "too subtle and too Vietnamese and the result was a very basic misunderstanding."[27]

Thieu procrastinated because he wanted to be anointed by his peers and blessed by the U.S. The Directorate, however, wanted a resolution, and when Thieu was rushed to the hospital on April 10 for an appendectomy, they acted. General Vien ordered Nguyen Duc Thang to visit Thieu in the hospital and ask him to step aside. Thang saw Thieu on April 18 and told him that most of the generals believed Ky had a better chance to win and that Thieu should instead command the military. Ky recounts that Thieu exploded in rage since he believed the generals were backing him based on the March 31 meeting. He shouted at Thang that he was lying. Thang in turn grew angry, and they "nearly had a fistfight."[28] Bui Diem describes that Thieu "felt deceived," but the generals denied telling "Thieu they would back him. They had just been polite about their attitude...[Nor had] they been deceitful; they just thought Ky had a better chance."[29] Thieu, however, did not believe their protestations, and Bui Diem said Thieu was now "deeply bitter and feels isolated and without support" and that "his personal prestige gave him no alternative but to stay in the race."[30] Oddly, in a conversation with his old friend, Ed Lansdale, Thang vehemently denied that he had spoken with Thieu.[31] It was an obvious refusal to inform the Americans about the general's innermost debates, and it would not be the last time the South Vietnamese chose to keep the U.S. in the dark about their deliberations.

A now frustrated General Vien decided he had given the two enough time. Vien publicly proclaimed on May 8 that since the military was not a political party, it would not nominate a candidate, and each serviceman could vote their conscience. Vien's masterstroke saved the generals from having to openly choose. For Ky, the ruling was a godsend. By refusing to formally vote for a candidate, Vien freed Ky from his earlier promises to Thieu. Thus, on May 9, Ky met with Thieu and told him of his intention to run for president. He asked for Thieu's approval. Thieu said his consent was not needed, since as per Vien's directive, each was now free to choose. Believing he had Thieu's implicit agreement, on May 12, Ky formally announced his candidacy.

Thieu continued to waffle, stating he had "doubts about the extent of his potential support and the belief that the Americans would accept only Ky as president."[32] Although Thieu felt he had no chance to win, a supportive visit by Westmoreland on May 7, the subsequent urging of Foreign Minister Tran Van Do, plus his belief that he still retained substantial military support convinced him otherwise. On May 20, Thieu told newsmen he intended to run, but he would delay a formal announcement for several weeks. Although he stressed that his candidacy would not threaten military unity, a worried Ambassador Ellsworth Bunker met with him to discuss that very point. Thieu informed Bunker that he "could reassure [Johnson] that he was a true patriot and that he would never do anything which would create division within the military or the country." The people, he said, "do not want another Diem. They want a freely elected President and Congress and they want the Armed Forces to stay out of politics and support the government."[33]

Given Thieu's announcement, on May 25, others also declared their candidacy. Tran Van Huong proclaimed his entry, joining Ha Thuc Ky and Phan Khac Suu as the main civilian contenders. Despite his poor relations with the Buddhists, in one of the odder pairings of Vietnamese politics, Huong had chosen a prominent Buddhist layman, Mai Tho Truyen, as his running mate.[34] Although Truyen had cooperated with Tri Quang and Tam Chau in the struggle against Diem, afterward he had broken with them over their ongoing political activity.

Thieu's announcement caught Ky by surprise. Believing Thieu had concurred with Ky's candidacy, Ky had made overtures to a wide range of

Vietnamese constituencies for their votes, and he had made considerable progress in organizing his election campaign. Thieu's dithering had also allowed Ky's confidant, Brigadier General Loan, to take the initiative among the province and police chiefs, a process that increasingly looked like vote rigging.

Fearing military disunity, Ky asked Bui Diem to intercede with Thieu and ask him to withdraw. On May 25, Bui Diem visited Thieu in "his lonely office." Despite his efforts, Thieu was adamant. Even if he only received his and his wife's votes, he intended to run. Thieu's motivations were undoubtedly a combination of ambition, encouragement from Westmoreland and Do, and pride. When Bui Diem informed Ky of Thieu's intentions, Ky remarked that "since we control the situation, we will move on without him."[35] Ky had closed the door on appeasing Thieu. He could not now abandon the race without losing considerable face. Thus, when Thieu made his formal announcement on June 14, the formerly close relations between the two men rapidly deteriorated, particularly over the crass methods that Loan was instituting to manipulate the election. Thieu was furious over reports that Loan had told each province police chief to produce twenty thousand votes apiece for Ky.

Thieu began giving press interviews demanding that the government hold honest elections, a direct shot at Loan's unsavory tactics. He also repeated that he was against military involvement in politics. Whether Thieu believed that or if his position remained fluid, it was a far cry from when he believed the military was the best option to govern South Vietnam. He promised that if elected, he would choose a civilian as his vice president and prime minister. Regarding his platform, he announced three planks: peace, democracy, and social justice. The words instantly became his election slogan, since to "rally the population, to bring it to cooperate with us, and to restore confidence, social justice must be promoted."[36]

While Thieu repeatedly called for free elections, it is difficult to confirm whether his democratic impulse resulted from personal growth, calculated pretense, or easily discarded campaign promises to garner votes. Perhaps Thieu sensed ambivalence in Ky over honest elections and saw it as a campaign wedge. If so, his instincts were correct. Reflecting years later, Ky claimed that, given the ensuing fall of South Vietnam, "I believe now the elections were a mistake." He judged that if he had maintained leadership, "many serious mistakes, including my own, might have been averted." In a more telling commentary, while Ky "was committed to the democratic process, I felt it important that a military candidate win the presidential election" since "the military must continue to have the primary role in government."[37]

Ky's shocking admission explains his subordinates' actions to slant the election, but how had he suddenly become oblivious to the enormous damage a fraudulent election would have on U.S. and Vietnamese public opinion? Or like previous Vietnamese leaders, had he suddenly become power hungry? If power corrupts and consumes, apparently it also infects. Bunker, however, would not permit Ky to steal the vote. Under heavy U.S. pressure and sensitive to public complaints from both Thieu and Assembly members about election tampering, Ky retreated. He committed to an honest election, convened a seminar of all province chiefs to reinforce his pledge, and reined in Loan. On June 27, he removed Loan from involvement in his campaign.

Saigon's political pond was suddenly roiled, however, when Duong Van Minh demanded to return from exile in Thailand. Fearing Minh's return might drain votes from him, Ky ruled against a Minh homecoming. Outraged, Minh declared his own presidential campaign and had his running mate, a lawyer named Tran Ngoc Lieng, file the necessary paperwork. Lieng was one of the southern ministers who had resigned from the government in November 1966 alongside Trieu. Unknown to Minh, however, Lieng was a covert Communist who would eventually form several neutralist groups that advocated a coalition with the NLF.[38]

At an AFC meeting on June 29, Ky again denied Minh's request to return, citing "national security" concerns. Thieu balked at Ky's decision and demanded the Directorate vote on Minh. Upset by Thieu's behavior, Nguyen Duc Thang "launched a blistering attack on Thieu for [Thieu's] trickiness and indecisiveness." Thang soon apologized, and an emotional Thieu broke down, "saying Thang was first general officer to apologize to him... after all the terrible things that had been said about him behind his back."[39]

This bitter exchange forced the generals to finally confront the Thieu-Ky impasse. Over the next two days, the Directorate hammered out a solution. The exact details of how Thieu achieved the political equivalent of a Hail Mary have never been disclosed, and it has remained one of the great mysteries of South Vietnamese politics. Ky published his account, which until now had been the prevailing version, but a complete picture has remained clouded, even for many senior-level Vietnamese. There was a good reason.

Based upon interviews with two Directorate members, plus confirming details from several of Thieu's closest advisers, a surprising tale of backroom dealmaking emerges. U.S. records generally agree that at the first day's meeting (June 29) with the larger Armed Forces Council present, both Ky and Thieu stated they would run, but they refused to run together. The council failed to find a solution despite heated and at times rather emotional arguments over the merits of each man.

Desperate to solve the rancor that was threatening military unity, that afternoon, General Vien brought the four corps commanders and several other top generals to his office to find a resolution. Of these men, three of the four corps commanders (Major General Hoang Xuan Lam, Lieutenant General Vinh Loc, and Major General Nguyen Van Manh) wanted Thieu, while Lieutenant General Le Nguyen Khang (III Corps) and the other five generals wanted Ky. After hours of fierce debate, they adjourned late in the evening of June 29 with an apparent agreement for Thieu to take over the military and for Ky to head the ticket.

What transpired next has remained hidden until now. It involved a joint effort by Thieu's main supporters, Vinh Loc and Hoang Xuan Lam, to wrestle the presidential slot from Ky. Their motivations were a combination of self-interest and old bonds. Loc and Thieu had been chummy since the incident on the bridge that had saved the Diem coup. Lam preferred Thieu, believing he had more integrity and was a better leader. Lam also wanted an army officer in charge, plus it helped that Thieu had obtained a third star for him in mid-June. Another important factor was the "fear that exiled General Duong Van Minh's chances of winning the election would be greatly enhanced if Thieu and Ky were on separate tickets."[40] This apprehension over Minh was confirmed by Thieu's close assistant Nguyen Van Ngan, who said postwar that "the reason that Thieu and Ky joined forces and ran on the same ticket is...because otherwise we would have lost to Minh."[41] Since many of the current senior officers had helped Khanh overthrow Minh in January 1964, they feared Minh's return to power.

Resuming the discussion in Vien's office on the morning of June 30, Loc and Lam dropped a bombshell. Loc proclaimed that he could not agree to let Ky lead the ticket because Ky would be susceptible to American blackmail due to drug smuggling by Ky's sister. Loc declared she was using Ky's former VNAF squadron to smuggle drugs from Laos into Vietnam. In Vientiane, Laos, heroin would be packed into Coca-Cola cans. Once the planes were over Dalat, the resort city in Loc's II Corps, the drugs would be parachuted to the ground, where local forces would recover them.[42] South Vietnam could not allow the U.S. to potentially control Ky. The solution was for Thieu to take the top spot and for Ky to run as his vice president.

An outraged Ky offered to return to the Air Force and let Thieu have the top spot. Given Ky's refusal to run as vice president, Lam tossed his three-star epaulets on the table and threatened to resign unless Ky agreed to run with Thieu. He and Vinh Loc then got up and left the meeting. Given this display, Le Nguyen Khang, Ky's former schoolmate, defected from Ky's camp. Khang was secretly disillusioned with Ky. His anger began, as it often did in politics, with a perceived slight. In early February 1967, when Vien and Nguyen Van Manh had received an additional star, Khang had not been promoted to permanent lieutenant general (he had been promoted in November 1966 to temporary lieutenant general, a Vietnamese rank structure) even though he commanded more troops than anyone else. The constitutional crisis in March further enflamed his irritation with Ky. He had been the most vocal general condemning the agreement to allow the assembly to continue after the constitution was accepted. When Lam and Loc stormed out, Khang also threatened to resign unless Thieu and Ky joined together.

At this point, General Vien broke the impasse. In a postwar account written for his daughter, Vien noted that he had asked Thieu and Ky to step outside so the Leadership Council could discuss the situation. Ky confirms in his memoirs that both men sat outside. Vien then hammered out a compromise. They agreed that both men should run together and

> that if either of them refused the decision of the Council, they should be expelled from the Leadership Council. After everyone agreed to this, Ky and Thieu were invited into the room. I announced the decision to them, telling them, 'The members of the Leadership Council have decided that the two of you must run on the same ticket. Thieu will be the candidate for President and Ky will be the candidate for Vice President. To compensate for this concession, the person that Ky chose to be his Vice-Presidential candidate [Nguyen Van Loc] will be appointed as the Prime Minister. If either of you refuses to accept the Leadership Council's decision, you will be expelled from the Leadership Council.' Faced with the firm, adamant position of all of the members of the Leadership Council, Thieu and Ky agreed to the decision.[43]

Lam then proposed a face-saving solution. They agreed to tell everyone that Ky had offered to give up the top spot since Thieu was the higher-ranking officer and already the head of state. In Vietnamese culture, class and date of rank are far more important than they are to Americans.[44]

There are corroborating details to support this smoke-filled-room version of events. In an interview with journalists three years later to refute charges Ky had made against him, Thieu "termed their union on one ticket a 'forced marriage' and said the facts refuted an allegation by Ky that he had 'yielded' the presidency to Thieu."[45] The commander of the Rangers, Colonel Tran Van Hai, who attended as part of the Armed Forces Council but was not in Vien's office, confirmed that "Ky made the decision to withdraw...when Khang, upon whose support Ky relied heavily, let it be known that he did not intend to back Ky."[46] Lam's embassy biographical study says that "Lam told an Embassy officer that he played the major role in talking Ky into accepting second place on the ticket."[47] Ky's memoir acknowledges Lam's role in his decision to accept second billing. Interestingly, Ky also refers to drugs and his sister. In his first book, he confirms that heroin was being refined in "Vientiane, from where it was flown to Saigon, often in Coca-Cola cans. Some was air-dropped from Laotian or Vietnamese military aircraft."[48] Regarding his sister, whom he called "the black sheep of our family," Ky states that she had moved to Laos and that they had not spoken in twenty years. Ky admitted, though, that during this "period it became common knowledge that many Vietnamese living in Laos were involved in smuggling gold or opium" and that because of his position, "rumors were spread that [she] and I smuggled drugs into Vietnam. It is possible she was involved, but I knew nothing about it then, and I know nothing about it now."[49]

Whether the drug charges against Ky were true or not, Vien and the four corps commanders had forced the two to join together. The Directorate had overridden the pair, setting a precedent that their collective voice would predominate in the future. Ky, of course, was furious, and many of his supporters were deeply upset. He had to find a way to explain his actions, and thus his postwar version—that he accepted the vice presidency on a spur-of-the-moment decision—fits neatly into the common perception of his impulsiveness.

Although Thieu had agreed that Ky would appoint the new prime minister and the cabinet, the deal's vagueness led Ky to seek something more concrete. On July 6, Thieu, Ky, and the other generals held a meeting to iron out the details. They signed an agreement that further spelled out that Ky "must approve any important government decisions...Thieu is satisfied with the agreement and understands his limited role as president."[50] The senior officers formed a covert group called the *Quan Uy Hoi* (Military Council) that Ky claims forced Thieu "to sign a secret protocol designed to keep him under military control...This council was responsible only to itself, and not bound by the constitution."[51] Basically, the current roles, with Thieu as a ceremonial figure and Ky holding the real power, would remain, constitution be damned.

The members of the secret Military Council, in typical authoritarian fashion, believed South Vietnam needed their continuing guidance since the "present stage of social and political development of the Vietnamese people and their political leaders do not permit establishment of a full democracy at this time." The country "must be assisted...to execute government programs and guided [to ensure] such programs are conceived and executed for the welfare of the people and the nation."[52] The general's disdain for the civilian presidential candidates, alongside ingrained self-interest, blinded them to the concept that Saigon's political legitimacy was as important as its military strength. Tran Van Huong was the only candidate they respected. Huong had taken a deeply unpopular stand in late 1964 against the militant Buddhists, then stood up to Khanh's back-stabbing maneuvers. Esteem, though, did not equate to submission.

A year later, Ky showed an aide the precise charter. Consisting of "two typewritten pages," the document affirmed that "the group's presidential candidate agrees that he will not make any major policy decisions as president without the advice and consent of the Council of Generals...Ky signed as Chairman and Thang signed as Secretary-General, while Thieu signed as a member, his signature appearing fourth...Ky told his aide that Thang had actually drafted the document."[53] The Directorate had secretly connived to undercut the constitution, and both Thieu and Ky had agreed to it rather than risk expulsion from the group. Both believed they had acted in the best interests of South Vietnam, and both men were wrong.

THE SLOW DANCE TOWARD UNITY

Despite the backroom political maneuvering, on the surface South Vietnam seemed to be moving forward. Militarily, the enemy had taken heavy losses, and recent PAVN offensives in I and II Corps had been blunted.

Economically, spending and money supply issues had been controlled, urban food supplies had increased, and prosperity was emerging in the cities and increasingly in parts of the countryside. Although inflation remained untamed, price increases had at least slowed from previous years.

Besides these positive indicators, other unseen and profound societal changes were occurring. The 1966 Buddhist spasm had convinced the ethnic and religious blocs that protest was ineffective against military repression. The Chinese, Catholics, Montagnards, and moderate Buddhists thus began a slow dance of accommodation with the GVN, leaving only the militant Buddhists as agitators. The movement toward constitutional government helped sparked the change, alongside the realization that the security situation had stabilized. While regional biases and religious disdain would never totally dissipate, overt tribalism had begun subsiding. Although many complex and seemingly intractable problems remained—primarily endemic corruption, weak local government, and the still considerable Communist military and political threat—the U.S. military shield had achieved its goal. While its critics were legion, South Vietnam had quietly regained a semblance of strength not seen since the early 1960s.

To build on the improvements from 1966, the GVN began planning for village and hamlet elections. Administratively, it was a challenging task, as South Vietnam had forty-four provinces, over 2,500 villages, and more than 11,000 hamlets. Saigon labeled about half of the villages and hamlets as secure, although in February 1967, the U.S. had made the first effort to statistically justify that claim with a new survey called the Hamlet Evaluation System (HES). Although its veracity was much maligned, the system was designed to uncover province-wide trends. Unfortunately, it quickly became the benchmark for showing progress, which meant pressure at the local level to show improvement regardless of the actual security situation.

The first village elections were held on April 2, and by the end of the month, almost a thousand had held elections, with 77 percent of the registered citizens voting. The security situation, particularly in northern I Corps, only permitted about one third of the total villages to participate. Hamlet elections occurred from mid-May to mid-June, with almost 4,500 hamlets joining. Thousands of people were elected to the new councils, a massive infusion of grassroots democracy in a country that had not experienced local rule for years. Another election phase was scheduled for July in areas that had recently been deemed secure. The NLF, despite killing twelve candidates, failed to disrupt the vote.

Legislatively, the assembly continued its working relationship with the Directorate, although mutual suspicion remained high. The main controversy was fixing the date for the Senate election. The assembly wanted to hold it in December, while the Directorate preferred it on the same day as the presidential vote. When the assembly refused, the generals overruled it, which generated significant animosity. Since the assembly's Election Committee was required to validate the various presidential and Senate lists, some members plotted revenge. When the validity of the Thieu-Ky slate was challenged on July 3 by former Economic Minister and presidential candidate Au Truong Thanh, deputies in the Election Committee seized the opportunity. On July 17, the committee rejected the military ticket, stating that the two leaders needed to resign from office to ensure a fair election. Concurrently, they approved Duong Van Minh's candidacy.

The generals balked, and after some ominous threats, the assembly backed down and approved the Thieu-Ky ticket. The Directorate also convinced them to ban Thanh from running by resurrecting the old accusations that he was a closet Communist since his platform, an immediate ceasefire and peace at any price, was seen as pro-NLF. Minh remained another sticking point. Since Minh was obviously not a national security risk, the Election Committee instead barred Minh's running mate Tran Ngoc Lieng on the basis that Lieng had once held French citizenship. Despite constant U.S. harping on the glaring need for fair elections, the generals' disdain for the messy cacophony of civilian oversight obviously remained unaffected.

While the assembly and the Directorate sparred, Vien followed through on his promise to keep the military from overtly interfering with the actual voting. On July 1, the JGS issued a directive prohibiting servicemen from either campaigning for a candidate or attempting to convince others within their units to support a specific ticket. Disciplinary action would be taken against anyone who did. To support that order, Major General Thang sent a letter to all RD cadres also barring them from actively supporting any nominee, while Ky also blocked civil servants. Additionally, Ky lifted all censorship restrictions, promised to provide equal transportation and media time to the other candidates, and invited the United Nations to send election monitors to certify the election. To show they meant business, several days before the election, Colonel Pham Van Lieu, the former director of police and now the commandant of the NCO Academy in Nha Trang, was placed under temporary house arrest after he used his officers to spread election leaflets for Phan Khac Suu. Regrettably, the move backfired since everyone interpreted the detention as attempting to silence the opposition.

Since May, Ky had made overtures to the various South Vietnamese constituencies to gain their support, and many seemed far more willing to cooperate than ever before. All except the militant Buddhists. Although they had remained quiet during the first months of 1967, by the spring of 1967, the militants had begun stirring in anticipation of the upcoming elections. While still badly weakened, An Quang was spurred to action when Thieu signed Decree 23/67 on July 18, 1967, which overrode the previous UBA charter and recognized Chau's Quoc Tu Pagoda as the official church leader. An Quang exploded, and the Buddhist supreme patriarch, the elected head of the church and a Tri Quang supporter, sent a letter to Thieu angrily denouncing the new charter. In August, both An Quang and Quoc Tu held dueling congresses, but most Vietnamese Buddhist organizations sided with Chau. They approved the charter and elected a new church leader, whereupon Tam Chau stepped down as head of the Institute for the Faith. Nevertheless, the two blocs continued to battle, and the charter controversy dragged on for years. When the assembly disqualified several militant Buddhist Senate blocs because of either neutralist leanings or because they had failed to provide the correct filing documents, the militants once more threatened to boycott the election and were once more ignored.

The other religions were also undergoing dramatic changes. In mid-May, Ky made a successful bid to gain the backing of the two bickering Hoa Hao factions. The Cao Dai, although torn by Pham Khac Suu's candidacy, quietly agreed to support Ky in exchange for several seats in the future legislature. The Catholics remained politically active but like the Buddhists were increasingly divided. With the demise of Father Hoang Quynh's multi-religion organization, laymen had taken control of Quynh's Greater Solidarity Force. More important, the church had modified its position on peace negotiations. In late September 1966, a special Vatican mission had visited Saigon carrying a letter from Pope Paul VI. The pope's message lead to a stunning Vietnamese Catholic reversal. On October 7, 1966, the Vietnam Council of Bishops formally requested peace negotiations. Completely overlooked by the furor over Ky's cabinet crisis and the Buddhist's own internal uproar, it was a sea change from the previous hardline stand of Father Hoang Quynh. By December 1966, the pope was publicly calling for negotiations to end the war. While the Catholics remained opposed to

NLF participation in South Vietnam's political life, they were careful not to contest the pope's peace appeal.

At the same time, Ky moved to bring the minorities into his camp. He signed a decree returning the community property to the Chinese that Diem had seized in 1960 as part of his assimilation efforts. While the Cambodians in the Delta remained passive, the Montagnards again sought out special treatment. Although the new constitution had enshrined minority rights, Lieutenant General Vinh Loc and Paul Nur, the special commissar for Montagnard affairs, continued to push, and in late June, a conference was held in Pleiku with two hundred delegates from various tribes. The All-Tribes Congress drafted a Statut Particulier, a degree conferring special rights for the hill people, including Montagnard landownership and improving schools and courts. Ky attended the closing ceremony and agreed to the recommendations, including upgrading the Special Commissariat to a full ministry. Although FULRO soon rejected the new law, the rebel group was increasingly marginalized. On August 29, Thieu and Ky signed the Statut Particulier at a ceremony in Ban Me Thuot. While Vietnamese racial bias would never dissipate, the Montagnards had achieved equal citizen status in South Vietnam.

As the time to cast one's vote neared, officials began evaluating the two South Vietnamese leaders' personality and character. Many had similar impressions but had come to different conclusions. While most U.S. mission personnel supported Ky, the two main American leaders, Ellsworth Bunker and General Westmoreland, backed Thieu. Bunker had "left his first meeting with Ky unimpressed with [Ky's] ability to think constructively [other than] flip sloganeering." Bunker felt "quite strongly that Thieu had greater ability and more depth than Ky...Thieu's intellectual powers were quite superior to Ky's. Thieu was also more straightforward, telling him when he did not agree."[54] Westmoreland felt Thieu was "a master of timing. He was patient, cautious, willing to take his time to block out his moves in advance behind the scenes, a deft handler of the leaders of the religious and sectional factions."[55]

Bui Diem, however, agreed that while Thieu "projected a serious mature image, in distinct contrast to Ky's unpredictable cockiness," he was "secretive and suspicious and calculating...[W]hat Bunker and Westmoreland saw as maturity, I felt as hesitancy and indecisiveness...[Thieu] was a hard worker...but he was not...a man of idea or vision...By nature, he was too careful, too aware of the angles, too convoluted in his thinking and indirect in his methods." Ky, on the other hand, was "quick to learn and enthusiastic about new ideas. And he had a certain fearlessness about him...[H]e was capable of taking tremendous risks without thinking much about the consequences of failure."[56]

Thieu's personality was in fact an odd duality. In public, he exhibited a stiff persona, a reserve called dignified by his supporters and standoffish by his detractors. He would listen attentively, taking notes and often agreeing with his visitor but rarely committing himself. This ability to listen but maintain reserve enabled him to avoid alienating or aligning himself with any group or course of action until he had extensively studied it. Many Vietnamese attributed this attitude to cunning self-interest, but his loyalists claim it was a shrewd strategy to determine if his interlocutor had hidden motives.

That intelligent people could make contrary appraisals was perhaps a reflection that judging character was as much about the observer as it was about the person. Yet in the hyper-politicized Vietnamese cauldron, such caution was ignored. Regardless, now began the campaign and vote to make South Vietnam the world's newest democracy.

12

"FROM THE MOMENT I TAKE OFFICE, I BELONG TO YOU"

Birth of the Second Republic

The election of September 1967 marked a watershed moment for South Vietnam as it completed the transition from a military regime to a democracy. As is often the case, the switch was met with challenges from various power groups that came close to derailing the entire process. Yet despite their growing personal antagonism, Thieu and Ky once again shepherded their country through its birthing pains. The inauguration of the Second Republic, however, brought them no respite. Thieu's personality, cautious and deliberative rather than bold, led to disgruntlement from both the U.S. and his own military. Thieu wanted to take his time and prepare, while the Americans pressed him hard to speed up the pace. Although many wanted him to exert strong leadership, the Military Council was watching his every move. No one would be happy.

CAMPAIGNING

The presidential campaign began on August 3. The presidential and senate elections would be held on September 3, the Lower House election on October 22. The election law contained the usual restrictions. Candidates had to be Vietnamese by birth and had to have lived in Vietnam for the last ten years. No Communists, neutralists, draft dodgers, or criminals could run. The assembly would examine and approve each ticket. Once the final list was confirmed, campaigning would begin on

August 3. After the election, the assembly would meet on October 2 and validate the results.

Thieu and Ky confirmed that their theme was "Peace, Democracy, and Social Justice." Suu and Huong also announced their platforms, which involved attacking corruption and fixing poor governmental performance. Despite the assembly's denial of Au Truong Thanh's ticket, peace quickly became the campaign's center issue. Each candidate separately emphasized that talks should only occur between Saigon and Hanoi, another jab at any designs Washington might entertain. They also demanded a withdrawal of Communist forces to North Vietnam. However, while the three men were willing to speak with Hanoi, none would bargain with the NLF as that might imply that the conflict was a civil war rather than external aggression by North Vietnam.

As part of his campaign manifesto, Thieu's initial peace plan reflected his tough position, but the campaign forced him to amend his peace plank. In early August, he offered direct talks with North Vietnam. By late August, he went a step further and dangled the possibility of a bombing halt, a tactic that he had previously opposed, but only if Hanoi agreed to negotiations. He even modified his position regarding talks with the NLF by offering to speak with any individual from the Front but only to discuss reconciliation. He would not speak with them as representatives of a separate political entity.

The nominees, though, differed on the tactics to achieve peace talks. Suu, for example, wanted to restart the Geneva conference. Thieu vehemently disagreed, arguing that there were now two Vietnams with distinct sovereign governments. For Thieu, Hanoi's agreement to directly negotiate with South Vietnam was the litmus test of Hanoi's sincerity. Agreeing to talk directly would validate the GVN's legitimacy by repudiating the Politburo's propaganda that the Nationalists were American "puppets" and that only the Front represented the South Vietnamese people. Regardless, Thieu did not think Hanoi would respond to an offer of direct talks. He believed Hanoi would negotiate only after it had concluded that it could not win militarily or to manipulate the U.S. elections. Otherwise, requesting negotiations was useless. The only worse outcome in Thieu's mind would be if the Americans took over.

The election campaign kicked off with a scheduled public appearance in Hue of all the candidates. However, severe weather diverted the plane carrying the civilian contenders to a nearby airport. Huong, Suu, and the others were stuck there and missed the opening ceremony with Thieu and Ky, who had taken a separate plane. The civilian nominees loudly declared that this was a deliberate government effort to embarrass them, and they threatened to withdraw from the race. The furor drew the attention of both the foreign and American media, and the U.S. press began pillorying the upcoming election as a fraud. Although the GVN had abolished press censorship on July 21 and had offered free transportation, money, and radio and TV time to all the candidates, the American journalists blindly repeated the candidate's harsh criticism. The press reproach in turn sparked U.S. congressional censure. On August 10, fifty-seven members of the House of Representatives signed a proclamation blasting Saigon over alleged campaign abuses. Making matters worse, the gaffe-prone Ky threatened a coup if a civilian who he believed was soft on Communism were to win. Thieu had to renounce any future military interference in the government. He declared that "if a civilian president is correctly elected, if we really have a fair election . . . the Army has no right to do a coup."[1]

The congressional denunciation also forced Bui Diem to do some damage control. The day after the congressional letter, he sat down for an interview with veteran journalist Carl Rowan. He claimed that Ky had been "misquoted" and that the government would not cheat. Expressing dismay that "Americans do not get the full story of what [the South Vietnamese] are doing in the war," he begged the U.S. public to maintain "steely determination." He predicted that Hanoi would fight on until after the September elections and might then reassess. He finished with a prophetic statement: "I feel 1968 might be a critical year for all of us."[2]

Campaign funding was difficult for every candidate. Although the Chinese business leaders had given Thieu and Ky significant amounts of money, other powerful benefactors had hedged their bets and split their financial support. Nguyen Cao Thang, the wealthy head of the powerful OPV company, provided the Suu-Dan ticket with six million piasters, a princely sum for the unfunded pair. Pham Van Lieu witnessed the check hand off to Suu and claimed that "Thang had also provided financial support to the Thieu-Ky slate and to Huong-Truyen. The amount of money he contributed to each varied, depending on the slate's odds for winning the election."[3]

As election day neared, many observers concluded that Thieu-Ky would win, but with ten civilian opponents, most believed the military ticket would win with less than 40 percent of the total. By late August, Phan Khac Suu had pulled into second place. He had gained traction in northern South Vietnam among the militant Buddhists by claiming that exiled Lieutenant General Nguyen Chanh Thi was supporting him. Huong had slipped to third place, even though General Minh and the widow of assassinated Assembly leader Tran Van Van had both announced their support.

The dark horse candidate was a prosperous lawyer named Truong Dinh Dzu, who was born on November 10, 1917, in Binh Dinh Province in central South Vietnam. A Buddhist, Dzu graduated from the University of Hanoi Law School in 1941 and moved to Saigon in 1947, where he represented several large French companies. He married the daughter of one of South Vietnam's wealthiest importers, and they had two children. His son, David Truong, would move to the U.S. and become a leading Vietnamese antiwar voice from the safety of America. He and a U.S. government official would be convicted in 1978 of passing classified materials to Hanoi. Dzu's law partner was the brother of Madame Ngo Dinh Nhu. Dzu was close to the Ngos, but like many prominent Vietnamese he eventually fell out with them. His running mate was Tran Van Chieu, a southerner who had fought the French but had returned to Saigon in 1947 after Communist troops mauled his Cao Dai unit. Chieu then bought a car parts business, which he developed into one of the largest commercial enterprises in Saigon. In early 1966, Chieu was named secretary-general of the Nationalist United Front, an old umbrella organization of various religious and small political factions that had supported Diem until Nhu undercut them. Dzu also joined this organization, where he was introduced to Nguyen Ngoc Huy's Tan Dai Viet (TDV) party, which was quietly spreading its tentacles across South Vietnam.

Few considered Dzu a viable candidate. Most commentators thought he might at best place fifth. He had a seamy reputation stemming from a variety of pending legal charges against him, including a bad check indictment in 1963, which he claimed was an attempt by Nhu to discredit him. Two U.S. servicemen he had defended accused him of demanding $10,000 to bribe the judge. Dzu was also under investigation for illegal overseas currency transactions, but the court temporarily halted the inquiry when he ran for president. Recognizing Au Truong Thanh's mistake, Dzu cleverly waited until after his ticket was approved before announcing his platform. As soon as the official campaign began, he demanded an immediate ceasefire and the opening of peace negotiations with both Hanoi and the Front. To reinforce his peace program, his campaign symbol was a white dove, although that was mainly directed at the international media since most Vietnamese were unfamiliar with the dove as a peace emblem.

Alongside providing free transportation and media time to each candidate, the GVN had arranged extensive election measures. Security precautions were wide-ranging, and local village officials were trained in election procedures. Millions of ballots were printed. Each contained the picture of the candidates and their symbols. They were shipped under guard to over 8,800 polling places around the country. Procedures were instituted to prevent voter fraud. To participate, each eligible resident had to submit their voter card and government ID. One corner of the voter card was then torn off to prevent them from voting again. The torn corners were compared against the number of ballots to ensure there was no double voting. The polling station was supervised by a local committee alongside poll watchers from the various candidates. President Johnson assembled twenty-two U.S. observers and dispatched them to Vietnam to monitor the balloting. Numerous foreign visitors also carefully watched for any irregularities. Ballot counting would be conducted by the local election committee and seconded by the poll watchers. A sworn statement confirming the tally would be signed by both groups, who would then telephone the results to Saigon, where an "unofficial" return would be announced. The ballots and the sworn statements would be sent to Saigon where the assembly would review the results and judge any irregularities. Once completed, the assembly would validate the results.

ANALYZING THE RESULTS

On election day, the Communists again attempted to disrupt the vote, mainly through attacks on polling sites. Several hundred civilians were killed or wounded. Their intimidation tactics failed as over half a million more people voted in the presidential and senate elections than in the assembly balloting a year earlier. Part of the gains came from improved security in the countryside, and part of it came from more refugees under GVN control. Eighty-three percent of registered voters cast ballots, representing 57 percent of the eligible pool. Thieu and Ky won 1.6 million votes, or almost 53 percent, while Dzu shockingly took second at 17 percent with 810,000 votes. Suu came in third with almost 11 percent, while Huong finished fourth at 10 percent. For South Vietnam, it was a monumental achievement while at war.[4]

Dzu's performance stunned everyone. The Cao Dai, for example, went heavily for him instead of Suu, perhaps because his running mate had served in the old Cao Dai militia. Dzu captured Tay Ninh, Binh Duong, and Hau Nghia provinces, all of which had Cao Dai and NLF influence. He also took Quang Ngai, supposedly a VNQDD hotbed. Suu won Thua Thien Province, along with Hue and Danang, mainly due to An Quang support. Thieu and Ky ran well in the Central Highlands, parts of the Delta, and the coastal provinces of central South Vietnam. Some accused the generals of having forced the Montagnards to vote for them by using army trucks to bus them to the polls, but that was the only means for the far-flung tribesmen to reach the voting booths. Plus, the government did not have to force the hill people to vote for Thieu and Ky. Their efforts in passing the Statut Particulier and Thieu's signing speech in a driving rainstorm in the city of Ban Me Thuot on August 29 in front of several thousand Montagnards sealed their support. Huong took Saigon but ran badly in I and II Corps. Surprisingly, he also did poorly in his native Delta, where he placed third behind Thieu and Dzu.

Numerous theorizers endeavored to divine Dzu's surprise showing. Most imprinted onto Dzu their own biases and agenda to account for his success. Many senior-level Vietnamese opined that Dzu's feat was due to money from either the nefarious French, the U.S. antiwar movement, or the favorite Vietnamese scapegoat, the CIA. When Bunker asked Thieu for his reading on Dzu's strong showing, Thieu remarked that the "principle reasons" were "the inevitable protest vote against the incumbents, the stress on peace for peace's sake, and the extensive financial support he had." Thieu alluded to "reports that Dzu's money" came from the French and U.S. sources, "specifically CIA and the 'dove' element" in America."[5] Bunker vehemently denied any CIA funding for Dzu, but many Vietnamese were unconvinced. Tran Van Don wrote in his memoirs that "the Americans enlisted...their Phoenix pacification program personnel to help get out the vote...[for] the obscure Saigon lawyer Truong Dinh Dzu," but that was totally false.[6] While the Vietnamese saw Dzu's second-place finish as the result of hidden foreign hands, the American media took the opposite tack and printed stories saying that Dzu's tally was mainly from covert Front backing. The U.S. antiwar movement then interpreted the vote for Dzu as proof of a "mandate for peace" among most South Vietnamese.

None of these speculations are correct. While both Dzu and Chieu believed they had received some small amount of NLF support, neither thought it had significantly added to their vote total. The "mandate for peace" was also an illusion. While the population was certainly war-weary, scholar Allan Goodman examined the 1967 election and concluded that "the magnitude of such a 'mandate' was limited since eighty-two percent...cast ballots for candidates who did not make peace more than a perfunctory campaign slogan and who expressed serious concern that a peace too hastily declared or one into which the Americans pressured the government would result in the takeover of the country by the Communists."[7]

Instead, Dzu's success was the result of the first employment in Vietnamese history of modern campaign tactics. An excellent orator, he was a Dale Carnegie devotee and had been voted director of the Rotary Club of Southeast Asia in 1961. He made effective use of radio and the rapidly growing reach of TV. Unlike the other candidates, he conducted numerous campaign rallies to introduce himself to rural Vietnamese. He stayed relentlessly "on message," combining his peace pleas with harsh criticisms of Thieu and Ky, which enabled him to capture the protest vote against the regime. His campaign was well financed, mostly from Chieu, his rich running mate.

More significant, Dzu claimed that he had been secretly forming a campaign organization since 1963, surely a bit of hyperbole but partially true. Like the Nguyen Khanh coup, once again the Dai Viets had slipped under everyone's radar and influenced events. Nguyen Ngoc Huy's Tan Dai Viets had deeply penetrated local administrations via the village and hamlet elections. They had decided to support Dzu, and they were the key factor in turning out the vote for him. Huy told the U.S. embassy that the "Tan Dai Viets supported Dzu in the election and probably comprised the most important element of Dzu's campaign machinery."[8] Huy states that although Suu and Huong "had contacted us for support...none discussed with us his policy and program of government in case of success. The only candidate with a precise program of government was [Dzu]."[9] The Tan Dai Viets wanted to back a southern-born civilian, but since Huong and Suu were urban French-trained elites long out of touch with both the rural and working classes, the TDV turned to Dzu out of convenience, not political harmony.

Although Huy was elated by the Tan Dai Viet's resurgence, Bunker dismissed his claims since none of Huy's people were elected to the Senate and only about a dozen to the Lower House. It was one of the few mistakes Bunker would make in analyzing the Vietnamese political scene. The 1967 election marked the return to prominence of the TDV, a program they had been working on for two years. After the two main Dai Viet factions had divorced in 1964, "the Tan Dai Viets had spread its organization [and by 1967], it was present in almost all provinces." Huy scoffed at those who claimed the NLF had voted for Dzu. When they pointed to Hau Nghia Province, an area of heavy Communist control won by Dzu, Huy skewered them by noting that Hau Nghia was "Nguyen Ton Hoan's native province, and the Tan Dan Viet controlled most of the village councils there."[10]

The Senate vote was held the same day as the presidential ballot. Much like the earlier election for the assembly, voting for the Senate was via a bloc of ten candidates, a nascent attempt to forge political parties. Only the top-six blocs would win. With forty-eight blocs competing, most people had little clue who was running. The most recognizable group was organized by former general Tran Van Don, who had joined forces with Dang Van Sung and Tran Quoc Buu's CVT labor union. Don received 980,000 votes, the most in the country. Like Dzu, Don's group was well organized, had a balanced regional and religious appeal, and campaigned throughout the country.

The Senate vote also offered a surprise. The Catholics did quite well in the Senate elections, winning four blocs, but each had some Buddhists members, giving the Catholics only thirty out of sixty senators. Catholic lay leader and attorney Nguyen Van Huyen came in second with 630,000 votes. With strong backing from his coreligionists, Huyen was elected Senate leader. Another winning Catholic bloc was led by Tran Van Lam, an easygoing southern lawyer who would eventually become Thieu's foreign minister. Former general and Diem favorite Huynh Van Cao—whose ten-man list included four Buddhists, a Cao Dai, and a Hoa Hao—came in fourth. Father Hoang Quynh's old Greater Solidarity Front, now under new leadership, placed fifth. Squeaking in last, only several hundred votes ahead of a Hoa Hao bloc, was Ha Thuc Ky's Revolutionary Dai Viets. Numerous other political luminaries had formed blocs, including one led by Tran Van Do and Tran Van Tuyen. They failed despite support from the VNQDD. Surprisingly, none of the blocs Thieu and Ky supported won.

The elections for the Lower House occurred successfully on October 22. The winning candidates were a mix of South Vietnam's social strata but leaned heavily toward urban residents. Several militant Buddhists won, as did former Kien Hoa Province chief Tran Ngoc Chau. One rising political star was Ly Qui Chung, who had worked in the old assembly. While fewer people voted than previously, an impressive number still went to the polls.

The 1967 election showed two major trends. First, the divisions long bedeviling South Vietnamese society were slowly losing their influence. None of the established regional, religious, and ethnic groups voted in unison; all split their votes among the various presidential candidates. Other than Huy's resurgent Tan Dai Viets, the old political parties were exposed for the rump organizations they were. Regionalism continued to play a significant role, but its sharp divides were slowly dissipating. Socially, the concept of top-down political control—mandarin, military, or otherwise—was roundly quashed. The candidates' often severe criticism of each other destroyed the aura of an untouchable ruling authority, consigning to the past the image of the virtuous mandarin governor. The peasants, who had formerly kept out of politics, now at least vaguely understood that the political leadership was accountable to them.

Second, the election amply displayed the inability of group identity to achieve national consensus. Factions such as the militant Buddhists or hard-line Catholics had devolved into single-issue protest cliques whose sway had diminished. Nor could candidates like Huong count on reputation alone to win a plurality. To achieve something close to a majority vote or broad national appeal, future candidates would have to transcend religious and regional labels. The key to future electoral victories would be to cobble together a winning coalition from the various interest groups. Thus, the election killed the career of long-established political figures like Phan Khac Suu. While he retained some influence with Thieu as a respected elder, he represented a dying breed, the Confucian mandarin trained to rule. The election was Suu's last hurrah. On May 24, 1970, he died from cancer. President Thieu awarded him the National Order Medal, 1st Class, South Vietnam's highest civilian honor.

Still, despite these emerging trends, South Vietnamese democratic tendencies remained embryonic. Substantial portions of the electorate were politically uninspired and maintained long-standing mistrust of authority. Worse, during the short one-month campaign period, the civilian candidates had spent most of their time carping about corruption or poor administration but had offered few practical programs on how to cure these ills. While the public debate was freer than during any other period in Vietnamese history, it did not produce a meaningful dialogue on the vital issues confronting the country. Only peace was discussed in any depth, but how exactly to induce Hanoi to talk with Saigon remained stubbornly unclear.

FINALIZING THE VOTE

Despite a prominent group of election observers as well as reporters from across the globe concluding that the election was fair and honest, the candidates immediately complained of irregularities and fraud. Among the loudest voices was Dzu. He claimed that the government had robbed him of victory in certain locales by printing ballots with his symbol but using pictures of Suu and Dan.

Dzu and the other candidates brought their charges to the Central Election Council, an independent body established by the presidential election law. The council's job was to investigate disputes and report its findings to the assembly's Special Election Committee. The council reviewed over thirty specific complaints, but they reported to the assembly committee on September 21 that it was unable to validate any grievance. The Election Committee reviewed the council's report and also examined the poll totals. Despite the council's analysis, on September 30, the Election Committee voted 16–2 to recommend that the Assembly invalidate the election.

The Special Committee's vote was not about election improprieties but was instead a power play by several assembly members. The main instigator was Hoa Hao leader Le Phuoc Sang, a close Ky supporter and a leading assembly voice.[11] Sang's Hoa Hao ticket had failed by several hundred votes to secure the last Senate bloc. Upset, Sang and several others had sought out Ky and offered to invalidate the election, thereby forcing a new vote and allowing Ky to run by himself. Ky immediately squelched that offer.[12]

Failing to convince Ky, Sang switched to Thieu. The price for Sang's acquiescence was one cabinet post and that each member of Sang's bloc receive 300,000 piasters. Thieu refused, and he and Ky set about persuading the deputies to approve the election. Ky told Bunker that "there are many ways to put pressure on, and they would use them including money, which unfortunately was an essential part."[13]

Sang's election maneuvering did not go unnoticed. On September 28, just before the committee's validation vote, Lieutenant General Khang reportedly "took Ky aside and told him privately that he did not know whether Ky had allowed the validation crisis to develop for his own political advantage, but if he had then...he would lose the support of the armed forces. Ky angrily denied having engineered the crisis for his own political advantage. Khang said he believed Ky [but] the military would not condone such activity."[14] To his credit, Ky's effort to refrain from political shenanigans maintained the election's integrity.

The full assembly debated the committee's report, and despite the pressure by Thieu and Ky, the outcome remained in doubt. Dzu's charges of election fraud had also sparked several hundred college students to demonstrate, which did little more than tie up traffic in Saigon. On September 30, however, tensions escalated after they broke into the assembly building and smashed some furniture. The police arrested forty students, investigated their backgrounds, and promptly inducted seventeen into the military for draft evasion. On October 1, Brigadier General Loan's police surrounded the assembly building to prevent another student protest from breaking into the building. Unfortunately, sealing off the building was viewed as an attempt to intimidate the assembly, especially when a pistol-packing Loan appeared in the visitor's galley, swigging beer and putting his feet up on the railing. Ky had sent Loan to sit in the assembly to ensure that Sang's faction did not act improperly, but the media, unaware of Sang's unsavory maneuvers, wrote that Loan's swaggering presence was overt intimidation by the military to force the assembly to legalize a fraudulent election. That was not the case, but Loan's thuggish reputation offered no alternative explanation. Finally, after several days of debate and backroom payoffs, the assembly voted 58 to 32 to validate the election. South Vietnam had its first democratically elected government, mainly because the two leaders had again steered the country to democracy.

After the election, the court resumed the trial against Dzu that had been postponed because of the election. The judge found Dzu guilty of illegal currency transactions by possessing an unauthorized account at the Bank of America in San Francisco and sentenced him to six to nine months in prison. Although Dzu remained out of prison by appealing his sentence, he appeared headed for jail. Many accused Thieu of persecuting the "peace candidate."

The postelection furor received another jolt when the An Quang Buddhists decided to join the fray. Thich Tri Quang, still angry over the revised UBC charter that Thieu had signed, sent almost a thousand monks and nuns in late September to Independence Palace to demand that the government rescind the new charter. When they set up a vigil in a park across the street, Thieu had the police cordon off the camp but otherwise left the Buddhists undisturbed. Thieu then sent emissaries to speak with both Tri Quang and Tam Chau and asked them to work out the issue together. Tri Quang refused and called Chau a "traitor."

Thieu smartly told the press that this was a religious question, not a political one, but he was willing to discuss it with them. He was also adroitly maneuvering behind the scenes, mainly by pressuring the assembly to approve the same An Quang candidates for the Lower House that it had earlier disapproved for the Senate race. Ignored by the public, within two weeks, the number of protestors had dwindled to less than a hundred. Thieu's restraint had squelched Tri Quang's effort to turn a small demonstration into a large, anti-government rally. Instead, he promised that if Tri Quang abandoned the protest, Thieu would reconsider the charter. On October 10, the fiery monk vacated his lonely watch and went back to the An Quang Pagoda. Shortly thereafter, Tri Chau issued a statement declaring the charter suspended until a new one could be created. Thieu had skillfully kept a volatile situation from escalating and had demonstrated that the once-mighty Thich Tri Quang was a spent force. He would never again appear on the streets.

THIEU MOVES CAUTIOUSLY

Despite the serious issues confronting the country, Thieu decided to delay announcing his programs until after the assembly had validated the election. Given the two-month delay between the election and the inauguration on October 31, the lack of new policies gave the impression that the government was adrift. Similar to the reaction to Duong Van Minh's slow start in November 1963, the Americans and many political-minded Vietnamese began carping about Thieu's sluggish pace, perceptions based on his personality and comparisons to the bombastic Ky.

Thieu was moving slowly for two main reasons. First, he remained hamstrung by the bonds imposed upon him by the Military Council. Second, he was trying to form his government. The most important choice was that of prime minister, the position responsible for handling the government's daily administrative work. Under the secret deal permitting Thieu to run for president, Ky would pick the prime minister. Ky had promised the job to Nguyen Van Loc. Loc was born on August 24, 1922, to a wealthy family in Vinh Long Province in the Delta. He served from 1945 to 1947 with the Viet Minh, where he was an editor for two newspapers. He returned to

Saigon in 1947, published several books, and then went to law school in France. After graduating in 1954, he returned to Saigon and quietly practiced law. A Cao Dai, he had few political ties other than his closeness to Ky.

While Ky wanted Loc, the decision was more complicated, reflecting the complex personal and professional issues among the leading politicians. In Saigon, personnel choices often required lengthy jostling to achieve consensus, which caused the leisurely decision-making that marked South Vietnamese politics. Although Ky had asked for Loc, after the election he took a less adversarial position and was willing to let Thieu make the decision. Yet despite Ky's newfound attitude, Thieu remained under considerable pressure to placate Ky. According to Thieu,

> Ky has indicated to him that as a matter of personal pride and prestige he would like very much to have Loc appointed as Prime Minister and indicated that if this should not work out after three to six months Thieu could of course replace him. Thieu said that the Generals also would like to have him take Ky's feeling in this matter into consideration. Thieu recognizes that Ky has been affected by being placed in position of No. 2 and giving in to him on the Loc appointment might help. Thieu said he recognizes also that it is essential that he have good relations with Ky... and this might be beneficial in this regard.[15]

Yet while Thieu thought Loc was a good man, he did not believe he was the right choice. Much of the delay in formally appointing Loc stemmed from Thieu seeking a substitute that Ky would find acceptable. Thieu had first offered the position to Tran Van Huong, hoping to bring a civilian into the government to balance the military, but Huong declined, pleading bad health. Health was a plausible excuse, but the real reason was that Huong disliked Ky and Ky's associates, particularly Loan. Ky's intemperate campaign remarks had wounded the proud old teacher, but more importantly, he thought Ky's associates were massively corrupt. After Huong refused, Thieu considered Nguyen Luu Vien, Nguyen Khanh's uncle and a respected southerner, and Tran Van Do. Neither was acceptable to Ky. He was still angry over Nguyen Luu Vien's flip-flopping during the October 1966 cabinet crisis, while the new vice president was upset that Do had supported Thieu over Ky. Stymied, on September 30, Thieu informed Bunker that he had chosen Loc.

Reports that Thieu had chosen Loc set off backbiting among Thieu's entourage. The sudden rancor forced Thieu to reevaluate his choice, leading to further delay. Unfortunately, the longer Thieu took to choose a prime minister, the longer it would take that man to confirm a cabinet, which in turn hampered the formulation of new government programs. Moreover, Thieu wanted to break with the recent past and appoint cabinet members "on the basis of honesty and ability rather than for political or religious affiliation." Thieu and Ky believed that appointing ministers to achieve regional, religious, and party balance had failed because the appointees had worked "for the interests of their organization rather than the country as a whole." But finding men willing to work "for the good of the country first" was proving time consuming.[16]

By mid-October, Thieu's older brother Nguyen Van Kieu, who acted as Thieu's personal liaison to a host of South Vietnamese interest groups, noted that picking the prime minister was still giving the new president "quite a headache." Since word had leaked that Loc was the front-runner, "all sorts of people had been advising Thieu not to appoint Loc, mostly due to a widely held belief that Loc's wife [was corrupt.]" Her illicit activities had drawn warnings from Tran Van Huong and "even from Tri Quang, [and] Thieu is holding up the appointment of Loc."[17] Despite the blowback, in late October, Thieu finally tapped Loc as prime minister.

The imbroglio over Loc and Thieu's decision to delay starting any programs until after the assembly had validated the election greatly annoyed the action-oriented Ky. Shortly after the election, Ky complained to Bunker that Thieu was moving too slowly. When the ambassador asked him about his future role in the government, Ky said he had not talked to Thieu and that Thieu "must decide these matters" but that "the first six months are decisive and if progress is not achieved, then there will be in trouble . . . Ky complained that he had been unable to get Thieu to act on critical matters . . . Ky said some leaders are discouraged and he mentioned General Thang [who] felt he was getting no support from Thieu. Ky said he had spent . . . most of yesterday trying to persuade Thang not to leave the government."[18]

A month later, Ky's annoyance had grown. On October 19, Ky "showed considerable emotion [over] Thieu's failures to make decisions and start acting." Ky wanted to immediately launch innovative programs since "the people hunger for signs of something different and better to give them hope for the future." Ky also attempted to allay Thieu's suspicions of him by telling him that he "did not necessarily want his 'own man' as Prime

Minister but did want [one] who would be able to carry out the new program vigorously."[19]

As elected president, Thieu faced a challenging new world. No longer wielding absolute power, he was learning how to exercise significantly reduced authority within the framework of a binding constitution, a structure that forced him, like all democratic leaders, to negotiate and compromise. He would face a recalcitrant congress and soon a Supreme Court legally armed to constrain his actions. This restraint on his power was new for him and for South Vietnam. Moreover, he confronted severe political headwinds. The simmering rivalry between Ky and him was handcuffing government progress, while the corps commanders and the Military Council remained unwilling to yield their prerogatives. The Americans were pressuring Thieu on numerous fronts, from broadening the government to speeding up pacification and reforming the military. To survive, he had to find a way to make it all work, a tall order for any leader. Still, Ky was right that the clock was ticking. The test of South Vietnam's fledgling democracy was about to begin.

THE RISE OF THE SECOND REPUBLIC

The Second Republic was officially born on October 31, 1967. After the inauguration, in front of dignitaries from a dozen countries and the unblinking stare of television cameras, Thieu spoke of his plans and hopes for the nation. He offered North Vietnam direct peace talks, and he thanked the allied nations for assisting his war-torn country. Then he frankly told the people that to win the war, they would have to practice austerity and carry a heavier load. He requested their help in building the country, and he assured them that he would "safeguard the fatherland, respect the Constitution, serve the interests of the nation and the people [and] do my utmost to fulfill the responsibilities" of president. Hearkening back to the 1963 coup, he acknowledged that since the Diem "revolution...the country has experienced many difficulties," but he promised that he would build democracy, restore peace, and improve society. Concluding, he pledged to devote himself to the country he loved: "From the moment I take the oath of office, I belong to you."[20]

Loc's cabinet only had three military officers, the lowest number since Diem. The U.S. embassy wanted more opposition leaders to broaden the government's base, but despite a vigorous outreach by Thieu, they all declined. Several current ministers remained, including Foreign Minister Tran Van Do. Despite Thieu's dislike of Loan, he retained him as director general of police to appease Ky. On November 17, Loc announced the government's programs. His speech attacked a wide range of social and government ills, but he offered few specifics on how to solve the myriad of issues confronting the country. While Loc's speech said all the right things, skeptical Vietnamese and foreign audiences would judge Saigon on concrete action rather lofty words.

The U.S. political system expects a new president's first hundred days in office to be a period of launching new policies, an exciting change from the old order. Many expected Thieu to emulate that, but his languorous pace continued due to a stifling combination of Loc's inexperience, the new assembly, and displeasure within the Military Council. Loc was completely unfamiliar with such a major governmental role, and the green new prime minister was groping his way forward. The legislature also had to start from scratch. It had to choose leaders, write governing rules, and establish various committees while sounding out each other to form pro-government or anti-Thieu political blocs. This process would take several months and left no time for legislative action on important items like the budget for 1968.

The generals were also giving Thieu pause. Although they had removed themselves from the country's day-to-day administration, the Military Council remained focused on reviewing and approving Thieu's main policies. For example, the council and Thieu had differing views on peace negotiations. Thieu's public offering for peace talks with Ho Chi Minh, along with Dzu's stunning "peace" vote, had unsettled the hardliners. Their opinion remained unchanged: if Hanoi wanted peace, any Communist could go north, leaving South Vietnam to the Nationalists. Infighting had also developed among the senior generals. Despite Ky's efforts to convince RD Minister Thang to remain, Thang wanted out. Resentment between Thang and Thieu still burned, and when he demanded the president fire Vinh Loc and Nguyen Van Manh for corruption and inferior performance, Thieu refused. Both corps commanders had backed Thieu in late June, and he was not going to eliminate the few supporters he had on the Military Council. Consequently, on October 2, Thang was reassigned to head up the RF/PF. A suggested RVNAF reorganization had also unsettled the council. Thieu wanted the prime minister to appoint province chiefs rather than the corps commanders. They fought against the shift since it directly menaced their power base. While no one threatened a coup, the military's discontent forced Thieu to tread delicately.

The Americans were also pressing Thieu to act. Bunker flooded him with various proposals for how to fix his country's problems. Aware of the enormous pressure on President Johnson, Bunker pleaded with Thieu to move quickly, trying to sway him by telling him that he "sensed an air of expectancy among the people." Bunker cited a recent statement by Phan Quang Dan that "this is a time for bold leadership" and that "few genuine Nationalists would oppose him." Thieu replied that he planned to outline his government's actions in a speech to the congress in early January.[21] Rightly or wrongly, Thieu was also trying to find his way in a new world, and his cautious, by-the-book nature prevented him from charging out of the proverbial gate.

The GVN's pacification efforts were a prime example. Before he left the RD Ministry, Thang wrote the 1968 pacification plan and backdated it to September 1 so the new congress could not modify it. While admitting that RD had again made a sluggish start, he still hoped to complete all of his 1967 goals. The combined hamlet-RD council concept had made "some relatively solid progress," but many weaknesses remained. Some local officials were still using the RD teams improperly, ARVN units had not always provided adequate security, and corruption continued to be a "plague." The plan for 1968 was not much different than the plan for 1967: improve the secure hamlets while slowly spreading GVN control to the insecure ones.[22] While the RD teams were improving, many were weak and unmotivated, mainly due to the arduous work and casualties they had sustained. In 1967, 720 members had been killed and another 1,312 were wounded.[23]

While Rome was not burning as Thieu fiddled, Johnson, buffeted by massive antiwar protests highlighted by a one-hundred-thousand-strong march on the Pentagon on October 21, 1967, needed action. One of Johnson's key advisors described the U.S. conundrum this way: "Can the tortoise of progress in Vietnam stay ahead of the hare of dissent at home?"[24] By mid-January 1968, pacification czar Robert Komer stated that the GVN was "simply not functioning at this time. The various ministries have [not] launched the new programs mentioned by Thieu in his inaugural address."[25] Further enflaming Komer, Thieu had now decided to wait until after the Tet holidays when Vietnamese culture permitted a fresh start to the new year. But under increasing American pressure, Thieu finally explained to a senior U.S. military officer the chief reasons for his slow pace. He outlined his conflicts with three major power groups: the assembly, the senior generals, and the Americans. The most dangerous were the generals. Fearing their backlash, "his approach apparently is to move…very slowly and thus gradually to diminish the powers of his military constituency…This all adds up to an absence of forward motion [and] Komer considers this to be intolerable, given the weight of U.S. investment in blood, dollars, and effort."[26]

With Bunker still pressing the new president to move with alacrity to solve his nation's many issues, an exasperated Thieu finally explained his viewpoint to the U.S. ambassador. "The Americans," he said, "had to understand that his administration was based upon the rule of law." Before he could just sign a decree, but now the National Assembly must be consulted. "The days of the 'rule of the warlords' has now passed. He realizes, that as his country's first president, he has the grave and time-consuming responsibility of establishing the 'rule of law.' He feels that it is not unreasonable that the government take a little time to organize itself, establish relationships, and develop a program." Bunker noted that Thieu "clearly understands, but does not completely accept, the current American desire for an increase in the pace of reforms."[27]

Having grasped the internal challenges that constrained Thieu, Bunker outlined to Johnson the new president's don't-rock-the-boat approach to his first months in office. Thieu, Bunker wrote, "could not move too fast without evoking a strong and perhaps unmanageable reaction from the military." He explained that Thieu had chosen Loc to "cement his relations with Ky" and had "retained in office" men he wanted to replace, such as Loan. Bunker appreciated that Thieu's go-slow methodology was the only way to break the "old system of power relationships among generals" and replace it with a constitutional government.[28]

Thieu was right about working in a new political environment. On October 24, when he signed a partial mobilization decree to expand the RVNAF that Bunker had pressed him to sign, the new legislature immediately condemned it as "unconstitutional" since it was approved before the members were sworn in and could review it. The unpopular decree extended service time for the military and lowered the draft age from twenty to eighteen. The Lower House summoned newly assigned Defense Minister Lieutenant General Nguyen Van Vy, the officer whom Tran Van Don had brought back from exile in late 1963 and a close Ky confidant, to discuss the new law. Vy appeared on December 18, marking the first time a government official had appeared for questioning to an elected Vietnamese legislature. Despite Vy's explanations, the Lower House, sensitive to constituent pressure, banned the decree until it could amend the law.

Economically, Nguyen Huu Hanh had been relatively successful in managing the markets, but as predicted, inflation in 1967 had proven intractable. Food prices had jumped another 30 percent. Fortunately, unemployment remained low, and higher prices for rice helped rural residents begin to see real income gains. For example, small water pumps to irrigate rice fields were now appearing among even poor farmers in the Delta, while one hundred imported Japanese tractors to till the paddies sold out almost immediately. The U.S. and Vietnamese navies had begun to clear the Delta's waterways of interdiction, but road travel on Route 4, the main artery from the Delta to Saigon, remained risky. While military campaigns had eliminated Communist roadblocks, trucks carrying rice and other foodstuffs to the capital were still subjected to mines and sniper attacks.

The program to increase imports had succeeded in soaking up the excess money supply, but this lever alone could not tame inflation. Worse, by the end of 1967, "the South Vietnamese economy had become more and more dependent on foreign aid." Exports had fallen, and "the value of imports had climbed to the highest value since 1955." The 1966 economic stabilization program had helped to control inflation, but conversely "could not effectively increase production."[29] These trends were unsustainable. The GVN was printing money to cover the budget gap, which in turn acerbated inflation. Washington repeatedly pushed the GVN to raise taxes, but Thieu shied away from what would surely be another massively unpopular act like the devaluation of 1966. Bunker recommended a pay increase for civil servants to help curb corruption and to raise taxes on petroleum products to shrink the growing budget deficit. Thieu declined, stating it would be difficult for him to develop popular support if he hiked government pay while currently demanding austerity from civilians.

Socially, perhaps due to the election providing a new sense of statehood, the Vietnamese press and others began voicing anti-American sentiments. The lifting of censorship allowed editorials to blast the Americans for a wide variety of social ills, such as rampant prostitution. Another claimed that Washington only wanted pliable "puppets so as to interfere more easily into Vietnamese national affairs."[30] The articles, although reflecting Vietnamese displeasure at a perceived U.S. dominance, were less anti-Americanism than a muscular reaffirmation of Vietnamese prerogative and identity. While the newfound sense of nationhood was partially responsible, U.S. media articles castigating the South Vietnamese military had lit the bonfire. On September 11, 1967, journalist Peter Arnett published a lengthy article describing the Vietnamese army as "shot through with inefficiency [which] often lacks the will for combat and is increasing prone to let the Americans do the fighting."[31] Arnett's blistering critique, supported by statistics and in-depth reporting, exposed ARVN's numerous flaws. While he cited Westmoreland's judgment that the ARVN were much better than a year ago, his article claimed that the U.S. soldier was carrying the brunt of the combat even though that was the intent in switching the bulk of the ARVN to pacification. Nor did Arnett grasp that the Communists' objective was to avoid combat with the ARVN and instead to "inflict as many casualties on U.S. troops as possible," hoping to wear down America and force peace "on terms foreseen as advantageous to the Communist side."[32]

A month later, *Newsweek* reporter Merton Perry published an even more inflammatory piece, this one entitled "Their Lions, Our Rabbits." Calling the ARVN cowards elicited a predictable response.[33] After South Vietnamese newspapers printed excerpts, the magazine was banned from sale in Saigon, the GVN threatened to expel the writer, and numerous angry editorials appeared. Yet instead of addressing both article's charges, the Vietnamese editors accused the U.S. of seeking to control South Vietnam's internal affairs and of moving forward on peace negotiations without consulting Saigon. They insisted that the constant peace offers were prolonging the war by encouraging Hanoi to hang on. The Vietnamese press also reprinted American articles on the widespread antiwar demonstrations that showed pro-Communist sympathizers waving NLF flags, further enflaming Nationalist fears of an American sellout.

While it was always easy to find flaws in the RVNAF, few American reporters traveled with South Vietnamese units or spoke the language. They relied mainly on American sources, who were understandably frustrated by perceptions of Vietnamese passivity, corruption, and refusal to hunt the enemy. Westmoreland, though, was outraged at what he considered biased reporting. On January 31, 1968, he published a report outlining numerous instances where the ARVN had recently either defeated a superior attacking force or had launched an aggressive campaign that had badly bloodied the enemy. He noted that in 1968, the "steady growth and modernization of RVNAF will enable all units to intensify the tempo of offensive operations."[34] Oddly, both sides were right; the RVNAF had come far since the dark days of 1965, but it still had a long way to go. The Tet Offensive, however, would prove the detractors wrong.

As South Vietnam began its traditional Tet holiday at the end of January 1968, the country was stronger than at any point in its history. Most senior Vietnamese officials were confident that they were winning the war, but they also believed this would be a crucial year. The country remained under considerable military, economic, and political stress. Tough decisions were needed on a wide range of issues, from removing the senior generals' interference in governmental affairs and improving pacification to fixing the economy. Although they were under no illusions that the Politburo would respond positively to peace offers, the South Vietnamese hoped the improved allied military posture might finally convince Hanoi to talk peace.

The Communist answer came early on the morning of January 31, 1968. While South Vietnam was sleeping off the first day of the sacred Tet holiday, Communist units launched the largest offensive of the war by attacking virtually every city in the country. Peace seemed further away than ever before.

13

"THIS IS OUR COUNTRY"

Defeating the Tet Offensive

A lthough the allies thought they were winning the war, the Politburo judged it a stalemate. To break the impasse, Communist party boss Le Duan in Hanoi decided to launch a massive surprise attack against South Vietnam's cities during the sacrosanct Tet festival. He believed it would spark a mass uprising like the Buddhist revolt in 1966. Backed by Communist units, it would overthrow the government and eradicate the GVN institutional fabric. Le Duan's gambit failed because the South Vietnamese people, despite having only the framework of a popularly elected government, fought for the survival of their embryonic state. Still, Hanoi's countrywide offensive delivered a strategic shock that radically altered the course of the war, inadvertently started peace talks, and reordered both the U.S. and GVN political landscapes.

Oddly, while the Tet Offensive destroyed President Johnson's desire to prosecute the war, it had the opposite effect on South Vietnam. After the allies had repulsed the attacks, and despite having no tradition or faith in democracy, a confidence arose among the South Vietnamese people. This newfound poise enabled Thieu and Ky to take bold new steps to strengthen and expand the state, one that had been painfully evolving since their ascendance in June 1965.

GOALS AND PLANS OF THE OFFENSIVE

Tet is far and away the most important Vietnamese holiday of the year. Commemorating the first day of spring and the Lunar New Year, which comes in late January or early February, it has no equivalent in the West. Of Chinese origin, it combines the ideals of Christmas, Thanksgiving, and New Year's Eve into one three-day festival. Prior to the holiday, shops bustle as people purchase gifts, food, and new clothing for numerous gatherings spent rejoicing with family, visiting friends, and attending temple. Spiritually, families pay homage to their ancestors, the emotional bedrock of Vietnamese religious beliefs. Tet is also seen as a fresh start, a purging of the previous year. Debts are settled, wrongs are forgiven, and houses are rigorously cleaned. Superstition underscores this tradition. Families seek to attract good fortune for the upcoming year while using dragon dances and banging gongs to ward off evil spirits.

Each year the two warring parties had declared a multiday ceasefire, but this time, Thieu had limited it to thirty-six hours after intelligence indicated the Communists might launch assaults. On January 29, fearing heavy Communists attacks in I Corps, he canceled the ceasefire for that military region. Still, roughly half of the RVNAF was on leave when the Communists struck early morning on January 31.

The driving force behind the Tet Offensive was Le Duan. Seeking to break the current bloody military deadlock and achieve a decisive victory, he pushed for a momentous shift in strategy: a sudden blow against the South Vietnamese cities and specific GVN centers of authority.[1] After sustaining heavy casualties in 1967, why risk assaulting the allies' strongest defenses? Postwar Communist histories concede that its forces could not defeat U.S. units. The Americans were simply too strong. Stymied, Le Duan sought a novel approach in 1968. Previously, all combat had occurred in the countryside, but under his prodding, the PAVN High Command now shifted "the direction of our primary strategic attack from the mountain and jungles and the rural areas to the cities, and especially toward Saigon, Hue, and Danang."[2] Le Duan believed that only by striking the enemy's lair could he secure a decisive victory. After reviewing South Vietnam's recent social, religious, and political spasms, he concluded that seizing the cities would allow the "oppressed masses" to revolt against government authority. This combination of a military occupation of the cities and South Vietnamese uprisings would overthrow the GVN and form a coalition government with the NLF. The new regime would then demand the U.S. withdraw. Once the Americans were gone, the new regime would unite under Hanoi's banner.

The Politburo had begun discussing a major incursion against the cities as early as April 1967. In July, they met to debate Le Duan's proposal for an all-out military-political offensive against the cities. However, the Politburo reserved judgment after both Ho Chi Minh and Vo Nguyen Giap seriously disagreed with the strategy, believing that it was suicidal to directly confront American firepower. Le Duan, though, eventually convinced the rest of the members to accept the concept. Subsequently, Ho and Giap left the country for medical reasons, and in mid-January 1968, the Central Committee approved the top-secret plan, known as Resolution 14. The attack would commence between the first and second days of Tet. Diplomatically, Hanoi would dangle peace talks to disguise their war preparations.

OVERVIEW OF THE RESULTS

Numerous volumes have described the heavy fighting that raged throughout the country, so it is unnecessary to recount it here.[3] It was the scale of the offensive that surprised the allies, and the Communists' ability to both hide and coordinate a massive assault was a major intelligence embarrassment. Almost every provincial capital was hit, along with about one quarter of the district capitals.

The attacks against Saigon began shortly before 3:00 a.m., January 31. Strict security precautions, however, hampered the assault units. Fearing leaks, the Communists kept the plan secret from local unit commanders until two days before the offensive was scheduled to begin, leaving them little time to prepare. For example, a local force battalion was ordered to destroy the South Vietnamese military command. According to General Cao Van Vien, the enemy penetrated the Joint General Staff compound but "mistakenly occupied the nearby General Headquarters Company building, mis-reading it for the Joint General Staff headquarters." Vien was extremely fortunate. At that point, as he explained, "there was nothing between them and me."[4] Since the Communist unit had orders to "hold at all costs the RVNAF Headquarters," it awaited reinforcement instead of expanding its perimeter.[5] Vien quickly ordered a nearby Airborne company to defend his position, and the enemy troops were driven off. The Communists had come exceedingly close to capturing the RVNAF's military commander, but the cost was extremely high. According to a

PAVN history, when the battalion that "stormed the JGS arrived back at its base it had only twenty-eight men left."[6]

Fortunately, the allies had indications that a major strike was planned for Tet and had made some preparations. As mentioned, Thieu had cancelled the ceasefire for I Corps while General Vien was at the JGS all night monitoring the countrywide situation. In Saigon, Police Chief Loan believed that the Front intended to attack the city, so he cancelled Tet leave for his men and remained at his headquarters. Similarly, General Westmoreland, on the advice of his field commanders, had pulled some American combat units closer to the capital. Their precautions probably saved Saigon.

Over the next several days, except in the former imperial city of Hue and parts of Saigon, the Communist troops that had conducted the initial assaults were decimated and driven out of the cities. NLF units in the first wave in III and IV Corps were local force battalions comprised mainly of southerners rather than main force regulars from North Vietnam. These local force units had taken heavy losses in 1967, but their ranks had recently been replenished with either North Vietnamese or part-time local guerrillas. Exposed and operating on unfamiliar city streets, they were cut to pieces by allied firepower. The total number of Communist troops in South Vietnam at the start of the offensive and the extent of enemy losses, however, has remained speculative. At that time, an analytical wrangle known as the Order of Battle controversy was raging between MACV and the CIA. The debate centered on both the complete number of enemy combatants and precisely who should be counted and in what category. MACV wanted to use stricter accounting procedures to drive the number lower. A higher number, or a figure that remained relatively static despite the U.S. claims of enemy casualties, would heighten the impression that the allied military strategy was failing. The CIA, however, argued that all personnel should be counted, even part-timers, which dramatically increased the overall figure and led to the disagreement.

Colonel Hoang Ngoc Lung, the J-2 (Intelligence) of the JGS, provided the RVNAF estimate. "At the end of 1967," he wrote, "total enemy strength in South Vietnam had reached approximately 323,000...[O]f this total, 130,000 were combat troops; [political cadres] and guerrillas accounted for [another] 160,000." The remaining were administrative or logistical.[7] MACV, on the other hand, listed enemy strength at 115,000 combat troops on the eve of the offensive, a number the CIA strongly disagreed with. A CIA review posited that "the actual number probably exceeded 160,000 by a substantial number."[8]

Allied estimates of enemy strength were wildly off. The official *History of the People's Army* states that at the beginning of 1968 they had 278,000 main and local force troops in South Vietnam.[9] Another official PAVN history agrees. Citing an internal report, the publication provides a breakdown: "220,000 main force troops and 57,000 local-force troops (not counting militia, guerrillas, or self-defense personnel.)"[10] Whether this solely meant combat soldiers, or included rear service units, is uncertain, as is the number involved in the offensive. U.S. intelligence estimated that 85,000 enemy soldiers participated in the attacks, but that is pure guesswork since no specific definitions were established on precisely whom to count.[11]

Allied claims of enemy losses from the offensive are also apparently erroneous. Colonel Lung asserts that the Communists lost 87,534 dead and 27,178 rallied to the South Vietnamese side in 1968 but does not venture how many were killed during the initial Tet attacks. U.S. commanders alleged around 40,000 enemy were killed during the offensive, the main reason MACV declared such a tremendous victory. However, an internal report from the PAVN's Combat Operations Department states that "our losses during the first wave [from January 30 to April 30] were 12,818 killed and 22,316 wounded."[12] A second document from the Ministry of Defense dated February 14, 1969, lists a total of 113,295 dead, wounded, and missing in 1968, not counting another 10,899 deserters. Of those, 44,824 were killed in action, and another 61,267 were wounded. According to this tally, 34 percent of those casualties, or 15,240 dead and 20,831 wounded, occurred during the first Tet attack.[13] There is no explanation for the discrepancy between the two documents, but the total casualty counts for both are close. Assuming PAVN accounting procedures are reasonably accurate, North Vietnam suffered over 35,000 casualties in those three months.

Hanoi, though, quickly made up these losses. It sent 141,000 men to the southern battlefields in 1968. Herein lies the war's quandary: if Hanoi could infiltrate more men in 1968 than the allies could eliminate from the field of battle, the war would remain stalemated. Even the strongest GVN could not survive with several hundred thousand North Vietnamese troops stationed on its soil, able to mass and strike at will. It was the fundamental reason why Saigon wanted the troops gone and why Hanoi refused to remove them.

The most significant Tet battle was the Communist occupation of Hue. Fighting against PAVN regulars, U.S. Marines and ARVN soldiers fought for nearly a month to recapture the city. The key element in holding a portion of Hue during the first days was the inspired leadership of Brigadier General Ngo Quang Truong, who had led the Airborne units in putting down the 1966 Buddhist crisis. Afterward, he was promoted and given command of the demoralized 1st ARVN Division, which he rebuilt into arguably the best regular division in the army.

Like Vien, Truong also decided to stay at his division headquarters on the first night. The only troops he had in Hue were his headquarters staff and the division Reconnaissance company, the famed Hac Bao, one of the elite ARVN units. When his division headquarters was attacked by a PAVN battalion, he formed an ad hoc defense comprised of clerks and guards. At one point, Truong's men were engaged in hand-to-hand combat sixty feet from his position. His soldiers stood their ground until part of the Hac Bao arrived to defend the headquarters.[14]

Numerous underground Communists agents and sympathizers, many of them students who had taken part in the 1966 Buddhist uprising, emerged from hiding and took control of the city. They immediately began a relentless purge of GVN civil servants, soldiers, and those deemed anti-communist. When allied forces retook Hue, they discovered that thousands of locals had been shot, clubbed to death, or buried alive. The senseless butchering of so-called "class enemies" became known as the Hue Massacre. The carnage stiffened South Vietnamese morale as much as the Communist violation of the sacred Tet holiday. The continued unearthing of mass graves into the fall of 1969, including the discovery of five hundred people who had been forced marched out of town and then slaughtered with automatic weapons along a creek, their bodies left there to rot, enraged the South Vietnamese.

The number of people executed in Hue remains the subject of considerable debate. Akin to Holocaust deniers, several antiwar authors claimed the deaths were the result of U.S. bombing. Most U.S. authors cite the number of dead at 2,800, a figure that was initially published but probably not updated as other mass graves were later uncovered. One important source that few have consulted is the South Vietnamese police officer who served as the Thua Thien Province (where Hue is located) Special Branch (intelligence) chief during the offensive. He led the postattack investigation and claims that the number killed was far higher. He states that

5,327 were murdered by the Viet Cong in their homes, on the streets, and many bodies of victims were later found in mass graves in the districts surrounding Hue. The number of people who disappeared permanently, without a trace, was 1,200...After Tet, in response to my instructions the district and village police offices worked closely with the district and village governments to help the people and the relatives of victims look for information and people that the Viet Cong had arrested and taken away. Each time a mass grave was found, whether it was a large one or a small one, all the details were recorded and then sent to the Province Police Operations Center. There we formed a sub-section to monitor and update all of this information every day to report it to the Regional Headquarters and the National Headquarters in Saigon.[15]

Meanwhile in Saigon, Police Chief Loan, the profanity-spewing, beer-guzzling poster boy for GVN repression, played the key role in defeating the first wave of Communist commandos who attacked installations in the city. Loan was many things, but no one ever questioned his guts, and he courageously led his men into every battle. Unfortunately, his bravery was ignored after photojournalist Eddie Adams captured him shooting a Communist prisoner in the head. The shocking image instantly became one of the most iconic photographs of the war and sparked global outrage. Although in later years Adams defended Loan, the picture appeared on the front page of virtually every U.S newspaper and helped turn American public opinion against the war. While undeniably a war crime, the South Vietnamese claim the man Loan killed—Nguyen Van Lem, aka Bay Lop—had been captured soon after he had murdered one of Loan's police commanders, his wife, and their four children.[16] In their view, Loan was meting out street justice to a terrorist. Loan told Thieu he had shot Lem in the "heat of anger, knowing all the deaths that [Lem] and his forces had caused in Saigon"[17] To this day, many South Vietnamese passionately defend Loan's conduct as moral symmetry and express anger at the worldwide damage to Saigon's reputation from the picture, particularly when compared to the thousands killed in Hue by Communist forces.

Despite its journalistic critics, the RVNAF and police stood and fought, taking twice as many casualties as U.S. forces. One leading U.S. historian of the Tet Offensive confirms that "notwithstanding the fact that most units had been seriously understrength due to the Tet holiday, South Vietnam's armed forces had performed remarkably well."[18] ARVN troops displayed an offensive spirit few thought they possessed by quickly retaking locations the Communists had captured, and they did so while being badly outgunned.

Communist soldiers had recently been equipped with Russian-designed RPD machine guns and B-40 rocket launchers alongside the well-known AK-47 rifle. Most South Vietnamese units were still using World War II–era M-1s and BAR automatic rifles, although some elite troops had lately been armed with the M16. While allied firepower dominated the battlefield, at the grunt level, Communist troops possessed a distinct advantage over South Vietnamese soldiers.[19] Tet forced the U.S. to modernize the RVNAF. To counter the disparity in weapons, by the end of May 1968, nearly 130,000 M16s were provided to the ARVN and police, with more to follow. The ARVN divisional structure was revamped to add mobility and more artillery. Equally important, personnel benefits such as dependent housing and commissaries were also improved.

However, like all armies, ARVN performance was uneven. Many units behaved passively or were overly reliant on firepower to kill the enemy, destroying countless homes and buildings through excessive shelling. Night operations remained desultory as South Vietnamese forces often retreated into defensive positions at dusk. Worse, ARVN's perennial weakness—poor soldier discipline—sparked considerable civilian backlash when troops openly looted abandoned homes in several cities. Vien responded by issuing a directive that RVNAF personnel caught looting would be court-martialed, and if warranted, executed.

The real disaster for South Vietnam was the terrible economic toll. Business confidence nosedived amid fears of further attacks, and imports, the driving force of GVN tax revenues, took a major hit. Communist units returned to interdict crucial Route 4 from the Delta, the area which produced two-thirds of South Vietnam's rice crop. Mined roads and destroyed bridges increased transportation costs and reduced deliveries to Saigon, causing food prices to skyrocket and puncturing the recent improvement in rural income. To alleviate the rice shortage, on March 11, the U.S. pledged to provide one hundred thousand tons of rice under the PL 480 program. To help its urban citizens and feed the army, the GVN sold this imported rice at a lower price than locally grown rice. This food subsidy helped urban consumers but hurt local farmer income.

Inflation soon added to the economic distress. Given the enormous GVN expenditures for reconstruction and other expenses, the budget deficit exploded. Slumping tax revenue forced the National Bank to print more money to cover the increased outlays, and as a result, Thieu was faced with two unpalatable choices: cut spending or raise taxes. By late March, he finally approved a tax increase on gasoline, which raised much needed revenue. But even with the rice subsidy, the cost-of-living index for urbanites continued its relentless climb. Although the military situation, and shortly peace negotiations, remained the country's principal concerns, the battered economy now directly threatened his popularity.

Caring for thousands of newly displaced refugees also strained GVN coffers. At the end of 1967, Saigon still had 810,000 refugees on its rolls. While national refugee coordination had greatly improved, province- and district-level efforts remained rife with corruption and inefficiency. Senator Edward Kennedy held hearings in 1967 that highlighted these shortcomings, and in early January 1968, he visited South Vietnam to inspect the refugee camps. After touring several locations, he met with Refugee Minister Nguyen Phuc Que. Kennedy acknowledged that GVN efforts were substantially better than he thought, but upon returning to the U.S. in late January, the senator reversed himself. Shocking Saigon, he gave a blistering speech about refugee conditions and the GVN's performance. Despite Kennedy's denouncement, when the offensive suddenly created over a half million more displaced people, the CORDS organization noted that Que's ministry "responded within hours of the initial attack to provide shelter and commodity support...including milk and vitamins, clothing, and blankets."[20]

The refugee count in Saigon alone was 172,000 people out of a population of several million. In the capital, the GVN quickly turned dozens of recently built schools into temporary centers, which halted primary education in the city for months. Government officials had little choice; property destruction was sizable. Allied firepower used to blast enemy troops had wrecked an estimated seventy-two thousand homes across the country. Although Cholon, the Chinese section of Saigon, suffered heavy damage, other cities fared much worse. One third of My Tho was ruined and Hue was devastated.

Although the countryside remained relatively untouched by the fighting, some ARVN battalions and RF/PF units were sent to defend the cities and district towns, leaving stretches of rural areas defenseless. Bunker and Komer pressed Thieu to immediately restore a military presence in the villages. Thieu agreed with the need to quickly reestablish GVN control in the countryside, but the JGS was convinced that the Communists were planning another attack on Saigon. Colonel Lung wrote that the enemy would "to try to surround and isolate the capital and that the enemy will make maximum use of his ability to shell us during the coming period."[21]

Thieu was disinclined to send ARVN battalions back into the country at the expense of defending Saigon, and his reluctance remained a contentious issue between him and the Americans.

Socially, the population had been stunned and frightened by the sudden offensive, but they quickly rallied. Military enlistments in February tripled over the previous February. Civic groups helped clear rubble, and for the most part, the population's confidence in themselves and their government grew after having withstood the Communists' best shot. Equally important, the Communist claim to the people's allegiance had been proven dramatically false. South Vietnamese civilians had refused Communist calls for an uprising and had often helped government forces by pointing out enemy hiding spots. The major question, though, was whether this civilian reaction was simply self-preservation, anger at Communist treachery for violating the Tet holiday, or whether the population had truly sided with Saigon? The answer undoubtedly included all three elements, but beneath the U.S. complaints about slow progress, corruption, and incompetence, two and a half years of pacification efforts and popular suffrage had quietly laid a political foundation.

For the moment, Saigon's leaders felt vindicated. Ky claimed the "Tet Offensive was my country's biggest victory, both militarily and politically."[22] More realistically, Phan Quang Dan said that "South Vietnam, with all of its weaknesses, is emerging from the [offensive] as a viable state with basically a loyal army, police, and population firmly committed to freedom."[23] Beneath these congratulatory judgments, however, raged the same theoretical conflict at the heart of South Vietnam's governing philosophy. Ky and senior leaders like Lieutenant General Khang remained convinced that only a strong, decisive leader unencumbered by an independent legislative branch could ensure the country's survival. Khang told a U.S. officer that "Vietnam could not afford democratic institutions at this time, and [America] had made a major mistake in forcing these on Vietnam ... [W]hat was needed now was strong leadership, which only the military could provide, discipline, and a benevolent authoritarian regime."[24]

Thieu on the hand, while aware of the need for resolute leadership, believed that it was vital for the country to move beyond the days of the strongman. He insisted on continuing the democratic tradition, no matter how messy or inefficient it might prove. While part of Thieu's vision was a sop to American sensitivities, he now believed that South Vietnam's ultimate victory over Communism depended upon upholding the constitution.

Future events would modify his views, but for now, the offensive had set in motion events that would enable Thieu to win the doctrinal battle inside South Vietnam.

As for Le Duan, like in 1965, he had gone for the kill again and failed. Not surprisingly, while his disastrous miscalculation of the mood and political disposition of the South Vietnamese people had resulted in a military debacle, a postwar Communist review of the Tet attacks shifted the blame from him to faulty reporting from subordinates. Apparently, Washington was not the only capital dealing with false reports. The offensive had flopped because

> the Central Committee's assessment underestimated the capabilities of the [South Vietnamese] army and government...The reason we did not assess the situation correctly was due, in part, to the fact that higher authorities were subjective in their analysis of both the enemy's situation and our own situation, and...to the fact that the reports...lower echelons sent up to their superiors were incomplete and inaccurate...The realities reveal that reports from lower levels...usually exaggerated accomplishments and did not report errors and shortcomings. These reports had a considerable impact. They caused higher level authorities to make incorrect and erroneous assessments of the situation, which in turn led these authorities to make policy decisions that were not in line with the situation.[25]

The Politburo designed the Tet Offensive to annihilate the GVN, but it had the unexpected consequence of instead destroying the U.S. government's will to "stay the course." After nearly three years of intense U.S. combat operations, the sudden and massive scale of the offensive shattered the administration's confidence and emboldened the antiwar protestors. Pessimism now permeated the highest echelons of the executive branch. Having previously touted that it was winning the war, and after spending billions of dollars, sustaining thousands of casualties, and under enormous domestic stress, the Johnson administration needed a public relations victory to push back against the raucous antiwar chorus. They wanted Thieu to provide them one. Senior American officials, especially Bunker, emphasized that to maintain the faith of the American people, Thieu needed to swiftly overcome GVN lassitude and show rapid recovery from the offensive. Thieu, though, continued to move gingerly, a combination of his ever-cautious personality and profound insight of sensitive internal Vietnamese political conditions. Nevertheless, while Bunker pressed the Vietnamese president to galvanize his country, the ambassador strove to present a balanced picture to Washington. Bunker noted that because of Thieu's "temperament, he does not give the picture of the dynamic, charismatic leader that we might think of as ideal." But, he added, "increasingly...he has made quick, sound decisions, pushed his ministers to rapid action, and in general, imparted more of a sense of urgency and confidence in the Vietnamese bureaucracy."[26]

While true, America had no patience for Thieu to find his footing as a new president. By March, opinion polls indicated that the American public was losing confidence in Johnson's Vietnam policy. Confronted by slipping poll numbers, enormous antiwar protests, and growing Congressional opposition, the American president concluded that the time had come to begin negotiations. The only way to do that was to accede to Hanoi's demands, at least partially. Whether he could find a willing partner in Hanoi remained the great unknown. Some outside observers judged that Le Duan used warfare as just a tool in his mainly political strategy to achieve unification, but the first secretary categorically saw military conquest as his chief instrument for victory. While he would talk peace, he would also continue fighting. Even after suffering thirty-six thousand casualties in the first assault, Le Duan was not done attacking the cities.

HOW THE SOUTH VIETNAMESE REACTED

Despite the disparate intelligence warnings collected by the allies, Thieu had left Saigon on the afternoon of January 29 to celebrate with his wife's family in My Tho, the capital of Dinh Tuong Province in the Delta. Like the Americans, the South Vietnamese were expecting attacks, but not a coordinated countrywide assault. The GVN had fallen victim to the same bureaucratic straitjacket experienced by other countries: failure of intelligence agencies to share information. Thieu would eventually correct this by accepting U.S. advice to totally revamp his Central Intelligence Office (CIO), the GVN counterpart to the CIA.

On January 31, Front troops seized part of My Tho. Major General Nguyen Viet Thanh, the former Long An Province chief and now 7th ARVN Division commander, had placed units in the city to protect the president. Mrs. Thieu's family home was in the middle of town and remained untouched, but with the city surrounded and under heavy attack, Thieu was stranded. After arriving in town, he had sent his helicopter back to Saigon, where it was currently parked on top of Independence Palace.

Meanwhile, Ky had stayed in Saigon to celebrate. The vice president was at his house on Tan Son Nhut Air Base when the attack happened. Although a commando team had seized the government radio station, Ky radioed Loan to recapture it. By 7:00 a.m., Loan had retaken the building, and Ky broadcast an appeal for the people to resist the attacks. In his memoirs, Ky denigrates Thieu by saying the president was incommunicado for days, but that is untrue. Thieu transmitted a message on January 31 declaring martial law, ordered a twenty-four-hour curfew, and directed that all bars and entertainment places be closed.[27]

Braving an uncertain enemy situation, Thieu's pilot flew the president's helicopter from Saigon early on February 1 and picked up the president and his family. Thieu ordered the pilot to fly low and fast and follow the river east to the coast to avoid enemy activity and then north to Saigon and the JGS compound. Thieu feared an assassination attempt by Ky, who had ordered two planes aloft to protect the president.[28]

Arriving at the JGS that morning, Thieu convened a cabinet meeting to reaffirm his decisions the day before. Two days later, Thieu and his senior principals met with Bunker, Westmoreland, and Komer. At Bunker's urging, they agreed to form a joint US/GVN task force to provide relief to the thousands of new refugees. Thieu appointed Ky to lead the project. On February 5, Ky announced that the committee's goals were to "restore security, regulate the food supply, assist war victims, and help the people organize an armed defense force."[29]

Thieu also planned to involve the legislature in his efforts as he "recognized that it was important to avoid the impression that a military regime was being re-imposed." Thieu invited the assembly leaders to join his cabinet meetings and "asked them, in accordance with the Constitution, to call a special joint session."[30] On February 9, Thieu spoke before the assembly. He demanded that they approve the partial mobilization that they had voted down in October, and he asked for decree powers for a year to deal with the economic consequences of the attack. While recounting the heavy South Vietnamese civilian and military casualties, he broke down in tears.[31] The government put civilian losses at over fourteen thousand killed and twenty-four thousand wounded. In a precursor to what would become one of his signature policies, the People's Self-Defense Force, all civil servants in

Saigon underwent basic military training, were issued a few weapons, and were ordered to defend their buildings.

As the security situation improved, Ky moved quickly to assist the thousands of refugees in Saigon. He brought in 2,500 RD members from Vung Tau to distribute food and man the temporary shelters. Then in mid-February, Ky recommended to Thieu that the task force be placed under the control of Prime Minister Loc as he claimed it was important for the various ministries to now take charge. Behind the scenes, Ky was upset that some of Thieu's supporters were spreading rumors that he was using the emergency committee to grab power. Although Thieu assured him that he did not believe it, Ky resigned as committee chair in a televised speech before even informing the president. Caught by surprise, Ky's stunt miffed Thieu.

Few outside observers understood that it was usually the two men's bickering entourages that caused the trouble between them. Despite the obvious temperamental differences that so often divided them, they had similarities as well. They had generally compatible views on the political and military issues confronting the nation. Both were stubborn, smart, tough, and determined to protect their country. Yet their associates' constant whisper campaigns aggravated their idiosyncrasies and sowed suspicion between them.

With Ky gone, Thieu took control of the relief committee. He visited Hue several days after the city was recaptured and again on March 9. After speaking with the locals and inspecting the destruction, Thieu pledged 10,000 piasters for each displaced family plus materials to help rebuild homes. In early March he also launched a National Recovery Fund to solicit donations to help subsidize reconstruction. Within days, over seventy million piasters in Saigon and Gia Dinh Province alone was collected to help rebuild houses.

The earlier criticisms of Vinh Loc and Nguyen Van Manh were proven correct, as both corps commanders performed poorly. On March 1, Thieu relieved them. He appointed Major General Lu Mong Lan to replace Vinh Loc in II Corps, and he assigned Nguyen Duc Thang to IV Corps. Following through on his "after Tet" schedule, he also reduced the power of the corps commanders and reorganized the bureaucracy. To stop corruption, Thieu declared that the interior minister would now appoint the province chiefs rather than the corps commanders since selling positions was a main conduit of bribery.

On February 9, Thieu had requested emergency powers from the assembly. After debating Thieu's request, on March 1, the Lower House overwhelmingly voted against it. Its members were not giving up what they had just been given. The largest bloc, which still had strong ties to Ky, had received no instructions from him. Thieu blamed Loan and by extension the vice president for not coordinating with the bloc. He saw their lack of action as an attempt to "undermine his power and prestige as president [and] a deliberate effort to embarrass him."[32] Thieu had learned his lesson. He asked his money man, Nguyen Cao Thang, to be his new liaison with the assembly.

He was also growing tired of placating Ky, especially after the vice president had resigned abruptly from leading the important task force. An exasperated Thieu told Bunker that "he had tried to be kind and friendly with Ky, noting that he had accepted Loc as prime minister and the retention of Loan because Ky insisted on them, and Thieu wanted to be cooperative [but] Loan's actions seeking to create 'two governments' made this very difficult."[33] Ky naturally saw the situation differently. He blamed Thieu, claiming that he often refused to schedule time together. Ky told everyone that he would gladly accede to Thieu's orders, but the president must put aside his suspicions and give him responsibility for certain duties. Faced with this intractable mess, there was little the Americans could do other than constantly plead for the two to work together while pointing out the great damage their infighting was causing to both countries.

FIRST INTERNAL CRISIS

The internal squabbling between the two leaders, Thieu's paring back the corps commander's power, plus losing the decree vote, sparked the first mini crisis within Thieu's government. In early March, Ky told an American visitor that senior officer dissatisfaction over "Thieu's failure to provide decisive leadership in the present emergency may lead to Thieu's ouster." Ky said while there were no concrete plans to overthrow Thieu as he realized the U.S. reaction to a coup would be "very bad." Regardless, Ky believed that "the government cannot afford the luxuries of debate…on urgent problems with the Viet Cong camped on the capital's outskirts."

Ky pointed to the mobilization issue as an example of Thieu's dithering. Ky had strongly recommended they immediately mobilize 120,000 men. When Thieu voiced concern over training and arming that many men all at once, Ky pushed back, stating that "American willingness to arm the new troops can be relied on since the U.S. would welcome this initiative to answer its domestic critics." Ky sneered and said that while Thieu had agreed, "three days later he had [still] failed to act."[34] Thieu knew they needed to expand the military, but he wanted a "formal U.S. agreement" to arm these men before the GVN implemented it.[35] After finally getting U.S. approval, and tired of waiting for the assembly to act, on March 31, Thieu announced his plan for a "general mobilization" of South Vietnam's manpower to dramatically expand the RVNAF. All males between the ages of seventeen and forty-five would be drafted. The assembly finally passed the bill on June 15.

Perhaps sensing democracy's faint foothold in South Vietnam, the Americans had been prodding the spectrum of Nationalist leadership to develop strong political parties, seeing these institutions as bulwarks against the Communists. Impressed by Park Chung-hee's success in South Korea, Thieu had been considering forming a government party but had "been very hesitant to build a political organization tied to himself personally because of Diem's unfortunate efforts."[36] Bunker's urgings, however, convinced Thieu, and he directed one of his government counsellors to develop an alliance of political parties but not a formal government group. Organizational efforts proceeded over several months, and a conference was scheduled for March that would bring together South Vietnamese religions, political parties, and factions.

Simultaneously, Senator Tran Van Don was diligently expanding his Senate bloc into something resembling a broad-based anti-communist organization. After the Tet attacks, Ky had encouraged Don to use this nascent organization to help rally the people. Although Don disliked Thieu, he met the president to apprise him of his efforts. While Thieu supported Don's plan, Thieu warned him that past efforts to form a broad coalition of Nationalists had failed. Regardless, on February 18, Don inaugurated his new National Salvation Front. Many leading political personalities attended, including Tran Van Huong and Ha Thuc Ky. In his opening speech, Don declared that the current "serious situation" required "unity and decisive action to save the country. No one can save us if we do not know how to save ourselves." While the Front would not be a "tool of the government," it would cooperate with Thieu when needed.[37]

On March 10, Don held a gathering of two thousand people to rally the diverse religious, ethnic, regional, and political factions. Although Thieu offered to continue supporting Don, the ever-suspicious president privately asked Lieutenant General Khang if the U.S. had secretly organized Don's group. He questioned whether Don's new Front might have "the ultimate objective of generating a coalition government with the NLF." Don's involvement resurrected the specter of the coup in January 1964. The past always hovered in the background, unseen yet cripplingly present. Since he was unsure, Thieu was simply "paying lip service to Don's requests for support while trying to counterbalance it with political efforts of his own."[38]

In late March, Thieu's own front, called the Freedom and Democracy Force, held its inaugural meeting. No politician of any standing attended, and Don claims that when he suggested they merge the two groups, Thieu's paranoia emerged. He accused Don of seeking to become prime minister, which Don vehemently denied. Don says Thieu was "jealous of a political activity that might create support for [Ky] even though the country was in great danger."[39]

The separate fronts further discouraged American hopes for South Vietnamese post-Tet unity and, by extension, political progress. CORDS czar Robert Komer, returning from a trip to D.C., met Thieu on March 18 to directly express Washington's dark mood. Komer

> dwelt heavily on the deep disappointment of the U.S. press and public, as well as a large segment of the U.S. Congress...[that] the GVN was...moving too slowly in reforming its machinery, in recovering the countryside, counterattacking the enemy, and rebuilding the cities...He emphasized that the constant reappearance of Thieu/Ky dissent gave the wrong impression of divided and uncertain management...The proliferation of efforts to organize different fronts was more evidence of the Vietnamese inability to pull together....[T]he U.S. position would be critically dependent on what the GVN itself did over the next several months to convince the administration, Congress, and the public that it merited [ongoing U.S.] support.[40]

Thieu promised improvement, but his response to Komer's blunt criticisms was to change the subject. He simply refused to upend Saigon's internal power structure in the forthright manner the Americans wanted.

Bui Diem returned to Saigon carrying the same grim message: the morale of the U.S. administration to prosecute the war had collapsed. Before leaving D.C., he had met with President Johnson and a bevy of senior congressional and administration officials. He found that their collective view of South Vietnam's prospects had become profoundly negative. He informed Thieu and Ky that "we [are] now looking directly at an American disengagement." The ambassador pleaded with Thieu and Ky to cooperate and said that South Vietnam needed to "show the American people that the Vietnamese were making greatest possible effort to defend themselves."[41] After the meeting, he made a surprising discovery. Unlike Washington, "Saigon had emerged from the offensive invigorated and optimistic." Morale was high. "Ironically," he wrote, the turnaround in Saigon "had come precisely [at] the moment when Washington had begun to lose heart."[42]

What the Americans had so desperately hoped for, a motivated South Vietnam, had finally begun to emerge, but it no longer mattered. Johnson needed to show he was "doing something." In early March, former CIA Saigon station chief William Colby returned to Saigon. He would become Komer's new deputy and eventually supplant him as head of CORDS. On March 22, after almost four years, Westmoreland was replaced as MACV commander by his deputy, General Creighton Abrams. Also in early March, Clark Clifford replaced Robert McNamara as secretary of defense, a decision Johnson had announced in mid-January. Clifford's first effort was to review Johnson's Vietnam policy. He soon recommended negotiations to extricate the U.S. from the war. It was irrelevant what Saigon thought about Washington's peace moves. On March 31, President Johnson, convinced he needed to change course, spoke to America in one of the most dramatic U.S. political speeches of the twentieth century.

"THIS IS OUR COUNTRY"

Although South Vietnam's peace policies remained unchanged, Thieu had tinkered with them. Despite Saigon's qualms about negotiations, in November 1967 he had sent a letter to Ho Chi Minh offering direct talks. However, Thieu's chief Asian allies, Taiwan's Chiang Kai-shek and South Korean's Park Chung-hee, were adamantly against any overtures to Hanoi. Their tough attitude on Vietnam peace talks reflected their own anti-communist experiences and fears regarding their heavy dependence on U.S. support.

Both countries had first warned the Americans against a precipitous peace with Hanoi during a visit by Vice President Hubert Humphrey in January 1966.[43] Park had further derided U.S. peace efforts at the Manila conference in October 1966. Nguyen Xuan Phong, Ky's former labor minister and at that time the chief of Ky's office staff, headed the Vietnamese delegation to draft the joint communiqué. Phong notes that the Koreans, under "strict instructions" from Park, asked to join future peace talks. When the Americans refused, the Korean delegate warned Phong that, based on their own war experience, "if peace talks ever came," the Americans would negotiate directly with Hanoi and "Saigon would not have much to say in the matter except to accept and comply."[44] Appropriately sobered, Phong cautioned Thieu, who said nothing.

Aware of Thieu's efforts to open communications with Hanoi, in late December 1967, Park sent a delegation to dissuade him. He also disagreed with Johnson's advice that Saigon "meet informally with the Vietcong as a starting point toward settling the Vietnam conflict." The South Korean leader preferred a clear-cut military victory and "strongly opposed any negotiations at this time." While Park understood Johnson's "domestic political reasons for making a peace proposal," he feared that any U.S. concession to Hanoi might weaken South Vietnam.[45] Park's opinion was based on his own country's history. The first South Korean president, Syngman Rhee, had long claimed that the "American hunger for peace during the Korean war betrayed him [and] his country." Park warned Thieu that, in his view, Rhee had been "bludgeoned by the U.S. into agreeing" to start truce talks in 1951 and that he was "bludgeoned again before he would accept the Korean armistice in 1953."[46] Thieu took heed. He soon said publicly that "Vietnam and its allies must avoid the error of Panmunjom."[47]

After the 1967 presidential election, many prominent Nationalists became alarmed at Johnson's pronouncements implying that Saigon should hold discussions with the NLF to end the war. Notwithstanding repeated American declarations that the U.S. would not force Saigon into a coalition, Thieu, playing to his domestic audience, criticized the U.S. peace efforts. In a speech on January 15, 1968, Thieu chastised Washington for succumbing to the "Communist stratagem of addressing themselves to the U.S. government only, while omitting the GVN." He pointedly reminded Washington that "this is our country." Saigon, he emphasized, should "have the central role in any developments relating to Vietnam . . . I regret to say that in the past our allies sometimes have not avoided . . . placing themselves at the center of peace efforts."[48]

Many thought Thieu was the driving force in Saigon's uncompromising anti-communist stand, but his policy was backed by most Nationalist constituencies, including the military, the press, and both houses of the assembly.

His inflexibility stemmed from both personal insight into the Communist mindset and a healthy desire to protect himself from either a coup or harsh criticism from his right flank. Yet while the Johnson administration had undertaken numerous in-depth internal reviews on how to achieve peace, Bunker feared that Saigon had not. Accurately foreseeing the future, Bunker predicted that the

> GVN will be very difficult to deal with in the matter of preparing for negotiations. Every move we make towards an accommodation with the Communists will raise lively and genuine fears of abandonment. [Bunker proposed to] focus on specific aspects of negotiations, discuss them in advance and in-depth with the top leadership...and try to bring them along as best we can without sapping their will to continue the struggle...This will be a painful experience requiring patience and understanding, but it is vital to our objective of finding a political solution in Vietnam acceptable to the broadest range of Vietnamese Nationalist opinion.[49]

In late March, as Johnson was contemplating new peace moves, Bunker warned him that getting Thieu to agree to U.S.-led peace negotiations would be difficult. While Thieu "has shown himself to be very responsive to our wishes and needs...in doing so, he has made himself vulnerable to charges of being unduly influenced by the Americans...Thieu could therefore find himself in a very delicate position if he should give his concurrence to our proposals unless Ky is equally committed."[50] Although Bunker's plan was sound, Johnson paid him no heed.

JOHNSON'S SPEECH SHOCKS ASIA

On March 31, the president spoke to the nation regarding his Vietnam policy. The speech was the culmination of weeks of debate within the administration. He offered to halt all bombing north of the 20th parallel if Hanoi agreed to peace talks. Then Johnson dropped a bombshell. He announced that he would not run for reelection. On April 3, Hanoi accepted his offer, and after acrimonious exchanges over a location, they finally agreed in early May to meet with the U.S. in Paris.

Johnson's speech shocked his Asian allies. Taiwan insisted that a "military victory is the only way to settle the Vietnam problem...Chiang said he feared [the bombing halt] could destroy the confidence of the South Vietnamese."[51] The South Koreans, panicked by the lack of U.S. response to the late January 1968 North Korean seizure of the USS *Pueblo* and the commando raid against Park's residence, also dreaded that a peace deal might signal "a pullback from Asia and a lessening of U.S. commitments to help defend South Korea." Park thundered that "talks will only [lead] to a U.S. withdrawal and a Communist takeover of South Vietnam."[52] He then backed Thieu by proclaiming that he agreed with Saigon's refusal to form a coalition government.

The Saigon leadership also dreaded the impact that Johnson's speech might have on South Vietnamese morale. Ky emphasized that what the GVN did in the next ten days was critical, and that

> it was important that the GVN demonstrate to the people that it was on top of the situation and working closely with the Americans. If the people got the impression that the U.S. was going it alone, most everyone would think that another 1954 Geneva agreement was imminent. The Communists will take full advantage of the situation to sow doubt and discord among the people. [Hanoi will try] to make the point that the war is over, that the US/GVN has lost, and that the VC will soon be taking over. If such a feeling should become widespread, it will become virtually impossible for the GVN to function.[53]

Scrambling to reassure South Vietnamese public opinion, Thieu held a press conference on April 2. He told the journalists that he accepted Johnson's policy but warned that this was the last time he would agree to bombing halt. He also cunningly targeted U.S. public opinion by proclaiming that with his recently announced general mobilization to increase South Vietnam's military capabilities, he hoped U.S. troops could begin withdrawing by the end of 1968.

Given the reports from Komer and Bui Diem, Thieu's immediate strategy was to maintain U.S. support while mollifying American antiwar critics. He knew that Saigon needed to display "concrete accomplishments" since it "may be the only thing that can influence U.S. public opinion and policy."[54] His mobilization demand was designed to demonstrate to "the world that the South Vietnamese are determined to fight alone if necessary."[55] Over a year before newly elected President Richard Nixon would announce "Vietnamization" with great fanfare, Thieu had broached the same concept.

Immediately after Hanoi accepted Johnson's offer, Bunker visited the president to alleviate Thieu's concerns over American plans. The South Vietnamese president, however, struck first. Dutifully explaining to the U.S. ambassador that Hanoi's intentions were simply to negotiate for a complete bombing cessation while "continuing policy of fighting and infiltrating and supporting South." This tactic, he remarked, "would not be acceptable" to Saigon. Thieu insisted that both governments "had to be very careful in our statements. If his people got the idea that the [Americans] were moving ahead without them, there would be most serious trouble in country and for him."

Bunker understood. Hearkening back to his previous comments about the best way to work with Thieu, he stressed to Washington policy makers "that it is of utmost importance that we not only keep them informed but that we consult, so that they have a sense of participation... There must not be appearance of unilateral action or unilateral statements." If Washington played it smart, he believed, "I am confident we can take them along with us and minimize their problems if we are sensitive to the requirements here."[56] Bunker's blueprint for patient explanation of U.S. policies would, over the next five years, essentially keep US/GVN relations from rupturing over a wide variety of issues, from economic policy and police repression to peace talks. His strategy, however, would first undergo a serious test.

14

"A COUNTRY THAT CANNOT ORGANIZE ITSELF IS NOT A COUNTRY"

Thieu Breaks His Chains

Scholars agree that the Tet Offensive was a key turning point for America in the war, as it led the Johnson administration to partially concede to Hanoi's demand to cease bombing in exchange for peace talks. The effects on South Vietnam, however, were also remarkably profound and yet little noticed. First, Tet exacerbated unresolved tensions in Saigon's internal structure and set in motion a fundamental power shift that allowed Thieu to gain control of the levers of government. He accomplished this feat by relying on the constitution. Second, his ascendency enabled him to take advantage of the Communist military setback by strengthening and extending Saigon's writ throughout the country. South Vietnam's Achilles' heel had always been the weak link between the government's mandate and the hamlets. Thieu wanted to bolster that connection and win the village war by forming a new part-time militia to defend the people and by attacking the Communist underground political cadres. Third, he sought to build a Nationalist political party for a future electoral contest. The results put Saigon in its strongest position since the war began.

THIEU GAINS CONTROL

Although Thieu had signed the document that gave the generals covert control, the constitution coalesced executive power in the presidency. Deciding GVN strategy after the Tet Offensive reopened the question of who held final policy authority, Thieu or the Military Council. The embattled president faced a stark choice: rule at the behest of a clique of generals or embrace his role as the elected representative of a constitutional government. This "internal contradiction," to borrow from Hanoi's Marxist viewpoint, came to a head in mid-1968.

In May, the nexus of power in South Vietnam remained diffuse. Ky supporters occupied most senior military positions. Due to their proximity to Saigon and command of significant combat power, the three most important generals in mid-1968 were RVNAF chief Cao Van Vien, Le Nguyen Khang—who commanded the Marines, III Corps, and the Capital Military District—and Nguyen Ngoc Loan, head of the police. Thieu was backed by the Americans and had the support of many division commanders.

Ky and the senior generals judged Thieu a weak and indecisive leader for many reasons, mainly because he refused to rule as a strongman.[1] Westerners assessed the generals as dictatorial, but they viewed themselves as patriots who, through experience and cultural imprint, had concluded that authoritarianism offered the best solution to South Vietnam's problems. Other Asian anti-communist leaders like South Korea's Park Chung-hee and Taiwan's Chiang Kai-shek had also deemed the people "not ready" for democracy, especially during a fratricidal war. Yet it was not just policy disputes that triggered friction between Thieu and the generals. Beneath the quarrels over governance, personality quirks and personal clashes often fueled the discord, a combustible mix of unresolved past grievances and ego-driven ambition. Khang observed that "personal relationships in Vietnam are very complicated and very important," perhaps even more than the official command structure.[2] Other unseen social currents also shaped policy decisions, particularly the enormous influence wielded by the wives. They ran their husband's "business affairs," which led to feuds over promotions and payoffs.

While South Vietnam struggled to recover from the Tet Offensive, for Le Duan in Hanoi, the defeat of the first wave did not give him pause. It simply meant he needed to continue the attack to achieve victory. Despite agreeing to meet to discuss peace, Hanoi had increased the flow of troops and material to the south under the well-known "talk-fight" strategy articulated by the first secretary in December 1965. More important, on April 24, 1968, the Politburo gathered to analyze the situation and discuss the next steps. Despite the failure of the first wave, "they decided to conduct a second wave of the general offensive and uprisings... [E]ven though we had suffered significant losses, our soldiers and civilians were still determined to continue the attacks and uprisings to win even greater victories."[3] Thieu's analysis had proven prescient.

Several days before the first meeting in Paris to begin peace negotiations, early on May 5, Communist troops launched a second round of attacks against the cities. Although 126 towns were struck by artillery and rocket fire, Saigon was the only city to face a ground assault. Often called "Mini-Tet," the fighting in the capital was intense, and the last diehards were not routed until mid-May. Follow-on battles flared again in late May, but COSVN finally halted further attacks on June 13. In Saigon and the suburbs, the urban combat generated 107,000 new refugees. Another 18,000 houses were destroyed. Still caring for 500,000 refugees from the first wave, the GVN's limited capabilities were now strained to the breaking point.

Enemy losses were again devastating. The main Communist military history for 1968 admits that "our soldiers suffered very heavy losses" in the second wave.[4] The PAVN document cited previously claims "Mini-Tet" accounted for 32 percent of their total losses in 1968, only slightly below the 34 percent for the first wave. Overall,

> during two successive waves of attacks (Tet and in May) our soldiers and civilians had suffered heavy losses of personnel, weapons, and ammunition... In addition, our secret forces concealed inside the cities and most of our agents and secret facilities—the places where we hid our weapons and equipment, the places where our troops were based, the places from which we had launched our attacks—had been exposed and had been virtually eliminated and destroyed. These were serious problems that would not be easy to overcome in a short period of time.[5]

These new attacks compelled the senior generals and Ky to meet with Thieu the next day to discuss the current state of affairs. Thieu claimed they were "very frank in telling him that his administration was weak, ineffective." But since Ky had insisted on Loc and had helped pick Loc's cabinet to ensure his policy role, the generals unknowingly provided Thieu with an opening. The president cagily replied that it was not "his government. It was theirs. Loc was not his choice, but a compromise to satisfy Ky and the generals." Now that the generals had "criticized, he would go ahead and take actions as required."[6] Previously, the Lower House in late April had roughly questioned Loc over the failure of GVN intelligence to uncover the offensive. Loc faced heavy criticism for the simplest of political reasons; the country needed a scapegoat because the enemy had successfully launched a surprise attack. After the generals upbraided him, Thieu sent his brother Kieu in mid-May to secretly convince the Lower House to vote "no confidence" in Loc.[7]

With Loc an obvious lame duck, Thieu finally convinced Tran Van Huong to accept the position of prime minister. Huong's price, though, was a free hand to eliminate corruption and to replace Ky's cronies like Loan. He warned Thieu, though, that he regarded himself as a "servant of the people and not the instrument of the president." Thieu agreed, and in turn Huong promised not to repeat his past mistake of loading the cabinet with his southern followers. He also reassured the president that he had "no ambitions of running again for office. When the situation has been restored...he will ask permission to resign."[8] Huong had put himself solely in service to his country and not his personal ambition.

Learning of Thieu's talk with Huong, on May 15, the Military Council again summoned Thieu. It reiterated that with the U.S. and the DRV meeting in Paris, and with Communist troops attacking Saigon, "the government must be strong, decisive, and tightly organized." The assembly should grant Thieu "full powers...[N]ow is not the time to experiment with concepts of civilian administration" that might work in peacetime but are inadequate in wartime. They claimed that the best way to influence U.S. public opinion "was to achieve solid military and political progress," and only a "strong and unified government led by the military" could accomplish this.[9] The council also requested that Thieu cancel his decree shifting the power to appoint province chiefs to the Interior Ministry, and it demanded to know his plans for Loc.

Democracy in South Vietnam had reached another crossroads, as had President Nguyen Van Thieu. To his credit, he rejected their ultimatums. He agreed that the assembly moved too slowly, but "he saw no alternative to working with it," nor would he "reverse any of his administrative reforms or change his plans to 'civilianize' the government." The president further refused to discuss his proposed change of the prime minister but said he "would make his intentions clear on May 18."[10] It was a key moment in the political history of South Vietnam. Thieu had faced Ky and his supporters alone, and the generals had blinked.

While most scholars believe the subsequent removal of Ky's supporters was a power grab by Thieu, that misses the deeper forces at work. Several of Ky's supporters were eliminated by combat action, others like Prime Minister Loc were obviously incapable, and the last tranche were fired to improve security in Saigon. Since the ramifications and true goals of how Thieu accomplished this authority shift have remained largely unexamined, some discussion is required.

The first Ky supporter to go was Saigon Police Chief Loan. On May 5, he was leading an assault against a Communist sniper when he was severely wounded in the right leg. Next in line was Loc, who resigned on May 18. That night, Thieu announced that Huong had accepted the role of prime minister and would form a new cabinet. Tellingly, Thieu did not inform Ky of the change in advance, and the vice president was in Nha Trang when Thieu made the announcement.

The senior generals met Huong's appointment with stony silence. On May 20, they convened with Ky and "decided to take no action against Thieu and adopt a wait-and-see attitude toward Huong." The generals "called the meeting because Thieu had not consulted them regarding Huong's appointment...The generals view Thieu's behavior as a violation of the agreement that the senior generals, including Thieu, signed after the 30 June meeting."[11] They decided to do nothing for now, but if Huong's government failed, they would use it as an excuse to regain power. Or they might attack Thieu on a more emotional issue, such as a peace settlement or a coalition with the NLF. These events—the near-death of Loan, the firing of Loc, and Thieu's gutsy stand against the Military Council—began the eclipse of Nguyen Cao Ky. Further happenings would accelerate his downfall.

On May 25, Huong assumed power. He was probably the most respected politician in South Vietnam. Even his former students still called him "Master." Yet his humble demeanor and unquestioned honesty concealed an innate stubbornness and inflexibility that those who knew him feared would doom his ability to lead a new government. They thought Saigon needed a man of vision and political cunning as it underwent its most challenging time since the 1966 Buddhist crisis. The renewed Communist attacks and the opening of talks in Paris had roiled the political atmosphere, one that was already under heavy strain from the Tet assault and Johnson's stunning announcement that he would not seek reelection. Moreover, the economy and pacification had been disrupted, the RVNAF was being revamped, and refugee care and rebuilding were overwhelming GVN resources.

Huong realized his limitations, so instead of focusing on policy, which was Thieu's domain, he saw his main purpose as establishing the state's moral mandate by firmly upholding the constitution and the law. He believed his country's principal problem was the absence of an ethical bond between the state and the people, the social contract between the government and the governed. By erecting the GVN on honorable ground, he hoped to win the people's allegiance. Corruption was his *bête noire*, and he zeroed in on Ky. He held Ky in disdain and appraised his allies as highly corrupt. He believed the old rumors that Ky was involved in "gold smuggling and the illegal traffic in opium and arms," although the U.S. embassy reported that Huong "had no hard evidence" to back his claim.[12]

Huong, though, saw Ky as only one part of the problem. The generals embodied "vested interests which continue to have grip on certain powers and prerogatives." Removing the generals (mainly Ky's supporters) from the cabinet was the crucial first step in convincing the people that the government truly represented them. Yet despite the clear obstacle they represented, Huong said "Thieu had been somewhat reluctant to move."[13] He was correct. While Thieu had broken the generals' hold over him, that was different than directly challenging them, and he intended to maintain the status quo. Huong, on the other hand, had concluded that the creation of a legitimate state meant reducing the army's control over it. The army served the state, not the other way around.

In foreign policy, Huong was also adamantly against a coalition. He believed that any non-communists were long gone from the NLF. Like many families, his view was not just political, it was a difficult personal choice. Huong's oldest son was a PAVN officer, one of only three southerners who had fought at Dien Bien Phu. When his son went north, Huong lost contact with him and believed he was dead. Like Big Minh's brother, in the mid-1960s the Communists had his son write a letter to reestablish contact, eventually hoping to influence Huong. Although he received the letter, Huong declined to respond. He would not see his son again until 1978.[14]

Thieu had also chosen the elderly southerner to "broaden the base" of his government, hoping it might encourage the fractious Nationalists to finally unify. As Huong formed his new cabinet, Thieu tried to convince the other political leaders to join. But they either demanded a senior position or refused, anticipating that the current government would fall and by some miracle they might achieve power. For example, RDV leader

Ha Thuc Ky declined to join when he was denied the Interior Ministry, the same position he had held under Khanh, who had fired him for corruption and coup plotting. However, Phan Quang Dan did accept, as did Mai Tho Truyen, Huong's former running mate. Truyen was a sop to the Buddhists, and it worked; the An Quang Pagoda announced their backing for the new cabinet, a rare instance of government support.

While Thieu is accused of replacing many Ky supporters, it was actually Huong who replaced them in the cabinet. The only Ky confidant retained was Defense Minister Lieutenant General Nguyen Van Vy. Surprisingly, Huong also replaced Tran Van Do. His new foreign minister was Senator Tran Chanh Thanh. Thanh's family were northerners, but his father had worked in Hue as the spokesman for the emperor. Thanh had received a law degree from the University of Hanoi and initially served with the Viet Minh, but like many Nationalists, he fled upon discovering Communist control. He had practiced law in Saigon until elected to the Senate in 1967.

The real shocker, though, was the nomination of Tran Thien Khiem to become the new minister of the interior. Khanh had sent Khiem out of the country in late 1964 as GVN ambassador to Washington. When Ky assumed power, he wanted his own man in D.C., so in October 1965, Thieu dispatched Khiem to Taiwan as GVN Ambassador. Many, especially in the U.S. embassy, assumed that the two men were close and that Thieu had brought Khiem back from diplomatic exile to strengthen his internal support. Both points are incorrect. In fact, they were barely on speaking terms at this time. Earlier Khiem had asked to return home to attend the funeral of his older brother. Thieu had declined but later relented. When Khiem finally arrived in Saigon, the death ceremony was almost finished. He recalls Thieu saying to him, "I do not even know where to put you now that you have returned to Vietnam."[15] Huong assigned him to the Interior Ministry.

Naturally, Thieu's personnel choices irked Ky. He felt Huong was too old, and he hated Khiem, calling him "devious, treacherous, and self-seeking... Khiem's true loyalty is to the Dai Viet Party."[16] Being kept in the dark also infuriated the vice president. Lamenting to a U.S. official, Ky bemoaned that many senior military officers were asking him what was going on. Ky "had to confess to them he did not know the president's intentions." He was clueless over who was in the new cabinet "until he heard the announcement on the radio." Then he revealed his true strategy. Like the other generals, Ky would simply wait for Thieu to fail. Then he would pounce. "Some," he said, "have approached me about a coup [but] I have told them a coup is out of the question. I tell them they must be patient...There are a thousand ways to destroy a leader without a coup."[17] Despite American pleas for unity, the gap between Thieu and Ky, and between Ky and the idea of constitutional government, continued to widen.

Much like the wounding of Loan, fate once again played a huge role in Thieu's ascendency. On June 2, a rocket strike from a U.S. helicopter accidently hit a command post in Cholon that was directing counterattacks against some recent infiltrators. The rocket killed six of Ky's top remaining lieutenants in the city. Wounded in the explosion was Colonel Van Van Cua, the mayor of Saigon and Loan's brother-in-law. Bunker apologized, and a thorough U.S. investigation indicated the helicopter pilot had mistakenly targeted the building. The Vietnamese press immediately mocked Bunker's claim that this was a friendly-fire mishap with banner headlines that the rocket was a deliberate American act to support Thieu over Ky.

Shortly afterward, the last two of Ky's chief supporters resigned. Lieutenant General Khang quit as III Corps Commander, as did Nguyen Duc Thang in IV Corps. In a letter to Thieu in early June, Thang said he had fixed the issues in the Delta and asked for reassignment. Thieu asked both men to remain, and Khang agreed to stay until Thieu could find a replacement. Despite his dislike of Thang, Thieu wrote Thang a letter "praising his work and said the work was not yet finished." On June 3, further trying to mollify Thang, Thieu promoted him to lieutenant general, but in mid-June, Thieu told Bunker that "the next thing I know Thang sends a letter to Vien saying he was in need of a rest."[18] On July 1, Thieu replaced him with Major General Nguyen Viet Thanh, the 7th Division commander. Thang would remain unemployed until the fall of the country.

The helicopter incident also allowed Thieu the opportunity to reshape the city of Saigon's administration. While the president was accused of packing the Saigon government with loyalists, that is only partially true. He was far more interested in improving the capital's defenses and local management. Ongoing enemy rocket attacks were disrupting efforts to rebuild, and Communist units remained poised near the capital. His main decision was to remove Lieutenant General Khang as commander of the Capital Military District (CMD). On June 4, he assigned Major General Nguyen Van Minh, the commander of the 21st ARVN Division in the lower Delta, to assume the leadership from Khang. He wanted a single overseer to concentrate on the capital's defenses. Minh, while an excellent division commander, was a mixed bag. Born in Saigon to a Buddhist family, he was a protégé of Major General Dang Van Quang, and like his mentor, anti-Ky and pro-Thieu. Minh, though, suffered from stomach ulcers, moodiness, and a deserved reputation for corruption resulting from his extensive "business interests" in the Delta. At the same time, Thieu assigned Colonel Do Kien Nhieu to replace Colonel Cua as mayor of Saigon. Nhieu, another southerner who had backed Huong, had mainly served in staff roles, but he was close to Major General Minh.

The quick replacement of so many of Ky's backers sparked a backlash. Lieutenant General Nguyen Van Vy, the last of the old guard generals, protested Nhieu's appointment. Vy was an ardent northerner and a major Ky supporter, having known the vice president since Ky was a child. Vy publicly claimed that Nhieu was highly corrupt and threatened to resign unless he was removed. The Vietnamese press quickly put the onus on north-south disputes. Thieu ordered an investigation, but when the inquiry failed to find any evidence against Nhieu, he retained him.

This was the last public spat over regional bias. The bubbling cauldron of regionalism and religious strife that had tortured South Vietnam had finally cooled. The sharp debates over South Vietnam's social and religious identity had led to a grudging cultural and political accommodation. Political scientist Allan Goodman saw the 1967 voting patterns for the assembly as the beginning of a "decline in the efficacy of religious and regional politics." People were less interested in identity politics and instead "increasingly demand[ed] that any organization provide tangible benefits to the people."[19] Unfortunately, in two years, schisms fueled by social and economic grievances would replace the ethnic and religious rivalries that had torn South Vietnam's unity.

With Thang gone, in early August, Thieu finally accepted Khang's resignation as III Corps Commander. Although Khang retained command of the newly formed Marine Division, his days close to the flame were over. Thieu replaced him with Lieutenant General Do Cao Tri, another diplomatically exiled general. Born in November 1920 near Saigon, Tri was one of ARVN's best field commanders. He commanded I Corps during the Diem coup but had been kicked out of the army by Khanh in September 1964 and sent abroad. While Tri was in exile, Thieu had quietly provided him money to survive. In May 1966, Thieu reinstated Tri into the army, and in mid-1967, Thieu sent him to South Korea as the GVN Ambassador. Tri took command on August 5, 1968. While a great combat leader, Tri was another mixed bag. His reputation for flamboyance and dalliance with the ladies nearly outshone Ky's, but he also was well known for corruption. Regardless, his loyalty to Thieu and his fighting prowess overcame the pall of corruption.

From early May to early August, by the whims of fate and deft maneuvering, Thieu had successfully broken the senior generals' hold over him and relegated Nguyen Cao Ky to the sidelines. While he had emerged victorious and had revamped his government, he now faced another stern test: rebuilding and expanding the state.

BUILDING UNITY

Bunker continued to advise Thieu to overcome the partisanship within the Nationalist camp and merge the two political fronts that had been created shortly after Tet. Thieu saw his opportunity in early May. Shortly after Huong announced his cabinet, Senator Tran Van Don published an open letter to Thieu calling on him to broaden his government. On May 27, Thieu summoned Don to the palace. Don says Thieu told him that "now was the right time to unify all nationalist political groups...[T]he peace talks in Paris made it evident that South Vietnam must show a greater degree of political unity." Thieu then asked Don to lead that effort, and he quickly concurred.[20] Thieu ordered his Free Democratic Force to merge with Don's National Salvation Front. While Don still distrusted Thieu, he agreed to "build a front in support of the government because this is what Vietnam needs."[21]

After a month of Don's energetic organizing, on June 29, Thieu held a meeting with two hundred political and religious representatives. He urged them to "create strong political alliances, even in opposition to the government" and said he would not consider an opposition party an enemy since "political activity is an important factor in building a true democracy." [22] Thieu then held a Q&A session, something Diem would never have considered.

Four days later, Don held the inaugural meeting of the new group, called the Front of Fronts for short. The embassy soon named it Lien Minh, the Vietnamese term for "alliance." Vu Van Mau, a staunch Buddhist who had once been Diem's foreign minister, joined the group, which lent the impression but not the substance of An Quang support. A mixed CVT/Hoa Hao group also merged with the Lien Minh. Others, such as the RDV and the Catholic Greater Solidarity Front decided instead to form their own voting bloc in the Senate, a right-wing group even more hardline on negotiations with the Communists than Thieu.

While Thieu recognized the embryonic nature of the effort, he hoped Don's "capacity for leadership and his political sense" would forge this current "loose alliance" into something more permanent. Thieu wanted Don to take the lead so he could remain behind the scenes, believing "an organization in support of him or his government would fail—the people were deeply suspicious of personal or government parties." Thieu hoped the Lien Minh would "support his government [but] not him personally." This, according to Thieu, was the "mistake of Diem, who had built Can Lao as a personal political party," and he would not repeat it.[23] To back his call for the Nationalists to build political parties, Thieu sent a proposed law on the formation of parties to the Lower House.

As with other efforts to organize the testy Nationalists, it failed. Within weeks, dissension among the old party leaders stymied cooperation. Many secretly appealed to the U.S. embassy for money to build their own front. Since the U.S. was already covertly supplying the Lien Minh with funds, all supplicants received the same response: "division among the Nationalists was a luxury the U.S. was not prepared to underwrite."[24] That argument fell on deaf ears, and the traditional curse of Vietnamese politics, individualism and opportunism, remained unbroken.

Although Don had committed to building the Lien Minh, his dislike of Thieu soon resurfaced. What had made Don suddenly change his mind? It might have been the result of an anti-Thieu whisper campaign conducted by Lower House Deputy Nguyen Van Dinh. A well-known Catholic southern politician, Dinh had served as Phan Khac Suu's deputy chairman in the Constitutional Assembly. He was also a long-time Communist penetration agent. He had been invited to the June 29 meeting with Thieu and was appointed to the Lien Minh's Executive Committee. Ordered to "neutralize" the new front, he decided to "concentrate his efforts on Don." Dinh believed that if "I pushed the right buttons, Don's resentment and anger [against Thieu] would burst forth into action that would benefit our side." Dinh held several meetings with Don and claims that by stoking the former general's simmering bitterness against Thieu, he convinced Don to forego any effort to assist in building the front.[25] It worked, and on July 16, Don left for Paris as part of a Senate delegation to "observe" the talks. He would not return until mid-September. In late October, Don openly criticized Thieu's negotiation gambit as too inflexible. It was the beginning of a ploy by Don to convince anyone who would listen that Thieu should be replaced, preferably by him.

EXPANDING THE STATE, AND THE BEGINNING OF VIETNAMIZATION

The Nationalists still wrestled with the question over the optimal governing arrangement in a time of civil war: an authoritarian strongman able to make quick decisions or one based upon the democratic ideal. Thieu wanted to use the constitutional foundation to erect a structure for South Vietnam's growth and expansion, but by training, inclination, and the need to react quickly to a ruthless enemy, he hoped for a little of both, and he moved to achieve that.

After losing the vote to give him decree powers to deal with the after-effects of the offensive, Thieu decided to strengthen his legislative affairs office. He certainly agreed with his fellow generals that the assembly should perform quicker and act less as a government irritant. He tapped the owner of the OPV company, Nguyen Cao Thang, as the conduit between the presidency and the assembly. Yet if he lauded the legislature's purpose, Thieu had hidden sins. Thang's role as legislative liaison chief was simple. If persuasion failed, Thang would resort to old-fashioned methods, i.e., bribery. In late June, Thang noted that the Senate presented few impedi-ments, but the Lower House was "another matter" because of a large bloc of opposition deputies. Thang was organizing a pro-GVN majority bloc in the Lower House, but it was "an expensive operation. While many deputies are inclined toward the president, they will not agree to join a disciplined pro-Thieu bloc without receiving something in return."[26]

One of the chief opposition Lower House members, Ly Qui Chung, confirmed that Thang had successfully manipulated most deputies. Thang, though, was not just a mere bag man. Chung admitted that Thang "was rather successful in his job not just because he had a lot of money to disperse but also because he was flexible and sensitive in the performance of his duties. His meetings and lobbying efforts were all conducted with the skill of someone who knew how to lobby in political backrooms." Yet despite Thang's largesse, Chung proudly asserted that "the voices of the opposi-tion deputies on the floor of the National Assembly were a constant source of pressure on the Thieu government. Those opposed to the government were still able to utilize this forum to denounce corruption, violations of democracy and justice, and even to oppose the war."[27]

While Thang would deal with the assembly, Thieu would focus on reclaiming the countryside. The heavy Communist losses presented the GVN an opportunity to enlarge its presence in the villages. Shortly after Tet, Komer and Bunker had pressed Thieu to expand the pacification effort and push the RD teams and the ARVN back into the hamlets, but Thieu had resisted, preferring to protect the cities. By the summer of 1968, however, he was reconsidering. His analysis suggested that since the Communists could not militarily win the war, the Politburo would soon switch to a political struggle via negotiations. The worst scenario would be if Hanoi suddenly requested a ceasefire, claimed half the country was under its rule, and demanded a coalition while keeping its troops in the south, precisely what it did in 1972. Thieu believed the U.S. antiwar crowd would find such an offer irresistible and would force Johnson's hand. He informed the cabinet on September 12 that "the GVN objective for the next year must be to consolidate its control" over 75 percent of the population.[28]

While many Nationalists demanded a military victory, Thieu realized that a diplomatic resolution followed by an election was the most likely means to end the war. His policies were simple. The PAVN and any die-hard Communists must leave South Vietnam, there would be no coalition, nor would he permit the NLF to participate as a Communist entity. The constitution forbade any Communist or neutralist participation in South Vietnamese political life, nor would he survive in power long if he offered such. He adamantly believed that Hanoi would view elections as war without guns, and they would attempt to manipulate the vote by sending agitprop cadres into the hamlets. He needed trained cadres in place to counter them.

In preparation, he undertook three programs, each part of a broad effort to expand the government into the countryside, defeat the insurgency, and prepare for a future electoral contest. Thieu wanted to mobilize the people to join several quasi-government groups, build a mass movement that he hoped would morph into a political party, and root out the Communist underground cadres.

Thieu saw the chance to accomplish all three goals with one organization. Although Diem had created an unpaid civilian self-defense program, it had been disbanded after the coup. It was reborn with Ky's village decree in December 1966, which stipulated the arming of hamlet inhabitants to free the RF/PF from mundane tasks like night-guard duty, but no action had been taken. In 1967, Komer had also pushed hard to improve the RF/ PF's fighting capabilities. He believed that "local security was paramount to pacification" and that enhancing territorial forces, who he believed bore the brunt of the fighting, "would be a quicker and easier way to expand... pacification."[29] His concept was also only partially implemented.

The Tet Offensive corrected that lassitude. The GVN's first move at local self-defense was to train Saigon civil servants in basic military skills and provide weapons to defend their buildings. The city government quickly organized over thirty-five thousand people into small defensive teams. Yet arming the citizens was not just a government initiative. When news spread about the Hue massacre, many civil and religious organizations, such as the VNQDD in I Corps and the Catholics near Saigon, immediately requested weapons to defend themselves.

This push from below gave Thieu the confidence to move forward. At his April 2 press conference discussing Johnson's bombing halt, Thieu announced a new nationwide civil defense program to provide rudimentary protection for the hamlets and villages. Ky had lobbied to run this civil defense program, and since Bunker had urged Thieu to give Ky a major project to manage, Thieu told him to oversee it. The goal was to halt small unit Communist incursions into the hamlets and turn territorial security over to the RF/PF, thus enabling the ARVN to replace U.S. troops in the mobile offensive role. Currently, the RF/PF had to defend the villages, the ARVN handled territory security, and the U.S. units took the fight to the enemy. This adjustment was one of Thieu's key policy shifts during the war and would form the basis for his views on the program that became known as Vietnamization.

In late July, Thieu was more explicit, stating that by mid-1969, "one division of U.S. troops can be withdrawn [given] the present evolution of the military situation." This, however, was predicated on "sufficient and modern arms and equipment" being provided to the RVNAF.[30] Given his comments, Thieu's strategy was clear: begin to de-Americanize the war. One of his main advisors confirmed that "the GVN was fully aware of the fragility of the U.S. position in the face of the mounting antiwar movements in the United States and widespread criticism of the U.S. role in Vietnam [and] the GVN made great efforts to assume a growing burden of the war to permit U.S. troop withdrawals."[31] Thieu, though, did not want a complete U.S. withdrawal, as he wanted a residual force to remain to deter future Communist offensives.

On May 2, Thieu signed the decree forming "People's Self-Defense Committees" that would organize the new part-time militia. In mid-May, Ky outlined the program's goals: "mobilize the entire population to take part in the war [and] give the rear areas a force to protect villages and city neighborhoods. All citizens will be part of the self-defense forces, and everyone will be assigned to an appropriate task," including women, children, and old men.[32]

Despite having requested the job, in typical fashion, Ky resigned a month later. On June 12, he sent a letter to Thieu giving the same excuse as when he had left as head of the Central Recovery Committee: the new self-defense program should be placed under the prime minister. Bunker was furious. He had practically begged Thieu to offer Ky a "constructive constitutional role," but Ky's second resignation "seems to be another example of his failure to follow through on duties even when they are given to him."[33] Many of Ky's supporters agreed. Lieutenant General Khang said that while Thieu was "slow and devious and did not trust his colleagues. Ky...while strong, was impulsive [and had] the bad habit of starting things and then just dropping them. He does not follow through, so there is much discouragement."[34]

The Vietnamese backlash was so great that Ky had to give a speech on TV to deny that he had resigned in a snit. As vice president, he said, he did not have the necessary powers to train and organize the new self-defense forces. No one believed him, and Ky's reputation was sullied. This new dustup, on top of the dismissal of the Loc government, the loss of his friends, and the failure of the Military Council, drove the mercurial Ky into bitterness. He left Saigon to drink and play mah-jongg with his friends, making only token appearances in the halls of government. He would not reengage until mid-September.

The general mobilization bill passed in June ratified the creation of the People's Self-Defense Force (*Nhan Dan Tu Ve*). It ordered all citizens ineligible for induction into the military to participate. A PSDF Directorate was created in the Interior Ministry to administer the PSDF committees that would extend from the national to the hamlet level. The PSDF force structure consisted of two sections: Combat and Support. The basic combat team was an eleven-person unit that would patrol near the hamlet. Team members elected their leaders. Support units were segregated into categories such as elders or women and provided first aid or other duties.

Many military and political leaders resisted the concept. Huong was ada-mantly against it, fearing that the various sects or other religious groups would turn the weapons against the government. William Colby, the new deputy to Komer, convinced him otherwise, but Huong was not the only doubter.[35] Writing postwar, Lieutenant General Ngo Quang Truong admitted "there was considerable debate…concerning the wisdom of arming civilians in rural communities. Could they really be trusted with weapons," or would they give them to the Communists? Truong noted how after the Tet Offensive, even though his unit had suffered heavy losses and he needed help, when the local VNQDD communities had asked for weapons, he politely refused. He admitted his mistake when he later saw how the people "responded to the program and participated in the defense of their own communities with genuine enthusiasm and effectiveness."[36]

Despite strong internal resistance, Thieu personally pushed the PSDF concept. On August 11 in Saigon City Hall, he inaugurated the People's Self Defense Month. In a short speech, Thieu outlined that the program was more than just protection against Communist attacks. It would "unite the people with the army in a common purpose…and will help to refute criticism from abroad that the people of South Vietnam are not willing to make the necessary sacrifices." Just as important, Thieu asserted, the PSDF cadres would "help social welfare action projects. A people who do not know how to organize themselves to better their lives," Thieu proclaimed, "cannot be said to constitute a nation."[37]

The PSDF grew rapidly. By the end of September, approximately five hundred thousand had joined. Despite hiccups in training and providing weapons, by April 1969, GVN statistics showed 1,215,030 people were involved. Of those, 742,000 had received some basic military training, and 205,000 weapons had been provided. Losses provide a clear gauge that the program was working. From Tet 1968 to the end of March 1969, 586 PSDF members were killed in action, with another 864 wounded and 344 missing. Around 536 weapons had been lost. They claimed 774 enemy dead, captured another 231, plus 315 weapons.[38] They had been bloodied, but they had punched back.

While Vietnamese statistics always inspired a whiff of skepticism, that the program had extended Saigon's reach to the people was undeniable. Granted, the security contributions of the People's Self-Defense Force were modest, but the ramifications at the local level were enormous. Previously, a small but armed NLF unit could enter a village at night, collect taxes, press-gang youths, spread propaganda, and execute government officials. The PSDF was designed to provide the villagers a means of defending themselves against these Communist depravations. The issuance of new weapons to the ARVN, primarily the M16 rifle, allowed them to transfer their old weapons to the PSDF. There were never enough guns to provide every PSDF combatant with one, so a checkout system was implemented that rotated weapons. The PSDF, combined with the "state building" aspects of the RD program and the expansion of the police into the villages, were increasing Saigon's rural authority. Even more crucial was the emotional signal. Arming its citizens was a dramatic gesture that Saigon had confidence in the loyalty of its people. That the people did not use those weapons against the GVN or give them to the Communists is perhaps the starkest example of where the people's loyalties truly lay. While land reform is acknowledged as Thieu's greatest political achievement, creating the PSDF was undoubtably his second.

While Thieu was launching the PSDF, he was also (Komer would say "finally") addressing the need to destroy the Communist political cadres in the countryside. Prime Minister Loc had signed a decree on December 20, 1967 creating local committees to share intelligence and operations, but the functional plan was not completed until mid-summer 1968. On July 1, 1968, Thieu signed a new decree that merged the various intelligence and police efforts into a coordinated whole at the province and district level. By the end of 1968, all provinces and districts had a functioning Phoenix committee, called *Phuong Hoang* by the Vietnamese.

The antiwar left in the U.S. would soon claim that the Phoenix program was riven by serious human rights violations, including torture, unlawful detention, and wanton assassination. While generally untrue, many abuses did occur, which only added to the overall image of a repressive GVN. Phoenix in 1968 also failed to achieve its goal, but it did make a dent in Communist ranks. Although almost sixteen thousand subversives were killed, captured, or rallied to the GVN side in 1968, a MACV study in March 1969 concluded that only roughly 13 percent of those were district-level or higher and that approximately eighty-two thousand enemy cadres remained. Yet despite its slow start, Phoenix would make life increasingly difficult for the Communist political cadres.

The third leg of the strategy to win the countryside was an American initiative. Following previous GVN policy, the ever-cautious Thieu planned in 1969 to continue building the secure hamlets, while the U.S. sought to push out into the contested areas. Both allies saw Tet '69 as the time frame when Hanoi might request a ceasefire and a coalition. To preempt that, Komer and Colby proposed a campaign that would run for three months, November 1968 to January 1969, and expand the GVN presence into a thousand hamlets considered insecure or Communist-controlled based upon the Hamlet Evaluation System (HES).[39] In what was known as the Accelerated Pacification Campaign (APC), Saigon would convert contested villages to relatively secure ones over the course of three months. APC was not simply a glorified land grab. It was a three-month sprint to increase territory, improve local government, and place Saigon in a strong position for peace talks and a future election.

After studying the situation, Thieu approved the plan. Kicking off the campaign on November 1, U.S. and South Vietnamese units quickly entered numerous insecure hamlets with little opposition. Unfortunately, results lagged in certain areas due to GVN inefficiency, while confusion reigned in ARVN circles over precisely how the army should conduct the APC in conjunction with the RD ministry. In response, Thieu took active measures to tweak performance. In November he formed a Central Pacification and Development Council to oversee GVN efforts, and he made numerous trips to the country to exhort local officials to improve performance. As one scholar notes, "Thieu's efforts...demonstrated his strong interest in pacification and his desire that local officials work harder to establish the government's presence in the countryside."[40]

No longer able to operate with impunity, local force Communist units were soon struggling to obtain supplies or help from the local people. A PAVN military history, describing the situation in the Mekong Delta in 1969, admits they were besieged.

It became very difficult to supply [our units] with replacement troops, weapons, and logistics and technical supplies...[O]ur underground agents, secret self-defense forces, and revolutionary mass organizations in many villages and hamlets had suffered heavy losses during 1968, and these losses had not been replaced. For that reason, not only was the movement to combat pacification in the Mekong Delta not able to grow, our revolutionary agents and organizations continued to suffer losses, our armed units suffered attrition, and in many locations our liberated areas and areas under our control began to shrink. This was a common problem in many areas throughout South Vietnam.[41]

These three programs—PSDF, the APC, and Phoenix—marked the expansion of the South Vietnamese state into previously contested tracts of the countryside. Extending Saigon's control over a clear majority of the population would enable Thieu to win a future electoral contest and defeat the insurgency. Thieu, however, was no policy alchemist. He had not suddenly concocted the perfect recipe of programs that would win the village war. It would also require a major policy decision by the Communists in July 1969 to disengage militarily before he could wrestle the rural areas away from the enemy. But for now, the South Vietnamese ended 1968 on a security high note, with almost 75 percent of the population living under their control.

DEALING WITH SOCIAL ISSUES

As in any pluralistic society, domestic politics usually require more executive time than foreign affairs. While Thieu was invigorating pacification, he also had to deal with a variety of critical internal matters. They ranged from Huong's anti-corruption drive, dissent, the courts, and the ever-quarrelsome Buddhists. The economy, unfortunately, received short shift, a mistake that would haunt Thieu for several years. Nguyen Huu Hanh had resigned as head of the National Bank in August 1968, dealing a blow to GVN efforts to handle inflation.

Although Huong initially made few overt moves against corruption, he did appoint Mai Tho Truyen to head the Inspectorate, a new anti-corruption agency stipulated by the constitution that was designed to collect evidence on venality. Unfortunately, the sinews of corruption ran deep and were hard to uncover. Corruption even struck close to him. In late August Huong dismissed his younger brother, who served as his special assistant, for involvement in a car theft ring.

Regardless, several anti-corruption efforts were already underway. Thieu had previously moved to destroy one channel for military corruption—payments flowing from district leaders to province chiefs to the corps commander—by firing about half of the existing chiefs and rescinding the corps commander's power to appoint new ones. He then instituted a training program for district and province officials that, while designed to improve bureaucratic efficiency, heavily promoted the anti-corruption drive. Interior Minister Khiem replaced two notoriously corrupt Ky cronies, the director of customs and the Saigon port manager. The port manager had been a main source of Ky's illicit funds. Even with these efforts, however, corruption still plagued the country.

While corruption badly tarred South Vietnam's image, its aura as a repressive state was equally damaging. Hanoi had successfully painted Saigon as a brutal military dictatorship while simultaneously avoiding a corresponding analysis of its own harsh police-state control. Although Saigon allowed Western journalists freedom to investigate every flaw, the GVN was often its own worst enemy. It saw dissent as "weakening the anti-communist spirit" of its combatants and people. With no legacy of press criticisms or the give-and-take of democracy, senior government officials were unused to reproach and often reacted harshly to it, usually in self-defeating ways.

Even after the worldwide condemnation from the picture of Loan shooting the prisoner in the head, Saigon remained stunningly tone-deaf. The city's elite were often unable to comprehend how outsiders viewed their actions. Equally destructive, they saw insidious Communist manipulation everywhere. While they were often correct, the GVN's inability to prove its claims turned world opinion against its actions. Antiwar critics fumed that Saigon's motives were not justified wartime caution but rightwing oppression of progressive reformers. It is a judgment that clouds opinion of South Vietnam even today. Although Saigon's failure to manage international public relations was not the sole reason for its low stock, and while Diem and Thieu had Vietnamese reasons for their actions, it does not excuse their inability to weigh deeds against results. It cost them dearly.

For example, in late February 1968, Saigon police arrested Thich Tri Quang, Truong Dinh Dzu, and Au Truong Thanh, claiming that the Communists might kidnap them. The real reason was to prevent them from publicly demanding peace talks. After seven weeks in "protective custody," Dzu and Thanh were released in mid-April after they staged a two-week hunger strike. Quang remained under wraps until June 30. The GVN never charged or even questioned them, and Dzu admitted upon release that "they treated us very nicely."[42]

Despite their jail time, neither man had changed their opinion that the NLF should be allowed to participate openly in an election. Two days after Dzu's release, the pudgy Dale Carnegie devotee gave a press interview in which he again advocated talks with the NLF. The GVN rearrested him in May for "violating national security." Then Phan Quang Dan, who was traveling in the U.S. visiting college campuses to promote South Vietnam and counter the antiwar narrative, was misquoted in the U.S. press as recommending direct peace talks with the NLF. When Vietnamese papers reprinted these stories, the hardliners in the assembly demanded that Huong fire him. Huong, fearing the possibility of a no-confidence vote and the fall of his government, removed Dan on June 15. South Vietnamese politics was so charged after the two offensives that even the hint of endorsing talks with the NLF was political suicide.

When Dan returned to Saigon shortly thereafter, he was not arrested, but Dzu was brought before a military court on July 24 and sentenced to five years' imprisonment. Bunker rationalized to Washington that Dzu's trial was "part of a broader effort to convey the image of a hard GVN position on the NLF and a coalition government." GVN leaders, he said, "apparently feel they must adopt such a posture to appease . . . the opponents of the government" who were charging them with being soft on Communism. Plus, it served to keep any left-leaning intellectuals "in line" while maintaining "a strong bargaining position" with Hanoi.[43]

Secretary of State Dean Rusk was unmoved. He complained to Bunker of the sharp reaction in the U.S. press to the Dzu trial. Bunker immediately visited Thieu, who blamed local fears about a U.S. sellout and ongoing rumors by the northern Catholics that he and Huong would agree to a coalition. "If the GVN merely stood passively on the sidelines" while people advocated for a coalition, Thieu opined, "there would be anarchy." Showcasing a worldview limited to his domestic audience, he noted that "there had been little reaction" inside Vietnam.[44] Thieu, however, assured the ambassador that he would offer Dzu a face-saving gesture. If Dzu asked for clemency, Thieu would grant it. Dzu refused, though, stating unequivocally that he was not guilty. He would become a cause célèbre for years. When Au Truong Thanh applied again for a visa to travel overseas, Huong "thought it best to let him leave. . . . If he made foolish statements or got into trouble here, he would have to be tried and we might have another Dzu trial on our hands."[45]

Press censorship and the courts were also often cited as examples of GVN repression. The U.S. embassy strongly disagreed, claiming that for a nation at war, South Vietnam had considerable press freedom. Newspapers, it asserted, "take editorial potshots at the GVN on a range of subjects."[46] While the embassy was correct about the press, it was on shaky ground with the courts. Thieu had attempted to adapt the court system to wartime conditions while enhancing the rule of law. Since the Tet Offensive, he had been wrestling with how to amend the state-of-war decree that he had signed on June 24, 1965. President Diem had placed the judiciary under the executive branch of government so that he could control the legal system. Thieu wanted to remove that control, but he also wanted to retain the ability to prosecute anyone violating "national security," an ambiguous rule designed to maintain a tight rein on those who might dare advocate a political solution with the Communists.

The first move came on October 30, 1967, when the government authorized a Mobile Military Field Court in Saigon to judge people in the Saigon area charged with violating national security. Much like what Khanh had instituted in August 1964, all national security cases would be transferred from the civilian courts to the new Mobile Military Court. Dzu was charged under that decree and in that court. Despite the furor over Dzu's trial, on November 5, 1968, Thieu quietly amended the 1965 decree to allow the police to search any home at any time without cause, and he banned strikes, boycotts, and "demonstrations of any kind." Moreover, "elements deemed to be dangerous to national security will be restricted to locations of residence or forcibly relocated to new living locations." Also forbidden was "the storage and distribution of all publications, documents, or leaflets deemed to be damaging to national security." Lastly, "All violations of national security will be tried by military field courts under emergency procedures."[47] The new decree essentially gave him the legal authority to crack down on any dissent.

Outside of "national security" matters, however, he eliminated government interference in the courts. The formation of the constitution and the National Assembly now prevented any leader from wielding absolute power, and the creation of a Supreme Court, the first independent court in South Vietnam's history, was the final piece to fully institute the rule of law. The constitution had radically changed the republic's court system with the creation of a Supreme Court that would control a unified judiciary. The assembly chose a group of lawyers who elected nine judges for the Supreme Court. On October 22, 1968, the judges were sworn in. Much like in the U.S., the Vietnamese Supreme Court would interpret the constitutionality of government laws and, if necessary, strike them down. The court began its first term on November 1. While the military courts were outside its purview, South Vietnam finally had a system of legislative and judicial checks on the executive, one of the hallmarks of Western governance. Its very first ruling determined whether the constitution required both houses of the assembly or just the Senate to approve sending a GVN delegation to the Paris talks. It voted in favor of a joint session.

Religious issues also continued, but they caused nowhere near the uproar as during prior years. In a notable display of how far Tri Quang's star had fallen, no one protested his detention or showed up for his release. With Quang's arrest, his chief lieutenant, Thich Thien Minh, had become the de facto head of the militant Buddhists. After Quang's release, the two former close friends began to jostle for control. Minh organized a congress at the An Quang Pagoda from August 18 to August 21 to vote for new leadership for the Propagation of the Faith. The Quoc Tu moderates refused to attend since Tam Chau was traveling to various countries to broaden relations with other major congregations, a clever ploy to outflank An Quang.

Although Tam Chau had declared the official UBC charter suspended, the GVN had not changed the law. The An Quang congress demanded a revision of the Buddhist charter anointing the Quoc Tu moderates as the officially recognized church. Afterward, forty members of the Lower House sent Thieu a petition requesting he abrogate the charter. Thieu immediately wrote back that modifying the decree should be handled by the assembly but that he was open to changing it. The Quoc Tu moderates planned their own congress for mid-November. More than a thousand delegates attended, as did several government figures such as Mai Tho Truyen, but its disagreements with An Quang remained deep. Thien Minh responded to the Quoc Tu congress by stating that they would continue fighting to get the charter revoked and that "as long as GVN supports Tam Chau, it will be difficult for Buddhists to contribute constructively to national life."[48] Although the militant Buddhists no longer commanded the street power of prior years, the old issue of the church's role in South Vietnamese society continued unresolved.

While the Buddhists were once more trying to sort out their issues, in early August the Lower House also petitioned Thieu to end the exile of Nationalist leaders, particularly Duong Van Minh. After consideration, Thieu agreed to allow Minh to return, and he sent Khiem to Bangkok to ask him to consider joining the government as an advisor. His gesture was not purely magnanimous; Thieu wanted to use Minh's popularity with the Buddhists and southerners to broaden his own government. Naturally, there was a price attached to his return: Minh could not be exploited by any political faction (meaning the militant Buddhists), nor could "he seek personal publicity for political purposes."[49]

After agreeing to Thieu's conditions, Minh returned on October 5. Despite Thieu's publicized offer to join him, Minh held the president at arm's length for almost ten days. Finally meeting him, Minh declined to join his government, dealing a blow to Thieu. Like Tran Van Don, Minh could not let go of the past. For now, Big Minh would remain a relic upon which the militant Buddhists and frustrated southerners superimposed their dreams of a path to power, but he was also a symbol of the inability of South Vietnam's political class to rise above its chronic divisions.

For Thieu, after "breaking his chains" and successfully wrestling power away from the military, he had embarked on Saigon's most critical effort: extending the state's control over the countryside. Yet while Thieu was focused on solving the social, religious, military, and economic issues that vexed South Vietnam, nothing hung more ominously over Saigon's future than the Paris peace talks. The negotiations had remained stalled for a variety of reasons, but unexpectedly in October, a possible breakthrough appeared. Now the contentious issue of who would take the lead role in negotiations—Saigon or Washington—required resolution. Peace, it seemed, would prove harder to manage than the war.

15

"THIS CONFERENCE WILL DECIDE THE FATE OF MY NATION"

Searching for Peace

October 1968, another tumultuous month in a year of upheaval. Five tragic years had passed since the momentous events of 1963 that had sealed President Ngo Dinh Diem's fate. Since then, South Vietnam had endured a cataclysmic war, shattering political trials, economic deprivations, and social calamities, but suddenly out of the maelstrom a faint hope for peace appeared. This was the third major episode of 1968. First had been the Tet Offensive. Next had come President Lyndon Johnson's stunning announcement of a bombing halt and his decision not to seek a second term, followed by a second wave of attacks and Thieu's victory over the Military Council.

For Thieu, the road to peace had always begun in Hanoi and ended in Saigon. Since his election, he had grown concerned over U.S. plans on how to achieve an accord. His myopic autocratic Asian allies had warned him that the Americans would "sell him out," which fueled Thieu's already sizeable paranoia. Fearing that the U.S. might force him into a coalition, he rejected NLF participation in any peace talks and instead demanded that his government lead the Paris talks and that Hanoi speak directly with Saigon. His tough stand stemmed from a combination of factors. He believed that Hanoi did not truly desire peace, and he had an overriding concern that most Nationalists would react with fury to any agreement that allowed NLF participation in the negotiations. When Hanoi balked at his demands, Thieu's subsequent refusal to attend the Paris talks would lead to a dramatic confrontation between the allies and create a political legend that presidential candidate Richard Nixon had secretly conspired with him to swing the U.S. election.

THE PEACE TALKS HEAT UP

On October 7, Thieu addressed the opening of the second regular session of the National Assembly. He stressed his dedication to constitutional government and asked for the assembly's assistance in establishing the rule of law. In terms of peace, he reiterated that he would not permit a coalition government, cede any territory, or allow the NLF to participate in elections as a political entity. Buttressing his confidence was his belief that the military equilibrium had swung his way. Mobilization was expanding his military, and new weapons were improving the firepower of his troops. In the countryside, the PSDF was rapidly growing, Phoenix was exacting a toll on the underground cadres, and the new pacification program would begin on November 1.

Bunker and General Abrams also believed the fortunes of war had turned in their favor. U.S. intelligence indicated that most Communist main force units had retreated across the Laotian and Cambodian borders to recuperate after suffering stinging defeats. Allied sweep operations had destroyed many Communist supply caches, robbing the enemy of his ability to mount future attacks. Analyzing Hanoi's battlefield strategy, Abrams concluded that the Politburo "had made a major decision to shift his emphasis from the military to the political" since the "cost of his struggle has been so great."[1]

Hanoi, however, did not view the situation similarly. If Bunker and Thieu felt that North Vietnam could not win militarily, Hanoi thought the same about the U.S. The Politburo judged that the conflict's mounting strains would soon force the Americans to end the war. Hanoi saw that the "imperialist/capitalist/neo-colonialists" were suffering severe financial stress and enormous social disorder, which were disrupting America's ability to maintain its other global commitments. These crushing burdens would force the U.S. to seek a way out. The Politburo claimed that Johnson's speech announcing a partial bombing halt was "a victory for us." They chalked up their triumph to the "ferocious struggles going on within American leadership circles, especially during the primary elections in the U.S., and because of powerful pressure from world and U.S. public opinion."[2]

Minister of the Economy Pham Kim Ngoc. *Photo courtesy of Pham Kim Ngoc*

Independence Palace. *Photo courtesy of Hoang Song Liem*

The author and Mrs. Nguyen Van Thieu, March 2013.
Photo courtesy of George J. Veith

Tran Quang Minh inspecting miracle rice in Long Khanh province, 1973. *Photo courtesy of Tran Quang Minh*

Left: Infantry Lieutenant Nguyen Van Thieu after graduating from the staff course in Hanoi, September 1952. Photo attached to his official French transcript. *Photo courtesy of the Vanuxem family*

Below: Ngo Dinh Nhu and his family at the Le Van Kim residence in Dalat in 1949. *Photo courtesy of Le Van Minh*

Above: Bao Dai in Dalat
in December 1949.
Photo courtesy of Le Van Minh

Right: Pham Duy Tat shortly
after being promoted to
Brigadier General.
Photo courtesy of Pham Duy Tat

Above: PAVN 122mm artillery captured in Quang Tri province, 1972. *Photo courtesy of Nguyen Thu Luong*

Left: Lieutenant General Cao Van Vien, probably in 1965. *Photo courtesy of Ly Thanh Tam*

Above: Tran Van Huong, Nguyen Van Thieu, and Major General Lu Lan, Pacification Conference, II Corps, 1969.
Photo courtesy of Lu Lan

Right: Campaign poster for the 1967 Thieu/Ky ticket.
Photo courtesy of George J. Veith

ĐỒNG BÀO HÃY DỒN PHIẾU CHO

LIÊN DANH DÂN-CHỦ

NGUYỄN-VĂN-**THIỆU**—NGUYỄN-CAO-**KỲ**

Ứng cử viên TỔNG-THỐNG NGUYỄN-VĂN-THIỆU   *Ứng cử viên PHÓ TỔNG-THỐNG NGUYỄN-CAO-KỲ*

ĐỂ

– XÂY-DỰNG DÂN-CHỦ

– GIẢI-QUYẾT CHIẾN-TRANH

– CẢI-TẠO XÃ-HỘI

Official portrait of President Nguyen Van Thieu after the presidential election of 1967. *Photo courtesy of George J. Veith*

Change of Command ceremony in I Corps, May 1972. From left to right: Major General Ngo Quang Truong, Lieutenant General Hoan Xuan Lam, General Cao Van Vien. *Photo courtesy of Ly Thanh Tam*

NGUYỄN VĂN THIỆU
Tổng-Thống Việt-Nam Cộng-Hòa

— S/gòn 25/4/7

Kính tặng
Tổng Thống Trần-văn-Hương

Thưa Cụ,

— Để thực hiện công tác dự phái
phó, tôi kính xin Cụ chấp thuận
cho những Sĩ quan sau đây, là
thành phần tối thiểu cần thiết
để phụ tôi, đi theo tôi trong suốt
thời gian công du :

1 — Đại-Tá Võ-văn-Cầm.
2 — Đại-Tá Nguyễn-văn-Đức.
3 — Đại-Tá Nhan-văn-Thiệt.
4 — Đại-Tá Trần-thanh-Điền.
5 — Trung-Tá Tôn-Thất-Ái-Chiêu.
6 — Bác-sĩ Thiếu-Tá Hồ-vương-M.

7 — Đại-úy Nguyễn-phú-Hải.
8 — Thục Dịch viên Nghi (Bình

— Ngoài ra, Cựu Thủ-Tướng Đại-Tướng
Trần-thiện-Khiêm cũng cần đem
theo những Sĩ quan và dân sự sau đây.
— Trung-Tá Đặng-văn-Châu.
— Thiếu-Tá Đinh-sơn-Thùng
— Thiếu-Tá Nguyễn-tấn-Phát
— Ông Đặng-Vui.
Đại-Tá Trần-thiện-Khiêm nhờ tôi
kính Cụ chấp thuận ./.

— Kính chào Tổng-Thống

Thuận
25/4/75
Hương

Thiệu

Left: This is a copy of Thieu's handwritten official request to be allowed to leave Vietnam for Taiwan, and the approval given by Huong. The English translation is on the opposite page.
Documents courtesy of Nguyen Tan Phan; translation by Merle Pribbenow

Saigon, 25 April 75

Nguyen Van Thieu
Former President of the Republic of Vietnam

Esteemed Elder [Tran Van Huong]
-To allow me to carry out the duties I have been given, I respectfully request that you approve the following list of officers, the minimum I need to assist me, to accompany me on this official foreign trip:
1. Colonel Vo Van Cam
2. Colonel Nguyen Van Duc
3. Colonel Nhan Van Thiet
4. Colonel Tran Thanh Dien [or Dieu - unclear]
5. Lieutenant Colonel Ton That Ai Chieu
6. Doctor, Lieutenant Colonel Ho Vuong M [sic]
7. Captain Nguyen Phu Thai
8. Aides Nghi + Binh
-In addition, former Prime Minister Tran Thien Khiem also needs the following officers and civilians to accompany him.
- Lieutenant Colonel Dang Van Chau
- Major Dinh Son Thang
- Mr. Dang Vu
General Tran Thien Khiem asked me to submit this list to you.

Respectfully

Thieu

Approved
25 April 75
Huong

This was Huong's handwritten response. *Courtesy of Nguyen Tan Phan; translation by Merle Pribbenow*

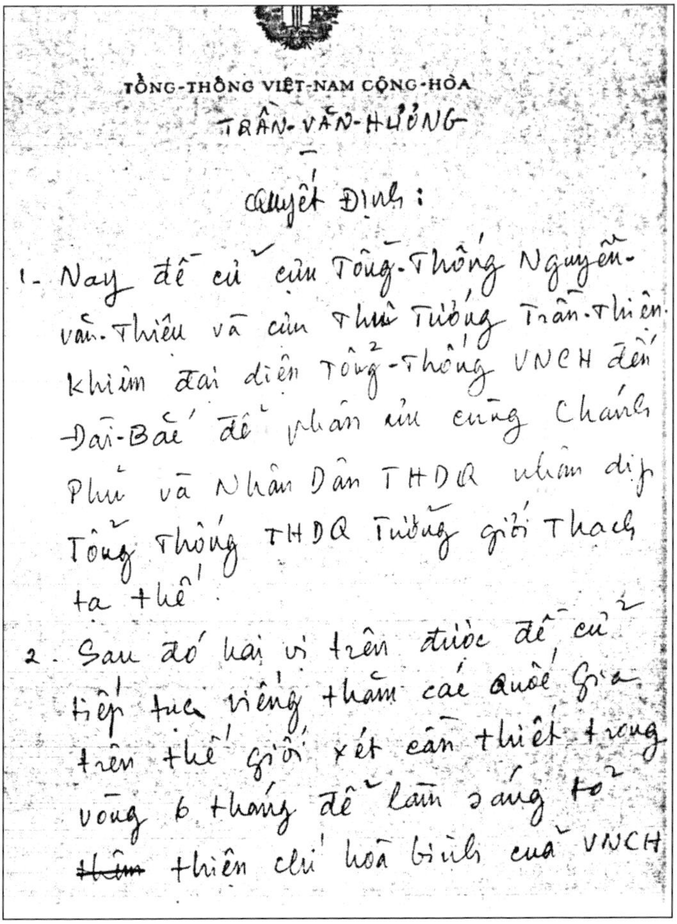

TỔNG-THỐNG VIỆT-NAM CỘNG-HÒA

TRẦN-VĂN-HƯƠNG

Quyết Định:

1.- Nay đề cử cựu Tổng-Thống Nguyễn-văn-Thiệu và cựu Thủ Tướng Trần-Thiện-Khiêm đại diện Tổng-Thống VNCH đến Đài-Bắc để phân ưu cùng Chánh Phủ và Nhân Dân THDQ nhân dịp Tổng Thống THDQ Tưởng giới Thạch tạ thế.

2. Sau đó hai vị trên được đề cử tiếp tục viếng thăm các quốc gia trên thế giới xét cần thiết trong vòng 6 tháng để làm sáng tỏ ~~thiện~~ thiện chí hòa bình của VNCH

PRESIDENT OF THE REPUBLIC OF VIETNAM

Tran Van Huong

1.-Former President Nguyen Van Thieu and former Prime Minister Tran Thien Khiem are hereby appointed to be sent to Taipei to represent the President of the Republic of Vietnam in offering condolences to the Government and people of Nationalist China for the death of Chinese President Chiang Kai Shek.
2.-These two representatives will then continue their travels on to other countries around the world as needed for a period of six months in order to inform these countries of the Republic of Vietnam's good faith desire for peace.

Addressees:
- Former President Nguyen Van Thieu
- Former Prime Minister Tran Thien Khiem
- Ministry of Foreign Affairs
- Ministry of Defense
  "For action"
- Prime Minister
  "For information"

Thieu and retired French general Paul Vanuxem visit the An Loc battlefield on July 7, 1972. *Photo courtesy of Ly Thanh Tam*

People protesting in Saigon against the Paris Peace Accords. *Photo courtesy of Hoang Song Liem*

Map of French Indochina. *Photo courtesy of Ly Thanh Tam*

The talks in Paris were currently stalemated over Hanoi's insistence that the U.S. unconditionally halt attacks on its territory as a prerequisite to real negotiations. Hanoi also refused to begin negotiations in exchange for a bombing cessation. There would be no reciprocity, only a U.S. admission that Hanoi's virtuous stance had defeated the "warmongering and criminal" American actions. Further, Hanoi rejected Saigon's attendance at the talks, claiming the GVN was merely an American "puppet." Only the NLF was the "true" representative of South Vietnam.

Although the U.S. had rebuffed the DRV's demands, Hanoi waited patiently, believing that America's "internal contradictions" would soon compel it to offer concessions. At the end of August, the Politburo provided its analysis of the situation to the 15th Plenum of the Central Committee. Its objectives remained unchanged: win a decisive battlefield triumph, force the U.S. to withdraw, or compel the U.S. and Saigon to talk with the NLF. Only then would it agree to settle "the Vietnam problem through negotiations." Nor had Hanoi's rulers modified their strategy. "Fighting and talking," they wrote, "are intimately connected to one another . . . [W]e are using the talks to conceal our preparations to make powerful attacks in South Vietnam." However, some reality was setting in. "Although we are in a stronger position than the enemy, we have not reached the point where we can force them to accept a settlement that meets our requirements. For that reason, it is inevitable that the Paris talks will last for quite some time."[3] Hanoi's tactics were not to seek peace but to stall until conditions were ripe to achieve victory.

Still, the Politburo's brief was as much exhortation to its depleted military as it was policy guidelines. The Soviets had secretly informed the U.S. in early June that Hanoi might finally be receptive to a complete bombing halt in exchange for serious peace talks. The Russians were correct, for despite its strident language in late August, the Politburo was flexible when necessary. On October 10, the Politburo informed COSVN that it had decided to exploit the U.S. election campaign by offering to trade Saigon's participation for a termination of the bombing of North Vietnam. Hanoi rationalized its sudden change by declaring that this offer would "de-Americanize the war," meaning it was the first step in removing the U.S.[4] Like Thieu, Le Duan was also searching for a way to remove the U.S. from the conflict.

After five months of DRV diatribes and stonewalling, on October 11, Hanoi's negotiators in Paris abruptly reversed course. They asked Averell Harriman, the chief U.S. negotiator, if the Americans would terminate the

bombing of North Vietnam in exchange for an answer on GVN participation. Johnson, however, did not leap at the bait. Despite Hanoi's first
semi-positive response, Johnson made three demands that had to be met
before he would agree: stop indirect fire barrages against South Vietnamese
cities, halt further attacks across the DMZ, and begin direct negotiations
with Saigon.

Hoping a breakthrough had finally appeared, Johnson promptly sent
Bunker to gain Thieu's concurrence. The ambassador explained the new
development to Saigon's leaders and asked for Thieu's agreement on moving
forward if the DRV accepted Johnson's three conditions. Surprisingly, the
South Vietnamese president said yes. "After all," he replied, "the problem
is not to stop the bombing, but to stop the war, and we must try this path
to see if they are serious."[5] Thieu then asked about the NLF's status at the
talks. Bunker said that the U.S. had informed Hanoi's delegates that it
would not accept the NLF's presence at the table, but after they refused,
Harriman had offered a your side–our side formula in which anyone could
be seated with either party. The U.S. plan was to sidestep Hanoi's demand
while rejecting NLF flags, nameplates, and other modalities that would
imply that the Front was a full participant in the talks.

On October 16, Bunker again visited Thieu and told him that Harriman
in Paris would soon meet with the DRV delegation. If Hanoi accepted the
three conditions, the U.S. would halt the bombing shortly thereafter. Bunker wanted Thieu to sign a joint communiqué announcing the initiation of
formal peace talks. Thieu immediately convened his newly formed National
Security Council (NSC) to discuss Bunker's request. He also invited the two
leaders of the Lower House and Senate to join them. Thieu's Special Assistant for Foreign Affairs Nguyen Phu Duc attended each NSC meeting and
took extensive notes.[6] He states that this "meeting was important because
it inaugurated the process of decision-making in the negotiating process on
the South Vietnamese side." While Thieu, Ky, Foreign Minister Thanh, and
Duc conducted the negotiations with Bunker, "decisions were taken only
after full consultations and discussions in the NSC."[7]

After Thieu explained the situation, Ky fumed that Johnson's true objective was to assist Humphrey's election rather than to help Saigon. Most
agreed with Ky's conspiratorial thinking, and after a short debate, the NSC
demanded that Thieu first clarify the NLF's status at the talks before signing
a joint communiqué. Thieu then sent Ambassador Bui Diem a cable ordering him to "insist with the State Department and the White House on the

disastrous consequences that NLF participation in the negotiations will have on the morale of our armed forces and our population...Such eventuality could even have dangerous repercussions on our political stability....Neither the National Assembly nor public opinion will accept a reversal."[8]

The next day, Thieu explained to Bunker his fears about his domestic audience. "If I and the prime minister accepted," he said, "to go into a meeting without the NLF status clarified, there could be a violent reaction here." Thieu was worried that the hardliners—the Revolutionary Dai Viets, the northern Catholics, and some military officers—would erupt. While he acknowledged that the world would blame him if Saigon declined to attend, he lamented that "I do not think I am strong enough to move; there are too many people here...who would use this as a pretext to make trouble."[9] Talking with the Front was a line Thieu would not, could not, cross. Saigon's position was that the NLF was a branch office of Hanoi and that if the GVN agreed to speak to the NLF as an equal, it would destroy Saigon's contention that the war was aggression from the north rather than a civil war. Like President Diem facing down General Nguyen Van Hinh, Thieu "was willing to risk everything rather than accept the NLF as a separate delegation."[10]

When U.S. press articles stated that the proposed bombing halt was "unconditional," Thieu spoke on Vietnamese television and radio on October 19 to reject any bombing cessation unless Hanoi publicly agreed to Johnson's three conditions. Thieu said he would not agree to a bombing halt that would allow Hanoi to continue shelling South Vietnam's cities and killing civilians. Further, he wanted Hanoi to publicly "recognize [that the GVN] is the only representative of the South Vietnamese people" and "manifest goodwill by deescalating the war." After all, "what is the use of ending the bombing...[unless] it leads quickly to peace?"[11] Otherwise, Thieu opined, Hanoi was just stalling, hoping the U.S. would force a coalition or give up.

Thieu sought these public assurances, which would upend Hanoi's propaganda, to determine if North Vietnam sincerely wanted peace rather than using the talks to spew invective. He wanted to avoid a "false peace," one where the Politburo would simply revert from armed clashes to intimidation and assassination, an effort to win by subversion rather than military conquest. Thieu's non-negotiable goal was the safeguarding of the Republic of Vietnam, and he wanted "the kind of peace which could preserve the freedom of South Vietnam" even if it meant "resisting...the demands of a hard-pressed ally."[12] Hence, Thieu required firm pledges that the DRV was not up to its old tricks. However, he was not demanding Hanoi's surrender. If Hanoi publicly agreed to speak seriously and directly with Saigon, Thieu was prepared to be "honest in our talks...from the moment we enter the conference room, we arrive for peace. We shall discuss any question with them...not as enemies but as compatriots."[13]

In response to Thieu's statement, two days later, Vice President Humphrey was asked on the CBS TV show "Face the Nation" about peace talks. He declared that the South Vietnamese "cannot exercise a veto" over the U.S. offer for a bombing halt. While he did not openly criticize Thieu, he opined that since America had borne a "heavy burden" helping South Vietnam, Thieu "should exercise great cooperation" with Johnson.[14]

The next day, Thieu issued a clarification, stating he was not categorically opposed to a bombing halt, but he would agree to it only after Hanoi had clearly indicated it would deescalate the fighting and speak directly with Saigon. Thieu then informed Bui Diem that his comment "does not mean a softer stand as interpreted by foreign and local press. But following Humphrey's speech, essential objective in that declaration is to repel any intention toward the desire of U.S. and world opinion to accuse us of belligerence or preventing any cessation of the bombing.... Declaration intentionally addressed to world opinion and the American people to prevent intoxication and to gain sympathy."[15]

Thieu then attempted to modify the language for the joint communiqué. He pressed for unambiguous terminology that explicitly denied NLF participation and verified that Hanoi was engaged in direct talks with the GVN. His motive was simple. If Hanoi failed to keep its promises, as it had so many times before, he wanted to decisively establish these provisions first so the allies could break off the negotiations without being condemned by international public opinion.

The Americans were instead trying to patch over the differences with the DRV on these issues. The vagueness of the U.S. prose in the communiqué was deliberate. The U.S. delegation in Paris believed that Hanoi would never publicly agree to Saigon's demands. The Soviets were reassuring Harriman that while the DRV would never publicly concur with the conditions, it would privately adhere to them. Harriman, who had spent much of his career negotiating with Communists, thought it was better to get started based on this "understanding" rather than remain deadlocked. After several more sessions between Bunker and Thieu, on October 28, the South Vietnamese, despite serious reservations, grudgingly agreed to the draft communiqué. Although Thieu had acquiesced, he secretly hoped that the joint message would become moot since Hanoi still had not responded to the U.S. offer.

Hanoi had in fact suddenly proven recalcitrant. On October 13, the Politburo sent a cable to Le Duc Tho, its chief negotiator in Paris, with tough new requirements. As much as Thieu wanted the DRV to publicly agree to Johnson's conditions, Hanoi was equally adamant that the U.S. stipulate in the communiqué that the bombing halt was "unconditional." Additionally, Hanoi wanted to wait an unspecified amount of time after the halt began before starting the formal negotiations, and it sought a four-power conference to inflate the status of the NLF. Le Duc Tho, aware that diplomacy is the art of the possible, believed these requirements were "excessive and impractical."[16] He knew the U.S. would not agree, and he immediately returned to Hanoi to confer. Due to the Politburo's cable and Tho's departure, the DRV negotiators in Paris stalled Harriman. The U.S. team was confused by their counterpart's sudden obstinacy. However, Tho convinced the Politburo to drop its demands, and on October 27, the Communist representatives assented to Johnson's three conditions. As the Soviets had indicated, they requested that the terms remain secret, as they would not admit to any reciprocity for a bombing halt.[17]

On October 29, Bunker informed Thieu that Hanoi had agreed. The U.S. thought Hanoi's capitulation to Saigon's inclusion in the conference was a major victory, and that the DRV had caved on the three conditions. Johnson planned to announce the bombing halt on October 31, and to offer to hold the first meeting on November 2. Bunker wanted Thieu's concurrence that he would send a delegation to attend the conference and that he would sign the communiqué.

After his meeting with Bunker, Thieu immediately convened the NSC. Thieu and his advisors were shocked that Hanoi had accepted right after he had agreed to the communiqué, and he was baffled by the American haste to start the talks. Frugal with his trust of U.S. and DRV assurances that they had an "understanding" on Johnson's conditions, Thieu viewed the timing with great doubt, and as the NSC debated Bunker's request, a stunning cable arrived from Paris. The chief GVN observer at the talks, Pham Dang Lam, wrote that Harriman had informed him that the U.S. could neither force Hanoi to engage in direct talks with Saigon nor prevent them from seating the NLF as a separate delegation. Both points contravened the language of the communiqué and every assurance Bunker had given the South

Vietnamese. The bombshell cable exacerbated Thieu's suspicions about U.S. motives, and he informed Bunker that he would not agree to participate in the talks until Harriman's remarks were clarified.

When Bunker cabled Rusk that Thieu was balking, the Secretary of State replied that Johnson "has decided that he must proceed on the basis of the joint position agreed between himself and Thieu as outlined in the joint communiqué." In the first inkling of what became known as the Chennault Affair, Rusk also told Bunker that "we have disturbing information from political circles that certain political elements in the United States have attempted to intervene in Saigon."[18]

While Saigon debated its response to the ambassador's ultimatum, Washington pressed Bunker to get an answer. He repeatedly visited Independence Palace over the next two days but made no headway. Then another incident heightened tensions between the two countries. Thieu's skepticism of Hanoi's promises was amplified when eight rockets slammed into Saigon on the night of October 31, the first attack in a month. Nineteen civilians were killed when one rocket hit a Catholic church. Thieu was furious, seeing it as a calculated violation of Harriman's "understanding" of Johnson's condition not to shell South Vietnamese cities. Bunker arrived at the palace shortly before midnight on October 31. He endured a torrent of South Vietnamese complaints, but under strict orders from Rusk, Bunker deflected the arguments and appealed for unity. Thieu was unmoved. Exasperated, he proclaimed that "this conference will decide the fate of my nation. We need time for that. If your government decides that it has no more time, that is up to you. But I have a responsibility to my nation and to my people."[19]

Duc admiringly notes that after Bunker left to confer with Rusk over more GVN modifications to the communiqué, Thieu calmly awaited Bunker's reply. Like other South Vietnamese leaders, Thieu secretly feared that if he refused U.S. requests, he would be replaced with someone more compliant. To prevent that, he claimed he had learned from Diem's mistake. He told Duc that he would not put himself "in front of a rolling American tank and get crushed but shall remain next to the driver and try to influence him."[20] Diem had chosen to defend his country's interests and stand in front of the moving tank, no matter the cost, and the image of Diem's bloodied corpse still haunted Thieu. The U.S., of course, had no plans to depose Thieu, but Bunker regretfully informed him on the morning of November 1 (Saigon time) that Johnson would not accept any further changes to the communiqué. Johnson would make the announcement at

8:00 p.m. on October 31. He would state that the bombing would stop the next morning and that the first meeting between the delegations would occur on November 6. Thieu did not buckle, and his answer remained no. But aware of the ramifications, he asked Bunker to tell Johnson that he had "the greatest gratitude to him and the U.S. government."[21]

On November 2, Thieu gave a speech to the National Assembly. He asserted that "the basic issue is not the end of the bombing" but "the end of the war." He proclaimed that the "GVN is ready to take any action which helps in restoring peace" and repeated his offer to negotiate directly with Hanoi. His voice rising, he then loudly declared that since those conditions had not been met, the "RVN will not attend" the meeting scheduled for November 6.[22] Thunderous applause greeted his remarks. After Thieu finished, a delegation of deputies marched to the palace to congratulate him. He had achieved the impossible; he had united the contentious political factions.

Thieu's decision was based on several factors. First, Thieu thought Johnson's haste to announce peace talks was to help Humphrey's election. Second, why rush to start a bombing halt when reports were pouring in that the enemy was badly hurt and a massive pacification drive was about to begin? Third, Thieu feared that talking with the NLF would cause the ARVN and government morale to collapse, not to mention his genuine concern over a coup or assassination by his right wing. Fourth, Thieu detested Averell Harriman, the chief American negotiator. The failure of the 1962 Laos Accords had enabled Hanoi to expand the Ho Chi Minh Trail, which the South Vietnamese had sarcastically christened "The Harriman Memorial Highway." They believed Harriman was too eager to make a deal with Hanoi. If Nixon won, Harriman would be replaced. Last, Thieu was not a man to make quick decisions, and the strong U.S. pressure caused him to dig in.

Regardless of his rationales, for President Nguyen Van Thieu, another moment of truth had arrived. Appealing to South Vietnamese national pride and standing up to the Americans had closed Vietnamese ranks behind him. Yet it had come at great cost: the dispute over the peace talks had created the worst crisis in U.S.-GVN relations since the last days of the Diem regime. Johnson on the other hand, believed that Thieu had previously conceded to U.S. demands but at the last second had reversed himself. Why had he abruptly altered course? Johnson speculated that the turnaround was due to a backroom deal between Thieu and presidential candidate Richard Nixon, a plot that became known as the Chennault Affair. Investigative journalists and writers have reviewed the evidence from U.S. records, but aside from Bui Diem's account, they have ignored the South Vietnamese records.[23] Here for the first time is Saigon's side of what happened.

THE CHENNAULT AFFAIR

According to the well-known story, Republican candidate Richard Nixon used Mrs. Anna Chennault, the Chinese-born widow of U.S. Major General Claire Chennault, commander of the famed World War II Flying Tigers, as a secret channel to Thieu via South Vietnamese Ambassador Bui Diem. Nixon's alleged message was that Thieu should refuse Johnson's request to attend the Paris talks before the election, and in turn Nixon would support Thieu's peace demands afterward. In this scenario, Nixon was desperately attempting to prevent a last-minute political bombshell by Johnson, called the "October Surprise," that would swing the election to Humphrey. Nixon believed that he had lost the presidency in 1960 to voter irregularities (he had not), and there is little doubt he was on guard against another attempt to steal the election.[24]

This assertion against Nixon is based on covert intelligence gathering that Johnson ordered in the final days of the 1968 election to uncover suspected intrigue between Nixon and Thieu. Although the U.S. government was already receiving precise intelligence on internal GVN discussions— the National Security Agency was intercepting and translating all South Vietnamese diplomatic traffic, and the CIA had installed listening devices in Thieu's office in Independence Palace—Johnson instructed the FBI to observe Chennault's movements and to tap Bui Diem's phone to unearth any conspiracy. The FBI's surveillance and the methods used to collect information from the South Vietnamese were so sensitive that Johnson directed National Security Advisor Walt Rostow to retain these reports when Rostow left the government. Although journalists began printing stories in early 1969 alleging Chennault's assistance to Nixon, Rostow did not give the file to the LBJ Library until mid-1973. Called the "X envelope," the library eventually declassified it. Other information detailing Johnson's discussions of the Nixon plot with political figures and his staff are contained in transcribed phone calls or meetings that were published as part of the State Department's *Foreign Relations* series. These two collections provide the documentary basis for Johnson's beliefs and a recounting of his actions.

The currently available U.S. records, which provide little evidence of a plot, have been thoroughly examined. The writers who insist that Nixon was involved in this scheme generally accept it because Johnson believed it and acted on his certainty. Most scholars, however, have judged that Thieu's refusal to attend the talks was related to his internal policies and not from Nixon's supposed entreaties. The South Vietnamese individuals who were involved adamantly confirm that assessment. In a rare postwar interview, Thieu also denied that he was directly influenced by a Nixon scheme. He insisted that his assembly speech on November 2 rejecting GVN participation was "my own statement, my own idea, it was my responsibility to present our position to our citizens, our National Assembly, our army. Nixon did not tell me to do it or push me to do it."[25] The fact that Thieu's behavior during the October 1972–January 1973 period, when the U.S. was trying to persuade him to sign the Paris Peace Agreement, closely paralleled his actions during this October–November 1968 period can be viewed as evidence that the Nixon's alleged request was not the determining factor in his decision in November 1968 to not attend.

Bui Diem has also repeatedly denied making any deals with the Nixon campaign to sabotage the peace talks. The only quid pro quo ever mentioned, he said, was a hint that Nixon would visit Saigon if he won the election.[26] Chennault has also rejected the allegations. Further, Thieu's foreign policy advisor, Nguyen Phu Duc, states that he knew Chennault from his time in Washington and that he often met her when she visited Saigon. If she had wanted to pass a message, Duc says, she could have contacted him, but she never did. Duc adds that "I received copies of all cables from Washington...I never heard [Thieu] or Foreign Minister Thanh mention at any time a message from Mrs. Chennault via Bui Diem, or another intermediary."[27]

Despite the denials from all sides, this story is far more complex than a simple Nixon conspiracy with Thieu. What has remained unexamined is the interplay between Thieu, his Asian allies, and the Nixon campaign. The stunning reality is that the writers who describe a Nixon plot have the conspiracy backward. Focused solely on U.S. evidence and forearmed with Nixon's later Watergate crimes, they have missed the possibility that Thieu and his Asian allies may have tried to manipulate the election for their own advantage.

How did Anna Chennault become the central figure for such a sensitive mission? A wealthy socialite and renowned hostess to Washington's elite, after her husband's death in 1958, she retained control of his aviation company, which had substantial contracts to haul cargo from America to South

Vietnam. She and her husband were extremely close to Chiang Kai-shek and his wife, and the Chennaults were members of the "China Lobby," an informal network of right-wing U.S. political elites working in collaboration with Nationalist Chinese officials to support Chiang's dream of recapturing mainland China. Chiang and his wife had a long history of attempting to influence American policy, either via well-funded publicity campaigns or odious political attacks against opponents of further aid to the Nationalist Chinese.

Given her contacts with the top GVN leaders, she was an invaluable source of information about South Vietnam. As early as July 1965, a Taiwanese archival document indicated she was reporting to Chiang Kai-shek on political developments in both the U.S. and South Vietnam.[28] In her memoirs, she describes how in the spring of 1967, Nixon asked her to provide him insights on the conflict and to act as a liaison between himself and the GVN. Impressed by Nixon's stated desire to win a military victory in South Vietnam, a key point given Nationalist Chinese opinions about the war, she agreed. Like South Korea, Taiwan believed that the Americans had "betrayed them" by not defeating the Communists.

By 1968, Chennault was vice chair of the Republican Women's National Finance Committee, a mostly symbolic role on an organization that supported Nixon. She was first introduced to Bui Diem in Saigon in 1965 when he was an assistant to Nguyen Cao Ky. After his arrival in America as GVN ambassador, he renewed the acquaintance as a means of meeting some of Washington's political movers and shakers. Although she met Ky several times, she claims she did not meet Thieu until shortly after his inauguration. At this point, she informed him that Nixon had asked her to serve as his informal liaison with the South Vietnamese leader.

When the U.S. election campaign began in earnest, Nixon held a comfortable lead over Humphrey in the polls. The news brought joy to Saigon. That the South Vietnamese leadership preferred Nixon over Humphrey was no secret. Thieu recalled his unpleasant conversation with the vice president at a meeting on November 1, 1967. In frank terms, Humphrey had expounded on the growing antiwar pressure facing the Johnson administration and expressed that the size of the U.S. commitment was unsustainable. He bluntly insisted that Thieu quickly improve his government and military. Thieu became convinced that Humphrey was not a strong backer of his country, a belief that was amplified during the U.S. presidential election campaign. Ky notes that "we never had any word from Humphrey [and] his enthusiasm for South Vietnam seemed to cool shortly before the election."[29]

In contrast to Humphrey, Nixon was a known GVN supporter and was considered a hard-line anti-communist. He had a long association with South Vietnam. Nixon had backed the French during the First Indochina War, and he had visited Vietnam on the eve of the Dien Bien Phu battle. In preparation for his expected presidential campaign, in April 1967, he embarked on a tour of Asian countries, including Taiwan and South Vietnam. In Saigon, he publicly "recommended a sharp increase in American efforts to win the Vietnam conflict," which sounded to Asian ears as supporting a military victory.[30] Thieu took notice.

After Hanoi's October 11 message, Johnson dispatched the U.S. ambassadors to each country providing troops to South Vietnam to gain their support for his peace initiative. He was particularly worried about South Korean President Park Chung-hee. After his March 31, 1968, speech, Johnson had traveled to Seoul in mid-April to meet Park and calm his fears. The South Korean leader told Johnson that Asians felt "shock" over Johnson's decision not to run for president. Park also expressed deep concern that U.S. "foreign policy toward Asia might retreat" after Johnson departed, and he was outraged about the restrictive U.S. military rules of engagement in Vietnam. Park clamored for an outright military victory, and he believed Johnson was tossing away success by limiting his military options.[31]

When the U.S. ambassador to South Korea informed Park about Hanoi's October 11 offer, the South Korean president responded that he would not object to peace talks but that he was skeptical that Hanoi would agree to the three conditions. He did not waste any time telling Thieu his views. On October 18, the CIA bug in Thieu's office recorded a conversation between the president and the South Korean ambassador to South Vietnam. After outlining his objections to the U.S. proposals, Thieu stated that he believed a bombing halt "would help Humphrey, and this is the purpose of it." Thieu knew that a cessation without his concurrence would only help Nixon. Hence, he believed Johnson would not attempt it without Saigon's agreement. More telling, Thieu said that since the "military and political situations within Vietnam are developing to our advantage, the longer we can delay the [bombing halt] the greater will be the advantage to the Vietnamese side." The Korean ambassador responded that "there is no difference in Korea's stand... and that of the [GVN]," and he proclaimed that Korea was "strongly backing [Saigon]" and that the two countries should work "closely together."[32] Nguyen Phu Duc claims that the South Korean ambassador "exhorted the GVN to be very careful, especially on the status of the NLF."[33]

Throughout October, both Thieu and Ky maintained contacts with high-level ROK officials, who encouraged the South Vietnamese to stay firm. Johnson remained concerned about Park's advice to Thieu. He told former Secretary of Defense Robert McNamara that "we've been watching what Korea said to South Vietnam."[34] While he did not elaborate, if U.S. intelligence was intercepting GVN cables and had a listening device in Thieu's office, it should not be surprising that the American government was engaged in a similar effort against South Korea. Years later, a scandal known as "Koreagate" erupted in which several South Koreans were charged with funneling bribes to some U.S. congressmen to reverse President Nixon's decision to withdraw troops from South Korea. The details of Park Chung-hee's involvement were discovered through electronic surveillance. News reports quoted unnamed U.S. government sources as stating that intelligence had "obtained electronic interception of Korean telephone and cable traffic between Seoul and Washington."[35] If information about the Chennault Affair was obtained from monitoring of the South Koreans (or Taiwan), no such intelligence has been declassified.

Park, however, was not the only one whispering in Thieu's ear. Taiwan's Chiang Kai-shek had been similarly upset by Johnson's declaration on March 31. Like Park, the generalissimo was extremely apprehensive that Johnson's announcement foreshadowed a U.S. withdrawal from Asia. Chiang also desired a military victory in South Vietnam. The Tet Offensive convinced him that America's policy of limited warfare could not defeat the Vietnamese Communists.

In late June, Chiang became further alarmed after a *New York Times* editorial urged that the U.S. improve relations with mainland China. Many saw the *Times* as a bellwether of U.S. policy. He believed that Humphrey might move closer to Beijing, while Nixon was a known hawk who had personally visited him and discussed national policy. Terrified that a Humphrey administration might abandon his island stronghold, he began an effort to "reawaken US support for [Taiwan], which has suffered a series of disappointments at American failure to uphold [Taiwan's] position on a variety of other issues." When the State Department declined to reject the *Times* editorial, the Taiwanese foreign minister became incensed. He bluntly told the U.S. ambassador that an official denial was a matter of "extreme urgency...to calm the people on Taiwan....Since Johnson's March 31 speech, Asian nations, particularly Taiwan, had become apprehensive about a U.S. withdrawal from Asia."[36]

It is critical to understand the mindset of both men regarding U.S. patronage. They viewed American action or inaction through the lens of their own perceived needs, and they blamed the loss of China and the division of Korea on a lack of U.S. support rather than their own inadequacies. While in Taiwan, GVN Ambassador Tran Thien Khiem often had dinner with Chiang Kai-shek, who he said repeatedly told him that "Vietnam and Taiwan were like members of the same family. Chiang used the relationship between the U.S. and the U.K. as analogous. He also said that since the U.S. abandoned him in 1949 and he had to flee, that the writing was on the wall for Vietnam."[37] Although both Asian autocrats supported South Vietnam's anti-communist fight, they did so mainly to protect their own interests. A precipitous U.S. withdrawal from South Vietnam would, in their view, encourage Communist aggression against them.

Moreover, their understanding of the complexities of American society and the weight of U.S. global obligations was shallow at best. For example, after Johnson's speech, in April and May 1968, Lieutenant General Wang Sheng, Taiwan's top political warfare officer, toured the U.S. to ascertain the U.S. commitment to Asia. Before his visit, his views undoubtedly reflected typical Nationalist Chinese dogma. Wang "often voiced his concern over the Administration's ability to hold course on Vietnam against the swell of domestic criticism of the U.S. war effort." He "consistently saw the dark hand of Communist subversion behind" the civil rights movement and student protests. The general condescendingly doubted U.S. competency "to lead the Free World against the Communist conspiracy, given the U.S. 'naivete' in not recognizing that almost all of its major problems at home and abroad were Communist-inspired."[38]

Thus, Thieu's two closest Asian allies held the same view: a fervent desire for a military victory in Vietnam and a wariness over the depth of the U.S. commitment combined with a deep-seated conviction that the Americans had "sold them out" and would do the same to Saigon. They both wanted Nixon to win the election, and most important, they encouraged Saigon to remain resolute and not cave to the U.S. demands. One Vietnamese official close to Thieu described the rapport that existed between Park, Chiang, and Thieu as an "older brother–younger brother" relationship, a term in Vietnamese society that implies a mentoring role by a wise family member. Their opinions clearly influenced Thieu, who told dinner guests on November 11 that Johnson's bombing halt was a "betrayal comparable to the U.S. abandonment of Chiang Kai-Shek."[39]

It would be incorrect, however, to think that Thieu listened dutifully to his "older brothers" without crafting his own agenda. On May 4, his Central Intelligence Office (CIO) provided a plan outlining how Saigon could achieve its goals during the peace talks. The CIO recommended that Thieu conduct allied proselytizing (*dong minh van*), a concept designed "to convince the U.S. to allow the GVN to take the lead role in the negotiations." The CIO endorsed targeting "other countries that are participating in this conflict, such as South Korea...to persuade them to provide the strongest support to Vietnam's position." In a harbinger of Thieu's future actions, the CIO advised adopting a blackmail policy, the kind that small, weak nations can use against powerful countries that have ties with small nations that cannot be immediately broken."[40]

The CIO also recommended two other critical activities. "Maintain close contact with our Asian allies—South Korea, Thailand, and the Philippines—who are now extremely worried about being deserted by the United States." The CIO then advised that Thieu should send out individuals to contact high-ranking Americans to flesh out the GVN's understanding of Johnson's policy. In a portent of things to come, they advocated conducting "exploratory feelers in the U.S....Only these kinds of unofficial individuals can do the best kind of work in feeling out the American position, because if we leave the task to our official delegations, U.S. officials may ignore them or avoid them. The individuals selected must be those whose identities have not yet become known on the Vietnamese political scene, but they must have sufficient English language capability and they must be knowledgeable of diplomatic techniques and tactics."

As these interactions between Thieu and his Asian allies were taking place behind the scenes, the unmasking of the supposed election manipulation occurred early on October 29. That morning, Rostow's brother telephoned him from New York to relay a message from Alexander Sachs, a prominent economist. Sachs had been told by a source in the Nixon campaign that the candidate was attempting to convince Saigon not to attend the talks. When Bunker simultaneously alerted Washington that same morning that Thieu was suddenly refusing to participate, Johnson saw connivance and ordered the FBI to wiretap Bui Diem and to follow Chennault. At a meeting later that day, Johnson and his staff discussed Nixon's alleged interference and why Thieu was balking. Rusk warned Johnson that if the GVN "cannot agree to a ceasefire before November 7 or agree to meeting before November 10, we know they are playing politics."[41]

Immediately after Johnson's October 31 speech, Chennault says she received a phone call from Nixon advisor John Mitchell. He called to express his concern about the impact of the announced bombing halt on the election. Mitchell said that he was speaking on behalf of Nixon and that he wanted her to communicate the "Republican position" to the South Vietnamese. She claims she was upset by Mitchell's demand as it would have changed her role from Nixon advisor to advocating a policy change with Thieu. On November 2, in probably the only damning piece of evidence collected, the FBI recorded a call from her to Bui Diem. She "advised him that her boss...wanted her to give personally to the ambassador" a message to "hold on, we are gonna win."[42] By "boss" she claimed she had meant Mitchell, but Johnson thought she had meant Nixon. When Thieu refused on November 2 to send representatives to attend the talks, that fact, along with the recording of the conversation, created the legend.

There are several flaws in this theory. First, despite Mitchell's urgency, Chennault did not pass Mitchell's message for two days. While true that the GVN embassy had hosted a major party to celebrate November 1, if she were using Bui Diem as a courier for messages from the Nixon camp, one assumes that a communication of this importance would have been delivered immediately. She does not mention this phone call in her memoirs, and the brevity and ambiguity of her call are unusual. Her language seems pro-forma rather than imperative. Equally important, the transcript of the call does not indicate any response by Bui Diem. He did not attempt to discuss or clarify her message, nor did he mention her call in any subsequent cable to Saigon. If he was the conduit, why did he not report her message? Coming on the heels of Johnson's speech, if he were passing messages, such an urgent contact would have been quickly transmitted back to Thieu. The NSA would have intercepted it and provided it to Rostow. Such a cable would have provided concrete evidence of the plot, yet no such document has ever appeared.

Bui Diem told the author that he did not report her message because "it did not mean anything or change the situation."[43] The only possible hint of her call came in a cable the next day from him to Thieu. His handwritten draft states that Thieu's Assembly speech has "received much comment here. Many are the friends who telephoned to compliment us or lend us their support."[44] The NSA intercept, however, adds the words "or ask that we remain resolute" to the end of that sentence.[45] The remainder of his cable details the latest events and his analysis of the current situation.

There is one suggestion that a cable from Bui Diem to Thieu mentioning her conversation does exist. On November 4, Johnson admitted to Rusk the tenuousness of the evidence. He explained that

> I don't know much more than I told the candidates themselves the other day...namely, these folks had tentatively agreed out there to go along and then they started having doubts because we had reports of some folks—the old China Lobby—contacting embassies, et cetera. Now, I cannot get much more specific than that, A, because of the sensitivity of the source...and B, because of the limited nature of the information. I did that on the basis of two things, one, the intercept from the Ambassador saying that he had had a call and the boss said wait and so forth, and second, this China Lobby operation, the Madame involved.[46]

Putting aside his devastating admission that much of his belief was based upon "limited information," whether Johnson is referring to her phone message to Bui Diem or a cable from the ambassador is uncertain. Since no cable has ever surfaced, Johnson probably misspoke and meant the phone tap, as he could not have seen Bui Diem's intercepted November 3 cable before his call with Rusk. That conversation was at 12:27 p.m., and the time stamp for the conversation on the NSA translation is 2228Z (10:38), or 5:38 p.m.

It appears, therefore, that Johnson, trying to comprehend Thieu's actions, and in the heat of the moment, had leapt to a conclusion based upon sheer coincidence. Regardless, with Johnson emphatic that Chennault was working with Bui Diem, the rest of the government fell into line. In a meeting on November 4, Clifford told staff members that "The mess we're in now is wholly of Saigon's making [and] is solely due to Republican pressure on Vietnam thru Bui Diem."[47]

Like all things political, nothing is straightforward. The truth of the matter, revealed here for the first time, is that Chennault did attempt to convince Thieu not to attend the Paris talks, but she did it at the behest of Chiang Kai-shek, not Nixon. Nor did she use Bui Diem as a conduit. She had other means to contact Thieu. According to Hoang Duc Nha, who was Thieu's second cousin and his private secretary in 1968, she used Thieu's brother, Nguyen Van Kieu, as her main conduit. Kieu at that time was the GVN charge d'affaires in Taipei, and he had long acted as his brother's go-between with various constituencies in South Vietnam, from the Dai Viets to the Catholics and others. Chennault's biographer confirms that "she was well acquainted with Thieu's brother, Nguyen Van Kieu."[48]

How then, did Chennault pass this message from Chiang? According to Nha, for a mission of this sensitivity, Chiang sent the message through a family member. Family is always the strongest bond, and he knew that Thieu was uncertain about Bui Diem's loyalty, given the ambassador's previous close connection with Ky. Thieu aide Nguyen Tien Hung confirms that Thieu was "leery of Bui Diem, whom he considered to be primarily loyal to . . . Ky."[49] Nha states that sometime after Johnson's speech March 31 speech, "the Taiwanese contacted Kieu . . . to arrange a meeting with Thieu and Anna. Kieu flew to Saigon. Thieu used me and Nguyen Phu Duc at this time for sensitive foreign policy stuff. Duc was not invited into this meeting, which is why he says it did not happen in his book."[50]

In a family-only meeting, Kieu passed the message from Chiang asking Thieu to meet Chennault to discuss the election. Thieu agreed to meet her, but he needed to do it away from prying U.S. eyes. She flew to Saigon, where Interior Minister Tran Thien Khiem met her. Khiem knew her well from his time in Taiwan. According to Khiem, "he picked her up at the airport and took her to Vung Tau by helicopter to meet Thieu. They met for two hours."[51] Khiem did not attend the meeting, and while he believes the message was that Nixon did not want Thieu to attend the peace talks, another South Vietnamese source who was very close to Thieu after the war says Chennault instead told Thieu that Chiang had recommended that Thieu not go and thus help Nixon win the election. According to this source, the president, in typical fashion, listened carefully and took notes but not did not commit himself to her request.[52]

Bui Diem agrees and states that he learned years later that the ever-suspicious Thieu believed her message but that "he did not really believe it," meaning he was unconvinced.[53] Thieu then attempted to contact Nixon to confirm that is what he wanted. A CIA bug recorded Thieu stating that "during the election campaign he had sent two secret emissaries to the U.S. to contact Nixon."[54] While Thieu did not elaborate, one emissary was certainly Mrs. Chennault. She recounts a conversation held with Thieu "as the campaign neared its climax" where he expressed "complaints" about the U.S. pressure to join the negotiations in Paris. After saying that he "would much prefer to have the peace talks after your election," she asked him, "[I]s this a message to my party?" She claimed that Thieu said yes and to "convey this message to your candidate."[55] Unfortunately, she does not reveal when this conversation took place, nor if she delivered it.

Following the CIO proposal to use Vietnamese who were relatively unknown in U.S. political circles, the other messenger was probably Huynh Van Trong, who was then assistant to the president for political and diplomatic affairs. Trong led a Vietnamese delegation to the U.S. in late September to mid-October. He carried a personal letter from Thieu authorizing his visit, which ostensibly was to assist Vietnamese students in the U.S. Secretly, though, Trong was instructed to observe the campaign and report back to Thieu. Trong deliberately avoided contact with Bui Diem to prevent the GVN embassy from monitoring his activities. Yet in an ironic twist, Trong was a Communist spy. He was arrested in the summer of 1969 and convicted of espionage. Trong's lawyer states that Trong had told him that "Thieu had sent Trong...to the U.S. to lobby the U.S. Congress, the press, and labor organizations."[56]

Despite all the backroom maneuvering, in late October 1968, Thieu had his own reasons to undermine American eagerness for talks with Hanoi. Every South Vietnamese who was involved in the negotiations insisted that they had not attended the Paris talks because of the political issues, not because of a request from Nixon. Nha asserts that "our initial refusal to go to Paris was because we were not aligned with the U.S. side on the strategy as well as the modalities for those talks."[57] Thieu's foreign policy advisor Nguyen Phu Duc concurs, writing that "the GVN felt that the future of South Vietnam should not be jeopardized" by the rush to begin talks. "That was the reason," Duc states, "and not the interference of the GVN in American politics...in the hope for a better deal with Richard Nixon."[58]

Bui Diem, while not passing messages, was nonetheless a smart and clever man who could read the tea leaves in Saigon. In a long-lost interview with the journalist Neil Sheehan in June 1975, the ambassador laid out his conjecture about what had transpired, one that is probably close to the truth. Although he did not tell Sheehan the basis for his conclusions, which came from later conversations with Nha and Thieu and reading press reports describing the conspiracy, he told Sheehan that "the Thieu regime did conspire tacitly with the Nixon camp" to help Nixon win the election. They did so "by holding back on cooperation" to attend the peace talks and "by simply taking advantage of the situation for what Saigon perceived to be its own interests." There was no reason to "weave a complicated plot" because the "dynamics of the situation were so obvious" based upon "Saigon's assessment of the positions of the candidates on Vietnam.... The basic reason Saigon favored Nixon" was due to Thieu's belief that "Nixon was 'firm against the Communists' while 'Humphrey was wavering.'"[59]

Bui Diem admits that Chennault did "call him several times and talk to him about the importance of Saigon supporting Nixon, but he never said anything to her which could leave him open to charges of conspiring." Like Thieu, "he would always just listen politely and then say, 'Yes, Anna, thank you very much,' without ever committing himself to anything." To be fair, when shown the Sheehan interview, he denied making these statements, claiming that Sheehan had misconstrued his words.

However, in later years, when rumors about her passing messages had already been printed by journalists, Bui Diem maintained contact with her.[60] In April 1971, when the South Vietnamese were angling to arrange a state visit by Thieu to the U.S., he cabled Nha to inform Thieu that "Mrs. Chennault told me yesterday that during her conversation with Nixon on Monday, on her own initiative she did mention why, when, and where of the 'fishing operation.'" Aware now that the Americans were monitoring his communications, he code-named Thieu's proposed trip as a "fishing operation."[61] Yet Chennault had little sway with Nixon. Although her visit to Nixon was to brief the president on her observations from an Asian trip, she then asked for a job or a title. Her request was met with awkward reluctance and was never acted upon.

Despite her limited influence with Nixon, Chennault has become the starring actress, a femme fatale manipulating two governments. While she was the initial go-between for Chiang, to call it the Chennault Affair is to give her far more credit that she deserves. She claims she only agreed to help Nixon because she believed that he would seek a military victory in South Vietnam, a point emphasized by Chiang. That her air transport company had major Defense Department contracts to haul freight also probably entered into her calculations, and one scholar has suggested that her main concern was her business.[62] Nor was she the only Chinese American that Nixon used to gain insight into the region. He also relied on Harold Lee, described by the president as a "close personal friend ... [who] is a perceptive observer of the Far Eastern scene whose views should be conveyed to [Nixon] on a personal and exclusive basis."[63] Ultimately, she was only a messenger, and trying to create causation from this tangled web is impossible unless more evidence surfaces.

While Nixon credited Thieu's action with helping him win the election, in his secret recordings, he never mentioned any communication to Thieu. In a remark about Thieu and the election, he told Kissinger years later that "what saved us, only by the scruff of our necks, was the fact that Thieu stomped on it the day before the election."[64] Like his Asian allies, Thieu had weighed the U.S. and found it wanting. He had refused to attend for his own political reasons, and if his delay also bought himself more time and a new American president, even better. But like the apocryphal Chinese proverb, "be careful what you wish for, lest it become true."[65]

16

"WE WHO RUN THIS COUNTRY ARE NOT WARLORDS"

Thieu Offers Peace

The US/GVN alliance had undergone a stern test, and the relationship remained uneasy for the remainder of President Johnson's term. Released from the constraints of the Military Council and bolstered by the outpouring of support following his refusal to bend to the U.S., the first six months of 1969 were among the most dynamic periods of Thieu's presidency. In particular, Thieu sought to influence the new Nixon administration by making multiple peace offers. Moreover, he would continue his efforts to unite the fractious Nationalists. His most important endeavor, however, was reinforcing earlier attempts to return power to the villages. He restructured GVN domestic strategy to focus on national development to improve the lives of the peasants through vigorous government programs. While not the top-down approach of President Diem, Thieu wanted to replicate the economic and political successes of Taiwan and South Korea. Although he did not copy the policies of his autocratic allies, he certainly wanted to achieve their results. Unfortunately, his increasing authoritarianism pushed his accomplishments offstage.

BLOWBACK

Reaction to Thieu's decision not to attend the Paris talks came swiftly. Standing up to the Americans instantly proved popular. When numerous legislators marched to the palace after Thieu's speech, an overly exuberant Nguyen Cao Ky addressed the crowd and denounced the U.S. for pressuring the South Vietnamese to sign a joint communiqué and attend the talks. Although a calmer Thieu thanked the U.S. for its aid and the "American blood which had been shed," he also got tougher. He asserted that if the U.S. "continued to insist on making all the decisions...the GVN would break its ties with the U.S. and develop stronger relations" with its allies like South Korea.[1] In response, Saigon's elite erupted in an oratorical frenzy. The assembly issued a fiery condemnation of Johnson's speech, calling it a "betrayal" and a violation of U.S. pledges to the GVN. Newspapers published editorials slamming the U.S. "unilateral action." The Catholic Greater Solidarity Force held a demonstration to support Thieu, while Buddhist leader Thich Tam Chau also loudly condemned the U.S. decision.

Since his Asian allies had strongly encouraged him not to attend the Paris talks or negotiate with the NLF, Thieu assumed they were completely backing him. He was sadly mistaken. After his assembly speech, his Korean partners abruptly distanced themselves. President Park Chung-hee called an emergency cabinet meeting to discuss the situation. His domestic audience often shaped his foreign policy just as Thieu's did. Park had to tread carefully between not irritating his own hardliners with too docile a response or publicly backing Thieu and thereby risking a break with his main benefactor. Park decided to straddle the fence. He sent Johnson a letter repeating what he had told the U.S. ambassador in early October: he supported the U.S. peace initiative but warned that Hanoi could not be trusted. Reading between the lines, Johnson's National Security Advisor Walt Rostow informed the president that the Koreans are "too conscious of their own interests to provide Thieu with satisfaction along lines he might currently desire."[2]

The Taiwanese reacted similarly. Chiang Kai-shek's opinion of Thieu's speech is unknown, but like Park, he was secretly playing both sides. In late December, he sent an emissary to Thieu urging him to join the negotiations, then promptly informed the U.S. ambassador of his action, remarking that "he considered full support to the U.S....in the Vietnamese situation to be the obligation of every ally."[3] In the first two months of 1969, Chiang passed several more messages to President Richard Nixon. In his opinion, the allies could achieve an honorable peace "if undue haste and impatience for immediate settlement can be avoided...[A]ny evidence of US-GVN over-eagerness at the conference table will inevitably be construed as a sign of weakness."[4] The message reinforced Nixon's thinking.

Within the Johnson administration, the response to Thieu's actions ranged from Rusk's calm demeanor to Secretary of Defense Clark Clifford's rage. Clifford, in a news conference on November 12, lashed out at Thieu and hinted the U.S. might attend the Paris talks alone. Bunker spent several days delicately defusing that landmine. Despite the difficulties between the two countries, the ever-positive ambassador continued to valiantly defend Thieu. Sympathetic to South Vietnam, he informed the senior U.S. leaders that Thieu's rousing speech on November 2 had enabled him to "shed the image of an American-appointed chief executive and became a leader in his own right. By catering to . . . nationalism, he has acquired the aura of a courageous patriot who is standing up to the foreigner."[5] Separately, Ky agreed with the ambassador, stating that "had Thieu yielded [to the U.S.], the people would have called Thieu's administration a U.S. puppet and Thieu might have been assassinated."[6] Rusk conceded Bunker's point, stating that "we do not wish to deny [Thieu] and South Vietnam such advantages as he and the Nationalists may have derived from this painful passage of self-assertation." Thieu, however, needed to quickly rethink his stridency. Rusk counseled the ambassador that "Congressional and newspaper awareness is building fast" and that "it is uniformly and powerfully negative."[7]

Despite U.S. assurances that Hanoi had agreed to Johnson's conditions, Thieu's foreign policy adviser Nguyen Phu Duc fumed that "the apprehensions of the GVN *were confirmed in every regard* by Hanoi's statements and actions."[8] Duc had warned the U.S. that without public confirmations, the Politburo would immediately renege on its promises. He was right. Hanoi promptly asserted that the halt was unconditional and that the talks include four parties. It continued sporadic rocketing of South Vietnamese cities.

Hanoi's declarations were not just external propaganda for foreign consumption. On November 9, the Politburo issued an update to its August 1968 resolution. The first sentence stated that it had met to assess the situation after "the U.S. was forced to unconditionally halt the bombing and . . . it agreed to enter into four-party talks." After a lengthy analysis in which the Politburo avowed that it still held the upper hand and that a military victory remained its primary goal, glimmers of a second option appeared. Hanoi would stir political agitation in South Vietnam to bring down the Thieu government. Nationalist dissent was often Communist inspired, even if Thieu's detractors refused to admit it. The Politburo asserted that now was an opportune time to

> intensify the political struggle in the cities. Struggle slogans are the key factor in mobilizing the masses to rise up. By inciting demonstrators to carry placards such as 'Negotiate with the NLF' or 'Restore Peace,' these protesters would attract all classes, all patriotic circles, all ethnic groups, and religions, particularly the Buddhists.…We must exploit every contradiction within the enemy's ranks…leading eventually to the toppling of the puppet government.…We must utilize every struggle method (legal, semi-legal, illegal), including conferences, presentations of demands, meetings, demonstrations, strikes, market boycotts, student class boycotts, etc., to boldly lead the people out into the streets to create a broad-based, wide-ranging revolutionary movement among the broad masses of the population. We must pay the utmost attention to utilizing leaflets and the press, including even the overt press. We must employ every type of legal activity in this effort.[9]

While the Communists had failed to marshal any demonstrations, it was the beginning of a temporary shift away from seeking an outright military victory to one in which political agitation would become central. Within a year, protestors would return to Saigon's streets. Some of the protest movements were created by Communist orders, while others were not. Le Duan could not admit, however, either externally or internally, that his military adventurism in 1968 had cost the Communists dearly. He remained fanatically determined to unite Vietnam under the Marxist banner. Peace remained a mirage.

NEXT STEPS FOR THE ALLIES

After Nationalist passions had cooled, they realized that a complete break with the U.S. was effectively a death sentence, and Bunker and Thieu began charting a new course for the allies. When Johnson decided against opening the talks on November 6, Foreign Minister Thanh made a counterproposal to Bunker on November 8, asking among other items if the U.S. would appoint the GVN as the chief of the allied delegation. If the U.S. took the lead, he said, it would give credence to Hanoi's propaganda that Saigon was a U.S. puppet while Ho Chi Minh was the standard bearer of Vietnamese independence. Although Rusk declined, he conceded on some procedural points to help Saigon save face.

After further wrangling, on November 27, Thieu agreed to send a GVN delegation to Paris. Thieu tapped Ky to "oversee" the negotiations, mainly to give him a job, but he designated former Foreign Minister Pham Dang Lam as the official head of Saigon's delegation.[10] Lam chose Nguyen Xuan Phong, Ky's former labor minister and an old friend of Lam's, as his deputy. Chief American negotiator Harriman despised Lam, but Phong considered Lam "intelligent and disciplined...the quintessential diplomat." Under no illusions about making progress with an obviously intractable Hanoi, Lam remarked to Phong that the talks would be a "conversation with the deaf." Both believed that Hanoi's negotiating position was unalterable: U.S. withdrawal and the "total elimination" of the Republic of Vietnam.[11]

As Nguyen Phu Duc had predicted, the two sides immediately stalemated over procedural issues. The main dispute became the size and arrangement of the conference table. Hanoi wanted a four-sided table, a clear attempt to use the shape to portray a four-sided negotiation. When Saigon refused, outside observers blamed Thieu for what seemed like a ludicrous impasse, yet he understood that procedural issues represented substantive ones. That table represented the sovereignty of South Vietnam, and he insisted on no markings to prevent Hanoi from promoting the NLF as a full attendee, and by inference, a partner equal in stature to the rightfully elected government. When Hanoi insisted, the talks remained stalled, unable to begin principal discussions until the logistics had been finalized.

On January 10, 1969, Bunker visited Thieu to convince him to halt further efforts to define the table. The ambassador explained that the American people and the incoming Nixon administration wanted to begin substantive talks. After listening, Thieu remarked that he was "no 'super-hawk'" and that two years ago he had stated that the war would not end with a military victory. While Thieu believed that one day in the future there would be a final reckoning with the People's Army, he thought that neither side could win militarily. "Eventually," Thieu said, "there would have to be political settlement involving competition with the Communists, a competition which would be decisive." True negotiations to achieve that competition could not start until Hanoi accepted this principle, an acceptance that seemed an impossible goal.

Thieu, however, left a key point unspoken. For years, Nationalist leaders had demanded a military victory. Even mentioning a political solution was "defeatist" and risked a visit from the gendarmes. Thieu now had to convince his people to accept an electoral arrangement, and

> that would take time.... The Vietnamese people now understand that there will be peace without victory, that they must expect a difficult contest with the Communists, and that the U.S. also wants and expects this. The question, therefore, has become how to make South Vietnam politically strong enough to win that looming contest.... the battle of propaganda is of the utmost importance. This is not only a matter of substance, it is equally, and sometimes even more, a matter of appearances, of face, of prestige.... Our common problem is how to win the political war and how to develop a propaganda position that will support that war.[12]

Thieu believed his public relations dilemma was to maintain optimism and determination on both sides of the Pacific. Hence, he needed to both satisfy U.S. opinion while maintaining the morale of the Vietnamese people to win a political settlement.

On January 15, a round, unmarked table was agreed upon by the negotiating teams. Thieu had grudgingly settled, mainly to curry favor with the new president-elect and to convince foreign observers that he was not the barrier to a meaningful compromise. Thieu knew that his worldwide image was badly tarnished, yet within South Vietnam his stock was currently high. Since his election, he had maneuvered skillfully among the discordant Nationalist voices to produce the most stable government since Diem. Although obsessed with secrecy and cautious to a fault, he had steered clear of the shoals upon which less capable Vietnamese leaders had foundered. After emerging victorious over the disgruntled generals, the public regarded him more as an adept maneuverer in the byzantine world of Saigon politics rather than an inspiring leader, one who had endured due to hard work, superb survivor instincts, and shrewd pragmatism. Bunker, however, saw in Thieu a leader growing into the role. The ambassador's increasingly close relationship with the South Vietnamese president, forged in the furnace of those difficult late October and early November days, would help Thieu in 1969 dramatically expand the state's reach into the villages.

BUILDING LEGITIMACY

While Thieu was consumed debating peace and restoring the pacification momentum, Prime Minister Tran Van Huong had worked diligently to establish that most amorphous of categories, the government's moral authority. Huong's age, often seen as a prerequisite for the exercise of power, and his reputation for honesty and devotion to his country had enhanced the government's stature. While he was not Thieu's closest confidante, he and the president worked well together and respected each other. Huong implemented government policy while Thieu, by force of personality and constitutional power, designed it. Thieu was seen as a competent chief executive, and Huong gave the government an eminence among the people it had not held since the early days of Diem.

For example, Huong's stature helped heal a national schism between the GVN and the Montagnard rebel group FULRO. Despite four years of seeking a compromise, the dispute remained unresolved. After an appeal by Huong to restart talks, on August 2, 1968, the FULRO leader Y'Bham Enuol left his jungle hideout in Cambodia and met GVN representatives in Ban Me Thuot. However, his demands remained unchanged: allow Montagnard units in the army, fly the FULRO flag alongside the South Vietnamese flag, and provide some autonomy for his people. Huong was willing to compromise and brought him to Saigon for further talks, but they stalled over autonomy. With no resolution, Y'Bham left Saigon on August 28. Huong, however, was persistent. While self-rule for the hill tribes remained nonnegotiable, Huong's personal assurances that Saigon could be trusted convinced Y'Bham. On December 12, 1968, the two sides finally reached agreement. The Montagnards were permitted to fly their own flag and to form their own militia units. On February 1, 1969, President Thieu attended a flag-draped ceremony at Ban Me Thuot where over five thousand returned FULRO fighters and family members pledged their allegiance to the Republic of Vietnam. Unfortunately, with Sihanouk's connivance, a small group of FULRO dissidents seized Y'Bham and retreated to Phnom Penh, where he was held captive to prevent him from signing the accord. Although they did not believe Saigon would grant these rights, FULRO would not confront the government again until late 1974.

Despite Huong's success, challenges still festered beneath the newfound stability. Although regional quarrels and religious strife were much reduced

from earlier years, new social and economic demons were arising to tor-
ment South Vietnamese society. Aware of South Vietnam's poor image in
the U.S., Thieu feared that America, like France, would tire of the war and
force a coalition. The Politburo would then use subversion to expand this
beachhead until it could take control. If South Vietnam were to survive, it
needed to prevent any U.S. efforts at a political shotgun wedding and to
convince Hanoi that destabilization was an untenable strategy. To achieve
both aims, South Vietnam needed to project unity and strength.

For Thieu, that meant restricting South Vietnamese discussions about
peace, political compromise, and dissent to narrow channels. His critics in
the West thought Thieu incapable of distinguishing between opposition
and sedition and thus viewed his actions as repressing free speech. Many
claimed Thieu's despotism mocked the contention that Saigon was a democracy, while others asserted that an elected government had a duty to
defend itself against an insurgency using terror and manipulation to gain
primacy. Unfortunately, these simple descriptions of complex events only
muddied the waters, especially when both views held elements of truth. Yet
when the GVN did provide proof of Communist activism, few believed it.
Saigon was damned for either having cried wolf too often or for a blanket
refusal to accept any of its explanations.

The first inkling of renewed troubles came from student discontent.
Saigon's universities, which had been quiet since some small disturbances
after the September 1967 election, began to simmer again. Passage of the
General Mobilization bill had sparked minor unrest, and Khiem's Interior
Ministry began monitoring the situation. When one student newspaper editorial embraced a coalition with the NLF, Khiem shut it down. On August
2, 1968, the recently enacted Mobile Military Court sentenced the paper's
editor and the head of the Saigon Students Union, Nguyen Dang Trung,
to ten years in prison in absentia for "weakening the anti-Communist spirit
of the people and the army." Trung, who was in fact an underground Communist agent, fled "to the liberated zone."[13] While Khiem had eliminated
one student Communist operative, an even more dangerous one, Huynh
Tan Mam, would take his place.

Government press restrictions intensified as interest in the Paris talks increased. In late December 1968, the Information Ministry began enforcing
press regulations by making papers submit articles in advance for review.
The ministry then made "suggestions" as to whether an article was untrue,
damaged the government's standing, or was advantageous to the Commu-

nists. The paper would then "self-censor," allowing the GVN to deny it was editing journalistic content. Regardless, on February 4, 1969, almost half the assembly signed a petition asking Thieu to liberalize the press policy. Thieu began formulating a new press law, but the GVN's heavy hand with the press contributed to its declining image abroad.

With the announcement that negotiations were beginning, several prominent civilians again appealed for talks with the NLF. The most prominent was Tran Ngoc Chau, the former Kien Hoa Province chief and now an elected legislator. On January 20, 1969, Chau publicly declared that the GVN should talk directly with the NLF. Six days later, Thich Thien Minh again called for peace talks. The police warned both men, but unlike Truong Dinh Dzu, they were not arrested.

Any indications that Thieu was moderating quickly dissipated when he spoke on February 6, 1969, at a pre-Tet news conference. Allied forces had captured Communist documents calling for increased political agitation, actions stemming from the Politburo's November announcement. With the peace talks starting, and aware of Communist efforts to spark political turmoil, Thieu claimed that South Vietnam was entering the most "dangerous period of its history." Stability, he warned, was "absolutely necessary" in this "period of political warfare," and he had no tolerance for anyone who threatened national unity.[14]

Lost amid the drama of press repression and social crackdowns, however, were several major new government initiatives for 1969, all designed to expand the state into the countryside. In early February 1969, Thieu announced four major priorities: pacification and reconstruction, strengthening local administrations, election of village leaders, and a "vigorous and truly revolutionary land reform program in the spirit of land to the tiller."[15] He conceded that previous land-reform efforts had fallen short due to security issues and the "reactionary" attitude of some government officials. Thieu mandated that all remaining lands in government possession would be distributed by the end of 1969 and that a new law would be submitted to the assembly. The new land-reform program had been quietly drafted by a U.S.-trained economist named Cao Van Than, who had begun working on it since shortly after the Tet attacks. The bill, however, would stall in the assembly for another year.

Just as Thieu announced his plans, the People's Army resumed the attack. Vo Nguyen Giap had begun planning in late July 1968 for renewed assaults in 1969.[16] This was the "talk/fight" pattern that Hanoi followed:

start negotiations with an offensive and hope that a victory would force their opponent to make concessions. It succeeded in Geneva with the Dien Bien Phu campaign, tried it again with the mini-Tet attacks and the first Paris meeting, and now Hanoi was repeating that model with the opening of formal talks. The 1972 offensive would cap this strategy.

Three days after Johnson's October 31 speech, the Politburo met to review Giap's plan. Hampered by its own poor internal reporting and ideological blinders, the Politburo still believed its forces had scored tremendous victories in 1968 and remained strong. While envoys in Paris were negotiating the procedures for peace talks, the Politburo decided to launch another attack.[17] After logistical preparations, on February 22, the Communists conducted assaults across South Vietnam. Unlike the previous year's attacks against GVN centers of power, these were aimed primarily at U.S. troops. The Politburo hoped that increased American losses would translate into U.S. compromises in Paris. Thumbing its nose at Johnson's conditions, Hanoi hit Saigon and other cities with rockets. Despite the provocation and internal calls for retribution, Thieu recommended against resuming the bombing of the DRV, wanting to see the U.S. reaction. He did not have to wait long. In retaliation for a rocket strike on Saigon on March 15, and to persuade the DRV to begin private talks, Nixon ordered secret B-52 bombing against PAVN sanctuaries in Cambodia.

Despite the Politburo's rosy assessment of its strength, the allies easily repulsed the Communist attacks. The first campaign continued until the end of March, followed by a second wave in the early summer of 1969. The results were the same as during Tet '68. Communist losses were staggering. According to the PAVN High Command,

during the first six months of 1969, our forces had suffered a total of 48,365 casualties throughout all of South Vietnam. This total consisted of 19,385 killed, 25,408 wounded, 522 captured, 2,915 missing, and 135 defectors. The battlefield that suffered the highest number of casualties was [the B2 Front], with a total of 25,934 casualties. We had suffered 19,400 casualties during the spring wave of attacks (22 February to 31 March 1969), representing forty percent of our total casualties; 19,030 casualties during the summer wave of attacks (11 May to 20 June 1969), representing thirty-nine percent of our total casualties; and 9,935 casualties during our regular, constant wave of operations, representing twenty-one percent of our total casualties.[18]

Hanoi coordinated its offensive with a wave of urban terrorism, seeking to spur infighting among Nationalist politicians such as had occurred after the Tran Van Van murder. On January 6, Communist assassins killed the GVN's minister of education by flinging a hand grenade into his car. Then in an even more brazen attempt, on March 5, a Saigon-based team attempted to kill Prime Minister Huong. A bomb was tossed under his car, but it failed to detonate. Several of the hit team were captured and sent to the prison on Con Son Island, where they were released in 1973.

Having repulsed the PAVN attacks, Thieu returned to his central goal for 1969, expanding the GVN's rural footprint. When the Accelerated Pacification Campaign was completed at the end of January, the GVN claimed that over one million people had been brought under its control and that 90 percent of the population was now living in areas that were "relatively secure" or better. Although CORDS believed the number was only 80 percent, Congressional antiwar critics harshly condemned the CORDS claim, which was based upon the Hamlet Evaluation System, or HES. In HES, "relatively secure" was a "C" rating. "A" was under total GVN control, while an "E" was under Communist rule. While HES statistics were often disputed, the Communists' own information agreed with CORDS. A PAVN report claimed that during the first six months of 1969 the Communists controlled less than 19 percent of the South Vietnamese population while admitting they had lost "1,015,594 people in comparison with 1968."[19]

Thieu's plan for 1969 reflected the increase in security and the population gain under GVN control. Building on the effort that Ky and Thieu had first started in December 1966 to restore local autonomy, the president designed the 1969 plan to strengthen local rule by assigning more power and responsibility to village officials. The "basic principle of the 1969 plan," he said, "is to develop community cooperation between the people, the government, and between government agencies." Each province would set its own goals, but since the village was "the traditional social community and basic administrative unit, the village will be restored to its traditional role of linking the government with the people."[20]

The first step was to create GVN rule in the recently secured areas by holding village and hamlet elections in these recaptured regions. District chiefs were now responsible for verifying voter rolls, creating the security plan, and ensuring the qualifications of the candidates. Saigon would only confirm the results. Following the 1967 election model, polling began on the first Sunday of March 1969 and continued every Sunday that month. Almost six hundred villages and over three thousand hamlets elected new officials and committees. Eighty percent of South Vietnam's villages and hamlets now had direct GVN administration. Voting was heavy, and highlighting the Communist's rural weakness, virtually no election violence was recorded.

Ecstatic over beating back the latest offensive and the successful elections, on April 1, Huong signed a decree amending the critical Degree 198 from December 1966 that had restored power to village and hamlet chiefs and committees. In a speech on April 21 at Vung Tau, Thieu articulated his revised design. Addressing the first in a series of training classes in 1969 for all sixteen thousand local officials, Thieu outlined his intention to expand grassroots democracy. To defeat the Communists, he said, "democracy must be implemented at every level in South Vietnamese life." The amended decree gave the village chiefs operational control over the Popular Force platoons, PSDF units, and RD cadres in each village. Thieu also announced that he was providing funds to each village council to spend on their own Self-Help projects. "With this new authority and these additional resources," Thieu emphasized, "local officials will be held responsible for providing good government to the people." Thieu was giving them the means and the power to "decide everything in accordance with the aspirations of the people. This is justice, this is democracy." Success, Thieu exhorted, "does not depend on me, but on you. We will succeed because you will do your tasks well."[21] The president added that he intended to implement national programs such as government-subsidized fertilizer and farm equipment to help farmers grow miracle rice.

Thieu's policy for increased local power was both farsighted and pragmatic. Unlike the other Vietnamese political parties, which viewed ruling as centralized power from "the top down," Thieu had embraced governing from "the bottom up." He believed that the NLF's cadre losses were so heavy that it would take several years to rebuild. Therefore, "our emphasis must be on meeting their competition in the hamlets and villages and districts. That is why I am concentrating on building our cadre force at this level, on improving local administration and improving the life of our people in the hamlets and villages."[22] By increasing security, adding a revolutionary land-reform program, and improving local government, Thieu intended to win any future political contest. After a decade of policy debates about which political program would best respond to the Communists' rural-based organizational threat, Thieu had answered with his own agenda: a radical mind shift in South Vietnam's governance.

First though, Thieu needed to get his house in order. On March 12, Huong announced some cabinet adjustments. The two key changes were the promotion of Cao Van Than, Thieu's assistant for developing the land-reform program, to the post of minister of land reform and agriculture. The other was elevating Tran Thien Khiem to deputy prime minister in charge of pacification and rural development. Khiem would replace Huong as head of pacification, but secretly Thieu was grooming Khiem to replace Huong. The prime minister's age and infirmities were hampering him, but while Huong had improved the government's status among the people, he had failed to build political bridges to achieve legislation or foster national unity. It would prove his downfall.

Seeking tight wartime discipline, Thieu once more began clamping down on anyone promoting a compromise with the NLF. On February 23, the day after the Communists launched their new offensive, Saigon police raided the headquarters of Thich Thien Minh's Youth Wing. The police claimed that recently captured NLF cadres had confessed that Communist agitators were operating out of the center. They were not, but when the police raided the center, they found a secret compartment in Minh's room where several draft dodgers were hiding. Other evidence discovered in the building included a pistol and some Communist leaflets. They arrested Thien Minh. His detention was immediately decried as "jailing the opposition."

Khiem took advantage of the amendment that Thieu had signed on November 5, 1968, that "all violations to national security are under the jurisdiction of the Field Military Tribunal."[23] Khiem transferred Thien Minh's case to the Mobile Military Court. On March 15, 1969, they sentenced the monk to ten years in prison, the harshest sentence ever handed out to a Buddhist opposition figure. Tri Quang, although at odds with Thien Minh, denounced the arrest but did not start protests, a telling indicator of both An Quang's weakened state and the bonze's dispute with his former protege. Wary of U.S. reaction, the next day, Thieu ordered Huong to place Thien Minh under house arrest rather than in prison and to provide him with medical facilities to care for his injuries sustained in the May 1966 grenade blast.

While these social, political, and military issues dominated Saigon, Thieu was fortunate that he had the time to focus on them as the new Nixon administration was clarifying its Vietnam policies. Despite journalists' speculation, Nixon did not have a "secret plan" to end the war, but he sought a strategy that lowered the U.S. commitment while not sacrificing South Vietnam. Thieu was about to give him one.

TROOP WITHDRAWALS

In January 1969, with a new U.S. president, Thieu changed his internal procedures to centralize all foreign policy decisions in his office. After the Harriman-Lam dustup in late October 1968, the U.S. had informed Thieu that all policy communications would come directly from the White House through Bunker. Copying the Americans, Thieu told Bui Diem and Pham Dang Lam on January 1, 1969, that henceforth foreign policy judgments would be strictly handled between him and Bunker. Bui Diem was not to "engage too much with U.S. government members and only speak on a personal level." He was to simply "gather the largest possible number of possible options...and report them to us...[Y]our information will be valuable but always wait for the results of work in Saigon."[24]

Following Thieu's directions, on January 13, Bui Diem provided his appraisal of American views, Nixon's probable course of action, and potential GVN responses. Regarding the stalled peace talks, Bui Diem noted that the U.S. public "aimed their criticisms at the Vietnamese government, saying that Vietnam has delayed the negotiations. Despite our efforts to explain our position on the procedural issues that Vietnam considers to be so important, the U.S. public believes that these issues are not important." Nixon "will be forced to make a choice in the next three months, and that policy choice will be based on the decisions that are made during the coming months." Mirroring Thieu's opinion, he recommended that South Vietnam proactively shape Nixon's policies. "Our government should publicize [troop withdrawal] first. We should not let the U.S. talk about it first, because the U.S. public and international public opinion will then get the impression that we are being forced into a position in which we have to agree."[25]

Thieu listened. In April 1968, he had first floated the possibility of U.S. troop withdrawals. His idea assumed new urgency when the U.S. provided its revised negotiating approach to him in early January 1969. The chief tenet was to achieve peace via mutual withdrawal of North Vietnamese and U.S. troops. Since Thieu thought it "very unlikely that Hanoi would accept," he considered the "key to preservation of freedom in the South" lay in RVNAF modernization.[26] To achieve that ambition, he sought new equipment and training.

Thieu thought the competency of his military was much greater than anyone else did. Although General Abrams was impressed by improved RVNAF performance, he did not believe the South Vietnamese were ready to defend the country against both well-trained regulars and guerrillas. Granted, the RVNAF had increased its personnel from 643,000 in 1968 to 820,000 at the end of January 1969. While Bunker claimed 160,000 of these new recruits were volunteers, undoubtedly a portion had joined local RF/PF units simply to stay close to home. Adding in the police and RD cadres, Saigon now had over a million men under arms, five percent of the population, one of the highest ratios in the world. Heavy fighting naturally increased casualties, and combat losses in 1968 totaled more than 87,000 men, double that of 1967. Desertions also added to Saigon's losses. Given the casualties and the stubbornly high desertion rate, to maintain its new force structure, Saigon had to induct and train over 150,000 new men into the armed forces each year.

Regardless, Thieu had been debating for a year over how to reduce the U.S. footprint in South Vietnam. Doing so would gut the Communist denigration of him as a U.S. "puppet" while also mitigating the pressure on Nixon from U.S. antiwar critics. On January 15, 1969, Foreign Minister Thanh broached the subject with Bunker. Thanh said that Thieu deemed that between his growing strength and the corresponding enemy weakness, "a limited replacement of American troops" should be possible. Thieu, Thanh said, cautioned that a sudden departure would rattle RVNAF morale, and he desired a residual U.S. force to help guarantee the peace, but he wanted to begin planning with Abrams for the departure of two U.S. combat divisions in 1969.[27]

Three days later, Thieu told a visitor that he was "serious about U.S. troop withdrawals." His purpose was to assist the U.S. government "in its relations with the American public, so that it may be able to maintain its program of assistance to South Vietnam, and not undertake a precipitous withdrawal." Thieu recognized "the political pressure faced" by Nixon, and he "wants to demonstrate his appreciation" by proving that South Vietnam was doing its fair share.[28] Bunker, however, attempted to dissuade Thieu from explicitly mentioning any precise figures or timetable. The current U.S. negotiating strategy required mutual withdrawal, and Bunker did not want to give Hanoi an excuse to simply wait and watch the U.S. unilaterally leave. Nixon also wanted the political gain by announcing it first to the American public.

By late January, Thieu had determined that the new U.S. president "would need some kind of solution" for Vietnam before the 1970 U.S. congressional elections. Seeking another means to shape Nixon's emerging policy, Thieu told Nguyen Phu Duc that he had decided to provide another proposal "to help the new U.S. administration face the fatigue of the war [and] that he was "contemplating a daring political initiative."[29] For Thieu, it was important "to keep ahead of what the U.S. would do in order to safeguard the essentials."[30] He planned to offer local elections "in which the Communists would be allowed to participate." If the situation continued to develop favorably, he believed, by June he would be ready for a settlement with the NLF. A shocked Duc asked him how he intended to overcome assembly reaction and the constitutional ban on Communist activity, but Thieu brushed aside his concerns.

Seeking to influence the new U.S. administration, Thieu told Bunker in mid-March to inform Nixon that Saigon no longer seeks "or speaks of complete military victory. We know the war cannot be won militarily.... Vietnam must do everything it can to relieve the burden which the American people are carrying...We who run this country are not warlords or warmongers seeking to prolong the war. This war has been imposed on us; we did not make it." Thieu was answering his critics; South Vietnam was under attack, and he was not deliberately stalling peace to maintain power.

A solution, according to Thieu, required two things: "[W]e need to be strong enough to win the political war with the Communists after peace is restored, and we must be assured that when we do make peace external aggression will cease...There can be no false solution as there was in 1954." To that end, the North Vietnamese must withdraw and provide guarantees against renewed aggression, and the RVNAF must be strengthened to enforce that guarantee. His greatest concern remained "American opinion about Vietnam. The Communists are counting on U.S. impatience and preoccupation with its internal difficulties."[31]

While popular history credits Nixon with crafting "Vietnamization," the process of withdrawing U.S. troops while improving the RVNAF, the concept had developed independently within the two governments. Ky claims that he coined the termed "Vietnamization" instead of "de-Americanization" in a meeting with Secretary of Defense Melvin Laird in early April 1969, but U.S. documents confirm the word was agreed upon at a National Security Council meeting on March 28.[32] While the idea originated with Thieu, he did not exert the influence on the formulation of Nixon's Vietnam policies that he had hoped. Still, he was preparing for the inevitable day when the Americans would pull out.

PEACE OFFERS

Despite Thieu's internal crackdown on anyone advocating talking to the NLF, he was open to the concept. In January 1969, Ky had mentioned to journalists that he was willing to privately meet in Paris with NLF representatives. Press coverage over this apparent turnaround in GVN thinking was extensive, and on March 2, Nixon quietly encouraged this effort. Nixon told Ky that it would be "very clever" if the GVN offered to speak with the NLF.[33] With Nixon's green light, on March 25, Thieu struck. In a dramatic announcement, he publicly offered to hold talks with the NLF in Paris without any preconditions. Further, even if rocketing of Saigon continued, he would not recommend resumed bombing as that would simply return everyone to the old status quo. To stymie any RVNAF backlash, Thieu held a luncheon two days later with General Vien and the other senior military leaders. After carefully explaining his thoughts, they agreed that the proposal was useful and had stolen "the NLF thunder and put the GVN in a good public light abroad."[34] The senior officer's easy acceptance of Thieu's previously heretical offer showed how much they now accepted his leadership.

Believing that military and public opinion backed him, on April 7, Thieu made a second bold proposal for peace. In his annual "State of the Nation" address to the assembly, he offered a six-point program for ending the war. In exchange for the withdrawal of North Vietnamese forces, a halt to violence, and their agreement to respect South Vietnam's constitution, the GVN would extend full rights to anyone in the NLF. If they did not call themselves Communists, they could form their own political party and run candidates for elections. International monitors would guarantee their rights. Thieu also called for the dismantling of PAVN bases in Laos and Cambodia, respect for the DMZ, and the reunification of the two countries through a supervised election. He had again accepted the NLF as a reality but not as a political entity.

Bunker had left Saigon in early April for consultations with Nixon. Upon his return, he briefed Thieu. Nixon, Bunker said, thought Thieu's April 7 speech was extremely helpful, and he agreed with Thieu's proposal for troop reductions "because of our public opinion."[35] Like Chiang Kai-shek, Nixon also believed that the allies should not "appear over-eager" in negotiations. Bunker emphasized that Nixon wanted to work closely with Thieu and harmonize their policies. Secretly, however, the new administration had begun planning to extricate the U.S. from the war. On April 10, in National Security Study Memorandum #36, Nixon "directed the preparation of a specific timetable for Vietnamizing the war."[36] The timetable would begin on July 1, 1969.

Nixon also supported Thieu's efforts to build a two-party system. Thieu's April 7 speech had called for building a more viable political party system in South Vietnam. Thieu believed that Tran Van Don saw the Lien Minh as a platform for him to become prime minister, and when that failed, Don's participation stopped. When Don's National Salvation Front publicly called on March 10 for changes in the Huong cabinet, Thieu saw this as a direct attack. He decided to move on without Don, and after a series of intense negotiations among various Nationalist organizations, Thieu launched his own front. Called the National Social Democratic Front (NSDF), it was comprised of Thieu's Free Democratic Force, the Revolutionary Dai Viets, part of the VNQDD, the Catholic Greater Solidarity Force, and the largest Hoa Hao bloc. Basically, Thieu had cobbled together various factions that were adamantly opposed to a coalition or compromise with the Communists. On May 25, 1969, Thieu addressed 1,500 delegates attending the NSDF's founding convention. Acknowledging that the Lien Minh had flopped, he emphasized that the new front's goal was to bring together all Nationalist groups to challenge the Communists. Unlike the first two efforts, this time Thieu agreed to be directly involved. But he repeatedly denied he was founding this front to become its leader, all too aware of the damage caused by the Can Lao Party.

Thieu's new front was not the only political party organizing. After years spent covertly expanding, the Tan Dai Viets were finally ready to show their face. While the TDV had covertly organized party chapters in many provinces, they were strongest along Route 1 from Saigon to southern Tay Ninh, which was often jokingly called the "Tan Dai Viet Road." Seeking to attract a broad range of people, Nguyen Ngoc Huy had named the new entity the Progressive Nationalist Movement (PNM). Given his TDV affiliation, Huy feared he would not be accepted as the head of this new party. Instead, he asked Dr. Nguyen Van Bong, the highly respected rector of Saigon's prestigious National Institute for Administration, the training college for GVN civil servants, to become the PNM leader. Bong agreed, and Huy would become his deputy.[37] Huy had petitioned the government in the summer of 1968 to grant official recognition of the party. In November, Huong gave permission for the local branches to begin quiet public operations. Huy then left for Paris as part of the GVN delegation, leaving Bong to finalize the party organization. Official recognition was finally granted in April 1969, and the PNM held an inaugural press conference. As Don had done with the Lien Minh, Huy labeled his party pro-government but not pro-Thieu.

Following the announcement of the NSDF, on June 19, 1969, the GVN proclaimed Law 009/69, which provided the legal foundation for political parties. The law was designed to weed out the numerous small parties, which usually consisted of several urban-based zealots and a handful of disciples. To achieve legal status as a party, each entity had to provide evidence that it had a certain level of support in at least fifteen provinces. By creating the NSDF and merging all the old non-communist parties that did not support him into a solid opposition, Thieu hoped the Nationalists would not fragment their vote in a competition with the Communists. Although Article 4 of the constitution prohibited Communist political activity, the left was now free to form its own party and offer candidates. Yet despite the very real Communist military and political threat, the Nationalists remained a house divided as Thieu prepared to meet the new U.S. president.

MEETING NIXON

Thieu's April 7 speech forced Hanoi and Washington to update their own peace proposals. On May 8, the NLF offered a ten-point peace plan for ending the war. It demanded the complete withdrawal of U.S. forces, the implementation of a coalition government, the drafting of a new constitution, and the holding of elections—in that order.

Nixon countered on May 14. Always cognizant of public opinion, in his first Vietnam discussion as president, his two themes were that the U.S. would not abandon Saigon and that the South Vietnamese people should determine their own future without outside interference. He publicly offered to withdraw U.S. troops over a twelve-month period if Hanoi did the same. After the mutual withdrawal, internationally supervised elections could be held. This was a retreat from Johnson's policy that Hanoi should withdraw first, followed six months later by a withdrawal of U.S. troops.

Thieu, always hyper-attuned to potential U.S. policy changes, some-how sensed movement toward a coalition government in Nixon's speech. Although Bui Diem told Thieu that Kissinger had "affirmed to me that the eventual transfer of military responsibilities to our forces is a sincere political move on the U.S. part and not a disguised policy of abandonment," Thieu wanted to hear it from Nixon.[38] He asked to meet, and the two presidents decided to convene on June 8, 1969, at the tiny island of Midway in the Pacific, site of the famous World War II naval battle.

Seeking support and negotiating advice, Thieu decided to first visit South Korea and Taiwan before seeing Nixon. Arriving in Seoul on May 27, thousands of flag-waving Koreans lined the road to welcome him. Thieu reportedly asked Park to join him in resisting any U.S. moves on either uni-lateral troop withdrawals or a forced coalition. Park, unfailingly consistent, urged him to seek a military victory rather than "invite an irretrievable disas-ter by falling prey to Communist trickery." Despite Thieu's decision to seek peace, however, Korea would "stand firmly by your side" until peace was achieved.[39] However, while supporting Thieu's two points, Park would not "exert any direct pressure on the U.S. in this matter." He drew a distinction between his agreement with Thieu and "a direct independent assertion" by him to Washington. Park remained firmly on the fence. He backed Thieu, but he would not risk alienating the Americans.[40]

Thieu next flew to Taiwan, where well-orchestrated crowds again lined the motorway from the airport. Chiang Kai-shek also strongly urged Thieu not to accept a coalition government under any circumstances. Chiang told Thieu that Nixon was "a staunch anti-communist...who had the interests of the free nations in Asia at heart" and that both countries "should have confidence in Nixon" and cooperate fully. At a state dinner that night, Thieu pointed to Chiang as an example of U.S. concessions that had led to a Communist takeover. But like Park, Chiang was also playing both sides. Several days after Thieu's departure, the U.S. ambassador was given a full briefing on the talks, with Chiang hoping that the information would be "conveyed directly to Nixon prior to his meeting at Midway with Thieu."[41]

Believing he had the firm support of his Asian allies, on June 4, Thieu made a televised speech declaring that he and the leaders of South Korea and Taiwan had agreed against any coalition government. Backed by his Asian allies, his assembly, and his military, Thieu flew to Midway. His strat-egy remained intact: dampen the antiwar pressure on the U.S. government by "de-Americanizing" the war through reducing the American combat role and shifting U.S. financial expenditures from military to economic aid. Thieu, though, was "very concerned that Nixon would give priority to the negotiating path, which the GVN knew would be sterile and illusory."[42]

Nixon on the other hand, wanted to calm Thieu's sensitivity regarding a coalition. Nixon confirmed that "there is currently a lot of speculation regarding American pressures for a coalition government and [it] is entirely unfounded."[43] Nixon's declaration appeased Thieu, and they jointly announced that twenty-five thousand U.S. troops—basically the two combat divisions that Thieu had proposed in January—would be withdrawn by the end of August. While Thieu's efforts had probably only slightly influenced Nixon's decisions, he certainly was not the passive actor silently raging at U.S. treachery or an autocratic puppet automatically performing Nixon's bidding. He had deliberately sought to shape Nixon's emerging Vietnam policy while gaining time and increased aid to compensate for the U.S. withdrawal.

In response to Thieu's earlier speeches, on June 10, the NLF declared the formation of a Provisional Revolutionary Government (PRG) to replace it. The spark was Vietnamization. According to Truong Nhu Tang, who had fled Saigon to COSVN headquarters,

> Vietnamization was a political maneuver meant to strike at us by hamstringing opposition to the war in the international and domestic American arenas. We decided to respond by countering this threat on precisely the same battlefields. We had long been developing plans to set up formal NLF governmental striations at the regional and lower levels; we now moved to create a central political entity that could compete with Saigon on the basis of formal, legal standing.... Our goal was to influence public opinion: domestically, where a non-communist government would give us added credibility with the South Vietnamese populace; internationally, where we would be able to compete with Saigon for formal recognition...and in the United States, where we would enhance our claim of representing the Southern people, giving the peace movement additional ammunition.[44]

Although the PRG announcement garnered worldwide attention, Thieu dismissed it as a "propaganda trick" and said that the NLF/PRG remained "part of the other side."[45] While outwardly contemptuous, Thieu knew he needed a riposte. He took two actions. Upon his return from Midway, he announced that South Vietnam was shifting its main priority from military action to the "political phase of the struggle for peace." The announcement of the PRG formation also made Thieu ramp up his efforts at suppression of any public discussions of peace. He warned that "those who spread rumors" advocating a coalition would be "severely punished on charges of colluding with the enemy [and] I will punish them in the name of the Constitution."[46]

He was incensed over the creation on June 4, 1969, of an opposition group called the National Progressive Force (*Luc Luong Quoc Gia Tien Bo*) by Tran Ngoc Lieng, Duong Van Minh's running mate in the 1967 election. Comprising a tiny group of Saigon-based intellectuals, this was the first organized left-wing rival since the Committee for Peace in March 1965, whose members the GVN had tried and jailed. In his June 4 statement, Lieng demanded the withdrawal of "foreign" troops while correspondingly leaving North Vietnamese troops on South Vietnamese soil, and an immediate ceasefire. Thieu saw Lieng not as a constructive oppositionist but a constant barb. He was right. "Our goal," Lieng wrote, "was to fight for the U.S. withdrawal, and we had no intentions of participating in any government." Following the Politburo's orders to stir opposition, "we sought ways to oppose all policies of the U.S. and Thieu governments, using many lively, vigorous methods, such as encouraging voters to burn their voters' cards during elections, having students attack and burn American vehicles, etc."[47] Thieu believed the formation of the PRG and Lieng's National Progressive Force was no coincidence, and he ordered the police to investigate it. Two weeks later, the police summoned Lieng for questioning. He was released with a stern warning, but leftists like Lieng would remain a weed in Thieu's garden that would prove troublesome to eradicate.

Seeking to reclaim political high ground, Thieu's next move was to offer the most far-reaching peace proposal of any South Vietnamese leader, one that he would adhere to for the next three years. Behind the scenes, Nixon had dispatched Bunker to discuss several ideas with Thieu, but he told Bunker not to pressure Thieu to include them. Nixon's main point was that if Hanoi had failed to respond to their peace overtures by September 1969, Nixon was considering strong military action to force a settlement. To make it clear that "we had no choice" for such an act, Nixon asked Thieu to be "very forthcoming" in his July 11 speech. Since the NLF had demanded that Thieu resign and his administration be replaced by a provisional government before elections could be held, Nixon suggested that Thieu offer to resign if the NLF agreed to participate in elections.[48] Thieu declined "because of the psychological effect of that word on the Vietnamese population and especially of the danger some might think he was getting ready to accept a coalition government."[49] Still a precedent had been set, and this trial balloon that Thieu resign prior to holding national elections with the NLF would have future repercussions between the allies.

Thieu addressed the nation on July 11. He detailed the Communists' ongoing violations of the understandings that had formed the basis for the allies to agree to the Paris talks. He pointed out that his prior compromise to permit the NLF as a separate entity in elections demonstrated his good-faith pursuit of peace. Thieu then made his offer: he challenged the NLF to hold internationally supervised elections, but only if the NLF renounced violence and pledged to accept the results. Further, he offered to let the NLF help set up and monitor the elections, promised that there would be no reprisals after the elections, and said the GVN would respect the election results no matter the outcome. He reiterated his earlier position that he was willing to hold private talks with the NLF without preconditions to discuss the election logistics. While Thieu was hedging on several points, everything was negotiable, except the concept of a free and general election.

Thieu had challenged the Communists to an electoral contest, but it was as far as he was prepared to go. He had reached his own limits and what was possible within Nationalist politics. After the devastating Tet Offensive and the start of peace talks, each side had begun maneuvering to enhance its position. Nixon wanted to reduce the U.S. military commitment to lower the pressure from antiwar protesters and Congress. Saigon was attempting to offer a peace settlement while strengthening its future electoral position against the Communists. Hanoi was hoping to hang on until it could rebuild its power. Peace ultimately depended on Le Duan, but he knew that the clock of the war-weary Americans was running out faster than his.

17

"LONG HAUL, LOW COST"

Thieu Proposes a New Strategy

After a tumultuous first half of 1969, Thieu entered the second part of the year determined to build on South Vietnam's successes. He still faced a relentless foe in Le Duan, but Nixon's reassurances of total support enabled Thieu to begin what Hoang Duc Nha termed "talking while building," meaning Thieu would seek a peaceful resolution to the war while developing the country. Unfortunately, while he was relatively effective in restructuring South Vietnam, an avalanche of political scandals beginning in April 1969 and continuing through 1970 overshadowed his domestic accomplishments. Much of this turmoil was self-inflicted, some it resulted from the usual disorder of a society in transition, and commotion in the U.S. accounted for the rest.

NEW STRATEGIES

Thieu's domestic critics immediately blistered his July 11 peace proposal. Senator Tran Van Don panned him for not offering more, while Saigon's press and other assembly leaders condemned Thieu for offering too much. They chastised him for tendering a valuable concession—the NLF could participate in elections—without receiving anything in return. Nationalist conspiratorialists thundered that Thieu had only made these offers under "American pressure." Buffeted from all sides, Thieu asserted that his six points were not concessions but "initiatives" to start negotiations. Foreign

Minister Thanh admitted that while Thieu's proposal would allow the NLF to participate in the elections, it could not partake as Communists given Article 4 of the constitution. When queried whether Thieu intended to amend Article 4, Thanh replied that if the Communists accepted the offer, all questions could be discussed. His comment, designed to convince everyone of Thieu's seriousness, instead created more Nationalist outrage.

Hanoi immediately rejected Thieu's deal, calling it a "deceitful move" and an "election farce staged...to maintain...U.S. neocolonialism in South Vietnam."[1] Thieu's reaction was restrained. Privately he told Bunker that we "must make it clear we are not angry or shutting any doors."[2] Publicly Thieu responded by asking the Communists to "think about" his plan while insisting that "I am a peaceful man who is trying to search for every conciliatory solution. I am not a war-like person, but neither will I surrender to the Communists."[3] He then declared that this was his last peace proposal. He had made a good faith offer; now it was Hanoi's turn to respond. Bunker, while acknowledging that the speech had triggered domestic difficulties for Thieu, observed that four months earlier it "would have been unthinkable" for Thieu to propose direct talks with the NLF. This speech was "impressive evidence of the evolution which has taken place in South Vietnamese opinion" regarding peace.[4] By previously establishing his Nationalist credentials, Thieu was able to offer peace without being deposed in a coup. Just as only a staunch anti-communist like Nixon could make a diplomatic opening to China, only a resolute Nationalist could propose elections with the NLF.

On an overseas trip shortly after the Midway meeting, Nixon proclaimed on July 25 what became known as the Nixon Doctrine. America would no longer insert combat troops in future fratricidal wars but would support friendly governments with aid and military training. Nixon then made a short stop in Saigon on July 30 to see Thieu and visit U.S. troops. To prepare for his visit, Thieu spent two days closeted with his advisors. His team developed what they considered an innovative approach that addressed U.S. government worries while supporting Saigon.

Opening their meeting, Thieu opined that he had offered "the maximum," such as elections and withdrawing U.S. troops, but "South Vietnam had come to a crossroads."[5] He could do no more. Nixon agreed that they should not provide further concessions. "We can't have you nibbled away," he remarked. Thieu, testing the new Nixon Doctrine, then proposed his own policy. Thieu claimed the allies now only had two options: seek a military victory or embrace a different path. Since an outright military triumph seemed beyond reach, he proposed "to make preparations for what he called a 'long haul, low cost' policy." He commented "that if the U.S. wishes to disengage, the best course is to help South Vietnam grow strong." Thieu wanted increased aid "to help the GVN to take over more of the war burden."[6]

In July 1965, Thieu and Ky had asked for U.S. troops to blunt the Communist summer offensive that was threatening to overrun South Vietnam. Four years later, Thieu was recommending a strategy to manage the U.S. withdrawal. His formula would dramatically reduce U.S. troop levels to calm an increasingly antiwar Congress, while modifying the GVN strategy and budget to face the dual challenge of combat and village development.

To accomplish his part, Thieu had taken two major steps. First, he had shifted the GVN's administrative philosophy to expand local statecraft, to build from the bottom rather than impose from the top. Second, Thieu had cast the U.S. withdrawals to his people "not as something forced on South Vietnam but as springing from its own initiative."[7] Thieu disparaged the term "Vietnamization," and he never used it in his speeches. Nor did he like the word "withdrawal," preferring "replacement" instead. However, Thieu envisioned a residual American commitment—logistical, financial, and military support like in Korea and Germany—to keep Hanoi at bay. Given such assistance, he would do the rest.

In principle, Nixon agreed. He reaffirmed his steadfast support for Thieu, promised to consult closely with him, and swore no further concessions. Yet several weeks later, and without informing Saigon, Nixon dispatched Kissinger to begin secret private talks with the North Vietnamese. Thieu, however, soon learned of these secret American meetings. In April 1969, South Vietnamese intelligence had tabbed an ARVN Special Forces Major named Mai Van Triet to take over the Central Intelligence Office station in Paris. According to Triet, after the first secret Kissinger meeting in 1969, "a French security officer, still upset about the failure of the U.S. to bomb in support of them at Dien Bien Phu, told my predecessor about the meeting. He promptly informed Saigon, so when Kissinger came to brief Thieu about the first secret talks, the president already knew but did not let on. After that, French intelligence provided me a [several] page document about every secret meeting between Kissinger and the Communists."[8]

Then on September 16, again without consulting Thieu, Nixon announced the withdrawal of a second tranche of troops, a move that was to be completed by December. Thieu wanted to time American withdrawals with the training and expansion of his own forces, particularly the local Regional Forces and Popular Forces. Instead, Nixon was centering his withdrawal timetable on his domestic political needs and not on conditions on the ground or Thieu's plan. Nor was he basing it on the simultaneous removal of PAVN units, which he had proclaimed as a condition for U.S. withdrawal in his speech of May 4. According to Thieu's close advisor, Hoang Duc Nha, in South Vietnamese eyes, "this was the beginning of the betrayal."[9]

If expanding his military and improving local government was crucial for Thieu, unifying the Nationalists to face the Communists in a political contest was next on his agenda. The two were intimately connected. For Thieu, national unity equaled national strength. Whether it was a chimera or not, it was a goal he sought with single-minded fervor. As Thieu told Nixon, his internal problem was "to hold back the super-hawks and to keep the super-doves from going too far." Moreover, there were "risks in the 'long haul, low cost' solution because the [Vietnamese] people do not yet have confidence in our ability to oppose the Communists politically."[10] However, before Thieu could consolidate the perennially divided Nationalists, a series of political scandals erupted that undermined his effort to convince the U.S. to engage in his "long haul, low cost," and "talking while building" policies.

SCANDAL AFTER SCANDAL

The tumult began April 6, 1969, with the arrest of Communist intelligence operative Tran Ngoc Hien, the older brother of former Kien Hoa Province chief and current Lower House deputy Tran Ngoc Chau. Hien revealed his intelligence net, and over twenty-five people were arrested. The most important collaborator was Nguyen Lau, the publisher of Bui Diem's English-language paper *Saigon Post*. Lau was a childhood friend of Hien's, had not reported Hien to the police when he discovered Hien's true purpose, and had accepted assignments to gather general information. However, the Hien case raised a huge political problem. Hien had also admitted to meeting with Chau eight times, but Chau had not reported these meetings to the government. Such gatherings were illegal if the government had not authorized them in advance. Chau, already in hot water for his call in January to negotiate with the NLF, was suddenly viewed with suspicion for not reporting his meetings with his brother, the Communist spy.

Hien was not the only spy case that damaged reputations. Shortly after the Tet Offensive, the Special Branch (SB), the police unit tasked with civilian counterintelligence, began examining how the NLF had acquired the detailed information used in the planning for its attacks on the Joint General Staff and Independence Palace. When U.S. forces later discovered copies of sensitive documents from Thieu's office in a sweep operation in Tay Ninh Province, the SB immediately suspected a spy.[11] It increased its monitoring of people thought to have covert Communist links. The Special Branch was currently watching a man living in Saigon named Le Huu Thuy. Under a pen name, Thuy had published articles that were critical of the government for a newspaper owned by Lower House deputy Hoang Ho, who was also a Communist spy. When the SB studied Thuy, they discovered that years earlier, Diem's police had arrested him for suspected Communist activity, but he had been released under Big Minh's blanket pardon of all political prisoners. Launching an operation codenamed "Projectile," the Special Branch sent an undercover agent posing as a repair man to befriend Thuy. When Thuy bragged to him about the number of spies inside the government, they began to surveil Thuy's house and placed a bug inside.[12]

In early 1969, the SB was shocked to discover that one regular visitor to Thuy's house was Vu Ngoc Nha, Thieu's advisor for religious affairs. Like Pham Ngoc Thao, Nha had originally fought with the Viet Minh and then "rallied" to the Nationalists. Nha was a northerner who converted to Catholicism and joined Father Hoang Quynh's parish in Phat Diem. After moving south in 1954, Nha settled near Hue, but in late December 1958, he was arrested for suspected Communist activity. Since Nha did not confess, Big Minh also released him shortly after the 1963 coup. Father Quynh eventually introduced Nha to Thieu, where he became a counselor to the president on relations between the GVN and the various religions.

Tailing Nha from Thuy's house, the SB spotted Nha meeting with Huynh Van Trong, Thieu's special advisor for political affairs, the man who Thieu had sent to America with a mission to study the U.S. presidential campaign. SB agents observed Trong pass an envelope to Nha. After Trong departed, the SB watched Nha hand the package to a woman courier. This case had now become highly politicized as both men were trusted advisors to South Vietnam's chief executive. When the CIA and SB briefed Thieu and recommended detaining the two men, an unhappy Thieu agreed but warned them that failure to prove their case would be disastrous. After gathering evidence, the SB apprehended Trong and Nha in July and found highly classified documents in their possession.[13] This time, Nha confessed to having been a Communist operative for twenty years. Trong affirmed that he knew Nha was a spy and that he had passed secret documents to him. Over fifty people were arrested as part of Nha's ring, including several journalists and two high-level officials in the Chieu Hoi Ministry, which was responsible for assimilating Communist defectors.[14] The subsequent trial and sentencing of Hien, Thuy, Nha, and Trong to life in prison made Thieu's government appear to be riddled with enemy spies.

As Nixon and Thieu were meeting at Midway, in early June a group sponsored by antiwar U.S. congressmen and led by Father Robert Drinan, dean of the Boston College Law School, arrived in South Vietnam to study political repression. Attempting to provide transparency, the GVN allowed Drinan's team to call on various political prisoners. In mid-June, the group visited Chi Hoa, the main Saigon prison, where they interviewed Truong Dinh Dzu. Drinan also saw Thich Thien Minh, while other team members visited Con Son Island, home to a large prison since colonial days. Although several weeks earlier Thieu had reduced Thien Minh's sentence to three years and he had met with Drinan's team to explain the reasoning behind the detentions, his explanations failed. Upon his return to America in late June, Drinan published a scathing exposé that received wide press coverage. He vilified Thieu for jailing "a non-Communist advocate of peace" like Dzu, "whose only subversive idea was to urge negotiation and conciliation with the hope of forming a coalition government."[15] This was the first major antiwar blast during Nixon's tenure. Drinan's broadside painted Thieu as a reactionary suppressing a political solution to the war, and it served to reopen the antiwar dam in the U.S.

Leaders of the antiwar movement, who had remained quiescent during Nixon's first six months, decided to act. On October 15, large demonstrations labeled the Moratorium to End the War in Vietnam were held throughout America. Bui Diem cabled Thieu about the resurgent demonstrations and asked him to address them. Aware that the antiwar protests were only one part of a tremendous cultural disruption rending American society, Bui Diem was tortured by the thought that his country's "future was being affected by social forces that we could not block and that only partly had to do with us." If Thieu wanted the American public to accept the "long haul, low cost" strategy, Bui Diem recommended reforming the GVN so that U.S. opinion would support a continued investment in American lives and treasure. Now cut out of the sensitive communications between Nixon and Thieu and painfully aware that his president did not fully trust him, Bui Diem judged he had failed to convince Thieu to see "events in

Vietnam through the prism of the great debate rocking American society."[16] It was his greatest regret, but Thieu's rebuff was more a function of the U.S. government's repeated message that the antiwar demonstrations would not influence Nixon rather than Bui Diem's inability to communicate the impact of American societal upheavals.

Nixon responded to the October 15 Moratorium on November 3, when he addressed the nation and appealed for support against the antiwar demonstrators from "the great silent majority of Americans." Undeterred, on November 15, a massive protest of a half million people marched on the White House. Yet despite the impressive crowd, a Gallup poll taken in mid-November showed most Americans backed Nixon. In fact, 74 percent opposed an immediate withdrawal, while 21 percent favored one.[17]

Hanoi instantly sought to capitalize on the Moratorium uproar in America by instigating more political agitation in South Vietnam. A cable was sent to its southern commands informing them that "the Politburo believes that we must begin to prepare immediately to incite a broad mass movement to respond to the upcoming struggle." The target was the South Vietnamese urban population. "Forces that can be mobilized for this effort include youth, high school students, college students, workers, Buddhists...We could employ different forms of struggle, such as meetings, seminars, drafting petitions, and street demonstrations to display support for the American people's struggle."[18] With its army in tatters, political agitation was now the Politburo's main tool for attacking the GVN from the inside and driving the Americans out.

The Moratorium protests, however, would pale in comparison to the incident known as the My Lai Massacre. In March 1968, a U.S. army infantry company was ordered to search for a local force battalion thought to be hiding in a Communist-controlled area in Quang Ngai Province that the Americans had sarcastically christened "Pinkville." After constantly sustaining losses from snipers and boobytraps, on March 16, 1968, the U.S. unit entered My Lai hamlet and went on a murderous rampage. Several hundred villagers were executed, and dozens of women were raped. Several helicopter pilots providing air support reported the massacre, but the division chain of command ignored their accounts. On November 12, 1969, journalist Seymour Hersh broke the story, which sparked vociferous demands for an inquiry. Although the Army investigated, only one officer, Lieutenant William Calley, was court-martialed. It was one of the worst stains on the honor of the U.S. Army in its history.

Nixon became deeply worried that the publicity about My Lai would affect U.S. and worldwide public opinion. He sought to downplay the incident, and so did the South Vietnamese government. Since Quang Ngai and its neighboring province Binh Dinh were probably the biggest Communist stronghold in the country, local ARVN leaders did not care that NLF supporters had been killed. Lieutenant General Hoang Xuan Lam, I Corps commander, initially denied anything had happened but eventually initiated an investigation. Thieu also expressed skepticism. He declared the area was "not just a peaceful stretch of countryside but a fortified VC area," and clamoring about My Lai did not help him implement his strategy to keep the U.S. engaged.[19]

A few Nationalists did not share Thieu vision; they only saw a chance to skewer the Vietnamese president. Senator Tran Van Don announced an investigation. He traveled several times to the area, and in mid-December, his National Salvation Front issued a statement condemning the massacre. Fearful of stoking U.S. antiwar emotions, the NSF declaration carefully avoided any reference that American soldiers had committed the atrocity. However, the NSF reproached the GVN for stating that no massacre had occurred. On January 5, 1970, Don's joint committee issued a report that confirmed that U.S. troops had killed some villagers but sought to deflect blame by claiming that Thieu was covering up the American involvement and "must be held totally responsible for the massacre."[20]

Thieu reacted with fury. He was already upset with Don after an earlier speech given by the retired general on October 30 to celebrate National Day. After a trip to the U.S., Don believed the Americans were on their way out and that his country needed to adapt. He wrote: "I realized that South Vietnam had to change course if it wanted to survive, because if it continued down the same old path it would be in danger."[21] Don's speech proposed a plan he termed "National Survival." After thanking America for its sacrifices, he demanded the withdrawal of all U.S. and DRV troops. Declaring Vietnamization a mistake, Don called for a "Third Force," ostensibly a middle group between the NLF and Thieu's anti-communists, to govern the country. South Vietnam would become a nonaligned country that would "remove ourselves from the international power game." Economically, he advocated a "regime of progressive socialism" that would redistribute the country's wealth.[22]

Don had been quietly working to convince his old friend, Duong Van Minh, to lead his Third Force concept. Since Don could never be president—the Constitution only permitted native-born Vietnamese to serve, and the former general had been born in France—Don promoted Minh, as did An Quang, although more reluctantly. Minh quickly added his voice to Don's clamor. On November 2, in his first public comments since returning from exile a year earlier, Minh told journalists he advocated a national referendum to determine the people's aspirations. Afterward, a "national convention" could form a "truly representative government for South Vietnam."[23] Characteristically, Minh waffled over the precise meaning of his remarks. His referendum idea was merely to "determine the aspirations of the people" to make the "struggle against the Communists" more effective. He was not advocating a coalition, he said, and he batted down Don's proposal by declaring that he had "no intention to form a third force."[24] Although outside observers claimed Minh was popular, especially among the Buddhists and southerners, his appeal had never been tested, a point avoided by those advocating Minh as Saigon's leader.

In response, Thieu viciously attacked those advocating the Third Force concept. In one speech, he called them "dogs." For him, the Third Force idea undermined Nationalist unity while also undercutting his effort to keep the U.S. aid flowing. On another level, it was tit-for-tat political bashing. To fully understand the Saigon political scene, one must recognize that some Saigon politicians did not differ with Thieu over policy; they were simply rival's for power. Many Nationalists suspected that Don, fueled by ambition and personal rancor for the president, secretly hoped that his proposal would entice the Americans to unseat Thieu. In today's political parlance, Don had gone "negative" in his messaging to convince the U.S. to remove Thieu. Believing the U.S. was desperate to leave, and since the U.S. had helped Don topple Diem, he hoped they might entertain the same notion with Thieu. To promote himself and Minh to embassy officials as an appealing replacement, Don constantly denigrated Thieu as a dictator who was unwilling to broaden his government or to seek peace. His condemnation was designed to test the American response, searching for any sign of U.S. displeasure. It was pure demagoguery since Don would undoubtedly cooperate with Thieu for a price, which was appointing him prime minister.

Since most of the leaders of the old political parties had similar outlooks, Thieu refused to bring them into the government until they had proven they would work for the country and not to promote their party. Unfortunately, Thieu saw people as either loyal or opposed, and he responded ruthlessly to real or imagined opponents. Thus, some of his response was simply a brass-knuckles takedown of a political adversary rather than repression. Discerning the difference, however, was almost impossible during that highly charged ideological era. The problem was all of this made it harder for Thieu to keep the support of the American public.

A unified Nationalist front also meant, in Thieu's mind, no press criticism, but silencing the press generated harsh international criticism. He had relaxed the press restrictions in May 1968, but he had in turn sought to codify the rules under which the press operated. To this end, the assembly passed a new law on December 30, 1969, that clarified media rights and responsibilities, especially regarding commentary on peace. With the passage in June of the law governing the establishment of political parties, the government had now enacted a second major bill safeguarding socio-political life in the Second Republic. Under the new legislation, the Information Ministry could censor an article or seize that day's issue, but it could no longer close a paper without a court order. Under the new guidelines, the U.S. embassy noted that from 1970 to 1971, "the South Vietnamese press enjoyed journalistic freedoms...[that were] impressive when compared on a world-wide scale of press freedom. However,...a small minority of newspapers...used their new-found freedom to launch vitriolic attacks on the Thieu administration and the U.S. government."[25] Hence Thieu attempted to modify the bill's section that allowed newspapers to print any comment by legislators without punishment. He feared liberal deputies would smear him. Since the constitution allowed Thieu to amend any law passed by the assembly, but it could override his changes with a majority vote of both houses. In a rare rebuke, it vetoed his change.

CHANGING OF THE GUARD

After meeting Nixon, and to get his local initiatives moving better, Thieu needed to replace Tran Van Huong as prime minister. His successor would be Tran Thien Khiem. Huong's fall on August 24 resulted from three issues: his battles with the assembly, his health, and his lack of expertise in pacification.

Rumblings about removing Huong to improve government efficiency, or gossip about disputes between him and Thieu, had occurred intermittently since Huong's ascension in May 1968. Thieu had ignored the rumors, but in mid-June 1969, the Lower House had sent the president a request to replace Huong. Its members were incensed over Huong's recent decree enacting tax increases on numerous imported luxury goods without first consulting the legislature. Huong angrily responded by publicly lashing out at the assembly. Deputies reacted by refusing to consider several pieces of crucial legislation, then demanded the ministers of Interior, Defense, and Justice appear to answer questions about allegations of arbitrary arrests, torture, and corruption in the Phoenix program, the effort to eliminate the NLF cadres in the countryside.

Testifying before the assembly on June 20, Interior Minister Khiem defended the program but agreed that abuses had occurred at the local level. Since gathering solid evidence on detainees was often difficult, he admitted that many suspects were harshly interrogated and could be held for up to two years without formal charges. With Vietnamese TV cameras broadcasting his grilling, Khiem pledged to remedy these mistreatments, but the appearance of the prime minister being questioned by the assembly both reinforced and encouraged the opposition to examine government missteps. In American governance, congressional oversight is mandated. In a young democracy like South Vietnam, this supervision was critical for its growth, but criticism was more often seen as a challenge to power.

On August 20, Khiem published new regulations tightening the procedures for holding suspects. In October, Khiem launched a national publicity campaign to explain the Phoenix program and asked for the people's help in reporting Communist underground cadres. Yet despite these efforts, Phoenix would continue to be pilloried by U.S. antiwar critics as, at best, a massive human rights violation, or at worst, a vile assassination program.

Phoenix, however, was not some James Bond license to kill, nor did the GVN triumph in halting abuses. Phoenix was another great idea that only half succeeded due to the failure to adequately train and manage the South Vietnamese who ran it. Giving community officials, especially local police, discretionary power to arrest and detain people was begging for abuse, and local personnel often took full advantage to settle vendettas or extort bribes. Phoenix proved to be a blunt instrument when a surgeon's precision was needed, but Communist security procedures often defeated knowing precisely where and how to cut.

Although the program seriously eroded the rural NLF political base, it never completely eradicated it, partly because of GVN inefficiency and partly because of a spy. In 1967, COSVN Security had inserted an agent into the

Police Special Branch. This agent eventually took command of Saigon's 6th Precinct Phoenix Committee, and he obtained

> information on the entire organizational structure of the Phoenix Committees and on the various Phoenix campaigns that were conducted. He attended the weekly meetings of the Capital Region Phoenix Committee...[He] obtain[ed] the list of investigative leads and of our cadres whom the enemy was watching, as well as the list of our cadres who had been arrested and were being interrogated by the enemy. Every week (from 1968 until early 1972), [he] sent these two lists and we were able to take timely defensive measures that limited the amount of damage done to our organization.[26]

With the new legislation halted, his ministers being grilled, and growing calls for improving government efficiency, Thieu realized that Huong's time was ending. Under the guise of "broadening the government," on July 19, Thieu announced he would change some cabinet members. After three weeks with no movement toward revamping the cabinet, on August 8, Thieu's National Social Democratic Front publicly called for Huong's removal, a pronouncement that many viewed as Thieu's covert way of signaling Huong that he needed to quit rather than force Thieu to fire him. Finally bowing to the inevitable, Huong resigned on August 24.

Thieu immediately asked Khiem to form a new government. The president had chosen a military officer as prime minister because he wanted someone to lead the critical pacification effort. It was a Faustian choice since a civilian might have defanged the claims that the GVN was a military dictatorship. Khiem, a rotund forty-three-year-old who wore thick frameless glasses, was considered by Vietnamese as a competent administrator but an endless intriguer. Colorless and reserved, he preferred working behind the scenes rather than leading. Less charitable Vietnamese called him an "arch-opportunist [with] an exceptional talent for flexibility in dealing with political shifts."[27]

On September 1, Khiem announced his new cabinet. While mostly technicians, his two most important choices were an energetic young man named Pham Kim Ngoc as economic minister and Senator Tran Van Lam to replace Tran Thanh Chanh as foreign minister. Lam, another in a long list of initial backers of Diem who had eventually fallen out with him, was a wealthy southerner and a leading Catholic layman who had long been associated with local Saigon politics. He was born in Cholon on July 30, 1913. He attended the elite francophone Lycee Petrus Ky, then graduated with a degree in pharmacy from the University of Hanoi in 1939. In 1967, Lam formed his own Senate slate, which finished fifth in the election. Urbane and fluent in both English and French, he was a jovial man who had a great interest in foreign affairs. In April 1968, he founded the Vietnam Council on Foreign Relations, which became a prominent nonprofit organization in South Vietnam. While never a heavyweight in policy formation, he would become Saigon's second-longest serving foreign minister.

Bunker instantly pressed Thieu to use this opportunity to bring in more "out" politicians, his usual refrain. Thieu tried once more to include in the cabinet some of the old-line politicians like Ha Thuc Ky of the RDV and Tran Van Tuyen of the VNQDD, but these men wanted top positions. When Thieu offered them slots they considered beneath them, they declined, so he opted for technocrats instead. Like other anti-communist Asian leaders, Thieu chose improving government efficiency over "broadening the government."

While this was a shibboleth for outsiders, Thieu was unconcerned. He knew that the peasants' main concerns were making a living and acquiring reasonably honest local government and security from depravations by both sides. The reality is that Thieu and his government's image among most South Vietnamese was generally balanced, except among Saigon elites who decried his every move. For example, in the first of a monthly series of public opinion polls conducted among villagers by CORDS using trained Vietnamese, 30 percent of those questioned agreed that the national government was strong and "strives hard to assist the people."[28] Yet other political aspirations did exist in the South Vietnamese political body, and Thieu needed to address them to build a national consciousness, especially regarding the inclusivity of democracy. For Thieu, though, it was an impossible philosophical leap during a fratricidal war. While he was determined to enshrine the rule of law, he believed a strong leader was necessary to guide the people and build his country, an echo both of his traditional rearing and his desire to emulate the economic successes of Taiwan and South Korea.

Unfortunately, Thieu's latest effort at merging the Nationalist parties to compete in elections had failed. Despite large infusions of covert U.S. cash from Bunker, the NSDF was moribund. This was a crucial letdown since uniting the Nationalists was key in Thieu's mind to win a subsequent election and convince Hanoi that it could not win the war. However,

Thieu's call for an opposition party had worked. Dr. Nguyen Van Bong's nascent pro-government party, the Progressive Nationalist Movement, was "showing more political energy and organizing drive than any of the established parties."[29] Although the party was growing, it was by no means broadly based. In late 1969, PNM membership was around thirty thousand people, primarily middle-class. Bong was concentrating on building a cadre organization that would win hamlet and village elections before attempting to induct thousands of people. Although Bong was building a countrywide organization, it was not yet strong enough to compete and succeed on a national level.

What South Vietnam needed was a mass-based party that could deliver Nationalist votes, and into that gap stepped Tran Quoc Buu's labor union, the CVT. On October 29, Buu's union filed the paperwork to form the Farmer-Worker Party (*Dang Cong Nong*). Given the union's large membership and strong anti-communist pedigree, it could provide an electoral bulwark against NLF recruitment among city workers. The Farmer-Worker Party was quickly approved under the new political party law, and Thieu asked Buu to speak with the other parties to merge with him. When Buu also failed to convince them to put aside their differences, Thieu began to entertain an idea first broached by the South Koreans but now proposed to him by Phan Quang Dan. In mid-October 1969, Dan recommended to Thieu and Khiem the formation of a government political party, much like the Kuomintang in Taiwan.

Dan, his earlier sins absolved, had returned to government employ when Khiem appointed him to the cabinet as minister of state without portfolio focused on foreign relations. Dan remarked to a U.S. embassy official that Thieu "has had a bitter experience with his allies in the NSDF." The Front's failure was the result of trying to "unite politicians. Thieu now realizes that an entirely new formula for political mobilization must be applied." Dan opined that "foreign observers" who had criticized Thieu for not "broadening the government" had failed to understand that "relying on the conventional political parties" was futile. Dan bashed the old politicians for "sitting on their hands waiting for Thieu to get into trouble so they could benefit from it. The obvious conclusion," Dan said, "is that political mobilization from the top has failed and that the government must now approach it from the bottom up." However, he was "frankly afraid that the constant carping of foreigners on the need to 'broaden the base' had obscured the real opportunity to mobilize the existing popular support for Thieu."[30]

Interested in politically mobilizing the people, and given the failures of the various "fronts," Thieu encouraged Dan to start thinking about a government party. At a cabinet meeting in February 1970, Dan stated that true Nationalist "political mobilization could only be obtained if government launches its own political party." The purpose of a government party was to ensure the "reelection of President Thieu."[31] Dan's idea was quickly dismissed, as Prime Minister Khiem said that they did not have enough time to form a party and develop cadres. Thieu, however, was intrigued. Shaking off his earlier reluctance about tying the presidency to a specific party like the Can Lao, Thieu gave Dan his blessing to begin organizational activity. From this would eventually emerge Thieu's Democracy Party, an attempt to mobilize the people using GVN employees as the party framework. This government party would also reinforce pacification by improving state services in the countryside, which in turn would lead to votes in an election.

In the meantime, Khiem moved to streamline the government. Khiem's first move, though, foreshadowed an issue that would severely damage the republic. On September 16, in his first speech as prime minister, Khiem never mentioned fighting corruption. Saigonese heard a clear message. Now only the toothless Inspectorate, the agency responsible for investigating government malfeasance, remained.

For suspicious minds, Khiem's action seemed timed to a recent Inspectorate judgment against Brigadier General Nguyen Van Toan, commander of the 2nd ARVN Division based in Quang Ngai. Toan had been charged with using military trucks in July 1967 to transport cinnamon bark from the province. The sale of the highly profitable bark had been banned in 1965 when the lone area where it grew fell under NLF control. Toan stated that he was simply helping a local businessman who had asked him to move the harvested bark to Danang, and he presented paperwork showing that the money he had received had been given to the transportation units involved, not pocketed by him. Regardless, the Inspectorate had recommended that Toan be removed from command and transferred out of I Corps. Several senior military leaders immediately protested, and Thieu refused to implement the recommendation. Toan became known as the "Cinnamon General," one of the few RVNAF senior officers caught red-handed. Thieu's failure to punish Toan, however, exacted a price. Many younger officers grew disenchanted by what they saw as Thieu covering up for one of his cronies. Contributing to their discontent was that these younger officers could not feed their families unless their wives also worked. Corruption at the senior levels would remain the cancer rotting the flesh of South Vietnam.

Not only was corruption bedeviling Thieu, but another ethnic tumult had erupted. In April 1969, Thieu disclosed that he wanted to improve diplomatic relations with various countries. He reinstated Saigon's ambassador to Laos, and he dispatched Foreign Minister Thanh to Indonesia to repair relations that had been broken since 1962. His most important initiative, however, was with Cambodia. Because Prince Sihanouk had recently admitted that the PAVN was violating Cambodian territory, both Nixon and Thieu hoped they could restart talks on defining the border and other matters that had been left dormant since 1964. Sihanouk, though, remained leery of embracing Thieu, and no progress was made on resolving the critical border issue.

Trying to convince Sihanouk of Thieu's good intentions, on September 18, Khiem signed a decree establishing a Directorate for Development of Vietnamese of Cambodian Origins. The Cambodian Buddhist church, the largest group in Tam Chau's Quoc Tu faction, had roused itself from its politically inert state and had begun pressuring Thieu since December 1968 for a separate agency with its own budget. Given the ethnic hatred between Cambodians and Vietnamese, Cambodians could not rise in Vietnamese society, especially in the military, and the bonzes wanted to end discrimination. When Thieu decreed an Ethnic Minorities Council on October 14 designed to advise him on issues or legislation relating to minorities, the Cambodians were somehow left out. Crimson-robed Cambodian Buddhist monks in Saigon immediately staged a nonviolent sit-in at Independence Palace. Although initially left undisturbed, on November 18, the police removed almost two hundred protesting monks. A month later, the Cambodian monks returned and this time clashed with the police. Using teargas and water cannons, the police broke up the demonstrations, but Thieu had had enough. On December 22, he added the Cambodians to the council. While the unrest died out in Saigon, Cambodians in the Delta continued to make small demonstrations in their southern strongholds, but they stopped after Lon Nol overthrew Sihanouk in March 1970. This was the last ethnic turbulence Thieu would face until 1974.

CONTINUING TO EXPAND THE STATE

Pacification remained the most critical program in Thieu's strategy to preserve the republic. Thieu began inspection trips to each corps, where he often up-braided local officials for poor conduct. His new pacification plan for 1970 had three major goals: end the war, build democracy, and achieve self-sufficiency. He particularly hoped to increase the income of peasant farmers by improving agricultural output. When a flood in late 1968 wiped out the harvest in the town of Vo Dat, a major rice producing area about seventy-five miles northeast of Saigon, USAID flew in bags of IR-8 "miracle rice" from the Philippines. Developed by the International Rice Research Institute, the new strain doubled the amount of rice grown per acre in a third less time. Although the IR-8 crop tasted worse than native rice, the miracle rice saved the harvest at Vo Dat.

Deeply impressed, Thieu expanded the program and began imploring farmers to use it. Around a hundred thousand acres were planted in 1968, and the Ministry of Agriculture quickly nicknamed the rice *Than Nong*, the name for the Vietnamese god of agriculture. Rice production increased in 1969 by almost a million metric tons over 1968. Thieu planned on making South Vietnam rice self-sufficient again in several years, but miracle rice required more fertilizer and pesticides, which were expensive for farmers. Soon, though, miracle rice would deliver a revolution in farm income.

Security gains also helped other critical government functions. By July 1969, elections had been held in almost all the villages and 80 percent of the hamlets. Thieu now planned for provincial council elections in 1970 to further cement local power. Refugees, a perennial GVN punching bag, had dropped from an all-time high of 1.4 million people in February 1969 to around 350,000 by the end of the year. Despite the usual problems of corruption and spartan camps, since 1965, the GVN had cared for almost four million rural and urban refugees, one quarter of the population. The refugee department of the Ministry of Social Welfare, almost nonexistent four years earlier, now had 1,600 employees. While the refugee problem was by no means solved, and the U.S. continued to pay the bulk of the resettlement benefits, the GVN had come a long way in four years.

Militarily, Thieu intended to shift each element of his armed forces—the People's Self Defense Force, the RF/PF, and the ARVN—to a different role to replace the departing U.S. forces. Critics had long stressed that overreliance on military force was self-defeating in what was primarily a political confrontation. While that was true in the early years of the war, a more conventional battle between larger units employing heavy artillery and armor was on the horizon, a change few saw coming. While Thieu was also not planning for a future conflict between heavily armed opponents, his plan was simple: the four million people enrolled in the PSDF would take over guarding the hamlets and villages from the Popular Forces. This would free the PF to patrol outside the villages, replacing the Regional Forces, who would then assume the pacification role from the ARVN. Improving the firepower and training of the RF/PF was decisive as they now accounted for 40 percent of the one million men under arms. Freed from static defense, the regular army would return to its original mobile role and take the fight to the PAVN.

The PSDF were not only the key to shifting the military roles, they were vital to the forthcoming political challenge at the ballot box. Hidden in Thieu's design was that the PSDF members would be trained in anti-communist doctrine and become the foot soldiers in the mass-based party he so desperately sought. "The concept," Thieu said, was "to train the PSDF not only in the use of weapons but to give them instructions in civics, to enhance their political motivation... and thereby make them effective exponents of the government and its policies. Fighting the Communists is not just a matter of defending against armed attacks... but of carrying the government's case to the people."[32]

Based upon the plan he had outlined to Nixon at their meeting in late July, and to support his military restructuring, on August 20, Thieu sent Nixon a massive aid request for 1970. He informed Nixon that the "GVN earnestly wishes to assume increasing responsibility in the Vietnam War... [but] the GVN needs U.S. help geared toward the strengthening of the country." Thieu wanted to add another 148,000 men to the RVNAF in 1970, and he asked the U.S. to provide their equipment and training.[33]

South Vietnam, however, was at the mercy of Congress, and Congress had soured on foreign aid. In October 1968, it passed the smallest foreign aid amount since the U.S. began giving aid after World War II. Shortly thereafter, in February 1969 the Senate launched an investigation into corruption and kickbacks among both South Vietnamese and American companies. Sensing the tide of U.S. congressional opinion shifting against him, Thieu decided to make a bold offer. In his annual address to the National Assembly, on October 6, 1969, he declared that "to help the U.S. government in its internal problems and reduce the U.S. people's burdens, we are determined to replace the majority of U.S. combat units in 1970."[34]

His offer was lost amid the Moratorium protests, but although Nixon on December 1 approved increased aid to Saigon, Congress again passed a much-reduced amount for 1970. Nixon would now have to drain aid money from other countries to support Thieu's plan since the principle U.S. economic goal for South Vietnam was to "insure that sufficient U.S. financial resources are available to assist the GVN in keeping inflation within manageable limits [and keep pressure] on the GVN to undertake monetary or fiscal measures essential to achieving this result." Without increased aid, "military and political advances may be seriously jeopardized if provisions are not made to maintain the economic underpinnings of the war effort as Vietnamization progresses."[35]

At the same time, though, Nixon announced another troop withdrawal, the third one in 1969. Thieu could only hope that his military plan would succeed before the Americans departed. As Kissinger later admitted, "After 1969 the war in Vietnam had turned into a race between our withdrawal, the improvement of the South Vietnamese army, and the ability of Hanoi to interrupt the process by launching offensives."[36]

Luckily for Nixon, the fortunes of war favored his withdrawal scheme. The Politburo had also decided to change strategy. Writing after the war, they acknowledged that by the end of 1969, Communist units were

> seriously weakened [and] almost all of our main force units either had to be recalled back to North Vietnam to regroup and refit or they had to be moved to the other side of the border. A few units had to be disbanded entirely. [This was] one of the two periods when we suffered the greatest losses in the history of the revolution in the South: the four years following the signing of the Geneva Agreement (1954–1958) and the two years following the Tet Offensive, from mid-1968 to early 1970. During this period, our casualties totaled more than 100,000 cadres, soldiers, and agents, a number approximately equal to our total casualties during the entire resistance war against the French.... In the two years 1968-1969 our losses in [the B-2 Front] alone were double our total losses during the previous seven years (from 1961 to 1967) and equaled one third of our entire troop strength in South Vietnam at that time. The enemy captured almost 3,000 more hamlets and gained control of an additional 3,000,000 civilians.[37]

Even infiltration was vastly reduced from 1968; only eighty-one thousand men were sent south in 1969. Given its terrible military predicament, in 1970, the Politburo would turn to its other weapon, political agitation. The U.S. antiwar protests and the new South Vietnamese social and political divisions offered the Politburo an opportunity it had not seen since the awful days of 1964 and 1966. The fires of protest would again come close to destroying South Vietnam.

18

"WE SELDOM UNDERSTOOD THE FINANCIAL COSTS OF VICTORY"

Finding Economic Security

Thieu planned in 1970 to cement his pacification gains by launching the most revolutionary land-reform program in human history. His grand design was to create an ownership society, raise the living standards of an impoverished agrarian society, and convert the peasantry to firm supporters of the Second Republic. Yet as he prepared to launch what became the signature program of his administration, economic malaise forced him to also focus on revamping South Vietnam's colonial economic structure. Concurrently, he needed to secure increased U.S. funding to bolster his finances and to feed his cash-strapped young soldiers. For the South Vietnamese president, it would be another year where his major domestic achievements were eclipsed by tremendous internal upheavals, including the trial and imprisonment of Tran Ngoc Chau, the former Kien Hoa Province chief and Lower House deputy.

THE TAXMAN COMETH

While historians have focused on the diplomatic and military ramifications of the 1968 Tet Offensive, the Communist attack had an equally important consequence: it triggered a severe recession in South Vietnam. Rural income declined, industrial production cratered, and imports dropped sharply. Hundreds of thousands were suddenly unemployed or homeless, and the loss of investor confidence over security concerns halted new capital investment.

By the fall of 1968, however, a combination of U.S. aid, foreign charitable donations, and South Vietnamese government spending produced an economic revival in the fourth quarter highlighted by a massive inflow of imports. The drop in consumer spending and U.S. aid had kept inflation within tolerable limits in 1968, far less than in similar war-ravaged countries like South Korea during the 1950–53 conflict. Prices in South Korea had soared 169 percent in 1952 but had dropped to 32 percent in 1953 after the U.N. command and the Korean leadership implemented tough anti-inflation policies.[1]

Although the economy was rebounding, the bear was still stalking Vietnam's market. Given the huge sums spent on refugee care and on RVNAF expansion, it was inevitable that the soaring spending would turbocharge inflation and the budget deficit. In May 1969, when prices jumped 11 percent, Prime Minister Tran Van Huong attempted to increase taxes to raise revenue, starting the turmoil that led to his removal. With economic indicators turning bleak, Bunker warned Thieu in June that the GVN would have to increase revenue and institute tough inflation controls to offset the higher spending.

Designing an overarching financial policy to accomplish these tasks was difficult because the country really had four separate economies. The first economic engine was imports, which were financed by a U.S. aid program called the Commercial Import Program (CIP). The U.S. funded imports by paying American businesses to send products to Saigon, while the Vietnamese importer who bought the goods paid into a counterpart GVN fund in piasters. This fund and the taxes applied to the imports were significant GVN revenue streams.

The second driver was agricultural products, which accounted for the bulk of South Vietnam's Gross Domestic Product. Rice was the chief measure of this market, but other commodities such as fish, pork, and vegetables were key as well. Given the war-related difficulties in growing rice and then transporting it to internal markets, the U.S. provided copious amounts of free rice to Saigon under the U.S. government's PL-480 Food For Peace program. The GVN then sold the U.S. rice to urban consumers and pocketed the revenue. Although improved security and miracle rice increased output in 1969 by 16 percent over 1968, it was not enough to keep up with demand, especially in the cities. The overall population, and urban dwellers especially, had grown dramatically since the early 1960s.

A third stimulus was a massive underground black market of pilfered goods from U.S. military stores. The wildly overvalued piaster, kept artificially low by the government to gain revenue, helped drive this criminality. The U.S. was buying piasters at the official exchange rate of 118 to 1 dollar, which Congress rightfully blasted as ripping off America since the black market value had soared to almost 400 to 1. When Congress again held hearings to investigate this drain on U.S. aid, Bunker was forced to confront Thieu. The ambassador told Thieu that corruption and black-marketing were an "open scandal." Thieu quickly dispatched the police to crack down on sidewalk vendors selling stolen goods, but they were often bribed to look the other way.

The fourth economic force was the U.S. presence. Hundreds of thousands of citizens either sold goods and services to the Americans or worked directly for the U.S. government or American companies. But as the U.S. footprint began to decline in 1969 and then in earnest in 1970, the loss of jobs or services had a tremendously depressive effect on income.

Into this storm stepped Pham Kim Ngoc. Appointed in September 1969 as South Vietnam's new economic minister, Ngoc was born on March 17, 1928, to a wealthy family in Hanoi. When the First Indochina War heated up, his parents sent him overseas to attend school, including graduate school at the prestigious London School of Economics. He returned to Saigon in 1955, where he led the Import Department of the Credit Commercial Bank of Vietnam, the lending arm of the National Bank. Ngoc was a protégé of former Economic Minister Nguyen Huu Hanh, and he joined the ministry as Hanh's deputy in 1967. Well known in Saigon's commercial banking circles, particularly with the wealthy Chinese merchants, Ngoc was also friendly with Nguyen Cao Thang of the OPV company. In August 1969, Thieu offered Hanh the economic portfolio, but Hanh declined and instead suggested Ngoc. Hanh believed he could run GVN economic policy from afar through Ngoc, but he had misjudged his proxy. Ngoc soon distanced himself from Hanh, believing Hanh had lost touch with economic conditions in South Vietnam. While Ngoc had powerful friends (Hanh, Thang, and the Chinese), he was a technocrat and had no political group to protect him. He survived because Thieu saw something in the energetic economist, and he backed Ngoc when many later demanded his removal. Thieu, who like Ky knew little about economics, gave him carte blanche to design economic policy.

Ngoc moved quickly to address the worsening economy. In a September 1969 speech, he opined that given South Vietnam's budget deficit, the country needed to reduce imports, lower expenditures, raise revenue, and increase exports. "We have been importing more than we need," he stated, and the new rule "will be austerity."[2] Ngoc was partially reacting to detractors who had been proclaiming that U.S.-funded imports were fueling an artificial consumer boom and that South Vietnamese society was living beyond its means due to the largesse of American taxpayers. In fact, imports only dampened inflation by replacing internal production lost from the fighting. While Ngoc's statements were designed to appease U.S. congressional critics, his chief goal was to restructure the economy. Ngoc wanted to implement a "Vietnamization of the economy" to pay for Thieu's massive increase in GVN defense expenditures to replace U.S. troops. As Ngoc later wrote, "we seldom understood the financial costs of victory."[3]

The GVN budget had two major weaknesses. First, 90 percent of its revenue came from indirect taxes, and two-thirds of that came from import levies. Second, rampant tax avoidance by the population cost the GVN millions of piasters each year in lost revenue. Consequently, the government was unable to finance itself, leading to high deficit spending, which increased inflation in South Vietnam. To address the deficit, in the summer of 1969, Prime Minister Huong offered Thieu an economic plan developed by Nguyen Huu Hanh. The U.S. was pressing Thieu to devalue the piaster, but Hanh disagreed. After the Saigon press had sneeringly dubbed him the "King of Devaluation" when he implemented the piaster reduction in 1966, Hanh now shied away from such a drastic action. He sought to boost import taxes, but he wanted to fine-tune the increase by raising duties 40 percent on specific goods while leaving taxes unchanged on essential items.

When Huong's government fell, Ngoc inherited Hanh's proposal. Thieu opted for Hanh's plan, which was essentially a devaluation but without the political baggage. Fearing a legislative battle, Thieu bypassed the assembly and signed a decree on October 23, 1969, implementing the tax increases. Urban citizens panicked as the cost of imports rose dramatically overnight. Gasoline taxes doubled, and food prices jumped. To prevent speculators from reaping windfall profits by hoarding goods and then selling after the announcement, the GVN had not informed the public in advance. Caught off guard and living on fixed incomes, Thieu's strongest political base— government workers and the military—reacted bitterly to the skyrocketing prices. Bunker called it "an act of high political courage but of poor political implementation."[4]

Thieu ordered Ngoc to appear on Vietnamese television and defend the program. After his appearance, the Vietnamese press immediately blamed the increase on him and called the decree the "Austerity Tax." The assembly roared that the decree was unconstitutional and requested that the Supreme Court decide its legality. In a sign of South Vietnam's growing democracy, the assembly was increasingly willing to challenge Thieu and assert its legislative prerogative. On December 12, 1969, the court ruled that only the assembly had the power to tax, but it waffled and did not overturn the decree. Ngoc, though, had learned a harsh lesson. His next reform would be done in conjunction with the assembly.

TRAN NGOC CHAU AND ONGOING FEARS OF A COALITION

At the end of 1969, Thieu was enduring his worst political storm since assuming the presidency. Between the austerity tax debacle, the spy ring fiascos, and his gnawing fear that Senator Don's naïve demand for a political accommodation with the Communists might sway a war-weary public, Thieu felt besieged. Determined to quash any cry for a coalition, he found a fall guy in Tran Ngoc Chau. The arrest of Chau's Communist spy brother, Tran Ngoc Hien, had put Chau in a bind. While Chau had informed several Americans of his meeting with Hien, for a variety of reasons he had not reported the contacts to Vietnamese authorities, which was a violation of the national security laws. Chau would now pay for talking with his "brother-enemy."

In November 1969, Thieu demanded that the Lower House lift Chau's parliamentary immunity so he could be prosecuted for meeting with Hien. Nguyen Cao Thang's aide, Nguyen Van Ngan, confirms that because Chau had

> become the defacto leader of the left-wing deputies...that was the real reason for stripping Chau's legislative immunity and for his arrest. If the government had failed to isolate Chau, the trend to seek a coalition with the Communists to end the war would have gained the upper hand in the Assembly, and this would have had a direct effect on the peace talks in Paris, on the internal political situation, and especially on the Presidential elections that were scheduled for 1971.[5]

Given Don's recent call for a Third Force, Thieu needed to make an example of Chau to quiet the Nationalist's demands for a coalition, but the subsequent heavy international criticism finally sobered the president. He confessed to Bunker that "he was aware of the difficulty the case was creating for him abroad [but] he was in a difficult position." He had to draw "a careful line between adverse effects in the U.S. and harmful effects in Vietnam... If he acted hesitantly... the people would question [his] motivations" and suspect that he sympathized with Chau. Thieu then cited one general who had said to him, "We doubted your determination after you moved so slowly against Chau, but now that you have taken action, we are very content. We have no fear of a coalition."[6] Thieu had a choice: suffer heavy international criticism or face a military terrified of a coalition. He choose to appease his domestic supporters, regardless of the worldwide damage.

After debating, the Lower House failed to muster the required three-fourths vote needed to remove his immunity. The vote was being obstructed by a group of southern deputies led by Nguyen Ba Can, a wealthy southerner who would eventually become chairman of the Lower House and then the last prime minister of South Vietnam. He had examined Chau's file and believed that the government's charges, while technically accurate, did not warrant prosecution. However, under pressure from pro-government deputies, Can requested Chau appear before his group. He would ask Chau one question: had he informed any government official about meeting his brother? "All that was required," Can later wrote, "was that Chau swear on his honor as a military officer and a member of the National Assembly that he was telling the truth." If he said yes, they would vote against stripping him. If he said no, then Can's group would vote against him. Chau, knowing he faced imprisonment if his immunity was removed, refused to lie. He admitted that he had not informed any GVN official. Chau's honesty impressed Can. He wrote that "my heart was filled with respect for the spirit of responsibility and honor... of my fellow legislator."[7] Can then outmaneuvered Thieu. The Lower House voted to continue examining the charge but refused to strip Chau of his immunity.

Thieu reacted badly. In a speech to the country in early January 1970, he railed against "political sorcerers" in the Nationalist ranks and those who advocated a Third Force.[8] The fallout was immediate. On January 16, Senator Don denounced the administration over its "failure" to solve the country's issues. At the same time, the political arm of Tran Quoc Buu's union withdrew from Thieu's NSDF, essentially killing it. The president fought back with more bluster. Since "the Communists no longer dream of military victory," Thieu said in his annual Tet message, they are using Nationalists "who have agreed to become their lackey." We must be "vigilant against these lackeys...Only we can defeat ourselves." Peace, Thieu proclaimed, "will only come through our own strength."[9] The foreign press uniformly condemned him for his harsh rhetoric.

Despite Can's roadblock, Thieu finally got his way. Nguyen Cao Thang engaged in some energetic bribery, known in the Lower House as the "Tran Hung Dao method," after Vietnam's national hero whose face was printed on the 500-piaster note.[10] In early February, the Lower House lifted Chau's immunity when two-thirds of its member simply signed a petition rather than hold a formal vote. It was Thang's last effort in the assembly. He immediately left for France for cancer treatment. Although Thieu asked the Mobile Military Court to try Chau, the Senate lobbied the Supreme Court to review the constitutionality of the petition. Chau went into hiding with several American friends who tried to convince him to flee the country. Chau courageously declined, and on February 23, he reappeared at the assembly. He refused to leave the building to attend his trial. Two days later, the Military Court found him guilty of "damaging national security" and sentenced him to twenty years in prison.

The next day, the Saigon police forcibly removed Chau from his office. The chaotic scene was publicized around the world. Despite his lawyer's vigorous defense, with Chau now present in court, on March 5, he was retried, but his sentence was reduced to ten years. Although Chau documented his contacts with the Americans, they denied meeting him, not wishing to undermine Thieu. His abandonment after colluding with the U.S. was not lost on many Nationalists, nor was Thieu's relentless persecution of Chau. Tran Van Tuyen, the VNQDD leader who had been one of Chau's attorneys, drew unflattering comparisons between Thieu and Diem. Tuyen remarked that "this trial was a test case of Vietnamese democracy, and democracy lost."[11]

On March 25, South Vietnam's third leg of government, the Supreme Court, finally took a stand. It ruled that the assembly's petition to strip Chau's immunity was invalid. A month later, it declared the Mobile Military Court unconstitutional, then in early May ruled that Chau could appeal his conviction. After employing restraint in its first year, the court, like the assembly, had also begun to exercise its responsibilities as a separate branch of government. The Supreme Court's judicial opinions, however, remained narrowly confined to answering constitutional questions but did not order any corrective action by the government. Although Thieu grumbled, he would propose new legislation to revamp the tax laws and reinstate the Mobile Military Court.

On October 31, 1970, the Supreme Court annulled Chau's conviction, but still treading carefully, did not order him released. When U.S. embassy officials queried Prime Minister Khiem on Thieu's plans, Khiem expressed frustration. He said that he had "no influence with Thieu in this matter, and when he had put forward objections in the past, he had been subject to the charge of 'following a soft line.'"[12] Thieu refused to release Chau, and although the case slowly faded from the front pages, Thieu's overseas image had suffered badly. He had assuaged his domestic base rather than appeasing his international detractors. But these devastating blows were accumulating just as he was seeking substantial amounts of new U.S. economic aid and as he was launching his most critical social policy, land reform.

LAND REFORM

With the Chau trial over, Thieu turned to other pressing matters. Since July 1969 he had been badgering the assembly to pass his land-reform legislation, a bill that would revolutionize property ownership in South Vietnam. Thieu had told Bunker that "he wanted to be remembered in Vietnam history as the person who had initiated" comprehensive land reform.[13] Others had tried, including Bao Dai in the early 1950s and Ngo Dinh Diem. Neither had succeeded. To understand the transformative nature of Thieu's land-reform program, one must review the dismal record of Saigon's previous efforts.

Historically, the number of actual landowners had been extremely low. In the 1940s, about a thousand families owned the vast bulk of the land in the Delta. The French once held sizeable tracts, but most remaining landlords were Vietnamese, many of whom had consolidated large holdings under the Nguyen Dynasty and had continued under the French.[14] The rents they charged tenant farmers to till the land ranged from moderate to exorbitant. Chinese merchants then bought the unhusked rice and shipped it to Chinese-owned rice mills in Saigon, where they sold the processed food for large profits. The lowly farmer, caught between these two monopolies, often barely made ends meet.

Bao Dai made the first attempt to correct land tenancy, but his efforts were stillborn due to the limited reach of his government during the First Indochina War. In October 1956, Diem's initial vision for land reform was called Ordinance 57. The decree was designed to lower land rents and to limit ownership to no more than 250 acres per person. The government would seize large tracts of land from wealthy property owners or French-owned properties and give it to the peasants.

His vision, however, was greater than mere economic improvement. Diem's concept of rural development was that it should provide both physical security against Communist encroachment and mentally immunize the peasants against the lure of Marxism. While he (mostly) appreciated American aid, as a leader with deep-seated, nationalistic pride, he strove to wean his people from foreign assistance by working to build a new society based on self-reliance. Diem hoped that with some initial government assistance, a Vietnamese self-help spirit would emerge from the communal beliefs that he thought infused the average peasant. He wanted to modernize and reshape the peasant worldview by infusing the Ngos' obscure philosophy of Personalism while retaining village traditions and cultural mores. His idea flowed from a desire to strike a path between the economic poles of communism and capitalism. Humans, however, are reluctant to change, particularly when forced instead of persuaded. Hence, Diem's concept foundered on the shoals of individual stubbornness, and he became another in a long line of rulers who had attempted to impose a new vision on an unwilling population. Only one hundred thousand families ever received a title to their fields.

Khanh had also begun land reform, mainly at the urging of Nguyen Ton Hoan, the Dai Viet leader. That effort also failed as the two men quickly had a falling out. By the time Ky and Thieu assumed leadership in June 1965, the situation in the countryside was so difficult that land reform had to wait until the security situation improved. Although Ky often spoke of restarting land reform and handed out some titles, his efforts were also minimal.

Thieu, however viewed land reform as Phase Two of his goal to transform the lives of the impoverished peasants and build political legitimacy for his republic. Phase One had been to restore authority to the village and to improve local security via the PSDF. Tenant farming was the largest occupation in South Vietnam, and cultivation remained primitive and mostly a family affair. By turning tenant farmers into landowners, improving agricultural production via mechanization, and introducing farming enhancements like fertilizer, pesticides, and miracle rice, Thieu sought to break the cycle of exploitation and back-breaking labor that had marked generations of landless farmers. Further, he wanted to continue expanding rural electricity, healthcare, and education to bring the countryside into the modern world. His vision was to create an "ownership society" by providing peasants with a means of production while instilling democracy and the rule of law, ideas that would stand in stark contrast to the Communists' collectivist offering.

On March 16, 1970, the assembly finally passed Thieu's legislation. On March 26, he signed the law in a ceremony in Can Tho, the capital of the Delta. Henceforth, he declared, March 26 would be a national holiday called Farmer's Day. With one stroke of the pen, Thieu had abolished years of traditional land tenancy for a people whose livelihood was tied to the soil. More strikingly, unlike the bloody land reform in North Vietnam, with its public denunciations, show trials and then executions of thousands of people, South Vietnam accomplished its program without one single person being killed or publicly humiliated.

Known as Land to the Tiller (LTTT), the law was the brainchild of Cao Van Than, the minister of agriculture and land reform. Than had been working on it since mid-1968.[15] Like Pham Kim Ngoc, Than had no power base other than Thieu's admiration. Along with Ngoc and Hoang Duc Nha (who in September 1969 had been appointed press secretary and well as Thieu's private secretary), Cao Van Than would become one of the three most important technocrats in the Second Republic and, oddly, the least known.

A quiet, self-effacing man, he was born on November 5, 1932, in Hoc Mon, a small town just outside Saigon. He received a French education yet concurrently learned English. He joined the Vietnamese National Army and graduated from officer school in 1953. He became close friends with Thieu when the Joint General Staff assigned him to the Dalat academy in 1956 to help translate American military texts into Vietnamese. After the Diem coup, Than left the army and went to study in the U.S. He earned a doctorate in economics at the University of Pittsburgh, then returned to Saigon in November 1967 when Thieu asked him to join his staff as an assistant for economic affairs. After many discussions about land reform, Thieu finally offered him the job of designing and implementing a new program. Than accepted, but he told Thieu to be patient, to let him study this complex problem and determine the best solution. Thieu agreed, and the president held off strident U.S. demands to implement land reform. Than examined all the previous GVN plans and compared them to the programs of Japan,

Korea, and Taiwan. He particularly scrutinized the Communist land-reform efforts as he wanted to beat the NLF at its own game.

Than kept his law simple. It was five pages long and only had twenty-two articles. Knowing he would face opposition in the assembly from wealthy landowners, he quietly asked the chief justice of the Supreme Court for his legal opinion. The justice confirmed it was constitutional. LTTT would dispense 2.5 million acres of free land to farmers, converting roughly six hundred thousand families from poor landless peasants to middle-class land-owners over a three-year period. This represented 60 percent of the land currently being farmed, greatly surpassing the acreage of other countries' programs, which were implemented far more slowly and in peacetime. A substantial majority of these families lived in the Delta, Vietnam's rice bowl. They lived from crop to crop, and the landlords could evict them at any time. A large share of their harvest was paid as rent, and they lived on or sold the rest to earn a living. Although the Front had eliminated rents in areas they controlled, their "taxes" on these sharecroppers often equaled landlord fees.

Like Thieu, correcting deep-seated rural poverty underlay Than's design. Farmers currently tilling the land received the priority, followed by the families of those killed in action or disabled veterans. To expand landownership, Than reduced the acreage that farmers in the Delta could own from Diem's 250 to seven, with a fifteen-year restriction on selling the land. In land-scarce central and northern South Vietnam, farmers were only given two and a half acres. Rather than outright government seizure, landowners would be compensated with 20 percent in cash and the rest in government bonds that paid 10 percent interest that would mature in eight years. The amount paid to the landowner per acre was two and a half times the annual paddy yield based on an average of the last five year's crop. The GVN would foot the bill, estimated at $400 million dollars. The cost was potentially budget-busting, yet while Washington had pushed Saigon for years to implement land reform, the U.S. would only provide $40 million in additional CIP money over the three years. The embassy feared accusations of "paying off" landlords.

Critically, Than would not create a massive Saigon bureaucracy to run LTTT. Like Thieu, he also believed in decentralization and giving authority to the village leadership. The first job was to delineate land boundaries and confirm the identities of people tilling the land. He tapped the RD cadres to finalize the property borders by using U.S.-supplied aerial photos instead of long-outdated village records. Once completed, he used the USAID computer to print land title certificates while simultaneously creating a national database of landownership. Previously, titles were hand-drawn, and the calligraphers could only make two per day. By mass producing certificates, Than was able to provide a thousand titles a day, dramatically speeding up the land transfer process. He then placed the onus on a newly formed Village Land Distribution Committee, led by the village chief, to arbitrate minor boundary disputes and distribute land titles. The committee entered the new landowners onto the village tax rolls, and new owners would be tax free for one year. To avoid landlords tying up the court system with litigation, he created Special Land Courts to adjudicate major land disputes.

Determined to subvert the NLF's rural program and swing apolitical peasants to the government, a crafty political strategy also underlined Than's plan. He let farmers keep the land given to them by the Front, but he ensured their ownership by providing them with a title to their plot. This was something the NLF had refused to do since Communist doctrine stipulated that land was collectively owned. He also deliberately chose a simple moniker for the program that the uneducated peasants would easily understand. The NLF called their program *Cai Cach Ruong Dat*, which translated as "reform farmland." The earlier GVN program name was *Cai Cach Dien Dia*, which meant "reform land." The last two words were Chinese in origin, and he believed the name was too formal. Than named his program *Nguoi Cay co Ruong*, or "person tilling has rice land."

In June, Thieu promulgated the decree outlining the procedure for tenants to apply for land. Displaying a bureaucratic synchronicity few thought the government could achieve, the first land titles were ready in late August 1970. The first payments to landlords were made in December 1970. Both men went out to the countryside to present the titles. Than deliberately stayed in the background so Thieu would reap the credit, plus he wanted Thieu front and center so that provincial and military leaders would get the point: the president was deeply interested in this program, it had his full backing, and local officials better get on board.

LTTT, however, was only step one in this rural renovation. Mechanization was also crucial. But where would impoverished farmers get the money to buy water pumps or mechanical threshers? Alongside miracle rice and landownership, providing credit to purchase tools to replace human or animal labor proved key to unlocking the Delta's vast potential. In preparation for land reform, Than wanted the Agricultural Development Bank (ADB) to open branches in the Delta to offer credit and banking services to the rural population. Currently there was no commercial banking presence at the local level other than Chinese lenders or the local Farmer's Association. Each only offered high interest loans to farmers due to the huge risk in the yearly rice harvest. The ADB balked; so in January 1970, Than fired the chairman and appointed the deputy economic minister, Nguyen Dang Hai, as its new chief. Than wanted to break the loan sharks' hold over the peasantry, but he also had a political motive. According to Hai, the ADB would become "a tool of the South Vietnamese government to promote agricultural production, combat poverty, and better the lives of the farmers, thus attracting [them] to the Nationalist government in the fight against Communism." Since the bank was not a "profit oriented financial institution," we could "grant soft loans with an extremely low interest rate."[16]

Than had crafted a self-reinforcing system. Funding for these new rural banks came from a joint venture between the government and private investors. If the landlords agreed to start a bank with the cash and bonds they had received for their land, Than would provide matching government funds. The GVN had compensated the landlords for expropriating their lands and then created a banking system where the landlords could deposit their money, whereupon the banks in turn lent it to the farmers. The rural banks provided small loans to farmers to buy miracle rice, water pumps, or other tools. Thirty-six years before Muhammad Yunus and the Grameen Bank in Bangladesh received the Nobel Peace Prize in 2006 for microloans, Than and the rural banks were doing the same exact thing. Over time, eighty-six rural banks were created, mostly in the Delta. Hai claims that the number of loans quadrupled from 1970 to 1974 and that the amount of money lent jumped from six billion piasters in 1970 to sixty-three billion piasters by the end of 1974. To ensure success, and limit corruption or thievery, both Than and Hai constantly ventured into the countryside, visiting banks and holding land-transfer ceremonies.

If creating property owners and providing credit to buy mechanical tools created the foundation to develop South Vietnam's agrarian society and build support for Thieu's government, next were enhanced agricultural methods and products. Miracle rice, now called "Honda rice" by the local farmers, who used their profits to buy imported Honda motorbikes, was the main program. Local rice varieties and weather patterns produced only one crop per year of roughly two tons of paddy per acre. Miracle rice, pesticides, water pumps, and fertilizer doubled yields and enabled some farmers to plant three crops per year. Farmers who had harvested two tons on one crop per year were now collecting four tons each on two or three crops. Rice production increased in 1970 by 11 percent over 1969. No longer having to pay exorbitant rent or high interest loans, farmer income dramatically rose.

Improved animal husbandry was another key. After rice, pork was the most important item in the Vietnamese diet. Farmers, however, only raised chickens and pigs on a subsistence basis, and losses were high due to disease. In 1967, the Ministry of Agriculture began an Accelerated Protein Program to improve Vietnamese nutrition. This new government program was led by Dr. Tran Quang Minh, one of the first two Vietnamese veterinarians trained in the U.S. Another technocrat, Minh was born in the Hoa Hao stronghold of Chau Doc Province in the Delta, and he had learned to raise chickens on his father's large chicken farm. In 1967, Minh was appointed to lead the program to increase protein production in South Vietnam. He brought robust foreign breeds of pigs, ducks, and chickens into the country to test and find out which could survive Vietnam's tropical climate. He also personally trained hundreds of agricultural cadres, who in turn taught farmers new techniques of animal husbandry. More importantly, Minh dramatically increased the number of inoculations produced in country, and by 1969, chicken and pig output had soared. Much like miracle rice, the breeds Minh choose considerably improved the supply of meat and eggs. In 1969, pork was the only food item that cost less than in 1968. His efforts earned him the nickname "Chicken Minh" (*Minh Ga*).

Farm animals were not the only improvements. Teams of Taiwanese technicians were brought in to teach vegetable production. Fishing also grew rapidly. Moreover, by mid-1970, the three rural electric pilot areas had been completed, and the country began rapidly expanding electrical capacity. By mid-1971, the totality of these programs had economically revolutionized the peasants' lives. The Saigon embassy visited My Thuan village in Vinh Long Province in the Delta to examine these changes. This village was first studied in 1960 by a visiting American team that found an "economic situation in which agricultural practices were not highly developed [and] the standard of living was low." The embassy wanted to examine the village eleven years later and compare the changes. In July 1971, it found that with

less acreage under cultivation, the village population is prosperous [and] the physical evidence of change is everywhere...[F]ootpaths are now paved with cement, monkey bridges made of poles have been replaced in many cases with cement footbridges. A majority of the houses now have tin or tile roofing and many of them are built of cement or brick. Hondas are ridden, all sampans have long-tailed motors, almost every house has a radio...The change that has occurred has been dramatic and is clearly recognized by the people...[T]he old village chief from 1960 said 'now almost everyone live the way the old landlords did.' [17]

The embassy report listed dozens of material changes, all attributable to "a revolution in agricultural methods" and breaking the "old cycle of debt to finance a crop [and then] harvest to pay off the debt." Millions of Vietnamese peasants owed their improved livelihood to Cao Van Than, who had transformed Thieu's vision of an ownership society into reality.

SENATE ELECTIONS AND A RESURGENT OPPOSITION

The constitution mandated that half of the Senate would stand for reelection three years after the 1967 election. Sixteen blocs of ten candidates each were running, but only the top three would win. Five slates were Catholic and four were Buddhist, including one supported by the An Quang Buddhist faction. The pagoda's anti-government ardor had dramatically cooled in 1969 after mass graves had been uncovered near Hue. Several identified victims had played active roles in the 1966 Struggle Movement, and when Hanoi Radio admitted that "the hooligan lackeys who had incurred blood debts...were annihilated by the southern armed force," An Quang was deeply affected.[18]

No longer believing that its "people power" could mitigate Communist influence, An Quang sought power the old-fashioned way: by running for office. Given the failure of its previous boycotts, the pagoda had decided to emerge from its sullen eclipse and resurrect its usual stridency. An Quang's tortured metamorphosis from outside agitator to potential government representative was a seismic shift in South Vietnam's political hothouse.

Senator Tran Van Don, while attempting to curry An Quang's backing of another Senate campaign, also met with Thieu on June 13, their first meeting in months. Thieu, aware that Don had been one of the unlucky senators picked for reelection, knew that Don was only meeting with him because he was in political trouble. Don's "various statements on neutrality and peace have lost him support in the military and on the right."[19] Thieu thought Don would not run, and he was right. On July 15, Don announced that he would not seek reelection. The head of the An Quang slate was Vu Van Mau, Diem's former foreign minister who had quit in protest over the August 1963 pagoda raids.

The Senate election law called for campaigning to begin in early August, leaving limited time for discussing the issues. Voter turnout for the August 30 elections was 65 percent, and NLF terrorism was rare. Much like in American politics, where the midterm elections often see a rejection of the president, especially during an economic malaise, Mau's opposition slate won the most votes. The two Catholic blocs led by former general Huynh Van Cao and Senator Nguyen Van Huyen came in second and third. A slate led by Nguyen Ngoc Huy of the Progressive National Movement came in fifth, the only political party displaying any degree of national support. Despite Mau's first-place finish, pro-government slates won about half of the total vote, with the opposition and independent slates winning one-fourth each.

There were a few scattered charges of election fraud. Hoang Duc Nha noted that "people always suspect the government of rigging the elections" but that if it had, "it certainly did a poor job of it since the Mau ticket ran first across the country." Analyzing the voting patterns for the upcoming elections in 1971, Nha said that "the basis of politics and thus of voting in Vietnam is really not by party but by personality and then religious and ethnic groupings." That had certainly proven true in the Senate vote. Religion had resurfaced as the chief polling factor due to the short election cycle. But if Thieu ran for president in 1971, he "would count heavily on the support of the country people. They now know the president as a person, but even more they believe their more prosperous and secure life is a result of the good work of the Thieu administration."[20] While Nha was looking to the future, the Senate elections had quietly produced an important consequence in South Vietnam's political life: An Quang would now have to exercise its opposition in the assembly rather than in the streets.

AN ECONOMIC REVOLUTION

Discussions of dry economic matters usually pale in comparison to hair-raising tales of battlefield clashes or intense high-stakes diplomacy. Yet while weapons create victory, "money is the nerve of war."[21] Thieu's design to expand the RVNAF to replace U.S. soldiers had an Achilles' heel: who was going to pay to arm, train, and feed all these new troops? Printing piasters inexorably led to inflation, and the sudden rise in the cost of living from the October austerity tax increase had struck the RVNAF lower ranks partic-ularly hard. Their pay could barely feed and house their families, and now the situation was turning critical. Aware of the growing discontent, on Jan-uary 12, 1970, Thieu asked the U.S. to underwrite food rations and family housing construction for the RVNAF enlisted. Secretary of Defense Melvin Laird was scheduled to visit Saigon in mid-February to assess the status of Vietnamization. After finding "cautious optimism" among the American commanders about RVNAF improvements, Laird informed Nixon that "the major constraint on U.S. involvement was now economic [and] the actual and prospective diminished U.S. funds available for national security are consistently narrowing our operational latitude in Southeast Asia. Compre-hension of that problem is vital to continued progress in Vietnamization."[22]

Pham Kim Ngoc absolutely concurred, and while he was determined to eventually wean South Vietnam from American charity, for now he desper-ately needed it. Given antiwar opposition and mounting U.S. congressional antagonism over aid to his country, he knew the republic could not depend forever on American money. After adjusting for inflation, U.S. imports in 1969 had fallen to their lowest levels since the onset of the aid program in 1954.

Concerned that the Supreme Court would invalidate the austerity tax decree, on April 3, 1970, Ngoc recommended that Thieu offer new legis-lation that would convert the austerity program from executive action into law. A chronic budget deficit hampered Thieu's ability to both create social programs and become self-sufficient. To achieve economic independence, Ngoc needed to improve the domestic savings rate, increase production, and add tax revenue. He hoped to boost revenue in 1970 by forty billion piasters, but even that would only partially cover the expected surge in spending from an enlarged RVNAF.

The U.S. mainly funded the defense budget as South Vietnam could not financially support its massive military apparatus. As much as 73 percent of the RVN defense budget went to salaries and allowances, and the only thing keeping it afloat was the Pentagon's sizable purchase of piasters for in-country use at the artificially low exchange rate. That gusher of money, however, would be soon reduced to a trickle given the drawdown of U.S. troops and U.S. congressional outrage over the exchange rate. With grow-ing military outlays and declining U.S. aid, the Republic of Vietnam was at a financial turning point: it had to either cut defense spending or raise taxes. Otherwise, Saigon was facing an inflationary spiral that Ngoc could not contain, one that could easily undermine the government's legitimacy as much as losing a major battle.

The U.S. wanted a piaster devaluation, which both Thieu and Ngoc rejected because the immediate and massive rise in prices might cause riots and collapse the government. Instead, Thieu's legal staff designed a Program Law to give the president decree powers for five months to deal with taxation, exchange rates, and the budget. However, even if the assembly accepted the legislation, the situation was grim. The government was staring at a minimum fifty-three-billion piaster deficit in 1970. Retail prices in Saigon had risen 30 percent since the October 1969 decree, confidence in the piaster was at an all-time low, and foreign exchange reserves had fallen to their lowest levels since early 1966. The CIA was sounding the alarm bell: "the cumulative effect of inflation and the government's failure to take decisive anti-inflationary measures have made economic problems a real factor in political stability for the first time."[23]

A public opinion survey in Saigon in early May 1970 noted that "sixty-three percent of public and eighty-four percent of college educated cited economic problems as the most important facing them."[24] The purchasing power of soldiers and civil servants was now 50 percent below 1967 levels despite a pay raise on July 1, 1969. Given that government wages comprised half of the GVN budget, the July pay hike amplified outlays, which in turn caused more inflation and defeated the wage increase. Consequently, rumors circulated that the piaster would be devalued, causing the black market exchange rate to soar. Ngoc recalled that he "had no choice but to look at a complete overhaul of the entire economic and financial structure. For too long, we had walked around the taboos of devaluation and taxation...[W]e resorted to piecemeal measures and avoided the tough decisions to devalue the currency to reflect market conditions, to adopt a realistic interest rate structure [and] to simplify the tax code."[25]

Nor could Ngoc simply mimic the economic plans of Saigon's Asian allies. Nguyen Duc Cuong, Ngoc's chief deputy and the man who would replace him as economic minister in 1973, states that while they wished to emulate the market-based successes of their Asian allies, "we did not follow any model. We had ministerial level meetings once a year with the delegations from Taiwan, or Korea, or Singapore to exchange ideas, share the experience, and discuss specific projects of interest. Their situation was so radically different from ours, i.e., a fulltime war versus peace, that there is not much we can learn from them except trying to achieve in our country what they have already achieved, particularly South Korea."[26]

In collaboration with the finance minister, Ngoc created a strategy to rescue South Vietnam's economy. On April 28, he presented his economic plan to Thieu. If the assembly passed the Program Law—which was hardly a given since it had rejected a similar measure in March 1968—he proposed radical changes. Ngoc recommended doubling tax collection, increasing interest rates to 24 percent to soak up excess cash, and reforming the exchange rate. He wanted to launch an innovative parallel market that would offer 275 piasters to the dollar for all foreign money transactions involving U.S. personnel stationed in country. Ngoc recommended "a vigorous plan to increase the collection of domestic taxes [by] reestablishing the center of tax policy around domestic taxes and direct taxes instead of import and indirect taxes." To pay for Vietnamization, Ngoc wanted to "levy income taxes on absolutely every income group...from the urban to the rural...because the entire population must share the burden of contributing to bring security to all."[27] If taxing everyone proved impossible, that left "only one possible measure—to decrease expenditures," which meant reducing the RVNAF just as Thieu was advocating military expansion to replace U.S. troops.

Ngoc recalled that in his meeting with the president to discuss his plan, Thieu quietly reviewed his memo, "red penciling here and there. He read my confidential report before me in fifteen minutes. I was subsequently dismissed with the report, without comments." Thieu, never the warmest of people, had oddly said nothing to Ngoc during this decisive meeting, yet he told Bunker that Ngoc had articulated the issues and provided a roadmap to solve them. Thieu intended to ask the Lower House to review the Program Law. Prime Minister Khiem told Bunker that "we learned a lesson [with the austerity decree] and do not mean to repeat that mistake."[28] On May 20, Thieu sent his proposal to the House. To placate the assembly, Thieu pledged to inform the assembly "at least twenty-four hours in advance" of any decrees he made with his emergency powers, and he promised that no decree would "create new taxes but can only modify the basic tax rates and procedures of levy of existing taxes which have been approved by the Assembly." Ngoc was thrilled; Thieu had "crossed the Rubicon and is now committed to reform measures."[29]

Opposition deputies, however, were adamantly against giving Thieu decree powers, and when the speaker of the Lower House called on June 21 for a final vote on Ngoc's bill, government and opposition deputies physically battled on the house floor. One deputy tossed rotten eggs at the house speaker. Despite the theatrics, on June 24, the bill passed with only minor changes, but twenty-five opposition deputies boycotted the vote, and another forty abstained or were absent.

The Senate proved more difficult. The senator in charge of the Finance Committee wanted Ngoc fired in exchange for his support. Thieu refused even though Ngoc's design to tax everyone to close the budget gap and spread the defense burden was, to put it mildly, political dynamite. No population welcomes sudden tax increases, regardless of circumstances, especially where tax avoidance and poverty are epidemic. With half of the Senate up for reelection, many refused to even consider the bill, and the senator at the Finance Committee held his ground.

Given the Nixon administration's desire that the GVN institute a piaster devaluation, congressional dismay over foreign aid to South Vietnam, and despite Laird's admonition about economic aid, the U.S. response to Thieu's requested aid for his soldiers in January had lagged. On May 4, Thieu wrote a letter to Nixon again pleading his case, and when Ambassador Bui Diem followed up on May 14, he was told that the "GVN proposals could not be considered in isolation from other economic matters on which action from GVN side was required."[30] Clearly, the U.S. was leveraging its aid to force Saigon to institute economic reforms, namely devaluation. In late June, the congressional committee that oversaw U.S. aid programs issued a report demanding that the GVN devalue the piaster and establish wage and price controls. Ngoc again refused and said that the "U.S. must choose whether it wants South Vietnam to replace American troops or American resources. I have made it clear we cannot do both." While acknowledging the generosity of U.S. aid, Ngoc lamented, "[W]hat is the use of giving M16 rifles to soldiers when they are suffering from malnutrition?"[31]

Nixon, although seeking GVN economic reforms and facing strong opposition to aid from Congress, was increasingly fearful that the harsh economic conditions among the RVNAF enlisted might jeopardize Vietnamization. Consequently, in early July he sent a letter to Thieu agreeing to provide $100 million to build twenty thousand dependent housing units per year for five years and to supply millions of canned rations to South Vietnamese troops. On July 18, Laird reminded Nixon that "our economic plans constituted the weakest link in the Vietnamization program."[32] Given the dire economic conditions, Nixon approved an additional $750 million to bolster Saigon's economy. Ngoc was relieved. While he despised having to ask for aid, "no one grasped the economic aspect of the Vietnamization program when it was inaugurated." As one senior GVN official remarked, "Politics often decides the economics."[33]

To disarm both Vietnamese and American congressional critics, in mid-July, Ngoc convinced the Finance Ministry to dispatch the tax inspectors to collect unpaid taxes from the rich. Tax audits, particularly of Chinese merchants and American contractors—perfect business and racial targets—dramatically increased. To improve compliance, Ngoc fed the Saigon press stories of the fines and back taxes assessed against rich businessmen, which they printed with glee. Tax revenues increased in 1970 by thirty-eight billion piasters, but expenditures continued to outpace collections. Ngoc lamented that "I was always chasing my tail. The problem was there was no industrial production to tax [and] no mechanism in the countryside to tax the farmers, plus there was the political and social implications of doing so. If you are trying to win [peasant] hearts and minds, adding a GVN tax did not help."[34] Lastly, in late September, he quietly doubled interest rates in the commercial banking system to enlarge domestic savings and forced the banks to increase their reserves to restrain lending, thus reducing the money supply.

After the Senate elections, Thieu offered a compromise on the stalled Program Law. He would not fire Ngoc, but he would limit his legislative request to only the parallel market. With many of the obstructionists now gone, the Senate finally agreed. Law 10/70 was passed on September 29 instituting a parallel exchange rate of 275 piasters outside official government purchases, which would remain at 118 to 1 dollar. The higher exchange rate enabled Thieu to placate his own base by not devaluing the piaster, while Ngoc had soothed U.S. congressional anger by enabling American servicemen to get a bigger bang for their proverbial buck. Moreover, he had preserved a key revenue stream since U.S. piaster purchases would continue at the old rate.

On October 3, Thieu signed the law. These changes enabled Thieu, at Ngoc's urging, to announce in mid-October another wage increase for the military, disabled veterans, war widows, and government workers. Although this added twenty-five billion piasters to the budget, the GVN money supply did not increase because people deposited their money into banks to take advantage of the higher interest rates that Ngoc had quietly instituted in early September. The reforms enabled the economy to absorb the wage hike without triggering new inflation.

Ngoc, however, was fully aware that this was only the opening round. Speaking to the press, he noted that "Vietnamization would not be decided by how the war was fought. It will be judged by how the war is sustained militarily, socially, and economically."[35] Unlike Than, who remained virtually anonymous, Ngoc had endured a deluge of criticism and repeated demands for his head, but his changes halted the worst inflationary period since 1966. By December, the black market rate for dollars had significantly dropped, and inflation had barely increased. Yet the parallel exchange could "restrain, but could not stop, inflation."[36] More was needed, but the architect of a series of profound economic changes, second only to land reform in its social impact, had provided a weapon to fight the Communists equally important as M16s: economic security.

19

"THE WAR WILL FADE AWAY"

Fanciful Notions and Other Thoughts

Many Nationalists hoped the war would fade away in 1970. As U.S. political scientist Allan Goodman wrote, "a sense of military progress and political advance, so long delayed and thwarted in the 1960's, had come to pervade discussion of Vietnam in 1970."[1] Instead, another internecine South Vietnamese battle erupted, one focused primarily on socioeconomic issues rather than the old devils of religion and region. Protests by disabled veterans for housing and other benefits were quickly followed by rampaging student demonstrations, political turmoil that was then compounded by the embarrassing exposé of prison conditions on Con Son Island. Although many observers consider the 1963 and 1966 Buddhist protests South Vietnam's gravest internal test, few realize that the eruptions in 1970 also severely tested the government. The war also returned in a ferocious fashion with an allied military attack against the Communist sanctuaries in Cambodia. This cross-border strike signaled that the small-unit war had transformed into a combined-arms clash, one that would become manifest in the massive 1972 and 1975 offensives.

CAMBODIA REDUX

Internal frustration with Prince Norodom Sihanouk had been building among the Cambodian military and political elite since the spring and summer of 1969. Corruption in the royal family and the country's economic

401

malaise were significant factors, but it was the prince's tacit permission to allow Communist Vietnamese troops to use Cambodian territory that created demands for a change in leadership. Consequently, a new government was formed in August 1969. While Sihanouk retained overall control, Lieutenant General Lon Nol became the new prime minister while also commanding the army, known as the *Forces armées nationales khmères* (FANK).

In early January 1970, Sihanouk departed Cambodia to visit Europe, Russia, and China. With the prince out of the country, on March 11, demonstrations suddenly erupted in Phnom Penh against the Communist Vietnamese. Secretly organized by anti-Sihanouk forces, the protests quickly turned violent, and the North Vietnamese and Soviet embassies were sacked. In mid-March, Lon Nol ordered Communist Vietnamese troops out of Cambodia within seventy-two hours, an ultimatum they ignored. On March 18, 1970, the Cambodian National Assembly voted to remove Sihanouk as leader. Lon Nol invoked emergency powers and subsequently terminated diplomatic relations with North Vietnam.

Within days of the coup, armed clashes erupted between FANK and Communist Vietnamese units, who easily defeated the lightly armed and poorly trained Cambodians. People's Army troops then seized most of the border provinces and began moving toward Phnom Penh. To rally the Cambodian people, the Lon Nol government stirred up a virulent anti-Vietnamese campaign. Racial animus, always close to the surface, exploded against the Vietnamese minority living in Cambodia, which led to ethnic slaughter rather than a successful military defense. When the Saigon press printed stories of the wholesale murder of Vietnamese civilians by the Cambodians, enraged Nationalists insisted that Thieu solve the problem.

Post-Diem, both Le Van Kim and Nguyen Khanh had prioritized improving Cambodian relations to solidify South Vietnam's porous left flank. The Cambodian border sanctuaries were a critical strategic military problem facing the allies. Without external rest areas, Communist main force units would have had difficulty surviving inside South Vietnam. Seeing an opportunity to eliminate the bases, Thieu immediately offered to assist Cambodia. Lon Nol responded positively, and shortly thereafter, Thieu sent Vice President Ky to initiate contacts and upgrade relations. By late March, Thieu had authorized several small military probes into the Cambodian border regions.

By mid-April, anger over the death and detention of thousands of ethnic Vietnamese finally forced Thieu's hand. On April 24, Foreign Minister Tran Van Lam publicly demanded that Lon Nol halt the killings. Lam also announced a dramatic change in GVN policy: Saigon would relocate thousands of Vietnamese back to South Vietnam. His denunciation, however, had an unintended consequence. University students, who were currently protesting GVN policies, suddenly reacted. At 10:00 p.m. on April 24, dozens of students seized the Cambodian embassy. Within hours, Phnom Penh accepted a delegation led by the GVN Minister of Social Welfare to visit and arrange for the return of Vietnamese living in Cambodia.

The U.S. was also focused on Cambodia. Earlier on April 20, President Nixon had announced that he would withdraw another 150,000 troops by the spring of 1971. His televised speech rebuked Hanoi by pointing out that it had "almost 40,000 Communist troops...conducting overt aggression against Cambodia, a small neutralist country that the Communists have used for years as a base for attack upon South Vietnam in violation of the Geneva Accords of 1954."[2] Nixon, though, had also been violating Cambodian neutrality. Back in March 1969, he secretly began bombing the Communist base areas in response to the continued rocketing of Saigon.

With PAVN forces poised to overrun the FANK, on April 30, the U.S. Army, in conjunction with ARVN units from III and IV Corps, launched a cross-border assault into Cambodia. The ARVN units, led respectively by Lieutenant General Do Cao Tri and Major General Nguyen Viet Thanh, advanced rapidly into Cambodia. Armored columns supported by infantry and artillery from Tri's III Corps quickly overran small Communist positions, while similar strikes from Thanh's IV Corps pushed up from the south. The war had become a combined-arms conflict, as both sides maneuvered and fought in large formations that included armor and artillery.

Protests instantly erupted on American colleges. After Ohio National Guard troops fired into a crowd of students at Kent State, killing four, a photograph showing a screaming woman kneeling next to a dead student won the Pulitzer Prize. Much like the pictures of the burning monk in Saigon in 1963 and Brigadier General Loan's execution of the prisoner during the 1968 Tet Offensive, the photo dramatized the war's divisiveness. The demonstrations and congressional opposition forced Nixon to announce that he would withdraw all American troops from Cambodia by the end of June. The U.S. Senate went a step further and passed the Cooper-Church Amendment, which disallowed any funds for U.S. military action in Cambodia after July 1, 1970. Although the bill failed in the House, congressional efforts to legislatively restrict Nixon's military actions in Vietnam were now a viable option for antiwar members. The House formed a Select Committee on Southeast Asia to travel to the area and investigate the war, a group that would make a discovery of enormous consequences.

Thieu announced that his forces were under no such restrictions. He and Lon Nol had agreed in late April to allow the South Vietnamese to conduct operations on Cambodian soil for an indefinite period. As the ARVN moved deeper into Cambodia, more serious battles erupted, but Tri's energetic command and lead-from-the-front mentality enabled his forces to smash the enemy defenses. The enhanced U.S. training had paid off, especially in III Corps, where the three ARVN divisions had long been considered among the worst military units in the world. Even the relentlessly antiwar *New York Times* admitted that Tri had performed well, exclaiming that a "combination of impatience and fearlessness has made General Tri the most conspicuous allied commander of the Cambodian operation."[3] South Vietnamese public and military confidence soared after the display of military prowess and the capture of thousands of tons of enemy supplies.

Behind the scenes, even bigger changes had occurred. An obscure ARVN Colonel named Tran Quang Khoi, a protégé of Tri's, had developed the III Corps armor plan. Colonel Khoi was part of an emerging new breed of South Vietnamese officers: U.S.-trained, disciplined, and tough.[4] Within a year, his decisive leadership would save a sizable ARVN force trapped inside Cambodia.

Ill fortune, though, always stalked South Vietnam, and the Cambodian incursion was no exception. On May 2, Major General Thanh, the former Long An Province chief and 7th Division commander whose incorruptibly and excellent leadership had dramatically improved security in the Delta, died in a helicopter crash. While both Thanh and Tri were excellent combat commanders, Thanh was reserved, devoted to his wife, and honest. He refused even small gifts like alcohol or fruit. Tri on the other hand, was flamboyant, a womanizer, and excessively corrupt. Thanh was soon replaced by Brigadier General Ngo Quang Truong, who had led the 1st ARVN Division during the Tet Offensive, but Thanh's death dealt a serious blow to a South Vietnamese officer corps that desperately needed men like him.

Despite these improvements, the ARVN remained heavily reliant on U.S. forces for supply support, vehicle maintenance, and helicopters. This dependence on logistics and airlift limited ARVN mobility, one of the key allied advantages over the PAVN. Even worse, Tri's undisciplined soldiers looted the Cambodian countryside, a damning comparison to Communist troops who had been trained not to steal from the locals. Reports of the "systemic plunder" of several towns and the "trail of pillage by two ARVN regiments" in late June exacerbated racial tensions already highly charged by the Cambodian treatment of local Vietnamese. These actions curbed the two government's efforts to cooperate against their common enemy.[5]

To discuss future military cooperation, on May 6, Lon Nol sent a FANK team to Saigon. After meeting the delegates, Nguyen Cao Ky flew to Phnom Penh, where both sides agreed to delineate a zone along the border that ARVN and FANK units could enter at any time without prior permission. More important, by the end of May, Saigon and Phnom Penh had reestablished diplomatic relations that had been broken by Sihanouk years ago. In mid-July, with U.S. troops withdrawn, Ky bombastically proclaimed that Saigon would ensure Cambodia's defense and offered a formal military alliance. Thieu quickly squelched that notion, hoping to preserve at least a fig leaf of Cambodian neutrality. While Thieu knew he could not allow Cambodia to fall, he would only clean "out the sanctuaries, protect Vietnamization and pacification, and by limited actions show that [the GVN had no territorial] designs in Cambodia."[6]

In early July, the Ministry of Social Welfare established a Special Bloc for the Relief of Vietnamese Repatriates from Cambodia. Led by Dr. Phan Quang Dan, almost two hundred thousand ethnic Vietnamese were repatriated, most of whom settled in the Delta. This was South Vietnam's second-largest refugee inflow; only the migration of nearly nine hundred thousand northerners in 1954 and 1955 was greater. Ultimately, with Sihanouk gone, relations between Saigon and Phnom Penh were much improved, but they would never achieve the close cooperation that Saigon desired or solve the long-standing issues that had pitted the two countries against each other.

THE VETERANS AND STUDENTS PROTEST

In April 1970, Thieu's government remained under tremendous strain. He had just launched the Land to the Tiller law, Cambodia was in a crisis, and he faced serious internal blowback over the economy. Amid these difficult issues, another outbreak of vocal and violent street protests suddenly flared up, shattering the relative street tranquility that had marked Thieu's first two years. This surge of anti-government unrest by two divergent groups, disabled veterans and students, was the worst internal strife the GVN had faced since the Buddhist agitation of 1966.

The announcement of the land-reform bill instantly created resentment among two almost invisible groups in South Vietnamese society: disabled veterans and war widows. Even though LTTT offered free land to this careworn group, few could take advantage of the bill's provisions. Living lives of extreme poverty in urban shantytowns and often too disabled to farm, they were society's most marginalized groups. Yet both Tran Thien Khiem and Thieu were acutely aware of the difficulties disabled vets faced, and as long-serving military officers, they were determined to find a solution. When Khiem became prime minister, he recreated the Ministry of Veterans Affairs as a separate ministry, then appointed former Major General Pham Van Dong as minister. Dong had served as mayor of Saigon during Khanh's regime but had been sacked for running an illicit gambling operation.

Dong immediately began to fix GVN services to this long-suffering group. In a speech on December 8, 1969, he noted there were approximately fifty-one thousand disabled veterans, ninety thousand war widows, and three hundred thousand orphans.[7] These figures would only grow each month with the ARVN shouldering more of the fighting. He cited his ministry's major challenges: poor pension processing, a lack of physical rehabilitation services, and limited vocational job training. Many disabled vets and their families lived on a government pension between $5 and $15 per month, which they often did not receive unless they paid a bribe. Chronic inflation constantly eroded this meager stipend, forcing many vets and their families to become beggars or thieves. In February 1970, Dong began preparing legislation to assist this forgotten segment of society by raising pension payouts, providing free medical care and housing, and helping with vocational training.

After the ministry's formation in 1968, a group of veterans created the Disabled Veteran's Association to press for improved benefits, but their efforts mostly failed. After the LTTT law was passed, the association sprang into action. They did not want land; they wanted housing. In Saigon, the disabled vets proclaimed the motto "Land to the tiller, housing to the disabled veteran."[8] In wheelchairs or on crutches, they mobilized hundreds in Saigon and occupied parks and streets, erected huts, and demanded that the government provide them with housing and jobs.

Caught off guard, Thieu ordered the police to leave them alone. Sympathetic to their plight, he also realized that the military would view harsh measures against them with dismay. On April 4, a group from the Disabled Veteran's Association marched on the National Assembly to present their petitions. From there, they trooped to Independence Palace to see Thieu. When the police prevented them from entering the palace grounds, vets began throwing stones at the police line. Minister Dong hurriedly came out to calm the mob and inform them about his bill to assist disabled veterans and widows. Not placated, they erected shanties on nearby streets to maintain their vigil to see the president. Over the next two days, the vets repeatedly attacked the police guarding the palace. After one skirmish where several policemen were badly hurt, they fired teargas to force the vets to retreat. Combined with newly resurgent student protests, after several years of peace, violence and instability had returned to Saigon's streets.

On April 7, Thieu appealed to the disabled vets to end their demonstrations and let the assembly review Dong's bill, and he requested that they not assault the police or block roads. In pleading tones, Thieu claimed he understood their cause. "I am myself a soldier who fought for twenty years.... and I will pay particular concern to your aspirations. I appeal for your understanding. For the sake of national interest, I must restore public order and make the laws of the land respected.... You must not mistake that you have won over the government, or vice versa. You must understand this and help me."[9] Thieu was in a tough spot. He knew the vet's grievances were justified, but finding the money to increase benefits was nearly impossible in a budget stretched to the limit. Still, his promises temporarily mollified the vets, allowing Thieu to attend to another looming crisis, the suddenly rebellious students.

After a small number of students in Hue and Saigon had openly helped the Communists during the 1968 Tet Offensive, the police seized the Saigon Students Union headquarters. Since then, the students had remained acquiescent. However, a sudden government tuition increase resurrected student discontent. On March 10, several schools went on strike. In response, the police arrested forty students, including Huynh Tan Mam, the chairman of the General Student Association (GSA), the overall student coordinating committee for the various universities. Mam's true name was Tran Van That, and he had been a secret Communist agent since 1965. He was not the only one; of the seven members of the GSA's Executive Committee, four, including Mam, were covert NLF cadres.[10]

While Mam was stoking the fire of outrage under COSVN direction, the vast bulk of the politically involved students were not Communists. Student activism was usually rooted in social welfare work rather than street demonstrations.[11] But enflamed by the arrests, university students demanded the release of their leaders. When the GVN refused, thousands boycotted classes at Saigon University, the country's main school.

Frustrated over the uproar by both groups, Thieu railed that the people must "not stab each other in the back but must unite." He claimed the Communists were "misusing democracy in an excessive manner. I want a disciplined and temperate democracy...The government must guide the people in their enjoyment of a democratic regime."[12] Several days later, he again called for a "disciplined democracy and warned that disorder could lead the people to support dictatorship...Disorderly democracy would discourage the people...[I]f someone were to establish a dictatorship, all the people would support it, since the law would be respected and the nation preserved."[13] Thieu's warning, echoed by other authoritarian Asian nationalist leaders, again shined a light into his thinking. Unity equaled strength, and order trumped discordance, particularly when facing an enemy who was a master at propaganda and insinuation to undermine the government.

Taking a page from An Quang, the students ignored Thieu's plea and launched a "struggle movement." They erected banners asking for "peace at any price," and insisted that the arrested students be tried in a civilian court rather than the Mobile Military Court. Marches continued, and several groups began using motorcycles to toss paint or Molotov cocktails at police or government buildings. Given the social tumult, the press and opposition politicians like Ly Qui Chung accused Thieu of "incompetence in dealing with national problems," citing "his failure to stabilize the economy, his handling of restive students and disabled vets."[14]

To defuse the worsening situation, on April 17, Thieu met with several student leaders. He promised not to send the arrested students to the Mobile Military Court, especially since the Supreme Court was about to rule on its constitutionality. Moreover, he agreed to investigate recent allegations of police torture of the arrested students. First leveled by *Tin Sang* (Morning News), the popular opposition paper, lawyers of the students then publicized details of the police viciousness. Afterward, several opposition deputies investigated. In a harbinger of the Con Son prison debacle, the deputies released a report claiming that the police beatings had left several students unable to walk or stand. Four policemen were subsequently charged with torture.

Thieu's attempt to placate the disabled vets and the students by agreeing to their demands while reining in overly repressive police tactics had flopped. The vets remained camped near the palace, and students were creating havoc in the streets. Opposition deputies skewered him, the assembly appeared unwilling to grant him economic decree powers, and the Supreme Court had ruled against him on three issues (austerity taxes, the military courts, and the Chau trial). The press railed over his failure to prevent atrocities against ethnic Vietnamese in Cambodia, and the Cambodian incursion had begun.

When some young An Quang Buddhist monks, taking advantage of the street chaos, forcibly seized the Quoc Tu Pagoda on May 3, the raid was the final straw for government hardliners. In a cabinet meeting on May 4, Thieu and his ministers decided to restore public order. Thieu's mantra, as voiced by him, was "Survival first." After the war was won, then he could enshrine democracy's insistence on civil rights. The cabinet voted to lower the curfew time, banned further demonstrations, brought in four battalions of army cadets to bolster the police, and closed all the schools. Early on the morning of May 5, riot police swept into the Cambodian embassy and arrested over seventy students. As crackdowns went, it was tepid but effective.

The clampdown, combined with news of military success in Cambodia, brought momentary peace to the capital, but not for Thieu. The president was trapped between warring perceptions of him and his actions. To outside observers, he was a tyrant. Yet while Thieu had chosen to impose stability, he had not yielded to harsher measures. The consequences of Diem's repression remained permanently etched in his mind. On the other hand, many Saigonese, frustrated by traffic jams, blocked streets, and the sting of tear gas, blamed Thieu for allowing the mayhem to continue. Against this backdrop of social chaos and economic discontent, his detractors were emboldened by his conciliatory approach and mounted further ripostes.

For Thieu, the war's disappearance—the thud of artillery rarely interrupted Saigon's sleep anymore—had allowed not just the students but democracy itself to run amok. Although the war had faded away, South Vietnam's ever-simmering social conflicts had replaced the roar of the cannons. In his mind, the press code he had recently signed allowed Saigon's newspapers to fully report and carp over every governmental shortcoming. The constitution provided cover for politicians to vent their complaints, criticism that he often viewed as a political threat. Fortunately for him, his opposition's habitual disarray left his power undented. Each group was focused solely on their own issue, and unlike during Diem's last days, they failed to rally a significant segment of society to their cause. More important, no one had even considered a coup to remove an "incompetent" Thieu. In fits and starts, the notion of the rule of law was maturing in South Vietnam.

The police batons finally calmed the situation. Still offering the olive branch, on June 13, Thieu ordered Huynh Tan Mam released. He also provided a building to the Saigon Students Union so they could reestablish their headquarters and directed the schools to reopen on June 22. As Mam walked out of police headquarters, Thieu's concessions were greeted by several hundred militants tossing Molotov cocktails.

On the same day, Thieu met with the leadership of the Disabled Vets Association and promised he would push for passage of the bill upgrading benefits. The assembly approved the measure on July 4. Several days later, a visiting Secretary of State William Rogers delivered a letter from Nixon offering $100 million over five years to help South Vietnam build housing and provide rations for the troops. On July 10, Thieu spoke on radio and TV. He insisted that he had ordered the security services to act gently and not tear down the squatter's shacks. The new law increased pensions, and Nixon's money enabled the government to build permanent housing or supply land and materials to those who wished to build elsewhere. For the most part, the veteran's protests ended, although a few emboldened elements began engaging in racketeering and other criminal activity. Thieu had swiftly tackled, with a large assist from U.S. coffers, a serious societal issue, but his successes were completely overlooked due to another firestorm: the exposé of prison conditions on Con Son Island.

CON SON

On July 7, news broke of a visit by a U.S. congressional delegation five days earlier to the former French and current GVN prison on Con Son Island. Located in the South China Sea, Con Son was South Vietnam's largest civilian prison. In July 1970, it held just under ten thousand inmates. Tipped off about inhumane conditions in one part of the prison, the group decided to investigate. On the flight to the island, the head of the small U.S. advisory team for public safety asserted to the group that Con Son was like a "boy scout camp." What the congressmen discovered was a boy scout camp from hell for four hundred prisoners. They found that the prisoners shackled en masse in concrete cells, were malnourished, and had limited water, sanitation, and medical treatment. Guards on open air walkways above the cells tossed burning lime on the inmates when they refused to obey prison rules. The congressman expressed outrage over the harsh detention methods and noted that the inmates called their cells Tiger Cages. The name and the conditions invoked images of a medieval-style horror chamber.

U.S. television immediately broadcast the claim. Shortly thereafter, *Life* magazine published photos taken during the visit from the walkways that gave the impression of a dungeon-like environment. Much like the photos of abuse at Abu Gharib prison in Iraq in April 2004, the pictures caused world-wide revulsion. Coming shortly after the Tran Ngoc Chau case, outrage over the Cambodian invasion and the subsequent death of four Kent State students, the Con Son story poured more fuel on an already raging fire.

However, like virtually everything else about the war, to fully grasp the prison exposé narrative, one needs background. In June 1969, the study team led by Father Robert Drinan had visited Con Son and other prisons to investigate conditions. Although they noted overcrowding at Con Son, they had tried but failed to confirm the existence of shackled prisoners held in Tiger Cages. They failed because there were none. The Red Cross had also inspected the prison in February 1970 and did not find any reprehensible treatment.

The GVN held three types of civilian prisoners: common criminals, military offenders, and Communists. The last were defined as civilians who were unarmed at the time of arrest. If they had weapons, they were considered military prisoners of war and sent to a POW camp under army jurisdiction. Communist political cadres, however, fell into a nebulous category. Neither civilian nor military, the GVN labeled them "criminals" to house them in civilian prisons. Outsiders called them political prisoners. The total GVN civilian prison population was roughly thirty-three thousand, with approximately 60 percent suspected or convicted Communist criminals, many of them waiting months for a trial in the military courts. There were only four major civilian prisons in South Vietnam, but each province and some districts had jails. Although the U.S. had spent money to upgrade the GVN penal system, the provincial ones remained inferior. According to one U.S. official responsible for assisting the GVN provincial detention facilities, "all were dirty, lacked reasonable sanitation and were in dire need of health delivery systems."[15] By GVN standards, Con Son was considered the best of the lot.

The section of the prison that had been nicknamed the Tiger Cages by the prisoners was a series of roughly nine-by-fifteen-feet above-ground concrete cell blocks built by the French seventy-five years earlier. The moniker "Tiger Cages" had no intrinsic meaning, as other prison areas also had nicknames. For example, one was called the "cattle cages," but it did not have similar concrete cells. In November 1968, the GVN camp commander at Con Son, concerned about poor housing for his guards and their families, decided to remove prisoners from the Tiger Cages and relocate the guard's families into them because they provided better accommodations. The guards and their families lived there for a year until over three hundred female prisoners were transferred to Con Son from Chi Hoa prison, the main detention facility in Saigon since colonial days. Considered the most hardcore NLF cadres, and highly skilled in political agitation, these female inmates caused disturbances at the other prisons by provoking the guards and inciting the other prisoners. The GVN decided to group them together at Chi Hoa to quiet the other prisons. It was a huge mistake. Brought together, they caused incredible commotion by attacking the guards and singing songs throughout the night. To prevent a planned riot, in late November 1969, the GVN transferred the three hundred females and about one hundred males to Con Son. Since this was the first group of female prisoners at the island, and to prevent a repeat of Chi Hoa, the camp commandant ordered the guard's families to vacate the Tiger Cage buildings. He used the concrete cells to house the females plus some of the males. Because the cells only had flimsy wooden doors, many were shackled to prevent escape or attacks against the guards.

After the Cambodian incursion, Congress had formed a House Select Committee and dispatched a team of congressmen to visit Southeast Asia. Only two members, Augustus Hawkins (D-Cal.) and William Anderson (D-Tenn.), joined by journalist Don Luce and congressional aide Tom Harkin, went to Con Son. Congressman Hawkins was vehemently antiwar, while Anderson was a highly decorated Navy submariner. Luce was the former head of the International Voluntary Services (IVS) in South Vietnam, a nonprofit agency that provided technical assistance on various projects in underdeveloped countries. In September 1967, Luce resigned in protest over U.S. policy, and he developed a singular hatred for the South Vietnamese government. He was currently working in Saigon as a journalist for the World Council of Churches while also teaching at Saigon University, where he was in close contact with the student protesters. Tom Harkin was then a congressional aide but would eventually become a U.S. Senator from Iowa. He had read about the Tiger Cages at Con Son prison in the Drinan report and was intrigued.

Upon arrival in Saigon in late June 1970, Harkin contacted Luce to discuss investigating GVN prisons, particularly Con Son. Luce introduced him to Cao Nguyen Loi, a student who had been held at Con Son but who had been released in late April 1970 with four other students. Loi was then living with Luce, but he was no innocent. Like Huynh Tan Mam, Loi was a secret NLF cadre. He had been arrested in July 1968 for protesting the General Mobilization Law. While in police custody, Loi said he had been beaten on the knees and feet so badly that he could not stand and that water had been forced down his throat. Despite this brutality, he refused to admit that he was a Communist, claiming he only wanted "peace."[16] He had been sent to Con Son and held in the Tiger Cages with the other hardcore Communist cadres. Loi's mother complained to assembly Deputy Dinh Van De about her son's imprisonment, and De arranged for her to visit Loi at Con Son. Taken out to meet her, Loi got a view of the camp, enabling him to provide Harkin a sketch of the Tiger Cage location. Returning to Saigon, she reported Loi's condition in the cramped cells. De intervened and got Loi and four others released. It was probably no coincidence that Loi's mother had chosen De. He was also a Communist agent, having converted to the revolutionary ranks in the summer of 1969. After talking to Luce, Harkin arranged for Hawkins and Anderson to meet Loi. After hearing Loi's story, the two congressmen agreed to visit the island to see whether it was true.

The five inmates that Deputy De had released published a report on prison conditions. They claimed that their "feet were shackled day and night. Most of our fellow prisoners were paralyzed, not to mention the ones suffering from chronic dysentery, tuberculosis [and] stomach disorders."[17] Nguyen Minh Tri was one of the five released students, and he was also an underground Communist agent. During one inspection, possibly during the Drinan team visit, Tri described how he "pretended to be a prisoner who had been paralyzed for six months."[18] After his release, Tri became the chief of Espionage Cluster A10, a network formed in late 1970 by the Communist Public Security section in Saigon.

Given the tremendous press coverage, the U.S. embassy immediately went into damage control and denied that prisoners had been tortured. That was true in the main prisons, but initial police interrogation methods, much like the CIA's "enhanced techniques," was institutionalized brutality designed to elicit confessions. Upon returning to the U.S., Hawkins and Anderson demanded an investigation and submitted a resolution to "condemn the cruel and inhumane treatment" of "tiger-cage imprisonment."[19] Prime Minister Khiem immediately sent an investigative team to Con Son. They agreed that the conditions in the cells were difficult but denied the main charges of torture and maltreatment. They decided to close the Tiger Cages and build larger facilities, but it failed to halt the indignation. In late July, Nixon sent another U.S. Congressman, Philip Crane (R-Ill.), to visit Con Son. His examination concluded that the reports of prisoners who were unable to stand due to constant shackling was untrue and that the vast bulk of the prison population was in good health, raising extra food, and engaged in making crafts. Crane publicly blasted the Hawkins and Anderson report as deeply exaggerated.

While Crane was correct and Luce and Harkins were deliberately looking for a way to embarrass the GVN, in this instance, the South Vietnamese had been caught red-handed. Embassy political officer James Nach said he received "a detailed report from Anderson immediately after his return from the island. He was shocked by what he learned and saw. Anderson was one of the smartest and most decent Congressmen I met during my career at State."[20] The GVN, however, was in a bind. While the harsh treatment was inexcusable, the prisoners, when brought together at Chi Hoa, had immediately instigated a riot. To keep them isolated from the other 9,500 docile prisoners and prevent a recurrence of Chi Hoa, the Con Son prison commander removed the guard's families from the buildings and put the new prisoners into them. This is what the American visitors found but did not understand.

The uproar and the various investigations destroyed prison discipline at Con Son. Many guards quit, and with the hardcore cadres no longer isolated, numerous prisoners who had previously cooperated were now being pressured into defiance. As news of Con Son spread, in October, the GVN Department of Corrections reported that "inmate disturbances, fires, hunger and work strikes occurred at the [prisons] at Chi Hoa and Thu Duc." At Con Son, there was a "total work stoppage" and other conflicts.[21] By December, even though the U.S. embassy had poured money into Con Son to improve the situation, the camp commander was forced to shackle over 1,500 inmates, which had been unnecessary before. The embassy immediately protested to Thieu "of the harmful effects of additional adverse publicity...both in Vietnam and in the U.S....It was imperative that confinement practices and facilities in Vietnam meet appropriate standards."[22]

Thieu agreed, but it was too late. He was not just being painted as a repressive dictator; South Vietnam itself was viewed as a cruel, tyrannical state, a gulag of torture chambers. For those ideologically inclined to damn Saigon, it was, to use a military term, a target-rich environment. The police brutality, the scandalous corruption, growing concerns over extrajudicial killings in the Phoenix program, and the shock over the My Lai Massacre, were destroying the underpinnings of America's commitment to South Vietnam. A virulent cocktail of Communist political agitation, Saigon's own missteps, and the inherent struggle of a nation trying to build democratic institutions in a country that had never known them had left it with few defenders internationally. The war had irreversibly jumbled who were the good guys and who were the bad guys.

STILL SEEKING PEACE

Faced with Hanoi's intractable stance in Paris, Nixon decided to propose something new. For months he had been ruminating over offering a cease-fire in Vietnam and then elections, hoping to tempt Hanoi to seek peace. Nixon was planning on pivoting American foreign policy away from its Cold War containment model and normalize affairs with China and the Soviet Union. He hoped to leverage better relations with both countries to gain their assistance in reining in Hanoi. While Nixon had no illusions about Hanoi's trustworthiness, to achieve his main foreign policy goal of improving bilateral relations with Russia and China, he needed to remove the Vietnam War as an irritant. U.S. diplomatic efforts regarding Vietnam were about to resume.

In early July 1970, Secretary of State Rogers visited Saigon to discuss Nixon's contemplated plan. He reassured Thieu that the "U.S. had no intention seek negotiating political settlement separately with North Viet-namese...and a coalition government...will continue to be unacceptable to the U.S." Equally important, "any political solution will have to be worked out by the Republic of Vietnam with the other side." Thieu replied that the GVN position of July 1969 remain unchanged even though his proposal "entailed risks" that the Communists might achieve "positions of authority through process of free elections." Thieu, however, doubted the Communists would accept a ceasefire. The war would more likely "just fade away."[23]

On July 31, Thieu informed his country that while he would accept the results of an internationally supervised election, he believed Hanoi would not agree to participate. He thought the chances for a negotiated settlement were "zero" since the "Communists never negotiate from weakness and they are losing now." Therefore, "the war will end...with our strength growing and their strength decreasing. It is only a matter of time."[24] However, with

U.S. intelligence warning Thieu that the Communists were planning a diplomatic offensive, in mid-September, he sent Vice President Ky to Paris to gain insight into the status of the talks.

Like Nixon, Hanoi was also planning a new gambit. On September 10, Le Duc Tho cabled the DRV team in Paris and said the Politburo had decided to mount a political offensive "to support the struggle movements in the cities of South Vietnam opposed to American aggression and demanding the removal of the Thieu-Ky-Khiem clique." This diplomacy was not to achieve peace but to sow "divisions within the ranks of the lackeys [and] help to stimulate the fall antiwar movement of the American people and the opposition faction in the U.S."[25] The Politburo was carefully watching the U.S. Congress, which had just defeated a bill by two senators to unilaterally withdraw all U.S. troops from Vietnam by the end of 1971. Coming on the heels of the Cooper-Church amendment disallowing any funds being spent on U.S. forces in Cambodia, Hanoi wanted to boost this antiwar groundswell by dangling a peace offer.

On September 17, Nguyen Thi Binh, the PRG Foreign Minister, publicized an "Eight-Point Clarification" of the PRG's Ten-Point program announced in May 1969. She said that if the U.S. withdrew all forces by June 30, 1971, removed "Thieu-Ky-Khiem" from power, and formed a three-party coalition (PRG, Saigon, and Third Force), then Front forces would not attack withdrawing U.S. troops, and they would discuss releasing captured American prisoners. Once a new government was formed, elections would be held for a new assembly that would write a new constitution. She rejected any elections if "Thieu-Ky-Khiem" were in power. Hanoi wanted to take advantage of what they believed was a resurgent U.S. antiwar movement, South Vietnamese war-weariness, and worldwide disdain for Thieu and Ky. They also hoped for a favorable response from South Vietnamese anti-government politicians by conveying the impression that peace could happen if they just got rid of three men. It was a brilliant strategy.

Although Saigon immediately rejected the PRG proposal, Thieu and Nixon knew they had to respond, and on October 8, Nixon presented a four-point response. He called for a ceasefire, an international conference to discuss the issues in Indochina, release of all POWs, and a timetable for withdrawal of all forces. Thieu repeated his offers of the previous year to negotiate with the PRG and to hold elections under the supervision of an international committee to ensure their fairness. Hanoi's response to Nixon's proposal was decidedly negative. COSVN informed its cadres that the U.S.

wanted "to commit aggression against Indochina and to keep its puppets in power in Southeast Asia. That was why the U.S. had ignored our main demands and had presented suggestions that were vague and peripheral. For that reason, COSVN requested that [its cadres] continue to struggle to demand that the U.S. withdraw its troops unconditionally and that it removes the fascist Thieu-Ky-Khiem puppet government."[26]

In early October, Xuan Thuy, the DRV's team leader in Paris, sent a cable to Le Duc Tho. He reported that while in Paris, Vice President Ky had made a surprising offer. Whether on his own or with Thieu's permission is unknown, but Ky had "made a request through Nguyen Khanh to meet with Madame Binh, but the request was not granted." Since his meeting request had been rebuffed, Ky passed a message to the Communists about a political solution for South Vietnam.

> The [Third Force] in the coalition government that Madame Binh spoke of in her eight-point plan is really insignificant...Therefore, to solve the second problem, the political structure in South Vietnam must be changed. This means a complete change of policy. But no matter what we do, we have the problem of who is the person to do it? Who is someone that our brothers on the other side can accept as someone they can talk to?...If they cannot accept Thieu, then get rid of him. Do the same with Khiem. And if they believe that I am an obstacle, then I am prepared to leave. If, however, they believe they need my help in finding a political solution for the problem of South Vietnam, when I am finished with my work and I leave, I am prepared to help.[27]

Thuy assessed Ky's statement as wanting "to shove Thieu aside to become the primary interlocutor with our side. The Ky faction will demand that the U.S. must withdraw and that North Vietnamese forces also must withdraw.... The meeting...may have been a personal initiative on Ky's part...or France may have asked Ky to do it, because recently France has endorsed pushing Thieu aside and is now paying attention to opposition forces in South Vietnam."[28]

France was indeed maneuvering again. In the early 1960s, having also let go of Algeria, President Charles de Gaulle had insisted that neutralism was the best option to halt the Vietnam War. After his resignation on April 28, 1969, French policy on Vietnam had become more restrained, although a Gaullist anti-GVN bias still dominated French policy. The various new peace offers, however, had reignited the French. While France saw Hanoi as the ultimate victor, South Vietnam's growing military might, embodied by the successful strike into Cambodia, had resulted in a more balanced view of the relative strengths of the two countries. Paris now offered itself as an "honest broker" between the warring parties, but it had to carefully dance between Washington, Beijing, Hanoi, and Saigon. Although it pressed the U.S. to set a fixed timetable for withdrawal and urged a "broadening" of the GVN—code for allowing the PRG a role in the government—Hanoi was not fooled by the French strategy. It covertly sought to manipulate France into pressuring the U.S. into removing Thieu. The French decision to expand its diplomatic role would not bear fruit for several more years, but eventually it would prove critical.

With Hanoi's outright rejection of Nixon's offer, Thieu returned to a harder line. In his annual speech to the National Assembly on October 31, he praised the military achievements of his government and painted a picture of near victory. He resumed his denunciations of those "cowardly and defeatist people" who advocated a coalition or "peace in neutrality." Our "military and civilians," he thundered, "must eliminate those cowards...I will never surrender to the Communists."[29] Thieu was playing to his base as much as he was proclaiming policy. A presidential election was a year away, and after these new peace offers, he needed to burnish his anti-communist credentials plus reassert his political dominance by projecting toughness.

For Thieu's political opposition, his rigidity remained anathema, and his South Vietnamese rivals played right into Hanoi's plan. Breaking a yearlong silence, Duong Van Minh rejected Thieu's hardline stand. In a speech the next day, Minh agreed that while the military situation had improved, "the political, economic, and social situations are in an apprehensive deterioration."[30] As long as the war continued, national sovereignty was "drastically impaired," meaning the Americans were overbearing. Solving Vietnam's problems, he said, "must be conceived by the Vietnamese in the interest of the Vietnamese people and nation."[31]

His appeal to Vietnamese xenophobia notwithstanding, many considered Minh's speech his opening gambit to run for the presidency in 1971. Foreign diplomats and Saigon politicians soon visited his home to ascertain the former general's thoughts. Minh's only solution, other than bemoaning that the people were destitute and miserable, was his usual vague pitch that South Vietnam needed "national reconciliation and solidarity." Notably absent from his bromides was a blueprint to solve the nation's problems. Regardless, he had staked out a position as the "peace candidate" in the election. Minh, though, was living in the past. He believed his reputation would carry him to victory. He had no campaign organization and limited funds. That formula had been tried in 1967 by Tran Van Huong and Phan Khac Suu and had failed, but Minh had not learned their lesson.

DOUBLE BLOWS

After his failed effort to speak to the PRG in Paris, Ky returned to Saigon. In late November, he visited the U.S., where he met Nixon and Kissinger. On the plane carrying Ky back home, Thieu's close advisor, Nguyen Cao Thang, died on December 8 of a heart attack. His death was the first blow Thieu suffered. Thang had not only been his main financial backer but also a confidant. Thang was replaced by his assistant, Nguyen Van Ngan, who would soon grow into another Rasputin-like figure in the administration. While Ngan did not have Thang's money, he matched him in deviousness, and he, too, would eventually play a key role for Thieu.[32]

With the withdrawal of U.S. and most ARVN troops from Cambodia, PAVN units began to slowly rebuild their old base areas. To prevent their return, and as a diversion for a top-secret planned assault into southern Laos in February 1971, Thieu ordered Lieutenant General Do Cao Tri to launch another cross-border operation. The objective was the destruction of enemy forces around Kratie, a town deep inside Cambodia. Along the way, ARVN forces would smash Communist sanctuaries in the Chup rubber plantation and at a major logistics base in the Dambe Valley. Route 7 was the only road into these areas.

Three ARVN task forces, spearheaded by Tri's protégé, Colonel Tran Quang Khoi, would lead the operation. Based on lessons learned from the first Cambodian incursion, Khoi had formed the 3rd Armored Cavalry Brigade. Borrowed from the American cavalry idea, it was the only such unit in the South Vietnamese army. Khoi had convinced Tri that a combination of armor, artillery, engineers, and Rangers in the role of mounted infantry could provide a lethal punch. The 5th Ranger Group, an ARVN strategic reserve unit, was the second task force, while an ad-hoc unit of Rangers and artillery formed the third. Reluctant to strip ARVN defenses in South Vietnam, Lieutenant General Tri had cobbled together a division-size element of Rangers and his own armor and artillery elements to conduct a mechanized strike over one hundred miles deep into Cambodia. By any measure, it was a daring operation.

Launching the attack on January 31, 1971, Khoi and the other two task forces moved decisively, fending off several counterattacks and breaking through enemy blocking positions. After several weeks inside Cambodia, Khoi had reached the Dambe Valley. Thieu then called Tri to the palace. The ARVN assault into lower Laos had encountered serious difficulties, so Thieu intended to replace Lieutenant General Hoang Xuan Lam in I Corps with Tri. On the morning of February 23, Tri's helicopter departed Tay Ninh to visit Khoi in Dambe and tell him the news. Then disaster struck Thieu a second blow. The helicopter exploded in midair, and Tri and everyone abroad perished. South Vietnam had lost one of its best combat commanders.

Thieu was shocked and deeply upset. He appointed Lieutenant General Nguyen Van Minh, the commander of the Capital Special Zone, to replace Tri. Corps command, however, was beyond Minh's skills. Synchronizing armor, infantry, and air power while managing logistics and intelligence proved too much for him, mainly because the individualistic command style of Vietnamese officers precluded using their staffs to handle many functions or to adequately plan. Hence, everything became an improvisational ballet rather than a carefully coordinated action.

Minh dithered and left Khoi's task forces sitting idle for a week in the Dambe Valley. Communist troops soon began to surround the encamped ARVN. On February 27, Minh ordered Khoi to withdraw to Vietnam along Route 7, but it was too late. Massing two divisions plus support troops, the PAVN attacked the next day. It blocked Route 7 and overran one Ranger battalion. The Rangers attempted to break out on Route 7 on March 1 but failed. When Minh ordered Khoi to retreat along the same route the next day, Khoi knew he was doomed if he attempted that plan. On the night of March 2, he radioed Minh and demanded to implement his own escape plan. Minh agreed and sent helicopters to remove Khoi from the encirclement, but Khoi refused to leave his men.

Using airstrikes as a diversion, he massed his tanks and launched an armor spearhead through the jungle instead of using Route 7. Surprised at first by an armor assault into dense vegetation, Communist forces soon reacted and rained fire onto his column. One recoilless rifle round hit Khoi's command carrier, but he switched vehicles and continued to lead his men forward. In heavy fighting, his armor broke through the enemy lines. He swung behind the roadblock on Route 7 and successfully retreated to South

Vietnam, evacuating all his wounded and dead.[33] Khoi's decisive leadership had saved almost a division of ARVN troops from annihilation. If he had been overrun, along with the emerging disaster in southern Laos, the combined military catastrophe may have proven fatal for Thieu politically. The death of Tri also had ramifications: if Tri had succeeded Lam, he may have averted or at least mitigated the calamity that almost befell I Corps a year later during the 1972 Easter Offensive. The war had not faded away; it had returned with even greater ferocity.

• • •

Since 1969, the Americans had been sending signals that they wanted to resume discussions with the Chinese, and by early 1970, Beijing responded. The Chinese suggested restarting the low-level discussions in Warsaw between the two countries that had been suspended since 1968. That fall, a back channel through Pakistan between Kissinger and Zhou Enlai was established, and in December 1970, Chou sent a message that he would welcome a visit by Kissinger.

These were not the only moves the Chinese were making. Unknown to the U.S., while Zhou was making a historic invitation to Kissinger, Nguyen Xuan Phong, still in Paris as the GVN deputy to the Paris talks, received a call from the Burmese ambassador to France.[34] He

> asked me to drop in for drinks at his residence. It was made clear that the invitation was strictly personal and not as a representative of the Saigon government! I reported this to President Thieu and had his clearance to go ahead. At that small gathering of diplomats, the Burmese ambassador took me aside and introduced me to Ambassador Huang Chen, the Chinese ambassador to France, who in turn presented me to another Chinese. The two of us then went to sit down for a very friendly and open conversation. I was made to understand that he was a member of Chou Enlai's office and he would like to have the opportunity to see me whenever he happened to be in Paris.[35]

At the end of the meeting, the man asked Phong, "Does President Thieu know who his real friends and foes are?" It was the diplomatic opening of the last great secret of the Vietnam War.

20

"THIEU OVERREACHED HIMSELF"

Laos, the Election, and the Beginning of the End

South Vietnam entered 1971 stronger than ever, but its strength proved unsustainable after the failure of a major attack in February against the Ho Chi Minh Trail in Laos and the shattering of any remaining international support due to the one-man presidential election. Both events, especially the Laotian debacle, marked the end of South Vietnam's ascension. Unseen at the time and not felt for several years, the defeat led directly to the 1972 Easter Offensive. The offensive in turn led to the 1973 Paris agreement, which set the stage for the fall of the country. Adding to South Vietnam's woes was the international debacle resulting from the botched presidential election and more internal trouble, including furor over drug use by U.S. soldiers. Combined into one maelstrom, they began South Vietnam's slide to defeat.

ATTACKING LAOS

In mid-1970, U.S. intelligence detected a PAVN military buildup in southern Laos adjacent to I Corps in northern South Vietnam. By early November, MACV had concluded that Hanoi intended to attack there during the next dry season, which would begin in mid-January 1971 and last until August. Since the U.S. would be withdrawing almost all its combat units from this area, Thieu and Nixon decided to launch a preemptive strike to disrupt the enemy plan and to eliminate the PAVN supply depots. The attack, designed to showcase that Vietnamization had succeeded, was aimed at the heart of the Communist infiltration system, the infamous Ho Chi Minh Trail in Laos.

In early January 1971, the South Vietnamese Joint General Staff and General Abrams began operational planning. They drew up a two-division ARVN attack to find and destroy the PAVN stockpiles. Code named "Lam Son 719," the operation would begin with U.S. units advancing to the Lao border to secure the South Vietnamese supply line, followed by diversionary feints by other American forces. The ARVN would then launch the main thrust, an infantry and armor assault along Route 9, a one-lane road that ran east to west from Dong Ha in South Vietnam into Laos. The ARVN would set up a series of fire support bases along the northern and southern sides of Route 9 to protect the exposed flanks of the advancing column. Lieutenant Hoang Xuan Lam, commander of I Corps, would lead the operation.

The American role inside Laos was restricted to providing firepower, air support, and helicopters. After the Cambodian invasion, Congress had attempted to outlaw U.S. forces from entering Cambodia or Laos. The initial effort failed, but a modified bill passed both houses in December 1970 and was signed in January 1971. The Cooper-Church amendment prohibited U.S. ground forces or advisors from entering either country. In comparison, the 1970 Cambodian operation was well planned, had U.S. troops involved, and had U.S. advisors with ARVN units. Lam Son 719 had none of these.

Although COSVN had predicted after the Lon Nol coup in March 1970 that the allies might invade Cambodia, it did not have any precise intelligence for such a move. The Laotian plan, however, was uncovered by several spies. One agent who exposed the operation was a Vietnamese operative who was employed at the Public Works Bureau in the Laotian capital of Vientiane. He knew the South Vietnamese military attaché assigned to Saigon's embassy. At a dinner party with the attaché and numerous high-ranking ARVN officers who were visiting Vientiane, he was able to review a top-secret folder in the attaché's office that laid out the plans for Lam Son 719.[1]

Hanoi did not need its spies to conclude that the allies might attack southern Laos. The Politburo had determined that the next logical allied offensive operation after the 1970 Cambodian incursion would be either a thrust across the DMZ into Quang Binh Province or an attack into southern Laos. Hanoi dreaded an assault against its prized infiltration system because the Politburo knew it could not win the war without it. The PAVN formed a temporary military structure called Group B70 to command its combat forces in this area. This was the first corps created by PAVN. It fielded three infantry divisions plus artillery and antiaircraft regiments.

Thieu, desiring to showcase his improved military capabilities, decided to launch two simultaneous campaigns: the one led by Colonel Tran Quang Khoi deep into Cambodia to destroy enemy supply caches and another into southern Laos. Unfortunately, the gods of war would not favor Nguyen Van Thieu. The Laotian operation would be ARVN's largest, most challenging battle to date. It would combine forces from I Corps such as the 1st Division with portions of the elite Airborne and Marine divisions from Saigon's General Reserve. These units would attack a heavily fortified area that PAVN troops would defend to the death.

Between the reduced U.S. support and the stiff PAVN defenses, the Laotian attack would prove more than the RVNAF could bear. The biggest problem was the inexperience of the I Corps leadership and staff in coordinating multiple units (Army, Rangers, Marines, and Airborne) that had different chain of commands into an integrated operation. This redundant military reporting system hindered coup plotting but reduced efficiency. The Marine and Airborne units would be operationally attached under Lieutenant General Lam, making the respective division commanders, Lieutenant Generals Le Nguyen Khang and Du Quoc Dong, report to him. Since they normally answered only to General Cao Van Vien or Thieu, they refused. Instead, they churlishly stayed in Saigon and dispatched their deputies to Lam's headquarters.

The offensive started off well. Launching the attack on February 8, 1971, ARVN armor and attached Airborne troops quickly punched into Laos along Route 9.[2] Within three days, the main column was halfway to Tchepone. Ranger units and the 1st Division provided flank defense. Route 9, however, was in terrible shape. Even armored vehicles could barely traverse the dirt road, leaving resupply mainly to helicopters. The terrain was also a major difficulty. Unlike Cambodia's relatively flat ground, this area was forest-covered mountains. The weather was also spotty. Although the dry season had arrived, early morning fog and low clouds often pushed air operations later into the day.

Compounding the difficulties, Lam was far from South Vietnam's finest combat commander. Thieu had kept him in command of I Corps as a reward for his support of the government during the 1966 Buddhist crisis and his backing of Thieu in the showdown with Ky in late June 1967. Unused to complex operations, fighting in the enemy's backyard, and hampered by the terrain and the weather, the operation bogged down. Even though Lam was an armor officer, he halted his advance on Route 9 to allow the 1st Division to catch up and protect the column's southern flank. For five days, the column remained stalled. Thieu then compounded the error by ordering Lam to delay the attack on Tchepone until the weather cleared enough to ensure adequate helicopter support.[3] It proved a deadly mistake, as it allowed the PAVN time to counter.

Local PAVN commanders at first reacted slowly, largely because their forces were scattered defending areas like the Plain of Jars and Quang Binh Province in North Vietnam. The Politburo pushed the High Command to forcefully respond, ordering that "we must win this battle, no matter how many men and how many resources we have to mobilize to do it, and no matter how many losses and sacrifices we must absorb, because this is a battle of decisive strategic importance....A victory in this counteroffensive battle will have a major impact on our cause of liberating South Vietnam."[4] The High Command ordered B70 to use every weapon it possessed, including some recently received Soviet-made T-54 tanks and heavy artillery.

In late February, PAVN forces counterattacked. They assaulted the stationary firebases protecting the flanks of the main column. ARVN casualties rose rapidly, especially when one Ranger battalion was overrun despite virtually destroying an attacking PAVN regiment. On March 3, with the largest battles since Tet 1968 raging along both flanks, Thieu ordered Lam to capture Tchepone. Speaking after the war, Thieu acknowledged that the operation was simply "a point of honor to show the Communists that we can go to Tchepone."[5]

Marshaling a tremendous amount of U.S. helicopters, several battalions of the 1st Division were air assaulted into Tchepone. They searched the deserted and ruined town, found nothing, and were quickly pulled out. Although Thieu had originally intended to leave his troops in Laos to block the infiltration corridor, with his losses growing, he ordered a retreat to Vietnam. The PAVN forces pressed hard against them, heavily shelling the firebases and conducting mass infantry assaults. Despite an enormous barrage of antiaircraft fire that inflicted a heavy toll on U.S. helicopters, American pilots flew harrowing missions to rescue isolated ARVN units. The retreat, difficult under any circumstances, became too much for some ARVN troops. Although many soldiers fought bravely without respite for forty-five days, others panicked and fled. Journalists published pictures of ARVN troops desperately clinging to the skids of helicopters, another photo that had hugely negative consequences for South Vietnam. By late March, the campaign was over. While not a resounding defeat, the battlefield loss had dangerous implications for the future.

Lam Son exposed modernization problems in both armies. Conventional warfare requires considerable logistics to sustain a proficient fighting force. Unfortunately, although the RVNAF had undergone significant upgrades, it still lacked the technological and managerial skills to field a modern military. Worse, while Do Cao Tri's units during the 1970 Cambodian operation had exemplified combined arms operations (the merging of infantry, armor, firepower), South Vietnamese operational tactics in LS 719 suffered tremendously from senior officer infighting. Serious personnel issues remained, including incompetent senior officers and a lack of qualified small unit leaders, while economic difficulties like poor pay lowered morale and esprit de corps.

The People's Army also struggled with the maturation to a fully conventional military. It had no concept of combined arms, a problem that would haunt it during the 1972 Easter Offensive. A dicey resupply system operating under withering bombing resulted in poor food and medical care that greatly sapped unit strength. The constant attacks had forced them into border sanctuaries, which meant the near abandonment of much of the South Vietnamese countryside. Plus, the People's Army's own morale had been reduced by heavy losses and the obvious ARVN improvements.

Conventional warfare increased casualties on both sides, but losses for Lam Son 719 are difficult to pin down. Major General Nguyen Duy Hinh lists ARVN statistics that claimed 13,601 enemy soldiers were killed, over 100 tanks were knocked out, and thousands of trucks destroyed. The PAVN, however, claimed that it suffered 2,163 killed and 6,176 wounded and that it only had a total of eighty-eight tanks in the operation.[6] ARVN losses are equally fuzzy. Lam, in a report to the Senate's Defense Committee, said they had lost around 1,400 killed and 4,700 wounded.[7] Hinh displayed a table claiming South Vietnamese losses were "1,146 killed, 4,236 wounded, and 246 missing."[8]

With major elections in six months, the next battle became shaping South Vietnamese public opinion about Lam Son 719. The people initially reacted with pride that their military was conducting two major operations simultaneously. A typical support-the-troops mentality arose, and many northern Catholic refugees resurrected calls for *Bac Tien* (March North) to reclaim their lost lands.[9] The initial glee turned somber, though, as newspapers began to report on the PAVN counterattacks and the growing ARVN losses. Poor explanation of events from the Information Ministry created cynicism, and as the operation wound down, people began asking hard questions, particularly about Thieu's decisions. There was no doubt that the president had made most of the significant military decisions. As Hinh later wrote, Thieu's "influence was obvious. It was he who approved the idea of the launching an offensive into lower Laos....On at least two occasions, the directives he gave to the I Corps commander clearly affected the course of the operation." The first was to have Lam remain encamped until the weather cleared, and the second was to capture Tchepone. Hinh did modify his veiled criticism of Thieu by remarking that the president had "listened carefully to the recommendations of his field commanders" and "allowed them the latitude in the execution of orders and plans that combat commanders must have."[10]

To bolster flagging public opinion and to prepare for the upcoming election, Thieu adamantly insisted that the attack had succeeded. He declared to the assembly on April 6 that the Laos operation had disrupted the enemy's presumed strategy of attacking I Corps in 1971. Thieu also reinforced his earlier decision to zealously crack down on any internal voices calling for peace talks. In late February 1971, the government convicted two progressive Catholic priests for printing articles promoting negotiations, claiming they had incited "subversion inimical to the fighting spirit of the army."[11] That Thieu would risk alienating one of his staunchest constituencies over minor editorials aptly demonstrates his fervor to suppress domestic calls for negotiations with the PRG. Like other repressive acts, it backfired. One jailed priest, Father Chan Tin, would become a relentless voice proclaiming that the GVN was holding thousands of political prisoners. Also, in late February, Thieu announced a new formulation for peace that quickly became known as the "Four No's:" no coalition, no neutralization, no land concession, and no Communist political activity. Thieu's "peace through strength" was both a starting point for when Hanoi decided to parley and a means for him to appease his right flank for the upcoming election.

Prepping for the election, he also began indirectly painting Duong Van Minh as soft on Communism. In his annual Tet message to the country, Thieu declared that since the Communists could not win a military victory, their only hope was for a "defeatist government" and the election of a leader who is "easy for them to fool at the conference table" or who would "surrender himself to the Communists by accepting a coalition [or] neutrality." The voters had a stark choice, peace with "freedom and prosperity" under him or "peace resulting from a weak settlement which gradually leads to the total loss of the country and eternal slavery for all Vietnamese."[12]

After Thieu declared victory, Nguyen Cao Ky decided to turn Lam Son 719 into an election issue. On April 20, he publicly broke with the president. Ky publicly ridiculed Thieu's victory claim and demanded that South Vietnam seek peace rather than engage in further combat operations. Ky denounced Thieu's government, calling it a "sinking boat with a deceptively good coat of paint, and the man [steering it is an] unfaithful, disloyal, dishonest, fellow."[13]

Hanoi saw events through its own lenses. The key indicator for the Politburo was that it had beaten South Vietnam's best troops, proof that the People's Army had rebuilt its strength. To take the fight to the enemy, however, the PAVN needed more weapons. Le Duan traveled to Moscow to attend the 24th Party Congress and to meet with Soviet leader Leonid Brezhnev. Like a magician, Le Duan attempted to conjure for Brezhnev a global strategic lesson from the victory in Laos similar to how COSVN propagandists had successfully converted the January 1963 battle at Ap Bac from a local tactical win into a thematic commentary on the war.

According to the Soviet ambassador to the DRV, on April 14, 1971, Le Duan bragged to Brezhnev that "the victory on Highway 9 is one of the greatest in the fight against the American imperialists." Le Duan stated that they were planning a "large-scale military operation" for next year's dry season "to strike a decisive blow during the presidential elections in the U.S. to remove Nixon." He boasted that "we will take down Nixon like we took down Johnson."[14] Defense Minister Andrei Grechko said to Brezhnev, "I think that the DRV has an advantage in forces. They will be able to reach their goals only by force. We are ready to provide them with the necessary support in the future."[15] The Russians began shipping more heavy weapons, mainly T-54 tanks and 122mm and 130mm artillery pieces. More important, it sent some advanced weapons such as the SA-7 Strella antiaircraft missile. China followed suit. Beijing had previously reduced aid to the DRV over its opposition to Hanoi's negotiations with the U.S., but "to convince the North Vietnamese that China's opening to America would not undermine their war effort, the Chinese leadership in 1971 substantially increased weapons shipments to the DRV, which had declined between 1969 and 1970."[16] Chinese aid, though, was mostly small arms, ammunition, and military gear rather than the more sophisticated weaponry the Soviets sent.

With new aid promised, in May 1971, the Politburo finalized its plan. It resolved to develop its "strategic offensive posture in South Vietnam to defeat the American 'Vietnamization' policy, gain a decisive victory in 1972, and force the U.S. imperialists to negotiate an end to the war from a position of defeat."[17] Hanoi was about to go for broke.

ECONOMIC REVIVAL

While peace was the main issue for the Vietnamese public, economic discontent was a close second. Monthly public opinion surveys conducted by trained Vietnamese interviewers for CORDS showed that pocketbook issues remained a pressing concern. The April 1971 report showed that while 43 percent of respondents thought the government had achieved economic progress, 37 percent believed it had failed.[18] Yet despite the economic woes, Bunker considered Economic Minister Pham Kim Ngoc "the best man they have got in the Cabinet."[19]

Notwithstanding the ongoing discontent, the macro-economic situation had improved. For example, land reform was a resounding success. By the one-year anniversary of the LTTT law, Cao Van Than's ministry had distributed over five hundred thousand acres to 162,341 farmers.[20] By any measure, it was a stunning achievement, conducted mostly at the village level. Than planned to divest an additional nine hundred thousand acres over the next year. By March 1973, his goal was to have completed the program and given away 2.5 million acres of land. The end result would hopefully foster the popular legitimacy in the countryside that the government sorely lacked.

For Ngoc, "the economy was as important as the war," something that very few realized at the time but was absolutely correct.[21] By March 1971, inflation had greatly slowed from its overheated pace in mid-1970, but the budget gap continued to widen. To address the need for more revenue, Ngoc planned on making significant economic structural changes in 1971 to solve South Vietnam's financial issues. Growth would remedy South Vietnam's economic misfortunes, and Ngoc's design rested on free-market principles, oil exploration, and industrial development. Whereas previous ministers like Nguyen Huu Hanh had relied on deficit financing, U.S. aid, and import taxes to bankroll the GVN, Ngoc's goal was to "divert the economy from its heavy dependence on foreign aid by mobilizing all efforts and resources towards financing the increasing war expenditures, and looking to the future, setting the foundation for sound economic development."[22] Both Ngoc and his deputy, Nguyen Duc Cuong, were determined to shift South Vietnam away from the centrally planned model favored by the French-trained bureaucrats who had previously dominated GVN economic planning.[23]

Ngoc was particularly eyeing oil exploration in South Vietnam's coastal waters. He secretly hoped that oil proceeds would solve Saigon's perennial revenue problem. After geological surveys indicated that South Vietnam's coastal waters might contain oil deposits, Thieu signed a law on December 1, 1970, authorizing exploration rights for foreign companies. He had decided to forego creating a national oil company and chose instead to let foreign companies take the risk and assume the costs. Ngoc tapped Tran Van Khoi, a young engineer in his department, to head South Vietnam's newly established National Petroleum Committee. Khoi traveled to Iran to study and develop an oil bidding contract, and he appeared on television to advertise the GVN's plans.[24]

Ngoc's great hope, however, failed due to forces outside his control. When he publicized in February 1971 that his ministry would begin accepting tenders for oil drilling rights, the antiwar left in the U.S. pounced. They proclaimed that oil was driving Nixon's Vietnam policy.[25] The furor forced Saigon to cancel the auction, but Ngoc announced on June 9 that bidding would resume. Numerous offers were provided, but Thieu allowed them to expire. The oil exploration bidding sat idle for the next two years. Not until early 1973, after Ngoc continued to pester Thieu, did he finally agree. The postponement was a huge mistake. If bids had been accepted in 1971, test wells would have been dug and by 1975 revenue from oil production might have helped stabilize Saigon's burgeoning budget deficit just as American aid was drastically declining. Moreover, Ngoc saw oil revenue as a psychological boost, something to give citizens economic hope rather than the grim despair of more taxes. What caused the delay?

Ngoc did not learn until years later that the suspension was due to a combination of factors. First, the clamor raised by the U.S. antiwar left had caused Thieu to pause to avert suspicion. Second, he secretly feared that the oil companies might corrupt government officials. Third, the 1972 Offensive and then the Paris talks consumed the government, relegating oil rights to a postscript.

Despite his grand design to use oil revenue, structural reform was Ngoc's immediate goal.[26] His first step was to improve tax collection, but given the backlash in October 1969 from suddenly increased import levies, Ngoc wanted to boost personal tax collection gradually to mitigate discontent. Yet the U.S. embassy, concerned about growing congressional ire at corruption and poor accounting for aid money, pressed him to immediately institute an across-the-board tax increase. Ngoc demurred, fearing it would incite street protests, but he convinced the finance minister to instead begin a tax census and audit in Saigon. Ngoc's instinct proved correct. After numerous businesses complained about the sudden appearance of tax inspectors, on February 25, 1971, Thieu called it off. The president then announced that civil servants and soldiers would remain exempt from income tax for the duration of the war. Thieu was clearly playing to his base, because in March he approved Ngoc's next round of economic reforms. These included the sale of GVN treasury bills, higher interest rates, and matching the price of imported rice with that of locally grown.[27] Ngoc's program was designed to help farmers, drain excess liquidity from the economy, cool inflation, and display economic changes to reassure aggrieved U.S. congressmen.

Ngoc's unpopular but necessary reforms, particularly the removal of the rice subsidy, which increased the cost of rice for urban consumers, raised a ruckus. On March 19, twenty-four senators signed a resolution demanding his removal. This marked their third call for Ngoc's head. Thieu ignored them. With the president's backing, Ngoc next turned to Saigon's chief economic problem, the badly overvalued piaster. The low official rate made it virtually impossible for South Vietnam to export goods. Moreover, the country's high customs duties, byzantine regulations, and foreign trade controls (a French legacy), on top of the security and corruption issues, severely restricted foreign investment. Ngoc needed outside financing to grow the economy. To do that, he had to reduce red tape and realistically price the piaster.

Ngoc, however, was forced to wait until after the presidential elections. Thieu did not want tough economic actions upsetting his reelection effort. Ngoc thus used the time to craft a new economic plan in conjunction with his close friend Ha Xuan Trung, the recently appointed finance minister.[28] With his help, Ngoc coordinated piaster and banking reforms. On November 15, Thieu announced fresh measures aimed at dramatically reshaping the country's exchange rates and tariffs. He tailored his public message to U.S. congressional concerns. Both actions, Thieu said, were aimed at reducing South Vietnam's dependency on U.S. aid. Any new assistance would be used to "develop and not consume."[29]

Ngoc eliminated one instrument of the centralized economic model favored by the French-trained bureaucrats. He transferred import licensing from the government to the banks. He also phased out tariff protection for domestic industries and reduced the number of import tax rates from two hundred to just four. He hoped to spark competition and spur new business creation. Ngoc knew that when the war ended, thousands of demobilized soldiers would need jobs. Furthermore, to encourage foreign investment, he raised the exchange rate to 410 piasters to the dollar, but the exchange rate would "float" on a daily basis rather than remain fixed, the system currently in vogue under the 1944 Bretton Woods agreement designed to regulate the international monetary system.[30] Alongside profound land reform and microloans, South Vietnam was among the very first countries to attempt such a radical monetary move.

While prices jumped in the short term and several GVN senators again screamed for Ngoc's dismissal, the results soon proved remarkable. Private money poured into the financial system, enabling the banks to purchase the new GVN bonds, which helped fund the budget. Inflation slowed tremendously, the black market in dollars was essentially eliminated, and production jumped. The year 1971 saw the lowest increase in inflation since 1964. Critically, Ngoc's monetary reforms were launched just as the U.S. Senate had again voted down the foreign aid bill and barely defeated an amendment to limit all Vietnam funds solely for a U.S. withdrawal.

Ngoc, aware of the tempest, immediately launched a public relations campaign. He told journalists that his "measures are taken [because] we want to show the American people, that we, the South Vietnamese, are really, sincerely working toward self-sufficiency and self-reliance." He then appealed for American help. Without U.S. aid, he said, "it will be difficult for South Vietnam to survive."[31] After the Nixon administration launched a major effort to restore the bill, Congress passed the legislation but still reduced funding. Just as Thieu was in a contest between improving his armed forces and the U.S. military withdrawal, Ngoc was in a race between economic reform and dwindling U.S. aid.

MORE SCANDALS

A National Intelligence Estimate published by the CIA in late April concluded that "the outlook for South Vietnam for the remainder of 1971 is reasonably good. The past three years have produced a more stable political situation, a marked improvement in security conditions, and considerable progress in Vietnamization."[32] But like all nations, the country struggled with a variety of ills. Vietnamese students were restless, the economy remained sluggish, and peace seemed unobtainable. For the Americans, the war appeared stalemated, congressional opposition was mounting, and as U.S. forces accelerated their withdrawal, American troop morale began to decline. Racial and disciplinary incidents were increasing when suddenly a new concern arose. Drug use and addiction among the soldiers, primarily from cheap, high-quality heroin, skyrocketed. From August to December 1970, ninety Americans died from suspected overdoses. In January and February 1971, another thirty-six died.[33]

In early February 1971, Secretary of Defense Melvin Laird brought it to Thieu's attention. The president remarked that "this was the first he had heard about it."[34] Much of the heroin came into the country via commercial flights from Laos to Saigon's Tan Son Nhut airport. Customs checks at the airport were nonexistent because the inspectors were either bribed to look the other way or were complicit in the smuggling. Under U.S. pressure, Thieu ordered heightened customs security at the airfield even though Prime Minister Khiem was indirectly tied to it. When Khiem had fired Ky's cronies at the Saigon port and at Customs Department, he replaced them with his own people. Khiem's younger brother was the director of the National Fraud Repression Division, the enforcement arm of the Customs Department. Under his tenure, smuggling in South Vietnam had soared, and GVN customs officials were obviously involved. On March 10, the police caught an Air Vietnam stewardess smuggling heroin from Laos. One week later, a Lower House deputy returning from Bangkok was nabbed at the airport while carrying heroin. The next day, a second deputy was caught by Thai customs in Bangkok attempting to bootleg gold into Saigon. This man, Nguyen Quang Luyen, was no small fish. He was second deputy chairman of the Lower House and head of the pro-Thieu Independence Bloc. Although Luyen was quickly released, his arrest and subsequent resignation was front-page news in the Vietnamese press.

After briefings by Abrams and Bunker regarding the growing drug addiction of American troops, on May 3, Thieu ordered his national security aide, Lieutenant General Dang Van Quang, to report to him within ten days with a plan to address the drug problem. The publicity also generated an immediate congressional response. Representative Robert Steele (R-Conn.) visited the country, and he proclaimed that over 10 percent of U.S. servicemen were addicted to heroin, a dubious claim. Congress exploded over Steele's declaration, and it added amendments to the foreign aid bill that restricted assistance to countries that did not institute narcotics controls. Realizing that failure to act decisively on heroin would directly threaten ongoing aid, Bunker reported that "Thieu intends to take personal charge of this program as he did in pacification."[35] On June 1, he cashiered Khiem's brother and the head of Customs and removed all Customs and baggage officials at the airport.

When Nixon declared his own War on Drugs on June 17, 1971, Thieu followed with a similar program. Although the police began making major drug seizures, and the smuggling at Tan Son Nhut was curtailed, controversy erupted again on July 7. Using unverified information acquired by the U.S. provost marshal that senior levels of the GVN were involved in the drug trade, Representative Steele publicly accused II Corps Commander Major General Ngo Dzu of heroin trafficking. Dzu disputed the charges, but his alleged involvement was overshadowed when NBC News broadcast a second bombshell. On July 15, Phil Brady, its Saigon television correspondent, claimed that both Thieu and Ky were using drug sales to finance their presidential campaigns. Brady, citing Vietnamese sources, claimed narcotics were entering Vietnam from Laos on Vietnamese Air Force planes, the old accusation against Ky. Although Brady said that neither man was directly involved, he alleged that Thieu's aide, Lieutenant General Quang (whom Thieu had ordered to investigate the drug and smuggling issues), was the "biggest pusher" in South Vietnam.[36] Thieu denied the story, as did Ky, who even defended Thieu. "Even though Thieu and I are no longer friends," Ky said, "I do not think he would be involved in something like this."[37]

While the smuggling scandal compounded the international belief that South Vietnam's government was riddled with corruption, in America, the idea that U.S. servicemen were being hooked on heroin by drug-pushing senior GVN officials made South Vietnam look like a narco-state.[38] Yet Thieu pressed forward, and on August 10, he asked the assembly to vote on a bill to institute the death penalty for importing or dealing drugs. The bill also created special trial procedures for users and moved major drug cases to the Mobile Military Court.

Smuggling and drugs, however, were temporarily pushed off the front pages when several U.S. congressmen hurled allegations that Phoenix was in reality a disguised assassination program. William Colby had just completed his tour as head of CORDS, and he was immediately asked to testify about purported violations in the Phoenix program. On July 19, he strongly rebuffed these charges, although he admitted that occasional abuses had occurred. The 1970 Phoenix plan, now mostly a Vietnamese operation, had assigned quotas to each district for capturing enemy cadres. While Phoenix was not a covert killing system, under presidential pressure to show results, district officials filled their quota by either fudging the numbers or rounding up anyone remotely suspected of collaborating with the Communists.

Such manipulations easily occurred because while the constitution had made it illegal to be a Communist or a neutralist, it had neither offered a definition nor stipulated what acts represented assistance to Communist plans. Hence, any activity not in accordance with government policy or against the whims of local officials could simply be branded "Communist," leading to harassment or arrest. The Lower House abolished the Phoenix Provincial Security Committees to halt the abuses, forcing Thieu to make legal modifications to the program to get the committees reapproved. In early August, Prime Minister Khiem signed a decree stiffening protections for accused subjects, sent prosecutors to the provinces to speed up trials, and required that "low-level elements who only support the VC" should be released if they "changed their behavior."[39]

While important, Phoenix was only one part of the overall effort in the countryside. Pacification remained high on Thieu's agenda, and the 1971 plan continued his efforts to improve local governance. He and Colby had developed three themes for 1971: local self-defense, local self-government, and local self-development. Since Thieu believed that he had recaptured the countryside from the Communists, he ordered the pacification title changed to Community Defense and Local Development to reflect his new priorities. He intended to improve security by further building up the People's Self-Defense Force, Phoenix, and police presence in the villages. Local rule, land reform, and agricultural development would also be strengthened and expanded.

In a speech, Thieu clearly explained his thinking; he had created an "effective anti-communist strategy...based on the people as the nucleus force. If we can control the countryside the communist cadres will stop functioning."[40] Colby noted that creating a national plan enabled Thieu "to impose a fundamentally political strategy on the South Vietnamese effort" by enlisting the people in fighting the Communist while concurrently building a better society and economy.[41]

Had Thieu finally concocted the fabled political strategy to defeat the Communists? Was this profound statement that the allies had retaken the countryside from the Communists after years of struggle accurate or wishful thinking? Did it mark a real shift in the war, or was it just one politician's hopeful opinion based upon fuzzy statistics and a desire to promote progress?

The answer usually depended upon who was asked, but Thieu based his conviction on his numerous visits to the countryside. He had increased his trips to the villages, mainly to hand out land titles, check on pacification efforts, and engage in ribbon cutting. While he was often accused of being a recluse in his office, the U.S. embassy noted that he spent "one and often two days outside of Saigon each week" visiting and checking on progress in the countryside.[42] Thieu frequently resolved "problems on the spot and gave implementing orders to the Ministers accompanying him." Thieu inspected PSDF units, met with local officials, and mingled with people in the market. Such encounters "appear to evoke a genuinely favorable response," and Thieu often made "an impromptu speech at each stop." His speeches always declared that he would not cede "one inch of South Vietnamese territory," nor would he accept a coalition. In 1967, Thieu's image was that of a reserved man uncomfortable in crowds. The embassy noted that now he was "markedly more outgoing and seems genuinely to like meeting people. He laces his speeches with humor" and "often plunges down a street not on his itinerary to greet the citizenry."

While the embassy acknowledged that it was "difficult to gauge the crowds' true sentiments," Thieu's visits to all forty-four provinces had made him and his government known to the rural people. While Thieu's outings were planned in advance, enabling local officials to showcase "progress," his barnstorming trips were designed to earn peasant votes and win the election. While Thieu would sweep the countryside in the 1971 election, without an opponent, it is difficult to gauge the real extent of his popularity. Still, given rising rural prosperity and the fact that people often vote their pocketbook, plus the difficulties for the Communist cadres to reenter the villages, it appears that Thieu was then far more popular than any current or former South Vietnamese politician. Whether that endured would depend on the economy and the war.

With Lam Son 719 over, on April 7, Nixon claimed that "Vietnamization had succeeded" and announced the withdrawal of another hundred thousand troops.[43] To compensate for the removal of American units from I Corps, Thieu formed a new division in the area. The 3rd ARVN Division was created by taking two regiments from the 1st Division and forcing other units to provide soldiers to fill out the rest of the new division. Typically, they sent their dregs, and the 3rd spent the rest of the year preparing to replace the departing U.S. troops. Eventually this newly created, untried unit was assigned to guard the DMZ in northern Quang Tri Province right next to the main PAVN troop concentrations. It was not the smartest military move of the war.

Despite Nixon's pledge to bring the troops home, the antiwar protests resumed. Part of it was sparked by his order moving Lieutenant William Calley to house arrest pending the appeal of his sentence on March 31, 1971, to life imprisonment for the My Lai massacre. A group of former Vietnam servicemen calling themselves the Vietnam Veterans Against the War were outraged that other officers were not convicted. In late April, they held a protest march in Washington, culminating in former Navy officer John Kerry's famous testimony before the Senate Foreign Relations Committee. On April 24, a massive antiwar protest was held in Washington. By early May, only the hardcore left remained, and activists went on a rampage in the capital. They blocked streets and government buildings, forcing the police to clear them.

Ambassador Bui Diem desperately tried to convey to Thieu the street pressure Nixon was facing. He wrote that "the image of thousands of young people bearing the Viet Cong flag, parading through the streets of Washington...will be like a mirror President Nixon will always have to look into whenever a decision on the Vietnamese question has to be taken."[44] Bui Diem saw a "deluge of congressional initiatives aimed at destroying the administration's capacity to carry on the fight...[E]ach day I lived with the constant erosion of support, and each night I attempted to translate the experience into a cogent message to Saigon."[45] After five years in Washington fighting for his country, a beleaguered, disillusioned, Bui Diembegan to contemplate retirement.

Other events also kept Vietnam on the nightly news. The release of the Pentagon Papers on June 13 fully engaged the American press over its various revelations. Although Hanoi had secretly embarked on preparations for a new round of fighting, on July 1, the PRG's Nguyen Thi Binh disguised its ambitions by proposing a new Seven-Point Peace Proposal, a slightly revamped proposition from her September 1970 offer. Nixon sent Kissinger to Saigon in early July to reassure Thieu that he had rejected her proposal.

Shortly thereafter, Nixon made a bombshell announcement on July 15 that he would visit China in 1972. Officially, Thieu welcomed the news, but behind the scenes he grew anxious that the U.S. might abandon South Vietnam via some "great power bargain," especially since Kissinger had not told Thieu (or the other U.S. allies he visited) about his trip to Beijing. Despite all these happenings, South Vietnam's forthcoming presidential election would soon dominate the headlines.[46]

THE 1971 ELECTIONS

The elections for the presidency and the Lower House presented another test of the democratic institutions so painfully created in South Vietnam four years earlier. Successful and honest elections with competitive candidates would enhance the luster of constitutional rule. A third lawful plebiscite would also showcase that military interference with the government was a relic of the past and that political opponents were now free to operate. Lastly, it would provide a referendum on Thieu's governance on a wide range of issues, from the war and peace to the economy.

Politically aware Vietnamese assumed that the race would be between three men: Thieu, Ky, and Minh. Even though the U.S. had declared strict neutrality to allay charges of interference in Saigon's affairs, no one believed it. Most urban Vietnamese highly exaggerated a supposedly nefarious U.S. influence on Saigon politics. They averred that clandestine American control had swayed numerous South Vietnamese leadership decisions. The publication of the Pentagon Papers, which was heavily serialized in Saigon's papers and showed deep U.S. involvement in Diem's overthrow, convinced everyone they were right.[47] Persuaded that Thieu was the "American" candidate and realizing the difficulty in running against an entrenched incumbent, the existing political parties, especially the Revolutionary Dai Viets and the Progressive Nationalist Movement, focused instead on winning seats in the Lower House. The Catholics and An Quang took the same approach.

As the unofficial campaigning began, each candidate had strengths and weaknesses. Long hawkish on talks between North and South Vietnam, the thirty-nine-year-old Ky was now staking out a position on peace and other issues that was squarely between Thieu and Minh. He defended his altered stand by claiming that given the U.S. withdrawal, the situation had changed. Ky also began accusing Thieu and his ministers of corruption, heavily criticized the Laos invasion, and revived his calls for social justice. He also cleverly appealed to anti-Americanism by painting Thieu as subservient to the U.S. while acknowledging that the country still needed U.S. military support and aid. Ky, however, had little ground organization to staff an election campaign, and his popularity was far thinner than he believed. While he retained some military backing, even his support in the Air Force had waned considerably. Some northerners, minorities, and youth groups viewed him favorably, but he remained anathema to the An Quang Buddhists and most southerners. He was a long shot, but he relished the spoiler role.

The fifty-five-year-old Minh had staked his candidacy on peace and his reputation as a true southerner, an honest man in a sea of corrupt politicians and a faithful Buddhist in a majority Buddhist country. A traditionalist, the retired general saw himself as a national figure above politics. Having to stump for votes was beneath him. Unable to comprehend modern canvassing, he naïvely believed that he would win by a spontaneous outpouring of national sentiment. Anything else was evidence that Thieu had rigged the election. Prestige, however, would no longer suffice in a transforming South Vietnam. He had not built any campaign organization in the countryside, nor had he articulated any policies to combat his reputation as a lazy, ineffective leader all too willing to strike a deal with the Communists. Peace was his only card. Thieu, he claimed, "believes peace can only be won by killing the last Communist. This cannot be done. The only way is to negotiate."[48] Minh, while convinced that the PRG would talk with him, sought a ceasefire and peaceful coexistence but not a coalition. It was an interesting policy nuance that, in typical fashion, he was unable to effectively articulate, especially since Thieu and the U.S. had already offered a ceasefire that the Communists had rejected. Plus, since the NLF had demanded a coalition before elections, this ultimatum made his proposal moot. For many ardent anti-communists, Minh was the Neville Chamberlain of his country.

After six years in office, first as chief of state and then president, the forty-eight-year-old Thieu had successfully transitioned from a general to a pragmatic politician. He was barnstorming the provinces, delivering speeches, and wooing the peasantry. The population at first respected him as a master competitor in Saigon's byzantine politics. Now they largely saw him as an effective chief executive: more stable than the mercurial Ky, more efficient than the inept Minh. Equally important, he had artfully balanced the rival demands of the Vietnamese public and the military and government bureaucracy while retaining critical U.S. support. He had rejuvenated the countryside, artfully managed the U.S. withdrawal, and overseen a vast strengthening of the state. To his credit, he had refused to court the religious groups or coopt the political parties by offering them government largesse in exchange for support. Any outreach efforts had been strictly to strengthen the bureaucracy. Still, like all leaders in developing countries, he faced seemingly insoluble problems. Corruption riddled the government, his hardline policy on negotiations alarmed a war-weary public, and he remained anathema to sections of the population. Tran Van Don summed it up by noting that "Thieu is a statesman but is not popular. Minh is popular but not a statesman."[49]

The constitution stipulated that the assembly must pass an election bill before every vote. As early as December 1970, Thieu had wanted to amend the law to "reduce the number of presidential candidates. Parties could not develop under the present law therefore it must be changed." Thieu thought a two-party system, "one on the left and one on the right," would enable a "more effectual and stable government."[50] Thieu had given Nguyen Van Ngan, his legislative advisor who had replaced Nguyen Cao Thang, carte blanche to run his election campaign.[51] To limit the number of fringe candidates that had diffused the vote in 1967, Ngan drafted a new election bill with a controversial provision. Although the election law basically mimicked the 1967 bill, a new Article 10 raised eyebrows. The article stipulated that a candidate must have the written endorsement of a minimum of forty senators or deputies, or 100 of the 554 provincial councilmen, at least sixty days in advance of the presidential election.

Known as the "40 or 100" provision, the Lower House passed the bill, but the Senate rejected it. Thieu resubmitted it, and on June 3, and the Lower House overrode the Senate veto. Opposition deputies charged that Thieu was trying to limit the candidates and that Ngan had bribed many deputies to get the necessary votes, accusations with some merit. Debate was so bitter that one deputy threatened to blow himself up with a hand grenade, while another pulled a pistol and threatened to shoot the speaker of the house. The election for the Lower House would occur on August 29, while the presidency was set for October 3. The bill, however, was not totally pro-Thieu. It restricted who could run for the Lower House by blocking current military or provincial officials, a clause impeding pro-Thieu candidates.

Despite the furor over the 40/100 provision, Thieu insisted that the new law was necessary. He repeated to a visiting Kissinger in early July "that he promulgated the law...not to allow fantasist candidates like 1967...[A]ny President, whether Minh, Ky or himself, should have sufficient prestige and not a 35% vote like before. This was important also for political stability." Further, Thieu said that the elections "would be well organized and fair; that his election law was not aimed at Minh or Ky, who had sufficient support, but rather to give the next president a real mandate."[52] Thieu also told a foreign journalist that the two biggest issues facing South Vietnam were the need "to enhance security and to secure political democracy." He wanted several candidates, "but not too many, so the winner would have a credible majority—we are waging war after all."[53]

Thus, Thieu sought a popular mandate for his peace policies while also defeating the Communist insistence that he be removed first before an election. Ngan confirms that

> Thieu never wanted to have a one-man election....[W]e wanted a fair and honest election, and we truly wanted Minh to enter the race, because then Thieu's victory would have given us Nationalists a strong position at the Paris peace talks...Further, he aspired to turn the election into a national plebiscite in which the people would have to choose between two completely opposite political solutions: on one side would be Thieu, representing the anti-communist Nationalists, and the other side would be Minh, representing those people who would accept a coalition with the Communists.[54]

Since the electorate's diversity fragmented the vote, how could Thieu put together a winning combination? What total could he reasonably win? To answer those questions, Ngan used the Joint General Staff computers to analyze the balloting from the August 1970 elections. He grasped that if Ky were not involved, Minh would poll around 45 percent, while Thieu would get roughly 55 percent.[55] However, when Ngan presented his study and his 40/100 plan to Thieu to eliminate Ky, he also speculated that Minh might drop out when confronted by the law. Despite the fears about Minh, Thieu approved Ngan's plan.

In March 1971, Thieu had considered Khiem to be his new vice president, but he changed his mind after the airport smuggling was revealed. Plus, he had become disillusioned with Khiem's performance as prime minister. They had clashed over the Tran Ngoc Chau case and the student-and-veteran protests, but the stench of corruption from the smuggling at Tan Son Nhut sealed Khiem's fate. Thieu reached out to Tran Van Huong, who agreed to be his vice president. Huong said that "although he and Thieu had had their differences he was in basic agreement with Thieu over the issues of war and peace and regarded Thieu as the best available national leader."[56] Thieu chose Huong for the same reasons that he had wanted him as prime minister: his reputation and the need to balance the ticket with someone who had deep ties with the southern elite.

Once the assembly passed the 40/100 bill, Ngan set in motion part two of his election strategy: corner every endorsement to prevent Ky from qualifying. Minh was certified by the requisite assembly deputies, but Ky failed to get the lawful number of signatures from the provincial council members. Ky cried foul, and he appealed to the Supreme Court, but it declared him invalid. The effort to sew up every endorsement was both a deliberate political sabotage of a rival and a personal vendetta against Thieu's former ally. Thieu, privately seething from Ky's savage criticisms, decided to publicly humiliate his vice president. Never a man to leave things to chance, Thieu and his campaign staff ruthlessly thwarted Ky's efforts.

With Ky suppressed, Minh also began to waver. Minh desperately needed An Quang to provide him with ground support, but when Minh supporter and assembly deputy Ly Qui Chung visited Thich Tri Quang to secure his backing, he found that the monk "was not very enthusiastic." While Quang hated Thieu and wanted "a government that was able to end the war and restore peace," he believed that Saigon needed a strong leader. Quang said that "Minh is not a real politician," a subtle way of passing judgment.[57]

When someone passed Ngan's covert campaign instructions to the province chiefs to Minh, the outraged general gave a copy to the U.S. embassy. The document outlined an impressive operational program combined with an equally notable design to suppress the opposition. Aware of Truong Dinh Dzu's surprise achievement in 1967, Ngan had created a novel (for Vietnam) plan to win based on detailed electoral voting analysis and superb ground organization. The plan delineated responsibility to the province chiefs for ensuring success and designated each campaign worker to determine the political leanings of around 350 voters. "The goal," Ngan wrote, was to "have an analysis for every village and [city] ward that provides clear knowledge of the tendency of each individual voter."[58] Moreover, the province chief should create a covert staff to "paralyze the activities of the opposition ticket." The "various tricks and schemes that can be employed to disrupt and paralyze the opposition elements" included bribery, threats, detention of "pro-Communists," and transfer of local officials working for the opposition. Mayor Richard Daley in Chicago would have been envious.

Minh was flummoxed by Ngan's modern political blitzkrieg. Rather than fight back, and with no backing from An Quang, on August 20, he withdrew. Bunker had tried to convince him the day before to remain for the good of the country and even offered him money to bolster his campaign, but Minh refused. The next day, in what was obviously another Thieu ploy, the Supreme Court surprisingly reinstated Ky. Bunker attempted to convince Ky to continue, but Ky also refused. Pride and self-interest in both men had supplanted any vestige of working for the national interest.

With Minh's withdrawal, and with Ky poised to announce that he would not run, Thieu needed to reassure the military that he was not turning into "Diem-lite." On August 23, he reconvened the moribund Military Council to gain its acquiescence to press ahead with the election. According to Ngan, Thieu offered to resign if the military would not support him. Everyone agreed to back Thieu except General Vien, who abstained to indicate his preference for the military to remain neutral in politics. Subsequently, on August 29, Thieu promoted almost thirty commanders one grade in rank. Among them was the notorious Ngo Dzu, an indication that domestic priorities for Thieu still far outweighed foreign opinion. He also outmaneuvered Ky by promoting the Air Force commander to lieutenant general, who now outranked the vice president. Ky also knew he could not employ the secret codicil both men had signed in 1967, the pact that gave the Military Council veto power over Thieu. "Using it against him," Ky wrote, would have "exposed the military to ridicule, and allowed our enemies to paint our real progress toward democracy as a sham. Making such a document public probably would have sent the Americans packing."[59] Thieu had secured the military against any plotting.

Despite the various political machinations capturing the headlines, elections for the Lower House went ahead. In early July, with over 1,300 candidates running, the GVN launched a large get-out-the-vote campaign by forming provincial teams to explain the voting procedures. The House was being expanded from 137 to 159 seats to account for population growth. Candidates did not run on party labels, and technically they did not represent a specified area but a group of fifty thousand voters within a district. Although most moderate opposition candidates had been left alone, local officials had harassed a few of Thieu's more ardent oppositionists. The Catholic firebrand Ngo Cong Duc had been disqualified by the Election Committee for supposedly being an NLF sympathizer. Duc was the publisher of *Tin Sang*, Saigon's chief opposition paper, and when the paper printed a story about Thieu's well-known mistress in Vung Tau, Duc's fate was sealed. Another foil, Duong Van Ba, also a Catholic southerner who was close to Mrs. Thieu's family, had barely qualified. Unlike Duc, Ba, who had been voted secretary-general of the Lower House during its first term, was in fact a secret NLF agent.[60]

Thieu's plan to use the PSDF as an anti-communist vanguard was bearing fruit. Following detailed plans first developed in June 1969 to use the PSDF to protect the village elections, in late July, the Interior Ministry issued another directive for the upcoming elections.[61] The PSDF were to mobilize the people to vote, protect them, and assist anyone who needed help getting to the polls. The PSDF would "launch a big campaign" a month ahead of time "to publicize the elections to ensure that the people clearly understand the importance of the elections and turn out to vote in large numbers." This included creating a security plan to prevent enemy attacks and assisting "old, weak, and disabled voters."[62] To prevent charges of voter intimidation, the PSDF were forbidden from carrying weapons to the polls. Despite Thieu's obvious wish to obtain a solid majority in the Lower House, the decree did not instruct the PSDF to proselytize whom to vote for but only to encourage voting as a "national duty."

Successful elections were held on August 29. Only a handful of more than seven thousand polling stations were closed due to Communist interference. With the PSDF "encouraging" people to vote, participation was high. Nationwide, 78 percent of eligible voters went to the polls, compared to 65 percent for the August 1970 Senate elections. Thieu was pleased with the turnout, believing it displayed national unity and strength, although many people had voted to avoid police harassment if their voter cards were not stamped.

Like the August 1970 Senate elections, An Quang made inroads. The Buddhists won twenty-four seats, mostly in I Corps, where they virtually swept the slate. While ballet box stuffing was rare, several opposition candidates like Duong Van Ba suffered blatant harassment and lost. The Supreme

Court tossed out the results in three provinces, including Ba's. Yet despite Minh's cries that Thieu was manipulating the election, forty-two newly elected deputies were known Thieu opponents, eighty-one were pro-Thieu, while thirty-six were politically unknown.

Nguyen Ba Can, the deputy who had attempted to defend Tran Ngoc Chau, was elected the new speaker, setting him on the road to even great-er power. Oddly, while only a minority of incumbents won, the election resurrected the careers of several well-known Saigon politicians, including Tran Van Tuyen, the VNQDD elder. Tuyen had failed to win in 1967, but this time he won a seat from Saigon. Another winner was former general Tran Van Don, who secured a position from Quang Ngai Province with backing from An Quang. Once elected, the cagey Don promptly switched his allegiance to Thieu. Don's about-face was a turning point in his career; while he destroyed his An Quang support, he secured the chairmanship of the Defense Committee, which would eventually provide him a springboard into the government.

The volatile Ky decided to fan the embers of public discontent. At first, he asked Thieu to resign and reformulate the election law. Many foreign observers also called for the election to be postponed. However, that would require a constitutional amendment by the assembly, a process deemed impossible given that the old assembly was over and the new one had not yet been credentialed. Rather than heed Ky's call for his resigna-tion, in a nationally televised speech on September 11, Thieu announced he would not resign. Ky then tried to persuade Vien to convene the Mil-itary Council to force out Thieu so they could organize a new election. Vien refused; he told Ky the army was out of politics.

Unable to stir the military, Ky turned to street pressure to compel Thieu to quit. He urged an election boycott, railing that Thieu was "selling out the country to foreigners," a surefire crowd pleaser.[63] Some prominent dissidents like Mrs. Ngo Ba Thanh picketed in front of the assembly, where she was promptly arrested and then tossed in jail for assaulting the judge at her trial. A few disabled veterans responded to Ky's call to arms, as did Huynh Tan Mam's radical student fringe. Under instructions from COSVN's Saigon City Youth Group, Mam asked Ky for help. Never a paragon of prudence, "Ky agreed to give them...office equipment, vehicles, and [two thousand] Mark 3 hand grenades used for training purposes."[64] On September 19, Mam's acolytes fought the police in downtown Saigon and used the gre-nades to destroy ballot boxes. A week later, they launched a campaign to firebomb American cars. The police rounded up the ringleaders, but Mam fled to Minh's villa. Unable to ignite a national response, he remained there in hiding until 1972, when he was arrested while sneaking out of Minh's sanctuary.

Despite the protests, Thieu pushed on. Since the constitution obligated him to hold the election on October 3, he announced he would instead consider it a referendum on his government. The vote would be either confidence or no confidence, and he would resign if he did not receive a minimum 50 percent confidence vote. He again informed the Military Council that he would resign if the U.S. cut off aid because of his decision.

Even the normally upbeat Bunker, in perhaps his most scathing report on South Vietnam, concluded that while each candidate "had behaved irresponsibly...I would hold Thieu most to account." In the ambassador's opinion, "Thieu had overreached himself."[65] Bunker wanted a vigorous campaign that showcased a free and fair election to eliminate the charge that Thieu was a dictator. Such a campaign would help maintain congressional and U.S. public support for the war and provide a distinct contrast to Hanoi's one-party rule. Instead, Thieu's decision gave the antiwar movement a bludgeon to use against him. The surest means to sway U.S. attitude against Thieu was to portray him as "anti-democratic."

The election went smoothly, and voter turnout was 88 percent, with 91 percent endorsing his continuation in office.[66] But rather than a display of democracy's strength in South Vietnam, the massive turnout instead showcased GVN population domination. While pockets of Communist sway remained, Saigon had unquestionably answered the question of who controlled the people and most of the countryside. Yet the elections showed that other trends continued. An Quang remained Thieu's chief opposition, critical but no longer implacably hostile. The old political parties, save the emerging PNM and Buu's Farmer-Worker Party, had again performed poorly. The senior military commanders, seeded with Thieu loyalists, refused to plot in the shadows. The countryside, while politically apathetic, recognized its self-interest in maintaining Thieu and voted accordingly. Only the urban elite remained disdainful of Thieu.

For better or worse, Thieu had become the pivot upon which South Vietnamese politics turned. After providing his country with four years of capable leadership, he had achieved a majority presidency. He had removed the onus of being an American pawn and braced himself for the war's endgame: negotiations, followed by elections that included the NLF. His goals were understandable; his methods were disreputable. The CIA's George Carver, an astute observer of Vietnam, articulated Thieu's miscalculation: "Thieu could have handily beaten any rivals...in a completely open and honest election. By doing so, he could have rendered virtually unarguable his own and his government's claim to constitutional legitimacy and put his critics and opponents—Communist and non-Communist, Vietnamese, and foreign—in a very awkward spot. Instead, he has blown it...[and given his] critics ample reason to argue plausibly (whether correctly or not) that he represents nothing but himself and whatever bayonets he can personally command."[67]

Why would Thieu, whose finely tuned political antenna made him far more aware of his worldwide detractors than he is given credit for, make such a tone-deaf error? Clearly there were unstated policy goals such as forcing a plebiscite with Minh over peace talks to strengthen his hand in Paris. But underneath lurked grave personal fears. Notwithstanding constant reassurances by Nixon, Thieu secretly sought a majority vote to prevent the Americans from bargaining him away in exchange for an honorable withdrawal. Ngan claims Thieu told him that he believed that the U.S. "wanted to replace me with Minh in the October election because if Minh won he would have asked the U.S. to totally end its intervention, which would have allowed the U.S. to abandon South Vietnam in a just and proper manner without fear of being accused of betraying its ally."[68]

Nguyen Ba Can, now the fourth-most-powerful politician in Saigon, held similar conspiratorial notions. He wrote,

> we knew very well that the U.S. was supporting Minh in this election, just as the U.S. had supported Truong Dinh Dzu in opposing Thieu during the first election campaign....Later, after reviewing the U.S.'s tricks and schemes in its policies toward South Vietnam, I concluded that the U.S. had arranged for Minh to pull out of the election and had allowed the media, and especially the U.S. media, to attack Thieu for his 'uncontested reelection' to put Thieu into a weak position that would then allow the U.S. to control and pressure him so that they could carry out their plan to sell out and betray Vietnam.[69]

Thus, when Kissinger visited him in July and then also met with Ky and Minh, Thieu's fears bubbled up. He connected Bunker's meeting to persuade Minh to remain in the election to U.S. support for the former general. What the U.S. intended as a public display of neutrality Thieu saw as American maneuvers. His spies were also telling him about U.S. contacts with other opposition figures, meetings which made Thieu's qualms seem plausible.

Then two alarming events happened simultaneously. Nixon aide Alexander Haig informed Thieu in September that the U.S. was going to offer Thieu's resignation as an inducement to get Hanoi to accept the U.S. peace offer. When about half of the GVN Senate on the same day as Haig's request also demanded that he resign because of the one-man election, Thieu saw it as proof of his suspicions. While Thieu did not think the U.S. was planning a military coup against him, he believed he had to do whatever it took to block a political coup.

While these fears swirled in Thieu's well-known mistrustful mind, unfortunately for his country, the growing pains of a young democracy had played out in the press and on U.S. television: the repression, the corruption, the Tiger Cages, and the heroin smuggling, to name but a few. The unrelenting scandals, the ideological critics, plus the toll of U.S. dead and wounded, had irrevocably weakened the American public's resolve to help South Vietnam. The one-man election was the final straw. A national survey taken by Harris at the end of October 1971 showed that 65 percent of the American people now thought the war was not simply a mistake but was "morally wrong."[70] The defeat in Laos eliminated any hope that Vietnamization could succeed. Around 53 percent doubted that the GVN could "keep the Communists from taking over after the U.S. has withdrawn its troops." Thieu's election gambit had veered into Greek tragedy, and with Hanoi secretly preparing a massive offensive to destroy pacification and "take out Nixon," these twin blows began Saigon's irreversible slide to destruction.

THE REVOLUTION STRIKES BACK

Aware they could not halt the elections, the Communists turned to their favorite weapon: killing Nationalist leaders to eliminate rivals and sow distrust among them. The first hit was aimed at fifty-seven-year-old Tran Quoc Buu, the leader of the CVT labor union and the Farmer-Worker Party. The Saigon "Party Committee ordered the T4 Security Section to kill Tran Quoc Buu."[71] It recruited a woman inside his headquarters who gave a local agent access to the building. On the afternoon of September 21, the cadres placed a bomb with a timer against the wall outside Buu's office. Buu escaped the explosion because he had left his office a few minutes earlier.

When it failed to kill the labor leader, the Saigon Party Committee set its sights on another prize, Professor Nguyen Van Bong, head of the Progressive National Movement and director of the National Institute of Administration, the training school for senior GVN bureaucrats. The Communists had accidently chosen the right target; secretly, Thieu intended to replace Khiem as prime minister with Bong.

Khiem was an able administrator whom Thieu had appointed as prime minister to run pacification, solve the economic issues, and repair relations with the assembly. However, given his coup-tainted past, and the constitutional dictates of the office, he deferred decisions to Thieu instead of taking charge. Hoang Duc Nha, whose insights on Khiem must be viewed with caution since the two men were mortal enemies, claimed Khiem would explain to Nha that "I am just an executor." Nha sneeringly called him "the greatest cover your ass guy I ever met."[72] Ngan concurs, stating that "Khiem avoided political responsibility, but in actuality he used his constitutional powers...to appoint his relatives and friends to cushy, profitable positions...to benefit himself personally and make money."[73] Khiem, however, preferred to privately discuss matters with Thieu. While it is uncertain how much he influenced the president on issues or policies, the available evidence indicates that he did not provide a counterbalance to Thieu's worst instincts.

According to Nha, with the rising chorus of criticism over the election, Thieu and he agreed that Bong, an incorruptible, highly respected individual, was the perfect choice to bring a responsible opposition leader into the government. Thieu wanted someone "who can really direct the government, a person that will be beyond reproach and that everyone will coalesce and support."[74] Nha confirms that Thieu's pick was as much about placating the U.S. antiwar critics as it was about broadening his government to prepare it for elections with the NLF. Typically, Thieu first sent his brother Kieu to discuss it with Bong. After Bong accepted, it was agreed that he "could [choose every cabinet minister] except Interior, Defense, and Economy."[75]

It was a stunning offer. Thieu, for the first time in modern Vietnamese history, was offering to turn over the bulk of the government to an opposition leader, one who was adamant about instituting democracy and constitutional law. According to Bong's wife, "his dream was to implement a democratic process in Vietnam...by establishing a political movement with progressive new changes, contrary to the old political parties...whose policies [were to] grab power [solely] for their own parties."[76] She noted that he had always turned down cabinet jobs because "Bong and I had promised ourselves that he should not accept any cabinet position unless he already had a strong political structure." With the PNM winning seats in the Lower House elections, and having established party chapters in most provinces, "Bong thought that it was the ripe time for him to step in, and not be manipulated by different forces."

Bong's appointment as prime minister would hopefully solve a plethora of issues, but it was not to be. Alerted by press reports that Thieu was considering replacing Khiem, the Saigon Party Committee, painfully aware that Bong's prestige and administrative abilities represented a tremendous danger to them, ordered his murder. At 11:50 a.m. on November 10, 1971, as he was leaving his office with his bodyguards to drive to Independence Palace to formally accept the role of prime minister, two assassins on a motorbike tossed an explosive charge under his car. The blast instantly killed the forty-two-year-old Bong and one of his bodyguards.

The murder achieved its purpose. It immediately set off a wave of recriminations. Nguyen Ngoc Huy and Bong's wife accused Khiem of orchestrating the murder. The T4 Committee further directed an "effort...to sow divisions in the enemy's ranks by planting stories in a number of newspapers...that said that 'They are killing each other in a struggle for power and then blaming the Viet Cong for the killings."[77] Finally, in late May 1972, the Saigon police arrested the two terrorists and in June presented them to the press, where they confessed. On September 4, 1973, the Military Field Court sentenced them to life imprisonment.

Bong was the perfect man to reenergize South Vietnam's voyage to democracy. His death represents the least known "what if" in South Vietnam's tortured political history. The people, Bong thought, would overlook Thieu's power grab if the new government showed administrative efficiency. The South Vietnamese were more tired of "corruption, administrative highhandedness, and loss of national sovereignty to the Americans" than Saigon politics.[78] Despite their war-weariness, he believed they remained afraid of a Communist takeover and that proper leadership would rally them. The world, unaware that Thieu intended to broaden his government with Bong, only saw more of the same. In turn, the world set its face against Nguyen Van Thieu, and by extension, South Vietnam, just as it was about to undergo its sternest test.

21

"ONLY A STEP BETWEEN
ME AND DEATH"

*The Easter Offensive and
the Paris Accords*

Behind the shield of U.S. firepower and financial largesse, and despite the tribulations of the previous four years, a fragile Nationalist political consensus emerged. This social agreement among most of the population, that the GVN was the legitimate guardian of the national interest, had permitted Thieu to strengthen and expand the state. But the edifice that Thieu had built remained menaced. Militarily, the People's Army remained a lethal threat, while politically, the main question was no longer a stark choice between the Communists or the Nationalists. Equally crucial was defining an inclusive political structure that resolved the antagonisms between Thieu and the other Nationalist political voices.

As 1972 began, Thieu set an aggressive agenda. He started preparing his country for several major challenges. These included fixing corruption, growing the economy, and completing land reform. More important, since 1969, Thieu had been preparing his country to win an electoral contest against the Communists. This goal accounted for so many of his actions, including attempting to secure a majority presidency, cracking down on dissent, and developing his own political party. His plans, however, were stillborn when Hanoi launched the largest offensive of the war. Early success by the People's Army once more called into question whether a Nationalist government could survive without U.S. assistance, but eventually the offensive was blunted. Peace talks then resumed, resurrecting the fears that had haunted Thieu over the U.S. negotiation strategy. Acrimonious discussions between the allies ensued, but eventually, a peace accord was signed. South Vietnam's golden years, essentially from March 1969 to March 1972, ended with the roar of PAVN artillery.

"THE CRISIS IS UPON US"—PREPARING FOR PEACE

Thieu's first order of business after his inauguration was dealing with venal officials. Corruption was more far-reaching than just crooked province chiefs stealing U.S. supplies and reselling them. Petty bribery was so widespread that people were constantly handing over cash, often called "tea money" or "coffee money," to get even simple paperwork accomplished. To combat corruption, on January 13, 1972, Thieu announced a decree giving Vice President Tran Van Huong the power "to conduct investigations and impose punishments on officials...for corruption, abuse of power, and actions harmful to the national economy and finances."[1] To signal his seriousness, two days later, Thieu fired recently promoted Major General Nguyen Van Toan, the commander of the 2nd ARVN Division. Toan, who had earlier been accused of corruption for smuggling cinnamon bark, was relieved of command for allegedly raping a teenage girl. When Toan was found not guilty, he sued the paper for libel and won, but he was shunted off to command the Armor School.

When many Vietnamese skewered the appointment of the infirm Huong as another empty declaration against corruption, the vice president responded by appointing Major General Nguyen Van Hieu as his deputy. While an average division commander, Hieu's honesty and integrity were unquestioned. Their first target appeared in early January 1972 when Pham Kim Vinh, a respected journalist and former ARVN officer, published an editorial in *Dieu Hau* (Hawk), a popular military magazine. Vinh exposed malfeasance in the Soldier's Mutual Aid and Savings Fund. The fund, enacted in 1968, deducted one hundred piasters monthly from each soldier's pay to provide a pension to injured warriors. The fund had accumulated around $10 million by the end of 1971. Vinh accused the fund's directors, five colonels in the Ministry of Defense, of using the money to create private companies to develop a postwar economic role for the military rather than provide payments to disabled veterans. Vinh scathingly criticized the Defense officials for "squandering" the soldiers' money on these companies.[2]

Vinh's editorial sparked furor among the RVNAF rank and file. Huong recounted that Thieu was "horrified by the situation," and he ordered the contributions stopped and demanded an audit.[3] The president sacked the five colonels, and on April 2, Defense Minister Nguyen Van Vy was placed on leave pending the investigation's results. On July 14, Hieu read his final report on national television. Although Lieutenant General Vy had not stolen any money, Hieu recommended disciplinary action against him and the colonels for failure to responsibly manage the fund. On August 5, Thieu replaced Vy as defense minister with Prime Minister Khiem. The fund's assets were sold, and the money was returned to the soldiers. Since Thieu had acted against corruption, Bunker once more pleaded with the president to provide "moral leadership." When Thieu did nothing further, a disappointed ambassador admitted that "no forthright position or effective action has been taken by Thieu."[4] The president remained hesitant to overly provoke the military, and corruption would remain a simmering issue, one that would explode in two years.

Although corruption probes garnered headlines, economic policy remained equally critical and equally ignored by the press. GVN economic leaders confronted difficult competing choices. They had to craft a fiscal policy that dampened inflation while simultaneously spending government funds to build new industries. At the same time, they faced a grim combination of reduced aid and great reluctance by the private sector to invest in major projects. Worse, macroeconomic trends were working at cross-purposes. Imports had boomed during the first quarter of 1972, sharply expanding the money supply. More cash in circulation always heralded a price spike. Concurrently, the U.S. drawdown had triggered high unemployment, while every year two hundred thousand new people joined the work force. To provide jobs for them and thousands of demobilized soldiers if peace came, Saigon needed to develop modern industries. Agriculture could not absorb everyone. It was a nearly impossible task in peacetime, let alone for a country at war.

Meanwhile, Thieu was carefully preparing for future electoral contests. While the PNM, Revolutionary Dai Viets, An Quang Buddhists, and Farmer-Worker Party had captured seats in the assembly, none had developed the organizational strength to successfully compete nationally. How then to achieve the goal of a powerful Nationalist political organization? Phan Quang Dan had earlier proposed the establishment of a government party. More recently, Thieu's brother and senior Dai Viet leader Nguyen Van Kieu had argued for "an organization built largely around certain existing moderate parties that could eventually become a vehicle for mass political participation," essentially a repeat of the failed Front experiments.[5] Labor leader Tran Quoc Buu states that Kieu had approached them before the 1971 election to discuss "a new political party to be based on CVT and PNM support." However, afterward Buu told U.S. officials that Kieu had moved "away from these earlier proposals" and was instead making "plans for a Democracy Party which resembled Diem's Can Lao organization."[6]

Hoang Duc Nha disputes Buu's assertations. He maintains that Thieu had again "enlisted Buu to be the point person to discuss this matter with the other political parties because [Thieu] got nowhere in his talks with the leaders of the key parties. They were suspicious about his intentions and did not want to put away their differences for the good of the nation."[7] Nha claims that Thieu decided to attempt to create a government party only after Buu failed to enlist the other parties.

While true, there were also other reasons. The triumphant presidential campaign had convinced Thieu that only the government apparatus could fully mobilize the population to win a political struggle. According to Nguyen Van Ngan, "Thieu decided to form a ruling party, but [it] would only be officially announced following the 1971 presidential election." The main purpose of the new party was "a way of dealing with the U.S. effort to end the war [by making] the governmental apparatus more effective in organizing the population."[8] The president saw a government party that gave him a solid electoral majority as a firewall against Communist demands that he resign, any U.S. plots to remove him, and future contests against the PRG.

Ngan quietly received a permit from the Interior Ministry on October 5, 1971, to conduct organizational and recruitment activity for a Democracy Party (DP) (*Dan Chu*). Thieu's initial plan was for Khiem to head the Democracy Party "so that Khiem could run for the Presidency in 1975. This was part of a plan to make sure that the Republic of Vietnam would be ready for the general elections that would inevitably be organized as part of an agreement to restore peace in Vietnam."[9] Thieu, however, soon changed his mind about Khiem leading the DP. In late February 1972, the first news reports surfaced about the party, but they also claimed that Thieu might amend the constitution to permit a third term.[10] The backlash against this obvious trial balloon was instant, and Thieu denied any plans for a third term. Like the cagey politician he was, the president was not telling the whole truth. He had simply decided to shelve a decision on a third term.

Although the Easter Offensive halted recruitment, by November 1972, most government officials had joined. Several prominent politicians from other parties also quickly defected to the new party. One was Senator Nguyen Van Ngai, a longtime member of the Revolutionary Dai Viets. He realized that "with the American withdrawal [we] must close ranks [and] unite behind our leader. The crisis is upon us."[11] Another was Tran Van Don. In November 1971, he had met with Thieu and offered to help him "organize a new government party." Don now fully supported Thieu, having concluded that Big Minh was "hopeless" while Ky is "temperamental and only works in spurts." Thieu, on the hand, was "well-organized…has learned a great deal about the country's problems, and he works hard."[12] Don also halted his sniping at Thieu for another reason. His younger brother was the press officer of the GVN delegation in Paris, and he told Don that the Communists "were exploiting my previous statements critical of the Thieu government in their presentations to the conference. For that reason, I stopped criticizing and opposing the government."[13] Don was now a full member of the "if you can't beat them, join them" club.

While Thieu was developing a tightly controlled statist party to defeat the PRG, pacification still topped his policy agenda. The pacification effort in 1971, which ended in February 1972, had produced excellent results. HES statistics indicated that most of the population now lived in relative security. The increased protection was the result of the "improved performance of the territorial forces" alongside the PSDF, Phoenix, and local police. Four million unpaid volunteers worked in the PSDF, while almost thirty-two thousand police manned the villages. Four years earlier, there had been neither. Lightly armed volunteers, though, were designed to defeat guerrillas and local cadres, not well-armed main force battalions.

Although the PSDF provided at best adequate security and the RF/PF remained the classic "work in progress," the HES statistics were not just wishful thinking. The national PAAS survey of Vietnamese indicated that 90 percent of those polled in December 1971 thought that security had greatly improved. Roughly 46 percent attributed this to better performance by the RF/PF, while another 37 percent claimed it was from decreased enemy effectiveness. Many thought that either there were no local Communist cadres in their area or that the number was greatly reduced. Around 62 percent said the enemy was unable to recruit new members or could only do so with great difficulty. Only taxation by the Communists still occasionally happened at night.[14] In short, the Communist rural presence was weak, one of Hanoi's main reasons for launching an offensive.

Other areas also showed remarkable progress. Refugee numbers had been greatly reduced, with over 300,000 people returned to their original homes and another 110,000 resettled elsewhere. Almost ten thousand homes, had been built for disabled veterans, while land reform had provided titles to another million acres of land.[15] While the majority still used animals to plow, 32 percent now had a tractor, an incredible improvement from prior years. Land Reform and Village Self-Help projects had progressed so well that the RD program was being transformed. Thousands of RD cadres had transferred to become village police or now worked on the local committees. Since its inception, the RD program had achieved mixed success, but the cadres had led the effort to improve GVN assistance in the countryside. Some 3,500 had died to support that endeavor.[16]

Judging pacification overall, however, was difficult since no province symbolized Vietnam as a whole. Each region had unique features that prevented a general characterization. For example, the Delta boasted 82 percent secure villages at the end of 1971. By comparison, HES showed that only 62 percent of the population along the coast from Quang Tri to Phu Yen Province were in relatively secure hamlets, a step down from secure on the HES scorecard. Much of the lower HES results in this area were due to two factors: parts of the coastal lowland had been under Communist control for years. An exhaustive postwar study of Binh Dinh concluded that despite one of the most innovative American pacification efforts in the country, the resilient Communists had maintained some of their local infrastructure.[17] The second key was the proximity of main force PAVN units. Without the constant sweep operations of American units, which had pushed the PAVN deep into the sparsely populated highlands, the Communists had returned to threaten the lowlands once more.

STILL SEARCHING FOR PEACE

Fearing a repeat of Lyndon Johnson's 1968 "October surprise," Thieu carefully monitored the forthcoming U.S. presidential election for signs of a sudden peace agreement. At a September 16, 1971, press conference, he stated that "one must not expect real progress in Paris. However, I am not against a compromise settlement. I am ready to pay a good price for a good peace." Thieu saw no sign that Hanoi was interested in an electoral compromise, not until after a final battlefield conflict. Eventually, though, the PRG would demand a general election. Foreshadowing his Democracy Party, "it is for this reason that we must be politically strong."[18]

Several days later, Nixon aide Alexander Haig visited Saigon to discuss a new U.S. peace proposal. He asked Thieu to resign one month before an election, a partial acceptance of Madame Binh's demand.[19] The request left Thieu "deeply humiliated," but he did not protest so as not to be seen "as an obstacle to peace."[20] Looking back, Kissinger remarked that "our strategy was either [of] us could make peace, [but the Nixon administration needed to] show movement to calm U.S. domestic concerns. Asking him to resign was a shade too clever. . . . It was a bad move by us telling the head of a foreign government to resign."[21]

When the U.S. then sought to meet privately with the North Vietnamese to discuss the new plan, Hanoi declined. To force Hanoi's hand and to head off potential opposition when Congress reconvened, Nixon decided to reveal the secret talks between the two sides. In early January 1972, Bunker informed Thieu of Nixon's decision. Thieu reacted with anger that he had not been consulted, and he demanded time to review Nixon's proposal. Although Bunker and Thieu's intelligence officer in Paris had kept the president aware of the secret talks between Kissinger and Le Duc Tho, Nha stressed that "this was the first time we knew the details of Kissinger's secret meetings with the North Vietnamese."[22] Thieu responded to Bunker that there were "a great many problems besides the issue of elections that I had not known about previously. If Nixon sticks to his intention to announce [this proposal] I cannot possibly jointly issue this text."[23] Bunker finally convinced him, but the president's dogged resistance presaged his response later that year when the peace accords were close to complete.[24]

On January 25, Nixon spoke to America. He revealed the secret talks, asked Hanoi for an immediate ceasefire and release of prisoners, and offered Thieu's resignation one month before internationally supervised elections that would include the PRG. In a radio address shortly after Nixon finished, Thieu restated Nixon's points, exclaiming that "I am always willing to sacrifice my personal interests for the great interests of the country and the people."[25] He again demanded that the PRG renounce violence before a vote.

Writing to Nixon, Thieu hoped that his agreement to resign and allow "the other side to participate" in an election would be "tangible evidence of my genuine desire for peace." Repeating his long-stated points, he penned that "on the basis of our experiences with Communist expansionism, I believe the ability of the RVN to defend itself is the key to a lasting peace [and not] a signed peace agreement with the Communists." Thieu noted that peace required effective guarantees but that creating them may be difficult "in view of the prevailing psychological and political climate in the free countries."[26] It was his subtle way of asking Nixon about a future U.S. military reaction when, not if, Hanoi broke the peace agreement. The recent announcement that the U.S. was reducing its manpower in South Korea by twenty thousand and withdrawing its troops from Taiwan after the U.N. had voted to remove the country from the organization had raised doubts about U.S. intentions.

After Nixon's speech, Bui Diem spent two weeks canvassing U.S. officials and monitoring the American press. His conclusion was bleak. He warned Thieu that "after revelation of the secret talks, the issue of Vietnam is stripped of illusion [and] is reduced to its basic alternatives. Which means that the problem is no more about withdrawal of troops but about the support to the GVN." He remarked that while Nixon remained committed, "the Democratic [presidential] candidates almost without exception are now calling for an end to the war even if that would lead to a Communist victory in a distant future."[27]

A distraught Bui Diem asked again for reassignment. In late February 1972, Nha informed him that Thieu had accepted his resignation. He would be replaced by a veteran diplomat, Tran Kim Phuong. Nha dismissed the idea that Bui Diem's old ties to Nguyen Cao Ky had played a role. Thieu instead wanted a new voice in the U.S., someone who could give the GVN "sensible advice" since they were "going into a delicate phase."[28] The U.S. embassy considered Phuong "by far the most able" GVN Foreign Service Officer.[29] The GVN Senate confirmed the new ambassador's appointment on May 10, and he arrived in Washington in mid-June. After five frantic years in Washington fighting for his country, an exhausted Bui Diem took a long vacation, finally returning to Saigon in August. However, he was not finished serving his nation.

After Nixon's speech, Bunker sent the president his predictions for 1972. He observed that the "consequences of our endeavors for many years in Vietnam will be on trial this year and next. We shall be navigating a narrow and dangerous strait between the enemy's still formidable capabilities and the political pressures in the U.S." Yet the ever-optimistic ambassador believed "we can draw encouragement from the advances made in 1971" by the South Vietnamese. They have "willingly shouldered the burden," but the American task "will be to retain the determination to stay the course and continue providing the essential support that will enable the Vietnamese to survive the coming tests."[30] Bunker's intuition was painfully correct. Since Tet '68, the Communists had been the hunted, and the allies the hunter. That was about to change.

HANOI STRIKES

The South Vietnamese called Hanoi's 1972 invasion the Summer of Fire (*Mua he do lua*). The Americans nicknamed it the Easter Offensive. Hanoi codenamed it "Nguyen Hue," the birth name of Emperor Quang Trung, the revered Vietnamese king who had defeated a Chinese army in 1789 and freed the country from Chinese domination.

The Politburo's goals were to destroy pacification, inflict a significant defeat on the RVNAF, and thereby force major concessions in Paris. On the eve of the offensive, Le Duc Tho, Politburo member and Hanoi's chief negotiator in Paris, provided his rationale for the offensive to the southern commanders. Tho and his brethren in the Politburo willfully ignored Saigon's achievements; they only saw South Vietnam's burdens. Economically, South Vietnam's "situation continues to deteriorate and there is nothing that can remedy that, no matter what kind of economic measures the enemy takes."[31] Militarily, he believed Vietnamization had failed, the withdrawal of U.S. forces had crushed South Vietnamese morale, and the loss of American firepower had left the RVNAF quantitatively weaker. Politically, "internal contradictions within the enemy camp are becoming increasingly serious." He viewed the airing of South Vietnamese political differences not as democracy's typical friction but as a sign the Nationalists were weak and in disarray, Thieu's precise reason for detesting dissent.

Tho also believed the American will to prosecute the war was flagging due to domestic turmoil from antiwar protesters. Although Nixon had attempted to pressure Hanoi through the Soviet Union and China, it would not work. In fact, Tho reported, Nixon's trip to China had presented them "no problems." Clearly, he stated, "we are in a posture of victory, we have the initiative, and we are on the rise, while the enemy is in a posture of defeat, he is passive and on the defensive, and he is on the decline. We have great prospects for winning a great victory."

It was Marxist dogma grafted onto Vietnamese circumstances. As it had in 1965 and 1968, the Politburo had convinced itself that Saigon would fold under the weight of a military assault and political agitation in the cities. Tho also informed the French Communist Party of another key Politburo goal: removing Thieu. The Politburo viewed Thieu both as the glue binding South Vietnam together and as the litmus test of U.S. resolve. Once PAVN forces surrounded Saigon,

> the political cadres, with the foreign press, will be able to bring the population...in favor of Hanoi [to] achieve Thieu's departure. He, and he alone, stands in the way of the implementation of our plans, which have not changed since 1945. We will reach our goals only by setting up another government in Saigon. All the rest only work toward this end. Thieu was responsible for Vietnamization. Without him, it will fall apart immediately....In addition, this is a test for us against the Americans. Through our demands, we know how much longer Nixon will support him. As soon as he drops him, we will have won.[32]

After months of preparation, the High Command decided to hurl most of its army against South Vietnam. This was Hanoi's third major military blitz to topple the GVN. First was the dispatch of a PAVN division to northern Central Highlands in late 1964 and early 1965 and the subsequent effort to cut South Vietnam in half. American troops had blunted that effort. Next was the 1968 Tet Offensive, which had resulted in a spectacular defeat and four years of retrenchment.

As Tho had articulated, they were convinced that this time would be different. Rather than using local force units to capture the GVN centers of power in the cities, the PAVN would instead send main force units to retake the countryside and defeat the South Vietnamese military. Soviet and Chinese aid had transformed the People's Army from light infantry into a combined arms dynamo. The initial assault would be made on three fronts by nine infantry divisions backed by hundreds of armored vehicles and heavy artillery. They would attack northern I Corps, the northern part of the Central Highlands, and from Cambodia along Route 13 leading to Tay Ninh Province and then to Saigon.[33] Eventually, fourteen infantry divisions would be engaged in South Vietnam, but General Vo Nguyen Giap kept some units in Laos, Cambodia, and at home.

On March 30, 1972, three infantry divisions attacked through the Demilitarized Zone (DMZ) and from Laos. Fortunately for Saigon, Hanoi had to launch its offensive from its redoubts across the border, giving the ARVN some defensive depth, space that would prove critical. The recently formed 3rd ARVN Division—pieced together from deserters, castoffs, and new recruits—guarded the DMZ. Two Vietnamese Marine brigades held the western approaches from Laos. Given Thieu's policy not to cede any territory, Lieutenant General Lam continued to occupy a string of American-built firebases close to the DMZ to defend the narrow plain between the mountains and the sea. After pounding the firebases with artillery, the PAVN launched infantry and armor assaults and quickly cracked the thin protective shield. Within days, the 3rd Division was in flight, and its 56th Regiment had surrendered. The division's retreat exposed the Marines' rear area and forced them to retreat. Approximately one hundred thousand refugees fled to the provincial capital, Quang Tri City.

When the PAVN halted to resupply, the South Vietnamese formed a hasty defensive line around Quang Tri City. Backed by devastating U.S. air and naval bombardment, the South Vietnamese held for the remainder of April, but continued enemy pressure forced the 3rd ARVN to abandon the city on May 1, the first provincial capital to fall into enemy hands since the French war. The retreat quickly turned into a disorganized stampede, and Thieu ordered the division commander arrested. Hue was the next city south on Route 1. When PAVN forces captured two firebases defending the city's western approaches and some ARVN looters set fire to the central market, the former imperial capital dissolved into panic. Fearing another Communist massacre, two hundred thousand people streamed out of the city. CORDS estimated that "two-thirds of Hue" departed for Danang sixty miles away.[34] Huge traffic jams snarled Route 1 and the critical Hai Van Pass between the two cities. Public services in Danang were quickly overwhelmed as the refugees doubled the city's population.

In the northern Central Highlands, PAVN troops routed the 22nd ARVN Division at Tan Canh and surrounded the city of Kontum. The 23rd ARVN Division, commanded by Colonel Ly Tong Ba, the armor officer who had led the assault at Ap Bac and against Diem's palace, was hastily pulled from the southern Central Highlands and ordered to hold Kontum. In III Corps, PAVN armor and infantry poured out of Cambodia, captured the district town of Loc Ninh in South Vietnam, and surrounded the 5th ARVN Division and local provincial forces and Rangers in the provincial capital of An Loc. By the beginning of May, two ARVN divisions had been destroyed (the 3rd and the 22nd), two were surrounded (the 5th and the

23rd), two were under heavy pressure in I Corps (the 1st and 2nd), and the elite Airborne, Marine, and Rangers had been bloodied. Over half of South Vietnam's ground forces were facing potential defeat.

Many South Vietnamese leaders quickly blamed Thieu for the battlefield reversals. RDV leader Ha Thuc Ky specifically criticized the president for "not making much effort to rally any of the Nationalist elements."[35] He was right. Though Thieu had spoken on the radio, he did not make his first public appearance until April 24. Instead of visibly leading the country to resist the invader, he had stayed in his office trying to manage the situation. He refused to embrace old antagonists like Nguyen Cao Ky, General Minh, or the An Quang Buddhists, fearing that such a gesture might provide political prestige for his rivals. Like Diem, Thieu saw them as usurpers rather than allies joining him to form a stronger government to fight the Communists. He squandered an opportunity to turn the national unity that arose in the days after the attack, similar to what had happened after the Tet Offensive, into the anti-communist political force he so desperately sought.

The former vice president also censured Thieu's leadership. At the start of the offensive, Ky had immediately flown to I Corps and II Corps to inspect the situation. For all his faults, Ky always ran toward the sound of the guns. He was intent on bolstering Vietnamese Air Force morale as he considered air power the key support to ARVN fighting spirit. Unaccustomed to conventional warfare, Ky claimed, the troops were wilting under "intensive artillery barrages [and] tanks and the 'fury' of the NVA attackers."[36]

Thieu, though, was not cowering in his office. If Ky was the hare, impulsive and excitable, Thieu was the turtle, slow and methodical. Temperamentally, Thieu was incapable of quick, decisive action, but the fall of Quang Tri City forced his hand. He decided to replace both Hoang Xuan Lam and Ngo Dzu. He summoned Major General Ngo Quang Truong from the Delta on May 3 and ordered him to take over I Corps. Thieu's military attaché, Major Nguyen Xuan Tam, recalls that shortly after Truong arrived in Danang, he called the palace to discuss how 3rd Division deserters were looting Hue. Tam says that Thieu "told Truong to shoot a couple of the trouble-makers, and Thieu would take responsibility."[37] Backed by Thieu, Truong ordered the military police to round up deserters and shoot anyone on the spot who resisted. He demanded all civil servants return to their posts, brought in trusted subordinate Brigadier General Nguyen Duy Hinh to rebuild the demoralized 3rd, and promised on local television and radio to hold Hue. Truong's forceful leadership and sterling reputation in the area and some timely reinforcements instantly put starch into the units in I Corps.

On May 10, Thieu replaced Ngo Dzu with Major General Toan, whom he had just fired as 2nd Division commander. Despite Toan's unsavory reputation, he was cut from the same cloth as Do Cao Tri. Both were excessively corrupt womanizers yet tough, hard-fighting soldiers. Thieu also replaced the old guard Airborne and Marine division commanders with younger, U.S.-trained leaders. After years as power brokers, Lieutenant Generals Le Nguyen Khang and Hoang Xuan Lam now just commanded empty desks at the JGS. Thieu also ordered "all government employees" and the PSDF to "defend the locations where they work without the use of RF/PF" and assist with refugee care. To that end, all government employees were told to remain at their jobs all day and night. "Stern disciplinary measures" were to be taken against any civil servants who fled, including trial in a military court.[38]

Thieu also told General Cao Van Vien to hold Quang Tri Province, Kontum, and An Loc "at all costs" because the "political and psychological repercussions of losing them would have destroyed South Vietnam." Losing Quang Tri would have unhinged Hue and Danang. Defeat at Kontum would have destroyed morale and made it "impossible to [defend] Pleiku or Binh Dinh."[39] Surrendering An Loc would have opened the gates to Saigon. Thieu believed that Hanoi wanted to seize Quang Tri and Thua Thien provinces, Kontum, and An Loc. Then it would accept Nixon's call for a ceasefire and demand a coalition. Given the American presidential campaign, he feared that the U.S. would agree, leaving South Vietnam in a gravely weakened position. This was Thieu's political reason for ordering Vien to hold these areas at all costs.

Stunned that the civilian population had fled instead of welcoming them as liberators, Hanoi's legions committed several horrific war crimes. The most well known was against fleeing civilians on Route 1 between Quang Tri City and Hue. U.S. advisors with a Vietnamese Marine brigade witnessed deliberate acts of carnage. On April 24, one advisor watched enemy troops rake a vehicular column "with small arms fire and artillery barrages which blew the convoy to pieces, littering the road and the fields surrounding with bodies of women, and old men, and children." Five days later, he saw PAVN artillery target thousands of civilians moving south on Route 1. He described it as "the worst sight I have even seen. The refugees were primarily small children and elderly... There were no weapons or ARVN in this exodus. The refugees packed the road shoulder to shoulder in a slowly moving mass," which stretched for four miles. The PAVN began firing 130mm shells with variable-timed fuses designed to explode above and rain shrapnel onto exposed troops. The airbursts "literally shredded to pieces the old people and their small charges.... The [PAVN] knew what they were doing. They had forward observers who were probably within a couple of hundred yards of the refugees.... This was just criminal slaughter of the old and the weak."[40] The PAVN fired hundreds of shells at the moving column, probably killing several thousand. When two South Vietnamese journalists were finally able to reach the area on July 1, they found decomposing bodies still strewn on the ground. They labeled that section of road the "Highway of Horror" (*Dai Lo Kinh Hoang*).[41]

On May 1, Abrams cabled the president that the enemy had broken through ARVN lines in I Corps and that the situation was grim. Hence on May 8, Nixon ordered Haiphong harbor mined to prevent further supplies from entering North Vietnam, and he increased the bombing to disrupt rail communications. He also repeated his call for an internationally supervised ceasefire followed by elections. South Vietnamese morale instantly soared; people were convinced that America would not abandon them.

Luckily for the allies, the People's Army was no juggernaut. By the end of May, dogged ARVN defenders, poor PAVN logistics, and relentless U.S. air strikes had turned the tide on all three fronts.[42] The High Command had made a terrible mistake. Once the initial assaults against Kontum and An Loc had failed, instead of bypassing them and striking less well-guarded areas, the PAVN commanders had massed their troops to capture them. Like Thieu, they believed that seizing these towns would destroy South Vietnamese morale. Yet massing provided easy targets for American bombers, which killed them by the thousands. How many, however, is unknown. The Communists have not released any casualty figures from the offensive.

These defeats exposed PAVN's chief failings: limited air defenses south of northern I Corps, terrible combined arms coordination, and pitiful command and staff tactical acumen. The PAVN lost hundreds of armored vehicles by attacking with poor infantry support and no air defense. Under sustained bombing, its logistic columns could not adequately supply its much larger formations, while inflexible battlefield tactics prevented it from exploiting ARVN defensive gaps. In 1972, the PAVN could not efficiently conduct modern warfare.

The ARVN and RF/PF also had issues. Leadership remained problematic, supply was unduly dependent on the U.S., and combat performance was mixed. Although the Vietnamese Air Force and Navy performed well, some ground units fought hard while others collapsed. For example, the RF in Binh Dinh bolted at the first sight of enemy units, but when three PAVN regiments probed Hau Nghia Province in III Corps to directly threaten Saigon's western defenses, the RF fiercely battled the main force regulars to a standstill and inflicted heavy casualties. In a province formerly infested with Communists, pacification in Hau Nghia had mostly succeeded.[43] As Truong Nhu Tang recounted, while Phoenix in other places was often "lackluster and ham-handed," in Hau Nghia, "the Front infrastructure was virtually eliminated."[44] While the collapse in Binh Dinh was a disaster, the RF defense of Hau Nghia was one of the most unheralded South Vietnamese victories of 1972.

The offensive forced Thieu to replace many unit commanders with those of proven fighting ability. Colonel Pham Duy Tat, the Special Forces officer who had almost stopped the Diem coup in November 1963, had transferred to the Rangers in 1970. For the last several years, he had commanded the Ranger units in IV Corps and was responsible for guarding the Cambodian border in IV Corps. In May 1972, he was sent to Pleiku to command the II Corps Rangers. His first mission in June was to break the siege of Kontum by clearing Route 14, the road between Pleiku and Kontum. As his units advanced, he drove a jeep to the top of Chu Pao Pass, the key terrain feature between the two cities. When he stopped and got out, an enemy soldier jumped up from behind a bush. Instead of killing Tat, the PAVN soldier simply ran away. A thought from Tat's youthful Bible study flashed into his head: "Yet as surely as the Lord lives and as you live, there is only a step between me and death."[45]

Much like his country, Tat had avoided the reaper's grasp. Saigon had survived Hanoi's knockout punch as much from allied resolution as PAVN ineptitude. Still, the People's Army would remain permanently encamped in South Vietnam, and the fall of Quang Tri City set in motion a series of events that would never be undone.

MARTIAL LAW, DECREE POWER, AND PLANNING FOR A CEASEFIRE

With South Vietnam facing defeat, in early May, Thieu made two moves he considered crucial to save his country. First, he would declare martial law. Second, rather than seize power, he would ask the assembly to grant him decree power for six months so that he could act rapidly to solve the current crisis. Although he hoped this would strengthen national resistance, in many ways his actions were a repeat of the demands made by Ky and the other generals in May 1968 for him to eliminate the assembly and rule by decree. Both were periods of intense enemy military pressure, but Thieu had resisted the urge to rule as a dictator even as Saigon faced severe tests.

Thieu spoke on television and radio on May 9. He asked that normal politics and opposition to his government be set aside due to the Communist offensive. The next day, his office declared martial law, effective at midnight. Meeting with Bunker, Thieu summarized that he would act in three areas: recruitment of new manpower, economic reforms, and mobilization of popular support. These actions included expanding the draft for males between the ages of seventeen to forty-three, closing the universities, and banning strikes and demonstrations. Thieu needed manpower to replenish his army's ranks. Official GVN statistics claimed that in April and May it had lost approximately twelve thousand killed, thirty-four thousand wounded, and fifteen thousand missing, with another twelve thousand deserted.

Economically, the offensive had triggered a severe recession and devastated Pham Kim Ngoc's economic plans. The financial debacles from the attack were staggering. Several major cities were in ruins, the destruction of physical infrastructure in the countryside was significant, and the offensive had suddenly put almost a million refugees and thousands of wounded soldiers onto government rolls. Heavy GVN spending to care for the refugees and wounded and repair the damage would inevitably lead to the same issues Ngoc had fought since 1969: higher inflation and a massive budget deficit. These blows would hit government coffers just as revenue had been drastically reduced from diminished U.S. in-country purchases, a lower piaster rate, and reduced imports. Ngoc begged for more U.S. aid. "I hope that Congress won't wield the axe," he said. "We have a case for the aid on the basis of human needs alone."[46] Among a variety of measures to raise money, Ngoc increased taxes on consumer goods like beer and offered low interest war bonds.

Thieu wanted to rapidly address these issues, but he also desired to retain a semblance of democracy. Rather than seize power, he quietly asked his Lower House supporters to petition him to assume full control. On May 14, the Lower House approved a bill granting Thieu unlimited decree power for six months. It was then forwarded to the Senate for confirmation. Although the Senate was usually the more pro-government of the two bodies, the bill ran into stiff opposition from that chamber. Thieu then made a mistake. After the one-man election, many senators were suspicious of his motives. When the Senate asked to modify the bill, he rejected any compromise. Thieu professed that he only wanted a unified display of support by the assembly. The CIA recorded him telling a visitor that "he had asked the Deputies and Senators if they wanted him to fail in the struggle against the enemy and lose the entire fatherland. He had explained to them that all he wanted to do was combat the Communists and that he needed the power to do so. During this difficult period, he needed...all the...parties, and the people 'standing behind him.'"[47]

Neither side convinced the other, and on June 2, the Senate rejected the bill. In a surprising move, the Catholics had allied with An Quang to defeat it. While both blocs feared a presidential power grab, other motives also interfered. An Quang thought Thieu was leading the country to defeat, while the Catholics dreaded allowing him unchecked economic power to pursue higher taxes on the monied classes.

With the Senate's veto, Thieu now needed to modify the bill since he did not have a two-thirds majority in the House to override it. A key player in convincing the House to redraft the bill was Tran Van Don. Thieu was cashing in on Don's promise to help, and the former general came through for him. After bitter debate, on June 10, the House sent to the Senate a modified bill limiting Thieu's powers to security, defense, finance, and the economy. The embassy noted that "Don had lobbied effectively for passage [which] Thieu evidently regarded as most important."[48]

Thieu, seeking to appease his detractors, sent a letter to Senate Chairman Nguyen Van Huyen promising that he would not eliminate the constitution or become dictatorial. When Huyen demurred, Thieu dispatched his legislative aide Ngan to engage in some chicanery. When Huyen failed to call a vote on the bill on June 27 and then left the building, pro-Thieu senators held a rump session without any opposition senators present and passed the bill by a vote of 26 to 0. Huyen declared it illegal, but Thieu ignored him and signed the legislation the next day. If Thieu sought Nationalist unity, this was precisely the way not to achieve it. While he had again resisted a dictatorial impulse, democracy had been set aside in the face of an enemy onslaught.

Thieu immediately began issuing decrees to institute a "more rational

manpower policy, sweeping tax reform [and] tightened controls over potentially subversive activities."[49] Economically, on July 8, he eliminated the
parallel market that Ngoc had formed in October 1970 and devalued the
piaster to 425 to the dollar. Ngoc also began drafting legislation for new
and surely unpopular income and property taxes. He had no choice. By the
end of July, costs from the offensive were estimated at 36 billion piasters.

Concurrently, Thieu intended to cut government expenses by reducing
head count in the countryside. Earlier in February, he had informed his
province chiefs that he planned to streamline the bureaucracy "from the
central to the local level."[50] He was also under pressure from the province
chiefs to permit them to directly appoint hamlet chiefs instead of holding
elections. They complained that many hamlet chiefs were incompetent or
would not submit to their control. When Bunker cautioned Thieu that
hamlet elections had proven popular, the president agreed. He was reluctant
to approve the change since that would be considered "anti-democratic."[51]

The offensive apparently changed his mind. On August 22, Prime Minister Khiem signed a decree repealing crucial Decree 198, the key legislation
that had authorized village and hamlet elections and set South Vietnam on
the path to democracy. The new decree enabled province chiefs to appoint
hamlet leaders and lowered the number of seats on the local councils, mainly
to "reduce expenditures and increase efficiency . . . and unify the chain of
command."[52] Thieu justified his actions by stating that the constitution
appointed the village, not the hamlet, as the lowest government echelon.
While true, the embassy believed he also wanted to exercise "tighter control
over the performance of [local] officials [plus] a desire to put people in key
positions in case a future ceasefire ushers in political competition with the
Communists."[53]

While Thieu's economic plans were rational, his comment about tightening "controls over subversive activities" proved foreboding. The offensive, the long and frustrating refusal of Hanoi to discuss peace, his failure
to rally the political class behind him, and a potential U.S. abandonment
had exacerbated the president's worst instincts. His plans would send him
down a dark path.

THE X-18 PLAN

After Nixon's January 25 speech offering a ceasefire, Thieu's perennial fears
that the U.S. would impose a coalition resurfaced. Believing he would face

a life-or-death struggle after the U.S. departed, Thieu ordered the drafting of plans that would increase the scrutiny and arrest of anyone suspected of being a Communist sympathizer. The offensive turned those plans into reality. On April 12, he signed a decree transferring all Phoenix activities to the National Police.[54] The police Special Branch immediately launched a national campaign to disrupt any local support for Communist military units by rounding up those suspected of Communist activity.

Since most Phoenix detainees were low-level and the new regulations that Khiem had instituted had forced the province security councils to release many captives for lack of evidence, on April 15, the Joint General Staff took an extra step. The JGS sent the top-secret X-18 Plan to the corps commanders and province chiefs providing instructions for actions to be taken just before and after an armistice. This was Saigon's first effort to create a coordinated response to various ceasefire contingencies. The directive ordered the military to showcase GVN territorial claims and protect government installations. While the plan was intended to marshal resources to defend the population, it contained a more menacing component. To counter enemy efforts after the ceasefire to "undermine and overthrow our government," and unencumbered by American moral sensibilities, the X-18 Plan ordered the provinces to "designate secret organizations or individuals to carry out special missions (such as assassinations of important enemy cadres) when necessary."[55]

Since no ceasefire materialized to implement the X-18 Plan, Thieu used his martial law power on May 18 to authorize the province chiefs to detain anyone they considered dangerous to national security. The Special Branch then reduced the Phoenix arrest criteria from three adverse reports against a person to one. Thousands more were arrested. In Thua Thien Province, Police Major Lien Thanh grabbed around 1,500 people that he believed were enemy adherents.[56] The press began reporting the mass seizures but noted that the GVN was "silent about the scope of the arrests," which included "house-to-house searches" in Saigon.[57] Thieu hinted in June at the plan's design when he admitted that the "elimination of Communist cadres is one of the government's duties" but that cases of abuse would be "appropriately punished."[58]

In late June, the Interior Ministry additionally ordered the provinces to reexamine the files of all convicted Communists who had completed their jail terms, rearrest them if necessary, and extend the sentences of all high-level prisoners indefinitely. In August, as the peace talks heated up,

Thieu ordered further planning regarding the military aspects of a ceasefire. Nha reviewed the X-18 plan but rejected it as too vague, and the plan was dropped.[59]

At the same time, Thieu exercised a heavy hand against his last detractors, the Vietnamese press. On August 4, he signed one of his most controversial decrees. He reregulated the press by requiring that each publisher submit a bond to guarantee payment of any court fines for libel and authorized the Interior Minister to shut down any paper suspended twice for "national security" reasons. The Saigon press reacted with fury, but fourteen papers, about half of Saigon's press, paid the deposit and remained open.

Additional ceasefire planning, however, would have to wait until Kissinger and Tho had ironed out the details of a peace plan. In late September, Kissinger again held extensive talks with Tho, and a peace pact seemed to be nearing a conclusion. To compensate, on November 19, 1972, the Interior Ministry ordered all provinces to detain medium- or high-level Communist cadres under criminal charges to prevent them from being released under a peace agreement.

This time, opposition South Vietnamese organizations began publicizing the seizures. Father Chan Tin, who had been arrested the previous year for publishing an article calling for peace talks, was the main proponent. He claimed that the GVN had two hundred thousand political prisoners, a ludicrous figure given that prison capacity was barely thirty-five thousand. The U.S. embassy went into spin mode and dismissed Father Tin's claims, citing that "under the Phoenix program, the total number detained, pending trial, and under investigation was 9,707 as of September 30."[60] Liberation Radio broadcast Father Tin's claims and accused Thieu of terrorizing opposition figures. Hanoi's negotiators in Paris quickly demanded that all detained civilians be released as part of a peace pact.

In hindsight, Thieu had badly overreacted domestically to the offensive, but in April and May, the military situation was decidedly grim. By November, however, that was no longer the case, and in the GVN's efforts to eliminate any Communist, it had swung a very wide broom. "Political prisoners" soon became the cudgel that foreign antiwar protestors would use to bash Saigon, a stick that Thieu had basically handed them. For now, though, peace was nearly at hand. The type of peace Saigon wanted, however, would be much different than the one it would get.

"SAME BED, DIFFERENT DREAMS" – PEACE IS AT HAND

In late June, I Corps Commander Major General Truong launched a counterattack codenamed "Lam Son 72" to retake Quang Tri Province. The Marine and Airborne divisions pushed forward along Route 1 against fierce resistance. A Vietnamese Marine brigade commander described the spectacle: "[T]he sky above Quang Tri was filled with dust and smoke. The noise of bombardments, shelling, and gunfire created a fearsome thunder. The ground literally shook beneath our feet."[61] Truong's units reached the outskirts of Quang Tri City on July 7. Thieu ordered him to retake it. Finally, on September 15, he succeeded, but his exhausted troops stalled at the Thach Han River north of the city.

Just as Le Duan and Thieu had long stated, the battlefield situation would dictate the peace terms. After losing Quang Tri City, Hanoi decided to conclude a peace agreement now and wait until a more opportune time to conquer the south. The Politburo wanted to exploit "the U.S.'s domestic problems" to "force the American government to accept a solution to end the war. Our soldiers...would secure an important victory with this solution by accomplishing our goal of 'fighting to make the Americans go home' so that we could then shift to a new phase in the struggle and continue to advance the cause of the revolution until we secured complete victory."[62]

After recapturing Quang Tri City, Thieu immediately rejected Hanoi's latest peace proposals, particularly one from September 11 offering a three-part coalition that included the PRG and the Third Force. He dismissed the Third Force as South Vietnamese "lackeys [or] opportunistic elements who are living in exile."[63] Bunker warned Thieu over his "increasingly un-compromising tenor" that "can play into the hands of our critics at home and abroad while we are engaged in a very delicate process."[64]

Did a viable Third Force exist, one that provided a political bridge between the Communists and the Nationalists? My answer is no, but one scholar, Sophie Quinn-Judge, disagrees. She confirms that Washington and Thieu's assessment was that the "idea of a neutral South Vietnam...has long been dismissed as a Communist ploy to get the Americans out of Vietnam." In her judgment, though, "the problem for historians to grapple with is that this solution appears to have had considerable appeal" among the South Vietnamese population.[65]

While true that many naturally longed for peace, the contention that a neutral solution held "considerable appeal" is based on anecdotal evidence that often depended on time period, region, and observer bias. The Third Force was a broad spectrum of groups, individuals, and political fancies ranging from An Quang to General Minh to the exile community in Paris to fringe leftists like Ngo Ba Thanh. Even if the GVN and the PRG could agree on the Third Force participants for a coalition, there was no hope that the Third Force could provide the political equilibrium, let alone the military muscle, to force the two violently opposed groups to cooperate. Moreover, the Politburo did in fact view the Third Force as a Trojan horse to abet its dream of overthrowing Thieu rather than an equal governing partner, a policy the anti-communists clearly understood.

Although the president's control of the government rivaled Ngo Dinh Diem's, that domination did not make the other influence centers irrelevant. Thieu sat atop a complex pyramid of competing power nodes ranging from the military to the religions to the assembly. Each had a voice but not a vote since the final decision rested with him. Yet his vision of peace was shared by the great majority of Nationalists, one that guaranteed the independence of South Vietnam and eliminated the Communist threat. He would not compromise on that goal, nor could he and survive.

In a lengthy and prophetic memo to Kissinger, the CIA's George Carver, who had watched Thieu for more than a decade, offered his opinion on Thieu's thoughts regarding peace. The president, Carver wrote, would approach a peace deal with "considerable skepticism, profound suspicion of Hanoi's motives, and more than a little suspicion of our motives." Thieu believed that Hanoi "would not budge on points of substance unless the Communists were really hurting." The allies "would be foolish to accept Hanoi's first real offers," and they should hold out for more. Thieu's domestic audience would play an important role, since in Vietnam, "political appearances transmute into political reality." Carver analyzed that Thieu's image of "independence vis-à-vis the U.S. is important to his psyche—and essential to his political survival—as his image of strength vis-à-vis the Communists."[66]

Carver was right, but while Thieu was willing to "pay a good price for a good peace," his opponent remained single-minded. Le Duan's decision to forge peace was simply to get the U.S. out, and he would not budge on removing his troops from the south. "The achievement of these two requirements," he said, "would lead to the recognition that, in practical terms, there were in fact two governments, two armies, and two zones of control. This would create a new balance of forces that would be extremely favorable to our side."[67]

With this mindset, in early October, Le Duc Tho switched from his previous obstinate demands and tabled his first compromise peace offer. He dropped the requirement that Thieu resign, but he still demanded a three-sided council that would prepare elections for a new government. The U.S. would get its prisoners back but must cease all bombing and withdraw from Vietnam. Communist troops would remain in South Vietnam.

Kissinger believed that Tho's acceptance of Thieu and the GVN was a major breakthrough, and he left for Saigon to inform Thieu and gain his concurrence for the deal.[68] He arrived in Saigon on October 19 to brief Thieu on the draft agreement. After listening to Kissinger, the president reacted with undisguised anger. Thieu's worst fears had come true: the Americans, in their rush to make an agreement, had foolishly accepted Tho's first offer. The year 1968 was repeating itself. Since 1965, when Phan Huy Quat's government had first articulated Saigon's peace terms, the main priority was the removal of Communist forces. Kissinger's proposed pact would allow enemy troops to remain, the DMZ would not be respected as a border, and the three-sided council was simply a stalking horse for a coalition. Thieu rejected the Kissinger-Tho plan and asked for significant changes to the draft agreement. After Kissinger informed Nixon, the president agreed to have him discuss these modifications with Le Duc Tho, but he warned Thieu that without a peace treaty, the U.S. Congress would most likely cut off aid.

Thieu was determined to hold his ground. Standing in the president's office early on the morning of October 23, Nha recalls that he and Thieu were

> waiting for Kissinger and Bunker [and] the two of us [were] looking out at the Thong Nhut Boulevard and the heavy traffic of cars, scooters, motorbikes, bicycles flowing like the Saigon river itself at this rush hour. President Thieu was silent for like ten minutes during which I stole a few glances at his face to gauge his mood. Finally, he told me 'we cannot let our country fall. Those people outside are happy as they start their day. It is my duty to safeguard our country and ensure that they can have the life they have always wanted and go about their daily chores.'[69]

His country was at war, and "survival first" was his lodestar. After Kissinger departed that day, Thieu met with his cabinet. Although Thieu had stood firm, he knew the "question was how to defend [his] position on peace and obtain popular support…while avoiding public confrontation with the U.S."[70] Fearing that Washington or Hanoi might spin the disastrous meeting and portray Saigon as the obstacle to peace, Nha convinced Thieu to speak to the nation on October 24. Nha wrote the speech and included what became Thieu's signature phrase: "Do not listen to what the Communists say, but watch carefully what the Communists do (*Dung nghe nhung gi Cong San noi ma hay nhin ky nhung gi Cong San lam*)." Thieu added the word *ky* (carefully) to the first draft of the speech.[71] He accurately claimed that Hanoi's proposal was simply a "cunning scheme…to keep their troops in the South to prepare for another offensive in the future." He outlined captured Communist orders that directed postwar attacks on the police and uprisings in towns and the planting of the PRG flag to claim territory. Thieu again demanded a PAVN retreat concurrent with the U.S. withdrawal.[72]

Like in 1968, the Vietnamese public again instantly backed Thieu. On October 30, ten thousand people in Danang "held a rally to support the GVN's position. On November 5, 15,000 Catholics…demonstrated in Saigon to protest the draft agreement."[73] The Lower House passed a resolution supporting Thieu's demands. Even An Quang grudgingly supported the president. Concurrently, he ordered that the cadets at the various military schools be trained on GVN policies and dispatched to the provinces to rally grassroots support for his policy. Five thousand cadets were sent into the country to tell the villagers about Communist military difficulties, the "just and reasonable GVN policies on the ceasefire and peace issues," and to "prevent the people from being fooled by Communist schemes and tricks."[74] Ngoc was told to spend 180 million piasters to purchase 1 million small flags to disburse to the provinces. All houses and buildings under GVN control must display the South Vietnamese flag. Anyone not flying a flag would be considered suspect.

Prime Minister Khiem, however, had begun a slow dance away from the president. For whatever reason, Khiem informed his embassy contacts that regarding peace, "he does not agree with Thieu" on virtually any point. He partially blamed Thieu's opinion on the president's staff and on Vice President Huong, labeling him "very stupid" and saying he "does not understand politics."[75] As the impasse dragged on, Khiem became even more adamant that the GVN should sign the accords on the "cold grounds of logistics alone." Khiem considered U.S. aid far more important than anything Kissinger had negotiated, and he was prepared to completely bend to American demands to maintain that flow. Khiem doubted that Thieu understood the ongoing aid fight between Nixon and the U.S. Congress. Thieu "comes from a very narrow background [and] he has been a soldier all his life" and he thinks Nixon can control Congress.[76] Khiem was an old coup plotter, and what he said had an ominous undertone: Khiem was positioning himself as a replacement should the Americans decide Thieu was blocking peace.

On November 7, Nixon won reelection. Thieu was ecstatic, and he decided to dispatch Nguyen Phu Duc to Washington to speak with him. He hoped to bypass Kissinger and appeal directly to the U.S. president. Thieu trusted Nixon. Conversely, he deeply resented Kissinger. He believed that Kissinger, by negotiating for the GVN, had made him "appear little more than an American puppet." Thus, he wanted Nixon to hear his petition directly rather than through Kissinger or Haig.[77]

Arriving in late November, Duc delivered a long letter from Thieu to Nixon. The missive lambasted Hanoi's intransigence and the "inevitable North Vietnamese duplicity and the essentiality of [a Communist] withdrawal and the inadequacies of the current language on the political solution." The letter laid out his efforts to craft a sustainable peace rather than a hurried rush to the exits by the U.S. that left PAVN troops stationed on South Vietnamese soil. Thieu also demanded an "elimination of the council, and no mention of the PRG in the text."[78]

Nixon reassured Duc that he would "respond with full force should the settlement be violated by North Vietnam and committed the U.S. to continued assistance in the post-settlement period."[79] Regardless, Nixon told Duc, without a peace agreement, Congress would cut off aid once it reconvened in January. While congressional opposition to the war was surging, blaming Congress was also a convenient straw man. By telling the South Vietnamese that they needed to sign before Congress cut them off completely, Nixon hoped to force Thieu's hand.

Duc failed to sway Nixon, and he returned to Saigon on December 3. He briefed Thieu at a meeting of the National Security Council (NSC). After listening to his remarks, Thieu asked him if he should sign. Duc replied that "if we sign the agreement as it is, South Vietnam will be lost." The NSC agreed, and Thieu dug in once more. Fearing his recalcitrance might incite a U.S.-sponsored coup, Thieu began an intensive round of discussions with leading political and military figures "to make the South Vietnamese people and the ARVN generals who might oppose him clearly understand the narrow choice with which South Vietnam was faced."[80] Much like his Democracy Party, his goal was to create strong social support to deter any U.S. plots for a coup.

To prepare for a post-ceasefire world, Thieu issued Decree 20, which amended the An Tri Law allowing for the arrest and detention of suspected Communist suspects. The new decree increased the grounds for detention to include violating "public order," a charge even more elastic than "national security." Since South Vietnam was in a declared state of war, this new decree would give the GVN wide latitude to deal with Communist agitators after a ceasefire.

The recent actions of his Asian allies had given Thieu some of these ideas on governing in a post-ceasefire period. Thieu had kept a close eye on political developments among his Asian neighbors. American détente with China and Russia had caused profound foreign policy changes among Asian countries. Foreign Minister Tran Van Lam summarized the situation, stating that while "there is tendency . . . toward peaceful coexistence with the Communist bloc," many Asian countries had "found it necessary to make their executive branches stronger so as to cope with" Communist subversion. Lam confessed that "this has exerted great influence on the Republic of Vietnam."[81] In Thailand, the military had staged a coup in November 1971 and announced martial law to fight a Communist insurgency. In the Philippines, President Marcos declared martial law on September 23, 1972, after Communist guerrillas attempted to assassinate the defense secretary.

South Korea, as usual, proved key. In 1969, President Park had amended the constitution to allow for a third term. After winning reelection in 1971, he had eliminated most opposition politicians, replaced key army commanders with loyalists, put strict restrictions on the press, and crafted economic policy by decree. On October 17, 1972, Park declared martial law. He suspended part of the constitution and dissolved the National Assembly to "reform the political structure of South Korea." He made the move because the announcement of a potential Vietnam peace treaty had resurrected the old fears of a U.S. retrenchment in the region. Park also justified his actions by explaining that South Korea had "attempted awkwardly to imitate democratic institutions . . . but had never divorced itself from factional strife and political intrigue," a situation akin to South Vietnam's.[82] To strengthen the executive to combat these "issues," Park submitted a new constitution for a popular vote. It won overwhelmingly, and he lifted martial law on December 13.

In early December, Kissinger and Tho resumed negotiations. They were close to a deal when Tho suddenly balked about restricting movement across the DMZ. Fearing such an agreement would do precisely what Thieu wanted—enshrine the DMZ as a national border—Tho refused. He then backtracked on a number of issues. By mid-December, Kissinger broke off the negotiations, and Tho headed back to Hanoi to confer with the Politburo.

With the breakdown, Nixon decided that only military pressure would force Hanoi to resume talking. On December 18, he sent waves of B-52s and hundreds of strike aircraft to pound North Vietnam. The Hanoi-Haiphong area saw the heaviest bombing of the war, and he mined Haiphong harbor again. In what journalists called the Christmas bombing, U.S. pilots inflicted heavy damage in the Hanoi-Haiphong area. U.S. defense officials opined that Hanoi was the "most heavily defended area in the world."[83] In reality, the PAVN had stripped most of its air defenses around the capital and had moved them south to defend its attacking columns. PAVN air defense units were roughly a third of what they had been in 1967 when the U.S. had last bombed Hanoi. The B-52s, attempting to avoid hitting civilian targets, followed the same exact flight paths for the first several nights, allowing the defenders to anticipate their movements. The PAVN fired almost 350 SA-2 missiles at the attacking aircraft, shooting down fifteen B-52s over a period of ten days.

Although Hanoi at first claimed it would not negotiate while under attack, on December 26, a spokesman stated it would resume the talks if the U.S. halted the bombing. When the U.S. accepted, the Politburo crowed that it had broken the back of U.S. military efforts. Declaring that their victory would lead to a peace treaty like the battle of Dien Bien Phu had in 1954, Hanoi's propagandists asserted that they had forced the Americans to cave. The U.S. stated the exact opposite, that the bombing had compelled Hanoi to return to the talks. The true answer remains unknown.

Writing to Kissinger after the Christmas bombing, Bunker opined that by refusing to sign in October, Thieu had strengthened South Vietnam while the Communists had grown weaker. In Bunker's opinion, Nixon had been "patient, lenient, and wise in giving Thieu every opportunity to present his case," but "we have fulfilled our responsibility to Thieu and Vietnam fully and completely. If we can get a reasonable settlement in Paris, I have no doubt that we should move ahead." Only when confronted by an adamant U.S. deadline will Thieu "decide to go with us."[84]

Bunker's prescience again proved uncanny. In January 1973, as Kissinger and Le Duc Tho resumed their talks, the two men and their staffs hammered out an agreement. Nixon sent several letters to Thieu promising to maintain economic and military aid and to respond with force to a breach of the ceasefire agreement. But he directly threatened to cut off all aid if Thieu did not sign the agreement. The question of removing Hanoi's troops was off the table. As Duc later wrote, "the GVN's opposition to the presence of NVA troops in South Vietnam had been shared by the U.S. for many years...and that was the basis for the common struggle." American and South Vietnamese views on peace were at loggerheads. The Vietnamese have a saying for couples who are estranged: *dong sang di mong* (same bed, different dreams).

In South Vietnamese minds, Nixon had traded the PAVN withdrawal for a peace settlement, the return of U.S. prisoners, and détente with the Soviet Union and China. While America had tired of the war, it was an unjust accusation given the enormous toll in U.S. blood, treasure, and civil discord. Like Taiwan and South Korea, Thieu often forgot that the U.S. had other world responsibilities besides South Vietnam. Ultimately, the Paris agreements reflected the facts on the ground and was the best agreement possible among bitter antagonists.

Under tremendous pressure, Thieu agreed to sign, and he convened the NSC to announce his decision. He recalled Nguyen Xuan Phong from Paris and met with him for an hour before the council session. Thieu lamented that the deal was "a sellout of South Vietnam to the Soviets."[85] Phong remarked that Thieu should consider asking Beijing for help, but Thieu said that "such a choice would be much worse that not having a U.S. military presence in South Vietnam."

The Paris Peace Accords were signed on January 27, 1973. With America leaving and PAVN troops on republic soil, Saigon now faced a precarious future. U.S. aid was being reduced, and Hanoi still dreamed of conquest. The 1972 offensive had destroyed years of hard-won state-building on both sides, but like two exhausted boxers, only one would finally land a knockout punch.

22

"WE MUST KEEP OUR HANDS FIRMLY ON OUR GUNS"

In the Shadow of Peace

A s South Vietnam entered the strange new world of peace, Thieu had to implement the complex agreement. Among its many articles, the accords mandated a ceasefire and established an International Commission of Control and Supervision (ICCS) made up of observers from four foreign countries to examine and report on ceasefire violations. It also created two joint military teams to organize the release of prisoners and finalize other military issues. Last, it ordered the formation of a "National Council of National Reconciliation and Concord" (NCNRC) between Saigon, the Provisional Revolutionary Government, and the Third Force neutralists to organize an election.

Surveying the devastation from the offensive and years of war, Thieu's first order of business was an ambitious reconstruction plan to rebuild the country, resettle refugees, and heal the economy. Taking stock, he believed that to win the peace, he needed to correct long-standing military and political deficiencies. Thieu entered the postwar period with three chief domestic goals. First, politically unify the Nationalists, even if it meant a shotgun marriage, to win an electoral contest against the PRG. He believed that the Communists would only win somewhere between 10 and 15 percent of the vote, but he was not taking any chances. Second, develop the economy to build a better life for the people to convince them to vote for him. And last, institute an Administrative Revolution to fix local government and eliminate corruption. Achieving these goals would cement peasant loyalty and help him win an election against the PRG.

While carefully watching the Communists' military and diplomatic actions to determine their intentions, Thieu hoped he could accomplish these policies during a year of peace. Instead, the PAVN continued to challenge him militarily while the PRG fought him politically. The year 1973 would mark another time of upheaval compounded by the resumption of fighting and desperate economic straits, calamities that accelerated South Vietnam's demise.

ASSESSING SOUTH VIETNAM

At the end of January 1973, the RVNAF's ability to defend the country without U.S. firepower remained problematic. While the PAVN had been badly weakened and Nixon claimed he had promises from the Soviet Union and China not to underwrite another massive rearmament, the People's Army now legally occupied parts of South Vietnam. It controlled northern Quang Tri, southern Quang Ngai, the mountainous area along the Lao border from the DMZ down to northern Kontum, and western Binh Long Province in III Corps. These and other Communist-controlled pockets, especially in remote, unpopulated areas, created what became known as a "leopard skin" ceasefire. When combined with ongoing local security issues such as taxation and assassinations, the leopard spots dramatically reduced internal security.

External defense was even more challenging. Geographically, the country had a long, ill-defined border region where the enemy could refit in unmolested camps. Neither Cambodia nor Laos had the military strength to attack the PAVN bases or interdict the enemy's supply routes. The terrain provided concealment that allowed Communist units to mass undetected and then strike with overwhelming combat power. Combined, these strategic disadvantages critically affected national defense and compounded other foundational deficiencies, such as an emasculated JGS and a total reliance on U.S. resupply.

The RVNAF also needed to fix deep-seated leadership woes, eliminate divisive corruption, remedy morale, and address desertions and benefits. Massive draft calls had kept its total strength at 1.1 million, the same number from January 1972 despite having suffered 150,000 casualties in 1972. However, only 290,000 of that total were regular combat troops.[1] About

400,000 were Regional/Popular Forces, while the remainder were combat support or administrative. The U.S. had replaced destroyed equipment under two resupply programs in late 1972 called Enhance and Enhance Plus, but much of the provided gear was worn out or nearly obsolete.

Thieu's order to defend every inch of the country, a political decision to affirm GVN sovereignty, had left the ARVN and RF/PF badly overstretched and often immobilized in static defense. Worse, the ARVN's two main General Reserve units—the Airborne and the Marine divisions—were now tied down in I Corps, which had the heaviest concentration of PAVN forces. This left only three Ranger Groups as reserves for the country and the Vietnamese Air Force as its main firepower differential. With so few reserves, a simultaneous PAVN attack in two or more military regions would make it almost impossible to reinforce multiple menaced ARVN units. With ARVN stretched thinly, one significant defeat might create a chain reaction and unravel the country's entire defensive posture, leading to a general collapse, which is precisely what happened.

Politically, Thieu had used the last six months of 1972 to increase government control. He had stiffened the An Tri procedures to detain Communists in peacetime, launched a roundup of suspected Communist sympathizers, and extended jail terms for some. The accords, however, forced him to release over five thousand civilians who had been arrested by the police in 1972. He had also restrained Saigon's raucous press and allowed the province chiefs to directly appoint the hamlet chiefs.

To prepare for elections, he launched the Democracy Party, which was basically an arm of the government. To force the Nationalists to unify, Thieu's signed his most controversial decree in the hours before his powers expired on December 27, 1972. Decree 60 amended the June 1969 Political Party Law by imposing much stricter organizational requirements on a party before it was given a license to operate. The old statute only required a party to have ten provincial chapters with five hundred members each. By mid-1972, the GVN had granted operating authority to twenty-four parties. The new regulations were far more stringent. Each party now needed a chapter in at least half of the provinces, plus one in Saigon. Each chapter must have 5 percent of the registered voters and have branches in 25 percent of the villages in that province. A party had until March 27, 1973, to meet the validation conditions.

Since the Democracy Party's cadres were mainly government workers, fearing comparisons to Diem's dreaded Can Lao Party, Thieu made a key change: the DP "would be expanded to [include] a mass base of support."[2] By early 1973, party leaders claimed to have several hundred thousand supporters. While many military leaders had registered, they did so covertly as the constitution forbade officers from joining a political party, another Diem specter. Some senior officers, however, refused to enroll. The most notable was Lieutenant General Ngo Quang Truong, who believed that the military should remain aloof from politics. Party finances, the Achilles' heel of Saigon political organizations, were provided by dues-paying members, corrupt money funneled from province chiefs, and reputedly a large sum provided by Thieu's bankroller, the Office Pharmaceutique du Vietnam (OPV), the country's large pharmaceutical company.

Opposition leaders grumbled that the law was designed merely to enshrine Thieu's hold on power, especially since the Democracy Party appeared to be the only one capable of achieving the prerequisites in the short registration period. Despite the discontent, the decree forced the PNM, the Farmer-Worker Party, and parts of the VNQDD to merge into a new party called the Social Democratic Alliance (SDA). The other major party, Ha Thuc Ky's Revolutionary Dai Viets, thumbed their noses at Thieu and returned to their clandestine roots. On the eve of peace, political unity remained a mirage.

The various religions took different paths. The Hoa Hao, after a personal appeal by Thieu, signed a unity proclamation on February 4 between its two warring factions. It also joined the SDA, as did the Cao Dai. Reflecting a seismic sociopolitical transformation, the two main religions, Catholicism and Buddhism, also changed course. If the Catholics had once been the GVN's buttress and An Quang the rebellious outsider, those roles were now somewhat changed. Although several Catholic politicians formed a Freedom Party by merging the Nhan Xa, the Lily Group, and the old Greater Solidarity Force, the Church hierarchy was done with politics. Archbishop Nguyen Van Binh refused to officially sanction the new party and insisted that priests refrain from joining, especially given the pope's neutral stand on the two Vietnamese belligerents.

The Buddhist An Quang Pagoda had no political party and little desire to create one. Internally, it was too divided over a conflict that raged between some militants who desired a Third Force role and a much larger moderate group that hated Thieu but feared the Communists even more. Plus, the deaths of its head of the Institute for the Faith and its Supreme Patriarch in early 1973 embroiled the clergy in jockeying for succession.

The Quoc Tu Buddhists remained supportive of Thieu but also did not form a party.

Regardless of appearances, Thieu intended Decree 60 not to consolidate his power but to finally force the badly splintered Nationalists to merge, the long-standing but so far unobtainable goal of South Vietnamese politics. He sought unity because the Paris agreement mandated that both sides were to establish the NCNRC by April 27 to organize an election. For Thieu, Decree 60 and the Democracy Party reflected his belief that the existing political parties were unequal to the task. If Thieu had to drag the intellectuals "kicking and screaming" into an electoral battle against the revolution, so be it. Plus, his contempt for South Vietnamese civilian politicians combined with his visceral hatred of the Communists had forced him into a maximum stand: one either sided with Saigon or Hanoi. There was no middle ground, and if one tried to occupy it, that meant you secretly sided with the enemy. He had made perhaps the supreme roll of the South Vietnamese political dice: he was betting that the people, properly instructed by government cadres, would vote overwhelmingly for him in an election.

Like Senator Nguyen Van Ngai from the RDV, Lower House Speaker Nguyen Ba Can, a high-ranking official of the Farmer-Worker Party, had decided to join the DP. Analyzing the situation, Can had yielded to Thieu's logic.

> It was impossible for a political force to 'stand in the middle' between the Communists and the administration. You have to be realistic about the nature of the political process in South Vietnam today. When people vote they have either a Communist-held knife at their backs or one held by the administration. In this situation, no Third Force group lacking physical force can hope to be effective in an election in South Vietnam.[3]

Political concord was only one part of Thieu's grand design to win an election. He also sought a better economy. Fortunately, Pham Kim Ngoc's steady hand on the commercial levers had enabled the battered economy to survive 1972. Although inflation came in at 24 percent compared to 17 percent for 1971, exports had almost doubled due to more realistic exchange rates. South Vietnamese markets, though, faced strong headwinds. The population had soared from fifteen million in 1964 to nineteen million in 1973. This growth, plus a flood of people into the cities, meant Saigon now had over two million inhabitants. These city dwellers needed housing and jobs, but businesses remained in a deep recession. Inflationary pressures were building as the price of rice had skyrocketed 30 percent in 1972 due to bad weather and the war. The piaster's value in January 1973 had fallen to 465 to the dollar and was continuing to sink. Although tax revenue had doubled from 1970, the budget had exploded to 435 billion in 1973.[4] Ngoc had narrowed the deficit but could not close it, and with a coming reduction in U.S. aid, the financial outlook for 1973 was forbidding just when Saigon needed it most. For Thieu, healing the wounds of war would be as challenging as winning the peace.

AFTER THE ACCORDS

Thieu's harsh view of the accords and his overriding suspicions of Communists intentions infected his subsequent actions and rhetoric. He fully expected Hanoi to violate the agreement, especially with several hundred thousand troops on republican soil. On January 23, he instructed all province chiefs and senior military commanders to "flood the territory with national flags in order to confirm and identify the territory and population of the Republic of Vietnam."[5] Thieu wanted to ratify his hegemony over the people and land before the ICCS arrived.

On the same day, Thieu ordered Ngoc to begin planning for a National Reconstruction and Development Plan and Program. Material prosperity was Thieu's key to winning the peace. Confucian morality and societal standing were now long-abandoned guideposts. The goal of

> our postwar economic efforts is to resurrect our economic activities and create jobs and livelihoods for our people in order to support the political struggle that will determine the survival of our free and democratic regime. During the postwar period, the nation must place the focus of its efforts on three main fields. We must restore normal life and activities during the first month after the ceasefire comes into effect in order ... to win the confidence and trust of the masses. Reconstruction to replace damage in order to prepare for the national development phase. National development to improve the lives of the people and to move forward to achieving economic independence and creating wealth.[6]

His policies were admirable but impossible to achieve. Like the 1968 Tet Offensive, the 1972 attack had wrought terrible physical destruction, cratered the economy, and enlarged the budget gap. The culprits were the enormous defense outlays and the reduction of U.S. military in-country purchases. In 1965 and 1968, the U.S. had paid to rebuild the country, but not this time. Thieu had no money to pay for his national reconstruction unless he printed it, which would only cause more inflation. If the cost of living became intolerable, GVN political stability might be seriously undermined.

First, though, Thieu had to deal with the shaky peace. After the signing ceremony in Paris, on January 28, he spoke to the nation. He thanked the U.S. and South Vietnamese military for their "blood sacrifices," but he cautioned his countrymen against undue optimism. Since Hanoi had failed to honor previous pledges, he warned everyone "to maintain utmost vigilance in the coming political struggle." He argued that whether the treaty evolved into a true peace depended on if the Communists abided by the ceasefire and if they showed "good intentions" in the upcoming talks. Until then, he stressed, the accords were simply "a ceasefire in place."[7] If peace did come, Thieu promised, the government would work to build a new life for the people.

Thieu viewed his enemy with paranoia, although both sides expected the worst and consequently got it. Hanoi's violations were plentiful, such as when the PAVN besieged the isolated Ranger camp at Tong Le Chan and attacked the ARVN border post at Hong Ngu in the Delta. These attacks and the continuing infiltration confirmed his suspicions about Communist intentions, but Hanoi did not receive the same worldwide condemnation as when Saigon made missteps. Perhaps if Thieu had publicly embraced the peace treaty, he might have secured a more favorable international response to the Politburo's obvious disregard for its written pledge, but South Vietnam's prior failings and misdeeds had left it with few international supporters.

After the signing, Nixon dispatched Vice President Spiro Agnew to visit South Vietnam and other Asian counties to explain the treaty and to reassure them that America was not abandoning them. In Saigon, Thieu informed Agnew of his chief concerns and plans. The offensive had wrecked years of development and required a colossal reconstruction effort. He needed to rebuild several cities and repair numerous destroyed bridges and roads. The GVN was also carrying a crushing social burden: caring for over one million refugees plus another 850,000 disabled veterans, widows, orphans, and wards of the state. He told Agnew that he had ordered his ministers to prepare a restoration plan for 1973 to "beat the

Communists politically in the next six months" since the "principal GVN problem in the months ahead was how to gain population support." To do so, he needed his main sponsor to bail him out. After listening, Agnew warned Thieu that Congress was opposed to more aid, but it would help if Saigon portrayed a "positive image" regarding peace.[8] Thieu "pledged to engage in sincere talks in order to reach a political solution; stalling would not serve the interests of the GVN."[9] Since 1965, the president had walked the same tightrope: appear diplomatically flexible to appease his American benefactors while sufficiently hardline to retain the support of key domestic audiences.

Just as Thieu had ordered flag's flown to demarcate GVN territory, in a clever move to annex land shortly before the signing ceremony, Communist units launched a highly coordinated campaign to seize hamlets, block roads, and plant the PRG flag to claim control before the ICCS arrived. Since Thieu could not allow the Communist blockades to undercut South Vietnam's economic and territorial integrity, he counterattacked. Although the ARVN swept out the enemy units, fighting was fierce and property destruction was heavy. Both sides suffered severe losses. In January and February 1973, RVNAF casualties were 7,545 killed and another 33,504 wounded.[10]

Given that the ARVN counterattacks occurred after the ceasefire, Hanoi's propaganda machine volubly insisted that Saigon had "massively violated" the ceasefire, which was true, but it was a response to the PAVN provocation. Unable to sort out the various claims and counterclaims, most foreign observers simply blamed both sides equally for the ongoing fighting. U.S. statistics compiled from January 28 to June 14 (the start of a second negotiated ceasefire period), however, showed a clear picture. "Ninety percent of incidents," they reported, "were enemy-initiated."[11] While Saigon had pushed into some contested areas, Hanoi's encroachments had created a security climate that necessitated an ARVN response. The PAVN had also breached the ban under the same pretext when they counterattacked after the ceasefire. It pushed out a Marine unit that had seized the river port of Cua Viet in northern Quang Tri Province in the last hours before the accords because it directly threatened its supply lines. The PAVN had also grabbed the small port of Sa Huynh in Quang Ngai Province shortly after the signing, a post-ceasefire violation that resulted in heavy fighting for a month until the ARVN drove them out.

More importantly, Hanoi deliberately flouted the accords when it secretly ordered the continuing infiltration of men and material into South

Vietnam, which the agreement had banned. The commander of Group 559, the unit responsible for the Ho Chi Minh Trail, writes that on February 5, the High Command ordered him to "step up its transport tasks, delivering about 80,000 tons of goods to various battlefields."[12] He then met with DRV Premier Pham Van Dong to brief him on expediting the flow of supplies into South Vietnam a week before Dong was to meet with a visiting Henry Kissinger to discuss implementing the accords, which specifically disallowed more infiltration. The deputy commander of Group 559 confirms that on the day the accords were signed "1,000 trucks assigned to our [Group 559] forces, all heavily loaded with supplies, crossed the Ben Hai River into South Vietnam."[13]

Despite the attacks, on February 17, Thieu ordered his commanders to strictly comply with the ceasefire except for self-defense.[14] Then, in an ominous foreshadowing of later troubles, three days later, citing the potential for reduced U.S. supplies of ammo and fuel, he restricted tactical air sorties and artillery use.[15] He was right; in March, upset at high ARVN artillery use since the armistice, the U.S. cut the artillery supply by 70 percent. In reaction, Thieu sent further instructions forbidding "major redeployments or movements of combat forces that could extend areas of control or would result in contact between opposing forces." He also prohibited patrols into enemy territory or any "hostile acts or counterattacks except for self-defense operations."[16]

Beside fighting the war, Thieu had to care for the people. The 1972 offensive had generated a total of 1.2 million refugees. The sheer numbers were swamping GVN services. By late January 1973, six hundred thousand were still in temporary camps, of which four hundred thousand were in I Corps.[17] The post-ceasefire fighting had created another two hundred thousand refugees, mainly in III Corps. Refugee support was not cheap. The Ministry of Social Welfare had to build temporary housing; provide medical care, food, and water; and clear sites for camps. In 1972, the ministry had spent three billion piasters (about six million dollars) in III Corps alone for roofing sheets, blankets, mosquito nets, and food. Remarkably, thousands of citizens had chipped in money or food to help the displaced people.[18]

Thousands had to be transplanted elsewhere since their homes had either been destroyed or were now in enemy hands. The ministry estimated that 250,000 refugees would have to be resettled from I Corps to points father south. Phan Quang Dan led the refugee resettlement program. In late April 1970, Thieu had appointed him to head the Inter-Ministerial Committee for

Repatriation of the thousands of Vietnamese from Cambodia. When Dan efficiently resettled the evacuees, Thieu had retained him. Now he told Dan to "clear the camps as soon as possible" either by resettlement or sending them home.[19] For Thieu, it was both a social requirement and a practical means to win peasant votes.

Pham Kim Ngoc was also trying to assist the refugees. While outside his domain, he felt compelled to help. In late November 1972, Ngoc and several U.S. embassy economic advisors traveled to Danang to assess the refugee situation. They found thousands of wretched people swamping the city and camped out on sidewalks and parks. Danang was suffering from massive unemployment and overwhelmed city services. Ngoc feared the situation might get out of control, so he created the most successful public works program in South Vietnamese history. He convinced USAID to provide one billion piasters (two million dollars) to pay refugees to repair culverts, dig drainage ditches, and clean up the city.[20] Ngoc designed the program not only to help the people but because he "wanted a change in the public perception of humanitarian relief, a new option between handouts vs. make-work. My U.S. counterpart recognized the latent socio-political explosiveness of refugee unemployment in Danang. I gave the U.S. Mission my assurance of competence and accountability. I secretly hoped [the program] would preserve the refugees' dignity in a desperate wartime situation."[21]

Called the Agency for Development of Danang Area (ADDA), it was an independent entity that reported to Prime Minister Khiem. A "modest title" was chosen "to create confidence and faith among the people, because in the past there have been many large, wide-ranging programs which have not produced the desired results." A "simple organizational structure" was developed to avoid "a heavy, clumsy administrative apparatus."[22] The ADDA was approved on February 20, 1973.[23] In a country notorious for a sloth-like bureaucracy, an issue that Thieu would shortly address, Ngoc's assistants developed and approved the paperwork and structure required to organize, manage, fund, and staff the organization in two months. To avoid bureaucratic foot-dragging, Ngoc decided against appointing a career civil servant to run the ADDA. Instead, he tapped Trinh Vien Dien, a respected manager with the Shell Oil company in Saigon.

Determined to keep Ngoc's promise to strictly account for the USAID funds, Dien designed the novel approach of paying the workers directly rather than employing contractors to hire people. By late March, Dien had about a thousand refugees engaged in sidewalk and road repair. Within two months, that number had doubled, and by September, Vien had 8,500 people working on numerous activities, including planting tree seedlings to reforest an area badly damaged by the fighting.[24] One of Ngoc's deputies later wrote that "the political, economic, and social impact of this program at the local level was notable. Politically, the program created tremendous confidence in the government. Economically, the program provided livelihoods to feed and house the people, forming the foundation for long-term economic development."[25]

He was correct as most of the major projects were designed to restore agricultural production that had been damaged in the fighting, particularly in war-ravaged Quang Tri. For example, by September 1974, the ADDA had twenty-six irrigation projects underway. A second program centered on Saigon was launched in August 1974. It quickly employed thousands of people in various public works projects. Both efforts were so successful that the GVN budgeted nine billion piasters for these programs in 1975.[26] By any measure, Ngoc's brainchild was a monumental success that allayed a humanitarian crisis and strengthened the GVN's political legitimacy.

Besides refugee care, Thieu also undertook a series of domestic psychological operations to prepare the country for a coming election. In November 1972, the GVN created information centers to coordinate an outreach program to the people. Personnel from the police, the military, RD, and Phoenix were formed into teams that went into the villages to explain the government's position on the accords. To improve this effort, on January 10, 1973, Thieu appointed Hoang Duc Nha to head a new Ministry of Mass Mobilization, replacing the old Ministry of Information. Nha reoriented the teams to conduct in-person discussions rather than rely on print or broadcast media. The teams held meetings, painted slogans on houses, and harangued people to avoid contact with the Communists. On January 24, Prime Minister Khiem issued instructions to turn the information centers into "Political Struggle Committees" in all "provinces (or cities, districts, and villages) in order to smash the Communist plot for a 'General Uprising' during the ceasefire."[27]

Given all the rhetoric, what did the South Vietnamese people think of the accords? The PAAS public opinion survey results for February revealed some remarkable insights. A whopping 91 percent of urbanites and 77 percent of rural people thought the ceasefire agreement was "good for the country." Although most agreed that the Communists "had not complied with the agreement," 84 percent of urbanites and 71 percent of rural folks thought the GVN had been wise to sign the accords. Moreover, a 64–46 split between urban and rural people thought Saigon had gained more from the accords than Hanoi.[28]

Providing security to the population remained high on Thieu's agenda. HES results for February 1973 showed that 80 percent of the population was under GVN rule, another 13 percent was contested, and the remainder were under Communist control. Thieu, however, wanted every South Vietnamese under his leadership, and he remained laser-focused on rebuilding to achieve that goal. At a cabinet meeting on February 28, he rejected the proposed 1973 pacification plan as "missing the mark." This year is different, he said:

> There will be no war. We have a political solution . . . [W]e will struggle with the Communists for the popular vote. If we want to win the voters, we must be successful in our social welfare activities, in our reconstruction . . . and in restoring our refugees to a normal life. We must develop our economy strongly in the postwar period. . . . In our 1973 plan, we must aim . . . at the population in order to win [against] the Communists in a political struggle.[29]

To showcase governmental success, on March 26, Thieu celebrated the third anniversary of the Land to the Tiller Law with a speech in front of sixty thousand people in Can Tho, the capital of the Delta. He had accomplished his ambition of distributing two and half million acres of land in three years. The land program, he proclaimed, had "dealt the Communists a deadly blow. The rural areas are ours, not theirs."[30] According to embassy statistics, in three years, land tenancy had dropped in the Delta from 60 percent to 15 percent. Personal income on average among farmers had risen 30 percent. Because income had grown, other industries were sprouting across the land. Compensation to landlords totaled 210 billion piasters, and the landlords in turn had deposited that money into local banks.[31] This money enabled the Agricultural Development Bank to almost double the number of piasters loaned in 1972 over 1971 and open over thirty rural banks in the previous two years. The embassy called this banking expansion "an ever more significant factor in the restoration and development of Vietnam's rural economy."[32]

Of all Thieu's programs, LTTT was a true rural revolution, a visionary remodeling of South Vietnam in the midst of war and without the bloodshed, mock trials, and public denunciations that had marked land reform in North Vietnam. LTTT was the bedrock of Thieu's popularity in the countryside. After his speech in Can Tho, he waded into the crowd, shaking hands and chatting with citizens at an agricultural fair organized to showcase new technologies. Nguyen Ba Can, seeing Thieu mingle with ease among the people, observed that the "silent majority of Vietnamese supported the president." Many politicians in Saigon, Can said, "think the average citizen opposes Thieu [but] most Vietnamese in the countryside backed him."[33]

Thieu planned a follow-on program to distribute abandoned land in contested areas, but an exhausted Cao Van Than asked to retire. While Thieu had received the accolades, it was Than who had devised and administered the project. He had worked virtually every day for the past five years. Recalling his time, he said, "I was grateful that Thieu had given me the unique opportunity to serve my beloved people, and to liberate them from slavery."[34] In October 1973, Thieu finally allowed Than to retire from government service, but first he asked him to become the GVN ambassador to Saudi Arabia. Than declined; he wanted to become a teacher. He sought a teaching job in the U.S., but "the antiwar professors kept me out. So, I applied in Paris and was immediately accepted."[35] Than left Saigon in April 1974. The architect of South Vietnam's greatest domestic accomplishment was teaching in Paris in obscurity when the country fell.

The day before, Thieu announced that the Democracy Party (DP) had met the legal requirements under Decree 60. At an inauguration ceremony in Saigon, Thieu proclaimed that the party had the "responsibility of creating, maintaining, and promoting democratic political activity in the country" and that the "party will not serve the interests of individuals."[36] Thieu was named chairman, and the leadership began calling it the "government party." The DP, however, was merely a façade. It had neither the discipline of a Marxist-Leninist organization nor the mass-based fervor of a Western party. It was an organization imposed from Saigon whose sole purpose was to convince the masses to vote for Thieu to ensure an election victory.

Yet if the DP was a mask, the Social Democratic Alliance and the Freedom Party were shells. Both had filed paperwork on March 21 but had only received permission to conduct organizational activities. They now had twelve months to meet the membership and chapter requirements. Since Thieu was on record affirming the need for an opposition party, particularly because the constitution encouraged a two-party system, he did not immediately enforce the decree. Finally, on May 17, the Interior Ministry ordered

all parties officially closed save these three. Now any election would be between Thieu's government machine, a weak middle, and whatever support
the Communists could muster. But first, elections had to be organized and
peace achieved, tall orders in a land of violence and guns.

BUNKER LEAVES AND THE FRENCH RETURN

In March 1973, the last U.S. and Korean troops departed Vietnam. MACV
was converted into the Defense Attaché Office (DAO), a small unit coordinating American supplies to South Vietnam. With the war technically
over, the long-serving Ellsworth Bunker asked to retire. Bunker's tenure as
ambassador paralleled the ascension of Thieu and South Vietnam. He had
championed the country's rise from a weak state to a maturing society with
a stable governing structure. Despite the difficult talks over negotiations in
1968 and 1972, the two men worked closely. Bunker had masterfully carried out the instructions and policies of two U.S. presidents while artfully
relaying Thieu's position on a variety of subjects. Although at times his
reports made him sound like he was Saigon's cheerleader, he had chosen
to accent the positive when so many others only saw the negatives. Overall,
there was little doubt that he had kept U.S.-Vietnamese relations from
self-destructing. Both sides had baggage. Saigon always suspected American
intentions, while three U.S. administrations had battled a latent desire to
rid itself of a financially costly, societally damaging, blood-soaked conflict
in a distant land.

On April 1, the White House announced that Graham Martin would
replace Bunker. Martin, a former Army officer who had served in the Pacific
theater during World War II, had begun his foreign service career in 1947.
He had previously served as ambassador to Thailand during the Johnson
administration and then did a stint as Nixon's envoy to Italy. Like Bunker,
Martin was tall, immaculately groomed, highly intelligent, and exceptionally
articulate. His personality, though, differed massively from Bunker's. While
Bunker was called *Ong tu lanh* (Mr. Refrigerator) by the Saigonese due to
his formal and reserved personality, Martin was chameleon-like, alternating
between graciously charming and brutally abrasive. In Nixon's eyes, Martin
was the perfect candidate to handle the most difficult post in the U.S. foreign service, and the president told his new ambassador in clear terms that
his sole job was to keep South Vietnam afloat.[37]

Martin did not disappoint. Hence the embassy, in numerous cables to

Washington and in briefings to the press and congressional visitors, was always "on message." That message was simple: the Republic of Vietnam was strong, Thieu had little political opposition, the Communists would not militarily succeed, and RVNAF morale was excellent. America simply needed to sustain South Vietnam with aid until Hanoi would negotiate peace seriously.

Regrettably, Martin was so implacable in his mission that opinions diverging from his own convictions regarding South Vietnam's strength, despite growing evidence to the contrary, were viewed as traitorous villainy. Given his predilection for scorning those who disagreed with him, his relationships with the press soon turned sour. His imperious pronouncements about South Vietnam were met with derision, and his detractors grew exponentially. His behavior reinforced rather than dispelled Thieu's image of a dictator using American-supplied arms to prevent a "political solution."

At the same time, France decided to restore full diplomatic ties with South Vietnam. Saigon had broken relations in 1965, but the two countries had kept their embassies open. French policy was to maintain relations with Hanoi and Saigon, a balanced posture designed to prevent accusations of neocolonialism and to allow Paris to expand its influence at U.S. expense. In early April 1973, the French offered to send ambassadors to both Hanoi and Saigon. The PRG negotiation team would become a "Permanent Mission" that would have no formal diplomatic status. Thieu, hoping for French aid and an improved international standing, was all too happy to approve a new French ambassador. In early July, French Ambassador Jean-Marie Mérillon presented his credentials to Independence Palace. Born in 1926, Mérillon was a first-rate diplomat. He had previously served as ambassador to Jordan in 1970 during the Palestinian Black September uprising, where he had won kudos for harboring Americans during the fighting. Mérillon would be a key player in the diplomatic dance during the final days.

Despite the previous furor over the accords, Saigon-Washington relations returned to normal, just as they had after the bad blood of late 1968. To coordinate future joint policies, Nixon invited Thieu to visit him in the U.S. Under heat from the widening Watergate probe and seeking to avoid anti-Thieu demonstrations, Nixon asked to meet him at his home in San Clemente, California, rather than in Washington. Thieu agreed and planned to heavily emphasize two key items: confirming the U.S. would react to a Communist offensive and the need for increased aid.

Meeting on April 2, Nixon asked Thieu for his analysis of the situation.

He responded that Hanoi's strategy "was to gain time... because they were not yet ready for either a political or a military contest." Thieu thought Hanoi might launch another offensive in the summer. If it did, how would America respond? Since Nixon had publicly warned Hanoi about its numerous violations of the accords, including its continuing movement of men and material into South Vietnam, he reaffirmed that "in the event of a massive Communist offensive the American reaction would be sharp and tough."[38] Nixon, however, did not define precisely what he meant, a point not lost on Thieu.

The next day, Thieu turned to economic matters. South Vietnam desperately needed help. He wanted to rebuild quickly, but with the PAVN camped on his soil, he had to maintain a sizable military, a force that Saigon could not afford. Given Thieu's policy to promote reconstruction to win a future political contest, the GVN economic team had devised an offer for the Americans: more money in return for a cutoff after a specific period. Thieu informed Nixon that his objective was "rapid economic development and self-sufficiency within a foreseeable time....We have done as much as we can [but] we feel this is the time for a new and bold 'Marshall Plan'...which will help us achieve 'Economic Vietnamization.'"[39] He asked for $4.038 billion spread over eight years. Given this sum—and peace—Thieu claimed that South Vietnam would grow faster than countries like South Korea. Nixon agreed to treat these yearly aid sums as goals, but he also warned him that Congress and the American people were bearish on aid, especially to Saigon. Still, Nixon decided to help, and he signed NSDM 210 on April 11, which increased economic assistance to South Vietnam.

Nixon had agreed despite his own serious economic issues. America had just suffered its second-ever trade deficit and the worst balance of payments in its history. President Johnson had created the problem by refusing to ask Congress for a tax increase in 1966 to pay for both his Great Society program and the war. Although Congress had passed a tax increase in 1968, the U.S. budget deficit had zoomed to $23 billion in fiscal year 1968. To compensate, Nixon instituted tight monetary controls that sent the U.S. into a recession from 1969 to 1970. Later he also removed the U.S. from the Bretton Woods agreement and devalued the dollar. When inflation rose to 6 percent in August 1971, he ordered a wage and price freeze. He devalued the dollar a second time on February 12, 1973. If World War II was an economic boon for America—lifting the country out of economic doldrums to full employment—the Vietnam War had been a terrible drain.

While South Vietnam was also asking other countries like Japan and France to provide financial assistance, it mainly looked to "Uncle Sugar" to finance its rebuilding. Unfortunately for Thieu, his request had come precisely when the U.S. was financially drained.

After meeting Nixon, Thieu visited Washington and then flew onward to Europe. He traveled first to Germany, where he was met with official coolness and huge protests. Flying to Rome to meet Pope Paul VI, anti-GVN demonstrations again greeted his arrival. The Holy Father pressed Thieu to reach an accommodation with the PRG and to release any political prisoners. A shocked Thieu proclaimed that only criminals and hard-core Communists were being held. The Communists, he explained, were aggressors, not a political opposition, and those who helped them were traitors. The pope was unconvinced. From there, he traveled to Seoul to thank President Park for South Korea's assistance during the war. He then visited Taiwan to consult with Chiang Kai-shek. He returned home on April 14. While the West had scorned him, at least in these two countries, he found considerable sympathy.

FORMING THE NATIONAL COUNCIL

If fixing the economy was problematic, finding a path to peace seemed unobtainable. To discuss creating the National Council, the GVN and PRG had agreed to meet in Paris at La Celle-St. Cloud, a chateau belonging to the French Foreign Ministry. The first meeting took place on March 19. The GVN delegation was led by Nguyen Luu Vien. Nguyen Xuan Phong was named deputy, while PNM chief Nguyen Ngoc Huy and former Foreign Minister Tran Van Do were also appointed to the delegation. Thieu believed that by choosing such distinguished members, in addition to Vien's former service with the Viet Minh and his well-established southern credentials, the PRG (and the world) would see that he intended to negotiate seriously.

The GVN's agenda was to form the National Council, quickly hold elections, and demobilize troops. This was Thieu's secret design to remove PAVN forces and save money. He wanted an agreement to hold a presidential election followed by the formation of the council to arrange the balloting. The accords, though, had not specified which election, the presidency or a National Assembly, leaving it to the GVN and PRG to negotiate.

The PRG countered by demanding Saigon first establish democratic liberties, form the council, and hold elections, in that order. The PRG insisted that ensuring "democratic liberties" was "fundamental and must be resolved before there can be progress on the other issues."[40] The mass arrest of thousands of people in 1972 had given Thieu's enemies the moral high ground. They also demanded elections for an assembly rather than for the presidency. The PRG's aim was polemical, not to mention ironic coming from people who espoused a totalitarian philosophy of government.[41] It was above all tactical, making sure that elections favored them or were delayed. "Democratic liberties" was a catchall phrase to condemn the GVN over the political prisoner issue and repressive ordinances such as the An Tri Law. In terms of prisoners, Saigon had provided a list of over five thousand names to release and had offered to discharge anyone the PRG said was a Communist. The PRG, on the other hand, had barely managed a list of four hundred people and refused to account for the sixty thousand civilians and officials who had been abducted during the war.

Meanwhile, Hanoi continued to pour troops into South Vietnam. Even with the Watergate scandal threatening to engulf him, Nixon could no longer look the other way. With all the U.S. prisoners returned at the end of March, in mid-April, he ordered the bombers aloft. Seeking to compel Hanoi to abide by its written pledges, U.S. aircraft struck targets in Laos for several days. It was a weak response, but Hanoi finally agreed to a request for Le Duc Tho to meet with Kissinger in Paris in mid-May to review the accords.

Hoping the Communists might now negotiate, on April 25, the GVN offered a stunning new peace offer. Thieu made several significant concessions. He offered general elections for an assembly, promised to remove the constitutional prohibition against Communist political activity within thirty days, and offered to "permit complete freedom for the Communists to wage their electoral campaigns."[42] After sixty days, both sides would convene a council to discuss the election and demobilize a portion of their troops. Within ninety days, the council would enact an election law, and a month later, a national election would be held that included all parties. The vote would be internationally supervised. The GVN proposed that if the PRG agreed to this offer and immediately formed the NCNRC and strictly implemented the ceasefire, and if the PAVN withdrew, Saigon would also "abolish the restrictions to the democratic liberties due to the war situation."[43] The PRG declined this deal and instead offered its own six-point proposal, which was basically a rehash of its earlier statements.

With the La Celle talks deadlocked, Kissinger and Le Duc Tho met in Paris in mid-May. After tense negotiations between all three sides, they finally agreed on a Joint Communiqué that was issued on June 14. Among its components, the communiqué, called Ceasefire II, ordered a halt to the fighting in South Vietnam, prescribed that zones of control be determined between the opposing armies, and instructed the release of civilian prisoners and the formation of the NCNRC. Fighting diminished but was not eliminated. Some prisoners were released, but no zones of control were delineated. North Vietnamese infiltration continued at a high pace. By the fall, PAVN ceasefire violations had resumed with an alarming regularity, reflecting Hanoi's secret decision in Central Committee Resolution 21 to seek victory through military means.[44]

Even with the joint communiqué, peace talks between the GVN and the PRG remained stalemated. Tran Van Do, the Nationalists' elder statesman, told the embassy that he and Nguyen Luu Vien had briefed Thieu on June 24. Their message was sobering. The PRG was "absolutely intransigent...[T]he NCNRC would never be created and the NLF would never participate in elections it was sure to lose. Do said he had tried to set up secret meetings with the other side but had been rejected." The Communists, he believed, would resume attacking but "maintain an offensive below the threshold at which the U.S." would intervene. This would force the GVN to keep a "million men under arms [and put] tremendous strains on South Vietnam" and discourage foreign investment. In this situation, Do and Vien forcefully told Thieu to "undertake a drastic house-cleaning which would help to assure the loyalty of the population." The bureaucracy was useless, and corruption was "rampant." Thieu said he was taking steps to address the issues.[45]

Meanwhile, the 1972 elections had finally given the antiwar opponents in the U.S. Congress a majority. As Kissinger and Le Duc Tho were hammering out a new ceasefire agreement, the Senate cut Kissinger's legs out from under him. The attack in Laos in April, combined with the recent revelation that the U.S. had secretly begun bombing Cambodia in 1969, had sparked Congressional anger. On June 4, the Senate passed the Case-Church Amendment to ban any funds for U.S. military operations in Indochina. The House concurred in late June, and with his Congressional opponents holding a veto-proof majority, Nixon was forced to sign the bill. It set August 15 as the terminal date for any U.S. military activity in Southeast Asia without the express consent of Congress. To deter any effort by Nixon to circumvent this restriction, in November, Congress passed the War Powers Act, which required the president to seek congressional approval to send armed forces into combat anywhere in the world. Nixon's promise to Thieu to respond forcefully to Communist violations was now subject to Congressional authorization, which everyone knew would not be forthcoming. Saigon's last, best hope to defend itself was military and economic aid.

THE FINAL STEP: THE ADMINISTRATIVE REVOLUTION

On March 6, Thieu disclosed to the cabinet another major domestic initiative for 1973: administrative reform of the civil service. He wanted to upgrade the GVN's weakest structure, the stodgy bureaucracy. Thieu proclaimed that "too many cases of administrative delay are due to laziness and inefficiency and corruption among administrative people. Local government has not responded well to the people, [it] is too cumbersome and inefficient."[46] Thieu again adamantly insisted that "if there are elections, we must win people's hearts, meaning win votes—we must do whatever is necessary to get the people to vote for Nationalist candidates. In order to do this...we must make the people sympathize with our regime and...love their local governments." However, "because peace is not yet guaranteed, we must keep our hands firmly on our guns."[47]

Thieu was distracted by the Kissinger–Le Duc Tho negotiations in Paris, and it was not until July 10 that he was able to publicly articulate his new Administrative Revolution. The goal was to cut red tape, move 70 percent of routine paperwork to the villages, and shift most bureaucrats from Saigon to the countryside. Thieu hoped to eliminate petty corruption, energize a sluggish system, and eliminate the harmful effects poorly paid bureaucrats, who often had to work two jobs, had on average citizens. Civil servants would be sent to a retraining program, and by the end of 1973, fifteen thousand of the estimated sixty-two thousand bureaucrats in Saigon had exchanged their shirts and ties for black pajamas at Vung Tau.[48]

Thieu was embarking on his final step to improve South Vietnamese governance. While America promotes federalism, where sovereignty is formally split between the central authority and the states, South Vietnam was a unitary state with no division of powers between Saigon and the provinces. Culturally and constitutionally, the leader held dominion, although historically, local affairs were handled at the village. Since the French and President Diem had uprooted this tradition, Thieu intended to restore rural autonomy through a variety of measures. Decree 198 in

December 1966 had begun this process. Then Thieu in 1969 had given village chiefs authority over the local security forces and had provided them funds to direct their own development projects. Next had come LTTT. In December 1972, he had forced local officials to become fiscally self-sufficient. He had decreed that new property taxes could be levied and kept by the village rather than sending the money to Saigon.

He had achieved this wholesale structural change because three fortuitous events had occurred simultaneously. First was his iron desire to permanently improve the lives of millions of poor villagers. While he wanted their allegiance, he had not compelled it via the barrel of a gun. He had attempted to win peasant trust via a genuine desire to create an ownership society where free people could choose their own destiny. He sought to modernize the village by alleviating disease and providing electricity, education, improved farming techniques, and a host of other enhancements. Second, the U.S. had given him the money, support, and protection to launch these programs. Third, after the Tet Offensive, the Communists had mostly retreated from the villages, lowering the security temperature enough that he could accomplish his goals. Overall, Thieu had laid the foundation for not just a state but a modern nation. If he could accomplish an administrative revolution, he would have completed the transformation of the countryside. He just needed peace and money to do it. Unfortunately, his accomplishments were subsumed by the war and the constant scandals, intrigues, and disasters that all young countries endure on the often-rocky path to maturity.

ECONOMIC MELTDOWN

On April 28, Ngoc and Finance Minister Ha Xuan Trung presented their plan to implement Thieu's reconstruction goals. Using Nixon's promised money, they proposed a short-term three-month program "designed to get the economy moving toward recovery and development by the end of 1973."[49] Ngoc and Trung, however, had overestimated the amount of U.S. aid they would receive. Since the piaster was tied to the dollar, Nixon's devaluation in February had lessened the buying power of the aid money by over 10 percent in real terms.

Even with the aid, Ngoc advised that the only way to achieve Thieu's reconstruction goals was to increase "the 1973 budget from 435 billion piasters to 490 billion. Of the extra 55 billion, 25 billion would be used for relief and resettlement and 30 billion for rehabilitation and reconstruction."[50] Ngoc intended to use the money to resettle refugees back onto their farms, provide them credit to increase rice production, and build low-cost housing for the urban poor. It was the classic economic stimulus: spend government money to restart the market. Ngoc and Trung hoped to keep inflation and the deficit in check with a slew of new taxes.

On May 20, Thieu declared his key plan for 1973. Based upon the hoped-for eight-year U.S. aid program, he announced a "National Economic Development Plan which laid out a growth path for the economy [after] the Paris Accords."[51] Hoang Duc Nha recalls that Thieu's strategy was to create "sound economic development so the people would realize that under democracy they can prosper instead of suffering under the Communists." The big questions, however, were "how are you going to leverage the support of the U.S., how are you going to grow your economy from economic aid as well as your own resources?"[52] Thieu created a National Planning Commission to run this reconstruction effort, one that would seek to coordinate economic policy between the Finance and Economic Ministries. Although Prime Minister Khiem recommended that Ngoc run the council, in early June, Thieu said no. This was the first indication that Thieu was considering a new postwar economic team.

While U.S. aid was paramount, South Vietnam desperately needed to increase its own revenue, but how to raise it after the country had been nearly bankrupted by the 1972 offensive? Under U.S. pressure, in 1971, the Finance Ministry had begun drafting a major tax reform proposal to replace the old French tax laws still in use. The ministry believed income taxes in a poor, rural society in the midst of war would be "too hard to collect."[53] With the memory of the Austerity Tax debacle still fresh, the ministry searched for a means to increase taxes without causing a national uproar. They believed they found one in a then-obscure European system called the Value Added Tax (VAT). Applied in only one or two countries in the world, the VAT was an indirect tax on consumption and production.

This was the third major financial innovation attempted by Saigon, with microloans and floating the piaster against other currencies the first two. As his decree powers were set to expire in December, Thieu enacted the ministry's new tax system into law. The ministry was given six months to teach the public and the Directorate General for Taxation the new system. Given that tax evasion was a deeply ingrained habit among South Vietnamese, the law also imposed strict procedures on merchants and retailers to account for all sales and taxes. The embassy reported that the net "effect should be a modern, fairly efficient set of tax laws which [should] set the stage for successful revenue increases."[54]

On July 1, the GVN instituted the VAT, which levied a 10 percent surcharge on all transactions. Finance Minister Trung claimed it would produce 20 billion piasters in revenue in 1973 and 55 billion in 1974.[55] While his math was correct, the tax instantly increased prices at the same time that inflation had exploded. Editorials and politicians sharply criticized Thieu and the government and demanded the VAT's repeal. At first he refused, but under heavy pressure, on August 9, he rescinded it. Trying to help consumers, he announced that the VAT would not be collected on retail sales but would still be applied to imports. Nha, who was beginning to take a larger role in overall policy formulation, recalls that "I personally led the charge to abolish VAT ... because the surveys my ministry had conducted pointed to a serious resentment and anger from the people. We needed the revenue, but the social cost was too high."[56] Yet for all of the uproar, the VAT did succeed. Tax revenue in 1973, even after adjusted for inflation, was 20 percent higher than 1972. Still, Thieu's economic plans were in serious danger of being derailed, not just by the uproar over the VAT but by a sudden shortfall in rice and the return of serious inflation.

Even with miracle rice and increased production in the Delta, the growing urban population, the war, plus a million refugees who needed to be fed and who were concurrently not raising crops, South Vietnam could not overcome its food deficit. Rice shortages had become so drastic that the first week of July saw the second sharpest price rise on record just as the VAT was introduced. By mid-July, overall inflation hit 31 percent since the beginning of the year.[57] People on fixed incomes, such as those serving in the military, government employees, and their dependents—perhaps one-quarter of the South Vietnamese population—were again being crushed by rising prices. By mid-August, the usual 100-kilogram bag of rice, which was 9,900 piasters on June 30, now sold for 14,500. In comparison, a sergeant with eight years of service with a wife and four children made 17,600 piasters per month, which included the two pay raises that Ngoc had orchestrated in 1973.[58] Rice was the economic weathervane that the government had faced since 1964. The stagnant economy was eroding morale and contributing to rising crime rates, absenteeism, and increased corruption. These economic strains compounded battle fatigue in overstressed army units, leading to poor military discipline that manifested itself in abuse of civilians.[59] South Vietnam suddenly faced a potential social implosion.

In response, and despite the previous success of Ngoc's free-market policies, some senior GVN officials wanted to impose a centralized economic model. They saw an opportunity when a British journalist in late March reported brisk trade with the enemy on the Cambodian border in Tay Ninh Province.[60] For years, GVN officials in Tay Ninh had not only ignored local people trading with enemy units, they had also profited from it. The Vietnamese Navy base at Ha Tien was notorious for smuggling fuel and food on nightly shipping runs to Cambodia. When the article was broadcast over BBC Vietnamese radio, these officials recommended an economic blockade of enemy territory in South Vietnam. Thieu agreed, and III Corps headquarters sent waves of police to suppress the trade, but it proved impossible to completely halt.

Consequently, in mid-June, Prime Minister Khiem issued instructions to each province to establish commodity control plans that included penalties for violators.[61] On July 21, the president went a step further and announced a countrywide "blockade of territory under temporary Communist control to prevent the movement of rice, sugar, and milk into these areas." The Communists were "draining needed commodities from the people in GVN-controlled areas."[62] On August 11, Khiem issued new instructions that each province establish a Central Commodities Control Committee. The purpose was to "thwart and neutralize the Communist tax collection channel" and prevent "commodity purchases, especially rice, salt, POL and medicines."[63] Every village was placed into a category based on their accessibility to Communist supply cadres. The most exposed families were only allowed to keep on hand a certain amount of rice for consumption, which did more to hurt GVN popularity than it did to prevent Communist purchases.

Military commanders, concerned about rising discipline problems from underfed troops, were unsatisfied. They claimed that rice shortages were not just due to illegal purchases by the Communists but also from farmer's hoarding paddy and price manipulation by Chinese merchants. They demanded to take control of rice collection and distribution from private traders to ensure an adequate supply for the enlisted. Thieu favored this approach, but Ngoc and Trung, fearing the overturn of their free-market approach, fought back. On August 16, a compromise was reached. The military would enforce an economic blockade of enemy territory and would collect all the rice or paddy being held by private citizens, while Ngoc agreed to provide rice to military families and to hold the official price of a 100-kilogram bag at 12,000 piasters.

On August 23, Thieu traveled to Can Tho to chair a conference with all the province chiefs in the Delta to finalize the plan for a militarization of rice procurement and a food blockade of enemy areas. Lieutenant General Nguyen Vinh Nghi, the IV Corps Commander and the most vocal officer proposing the elimination of the private rice market, was placed in charge of procuring the harvest and ensuring its delivery to Saigon. The RD cadres in the villages were ordered to catalog all rice paddy in private hands. After the inventory, Nghi instructed the village chiefs to sell their rice stocks to GVN officials instead of the Chinese merchants. This was to both ensure that it did not fall into Communist hands and that Saigon had enough rice to sustain it until new U.S. shipments arrived in the late winter. The sale fee would be at the official GVN purchase price, which was well below the market amount. The rice was then shipped to Saigon. Families were only allowed to keep a one-week supply of rice and were forbidden from transporting paddy. Nha's ministry couched the effort as a "rice war" to deny food for the enemy and prevent them from launching another offensive.

Over the next two months, Nghi procured enough rice from Delta farmers and wholesalers to feed Saigon and the troops, but farmers were furious at seeing their livelihoods disrupted. Many threatened to reduce plantings for the next season. Seeing one of his main constituencies outraged, Thieu ordered Nghi in November to halt his collection efforts but to maintain the blockade. The damage, however, had been done. One embassy economic advisor, after touring the Delta, noted

deepening popular disaffection with the government's handling of the economy and a corresponding decline in public confidence in the ability of the administration to govern effectively. The smattering of official and private citizens whom I talked to express a sense of hopelessness... toward their economic plight that I have not encountered in such intensity... since 1969.[64]

The failure of the accords to halt the fighting also played a huge role in this discontent. Security in the Delta, South Vietnam's breadbasket, began to deteriorate as much from economic discontent as Communist attacks. Between the sudden VAT increase, the inflation spike, the rice shortages, the high unemployment, the staggering costs for refugees, and the sharp rise in world commodity prices, South Vietnam was nearing financial collapse. Thieu's grand reconstruction scheme was dead.

On September 28, Hoang Duc Nha submitted a report that concluded that

> eight months after the signing of the Paris Agreement we have made no significant progress on national development. We can frankly state that the reconstruction and development that we launched with such fanfare has clearly become a failure.... This means, in the economic area, that our resources are increasingly shrinking because of increasing expenditures combined with the significant decrease in direct and indirect US aid since 1971.... In summary, in 1974 our economy will gradually come under great inflationary pressure, prices will continue to increase, there will be a serious budget deficit, we will lose foreign currency, and in the meantime our production capabilities may increase only very slowly.[65]

Facing economic disintegration, Nha laid out his vision for a new national strategy. "In the current domestic political atmosphere and in the current international political climate [our] ultimate goal must be to create for ourselves the ability to survive and to demonstrate that viability to the outside world, especially to the United States." For Nha, "economic development is a political action with a defined goal." Much as Ngoc had done, Nha wanted to show the U.S. that Saigon was getting its proverbial act together and thus deserved more aid. To do that, he was recommending that the GVN adopt centralized planning. Stabilizing the economy would help achieve its political goals. These measures included rice subsidies, price and wage controls, and nationalization of the rice distribution system from the Chinese merchants.

Charles Cooper, the senior economic advisor at the embassy, hurriedly informed Kissinger that "economic problems have again become of critical importance to the survival of the GVN." Cooper reported that these economic pressures "are causing senior GVN officials to question the viability" of free-market policies that the "Ngoc economic team has pushed with our guidance for the past three years."[66] Ngoc and Trung were facing a complete reversal of the economic policies they had implemented and which had brought a degree of prosperity to the country.

"OUR HOPES HAVE BECOME BITTER DESPAIR"

Despite the requirement to form the NCNRC, in March 1973, the GVN decided to restart village council elections that had been postponed by the offensive. By the end of 1973, those village councils whose term in office had expired in 1972 or were up in 1973 had elected new ones. The DP won a majority of the village seats, but the other parties held onto their strongholds. Roughly 90 percent of the population voted, and there was no violence, indicating again the tremendous reduction in enemy control of the population despite intense Communist proselytizing to join them.

The National Assembly reopened on April 2. It held two sessions per year: one from April to June, the second from October to December. It passed a new election bill for the next round of Senate elections in August 1973, which Thieu signed on June 11. In the August 1970 Senate elections, sixteen slates had run. Thieu was determined to reduce this pack to a more manageable number. Hence another controversial election law was passed. It mandated that each slate have fifteen candidates and required a two-million-piaster deposit that would be forfeited if the slate received less than 10 percent of the vote. Election day was set for August 26, and the top two slates would win.

Thieu, however, rescinded the requirement under Decree 60 that each slate be sponsored by an authorized party. It was an olive branch to the opposition despite his pressing need for both slates to be pro-government so he could achieve a majority. Four slates applied. Two were pro-government, while the other two contained little-known personalities. Even though Thieu covertly sent DP leader Nguyen Van Ngai to convince the SDA and Freedom Party to run slates, they refused, claiming it was hopeless to run against the government. Plus, they had little money and remained unwieldy alliances rather than well-organized outfits.

Thieu sought a loyal lieutenant to head the Senate. He asked Tran Van Lam to resign as foreign minister and run for the Senate, his original government position. On July 9, Thieu appointed Nguyen Phu Duc to temporarily replace Lam. On August 26, the elections went off without a hitch. Only four terrorist incidents were reported. Voter turnout was 93 percent of registered voters, far surpassing the vote totals in the August 1970 Senate elections.[67] The two pro-government slates easily swept to victory, giving Thieu his majority. When the assembly reconvened in October, Nguyen Ba Can was reelected speaker, while Tran Van Lam was voted in as Senate chairman. For South Vietnam, elections had become a routine, institutionalized process, one apparently free of fraud. It was a remarkable achievement.

With the Senate elections over, Thieu decided to revamp his cabinet. On October 23, the palace announced major changes. Ngoc and Trung were swept out. They shared the onus of the VAT debacle, the rice shortages, and the infighting over government control of the rice trade. Trung was fired, while Ngoc was placed in charge of GVN planning, the job he had not been given in June. Ngoc had been South Vietnam's longest serving economic minister. He summed up his tenure by saying that "in the face of a run-away defense budget, our monetary and fiscal juggling alongside market liberalizations was not good enough without U.S. aid and economic growth. I could not 'pull a rabbit out of the hat' in 1972/73."[68]

Nha tapped Ngoc's deputy, Nguyen Duc Cuong, as the new minister. The choice signaled that Thieu had sided with the free marketers. Cuong was close to Ngoc and shared his vision of a market-based economy. Cuong, another technocrat with no political aspirations, was born in Hanoi. A Catholic, his family had joined the southern exodus. A brilliant student, he had received a USAID scholarship and studied in the U.S. Upon his return, he joined the Economic Ministry and rose in the ranks. Like Ngoc, Cuong noted that he "rarely discussed with Thieu anything serious about economic policy. His attitude was, I do not know anything about [economics], I worry about the military and political situation, you take care of this situation."[69]

Three other major changes occurred. Cao Van Than quietly retired, but Tran Quang Minh, Cao Van Than's agricultural deputy who had been instrumental in improving veterinary care and increasing protein supplies, was appointed to head a new National Food Agency. The severe rice crisis of late summer and fall had convinced Thieu that he needed someone other than the army to directly manage the rice supply. Summoning Minh to the palace in early December, Thieu said

> I have heard you are a vigorous implementer of vital government agri-cultural development programs. You will be put in charge of another no less important duty to carry out....All I am interested in that endeavor is that you do everything possible to stabilize the rice market so that the soldiers and the civil servants could put all their heart and mind in fight-

ing Communism instead of worrying about food for their family on a daily basis. I think that a strategic rice stockpile is a must for that effort.[70]

According to Minh, he had one job: "concentrate on rice procurement, transportation, stockpiling, and distribution on a nationwide basis with a view of privatizing all these operations as soon as possible." The highly energetic Minh, who now reported to Cuong, was given a budget of 34 billion piasters. Only Defense's budget was higher. During 1974, Minh developed a

strategic rice stockpile that would last a year until the next harvest for our military and civil servants in each military region. The private sector in rice marketing was thriving, and the Chinese rice speculators were at bay because every time the price shot up or supply diminished my Agency threatened to open our vast warehouses wide open. Every time the Council of Ministers meet at the Palace with the military region commanders, I was invited to report about the rice situation first. The president was that adamant about fixing the rice situation. . . . Any time Thieu heard a military commander complain about the non-subsidized price of rice, he invariably brushed that aside and stressed the fact that they can count on an ample supply of rice in his region.[71]

The third major cabinet change was replacing Duc as foreign minister with Vuong Van Bac, who had been the GVN ambassador to the United Kingdom since July 1972. Another northerner, Bac was one of the most prominent Vietnamese lawyers in Saigon. He had been a member of the GVN delegation to the Paris talks until 1971 and then had served as Prime Minister Khiem's legal advisor before taking the UK posting. While the amiable Bac would have limited latitude for independent action, he would launch a diplomatic offensive in 1974 to counter Hanoi's efforts to convince the U.N. and other world bodies to treat the PRG and the GVN on an equal footing.

While Minh was focused on fixing the rice issue, Economic Minister Cuong suddenly had another devastating economic issue to deal with: the skyrocketing cost of gasoline. The October 1973 Yom Kippur War in the Middle East had caused the Arab states to declare an oil embargo against countries supporting Israel. Under Arab pressure, Singapore, which refined almost all of South Vietnam's fuel, refused to sell gas to Saigon. The effect was soon felt. On November 20, Cuong announced a dramatic price increase in gas to reduce civilian consumption by 25 percent in two months. Gas prices, which had already gone up 50 percent since January, now doubled again. Coming on top of the steep rise in rice, the surge in gas prices threatened to derail the already wobbly economy.

The Communists, adept at economic warfare, found a way to retaliate for the rice embargo. On the night of December 3, a handful of sappers slipped into Saigon's main petroleum holding facility at Nha Be and destroyed many storage tanks. About one-third of the nation's gasoline stock went up in flames. Although the U.S. bypassed Singapore and shipped gas directly to the RVNAF to keep combat units operational, the Nha Be depot fueled the civilians in Saigon. Cuong immediately instituted rationing. He was most concerned about keeping transportation moving. Trucks carried Saigon's food and ferried most of its freight. A trucking shutdown would literally starve the capital.

The disaster at Nha Be capped a tremendously difficult year for South Vietnam. The country's great hopes had turned into ashes. Earlier, Thieu had spoken to the nation. He reviewed the failure of the accords and charged that the Communists were preparing for another offensive in 1974, his usual means of trying to rally the country. He promised to defend the nation, improve food production, and implement the first phase of a "vigorous and far-reaching Administrative Revolution." However, looking back at the events of the past year, Thieu felt angry and frustrated. The "hopes of our entire people," he lamented, "have now become bitter despair."[72] It would only get worse.

23

"THE WAR HAS BEGUN AGAIN"

South Vietnam Starts to Unravel

E very year since 1968, Thieu had set ambitious goals to reshape and develop the country. The year 1974, however, was different. He simply sought a continuance of 1973's efforts, a reflection not only of the dire economic situation but the lack of good available options. Many Vietnamese viewed America as washing its hands of South Vietnam. While he paid lip service to peace efforts, Thieu still did not believe Hanoi would agree to hold elections that included the PRG. His prediction seemed proven when the People's Army launched strong attacks in the three northern corps and chipped away at territorial security in the Delta.

As the year progressed, the combination of U.S. aid cuts, the forbidding outlook for peace, and the economic malaise accomplished what had been unthinkable even one year ago: South Vietnam's social contract began to fracture. This rupture unleashed the first real challenge to Thieu's political power since May 1968. Populations with an implacable enemy at their throats often seek new leaders, hoping that someone else might save them. Such was true for South Vietnam. This impulse for security resurrected a desire for autonomy among certain religious and racial groups. When combined with serious economic discontent, South Vietnam's social framework was stretched to the breaking point.

"IT IS WE WHO MUST SAVE OURSELVES"

On October 15, 1973, the Communist military B-2 Front in South Vietnam announced that it would seize areas "illegally occupied by the enemy."[1] It was the first overt sign that North Vietnam was returning to war. On January 4, 1974, Thieu responded to Hanoi's bellicosity. Speaking to a crowd in Can Tho, he blamed the renewed fighting on Hanoi and threatened "retaliatory measures against the northern invaders," including "attacks on their base areas." The war, Thieu charged, "has begun again," but "it is we who must save ourselves."[2] His war-weary and economically stressed people met another of his clarion calls with indifference.

Concurrent with the resumption of fighting, the situation in the South China Sea—the Vietnamese call it the East Sea—also suddenly erupted. Both China and the Republic of Vietnam had territorial claims over several small island groups, particularly the Paracels. In early January 1974, the Chinese landed fishermen on several islands in the Paracel group. Saigon responded by dispatching naval vessels to the area, which sent in RF troops to remove the people. The Chinese answered by sending armed ships that aggressively shadowed the Vietnamese Navy craft. On the morning of January 19, the two sides exchanged gun and missile fire. One VNN ship was sunk, three were damaged, and two Chinese ships were set on fire and possibly sunk.[3] The Chinese sent soldiers ashore and captured the RF troops and one visiting DAO contractor. Despite pleas from Saigon for the U.S. Seventh Fleet to assist, the White House refused to intervene. When the Chinese moved a naval task force into the area, the VNN retreated. Its cast-off hulls from World War II could not fight an armada, while VNAF fighters barely had enough fuel to reach the islands and return to Danang. The U.S. failure to respond left South Vietnam feeling more alone than ever.

The increase in combat in South Vietnam in late 1973 came at precisely the moment when the U.S. began to reduce military funding. America's military warehouses were drained from resupplying Israel during the Yom Kippur War, and it faced Congressional mandates to reduce support to South Vietnam. In mid-December 1973, the hammer fell. The U.S. Army cut all remaining operational funds for Fiscal Year 1974 (October 1973–September 1974). Major General John Murray, head of the Defense Attaché Office, the unit responsible for managing ongoing military aid, strongly protested. When he attempted to ascertain how much money remained, the Pentagon could not provide an accurate amount. Frustrated, Murray asked

Ambassador Graham Martin to inform General Cao Van Vien to reduce the consumption of supplies, but Martin denied his request. The ambassador hoped to convince the administration to restore the funding without telling the South Vietnamese.

Martin then asked Kissinger to request a $250 million supplemental aid package from Congress, but Kissinger declined. He informed Martin that congressional "reaction to foreign aid...is more negative than usual." He further warned that Cambodia also desperately needed money, creating a policy dilemma over how to allocate scarce funds. While Kissinger recognized that "these funding levels will create real problems in Vietnam," he feared that a rejection by Congress of an additional funding appeal "could be a major psychological defeat for our Indochina policy."[4] Martin insisted, but Kissinger proved correct. On April 3, 1974, the House rejected a supplemental arms request for Saigon. Martin was ordered to have Murray immediately inform Vien to reduce expenditures, but the damage had been done. The RVNAF had spent four months burning through supplies, unaware that replacements were not being filled.

The news only got worse. In late May, the congressional committees responsible for reviewing FY75 defense funding recommended a massive reduction in military aid for Saigon. The antiwar crowd claimed that Thieu was the obstacle to peace and that slashing fiscal support would, in their view, force him to compromise on a political solution. They seemed blissfully unaware that the ARVN and RF/PF, thinly stretched over numerous positions, relied on firepower and mobility to defeat enemy attacks. These attacks were now conducted mostly by conventional forces that included artillery and air defenses. The days of the hit-and-run guerrilla were long gone. The ARVN were weakening while the People's Army was regaining strength.

President Richard Nixon, crippled by the Watergate scandal, could not fight Congress over the cuts. Under enormous pressure, on August 9, 1974, he resigned and was replaced by Gerald Ford, a long-serving member of the House of Representatives who had become vice president after Spiro Agnew quit over charges of felony tax evasion. Saigon's chief ally was gone, and the South Vietnamese government and press reacted with justifiable trepidation. While the embassy reassured Thieu and Khiem that U.S. policy would remain unchanged, both men undoubtedly realized that they were entering uncharted waters.

In late August after Nixon departed, Congress voted to reduce the administration's $1.6 billion military aid budget for Vietnam to $1 billion.

Congress then decided to only appropriate $700 million of the $1 billion that it had authorized. Worse, it ordered that all costs associated with Vietnam must be charged to the $700 million, reducing overall funds even more. Just as the PAVN was launching large-scale assaults, Congress had ordered a two-thirds reduction in military aid.

Murray, who had a writing style any observer would call scathing, was furious. Although his tour was almost over, he valiantly attempted to rally the Pentagon leadership to fight the cuts by outlining their impact. In a farewell call on Lieutenant General Nguyen Van Nghi in IV Corps, Murray reported that Nghi had plunged in the "statistical needle." The corps commander told Murray that "before the ceasefire he was getting 248,500 rounds of 105mm [artillery ammunition] a month to offset [thirty-five] enemy attacks per day. Now he is getting 45,000 rounds to offset 70 attacks per day, while 155mm ammunition was cut 72 percent." Equally worse, SA-7 AAA missiles had forced the VNAF to bomb from "over 10,000 feet, and targets are consistently missed, so more artillery is needed" to compensate for the loss of effective airpower.[5] It was to no avail; DOD, having read the political winds, declined to appeal to Congress.

In his final meeting in mid-August 1974, Murray accompanied Admiral Noel Gayler, the U.S. military commander for the Pacific, to visit General Vien to discuss the funding cuts. Even though Vien had followed Murray's recommendations in April and ordered deep reductions, he said the strong enemy attacks were forcing the ARVN to fire "twice as much ammo as they have money." Gayler suggested that Vien pull exposed units from isolated posts and use these troops to defend the populated areas. Vien agreed but replied that such "a change of strategy would have political implications," meaning Thieu's decision to hold all territory remained sacrosanct. Gayler concluded his report by noting that "if the intent of Congress ... is to force Thieu to negotiate ... he will not negotiate from strength, nor even parity, but as a loser."[6]

Vien briefed Thieu on the aid reduction. The president ordered the RVNAF commander to "fight a poor man's war" and confirmed his earlier assessment that "giving up any real estate creates psychological problems for the GVN."[7] Vien made further decreases in artillery use and cut the Vietnamese Air Force to the bone. He told the corps commanders that "funds allotted for flying time in FY75 come to only $44 million as compared to $100 million for FY74." Since the cost of one hour's flying time had risen 20 percent because of the jump in oil prices and it had already spent $20 million beating back enemy attacks that summer, the VNAF was ordered to mothball older planes and sharply cut flight time for each military region. He told the commanders that "Air Force assets should be used only when absolutely necessary...In view of this situation in which funding is more and more limited...the JGS urges all units to give the most serious regard to all directives concerning utilization of air assets...to economize the national budget."[8] Vien had placed the military on starvation rations. One doctor in the Danang military hospital, surveying the more than one thousand wounded in his ward from recent battles, lamented that "we are short everything—except wounded men."[9] South Vietnam would indeed have to save itself.

CHANGING THE CONSTITUTION
AND THE DEMISE OF THE DEMOCRACY PARTY

On January 15, 1974, pro-Thieu legislators in the assembly submitted three constitutional amendments. The first would change the way that Supreme Court justices were appointed. The National Assembly, rather than the Bar Association, would approve all Supreme Court justices. The second would allow the president to continue to appoint province chiefs rather than hold elections for the office. The third, however, was the long-rumored change to permit the president to serve a third consecutive term in office. It would also extend the president's time in office from four years to five.

Thieu informed Martin that he want to reform the "totally corrupt" judiciary. Electing province chiefs in this period of escalating violence would only add "uncertainty and instability" even though South Vietnam had successful held local elections multiple times.[10] The third presidential term, he said, was also to maintain stability during this difficult time. Wary of domestic reaction, he had offered the amendments shortly before the Tet festival because the Vietnamese public would be distracted by holiday preparations. The assembly leadership convened a special session and passed the three changes on January 19. Nguyen Van Ngan secretly persuaded Nguyen Ngoc Huy's PNM Lower House deputies to vote for the amendments in exchange for Ngan's help in legalizing the Social Democratic Alliance party under Decree 60. The Catholic and Buddhist blocs in the Senate protested, but to no avail. Catholic Senator Nguyen Van Huyen dissolved the Freedom Party, but An Quang remained too riven by its internal battles to mount much opposition.

Thieu had other reasons for the third-term amendment besides the one he told Martin. Ngan, who had authored the amendments, recalled that the decision to seek this change was made after Thieu's trip to San Clemente in April 1973. He said that despite Thieu's outward happiness over the meeting, secretly he had little confidence in Nixon's promises. "The goal," Ngan wrote, "was not really a third term for the President. The true goal of the amendment was to demonstrate the trust and confidence of the people through the actions of the Legislature in order to 're-equip' [re-strengthen] Thieu's leadership position so that he could deal with the new situation." Ngan feared that Thieu would soon become a lame-duck president, increasingly unable to control a highly volatile situation. The change from a four-year to a five-year term was made because "we wanted to place some distance between the U.S. presidential election and Vietnam's presidential election. The American president's term of office was also four years, and every four years America underwent a period of political upheaval that had a major influence on the presidential election in Vietnam."[11] However, Thieu and Ngan had to wait until after the August 1973 Senate elections, which gave the president the two-thirds majority they needed to pass the amendments.

After winning the constitutional battle, Thieu moved to streamline the government and force Prime Minister Khiem to take more responsibility for executing government policies. The Thieu-Khiem relationship, the most sensitive in the government, had had its up and downs over the years. Since the one-man election of 1971, Thieu had increasingly taken control from Khiem of even routine administrative matters. Khiem had complained about this situation, so now the president was restoring that balance. On February 16, 1974, Thieu made his first move by asking the cabinet to resign. Two days later, he appointed his smallest cabinet ever, which included three deputy prime ministers. Nguyen Luu Vien kept his position as head of the peace talks, while Pham Quang Dan was promoted to deputy prime minister heading all social programs, including the refugee program. Surprisingly, the third deputy prime minister was Tran Van Don, who was given the amorphous job of "inspecting" national development. Don later wrote that he realized that Thieu "wanted my name in the government as a show of national concord."[12]

Most of the incumbents were reappointed, including Nguyen Duc Cuong and Vuong Van Bac, but Thieu finally shuffled off Pham Kim Ngoc. He was replaced as head of National Planning by Nguyen Tien Hung, a northern Catholic who had been educated in America. Hung taught economics at Howard University in Washington, but he had returned to Saigon in July 1973 and joined Thieu's staff as a special assistant. Other key moves included firing Minister of Veterans Affairs Pham Van Dong after his wife was arrested for running an illegal gambling operation. Dong had been cashiered for the same reason in 1965 when he was mayor of Saigon. A week later, Thieu made a second move. He forced the resignations of over twelve generals, including Hoang Xuan Lam, Nguyen Van Vy, and the officer accused of heroin smuggling, Ngo Dzu.

Thieu's principal change, however, was clipping the wings of his two chief aides, Hoang Duc Nha and Ngan. It was a bureaucratic victory for Khiem, who had long chafed at their direct access to Thieu. After the prime minister badgered the president about Nha's meddling in other ministries, Thieu solved the issue by changing Nha's title to minister and placing him directly under Khiem. At the same time, Thieu also scaled back Ngan's and the Democracy Party's roles in the administration. Thieu had secretly decided to reduce the party's involvement in government affairs. According to DP leader Nguyen Van Ngai, Thieu only told Khiem, Ngan, and him. Thieu viewed the DP as a get-out-the-vote machine, but Ngan had dreams of it controlling government policy and rooting out corruption. When Ngan disagreed, Thieu did nothing, but he waited for an opportune time for the ambitious Ngan to overreach.

One reason that Khiem had complained about Ngan was that Thieu's aide had developed a covert Democracy Party conduit called the Red Channel that stretched from Thieu through Ngan to the military commanders and the province chiefs. Many policy instructions were now passed through the Red Channel rather than via normal government paths. In late November 1973, Khiem told Thieu that Ngan exercised "too much influence on domestic political decisions." He was also concerned that Ngan was trying to "eliminate all rival political groups," which Khiem believed "was a mistake." Khiem hoped to convince Thieu that the "national situation had changed since Decree 60 was enacted."[13]

When Ngan then began contemplating the establishment of DP military committees, much like the ones instituted by Ngo Dinh Nhu and the Can Lao Party, General Vien objected bitterly. He told his old friend Khiem that the generals were adamantly opposed to resurrecting anything resembling the Can Lao committees. Khiem informed Thieu that "if the Ngan situation was not resolved, then the army would take action to resolve it," meaning a coup.[14] Given Khiem's history, Thieu could not ignore that comment.

According to Nguyen Ba Can, Thieu quickly called a meeting with the cabinet and the legislative leadership and waved the white flag. The DP would no longer interfere in government business. He ordered the Red Channel closed and told the province chiefs to end direct involvement in the party. Ngan was also no longer able to see Thieu directly, and in late May 1974, Saigon's éminence grise was fired. Tran Van Don was soon appointed the new liaison with the assembly but would report to Khiem. Don, no longer flaying Thieu from his safe perch in the assembly, was now proselytizing for the administration. Even in a city seasoned by irony, his political U-turn was not lost on the gossips lounging in Saigon cafes.

To further mollify the military, on June 19, Thieu publicly ordered all military or civil servants to no longer participate in political activity. It was a seismic change from the frantic days of late 1972 and early 1973, when Thieu was laser-focused on building a state party for a potential future political contest against the Communists. Although he later clarified that he was not downgrading the party, only that he was transforming it into a mass-based organization rather than one comprised of government cadres, his pronouncements were laughable. Regardless, his June 19 speech essentially ended the Democracy Party. By November 1974, embassy reps in III Corps, after canvassing local DP buildings, found that the "Democracy Party is totally inactive and . . . there are no meetings, no activities, and that party headquarters are deserted."[15] Government workers had a complete lack of enthusiasm for the party and had only joined because they feared for their jobs. Thieu's grand design to mobilize the masses to win an election was dead. The Democracy Party had died just as it had been born: by fiat from Thieu.

DOMESTIC WOES

With congressional votes on aid looming, Thieu sought to curry U.S. favor by releasing some cause célèbre prisoners. In mid-February 1974, Communist intelligence operative Tran Ngoc Hien, the brother of Tran Ngoc Chau, was released to the other side. Hien, however, was not greeted with comradely warmth. He was stripped of his party membership and his military rank for having failed in his mission to recruit his brother.[16] Convicted spies Huynh Tan Mam and Huynh Van Trong refused to go to the other side and were transferred to the Chieu Hoi Ministry. As part of the accords, by mid-1974, the GVN had released almost twenty-seven thousand healthy military prisoners and over five thousand civilian prisoners. In return, they received roughly 5,400 military and 600 civilians, most of whom were in poor physical condition after being held in jungle prisons.[17] Many more remained secretly held in North Vietnamese jails.

Tran Ngoc Chau was freed from his prison term early after he agreed to avoid the press and not to condemn the government. He remained silent, but Mrs. Ngo Ba Thanh, who had been released on September 21, 1973, took the opposite tack. After completing her third sentence since 1965, she promptly resumed her dissent activities. She staged small demonstrations in front of the assembly and gave numerous interviews to the foreign press that harshly criticized the GVN. With Duong Van Minh somnolent, she also declared herself the leader of the Third Force. She vociferously blamed Thieu for the lack of peace due to his "failure to properly implement the accords."[18] Since her peace demands closely mirrored the PRG's, Mrs. Thanh had become the embodiment of radical opposition politics in South Vietnam.

Peace, though, was a mirage. The surrounded Ranger unit at Tong Le Chan, under siege for over a year, had become a bright symbol of South Vietnamese military resistance to Communist ceasefire violations. But after enduring near-daily shelling and repulsing numerous ground assaults, with the unit's supplies running low and casualties mounting, the outpost commander decided to retreat. On the night of April 11, 1974, his unit slipped though the enemy cordon and escaped. The fall of the base generated heated commentary in the South Vietnamese press, anger that was already stoked from the Communist mortaring of a school in the Delta.

A Communist 82mm mortar shell had struck a school yard in the village of Cai Lay on March 9, killing thirty-two children and wounding dozens more. In response, Thieu ordered the GVN delegation in Paris to suspend its participation in the talks until the PRG "has proven their goodwill for peace through concrete actions," meaning a true ceasefire.[19] When a second school was shelled in the Delta on May 4, killing seven children and wounding thirty-six others, Thieu refused further talks. The ICCS investigated Cai Lay, but the Communist members declined to sign the report, preventing its release. When the GVN publicly condemned the PRG for this second massacre, the PRG announced it would also boycott the meetings. The La Celle talks were dead.

Speaking to his cabinet several days later, Thieu lamented that the PRG is not "seeking a solution through negotiations. It wants to resolve the problem [using] North Vietnamese forces. No country in the world can hold free democratic elections with a huge modern hostile army active within its borders.... The current negotiations resemble the 1954 peace talks in that the Communists are waiting... for decisive changes that will be in their favor in 1974–76." Saigon could not expect U.S. military help: "Forget about that possibility," he said. Eventually, when Hanoi sensed that South Vietnam had lost "American moral support, political support, and material support," it would launch its final assault.[20] His contentions would prove accurate.

Even with the main force war heating up, Thieu was intent on maintaining the GVN's hard-won control of the villages. In Thieu's annual Tet speech in early 1974, he mentioned the major pacification tasks for the new year: strengthen territorial security, boost agricultural production, and improve the government machinery via the Administrative Revolution.[21] On February 25, Thieu held his annual pacification conference. The 1974 plan emphasized bureaucratic de-centralization under the Administration Revolution. Since USAID funding for Rural Development was ending, he abolished the RD ministry and directed the remaining RD teams to help the village councils achieve their objectives for 1974. This key GVN program, begun with such fanfare under Lieutenant General Nguyen Duc Thang in 1966, had accomplished its mission. Pacification was now ingrained in the South Vietnamese government fabric.

As proof, in one year, Phan Quang Dan and the military staff in I Corps had quietly rebuilt the portion of devastated Quang Tri Province still under South Vietnamese control into a functioning entity. They had recreated the provincial administration, reestablished the RF/PF/PSDF units, and provided half a billion piasters to jumpstart agriculture production and repair war damage. To comprehend the scale of this project, in October 1972, there were more than 540,000 refugees in I Corps. By June 1974, that number was twenty thousand. According to the U.S. Consulate in Danang, of that group, 130,000 people were returned to Quang Tri.[22] Given the rising cost of materials, it was an impressive accomplishment. While the makeshift refugee camps the GVN had established to house the refugees from the 1972 offensive were often spartan and riddled with corruption, very few people migrated from government zones to Communist areas.

Thieu also continued to press the Administrative Revolution as an integral part of pacification. While improving local government seems like boring policy wonkiness, it was a perennial weakness often cited as a main reason for the peasantry's indifference to the GVN. While many American over the years had suggested this mission, in scope, funding, and implementation, this new effort was strictly a Vietnamese affair. Thieu still wanted to reorient the civil service to be more efficient and responsive to the people, a major undertaking that would require a great deal of experimentation, time, and patience. It was as much about changing the bureaucracy's mindset as it was rearranging its structure. Thieu's goal was to "give the people better service by means of a single-manager system at each level [and] which embraces all civil servants as 'National Cadres.'"[23] Thieu realized he was saddled with a colonial-style apparatus staffed by self-serving bureaucrats. With the military situation stalemated, future competition with the Communists would be at the economic and political level. Without a major overhaul of the administrative structure to provide better service to the people, the continued allegiance of the population—and hence the viability of the republic—was in doubt. As Thieu said in a speech on July 10 honoring the first anniversary of the Administrative Revolution, "if hamlets and villages stand fast, our country will stand fast," which was true against lightly armed political cadres but not against main force battalions.[24]

Formalizing the program took much longer than expected, but by mid-December 1973, a pilot program was begun in two provinces. The decree directed that the local offices of the various ministries would now report to the province chief. Previously they were autonomous units that received instructions and funding from Saigon. Improving overall efficiency was the first job. Performance in these local offices varied by province and ministry. For example, a survey of a thousand people in III Corps in mid-1974 revealed that Education, Public Health, and Social Welfare were generally regarded as the GVN's best efforts. Public Works and the police were derided as cesspools of corruption or poor performance.[25]

While the two test beds showed improvements in processing time for simple paperwork like ID cards, embassy surveys in late April revealed that little had changed in the other provinces. People still complained that local officials "exploited their offices for personal gain," devoted "little effort to helping the people," and were often "incompetent to conduct even routine matters."[26] Worse, the sluggish economy had exacerbated absenteeism. Restructuring local government would not be easy, especially with the war heating up. The Administrative Revolution, like so many other well-intentioned government programs, would fail to achieve its goals due to rising insecurity in the countryside and the sheer enormity of the task.

The rice blockade also remained a government priority, but its results were similar to the Administrative Revolution. Creating numerous police checkpoints and forcing farmers to obtain permits to ship rice from the provinces to Saigon had harmed the South Vietnamese economy more by restricting the free flow of goods than it succeeded in cutting off commodities to the enemy. To restart the rice trade, South Vietnam's most critical industry, on January 3, 1974, Khiem issued an order to remove the checkpoints. He also abolished the permit requirements and allowed private traders to resume direct purchase of Delta rice. However, he repeated his directive from June 1973 to maintain "tight control and appropriate blockade measures."[27] The blockade proved only partially successful. Enemy units in the Delta acquired food by taxing local farmers, growing their own food, or obtaining it in Cambodia. Although the GVN restrictions, the shortfall in Delta rice in late 1973, and serious rice shortages in Cambodia due to the fighting had severely hampered rice acquisition by Communist forces, the U.S. embassy concluded that "the economic blockade has not succeeded" in preventing rice from reaching enemy hands.[28]

The situation was similar in II Corps, an area that experienced a significant annual rice deficit. In 1974, the region produced roughly 350,000 tons of rice but required 550,000 tons. Imports of U.S. rice under PL-480 made up the shortfall. Communist forces in II Corps were estimated to procure 80 percent of the thirty-one thousand tons of rice they needed from GVN sources. Most of this trade occurred in the coastal areas as little rice was grown in the highlands. Nor did North Vietnam supply much food as the DRV could barely feed itself. The U.S. embassy reported that while the Communists were "experiencing shortages" and that ralliers were often malnourished, the GVN had failed to halt the flow of food to them.[29] Local farmers were intimidated to leave paddy in the fields for Communist forces to recover, and merchants and GVN officials continued to trade with the enemy to make a handsome profit.

ECONOMIC WOES

Adjusting the rice blockade was only one part of reviving the moribund economy. Despite the gloominess, there was some welcome news. The rice harvest for 1974 was the best on record, but the GVN still had to import 255,000 tons. In 1973, numerous oil companies had tendered bids, of which four were accepted. Government coffers received $17 million for exploration rights. A second round was completed in 1974, and another $30 million was received. The first oil strike was made on August 28, 1974. Tax receipts, which in 1973 had almost doubled over 1972, were up sharply again for 1974. The VAT, for all the political outrage, was quietly working, but inflation had eroded these gains.

Saigon, though, continued to chase its revenue tail. The 1973 budget had soared to 505 billion piasters, mainly from massive defense expenditures and refugee costs. The budget for 1974 was 700 billion piasters, and the budget for 1975 was 785 billion. Salaries for civil servants and the military still comprised almost half the budget. To pay for this massive government structure and repair war damage, the budget had doubled in five years, creating a deficit of 120 billion piasters in 1973 and again in 1974. The increased taxes could not fill the budget gap. The rest was financed by aid or deficit spending. No country in the world could sustain government largesse of this magnitude, and the results were obvious. Unemployment remained stubbornly high, even though the GVN was employing twenty-five thousand people in various ADDA-style projects.

For the first time in a decade, expenditures for civilian concerns had outpaced the ruinously expensive military outlays. Much of the civilian increase came from Tran Quang Minh's National Food Agency. Minh had achieved Thieu's goal of stabilizing South Vietnam's rice deficit areas, basically everything north of Saigon. He had also bailed out the military, civil servants, and refugees by supplying either free or heavily discounted rice to their commissaries. The price, though, was steep. The GVN had spent over seventy-six billion piasters to buy and ship hundreds of thousands of tons of rice in 1974 to feed its people.[30]

While 1974 was another bad year, especially for the urban poor, the second half of 1974 saw the economy stabilize, although at a low level. Basically, it had bottomed out, which was cold comfort to parents trying to feed their families. In December 1974, the GVN signed an aid deal for Paris to provide 130 million francs, although France had also signed a similar deal with Hanoi. Exports were increasing somewhat despite declining external demand. Pham Kim Ngoc's plan to shift South Vietnam away from a market heavily dependent on imports was subtly working. Two industries—steel and sugar—were nascent but growing.

Cuong continued to make small devaluations of the piaster, and by the end of 1974, it was over 700 to the dollar. He had little choice. OPEC price increases had forced him to increase the cost of one liter of gas from

85 piasters in August 1973 to 235 piasters in February 1974. Inflation increased 67 percent in 1973, the worst year since 1966, and was up 40 percent in 1974. Two-thirds of the increase was caused by higher prices for imported goods, primarily gasoline and other commodities. High inflation also sapped government effectiveness as many employees augmented their income by working other jobs. South Vietnam faced the harsh reality of being an economically developing country in a long, debilitating war.

Despite South Vietnamese belt-tightening, several factors played an outsize role in the country's economic life. The first was the fighting, which directly influenced both production and foreign investment. The second was the amount of external aid. Lastly, the GVN's inability to develop new industries to create jobs, feed itself, and raise revenue to pay for its massive civil and military structure. Although the people had not taken to the streets in protest after two years of hardship and stress, discontent was bubbling. It just needed a catalyst, and it soon got one.

"TORCHES FOR PEACE"

The self-immolation by Buddhist bonze Thich Quang Duc in the summer of 1963 sparked worldwide revulsion against the Diem regime. Although the grisly deed inspired other Buddhists to also sacrifice themselves to protest social and religious grievances, the others attracted little attention. But now, everything old was new again. On July 11, 1974, a former Buddhist monk and disabled ARVN soldier named Buu Phong sat down in front of the ICCS headquarters in Saigon. He placed several letters near him protesting North Vietnamese attacks, then lit himself on fire. His death motivated three other disabled ARVN veterans to also self-immolate to protest Hanoi's actions. The South Vietnamese press called them "torches for peace" and lauded them as heroes.[31] When two civilians did the same shortly thereafter, Thieu publicly asked that they stop. "The sound of the alarm bell has been listened to," he said.[32]

Unfortunately, those who heard it, rather than unite, did the opposite. The torch was going out throughout South Vietnam as old rivalries re-emerged and groups begin quitting the republic. Religious, regional, and ethnic animosities had long bedeviled South Vietnam, but time, government outreach, and the occasional police beating had reduced passions. The last uproar was four years ago with the Cambodians in the Delta, but now, with a visibly weakened GVN, old tendencies reappeared. South Vietnamese society was imploding; when the enemy is at the gates, the impulse is to save yourself either through accommodation or retreating behind your own walls.

First into the limelight were the Hoa Hao in the Delta. In late January 1974, Lieutenant General Nghi had ordered the Hoa Hao Defense Force, a group of deserters armed with a mishmash of weapons and congregating at the temple of the main faction, to disarm and integrate into local RF/PF units. When they ignored his order, Thieu told Nghi to leave them alone. The reason was political. The key Hoa Hao leader was Luong Trong Tuong, and his chief backer was Le Phuoc Sang, Nguyen Cao Ky's former legislative partner in the old Constituent Assembly. After Thieu helped Sang open a Hoa Hao University in November 1970 and appointed him rector, the Hoa Hao fully supported Thieu in the 1971 election. Since then, relations between the Hoa Hao and the GVN had remained amicable except for the issue caused by deserters.

Although the two main Hoa Hao factions had agreed in February 1973 to settle their old scores and merge, the signed pact was stillborn. The dispute broke into open warfare again when unknown assassins ambushed Sang's car on April 1, 1974, killing two bodyguards. Sang was unhurt, but Thieu was furious over the incident. He ordered the Defense Force disbanded, saying that the GVN "could not accept the existence of an armed organization outside of the RVNAF."[33] Rather than capitulate, Tuong demanded that Thieu provide draft deferments for Hoa Hao "monks." The old issue of Hoa Hao independence, which Diem had crushed in 1956, was resurrecting itself. Thieu met with Tuong on June 21 and agreed to officially recognize him as the church leader, but he wanted the weapons returned. Some guns were turned in, but Tuong reneged and kept the bulk of his arms by claiming that his Defense Force was now a PSDF unit.

Thieu again ignored the issue, and it lay quiet until December 1974. However, when the PAVN overran Phuoc Long Province in early January 1975, Tuong decided to press the issue of an independent militia. The Hoa Hao leader offered to provide seventy-five thousand of his followers to defend Hoa Hao territory if the ARVN gave them weapons. Although Tuong insisted that he still supported Thieu, he thought a desperate GVN would acquiesce. He had misjudged the president. Thieu's patience was over, and when the Cao Dai sect also stated that month that it was adopting a policy of neutrality, he acted to prevent an erosion of government dominance. He ordered the police to begin arresting Hoa Hao deserters. On January 30,

1975, the police captured some Defense Force leaders, then began a major roundup. By early February, several Hoa Hao had been killed in armed clashes, six hundred had been arrested, and almost two hundred weapons were confiscated. The remainder retreated to Tuong's pagoda in the Hoa Hao heartland, but the police, hoping to calm the situation, did not seize the temple. Tuong remained surrounded in his pagoda, his dreams of Hoa Hao independence in ruins. That his ragtag militia could not even resist the police shattered his military fantasies.

Meanwhile, another old thorn, the Montagnard rebel faction FULRO, had returned. In the summer of 1974, a small FULRO band left their base in Cambodia and traveled to the Rhade tribal stronghold of Darlac Province in the Central Highlands. They began raiding Vietnamese farms and played on the old Montagnard anger over Vietnamese interlopers stealing their land. They pointed out that Vietnamese logging companies (a key export industry) were cutting down swaths of forest. Moreover, despite previous promises, the government had been unable to provide adequate services to the tribesmen, and II Corps had forced them into large resettlement camps to protect them from PAVN attacks. The FULRO agitation worked, and disenchanted PF troops began to desert, taking their weapons with them. The Darlac Province chief reported that the Montagnard "RF/PF under his command could not be counted on to act against their Montagnard brothers." Further, the province command confessed they were no longer receiving "reliable intelligence" on the location of Communist forces."[34] By the end of 1974, FULRO ambushes had increased to the point that the ARVN were forced to dispatch several Ranger battalions to hunt down the rebels. While FULRO was never more than a nuisance, that RF/PF morale had dramatically dropped due to Montagnard dissatisfaction with the GVN was an ominous sign. Worse, that the province command was no longer receiving intelligence on Communist movements would prove the undoing of the Central Highlands and South Vietnam when the PAVN attacked and captured the city of Ban Me Thuot in March 1975.

The Cao Dai religious sect in Tay Ninh Province along the Cambodian border had also become restless. The fall of remote Phuoc Long Province to its north and the subsequent capture on January 6, 1975, by PAVN forces of an ARVN communications facility on the peak of Ba Den Mountain (the seat of the Cao Dai church) forced it to reassess its position. In mid-January 1975, the Cao Dai pope informed Khiem that their territory should be considered a "no fight zone."[35] While they would not oppose the GVN, they would no longer actively support it. The Cao Dai were returning to their policy from the Diem years: peaceful coexistence between the two sides.

Between the Hoa Hao, FULRO, and the Cao Dai, South Vietnam's old centrifugal tendencies were returning, exacerbated by forces outside Thieu's control. A sense of public pessimism had emerged because of Communist military pressure, poor prospects for peace, a ghastly economy, and declining U.S. aid. With next year's presidential election looming, the politically active began to maneuver by challenging Thieu's ability to solve the nation's various dilemmas. The first dagger would be corruption.

CORRUPTION WOES

Nguyen Van Ngan's dismissal was not just a bureaucratic turf war but was also the result of another factor: a corruption investigation that threatened the Thieu family itself. First, however, came two well-publicized corruption scandals that touched the highest echelons of his administration. The most titillating was the seizure on the night of January 31, 1974, of a convoy of ARVN trucks filled with foreign-made cigarettes and Martell cognac on its way to Saigon from a dock in Long An Province, where the smuggled goods had been unloaded. Journalists wildly speculated over the convoy's financial organizer, but only the lower-level officers caught red-handed were charged. Then the police arrested Minister Pham Van Dong's wife in mid-February for running an illegal gambling den. After that, rumors of commodity hoarding—long a practice by importers to reap windfall profits—began spreading. Trying to distract the public's attention, on April 17, Thieu agreed to Ngan's suggestion to ask the Senate to create a committee to investigate fertilizer distribution problems. Miracle rice needed high amounts of imported urea fertilizer, yet despite sizeable imports, farmers were forced to buy it from middlemen at exorbitant rates since government stores were empty.

The Senate took their job seriously and discovered that several import companies had been falsifying sales receipts to the government and had then channeled the fertilizer to the black market. One major profiteer was the Hai Long Cong Ty Company. The Senators were shocked to discover that the company owner was Nguyen Xuan Nguyen, who just happened to be the husband of Mrs. Thieu's older sister.[36] When they reported their findings to Thieu in mid-May, the president concluded that Ngan had maneuvered the investigation to discredit his family and himself. Thieu convinced the

Senate to not highlight his family's involvement by claiming that U.S. antiwar critics would use it as an excuse to cut aid. Then he fired Ngan. On May 31, the Senate released its report, naming three Lower House deputies and thirty businesses for involvement but downplaying the role of the Hai Long company.

Senator Truong Tien Dat, a maverick Catholic opposed to the Thieu government, railed against the whitewash. On June 14, he issued a letter demanding Thieu fire eight senior officers for corruption. His actions encouraged a group of Catholic priests to hold a rally several days later at a church outside Saigon to publish a manifesto they had written denouncing corruption's corrosive effects. Although the police stopped them, Thieu could not ignore one of his most important constituencies. On June 19 and again on July 10, he ordered a crackdown on venality.[37]

Little did he know that his orders, so often proclaimed and so often ignored, would haunt him. A match had been lit, and much like Hue in 1963, that city would again provide flammable ground for a national protest movement. This time, however, it would be the Catholics rather than the Buddhists who would take to the streets seeking new government leadership. While regionalism had retreated from South Vietnam's political consciousness, religion's grip was still felt. Although the leadership of the main faiths in South Vietnam, the Buddhists and the Catholics, had withdrawn from the political ramparts, the heat still burned in certain segments of both churches.[38] They found a trigger in corruption.

After the police stopped the priest's petition, the group formed the People's Anti-Corruption Movement. Known by its initials PACM, it was led by Father Tran Huu Thanh, who had been born on August 8, 1915, in Quang Tri Province. Ordained as a priest in 1942, his first pastorate was in Hue. When he went to Saigon after the First Indochina War, President Diem appointed him to form the Republican Youth and eventually lead the School of Personalism. He ran afoul of the Ngo family when he accused Diem's brother, Ngo Dinh Can, of corruption. He left Saigon for Belgium, but upon his return, he taught anti-communism at the Dalat Academy for many years.[39] While he endorsed social justice and helping the poor, his virulent anti-communism and acquaintance with thousands of RVNAF officers meant Thieu would have difficulties dismissing him as a Communist stooge.

South Vietnamese Catholics were not the only ones chafing about political and social injustice. South Korean President Park Chung-hee had instituted heavy repressive measures in October 1972, including martial law and the death penalty for some protesters. On July 7, 1974, the ROK police arrested Bishop Daniel Chi, one of South Korea's most prominent religious leaders, for giving money to a dissident who had earlier in the year masterminded anti-government protests. While under arrest, Chi issued a "statement of conscience" that accused Park of stifling "fundamental human rights…through emergency decrees." He also decried Korea's military courts (similar to South Vietnam's) that had sentenced fourteen people to death and many others to long prison sentences.[40] Park made Thieu look like a choir boy.

The day after Bishop Chi's arrest, two thousand Catholics held a mass to protest his detention. The Park government responded and said that these people were just a "handful of disgruntled dissents" and that Park's repressiveness was due to Korea's "Confucian heritage" that honored duty over individual rights.[41] Park's position was not threatened because, like Thieu, he had carefully cultivated military loyalty. Whether South Vietnam's Catholics were inspired by the events in Korea is unknown, but they surely noticed. Thieu certainly did when the news broke that an assassin had shot at Park on August 15 but had missed and killed his wife. The assassin confessed that he was a Communist, but the social unrest undoubtedly provided perfect cover for the attempt. A month later, a chastened Park began lifting the decrees.

Thieu was not oblivious to the growing unrest over corruption. In speeches he called corruption a national dishonor, and he fired two division commanders on September 7 for thievery. With the president's action as backdrop, Father Thanh struck the next day. He led a crowd of five hundred people toward the town center in Hue, but police threw teargas grenades to disperse the group. Like Bishop Chi, Thanh responded by issuing a searing condemnation. Thanh published "Indictment No. 1," which accused Thieu of misusing his office for personal gain. He alleged that Thieu had purchased expensive properties, highlighted the Hai Long company's involvement in the fertilizer scandal, skewered the Vi Dan Hospital (Mrs. Thieu's pet charity) for its refusal to accept poor people, and charged that Hoang Duc Nha's mother (who was a well-known rice trader) of stealing government rice.[42] It was the most dramatic set of charges leveled against Thieu since he was accused of abetting heroin sales. That Thanh had inside knowledge of the Hai Long company's involvement in the fertilizer scandal implied that a senior GVN official had leaked the information to embarrass the president. While suspicion fell on Khiem, it was never proven.

Thieu immediately denied the allegations and gave orders not to suppress the protests. He then fired the province chief for the police actions in Hue. Instead, Thieu secretly convinced senior Catholic leaders to isolate Father Thanh. His ploy worked, and Thanh's group, however well-intentioned, failed to receive church blessing. The church hierarchy still backed Thieu, although their affinity for him had waned since 1972. Since Thieu represented the government, Archbishop Binh, while acknowledging the public's indignation about corruption, was far more afraid that Father Thanh's efforts would destabilize the government just as PAVN attacks were increasing.

The An Quang Buddhists also remained on the sidelines. They too feared that a "change in government leadership at this dangerous time in country's history" would only help the Communists.[43] Both churches were walking a fine line: they detested corruption but did not want to associate themselves with personal attacks on Thieu. The other two major protest groups, the disabled veterans and the students, also stayed silent. The students, long shorn of their pro-Communist leadership and now thoroughly infiltrated by government spies, remained focused on social work and the classroom.

Some groups, however, did join Father Thanh, especially the Vietnamese press after Nha's Information Ministry confiscated papers and sued three publishers that had printed Indictment No. 1. The ministry claimed that the revised press law banned false accusations. Journalists immediately protested his action and the stringent press law by burning newspapers in the streets. Their actions convinced the Revolutionary Dai Viets to also back Thanh, while Senator Vu Van Mau created a Buddhist National Reconciliation Force to demand both sides seek peace. While these various organizations did not unite, South Vietnam's body politic was starting to fracture.

Seeking to defuse the situation, on October 1, Thieu spoke to the nation. He again insisted that the country prepare for a massive attack by Hanoi and that he had taken steps to address corruption by dismissing the two division commanders, and he pointed out that over the summer he had directed the JGS to investigate "ghost soldiers" in RF/PF ranks in IV Corps. Although he again denied Father Thanh's allegations, he stumbled badly when he claimed that "those making such allegations are probably puppets of the Communists or foreigners."[44]

It was the worst speech of his presidency. Calling Thanh a Communist puppet instantly backfired, while many thought he had rambled and did not offer any solutions to South Vietnam's issues. Even the embassy conceded he had failed to rally "his own forces while giving the extremist opposition some specific points to renew their attacks."[45] Father Thanh quickly held protest masses in churches denouncing Thieu. He then ratcheted up the pressure and demanded the president resign. Other groups joined in, including some who had been on the sidelines. On October 10, around two hundred journalists and their supporters demonstrated in Saigon, where the irrepressible Mrs. Ngo Ba Thanh quickly joined them. Several days later, thirteen Saigon papers suspended publication for one day to protest the press law. The Disabled Veterans also released a letter demanding government reform, and on October 20, a small gang of rock-throwing students assaulted the National Assembly building. Breaking windows and overturning furniture, they also demanded Thieu resign.

With calls mounting for his resignation, Thieu was facing his most explosive domestic issue since April 1970. He needed to confront his opponents firmly enough to demonstrate his continuing control yet not create martyrs or generate opposition from the still politically inert urban population. In late October, when several prominent newspaper publishers demanded that Nha resign, it gave Thieu a way out. To temper rising criticism, on October 24, he fired four cabinet ministers, including Nha and Nguyen Duc Cuong. Both had become lightning rods for the administration. Thieu pledged to improve press relations and stated his rationale for changing economic ministers was to help the poor. He asserted that the economy "must be realistic and fair to the whole people" and that "development policy must be based on private business under the guidance of the government to meet the interests of the majority of the people."[46]

Losing Nha left Thieu isolated. Only a small coterie of men whom Thieu trusted, like his intelligence chief Nguyen Khac Binh, remained in the government. As the GVN's chief censor, Nha was ostensibly sacked for his abrasive relations with the press, but in reality, Khiem had threatened Thieu with his resignation if Nha was not removed. Cuong was a convenient scapegoat for the fertilizer scandal. Khiem picked a well-known banker, Nguyen Van Diep, to replace Cuong. Diep, though, was a secret Communist cadre.[47]

Thieu had also appointed Nguyen Van Hao as the new Deputy Prime Minister in charge of economic development. For the first time since 1966, Thieu had created a "super-minister" to oversee the economy. Hao, though, did not possess a new vision to revive the economy, nor was he able to convince a recalcitrant U.S. Congress to provide more aid.

After the cabinet shakeup, Thieu continued housecleaning. The next day, he discharged 377 officers from the RVNAF for a variety of ills, mostly corruption. Later that week, he also fired three of the four corps commanders. The only commander to remain was Truong in I Corps. Major General Pham Van Phu replaced Toan in II Corps, and Major General Nguyen Khoa Nam took over from Nghi in IV Corps. None of this satisfied the strident opposition. Rather than lower the political temperature, Thieu's sacrificial offerings only encouraged new ultimatums from them. The PACM launched a demonstration on October 31 that resulted in the first clash with the police. Afterward, Father Thanh pledged a nonviolent struggle, but he again called for Thieu's resignation. Although An Quang refused to openly side with Thanh, they now also demanded Thieu's resignation. Two weeks later, a group of forty-five opposition senators and deputies also requested Thieu resign, citing a loss of confidence in the president.

The president then suffered another blow when labor leader Tran Quoc Buu gave a speech demanding the eradication of corruption and then strongly criticized both sides for failing to achieve peace. Long seen as pro-government but not pro-Thieu, his word still carried weight with many people. Although he did not publicly call for the president's head, it was definitely a shot at Thieu. His speech asking for peace, though, was not just political opportunism; he was also suffering from a broken heart. His eldest son had recently been killed in combat. On October 18, Buu's son was leading a column to retake an outpost that had just been overrun when his unit was ambushed. He was not the only senior GVN politician to have lost a child to enemy fire. On April 6, 1972, one of Phan Quang Dan's sons, a South Vietnamese Air Force pilot, was shot down over Quang Tri Province while attacking enemy tanks. Reports indicate he had already destroyed several tanks when he was hit by a missile. The war had spared few South Vietnamese families.

While a respected figure like Buu could get away with indirectly condemning Thieu, demanding the president's resignation punctured Father Thanh's movement. He was unable to attract support from the country's major power groups, and PACM soon ran out of steam. His next protest effort was on November 28, but the number who attended dropped significantly from the earlier demonstrations. Only the Vietnamese press still backed him, but it was only promoting him as a means to convince Thieu to repeal the press law. When the PAVN attacked Phuoc Long in December, the focus instantly returned to the Communist enemy.

Although Father Thanh had spotlighted the key issue damaging South Vietnamese society, lost in the tumult was the recognition that the ability to engage in free speech and organize without interference were the core rights of a democratic society. Although Thieu had rightfully not sent the police to persuade the good father, he saw Thanh's protests as aiding Hanoi. Thieu's fear of Communist aggression overrode his sympathy for a people wearied by dashed hopes for peace and frightened by pitiless military and economic conditions. For Thieu, dissent only helped the Communists. He told Vice President Tran Van Huong in late November that "those elements of the Catholic opposition who...seek a compromise with the Communists as a shortcut to obtaining power themselves [are] pseudo-communists... [I]f the political programs advocated by these naïve individuals were ever put into effect, the Communists would quickly dominate the government."[48]

Thieu desired Nationalist anti-communist unity to convince the Politburo it could not win. He was correct in that Hanoi, bound by a dogma that an infallible party led the North Vietnamese state and people, defined protests in South Vietnam as "internal contradictions" that highlighted Saigon's weakness. Yet his failure to incorporate the political middle weakened the country as much as South Vietnam's economic doldrums. These grand political questions, however, were about to become moot. The People's Army was gathering for its final assault.

24

"I WILL DRAW OUT
MY SWORD"

Diplomacy's Final Dance

A fter the surprise North Vietnamese attack on March 10, 1975, against Ban Me Thuot, the capital of the southern part of the Central Highlands, President Thieu ordered his military forces in II Corps to retake the city. The repositioning ARVN column was destroyed, setting off a chain reaction that led to the chaotic disintegration of I Corps and the capture of Hue and Danang. The collapse of the northern half of South Vietnam enabled the Communist military commanders to concentrate virtually their entire army against Saigon.

Numerous books have detailed the final days. Many have concentrated on the U.S. evacuation or the military campaigns, but few have delved deeply into the last-ditch diplomatic efforts by the French to create a new South Vietnamese government. Paris wanted Thieu to resign so a coalition with the PRG could be forged to prevent a complete takeover by Hanoi. The French policy was based on information from Hanoi and the PRG that they would agree to a ceasefire if Duong Van Minh replaced Thieu as president. Despite this clandestine diplomatic effort, on April 30, Communist troops entered Saigon, and the war was over.

"MAKE THEM EAT THEIR WORDS"

Regardless of his outrage over the mortaring of the two schools in the

Delta in May 1974, Thieu decided to reoffer negotiations to prove that he was not the obstacle to peace. On July 20, the twentieth anniversary of the Geneva Accords, he called for direct talks between Hanoi and Saigon. The Politburo immediately rejected any dialogue. Diplomacy remained quiet until October 8, when the PRG attempted to capitalize on Father Thanh's call for the president to quit by announcing that it would only resume negotiations if Thieu resigned.

Between Nixon's departure, the aid cutbacks, the street agitation, and the growing combat, Thieu felt isolated. Believing a major offensive loomed, he furtively made a momentous decision to try to save his country, one that has been unknown until now. The first inkling appeared on October 23, when Nguyen Xuan Phong, now leading the GVN negotiation team in Paris, requested an audience with the Americans. Phong, obliquely responding to the recent PRG statement, told the U.S. officials that "the time may soon be ripe for the GVN side to offer something new to the Communist side." This proposal would "blunt the political unrest in South Vietnam" and would "be specific and tempting." While not offering specifics, Phong opined that since the PRG had just "stated publicly that they would not negotiate" with Thieu, this new proposition "might make them eat their words." Moreover, although the GVN viewed the NCNRC "as a subversive element," the GVN "must consider the extent to which it can tolerate...this subversion...to maintain its overall authority."[1] Since Hanoi would surely reject Saigon's entreaties, Phong hinted that the U.S. must pitch this idea to the Russians and the Chinese. With President Gerald Ford meeting the Russians in Vladivostok in late November, followed shortly thereafter with a visit by Secretary of State Henry Kissinger to Beijing, Phong hoped that the U.S. could convince Hanoi's allies to pressure the Politburo into accepting it.

Although the U.S. failed to act on his request, in the first of two highly classified diplomatic initiatives that Phong was involved in during the final months, Thieu made an abrupt and dramatic change in policy. In secret desperation, Thieu informed Phong that he was prepared to resign in exchange for Hanoi's guarantee to maintain the existence of South Vietnam's government. Phong relates that

Thieu was no longer sure he could hold on. He sent me a cable...and told me he would 'not be an obstacle to peace.' He told me to feel everyone out, what they would think. He did not expect much of a response from Hanoi. 'Who would be acceptable to them?' was his main question. My intention was also to probe the U. S. reaction to a possible 'international solution.' He hoped I could salvage a South Vietnam distinct from North Vietnam.[2]

To accomplish his mission, Phong needed to find a formula that would be acceptable to both the South Vietnamese military and the Communists. Although Thieu did not envision a coalition, Phong knew this was a disguised surrender. While the president viewed it as trading himself for a political settlement, Phong believed the offer, if accepted, would simply buy time, a chance for the republic to perhaps save itself. Regardless, the idea was not mentioned by either Ford or Kissinger to Hanoi's allies. Part of the reason was that Thieu had kept this change closely held. Foreign Minister Vuong Van Bac stated later that "I would have resigned if [I] knew."[3] Hoang Duc Nha, however, confirms Phong's account. Nha termed the offer a "gamble to see the reality" of Hanoi's willingness to talk peace. Thieu, though, felt "it would be very irresponsible to resign without...knowing what the enemy would do," meaning he would not resign without a guarantee.[4]

At the same time, the GVN publicized another diplomatic offer. On November 7, Bac renewed the GVN's proposal to negotiate, but he vetoed the PRG demand that Thieu resign as a precondition for talks. When the PRG rebuffed Bac, Thieu publicly suggested it delineate areas of control and establish the NCNRC. Once more the PRG refused, calling Thieu's proposal a "deceptive trick."[5] With no traction, Phong again visited the Americans. For a second time he hinted that a "packaged deal" should be offered, one that would "give a tempting concession to the Communists in return for their adherence for a 'real ceasefire.'" Any GVN compromise, though, should "not damage the RVN's authority unduly."[6] The U.S. again ignored Phong, and in late 1974, the Politburo finalized its plans for a spring offensive.

However, France had discerned Phong's insinuations, leading it to resurrect its long-standing push to neutralize South Vietnam. Paris had pursued this goal intermittently since 1954, often with Hanoi's encouragement. A Politburo cable from 1968 spells out their thinking:

The diplomatic struggle must make a positive contribution to our effort to pressure the U.S. to replace the current puppet leaders [and] to talk directly to the [NLF]. We must tell the Americans that only if they do these things can there be a resolution of the South Vietnam problem....One critical issue at present is to establish a government in Saigon whose goal is to discuss political issues with the Front and that will work with the Front to form a coalition government that will demand that the American imperialists withdraw their troops...To accomplish this, we must utilize the role of France and the pro-French faction [in South Vietnam]....We must...coordinate the political and diplomatic struggles and the stratagem we use with France [along] with an extremely active, vigorous military plan in order to win the highest level of victory.[7]

French policy after the accords had been to recognize only one government in South Vietnam, but it viewed that entity as a coalition government that included the PRG and the Third Force. French officials repeatedly told Phong was that "France was in a unique position to act as an effective 'go-between' for all the parties involved [and] could provide the 'cement' for a negotiated settlement between North Vietnam, the PRG, and South Vietnam."[8] However, the French needed a partner, and they sought one in the Chinese.

President Georges Pompidou had continued Charles De Gaulle's neutralist policy. In a statement Pompidou read on October 1, 1971, to a visiting Chinese Communist delegation, he affirmed that France "was still loyal to the policy of neutralizing Indochina." GVN Foreign Minister Tran Van Lam informed Prime Minister Khiem that

> according to sources in Paris that are well-informed about the French political scene, the reason that Pompidou made the statement is that he wants Communist China to recognize that France will play a role in resolving the Indochina problem, especially now that Nixon is preparing to visit Beijing. However, the Chinese Communist delegation's total silence on this matter demonstrates that they only want to talk to the United States about this issue.[9]

Pompidou continued to pursue ties with China, and he traveled to Beijing in September 1973 to improve trade. The discussions on international affairs mostly revolved around finding a solution for Cambodia, but they set the groundwork for future cooperation on Indochina.[10] Long-time French Director for Asian Affairs Henri Froment-Meurice informed the

Americans after the meeting that France is "very interested in developing China relations and Chinese have begun to consult more frequently with French on various issues."[11]

With the death of Pompidou in April 1974 and the subsequent election of Valéry Giscard d'Estaing, French policy moved from acceptance of the status quo in Vietnam to a more proactive role. Froment-Meurice saw the growing street protests in Saigon as an opportunity to remove Thieu, and he duly informed the North Vietnamese. In early November, the chief PRG representative in Paris cabled DRV Foreign Minister Nguyen Duy Trinh that

> France is considering the possibility that Thieu will be replaced and realizes that we are determined to overthrow Thieu.... The French President is trying to explore our attitude on this, both our attitude for the immediate future and our attitude about things over the long run. Fundamentally, French policy has not changed, but France wants to take advantage of this opportunity to bargain with the U.S., and...to give France some kind of a role to play in South Vietnam. We think that we might be able to use France in some fashion to add impetus to Thieu's downfall.[12]

Hanoi's stratagem to use France to achieve its goals was finally bearing fruit. But just as Hanoi's diplomats had discerned France's intentions, Le Duan was equally suspicious of China's ambitions. After a Politburo meeting in October 1974 to discuss the new offensive in 1975, he wrote a letter to COSVN. Explaining the international situation, he posited that a "number of major powers...are quietly working to become rulers" of Indochina. They "view a unified, independent Vietnam...as a major obstacle to their schemes. For that reason, they are trying to block Vietnam's efforts to advance and to prolong the time during which our country is still divided in order to weaken us. To accomplish this goal, the U.S. hopes China will pressure us to stop after we signed the Paris Agreement."[13]

Le Duan believed China secretly desired to prevent a unified Vietnam. This reason, one among several, is why he pushed for another offensive. He wanted to act before China could intervene to deny him victory. His assessment that Beijing dreaded a unified Vietnam was correct. With a nuclear-armed Soviet army camped on its northern border, if Hanoi allied itself with the Russians, China would be surrounded. Beijing, aware of the Politburo's plans for a massive spring attack, had warmed to France's policy of a coalition government in South Vietnam to prevent a North Vietnamese takeover. Phong was also told independently that Hanoi's fear of China preventing it from conquering Saigon was a main rationale for the spring offensive. China's actions in the last days would confirm Le Duan's fears.

CUTTING OFF U.S. AID

On the second anniversary of the Paris Peace Accords, South Vietnamese losses continued at an appalling rate. The GVN released a statement claiming that they had suffered "nearly 160,000 casualties since the ceasefire agreement was signed."[14] A combination of Thieu's pleas, Martin's strident messages, and the increasing sound of the guns convinced President Gerald Ford to ask Congress to restore the $300 million in the $1 billion FY75 aid package for South Vietnam that it had not appropriated.

The money was desperately needed. Congress had mandated in the aid bill that costs for South Vietnam normally expensed out of the Pentagon's operating budget must be charged against the allocated $700 million. That left only $470 million for regular supplies like fuel and ammunition. General Cao Van Vien poignantly explained in late January 1975 the debilitating consequences of this fiat. Even after draconian reductions in RVNAF expenditures in FY74, $470 million "will only satisfy thirty-eight percent of our operating expenses" in 1975. In the face of the "increasing pace and intensity" of enemy attacks, further reductions "will have a serious effect on the combat capabilities of the ARVN and on the morale of our soldiers." By the end of the year, Vien projected that artillery ammunition reserves, critical stockpiles that were maintained in case of a countrywide offensive, would be reduced to a thirty-seven-day supply. The lag time between the order and arrival of U.S ammunition was sixty to ninety days. Worse, "our fuel supply will be completely gone by the end of December."[15]

Although General Vien cogently explained the devastating impact of the aid cuts, his arguments fell on deaf ears. The November 1974 U.S. midterm congressional elections had resulted in an even larger Democratic Party majority, one that was stridently anti-Thieu. Between U.S. economic doldrums and strong antiwar sentiments, the request never stood a chance. Congress, however, was not solely to blame. A Gallup poll conducted in early February 1975 found that 78 percent of the U.S. population opposed further aid.[16]

Years of American social conflicts over Vietnam and perceptions of Saigon as a corrupt hellhole had eradicated support for the war.

Ford then asked a congressional delegation to tour Indochina and write a report. He hoped a review detailing the ominous situation would spur Congress to rethink its opposition. Congressman John Flynt (D-Ga.), led the group, which arrived at the end of February. After meeting South Vietnamese leaders and U.S. officials, Flynt encouraged Thieu to open his government to more opposition figures, a U.S. proposal since the Diem era.

Thieu responded with his usual mantra: "For the present time, Vietnam's first priority must be its survival." Many people criticize, and "sometimes that criticism is justified," but it is "easier to criticize the government than it is to actually hold responsibility for governing." To achieve peace, he had offered to allow the PRG to "participate in the political life of Vietnam. That is not an easy proposition to advocate for a man who has been fighting the VC for so long." Regarding aid, Vietnam was not a "bottomless pit." The country just needed another three or four years until "it can stand on its own feet. In the 1960's Vietnam was forced to call upon U.S. troops to help defend it [but we] will never need your troops again, only your material support."[17] Neither Thieu's arguments nor the team's report swayed many voters. On March 12 and 13, just after the Communists had launched their new offensive, the U.S. Congress voted overwhelmingly against more aid. Brigadier General Tran Van Hai, who commanded the 7th ARVN Division, bitterly remarked, "We will fight lonely and desperate."[18]

PRESSING THIEU TO RESIGN

Military aid was not Saigon's only issue. Internal fissures like corruption and the stubbornly high unemployment rate continued to generate social turmoil. On February 1, 1975, Father Tran Huu Thanh published another blistering denunciation of Thieu. Known as "Indictment No. 2," he called for Thieu to stand trial for "high treason" because the president had "destroyed the Nationalist cause." Moreover, Thieu "cannot possibly bring peace to Vietnam" since he was using "the war as an excuse for consolidating his own personal power and wealth."[19]

Upset, Thieu immediately closed five newspapers that had printed Indictment No. 2. Over twenty journalists, many already secretly under investigation for Communist ties, were arrested. The detentions, right before the

U.S. congressional hearings on aid, were singularly unhelpful, as Thieu was again viewed as oppressing freedom of speech. Several journalists, however, were in fact covert Communist cadres. One reporter, Nguyen Van Hong, belonged to the Public Security A10 espionage ring. Assembly deputy Ly Qui Chung confirmed that the chairman of the South Vietnamese Journalists Union and several others "were full-fledged Communist cadres."[20]

Thieu's dedicated opposition was instantly outraged over his response. Senator Vu Van Mau opined that Thieu was "going to follow Park Chung-Hee [and] clamp down completely on his opponents," a comment revealing how closely events in South Korea were followed.[21] Duong Van Minh and over forty deputies signed a letter in blood demanding Thieu resign.

The main schemer, however, was Tran Quoc Buu. The labor leader normally stayed in the shadows of Saigon's political arena, but the grave situation had forced him to strongly consider a run for the presidency in the upcoming election. After his speech in late 1974, Buu's next step was to forge a committee of "very prestigious Vietnamese" that would make a "strong call to all Nationalists to come together under the leadership of this committee to protect South Vietnam from the Communist invasion."[22] Bui Diem, Tran Van Do, and Dang Van Sung were committee members. Alarmed at South Vietnam's rapid deterioration, the men were determined to press the president to craft a broader government to rally the people before the Communist hammer fell. They sent a letter to Thieu "proposing that he invite all opposition groups to discuss [forming] a Government of National Union," which included "a cabinet reorganization and serious reforms."[23] If he refused, they would publicly call for his resignation. However, Buu immediately left for the U.S. to convince Congress to loosen its purse strings. When he returned, the Communists had launched their offensive. Demands for Thieu to resign or add opposition figures into his government were mounting again. Soon they would blossom.

Several days after the U.S. congressional delegation departed Saigon, PAVN forces cut the three main roads in the Central Highlands, signaling the opening of the spring offensive. For the fourth time, Hanoi had launched an attack because it thought Saigon was an easy pushover. Just as it had in prior years, the Politburo believed South Vietnam was weak and in disarray. Since Hanoi had been wrong the first three times, this time it was more cautious. While it did not believe this attack would collapse its mortal enemy, it hoped to conquer large tracts of the countryside and force Thieu out of office. Just as Le Duc Tho had opined in Paris in 1972, the Politburo saw removing him as the surest way to defeat South Vietnam. Eliminating Thieu would be Hanoi's chief diplomatic strategy to complete its conquest.

There was, however, one mortal difference between 1975 and prior years. The People's Army, while not the powerhouse of 1972, had inculcated the bloody lessons from the offensive. This version of PAVN had spent two plus years rebuilding its devastated divisions. Equally consequential, it now excelled in key aspects of military undertakings: well-crafted staff plans, superb communications, logistical preplanning, and tactical flexibility. Air defenses had been extended far south, as had roads, a fuel pipeline, and supply storehouses. Without U.S. bombers raining destruction on them, and seeing a demoralized RVNAF, Hanoi once more threw its army at South Vietnam. This time, it was right.

After cutting the roads, on March 10, the Communists attacked and overran the city of Ban Me Thuot.[24] In III Corps, heavy attacks threatened to isolate Saigon, while in northern I Corps, enemy units assaulted Quang Tri Province and south of Hue. Civilians by the thousands in Quang Tri instantly fled toward Hue. Faced with this onslaught, and with news of the aid defeat, on March 13 and 14, Thieu made two military decisions that sealed his defeat. First, he told Lieutenant General Ngo Quang Truong to return the Airborne Division from I Corps to Saigon to bolster the capital's defenses. In 1972, he had ordered General Vien to hold Kontum and retake Quang Tri because losing those areas would have possibly unraveled the nation. Thieu's decision to stand fast was bolstered by enormous U.S. firepower and logistics. Realizing that the B-52s would not return, and with limited supplies, he believed his only hope was to change strategy. He decided to withdraw to more defensible positions in the northern half of the country to free forces to protect the prosperous southern half, a plan he called "Light at the Top, Heavy at the Bottom." However, the withdrawal of the Airborne forced Truong to shift his forces to compensate, which tore holes in his lines and created civilian panic. Worse, a toxic rumor spread that the "great powers" had ceded most of I Corps to Hanoi. Between the Airborne withdrawal and the rumor, people panicked, and several hundred thousand civilians stampeded toward Danang.

The next day, Thieu ordered II Corps Commander Major General Pham Van Phu to retake Ban Me Thuot. With the only road from Pleiku to the city blocked, Phu chose to move his forces along a little-used and badly maintained road that led to the coast. From there, he intended to attack west along Route 21 and recapture Ban Me Thuot. His poorly planned maneuver disintegrated when thousands of local civilians followed the withdrawing column. Communist units closed in and annihilated Phu's forces.

The loss of Ban Me Thuot instantly renewed calls for Thieu to resign or relinquish power. Hoping to rally the opposition to support the GVN, on March 15, Bui Diem, Tran Van Do, and Tran Quoc Buu visited the president. Do told him told that "a gulf exists between the government and the population [and] that it was now necessary to do something." They recommended a cabinet change that would bring into the government "members of the 'real opposition.'"[25] Thieu agreed, as he always did, but he asked for a written recommendation, mainly to stall.

The rapidly worsening military situation, however, forced his hand. On March 25, he directed Khiem to form a new cabinet. Lower House leader Nguyen Ba Can reports that Thieu wanted to reorganize the "cabinet to bring in a large number of different political parties, associations, and groups from around the country. He wanted to achieve national solidarity so that we could mobilize the spirit of patriotism...of the population and give top priority to supporting the front lines."[26] For a week, Khiem met with numerous representatives, but he failed.

Tran Van Do, however, believed Thieu was not seeking a broader government but maneuvering to bypass his group. Do had been quietly talking with Nguyen Cao Ky, an indication of how much South Vietnam's elder statesman feared for the future. Do had urged Thieu to run for president in 1967, and he and Ky had been long-time antagonists. Yet now he pressed Ky to emerge from retirement and return to the political stage. Ky agreed, and on March 26, he held a press conference to announce the formation of a National Salvation Committee, a version of Buu's proposed Government of National Union. Joined by many opposition figures, Ky insisted that Thieu either resign or turn power over to his group so they could rally the country. Ky wanted authority to lead the armed forces, believing that he could inject leadership into a badly demoralized military. Ky insisted that he was not advocating a coup, nor did he seek power; he only wanted to save the country. Once the situation had stabilized, he would open negotiations with Hanoi or the PRG. The Interior Ministry responded that night by arresting ten opposition figures for coup plotting, which only stiffened the opposition's refusal to join the government.

With the fall of I Corps on March 31 and the broadcast of horrific scenes of frantic people attempting to escape Danang, the last remnants of Thieu's credibility evaporated. His political rivals and even his supporters began to circle. The first blow was a private letter from Buddhist leader Thich Tam Chau on April 1 asking Thieu to resign. The next day, Duong Van Minh again called for Thieu's resignation so that "a new government can be formed...to make peace." Minh, however, was not supporting the effort by Buu and Do. Still beholden to An Quang, he stated that "the Buddhists want nothing to do with this formula." Nor was he backing Ky "after everything he did to the Buddhists in 1966."[27] At the same time, Senator Tran Van Lam mustered a nonbinding "no confidence" vote in the Senate. He then visited the president and asked Thieu, Huong, and Khiem to step down. Constitutionally, Lam would succeed Thieu and Huong, and he claimed that a new government led by him could negotiate a coalition with the PRG. He also wanted to give Ky military authority. Finally, Archbishop Nguyen Van Binh published a statement adding his voice to those demanding a new direction. Virtually every power bloc in the country save the military had now demanded Thieu's resignation.

Thieu spurned them all. He was able to cling to power for four reasons. First, while some younger officers were making wild threats, no senior officer considered a coup. The generals wanted Thieu's removal via the constitution. Second, the U.S. appeared committed to Thieu or had at least not voiced displeasure. Third was his notorious stubbornness. He refused to be pushed from power, especially by Ky or Minh. Last, his opposition remained weak. That, however, was about to change.

Thieu's usurpers moved to knock out the regime's last prop: the army. Ky was the main instigator. Ambassador Martin was called to Khiem's office on April 4 to meet with General Vien and the prime minister. They had two messages for the ambassador. First, Vien said, Ky had approached him to ask Martin to recommend to the president that Thieu, Huong, and Khiem resign so that Senator Lam could assume power and appoint Ky as prime minister to run the war. When Martin declined, Vien then asked him to speak to Ky and warn him against a coup. When the ambassador again demurred, Vien told him that Thieu had authorized him to see Ky.

With Thieu's blessing, Martin visited Ky. The former vice president reemphasized his earlier points to Martin. "In order to boost morale," Thieu and Khiem had to go. Ky would become prime minister, and once the front was stabilized, negotiations could begin. Ky insisted, though, "there must be no coup" because only the Communists would profit.[28] Ky was dissembling; he had asked Vien on April 2 to support a coup, but Vien had refused. Vien promptly told Khiem, which triggered their request to see Martin. The ambassador's admonition worked, and Ky stood down his coup plans.

Ky, though, was not the only conspirator. Earlier that morning, Thieu's former legislative advisor, Nguyen Van Ngan, was arrested for coup plotting. Thieu accused Ngan of having colluded with Senator Lam to convince the Senate to pass the no confidence vote on April 2. That was true, but Ngan's maneuver was motivated more by revenge for having been pushed out a year earlier than his desire for a coup. Despite his meeting with Martin, Khiem was also secretly plotting to remove Thieu. The prime minister had sounded out various senior officers, including Vien, but they had declined.

Catching wind of Khiem's intrigues, after Martin left the palace, Thieu summoned Khiem to his office. Before Khiem could speak, Thieu told him to resign. Khiem has denied this, stating that he resigned at the suggestion of Tran Van Do rather than being forced out by Thieu. Khiem "foresaw the need for negotiations with the Communists," and his presence made that impossible.[29] Whatever the truth, the long-serving prime minister was gone. Thieu then announced to the nation that Nguyen Ba Can would be the new prime minister to head a government of war and national union, precisely what Tran Van Do had suggested three weeks prior. Hoang Duc Nha claims that the president was trying "to meet the Bui Diem/Buu/Do folks halfway...a desperate move by Thieu to prevent the U.S. from deposing him."[30] Thieu, though, was whistling in the dark, and his "desperate move" would nearly be his last.

END OF AN ERA

Early on the morning of April 8, First Lieutenant Nguyen Thanh Trung taxied his F5E fighter plane onto the Bien Hoa Air Base runway. Armed with two bombs, Trung's mission that morning was support for an ARVN unit. Trung, though, had a different plan. After signaling his wingman that he had an electrical problem and needed to return to the hanger, the other plane departed. Trung waited ten seconds, and then he pushed his throttles forward and lifted off. But instead of heading west, he turned east toward Independence Palace. Trung had secretly joined the NLF in 1960 when he was only thirteen, and on his own initiative, he decided to kill Thieu.[31]

Trung quickly reached the palace. Coming in low, he dropped his first bomb. The bomb missed the reinforced helicopter pad and punctured the roof. It entered the fourth floor but did not explode. Trung swung around and released his second bomb, which hit the palace grounds and exploded, shattering numerous windows. Trung then departed and landed at a captured air base in Phuoc Long. The bombing, reminiscent of the attempt in February 1962 on President Diem, had one other odd similarity. Both initial bombs had not exploded. If they had, each attack would have killed the president. Based on interviews with Thieu's chief military aide, the palace's head of security, and Hoang Duc Nha's military aide, here for the first time is what happened inside the building.[32]

As he did every day, Thieu was eating breakfast on the fourth floor. His military aide, Major Nguyen Xuan Tam, provided the president two reports each morning, which Thieu read during his meal. When he was finished eating and had read the two reports, Thieu then went to his office on the second floor. Since Tam had not yet received one report, Thieu finished his bowl of soup and went downstairs. Seconds after he left, Trung's first bomb hit the roof. It "broke into two pieces," one missing where Thieu had been sitting by "ten meters." The other half rolled down a staircase and caught some curtains on fire. Tam rushed Thieu downstairs to the reinforced bunker in the basement. Meanwhile, Colonel Tran Thanh Dien, commander of the palace security unit, had been outside inspecting the guard posts when the first bomb hit. Dien jumped into a recently dug bunker. When Trung flew off, Dien ran toward the palace. Just as he arrived, Thieu and Tam were exiting the stairs. Dien recalls that Thieu laughingly said to him, "Where have you been?"

Thieu told Tam to find his family. Tam went upstairs to the bedroom, but the door was locked. He broke it down and found Mrs. Thieu and the couple's oldest daughter hiding in the corner, terribly frightened. Thieu ordered Tam to have them flown to Can Tho. Thieu then asked Tam, "How can Minh [VNAF Commander Lieutenant General Tran Van Minh] drop a bomb on my place?" Tam called Minh and told him to report to the palace. When Minh arrived, another military aide, Captain Doan Huu Dinh, went to escort him to the president. Spotting Dinh, a "heavily sweating" Minh dropped his pistol belt and weapon onto the floor and loudly proclaimed, "I had nothing to do with it!" Suspicion then immediately fell on Ky, who also vigorously denied any involvement.

Although the bomb had missed killing Thieu by seconds, no one was hurt except one officer who slipped on broken glass and broke his arm. If Trung's first bomb, which Colonel Dien said did not detonate because it had an armor-piercing fuse, had hit the helicopter pad, it would have exploded and killed Thieu. If it had been contact-fused instead, it also would have burst when it hit the roof. If he had still been sitting at the breakfast table when the first bomb hit, he might have been killed. By the narrowest of margins, Thieu had escaped death. While an isolated incident, the impression had been made that the RVNAF was fracturing. More importantly, Trung's failed attempt began the countdown to Thieu's removal.

Like Khiem, Nguyen Ba Can also had difficulty forming a cabinet, but finally, on April 14, he announced his new government. It had taken Can ten days to piece together this group, ten days in which the military situation rapidly deteriorated as the PAVN rolled down the coast, leaving only part of III Corps and all of IV Corps still in ARVN hands.

Cambodia was also undergoing its death throes. The Khmer Rouge (KR) had overrun much of the country and had surrounded Phnom Penh. On April 1, Lon Nol resigned as head of the government in the forlorn hope that peace talks might ensue. The Khmer Rouge rejected negotiations, and heavy fighting engulfed the remaining Cambodian army positions. On April 17, the KR overcame the army's last lines of resistance and entered the city. Cambodia had fallen. The KR rounded up numerous Cambodian military personnel and government officials, and shortly thereafter, executed them. During the next few years, a genocidal wave swept the country. Over a million Cambodians perished.

That same day Phnom Penh fell, French Ambassador Jean-Marie Mérillon met with Thieu. He had come to press Thieu to resign. Mérillon remarked that "the moment was emotional. Even a diplomat could feel it. But my job was to analyze the political situation with realism." He urged him to resign so that negotiations might begin. France was intervening in South Vietnam's internal affairs because "we had an overall view of the problem [and] we were the only ones in a position to converse directly, and in confidence, with the Americans, the Soviets, the Chinese, the North Vietnamese and the Viet Cong."[33]

Thieu, according to Mérillon, said little. Several days later, with Thieu still dallying, Ambassador Martin also visited him. He was carrying the same message: Thieu needed to leave. Martin told him that the military situation was hopeless, that U.S. aid would not magically appear, and that "time was the essential commodity." While only a faint hope existed for negotiations, Martin, like Mérillon, wanted to try. Thieu said he would do what was best for South Vietnam. The ambassador's report to Kissinger ended by expressing that afterward he had showered and had "scrubbed very hard with the strongest soap I could find."[34]

With the "Mandate of Heaven" withdrawn, the next day, Thieu gathered his closest advisors. He had decided to resign, but he wanted to abide by the constitution. In a postwar interview, Thieu claimed he knew the demand for his resignation to start talks was a "Communist trick," but he wanted "to prove that I was not trying to hang on to the presidential chair. Then people would say that because of me and my stubbornness they could not negotiate a peace agreement."[35] Since maintaining the constitution was crucial, he would turn power over to Huong, not to Minh. Prime Minister Can resigned as well, but he was asked to remain for a short time.

On the evening of April 21, Nguyen Van Thieu spoke to his country for the last time. In a fiery speech, he denounced the Americans for abandoning his people. The man who had been intertwined with South Vietnam's fate for over a decade was gone. He had overseen the birth of the Second Republic, nursed it through two major attacks, managed the U.S. withdrawal, and offered a lasting peace. Yet he seemed forever tarred for allowing corruption to flourish, and he was denounced for a warlike attitude and pilloried for authoritarianism. Those charges miss the mark. He fought South Vietnam's long battle with courage and determination, force-fed the concept of constitutional law to a skeptical elite, and survived crises that would have trampled a lesser man. Despite being trapped between the crushing levers of a fratricidal war and South Vietnam's centrifugal tendencies, he devised and led the modernization of his country's economic, governmental, and administrative structure, the essential building blocks for a viable state. He transformed his country while ignoring the constant carping of the coffee-house malcontents while simultaneously fending off the arm-twisting of a disengaging ally. In the minds of those who knew and worked with him, he was a patriot. Others believed he was responsible for South Vietnam's defeat. Both views have merit.

After Thieu finished his speech, Huong was sworn in. On April 26, Thieu, Khiem, and their aides left for Taiwan. Despite the rumors, Thieu did not take some of South Vietnam's gold with him. But now that he was gone, the last diplomatic dance could finally begin.

A CLEVER SMOKESCREEN

With the growing military debacle in I and II Corps, Nguyen Xuan Phong attempted a third time to enlist the U.S. to help find a diplomatic solution, but now he was feverishly trying to stave off the republic's total defeat. On March 20, Phong offered "his conviction that the GVN should undertake a major political activity very soon." He proposed "a broader role for the NCNRC or a political evolution toward a transitional government of national union." Phong's desperate plan would grant the NCNRC far more power than just organizing elections: "[T]he current GVN would be replaced by a broader based grouping of the Nationalists...This government would then call for the PRG to join to enlarge it further." Repeating his earlier pleas, Phong said he needed "strong U.S support" to convince Hanoi that it "was not just a gimmick. U.S. intervention with Moscow [and Beijing]...would help pressure the Communists into accepting the proposal." Phong had no illusions that Hanoi had given up its dream of conquest, but "hopefully the arrangement...would last a few years," enough to give the Nationalists "some breathing space."[36] Kissinger brushed off Phong's approach, stating that "whatever diplomatic opportunities may arise, we would look to the Vietnamese parties to deal with the issues he raises."[37] The secretary of state was going his own route with the Soviets.

Even if Phong had convinced the Americans to help, would he have found a willing partner in Hanoi? The answer is no. The Politburo's diplomatic strategy after the accords was focused on three concepts. The first was to smear Thieu by utilizing the "favorable provisions of the Paris Agreement [demanding democratic liberties] to incite a worldwide movement denouncing the [GVN's] systematic actions to sabotage and resist the newly-signed Peace Agreement."[38] Second, by painting Saigon as the aggressor, Hanoi sought "to win sympathy, approval, and eventually positive support for our use of political violence and armed force in our struggle to overthrow the puppet regime." In other words, Hanoi attempted to convince the world that its military actions in South Vietnam were justified. Third, after launching the 1975 offensive, "the primary role of diplomacy was to monitor the possibility that the U.S. might again intervene militarily and to fight to block such a possibility."[39]

After the Ban Me Thuot victory, the Politburo launched a fourth effort. Le Duan believed that Thieu's strategy was to make a stand in III and IV Corps and negotiate a ceasefire. Le Duan, though, was adamantly against talks, and the Politburo had devised a diplomatic deception plan to prevent another American intervention and disguise its true intentions for a military victory.

The outlines of this scheme were revealed postwar by Ha Van Lau in an interview with French journalist Olivier Todd. Lau had been a senior member of Hanoi's delegation to the Paris talks, and when he spoke to Todd, he was Vietnam's ambassador to France. Lau said that on March 15, 1975, the Politburo had created a secret cell that would devise a strategy to "take advantage of all contradictions in the enemy camp and give adversaries the impression that there is a slight slippage between the DRV's position and the PRG's."[40] The concept was to exploit France's desire for a ceasefire by making it appear that the southern-based Communists were interested in peace via a coalition while Hanoi was not. By dangling a political solution which required the toppling of Thieu, the Politburo hoped to destroy Saigon's ability to resist. Afterward, Hanoi would assume control in a bloodless coup.

Initially, Hanoi wanted Tran Van Don to replace Thieu. After conquering I Corps, however, Hanoi shifted to Duong Van Minh. A postwar article, heavily sourced to French diplomats, agrees that after the opening attacks, the Communists confirmed that a "senior Saigon personality [like Don]" was acceptable to "negotiate a coalition with the PRG." After the fall of Hue, [Don] was "discarded as unnecessary," and the PRG then insisted on Minh. Interestingly, the article contends that the PRG "preferred negotiations for fear of being eclipsed and left powerless" if Hanoi won an outright military victory, which was precisely what occurred.[41]

The first instance of Hanoi's diplomatic offensive came on March 21 when the PRG demanded that Thieu be replaced by a government that supported "peace, national reconciliation, independence, and democracy."[42] Although the Politburo had secretly decided on March 18 to conquer South Vietnam in 1975, the PRG broadcast the opposite. It was "ready to negotiate with such an administration with a view to promptly solving South Vietnam's problems." While a repeat of its offer in October 1974, the proposal seemingly offered a means to halt the killing.

The second effort came the next day. At a banquet in Hanoi, DRV Prime Minister Pham Van Dong pulled aside the French ambassador, Philippe Richer, to confer. Dong stated that France should help end the tragic situation in South Vietnam by removing Thieu so negotiations could begin. Richer believed that Dong's "briefing" provided multiple messages. According to Richer, Dong claimed Hanoi had won the war, and he wanted to achieve his objective without further bloodshed. Richer felt that Dong "was asking us to adopt an active role." Basically, "one must even go further and interpret the insistence of the prime minister as a discrete reminder that we should...modify our position regarding the government in Saigon before it is too late." Naturally, "if we try to convince the Americans to abandon Thieu we would be taking sides with Pham Van Dong." This would risk a rupture with the Americans, but it "seems to me that our degree of influence in Hanoi within the future context of Indochina depends on what we decide to do or not to do in the near future." Richer subtly asked Paris to decide by concluding "who knows when the last train leaves?"[43]

That Dong wanted to peacefully take over South Vietnam was ludicrous. At a Politburo meeting on March 25, he pressed for a rapid victory. Dong was handling Richer precisely according to the game plan, while the PRG was also playing its role. On March 25, the PRG held another press conference in Paris and repeated its statement of March 21 that if Thieu were removed, the PRG was ready to talk.

Richer's report, the heavy fighting, and the PRG statement set in motion serious efforts by France to replace Thieu with a coalition. In late March, the French believed the PRG assurances that they would accept Don as the head of a revamped South Vietnamese government. The French quietly informed him that they would serve as an intermediary between the opposing sides but only if Don were involved. But with the fall of I Corps on March 31, Hanoi discarded Don in favor of Minh. The PRG's Madame Nguyen Thi Binh also knew her lines. On April 2, she announced in Paris that the Front would talk with Minh about peace. Don was no longer mentioned.

With Madame Binh's declaration, the French began to publicly engage. On April 5, Paris broadcast that it would supply humanitarian aid to both sides and asked for a peaceful solution to the conflict. Three days later, the French Foreign Ministry outlined for President D'Estaing that

> the evolution of power in the South has forced us to re-examine our relationship with the various South Vietnamese parties in an attempt to re-establish a balance.... The French government intends to actively contribute to a process which will result in a political settlement in the South in conformance with the Accords. Our contacts with the Third Force in Saigon and particularly with the PRG and DRV representatives in Paris have been intensified.... [T]he departure of President Thieu seems to us a precondition for finding a solution following the Paris Accords. Furthermore, we have deemed it useful to inform the Soviet Union and China of the general nature of our action and position. It seems that if President Thieu were to give way

to an acceptable new team, a chance would be offered, admittedly a slim one, for preserving the nature and the individuality of a South Vietnam separate from the North.[44]

The next day, the French president publicly demanded a political settlement via the Paris Accords. While not openly calling for Thieu's ouster, that was the intent. Thieu was furious, and when Mérillon requested an audience, Thieu refused. A week would pass before he granted him a meeting. Despite Thieu's anger, Mérillon's intelligence officer in the French embassy in Saigon, Pierre Brochand, began contacting Third Force personalities to convince them to join a Minh government. For Brochand, French policy boiled down to two simple goals. First, it was a

noble attempt to save some aspect of a non-communist South Vietnam. Second, it was a humanitarian effort. We had 15,000 French citizens in Saigon, and the French government did not want to evacuate them. To protect our people, we wanted to avoid another Danang-type panic in Saigon, so we strove for an orderly transition. People believe that the PRG played us, but we well aware that they were not separate from Hanoi.[45]

The French, however, were not the only coalition game afoot. Thomas Polgar, the CIA Station chief in Saigon, was in contact with a senior officer in the Hungarian ICCS delegation, who was whispering the same story to him that the PRG was peddling to the French. If Thieu left, a new Minh government was installed, and the U.S. pledged no further interference, a deal might be struck. At the same time, the Polish ambassador to the ICCS was slipping Martin similar fanciful tales. It was a well-coordinated diplomatic smokescreen. As CIA analyst Frank Snepp pointed out, information he had received on April 8 from the agency's best spy in the south confirmed that Hanoi was going for the kill. Negotiations for a coalition government were "merely a ruse to confuse the South Vietnamese and sow suspicion between them and the Americans."[46]

Kissinger, meanwhile, was trying to convince the Soviets to restrain Hanoi by offering the same package: removal of Thieu and a coalition government. He concurrently resisted the French tactic, preferring to let the Soviets take a shot. As he saw it, "to make the Soviet approach work, we will need a structure in Saigon that can be transformed after our approach has been accepted." The French proposal, wrote Kissinger, "requires precisely the opposite," a dismantling of the government.[47] The Soviets, like the Hungarians and the Poles, strung the U.S. along, keeping a solution just out of reach until Hanoi's army was fully positioned around Saigon.

When Huong sought to preserve the GVN's constitutionality and declined to step aside for Minh, this sparked fruitless maneuvering between Huong, Minh, Don, and other South Vietnamese over who would replace Can as prime minister. Khiem was sent to persuade "Minh to serve as prime minister under Huong to see if the other side would accept such an arrangement. This was because the condition...that Minh replace Huong, would mean ripping up our constitution and would destroy the legal, constitutional foundation of the Republic of Vietnam."[48] Minh refused the offer, and when the Communists declared that Huong's government was no different than Thieu's, Huong finally succumbed. On April 26, he summoned the assembly and asked them to decide whether Minh should assume the presidency. The next day, the deputies concurred, and Senator Lam scheduled a session for April 28 to formally appoint Minh. Shortly after 5:00 p.m. on Monday, April 28, 1975, Duong Van Minh was sworn in as South Vietnam's last president. Declaring that for several years he had been advocating a government of peace, he was now prepared to forge a union with the PRG to halt the fighting. In response, Hanoi's divisions, which had launched their attack against the capital on April 26, only pressed harder against Saigon's defenses.

A week earlier, Phong had received a short, emotional cable from Saigon: "Huong needs to see Phong."[49] Before departing, Phong informed the U.S. ambassador that "he would push vigorously for rapid implementation of the ideas he had outlined previously....He believes the PRG...may be prepared to permit the continuation...of an independent, neutralist and non-communist South Vietnam." Phong told him that Paris "could be of considerable use" to convince Hanoi to agree to a ceasefire. Clearly, the ambassador wrote, "Phong has been talking" to the French.[50] Phong was not only talking with the French. As he boarded the last Air France flight to his embattled capital, Phong was carrying with him the last, great secret of the Vietnam War.

THE FINAL ACTOR: CHINA

The following revelation has been drawn from over a decade of interviews and email exchanges with Nguyen Xuan Phong until his death in July 2017. For over thirty years, he told no one of his last clandestine mission to save his country. He noted that while in prison after the war, "I was interrogated for two years to find out what had happened with the Chinese, but I would not tell them."[51] One time, his guards beat him severely and broke two of his ribs, but he continued to deny any knowledge of Chinese interference during the last days. While an urbane, gregarious, and witty man who often spiced his conversations with 1960s slang, only after providing him with numerous declassified French and U.S. documents detailing both countries diplomatic efforts in April 1975, did he finally reveal the substance of his secret message. Based on these discussions, further research pieced together a second set of evidence that seems to substantiate his account, but unfortunately, no documentary proof has been released to confirm it. This narrative contains the key points of his fascinating story, one that upends the accepted history of the war's final days.

As Phong flew to Saigon, he was determined to prevent a "battle for Saigon." DRV representatives had passed word to him, the French, and others that if Minh were not installed by April 26, they would level Saigon with twenty-thousand artillery shells. Whether it was a bluff is uncertain, but it was a deadly threat, one that Phong had to take seriously. When Phong arrived, he immediately went to see Huong. Because he had known the ailing president for years, he was unable to directly tell his old friend to step down. Instead, he only confirmed there was no hope for negotiations with him in office. Huong listened carefully, and the next day, he summoned the assembly. Phong did not mention the message he was carrying, since he knew that the triggering event was for Minh to assume power and accept a coalition with the PRG.

Several days later, Phong met with Tran Van Don and a representative from the PRG to discuss the possible coalition. Tran Ngoc Lieng, the secret Communist agent, was present as Minh's representative. Phong subtly informed the PRG official at this meeting that France and other countries would help the new government, but he was deliberately vague. This was Phong's only attempt to pass on his explosive missive. The next day, Minh was sworn in, but the PAVN advance quickly overwhelmed the ARVN defenses around Saigon, and the war was over.

What message was Phong carrying? The Chinese, he said, desperately wanted the PRG to assume power via the French formula to prevent a North Vietnamese takeover. After a coalition was formed, Minh would issue an appeal for help. The French would respond that an international force would enter South Vietnam to protect the new government. The initial "muscle," as Phong termed it, would be "two Chinese Airborne divisions into Bien Hoa." Beijing asked for four days to marshal their troops and shuttle them to the air base.[52] Phong explains their thinking:

> Beijing could not come forward and do this work directly, but they let people know that they were...letting the French do this work! Because of international politics...Beijing could not blatantly intervene militarily in South Vietnam. France would need to appeal to a few nations to participate in an 'international force' (with France serving as the spearhead) in order to allow Beijing to intervene. A number of problems faced Beijing at that time: What number of Chinese military forces should be employed, and how long would they have to stay in South Vietnam to contain and suppress North Vietnam's army? They promised that they would stay as long as the situation required, but they thought that between three and six months would be the maximum length of time they could participate...because they did not want to be accused of militarily occupying South Vietnam.

Why would China militarily intercede to thwart a North Vietnamese victory, especially after years of supporting Hanoi? China wanted a neutral South Vietnam solely to prevent being surrounded by a potential Moscow-Hanoi pact. One historian affirms that the "scholarly consensus is that by 1973 Chinese leaders were increasingly concerned about Hanoi's tilt toward Moscow."[53] While relations between the two Communist powers had been poor since the early 1960s, China had begun to fear Russian military intervention after the invasion of Czechoslovakia in 1968. The subsequent proclamation of the Brezhnev Doctrine claiming the right to overthrow any Communist government diverging from Moscow's orbit further concerned Beijing. In March 1969, armed skirmishes broke out along the Soviet and Chinese border, and the Russians attempted in May to convince India and North Korea to join an anti-Chinese alliance. Although the Russian effort failed, this move alarmed Beijing. According to Phong, his meeting with Zhou Enlai's emissary in December 1970 was Beijing's opening gambit to Saigon to prevent a unified Vietnam.

No one was more shocked to learn of this sea change in Chinese policy than U.S. presidential envoy Alexander Haig. Meeting Zhou Enlai in 1972 as part of the advance team for Nixon's visit, Zhou informed a stunned Haig: "Do not lose in Vietnam." Despite all the harsh anti-Saigon rhetoric emanating from Beijing, the "last thing China wanted," Zhou explained, "was an armed and militant Soviet client state on it southern frontier."[54] Haig reported that Zhou "regarded an American defeat and withdrawal from Southeast Asia as…dangerous to China…[H]e seemed particularly determined that I understand his meaning regarding the war in Vietnam."[55]

Nayan Chanda, the highly respected correspondent for the *Far Eastern Economic Review*, extensively detailed the Chinese dread of a unified Vietnam. He writes that Beijing has "consistently followed the policy of maintaining by all the means at its disposal a fragmented Indochina free of the major powers. These means included quiet diplomacy, economic persuasion, and, of course, use of its military might."[56] Chanda further notes that

> the Vietnamese claimed that [Beijing] urged Hanoi in April 1975 not to launch the final offensive on Saigon. That claim, like so many others put out by the Vietnamese since their open break with China, could [be] propaganda. But Philippe Richer, who served as French ambassador to Hanoi in 1973–75, later confirmed that on April 20, 1975—nine days before the capture of Saigon—[Beijing] did indeed warn Hanoi of the danger of 'stretching the broom too far,' using the metaphor that Mao used in 1972.[57]

The Chinese also allegedly approached Nguyen Cao Ky. In an interview with William Buckley on *Firing Line* in September 1975, the former vice president claimed that sometime in late 1972, Chinese agents had come to his house in Saigon. Ky said they asked him to overthrow Thieu and "declare South Vietnam neutral, not siding with the Russians or the Americans." If he did that, "the Chinese will support you because we already have trouble on our northern border with the Russians. We do not want to see our south flank occupied by a Russian satellite."[58] Ky repeated this story in a speech in December 1975 in the U.S., claiming that "a group of Chinese agents came to his home…and proposed a Chinese-supported coup to overthrow Thieu."[59] Why Ky never mentions this incident in either of his books, however, is troubling.

Since Thieu had not responded to the initial Chinese overtures, when China seized the Paracel Islands in January 1974, Beijing used the incident to attempt to contact him again. When the Chinese repatriated the captured South Vietnamese through Hong Kong, they asked the GVN counsel general to pass a message to Thieu requesting a clandestine meeting. While Phong was not involved with that effort, he was told about it, plus a second attempt by the Chinese in the summer of 1974 with the GVN embassy in London.[60] One confirmation of the Hong Kong channel comes from Jim Eckes, a close friend of Phong's who, at the time, was the Saigon manager for a charter airline. Eckes' family lived in Hong Kong, and he traveled back and forth. The GVN counsel general asked Eckes to pass the message to Thieu, but Eckes instead relayed it to Ambassador Martin. "The message," Eckes said, "died with Martin."[61]

Although Phong had informed Thieu of China's overtures, the president had rejected the Chinese proposition. Phong states that by early 1975, the Chinese "were disgusted by the 'complete lack of comprehension'" by Thieu. With the loss of Phuoc Long, however, "Chinese efforts became hectic in the last few months...with repeated messages to me in Paris."

By March 1975, the U.S. was becoming aware of Chinese discomfort over Hanoi's military adventurism. The CIA analyzed that "Chinese leaders almost certainly recognize that [a Hanoi victory] would bring [Beijing] into even more direct and costly competition with both Hanoi and the Soviets."[62] In early April, Ambassador Martin informed Kissinger that he was receiving "bits and pieces of diplomatic and intelligence traffic that indicate Chinese and Soviet unhappiness at...North Vietnamese aggression. I am inclined to believe the Chinese do feel this way."[63] This intelligence came from meetings with Chinese officials and newsmen in Hong Kong.[64]

Phong recalls that by March 1975, China was losing hope that it could convince the PRG to accept its offer, it was upset at Thieu, and it feared the U.S. would turn Vietnam over to the Soviets to improve détente. But the rapid PAVN advance forced China to move quickly to keep a separate South Vietnam. Beijing and Paris wanted Minh to lead a coalition government because it needed an ARVN general to keep the South Vietnamese military onboard, Minh was acceptable to the PRG, and China did not want to dismantle the government. According to Phong,

the 'political coalition' (one that was not pro–North Vietnam) in South Vietnam must be capable of defending its own national security. Beijing swore on the heads of their children that the last thing they wanted was [to be] a force of occupation in South Vietnam. For that reason, they said that only ARVN was capable...of carrying out this mission. The problem was that since ARVN had no supplies or equipment left, what could it do? They said that the presence of an 'international force' in South Vietnam [could] resolve this problem....What I can also tell you is, Hanoi's suspicion of a possible intervention by the PRC...was, for me, the main reason why Hanoi would not go for a ceasefire and some civilized way to end the war by a resounding diplomatic victory instead of a dreadful military victory.

If Phong was the only courier bearing this message, he might be easily dismissed. He was not. Retired French *Général de Division* Paul Vanuxem had known Thieu and other senior Vietnamese military officers since the First Indochina War. He had visited Thieu occasionally over the years and had returned to Vietnam in the last days as a correspondent for the French weekly magazine *Carrefour*. Vanuxem published a slim book in 1976 detailing the final days of the war. He notes that he was present at Independence Palace on April 30 to speak with Minh. While he alluded to his purpose, stating that "all the minds were paralyzed with fear and incapable of receiving the overtures which were then being made and which could have saved everything," he left out the critical details.[65]

There are numerous firsthand witnesses that Vanuxem spoke to Minh and relayed a message similar to Phong's. While these men relate slightly different versions of the conversation, all were in the room, and several were secret Communist agents. ARVN Brigadier General Nguyen Huu Hanh provided the first revelation in 1981 in a recorded interview for the PBS series *Vietnam: A Television History*. Hanh, whom Minh had called out of retirement, was a longtime Communist penetration agent. He was with Minh in Independence Palace on April 30. Hanh recounted

the very first thing Vanuxem said was that he had just come from Paris. Before he came, he met with many personalities, including members of the [Beijing] embassy. He suggested that Minh announce that he would leave the Americans and would come to the side of China. According to him, if we did that China would put pressure on Hanoi to have a ceasefire in the southern part of Vietnam. After having thought it over, Minh rejected the proposal. And when Vanuxem pleaded with Minh to prolong the whole thing for another twenty-four hours, the latter also rejected the idea. After Vanuxem left, we announced the transfer of power.[66]

Nguyen Van Diep, the economic minister and underground mole, agrees that "Vanuxem had come to see Minh to try and encourage Minh and to persuade him that the situation was not yet hopeless. Vanuxem arrived just after General Minh finished tape-recording his surrender statement." After Minh told him the situation was hopeless, Vanuxem replied that "It is not hopeless. I have already arranged for this in Paris. I request that you publicly ask for Nation C [China] to protect you." Vanuxem asked Minh to hold out for three days, but Minh refused.[67]

Opposition deputy Ly Qui Chung, whom Minh had appointed minister of information, confirms that

> Vanuxem said that he wanted to offer a plan to Minh to save the hopeless situation that the Saigon regime faced. Vanuxem said that Minh should speak out to appeal for a powerful country to intervene, and that if the South Vietnamese government issued an official request this powerful country would intervene immediately. Minh gave a bitter laugh and said, I thank you for your good intentions, but during my life I have already served as a lackey for the French and then as a lackey for the Americans. That is enough. I do not want to be a lackey again.[68]

Others provide similar accounts. Nguyen Huu Thai, a longtime student leader and secret Communist agent who was also at the palace, states that "Vanuxem asked to speak to General Minh. Vanuxem told the group, 'You must withdraw down to Can Tho and try to defend [IV Corps]. In a few days China will impose a solution that will neutralize South Vietnam.' General Minh made the same complaint: 'First the French and then the Americans, and now they want us to become the lackeys of the Chinese!'"[69] Minh's military aide, Major Trinh Ba Loc, who had served Minh since 1957 but was not a Communist agent, confirms that Vanuxem asked Minh to "suspend the order to surrender. The French Government and I will appeal to the Government of the People's Republic of China to intervene. With a stern look on his face General Minh replied, 'We have just asked the Americans to leave Vietnam within the next 24 hours. We cannot ask the Chinese Communists to intervene in Vietnam's internal affairs.'"[70] French journalist Olivier Todd also reported Vanuxem's comment. Todd writes that Vanuxem proposed that Minh "should ask China to invade North Vietnam. Then Paris could serve as mediator."[71]

Given its spies at the meeting with Minh, Hanoi learned of Vanuxem's proposal. Van Tien Dung, the PAVN general commanding the offensive, wrote that "Vanuxem...came hurriedly from France to Saigon." On April 30, he attempted to "intercept the tape [Minh] had recorded...and presented a plan to block our general offensive into Saigon," although "it is not yet convenient to say much about them."[72]

Unsurprisingly, Chinese-Vietnamese postwar relations quickly soured. Meeting Le Duan in September 1975, Chinese leader Deng Xiaoping bashed him for recent Vietnamese propaganda that painted China as "the threat from the north....We are not at ease with this."[73] Whether Deng's comments, which condemn anti-Chinese propaganda, also reflect an unspoken fear that Le Duan knew about the Chinese scheme, is unknown. However, after China and Vietnam fought a short but intense border war in February 1979 (for reasons not related to April 1975), Hanoi published a book denouncing China's "schemes" against Vietnam. They alluded to the Vanuxem incident by stating that China "sought to induce many Saigon generals and government officials to cooperate with them, and they even sent someone to try to persuade General Duong Van Minh...to continue to resist the general offensive and uprising of the soldiers and civilians of South Vietnam."[74]

Le Duan, speaking after the February 1979 border war, claimed that he had always been aware of China's designs on his country. In a document unearthed by historian Christopher Goscha, Le Duan said, "[W]hen we won in southern Vietnam, there were many [leaders] in China who were unhappy....After defeating the Americans we kept in place over one million troops, leading Soviet comrades to ask us: 'Comrades, whom do you intend to fight that you keep such a large [standing] army?' I said: 'Later, comrades, you will understand.' The only reason we had kept such a standing army was because of China's threat to Vietnam. If there had not been [such a threat], then this [large standing army] would have been unnecessary."[75]

On the tenth anniversary of the fall of Saigon, Hanoi finally acknowledged China's attempted intervention. An official stated that "the Chinese authorities nursed an extremely sinister scheme. As Duong Van Minh, the puppet regime's last president revealed: On the morning of 30 April 1975, through the intermediary of Vanuxem...China requested that Minh carry on the fighting for at least another 24 hours so as to have enough time to announce a disassociation from the U.S. and an alliance with China. China would then bring pressure to bear, including introduction of troops into Vietnam to end the hostilities to China's advantage."[76]

While numerous witnesses attest to Vanuxem's statement, several key persons dispute that he was carrying a message from the French government. Phong said he was unaware of Vanuxem's effort, although when informed by the author, he states that Vanuxem was "with me on the Air France flight to Saigon before the city fell. I am sure he must have heard something about what was going on at the time, but I am also sure he was not part of it, although he might have been of some help in the French efforts [to form a coalition]."

Vanuxem's family also does not believe that the French government would use him as a messenger. They contend that his involvement in the failed French army coup of April 1961 made him a pariah to the French government. Vanuxem was jailed for two years afterward, his property was confiscated, and his children were not permitted to attend school. He traveled to South Vietnam simply as a journalist, and he never mentioned this incident to the family.[77] Pierre Brochand adamantly insists that Vanuxem "was not a French emissary. While an old Indochina hand, he had no relations with the embassy, and I never met him." While he concedes that the "Chinese were not happy that Hanoi was taking control," Brochand does not recall any contacts with China, nor does he believe that Beijing would have attempted a military foray into Bien Hoa. "The situation was hopeless by then," he said.[78] Mérillon's wife also states she never met Vanuxem and that Brochand was close to her husband.[79]

Could Vanuxem have conjured this effort on his own? Frank Snepp at the U.S. embassy writes that on the morning of April 25, Saigon Radio blasted out that "Le Duan murders his chief political rival in Hanoi! Chinese troops pour across the border into North Vietnam to avenge the death! . . . But of course, they were nothing more than a hoax, a piece of psychological warfare conjured up by the Saigon authorities to confuse and demoralize the North Vietnamese troops on their doorstep."[80] If Vanuxem was on the plane that landed on the afternoon of April 25, he might have heard these spurious reports and thought they were real. However, given the specific details in his message, that scenario seems unlikely. He never mentioned the radio broadcast, nor the supposed death of Le Duan, and his comments were eerily similar to Phong's information.

Assuming that Vanuxem's pariah status with the French government remained intact, it is doubtful he was carrying a message from the French government, especially since it had Mérillon in Saigon. What seems more likely is that the Chinese sought another emissary besides Phong. Phong was a civilian diplomat, while Vanuxem had close ties to the ARVN generals, and he had a long history of supporting the republic. He would be the perfect envoy to convince anti-communist ARVN generals to accept Chinese and French help, especially such a bold offer as this. Moreover, as a lone courier, he was also deniable if necessary.

That Vanuxem made the statement seems indisputable. Whether his or Phong's information was actually China's true intent is unresolved. Could this have been another diplomatic smokescreen? Forging a coalition government to remove Thieu during the last days was certainly Hanoi's ploy, one that the Politburo's allies happily assisted. Hoang Duc Nha believes that it was. He confirms that Mérillon had told him, as part of a plea for Nha to become the new prime minister, that "the Chinese are going to bring in some divisions to stop the North Vietnamese," but Nha suspected this was a Chinese trick to sell them on a coalition government.[81] Given all the diplomatic maneuvers to remove Thieu, the idea cannot be discounted.

Vanuxem died in 1979, leaving his actions unexamined, while Phong never discussed the possibility that he was being used. Moreover, while Hanoi has apparently accepted the Vanuxem story, it cannot be confirmed without documentary evidence or an official Chinese or French government admission. Whether China and France, each for its own national interests, had colluded to create a neutral South Vietnam and deny Hanoi its long-sought victory remains an intriguing possibility, but one that, for now, remains the last great secret of the Vietnam War.

CONCLUSION

The history of South Vietnam is more than just an acrimonious war, the intrigues of great powers maneuvering in the diplomatic shadows, or an effort to shed colonialism. It is equally about the Nationalists' struggle to build a viable state where one had not previously existed. That monumental effort has been ignored or, worse, treated with contempt. This book has sought to redress that by showcasing the Nationalists' tormented path to something resembling a modern state, to tell the tale, as much as possible, from their perspective.

The Second Republic gave the South Vietnamese people a chance to create viable institutions and construct their country. Yet for all of Thieu's structural achievements like land reform and local governance, nearing defeat, Saigon's political leaders clung to the constitution. It provided political legitimacy, served as the country's legal foundation, and defined the existence of the National Assembly, the courts, and the need for popular suffrage. Furthermore, the constitution provided a distinct reminder of the differences between Diem's one-man regime, Communist one-party dictatorship, and the emerging rule of law in the Second Republic.

Saigon tried to accomplish two simultaneous goals: defeat the Communists and build a modern state. It accomplished neither because the failure of the first prevented the second. That it came achingly close to the second is only due to the failure of the first goal. Whether it could have achieved the first aim remains unclear, especially without having forged a more unified country. Equally important, while the enemy offensives of 1965, 1968, and 1972 did not inflict mortal blows on South Vietnam, each assault wounded it. The difference is that after the first two attacks, the U.S. provided the financial means to rebuild and a security shield to guard the reconstruction.

America did neither after the 1972 offensive. By 1973, the U.S. was gone, Saigon had few international friends, and South Vietnam could not rebound from the devastation wrought by the Easter Offensive like it had from the earlier assaults. Although the GVN valiantly tried to recover, between fighting an enemy army on its soil and burdened by a floundering economy, the country was on the wrong end of the economic cycle when a well-planned, brilliantly executed assault in 1975 against a demoralized and badly weakened South Vietnamese military finally accomplished what the previous offensives had failed to do: achieve victory.

For America, it could hardly have chosen a more difficult battleground upon which to invest so heavily. Americans think of the war as an unwinnable conflict where enemies battled without fixed lines in a pitiless jungle that defeated even the best generals and technology. That was only one piece of the equation. The other was the incredible difficulty of building a functioning state while it was under attack, compounded by the often insurmountable social, language, and cultural gaps between allies. Thus, when the scandals of a young democracy played out under the microscope of a foreign press, the barrage of tragedies, apparent government repression, and political lethargy ostensibly confirmed South Vietnam's image as an unsalvageable wreck.

This is not to suggest that the press "lost the war." The Nationalists were unable to properly explain themselves to faraway foreigners. They failed to articulate to the American public an acceptable alternative to the Western forms of governance and national cohesion that were so noticeable by their absence. Saigon botched the information and propaganda field where Hanoi, by sheer dint of repetition, eventually succeeded. Worse, with the severe disadvantages of geography and deep aid cuts, the republic failed to develop a military posture that could withstand a PAVN offensive. Whether there was such a stand-alone strategy remains unknown.

That, however, is not South Vietnam's epitaph. Despite having fought with great endurance, the republic fell because PAVN tanks crushed it before this fledgling state could finish developing. Yet many exiled South Vietnamese still feel the weight and judgment of history as if their bitter fate encapsulated the Biblical phrase "I will turn my face against you so that you will be defeated by your enemies... I will scatter you among the nations and will draw out my sword and pursue you."[82] For years, history has judged that they were cast out of their lands for their sins of kleptocracy, despotism, and poor military decisions. Perhaps now history will judge more fairly.

SELECTED BIBLIOGRAPHY

NATIONALIST PUBLICATIONS IN VIETNAMESE

Cao The Dung and Luong Minh Khai (pseudonym: Tran Kim Tuyen), *Lam The Nao De Giet Mot Tong Thong* [*How to Kill a President*]. San Jose, CA: Co So Van Hoa Dong Phuong, 1988. Reprinted from Mua Dong, 1970.

Chinh Dao, ed., *Nhin Lai Bien Co 11/11/1960* [*Looking Back at the 11 November 1960 Event*]. Houston, TX: Van Hoa Publishing, 1997.

Do Tho, *Nhat Ky Do Tho: Tuy Vien Mot Tong Thong Bi Giet* [*The Diary of Do Tho: Aide to a Murdered President*]. Garden Grove, CA: Dai Nam Publishing, 1982. Reprinted from Dong Nai, 1970.

Ha Thuc Ky, *Song con voi Dan toc: Hoi Ky Chanh Tri* [*Life and Death with Our Nation: A Political Memoir*]. Sacramento, CA: Phuong Nghi, 2009.

Hoang Linh Do Mau, *Viet Nam: Mau Lua Que Huong Toi* [*Vietnam: War in My Native Land*]. Garden Grove, CA: Self-published, 1986.

Huynh Van Cao, *Tron Mot Kiep Nguoi* [*A Full Life*]. San Jose, CA: Self-published, 1993.

Huynh Van Lang, *Ky Uc Huynh Van Lang, Tap II: Thoi ky Viet Nam doc lap (1955–1975)* [*The Memoirs of Huynh Van Lang, Volume II: The Era of Vietnamese Independence (1955–1975)*]. CA: Self-published, 2012.

Lam Le Trinh, *Ve Nguon Sinh Lo Cho Que Huong* [*Back to Our Roots: The Road to Life for Our Homeland*]. Huntington Beach, CA: Human Rights Bookshelf, 2006.

Lien Thanh, *Bien Dong Mien Trung: Nhung bi mat lich su ve can giai doan 1966 – 1968 – 1972* [*Upheavals in Central Vietnam: Historical Secrets about 1966, 1968, and 1972*]. Westminster, CA: Self-Published, 2012.

Ly Qui Chung, *Hoi Ky Khong Ten* [*Untitled Memoir*]. Saigon: Youth Publishing House, 2004.

Ly Tong Ba, *Hoi Ky 25 Nam Khoi Lua; Cam Nghi Cua Mot Tuong Cam Quan Tai Mat Tran* [*Memoir of 25 Years of War; Thoughts of a General Who Commanded Troops on the Battlefield*]. San Marcos, CA: Self-Published, 1999.

Nguyen Ba Can, *Dat Nuoc Toi: Hoi Ky Chanh Tri* [*My Country: A Political Memoir*]. Derwood, MD: Hoa Hao Press, 2003.

Nguyen Chanh Thi, *Viet Nam: Mot Troi Tam Su* [*Vietnam: Confiding a Sea of Memories*]. Los Alamitos, CA: Xuan Thu Publishing, 1987.

Nguyen Mau, *N.D.B.: Nganh Dac Biet, Tap I* [*S.B.: The Special Branch, Volume I*]. San Jose: Self-Published, 2007.

Nguyen Tien Hung, *Tam tu Tong Thong Thieu* [*President's Thieu's Thoughts and Concerns*]. Westminster, CA: Hua Can Publishers, 2010.

Nguyen Van Chau, *Ngo Dinh Diem va No Luc Hoa Binh Dang Do* [*Ngo Dinh Diem and the Unfinished Peace Effort*]. Los Alamitos, CA: Xuan Thu Publishers, 1989.

Pham Van Lieu, *Tra Ta Song Nui (Hoi Ky, Tap 2: 1963–1975)* [*Give Us Our Country Back (A Memoir, Volume II: 1963–1975)*]. Houston: Van Hoa Publishing, 2003.

Quang Minh (pseudonym: Truong Tu Thien), *Dai Viet Quoc Dan Dang: Cach Mang Viet Nam Thoi Can Kim* [*The Dai Viet Quoc Dan Party: The Vietnamese Revolution in the Modern Era*]. Westminster, CA: Van Nghe Publishing, 2000.

Thich Tam Chau, *Vu Van De Chia Re Giua An Quang Voi Viet Nam Quoc Tu* [*White Paper On the Split Between An Quang and Vietnam Quoc Tu*]. Montreal: Tu Quang Temple, 1993.

Ton That Dinh, *20 Nam Binh Nghiep* [*My Twenty-Year Military Career*]. San Jose, CA: Chanh Dao, 1998.

Tran Do Cung and Mrs. Nguyen Ton Hoan, *Ong ba Nguyen Ton Hoan trong dong su Viet* [*Nguyen Ton Hoan and His Wife in Vietnamese History*]. CA: Self-Published, 2012.

Tran Van Don, *Viet Nam Nhan Chung: Hoi Ky Chanh Tri* [*Vietnam Witness: A Political Memoir*]. Los Alamitos, CA: Xuan Thu Publishing, 1989.

Tran Van Khoi, *Dau Hoa Viet Nam, 1970-1975: Nhung Ngay Con Nho* [*Vietnam's Oil, 1970–1975: I Still Remember Those Days*]. Houston: Self-published, 2002.

Van Van Cua, *Mong Khong Thanh* [*The Unfulfilled Dream*]. Westminster, CA: YTE Distributors, 2000.

Vo Long Trieu, *Vo Long Trieu: Hoi Ky, tap I* [*Vo Long Trieu: A Memoir, Volume I*]. Fresno, CA: Nguoi Viet Publishers, 2009.

Vuong Van Dong, *Binh Bien 11-11-60, Khoi Diem Mot Hanh Trình* [*The 11 November 1960 Mutiny, the Beginning of a Journey*]. Paris: Self-published, 2000.

NATIONALIST PUBLICATIONS IN ENGLISH

Bui Diem, with David Chanoff, *In the Jaws of History*. Bloomington: Indiana University Press, 1989.

Nguyen Anh Tuan, *South Vietnam: Trial and Experience*. Athens, OH: Ohio University, 1987.

Nguyen Cao Ky, *Buddha's Child: My Fight to Save Vietnam*. New York: St. Martin's Press, 2001.

Nguyen Cao Ky, *Twenty Years and Twenty Days*. New York: Stein and Day, 1976.

Nguyen Dang Hai, *Get Up One More Time: A Personal Odyssey*. Ellicott City, MD: H&T Publishers, 2007.

Nguyen Ngoc Huy and Stephen B. Young, *Understanding Vietnam*. Amsterdam: The DPC Information Service, 1982.

Nguyen Huu Hanh, *Brushing the World Famous: The Story of My Life*. Lincoln, NE: iUniverse, 2005.

Nguyen Phu Duc, *The Viet-Nam Peace Negotiations: Saigon's Side of the Story*. Edited by Arthur Dommen. Christiansburg, VA: Dalley Book Service, 2005.

Nguyen Tien Hung and Jerrold Schecter, *The Palace File*. New York: Harper & Row, 1986.

Nguyen Xuan Phong, *Hope and Vanquished Reality*. New York: Center for a Science of Hope, 2001.

Phan Nhat Nam, *The Stories Must Be Told*. Westminster, CA: Nang Moi Publisher, 2002.

Pham Van Minh, *Vietnamese Engaged Buddhism: The Struggle Movement of 1963–1966*. Westminster: Van Nghe, 2002.

Phan Quang Dan, with Ray Fontaine, *The Dawn of Free Vietnam: A Biographical Sketch of Dr. Phan Quang Dan*. Brownsville, TX: Pan American Business Services, 1992.

Tran Ngoc Chau, *Vietnam Labyrinth: Allies, Enemies, and Why the U.S. Lost the War*. Lubbock, TX: TTU University Press, 2012.

Tran Van Don, *Our Endless War*. Novato, CA: Presidio Press, 1978.

COMMUNIST PUBLICATIONS IN VIETNAMESE

Bien nien su kien: Bo tong tham muu trong khang chien chong My, cuu nuoc, tap V (1968) [*Chronology of Events: General Staff During the Resistance War Against the Americans to Save the Nation, Volume V (1968)*]. Hanoi: People's Army Publishing House, 2005.

Chien Dich Phan Cong Duong So 9 – Nam Lao Nam 1971 [*The Route 9-Southern Laos Counteroffensive Campaign, 1971*]. Hanoi: Military History Institute of Vietnam, 1987.

Chung Mot Bong Co (ve Mat Tran Dan Toc Giai Phong Mien Nam Viet Nam) [*Under One Flag: The National Liberation Front of South Vietnam*]. Ho Chi Minh City: National Political Publishing House, 1993.

Cong An Nhan Dan Thanh pho Ho Chi Minh: Bien mien su Kien l ch su (1954–1975) [*Ho Chi Minh City People's Public Security: Chronology of Historical Events (1945–1975)*]. National Political Publishing House, Hanoi, 2002.

Cong An Nhan Dan Viet Nam: Lich Su Bien Nien (1954–1975), Quyen II [*Vietnam's People's Public Security: Chronology of Events (1954–1975), vol. II*]. Hanoi: People's Public Security Publishing House, 2000.

Cong Tac Chien Dich Duong 9 Nam Lao (Tu 28/2 Den 23/3/1971) [*Route 9-Southern Laos Campaign Rear Services Operations (28 February–23 March 1971)*]. Hanoi: General Rear Services Department, 1987.

Dai Su Ky Chuyen De: Dau Tranh Ngoai Giao va Van Dong Quoc Te Trong Khang Chien Chong My Cuu Nuoc, 1954–1975, Tap 4 [*Major Events: The Diplomatic Struggle and International Activities During the Resistance War Against the Americans to Save the Nation 1954–1975, Volume 4*]. Hanoi: Ministry of Foreign Affairs, 1987.

Duong Van Ba, *Nhung Ng Re: Hoi ky* [*Forks in the Road: A Memoir*]. Viet Studies website, at http://www.viet-studies.info/kinhte/DuongVan-Ba_1.htm, accessed 30 July 2016.

Huong Tien Cong Saigon-Gia Dinh (Nam 1968) [*The Offensive in the Saigon-Gia Dinh Sector (1968)*]. Hanoi: Military History Institute of Vietnam, 1988.

Le Duan, *Tho Vao Nam* [*Letters to the South*], 2nd ed. Hanoi: Su That Publishing House, 1986.

Lich Su Bien Nien Xu Uy Nam Bo va Trung Uong Cuc Mien Nam (1954–1975) [*Historical Chronicle of the Cochin China Party Committee and the Central Office for South Vietnam, 1954-1975*]. Hanoi: National Political Publishing House, 2002.

Lich Su Khang Chien Chong My Cuu Nuoc, 1954–1975, Tap V: Tong Tien Cong Va Noni Day Nam 1968 [*History of the Resistance War Against the Americans to Save the Nation, 1954–1975, Volume V: The 1968 General Offensive and Uprising*]. Hanoi: National Political Publishing House, 2001.

Lich Su Khang Chien Chong My Cuu Nuoc, 1954–1975, Tap VI: Thang My Tren Chien Truong Ba Nuoc Dong Duong [*History of the Resistance War Against the Americans to Save the Nation, 1954–1975, Volume VI: Defeating the Americans in the Three Nations of Indochina*]. Hanoi: National Political Publishing House, 2003.

Lich su Nam Bo Khang chin, tap II, 1954–1975 [*History of the Resistance War in Cochin China, Volume II: 1954–1975*]. Hanoi: National Political Publishing House, 2010.

Lich Su Saigon-Cho Lon-Gia Dinh Khang Chien (1945–1975) [*History of the Resistance War in Saigon-Cho Lon-Gia Dinh (1945–1975)*]. Ho Chi Minh City: Ho Chi Minh City Publishing House, 1994.

Long An: Lich Su Khang Chien Chong My Cuu Nuoc (1954–1975) [*Long An: History of the Resistance War Against the Americans to Save the Nation (1954–1975)*]. Hanoi: People's Army Publishing House, 1994.

Mot So Van Kien Cua Dang Ve Chong My, Cuu Nuoc, Tap I (1954–1965) [*A Number of Party Documents Regarding the Resistance to the Americans to Save the Nation*]. Hanoi: Su That Publishing House, 1985.

Ngoai Giao Viet Nam: 1945–2000 [*Vietnamese Diplomacy: 1945–2000*]. Hanoi: National Political Publishing House, 2002.

Quang Nam-Da Nang: 30 Nam Chien Dau va Chien Thang, 1945–1975, Tap II [*Quang Nam-Da Nang: 30 Years of Fighting and Victory, 1945–1975, Volume II*]. Hanoi: People's Army Publishing House, 1988.

Tong Ket Cuoc Khang Chien Chong My Cuu Nuoc: Thang Loi va Bai Hoc [*Review of the Resistance War Against the Americans to Save the Nation: Victory and Lessons*]. Hanoi: The Guidance Committee for Reviewing the War, Directly Subordinate to the Politburo, 1995.

Trinh Dinh Thao, *Suy nghi va hanh dong: Hoi ky* [*Thought and Action: A Memoir*]. Ho Chi Minh City: Ho Chi Minh City Publishing House, 1985.

Tuoi tre Sai Gon Mau Than 1968 [*Saigon Youth: Tet Mau Than, 1968*]. Ho Chi Minh City: Tre Publishing House, 2003.

Van Kien Dang, Toan Tap, Tap 21, 1960 [*Collected Party Documents, Volume 21, 1960*]. Hanoi: National Political Publishing House, 2002.

Van Kien Dang, Toan Tap, Tap 25, 1964 [*Collected Party Documents, Volume 25, 1964*]. Hanoi: National Political Publishing House, 2003.

Van Kien Dang, Toan Tap, Tap 26, 1965 [*Collected Party Documents, Volume 26, 1965*]. Hanoi: National Political Publishing House, 2003.

Van Kien Dang, Toan Tap, 29, 1968 [*Collected Party Documents, Volume 29, 1968*]. Hanoi: National Political Publishing House, 2004.

Van Kien Dang, Toan Tap 30, 1969 [*Collected Party Documents, Volume 30, 1969*]. Hanoi: National Political Publishing House.

COMMUNIST PUBLICATIONS IN ENGLISH

Military History Institute of Vietnam, *Victory in Vietnam: The Official History of the People's Army of Vietnam, 1954–1975*, trans. by Merle Pribbenow. Lawrence, KS: University Press of Kansas, 2002.

Truong Nhu Tang, *A Viet Cong Memoir: An Inside Account of the Vietnam War and its Aftermath*. New York: Vintage, 1986.

U.S. PUBLICATIONS

Ahern, Thomas L., Jr. *CIA and the House of Nho: Covert Action in South Vietnam, 1954–1963*. Washington, D.C.: Central Intelligence Agency, 2000.

Central Intelligence Agency, *CIA and the Generals: Covert Support to Military Government in South Vietnam*. Washington, D.C.: Central Intelligence Agency, 1998.

Bordenkircher, Don. *Tiger Cages: An Untold Story*. Cameron, WV: Abby Publishing, 1998.

Colby, William. *Lost Victory: A Firsthand Account of America's Sixteen Year Involvement in Vietnam*. Chicago: Contemporary Books, 1989.

Dommen, Arthur. *The Indochinese Experience of the French and the Americans*. Bloomington: Indiana University Press, 2001.

Goodman, Allan. *The Lost Peace: America's Search for a Negotiated Settlement of the Vietnam War*. Stanford, CA: Hoover Institution Press, 1976.

Hammer, Ellen. *A Death in November: America in Vietnam, 1963*. New York: E. P. Dutton, 1987.

Higgins, Marguerite. *Our Vietnam Nightmare*. New York: Harper and Row, 1965.

Hunt, Ira. *Losing Vietnam: How America Abandoned Southeast Asia*. Lexington: University Press of Kentucky, 2013.

Hunt, Richard. *Pacification: The American Struggle for Vietnam's Hearts and Minds*. San Francisco: Westview Press, 1995.

Kahin, George McT. *Intervention: How America Became Involved in Vietnam*. New York: Knopf, 1986.

Kissinger, Henry. *White House Years*. New York: Little, Brown and Company, 1979.

Kissinger, Henry. *Ending the Vietnam War: A History of America's Involvement in and Extraction from the Vietnam War*. New York: Simon and Schuster, 2003.

Logevall, Fredrik. *Choosing War: The Lost Chance for Peace and the Escalation of War in Vietnam*. Berkeley: University of California Press, 2001.

Miller, Edward. *Misalliance: Ngo Dinh Diem, the United States, and the Fate of South Vietnam*. Cambridge: Harvard University Press, 2013.

Moyar, Mark. *Triumph Forsaken: The Vietnam War, 1954–1965*. New York: Cambridge University Press, 2006.

Phillips, Rufus. *Why Vietnam Matters: An Eyewitness Account of Lessons Not Learned*. Annapolis, MD: Naval Institute Press, 2008.

Pike, Douglas. *Viet Cong: The Organization and Techniques of the National Liberation Front of South Vietnam*. Cambridge: The MIT Press, 1966.

Pike, Douglas, ed. *The Bunker Papers, vols. 1–3*. Berkeley, CA: Asian Foundation, 1990.

Porter, Gareth. *Vietnam: The Definitive Documentation of Human Decisions, vol. 2*. Stanfordville, NY: Earl Coleman Productions, 1979.

Quinn-Judge, Sophie. *The Third Force in the Vietnam War: The Elusive Search for Peace 1954–75*. New York: I. B. Taurus, 2017.

Scotton, Frank. *Uphill Battle: Reflections on Viet Nam Counterinsurgency*. Lubbock: Texas Tech University Press, 2014.

Villard, Erik. *Combat Operations: Staying the Course, October 1967 to September 1968*. Washington, D.C.: Center for Military History, 2017.

Westmoreland, William. *A Soldier Reports* New York: Doubleday, 1976.

Wiest, Andrew. *Vietnam's Forgotten Army: Heroism and Betrayal in the ARVN*. New York: New York University Press, 2008.

NOTES

INTRODUCTION

1 Nguyen Tien Hung, *Tam tu Tong Thong Thieu* [*President Thieu's Thoughts and Concerns*] (Westminster: Hua Chan Minh Publishers, 2010), 373. According to Hung, this book on Thieu's "thoughts" is a rehash of information he gleaned from other authors and what the president told him for his earlier book, *The Palace File*.

2 Brett Reilly, "The Origins of the Vietnamese Civil War and the State of Vietnam," Dissertation. University of Wisconsin-Madison, May 2018.

3 Mark Moyar, *Triumph Forsaken: The Vietnam War, 1954–1965* (New York: Cambridge University Press, 2006). Edward Miller, *Misalliance: Ngo Dinh Diem, the United States, and the Fate of South Vietnam* (Cambridge, MA: Harvard University Press, 2013). Jessica Chapman, *Cauldron of Resistance: Ngo Dinh Diem, the United States, and 1950s Southern Vietnam* (Ithaca, NY: Cornell University Press, 2013). Geoffrey Shaw, *The Lost Mandate of Heaven: The American Betrayal of Ngo Dinh Diem, President of Vietnam* (San Francisco, CA: Ignatius Press, 2015).

4 Martin Clemis, *The Control War: The Struggle for South Vietnam, 1968–1975* (Norman, OK: University of Oklahoma Press, 2018); Andrew Gawthorpe, *To Build as Well as Destroy: American Nation Building in South Vietnam* (Ithaca, NY: Cornell University Press, 2018); Heather Marie Stur, *Saigon at War: South Vietnam and the Global Sixties* (New York: Cambridge University Press, 2020).

5 The terms "state" and "nation" are often used interchangeably, but there is difference. A state is a territory with its own defined boundaries, sovereignty, and population; a nation is a group of people who inhabit and are connected by a shared history, language, culture, and customs.

6 Michael Howard, *War in European History* (Oxford: Oxford University Press, 2009), xi.

7 Oddly, personal misdeeds seemed to have had little impact on South Vietnamese views of Thieu. The president had several children out of wedlock, including one from a well-known affair with the owner of the Cyrnos restaurant in Vung Tau. While I will not discuss his extramarital dealings and dalliance with fortune-telling, such revelations would have devastated an American president. Most South Vietnamese simply shrugged.

8 Email from Richard Boylan, retired senior archivist with the National Archives, who worked closely with U.S. military records for almost thirty-nine years, September 1, 2014.

9 Letter from Antoine Boulant, chief of public relations, Service historique de la Defense, August 25, 2014.

10 One scholar who has combed the former GVN records has found few documents outlining Thieu's direct thinking. Email from Dr. Sean Fear, March 5, 2019.

11 Tuong Vu and Sean Fear, eds. *The Republic of Vietnam, 1955–1975: Perspectives on Nation Building* (Ithaca, NY: Cornell University Press, 2019). Keith Taylor, ed. *Voices*

from the Second Republic of Vietnam (1967-1975) (Ithaca, NY: Cornell University Press, 2014).

12　William Shakespeare, *Henry V*, Prologue, Arden Shakespeare, Third Series.

CHAPTER I

1　Christopher Goscha, *Vietnam: A New History* (New York: Basic Books, 2016), 55–122.

2　Fredrik Logeval, *Embers of War: The Fall of an Empire, and the Making of America's Vietnam* (New York: Random House, 2012), 71.

3　Fox Butterfield, "Nguyen Van Thieu is Dead at 76; Last President of South Vietnam," *New York Times*, October 1, 2001, 6.

4　Thomas Bass, "Exile on Newberry Street," *New York Times Magazine*, December 30, 2001, 25.

5　Interview with Mrs. Nguyen Van Thieu, February 6, 2014, Irving, CA. Translator: Tran Quang Minh. Until now, Mrs. Thieu refused all interview requests after the end of the war. This was the second interview with her conducted by the author. The first, at her home in Irving, CA, was on March 6, 2013, and was arranged by Cao Van Than, Thieu's minister of land reform. Than served as translator for the first interview. The author thanks Mrs. Thieu for welcoming the author into her home and graciously answering questions.

6　According to a study by Saigon embassy officer Calvin Mehlert, Thieu's birthday is astrologically "exceptionally auspicious…Thieu was born at the hour, day, month and year of 'Ty,' a rare four-fold confluence that in Vietnamese astrology is an exceptionally good omen. In Vietnam, many people in public life, including Thieu, consult soothsayers. Astrologers are used to determine days for inauguration of political parties, for change of command ceremonies, and for initiation of military operations." "Some Aspects of Personal Relations among Senior RVNAF Officers," Saigon Embassy Airgram A-131, August 13, 1971, RG 59, Subject Numeric Files 1970–1973, Box 2808, National Archives and Records Administration (NARA), College Park, MD. Mehlert drew much of his information from Colonel Pham Van Lieu, a bitter foe of President Thieu. Email with Calvin Mehlert, October 26, 2009.

7　Larry Engelmann, "The Man Who Lost Vietnam: Interview with Nguyen Van Thieu," April 9, 1990.

8　Nguyen Tien Hung, *Thieu's Thoughts*, 359.

9　Engelmann interview with Thieu.

10　Hoang Linh Do Mau, *Viet Nam: Mau Lua Que Huong Toi* [*Vietnam: War in My Native Land*] (California: Self-published, 1986), 767.

11　Interview with Hoang Duc Nha, June 4, 2009, Falls Church, VA. Their grandmothers were sisters.

12　"Biographic Data on Hoang Duc Nha," Saigon Embassy Airgram A-104, May 20, 1974.

13　"South Vietnam: A Vote for the Future," *Time*, September 15, 1967.

14　Ibid.

15　The Central Intelligence Agency (CIA) produced two short sketches of Thieu, one on January 29, 1965, and a second on June 24, 1965. In July 1968, the Defense Intelligence Agency, as part of a broader biographical analysis of the Vietnamese military leadership, created a more detailed review of his career.

16　After the war, Thieu provided a handwritten note to his chief military aide, Major Nguyen Xuan Tam, listing his career from his entrance into the Hue military academy until 1965. He does not list the 21st Division. However, on June 15, 1965, the government-sponsored *Vietnam Press* published a short biographical sketch of Thieu that included this information. A biography written in early 1973 by South

Vietnamese Ministry of Information official Nguyen Ngoc Bich for President Thieu's trip to the U.S. also included this claim, but Bich wrote it based upon the *Vietnam Press* information and the files in the South Vietnamese embassy in Washington. The claim remains a mystery as it seems odd that a semiofficial government news agency would print such an egregious error.

17 Out of fifty-three attendees, nine of Thieu's classmates reached General Officer rank. Thieu claimed that some graduates of his class joined the Communists, but he did not say who.

18 "Officer Record for Lieutenant Nguyen Van Thieu," *Archive de General de Division* Paul Vanuxem, Lyon, France. According to this file, Thieu entered service on October 1, 1948. There are some minor discrepancies in dates between his French file, the dates listed in U.S. records, and South Vietnamese information. The author wishes to thank the Vanuxem family for permission to use this record.

19 This was the École de L'infanterie school next to Saint Cyr, the main French military academy, and not Saint Cyr itself, which is a three-year school. Vanuxem's file says that Thieu "stayed in France from September 1, 1949 to July 1, 1950," and that he graduated third out of twelve, not tenth as related in South Vietnamese records.

20 Saigon embassy cable #17454 to Department of State, July 28, 1969, Record Group 59, Subject Numeric Files 1967–1969, NARA. Hereafter Saigon and the cable number.

21 Interview of former Prime Minister Tran Thien Khiem by Lan Cao, June 11, 2017. Like Mrs. Thieu, Khiem has refused all postwar interviews, but he agreed to speak to Lan Cao, the daughter of his close friend, General Cao Van Vien. The author wishes to thank Lan Cao for her assistance interviewing General Khiem. Lan Cao is a well-known lawyer teaching international law and a celebrated author in her own right. For an excellent (and semiautobiographical) novel of her family, see Lan Cao, *The Lotus and the Storm* (New York: Viking, 2014).

22 "President Nguyen Van Thieu of the Republic of Vietnam," n.d., Folder 13, Box 8, Douglas Pike Collection: Unit 11 - Monographs, The Vietnam Center and Archive, Texas Tech University, Item #2390813001. Her Christian name is Christine-Helene. Thieu's Christian name was Martino.

23 Taipei #3192, June 6, 1975.

24 "Mme. Thieu Shuns Politics," *Los Angeles Times*, March 24, 1970.

25 "Scores on the Aptitude tests during the period of Instruction from June 25, 1952 to September 25, 1952," September 25, 1952, *Archive de General de Division* Paul Vanuxem, Lyon, France.

26 Interview of Mrs. Nguyen Van Thieu, March 6, 2013, Irvine, CA. Translator: Cao Van Than.

27 "Who's Thieu," *Washington Post*, October 3, 1971, B1.

28 "Savior of Vietnam," *The Jerusalem Post*, October 31, 1971, 7.

29 "Navarre Doubts Delta Drive Now: Admits Failure in Central Annam," *New York Times*, June 8, 1954, 3.

30 "South Vietnam: A Vote for the Future," *Time*, September 15, 1967.

31 Engelmann interview with Thieu.

32 Tran Ngoc Trong, Ho Dac Huan, and Le Dinh Thuy, *Luoc su Quan luc Viet Nam Cong Hoa* [*Summary History of the Armed Forces of the Republic of Vietnam*] (San Jose, CA: Huong Que Publishing, 2011), 45.

33 Do Mau, *War in My Native Land*, 767.

34 1 Corinthians 13:12.

35 Decree signed by Vo Nguyen Giap, minister of interior, September 5, 1945, in *Vietnam Dan Quoc Cong Bao*, September 9, 1945. The author thanks Dr. Stephen Young for providing this document.

36   Nguyen Ngoc Huy, "Political Parties in Vietnam," *The Vietnam Council on Foreign Relations*, November 16, 1970.

37   Edward Lansdale, Calvin Mehlert, and Charles Sweet, "Nationalist Politics in South Vietnam," U.S. embassy, Saigon, May 1968, 6.

38   Huy was born in Saigon, but he spent his youth in Bien Hoa Province. He left school at seventeen after his father died, and he found work as a civil servant. In 1945, he met Nguyen Ton Hoan and was introduced to the Dai Viet Party. Diem exiled them both in 1955 to Paris, where Huy went to school and graduated with a doctorate in political science.

39   Dang Van Sung, "To the Vietnamese Nationalist Leaders," 7.

40   "Biographic Data on Tran Quoc Buu," Saigon Embassy Airgram A-167, July 31, 1974.

41   For a more detailed discussion of the Buddhist movement, see Mark Moyar, "Political Monks: The Militant Buddhist Movement during the Vietnam War," *Modern Asian Studies* 38, 4 (2004), 749–784; Robert Topmiller, "Struggling for Peace: South Vietnamese Buddhist Women and Resistance to the Vietnam War," *Journal of Women's History* 17, 3 (2005), 133–157; James McAllister, "Only Religions Count in Vietnam: Thich Tri Quang and the Vietnam War," *Modern Asian Studies* 42, no. 4 (2008): 751–782.

42   Chau was born November 2, 1921, in Ninh Binh Province, North Vietnam. He came south sometime in the early 1950s, where he was a founding member of the Vietnamese Buddhist Association of Hue. When the Unified Buddhist Church (UBC) was formed in January 1964, he was chosen to be the Chairman of the Church's Institute for Propagation of the Faith, a position he held until 1967.

43   Francois Guillemot, "Autopsy of a Massacre: On a Political Purge in the Early Days of the Indochina War," *European Journal of East Asian Studies* 9 (2010): 225–265.

CHAPTER 2

1   Nguyen Tuan Cuong, "The Promotion of Confucianism in South Vietnam (1955–1975) and the Role of Nguyen Dang Thuc as a New Confucian Scholar." *Journal of Vietnamese Studies* (2015) vol. 10, Issue 4, 43.

2   Miller, *Misalliance*, 32.

3   Ton That Dinh, *20 Nam Binh Nghiep* [*My Twenty-Year Military Career*] (San Jose, CA: Chanh Dao, 1998), 50. Dinh commanded the 32nd Mobile Group, a prestigious assignment. Dinh was born in Hue, and the family name Ton indicates he was a member of the royal family.

4   Nguyen Van Chau, translated by Nguyen Vi Khanh, *Ngo Dinh Diem va No Luc Hoa Binh Dang Do* [*Ngo Dinh Diem and the Unfinished Peace Effort*] (Los Alamitos, CA: Xuan Thu Publishers, 1989), 52.

5   "Central Intelligence Bulletin," CIA, November 10, 1954.

6   Hinh was not the only officer who left under a cloud. Another Vietnamese officer, Captain Tran Dinh Lan, who had long been suspected of covertly working for French intelligence, also left for France.

7   Tran Ngoc Chau, *Vietnam Labyrinth: Allies, Enemies, and Why the U.S. Lost the War* (Lubbock: Texas Tech University Press, 2012), 139. Chau saved Mrs. Thieu's life by rushing into a burning building at their shared quarters in Dalat to rescue her.

8   Interview with Lieutenant General Lu Mong Lan, December 3, 2016, Falls Church, VA.

9   Pham Van Lieu, *Tra Ta Song Nui (Hoi Ky, tap 2: 1963–1975)* [*Return Our Land to Us (A Memoir, Volume II: 1963–1975)*] (Houston: Van Hoa Publishing, 2003), 58. Lieu was a northerner who came south and graduated with the famous 5th class at the Dalat military academy. He knew many of the senior RVNAF officials.

Lieu was a close supporter of Lieutenant General Nguyen Chanh Thi. James Nach, another Saigon embassy political officer who spoke often with Lieu, said Lieu had an "encyclopedic memory." Lieu's three-volume memoir, if used carefully, remains one of the most insightful sources into Vietnamese politics.

10   Ha Thuc Ky, *Song con voi dan toc: Hoi Ky chanh tri* [*Life and Death with Our Nation: A Political Memoir*] (CA: Phuong Nghi Publishing, 2009), 351.

11   Lan Cao interview with Khiem, September 22, 2017.

12   Huynh Van Lang, *Ky Uc Huynh Van Lang, Tap II* [*The Memoirs of Huynh Van Lang, Volume II*] (CA: Self-published, 2012), 242. Lang notes that within a year, Pham Ngoc Thao joined the Can Lao party and that the three men—Lang, Khiem, and Thao—became close.

13   "Biographic Data on the Prime Minister Tran Thien Khiem," Saigon Embassy Airgram A-155, August 13, 1974.

14   Lan Cao interview of Khiem, February 23, 2018

15   Several of Khiem's classmates would be promoted to General: Nguyen Khanh, Le Van Phat, Duong Van Duc, Nguyen Van Kiem, and Cao Hao Hon.

16   Pham Van Lieu, *Return Our Land*, vol. II, 308.

17   "Pham Ngoc Thao—Silent Heroism," *Thanh Nien*, December 20, 2012.

18   Interview with Mrs. Thieu, March 6, 2013, Irving, CA.

19   Ellen Hammer, *A Death in November: America in Vietnam, 1963* (New York: E. P. Dutton, 1987), 287.

20   Kim was born on November 21, 1918, in Binh Dinh province. His parents moved to France when he was young, and he joined the French army in 1939. He fought against the Germans, but he returned to Vietnam in 1943. When the VNA was formed in 1949, Kim, then a major in the French army, transferred to the VNA. Don joined as a captain, and Duong Van Minh joined as a first lieutenant. By June 1953, Kim was one of only ten colonels in the VNA. When Diem assumed the presidency, he was highly suspicious of Kim's French ties, and Kim's career soon lagged.

21   "Biographic Data on Duong Van Minh," Saigon Embassy Airgram A-162, August 14, 1973.

22   "Debriefing Report of Lieutenant Colonel John Geraci," November 7, 1963, "Subject Files of the Vietnam Working Group, 1963–1966," Box 3, Rebellion Coups, RG 59, NARA.

23   The 21st Division was formed on June 1, 1959, from the 11th and 13th Light Divisions. In early 1960, it had regiments deployed from Tay Ninh province to Ca Mau, the tip of South Vietnam. It was eventually concentrated in the lower Mekong Delta in late 1961.

24   Tran Van Don, *Viet Nam Nhan Chung: Hoi Ky Chanh Tri* [*Vietnam Witness: A Political Memoir*] (San Jose, CA: Xuan Thu Publishing, 1989), 149–150.

25   Do Mau, *War in My Native Land*, 301–302.

26   The region designation changed on April 13, 1961, to the 1st Tactical Zone, more commonly known as I Corps.

27   Thi claims in his memoirs that coup plotting began in July 1960 and that he was deeply involved. See Nguyen Chanh Thi, *Viet Nam: Mot Troi Tam Su* [*Vietnam: Confiding a Sea of Memories*] (Los Alamitos, CA: Xuan Thu, 1987). Dong and others strongly deny Thi's account. Vuong Van Dong, *Binh Bien 11-11- 60, Khoi Diem Mot Hanh Trinh* [*The 11 November 1960 Mutiny, the Beginning of a Journey*] (Paris: Self-published, 2000).

28   Interview with Colonel Ngo Thanh Tung, September 27, 2017, Orlando, FL. Tung, born in Hanoi, was arrested after the effort collapsed. He spent three years in jail on Con Son Island but was released after the November 1963 coup.

29 "Biographic Data on Nguyen Khanh," Saigon Embassy Airgram A-125, June 14, 1974.

30 "Biographic Data on Khiem," 3.

31 Interview of Mrs. Loan Dommen, July 9, 2018, Bethesda, MD.

32 Rufus Phillips, *Why Vietnam Matters: An Eyewitness Account of Lessons Not Learned* (Annapolis, MD: Naval Institute Press, 2008), 102.

33 "Biographic Data on Tran Van Don," Saigon Embassy Airgram A-158, July 25, 1974.

34 "Politburo Cable No. 20-NB," November 12, 1960, in *Van Kien Dang, Toan Tap, 21, 1960* [*Collected Party Documents, Volume 21, 1960*] (Hanoi: National Political Publishing House, 2002), 1019–1021. Hereafter *Collected Party* and the year.

35 Nguyen Chanh Thi, *Sea of Memories*, 165. Lieu claimed that Tran Dinh Lan flew in from Paris to visit them. After first talking to Dong, he then met with Lieu and Thi. Lieu states that Lan was "wearing the rank of a captain in the French Army" and that Lan claimed that his anti-Diem group "had the whole-hearted support of both the French government and the Cambodian government." Lieu, *Return Our Land*, vol. 1, 429.

36 Pham Xuan Tich, "Vuong Van Dong and the 11 November 1960 Mutiny," in Chinh Dao, ed., *Nhin Lai Bien Co 11/11/1960* [*Looking Back at the 11 November 1960 Event*] (Houston: Van Hoa Publishing, 1997), 165.

37 Upon Diem's death, Cu returned to Saigon, and rejoined the VNAF. He served in the Air Force for the rest of the war. Quoc was imprisoned until the coup, whereupon he was released. He also rejoined the VNAF but was shot down and killed on April 19, 1965, while leading an airstrike against North Vietnam.

38 Ly Tong Ba, *Hoi Ky 25 Nam Khoi Lua* [*Memoir of 25 Years of War*] (San Marcos, CA: Self-published, 1999), 56.

39 Huynh Van Cao, *Tron Mot Kiep Nguoi* [*A Full Life*] (San Jose, CA: Self-published, 1993).

40 In January 1965, soldiers from the 7th ARVN Division trapped and decimated an NLF battalion at the same village, killing over 150 enemy, the largest number in a single engagement since the war began. ARVN losses were relatively light, and it was a dramatic payback for the defeat two years earlier. Although the first Ap Bac battle was broadly reported and analyzed, Ap Bac II, as the ARVN called it, was barely mentioned in the American press, which was focused on the latest Saigon turmoil.

41 Quang was born in 1922 in Quang Binh, the province directly above the DMZ. Well educated, he studied for the clergy in the 1936–45 class of Buddhist aspirants at the Bao Quoc Pagoda in Hue and finished first in his class.

42 Pham Van Minh, *Vietnamese Engaged Buddhism: The Struggle Movement, 1963–1966* (Westminster, CA: Van Nghe Publishing, 2002), 164.

43 Ibid.,191

44 Interview with Pham Duy Tat, November 5, 2017, Falls Church, VA.

45 Tran Van Don, *Our Endless War* (Novato, CA: Presidio Press, 1978), 90. This is Don's English-language book.

46 *Foreign Relations of the United States*, 1961–1963, volume III, Vietnam, document 281, Hereafter *FRUS,* the year and volume number, and # for document number. All citations are to Vietnam volumes, unless otherwise noted.

CHAPTER 3

1   "French Writer Describes 1963 Peace Bid," *Los Angeles Times*, December 15, 1968, quoting an article by French writer George Chaffard. The piece accurately describes Nhu's efforts to contact Hanoi through various means and provides other unconfirmed details.

2   Ton That Dinh, *Military Career*, 433.

3 Do Mau, *War in My Native Land*, 780.

4 Thomas L. Ahern, Jr., *CIA and the House of Nho: Covert Action in South Vietnam, 1954–1963* (Washington, D.C.: Central Intelligence Agency, 2000), 175.

5 Memcon with Nguyen Ngoc Tho, December 6, 1969. The author wishes to thank Mrs. Loan Dommen for access to the files of her late husband, the journalist Arthur Dommen. It is uncertain who conducted the interview with Tho as there is no name attached to the typewritten document.

6 Nguyen Tien Hung and Jerrold Schecter, *The Palace File* (New York: Harper & Sons, 1986), 76.

7 "Vietnam Hindsight. Part II: The Death of Diem," Transcript of NBC News Broadcast, December 22, 1971, 11–12.

8 *FRUS*, 1961–1963, vol. II, #239.

9 Moyar, *Triumph Forsaken*, 163.

10 "On Revolutionary Operations in South Vietnam," Politburo Resolution, February 25–27, 1962, in *Mot So Van Kien Cua Dang Ve Chong My, Cuu Nuoc, Tap I (1954–1965) [A Number of Party Documents Regarding the Resistance to the Americans to Save the Nation]* (Hanoi, Su That Publishing House, 1985), 157.

11 "Four Urgently Needed Policies to Save the Nation," July 20, 1962. Item #23119048001, TTU.

12 "On the Big Political Attack on the Occasion of July 20th," July 24, 1962, Item #2310104013, TTU.

13 "COSVN Current Affairs Committee Issues Directive on Propaganda and Directs the Implementation of the Stratagem Slogans of the Front," July 10, 1962, in *Lich Su Bien Nien Xu Uy Nam Bo va Trung Uong Cuc Mien Nam (1954–1975) [Historical Chronicle of the Cochin China Party Committee and the Central Office for South Vietnam, 1954–1975]* (Hanoi: National Political Publishing House, 2002), 322–323. Hereafter *COSVN Chronicle*.

14 "Comrade Le Duan Sends Letter to COSVN Providing Additional Thoughts on Directing the Opposition to the Enemy's 'Special War' Strategy," July 18, 1962, *COSVN Chronicle*, 324.

15 Pierre Asselin, *Hanoi's Road to the Vietnam War, 1954–1965* (Berkeley: University of California Press, 2013), 124.

16 *FRUS*, 1961–1963, vol. 24, Laos Crisis, #361.

17 "De Gaulle Offers to Help Vietnam End Foreign Rule," *New York Times*, August 30, 1963, 1.

18 For an excellent examination of the Kennedy and Johnson administration's reaction to De Gaulle's proposal, see Fredrik Logeval's *Choosing War: The Lost Chance for Peace and the Escalation of War in Vietnam* (Berkeley: University of California Press, 2001).

19 "Secret Telegram from Maneli (Saigon) to Spasowski (Warsaw) [Ciphergram No.11424]," September 4, 1963, History and Public Policy Program Digital Archive, AMSZ, Warsaw; 6/77, w-102, t-625, translated by Margaret Gnoinska. CWIHP Working Paper No. 45, http://digitalarchive.wilsoncenter.org/document/118971.

20 *FRUS*, 1961–1963 vol. IV, #119.

21 "Cautious Optimism for Vietnam's New Regime," *Globe and Mail*, November 18, 1963, 18.

22 Interview with Tran Van Don in *Vietnam: A Television History*, May 7, 1981.

23 Nguyen Ngoc Huy and Stephen Young, *Understanding Vietnam* (Amsterdam: DPC Information Service, 1982), 95.

24 "Memorial Rite to Honor Writer-Martyr Nguyen Tuong Tam," January 4, 1964. Item #2361205115, TTU.

25 Interview with Mrs. Thieu, March 6, 2013, Irving, CA. Mrs. Thieu further relates

that her husband's main condition for joining the coup was that no harm befall Diem. Removal and exile was the preferred option.

26 Nguyen Tien Hung, *Thieu's Thoughts*, 372. This timeframe would have been in early October 1963, shortly after the U.S. announced an aid cutback to the South Vietnamese in response to the pagoda raids.

27 "Thieu Defends Role in '63 Overthrow of Diem," *Los Angeles Times*, July 20, 1971, 10.

28 Ibid.

29 According to Thieu's future military aide, Major Nguyen Xuan Tam, on the day of the coup, Thieu misled his U.S. advisor by telling him that he was traveling to Ba Ria, a town near Vung Tau. The American departed in his jeep for Ba Ria, and Thieu went in the opposite direction, toward Saigon. Thieu maintained radio contact with his advisor during the day, telling him he was "right behind him." Moreover, he had covertly sent his division chief of artillery into Saigon a few days before to scout direct firing positions for a battery of 105mm guns. Thieu left his chief of staff, Major Pham Quoc Thuan, in charge of the 5th Division base camp while placing his division deputy commander under guard.

30 Huynh Van Cao, *A Full Life*, 103.

31 Tat interview.

32 Tat said the deputy commander did not provide a reason for ordering him not to attack.

33 Ton That Dinh, *Military Career*, 448.

34 Ibid., 447.

35 Do Tho, *Nhat Ky Do Tho: Tuy Vien Mot Tong Thong Bi Giet* [*The Diary of Do Tho: Aide to a Murdered President*] (Garden Grove, CA: Dai Nam Publishing, 1982), 219–220.

36 Ly Tong Ba, *Twenty-Five Years of War*, 98.

37 Marguerite Higgins, *Our Vietnam Nightmare* (New York: Harper and Row, 1965), 217.

38 It is uncertain if Dinh is referring only to the palace assault or total casualties.

39 Lou Conein confirmed Mau's account regarding this officer to U.S. embassy political officers Jim Nach and Cal Mehlert at a meeting in Saigon in 1970. Conein, while not on the balcony, also stated that it was a group decision to kill Diem and Nhu. Email from James Nach, June 14, 2014.

40 "Forces at Work in Generals Committee of Vietnam," November 5, 1963.

41 Tran Van Don, *Vietnam Witness*, 231.

42 Higgins, *Our Vietnam Nightmare*, 218.

43 Duong Hieu Nghia, "Report on the Death of President Diem." Nghia's account must also be taken with the proverbial grain of salt. Given the close confines of an M-113, in which the author has ridden many times, it would make sense to use a knife instead of firing an automatic weapon inside a metal box.

44 "Vietnam Hindsight. Part II: The Death of Diem."

45 Interview with Le Minh Dao, May 30, 2014, Hartford, CT.

46 Cao The Dung [pseudonym: Tran Kim Tuyen] and Luong Minh Khai, *Lam The Nao De Giet Mot Tong Thong* [*How to Kill a President*] (Dong Phuong Foundation, San Jose, CA, 1988). The book was first published in Saigon in 1970.

47 "Thieu Accuses Junta Chiefs in Diem Death," *Los Angeles Times*, October 3, 1970.

48 "Using History for Politics: The Case of Tran Van Don," Saigon Embassy Memorandum, August 18, 1971, RG 84, Saigon Embassy Mission Files, U.S. Consulate General Danang: Economic and Political Files, 1971–1973, Box 2. Hereafter the originating agency and Memo.

49 "Thieu terms Minh a Liar, and Defends Role in Diem Coup," *New York Times*, July 20, 1971, 1.

CHAPTER 4

1 The most notable exception is George Mcturnan Kahin's *Intervention: How America Became Involved in Vietnam* (New York: Knopf, 1986). Kahin accurately reflects Minh's efforts to change the course of the war. However, he mistakenly takes at face value the views of senior South Vietnamese participants, such as Don, Minh, and Tho, who blame the subsequent Khanh coup on "American interference." Don knew differently.

2 "Meeting with General Do Mau on 9 November 1963," CIA Memo, n.d.

3 *FRUS*, 1961–1963, vol. IV, #243.

4 Tho was born in 1908 to a wealthy family in what was then Long Xuyen Province in the Delta. He became the private secretary to Vice Admiral Jean Decaux, governor general of French Indochina. He had been an early supporter of Diem, and to achieve regional balance in his administration, Diem appointed him vice president.

5 Interview with Le Van Minh, November 16, 2016, Paris, France.

6 "Cong Luan Interviews 'Big' Minh," Saigon Embassy Airgram A-947, October 17, 1968.

7 Huy and Young, *Understanding Vietnam*, 107.

8 *FRUS*, 1961–1963, vol. IV, #349.

9 Thomas Ahern, Jr., *CIA and the Generals: Covert Support to Military Government in South Vietnam* (Washington, D.C.: Central Intelligence Agency, 1998), 9. On November 30, Lodge changed his mind. He reported that Minh wanted a U.S. "brain trust" team to help him develop policies.

10 "Statute of Council Notables Fixed by Decree of Chairman of MRC," *Vietnam Press*, November 24, 1963.

11 According to Rural Affairs chief Rufus Phillips, Diem did not want an independent judiciary as he "felt communist subversion was such a danger that he needed to be able to act by decree, without reference to the legislature or judicial review." The Americans attempted to instruct Diem on the "checks and balances" in the U.S. Constitution, but Diem was "not convinced." Phillips, *Why Vietnam Matters*, 87.

12 Minh would later tell an American official that he regretted allowing Duc to return since Duc was "incompetent and crazy." *FRUS*, 1964–1968, vol. I, #75.

13 Tran Van Don, *Vietnam Witness*, 255.

14 Hoang Van Lac and Ha Mai Viet, *Blind Design: Why America Lost the Vietnam War* (Houston: Self-published, 1996), 138.

15 Ibid.

16 Frank Scotton, *Uphill Battle: Reflections on Viet Nam Counterinsurgency* (Lubbock, TX: TTU University Press, 2014).

17 "Politburo Cable to COSVN and Region 5 on Strengthening Our Leadership of the Movement following the American Coup against Ngo Dinh Diem," late November 1963, *COSVN Chronicle*, 405.

18 *Cuoc Khang Chien Chong My Cuu Nuoc Cua Nhan Dan Ben Tre* [*The People of Ben Tre's Resistance War against the Americans to Save the Nation*] (Ben Tre: Ben Tre Province Military Headquarters, 1985), 105.

19 Thomas L. Ahern, Jr., *Vietnam Declassified: The CIA and Counterinsurgency* (Lexington: The University Press of Kentucky, 2010), 26.

20 "Junta says Ngo's Hurt War Effort," *New York Times*, November 9, 1963, 4.

21 Rufus Phillips, "Conversation with Duong Van Minh," November 20, 1963, Item #23970202017, TTU.

22 Jeffery Race, *War Comes to Long An* (Berkeley, CA: University of California Press, 1972), 130–133.

23 Interview with Le Minh Dao, July 22, 2014, Hartford, CT.

24 While the University of Michigan during Diem's reign conducted a series of studies on the administrative structure of a hamlet, district, and province, Scotton's survey effort was the first to analyze the political and security aspects that had occurred over the past couple of months for an area.

25 Kahin, *Intervention*, 185.

26 "Saigon Asks Sect to Fight Viet Cong," *New York Times*, November 27, 1963, 7.

27 "Saigon is Mending Ties to Cambodia, *New York Times*, December 16, 1963, 2.

28 "Excerpts from speech of General Duong Van Minh," *Public Administration Bulletin* #11, January 10, 1964, Item #1070107011, TTU. Hereafter *PAB*.

29 "Neutralists in Exile Barred by Saigon," *New York Times*, December 10, 1963, 11.

30 *FRUS*, 1961–1963, vol. IV, #359.

31 Ibid., #383.

32 "No Neutralism—Duong Van Minh," *Saigon Post*, December 26, 1963, Item #2300218008, TTU.

33 "France Seeking a Larger Role in Asia," *New York Times*, January 19, 1964, E4.

34 "PsyWarriors Gathered for Sessions in Saigon," *Saigon Daily News*, January 9, 1964, Item #2274203012, TTU.

35 "Saigon Reforms Pledged; Resources are Limited," *Christian Science Monitor*, January 10, 1964, 2.

36 "Dien Huong Plan," MACV #196 to CINCPAC, January 9, 1964. The author believes the correct spelling is Dien Hong, after a famous conference in Vietnamese history that was convened by Vietnam's king to poll his nobles and elders about whether to fight the latest Chinese invasion of Vietnam.

37 "A Viet Cong Defeat by 1965 Predicted," *South China Morning News*, December 30, 1963, 7.

38 Douglas Pike, *Viet Cong: The Organization and Techniques of the National Liberation Front of South Vietnam* (Cambridge: The MIT Press, 1966), 362.

39 Interview with Senior Colonel Nguyen Van Tong, in "*Ve hanh dong cua ong Duong Van Minh trong ngay* 30/4/1975" [Duong Van Minh's Actions on 30 April 1975], *Hon Viet*, May 2008, 16. Minh was the oldest of seven children; Nhut was the second. Nhut had joined the Viet Minh in 1944 and regrouped to North Vietnam in 1954. In December 1960, at the request of COSVN, the North Vietnamese sent him south to recruit Minh. In August 1962, Nhut reestablished contact with his family, but he did not meet Minh until later.

40 Ibid.

CHAPTER 5

1 Tran Van Don, *Our Endless War*, 93.

2 Huynh Van Lang, *Memoirs*, 445.

3 Tran Van Don, *Our Endless War*, 94.

4 Huynh Van Cao, *A Full Life*, 104.

5 Interview with Nguyen Khanh by Geoff Shaw, June 16, 1994, 45; interview of Nguyen Khanh by Paul Van and Bui Duong Liem, June 14, 2009, http://www .youtube.com/watch?v=xjTXJow2ZnI&feature=youtu.be. Khanh ignores, or perhaps forgot, that his 43rd Regiment was then based in Lam Dong Province, about a five-hour drive from Saigon.

6 Leonard Maynard, "Unofficial translation of Prime Minister Decree #12TTP/TSNT: Concept, Principles, and Program of New Rural Life Hamlets," January 23, 1964, Item #23970108003, TTU.

7   Tran Van Don, *Vietnam Witness*, 260.

8   "Viet Leader Denies Plan to Replace Tho," *New York Times*, December 18, 1963, A19.

9   Huy and Young, *Understanding Vietnam*, 108.

10 Pham Van Lieu, *Return Our Land*, vol. II, 64–65.

11 Kim's son Le Van Minh denies his father was close to Tran Dinh Lan. Minh recalls that his father was not impressed by Lan, believing he was "all talk and no action" and that "upon Lan's return from France, he was making big talk to make himself sound important."

12 *FRUS*, 1964–1968, vol. I, #75.

13 Interview with Bui Diem and Le Van Phuc, July 18, 2014, Rockville. MD. Interview with Nguyen Minh Chanh, October 23, 2014, Garden Grove, CA.

14 Bui Diem, with David Chanoff, *In the Jaws of History* (Bloomington: Indiana University Press, 1989), 107.

15 Quang Minh [pseudonym: Truong Tu Thien], *Dai Viet Quoc Dan Dang: Cach Mang Viet Nam Thoi Can Kim* [*The Dai Viet Quoc Dan Party: The Vietnamese Revolution in the Modern Era*] (Westminster, CA: Van Nghe Publishing, 2000), 247.

16 Ibid.

17 "Political Theories of Dai Viet," in *PAB* #12, February 28, 1964.

18 Huy and Young, *Understanding Vietnam*, 114.

19 Nguyen Chanh Thi, *Sea of Memories*, 232.

20 Embassy of France in Vietnam, cable #168/169, to the Ministry of Foreign Affairs, January 31, 1964, Serie Asie Oceanie, sous serie Vietnam du Sud, 1954–1964, Section 150qo, Folder 19. Translated by Le Van Minh. Hereafter French embassy to MFA and the cable number. Georges Perruche was the deputy ambassador since Saigon had refused to accept a replacement for Roger Lalouette, who had departed in September 1963.

21 Pham Van Lieu, *Return Our Land*, vol. II, 65.

22 Huy and Young, *Understanding Vietnam*, 109.

23 *FRUS*, 1964–1968, vol. I, #322.

24 Tran Van Don, *Vietnam Witness*, 300, 306.

25 "Coup of January 30, 1964," French embassy to MFA, #529, September 18, 1964.

26 Nguyen Chanh Thi, *Sea of Memories*, 216.

27 Harkins to Taylor, MAC #0325, January 30, 1964.

28 French embassy to MFA, #238, February 17, 1964.

29 Ted Gittinger, "General Paul D. Harkins," *Association for Diplomatic Studies*, November 10, 1981, 29.

30 *Pentagon Papers*, part IV, Nov 63–Apr 65, 27.

31 Nguyen Chanh Thi, *Sea of Memories*, 220.

32 Cao Van Vien was born on December 11, 1921, in Vientiane, Laos. He joined the French army as an enlisted man in July 1946 and was commissioned a second lieutenant in 1949. After Hung Yen, he was given command of a VNA battalion. In early 1958, he was appointed chief of staff of Diem's Personal Staff, where he became close to the president. He was promoted to colonel on October 26, 1960, and his loyalty was rewarded when he was assigned as commander of the Airborne Brigade after the failed November 1960 coup.

33 "Conversation with General Cao Van Vien," in Lam Le Trinh, *Ve Nguon Sinh Lo Cho Que Huong* [*Back to Our Roots: The Road to Life for Our Homeland*] (Huntington Beach, CA: Human Rights Bookshelf, 2006), 271.

34 Arthur Dommen, *The Indochinese Experience of the French and the Americans* (Bloomington: Indiana University Press, 2001), 620–621.

35 Tran Van Don, *Endless War*, 123.

36   Huy and Young, *Understanding Vietnam*, 111.

37   "Cong Luan Interviews 'Big' Minh," Saigon Embassy Airgram A-947, October 17, 1968.

38   Lan Cao interview with Khiem, September 22, 2017.

39   Saigon #1442, January 30, 1964.

40   Tran Do Cung and Mrs. Nguyen Ton Hoan, *Ong ba Nguyen Ton Hoan trong dong su Viet* [*Nguyen Ton Hoan and His Wife in Vietnamese History*] (CA: Self-published, 2012), 172.

41   Quang Minh, *Dai Viet Party*, 250.

42   "On the New Coup in South Vietnam," Politburo Announcement No. 50/TB/TW, February 1, 1964, *Collected Party Documents, 1964*, 50–51.

43   "Politburo Cable to COSVN and Region 5 Party Committee on Exploiting the Deep Internal Crisis Within the Puppet Government and Developing Revolutionary Strength," January 31, 1964, *COSVN Chronicle*, 422.

44   "Policy and Program of the Republic of Vietnam," Embassy of the Republic of Vietnam, March 9, 1964, 4.

45   Wesley Fishel, "The Eleventh Hour in Vietnam," *Asian Survey*, vol. 5 (2), February 1965, 98.

46   Ahern, *CIA and the Generals*, 19.

47   Huy and Young, *Understanding Vietnam*, 115.

48   Do Mau, *War in My Native Land*, 839.

49   Military History Institute of Vietnam, *Victory in Vietnam: The Official History of the People's Army of Vietnam, 1954–1975*, trans. by Merle Pribbenow (Lawrence, KS: University Press of Kansas, 2002), 459, endnote 41.

50   Nguyen Ngoc, *Co mot con duong tren Bien Dong* [*There Was a Trail on the South China Sea*] (Hanoi: Hanoi Publishing House, 1994), 111.

51   *Quan Khu 8: Ba Muoi Nam Khang Chien (1945–1975)* [*Military Region 8: Thirty Years of Resistance War (1945–1975)*] (Hanoi: People's Army Publishing House, 1998), 487.

52   "Survivors of Massacre Fear New Viet Raid," *Los Angeles Times*, April 17, 1964, 2.

53   *FRUS*, Mainland Southeast Asia, vol. XXVII, #107.

54   Khanh interview, June 14, 2009, http://www.youtube.com/watch?v=xjTXJow2ZnI&feature=youtu.be.

CHAPTER 6

1   *FRUS*, 1964, vol. 1, #136.

2   Ibid., #140.

3   Ibid., #152.

4   Khanh interview, June 14, 2009. Khanh made the same claim in the PBS television series "Vietnam," April 29, 1981. In Central Vietnam, the monks practiced the Mahayana form and wore robes of dark maroon or brown.

5   "No Fresh Religious Crisis," *South China Morning Post*, June 9, 1964, 22.

6   "Khanh Calls on Vietnamese to Close Ranks, Save Nation," *Washington Post*, June 14, 1964, 20.

7   Robert Shaplen, *The Lost Revolution: The U.S. in Vietnam, 1946–1966* (New York: Harpers & Row, 1966), 256.

8   Khanh confirmed to Arthur Dommen that he had "no actual evidence of a French-inspired conspiracy." Dommen, *Indochinese Experience*, 620.

9   Tran Van Don, *Vietnam Witness*, 301.

10   "Dr. Dang Van Sung's Adverse Reaction to the Release of the Generals in Dalat." CIA Intelligence Information Cable (IIC), June 5, 1964. Hereafter CIA IIC.

11 Truong Nhu Tang, *A Viet Cong Memoir: An Inside Account of the Vietnam War and its Aftermath* (New York: Vintage, 1986), 91.

12 *FRUS*, 1964, vol. 1, #242.

13 State #70, July 8, 1964.

14 Khanh interview, June 14, 2009. Hoach had relatives who were senior NLF leaders.

15 *PAB* #17, October 31, 1964, 5. Item #1070108001, TTU.

16 "Decree Law 18/64," *PAB* #15, August 31, 1964.

17 Saigon #613, August 29, 1964.

18 Saigon #564, August 26, 1964.

19 Quang Minh, *Dai Viet Party*, 251.

20 "Some Aspects of Personal Relations among Senior RVNAF Officers," Enclosure #2, 11.

21 Quang Minh, *Dai Viet Party*, 251.

22 "Details of the 26 and 27 August 1964 Meetings of the MRC," CIA IIC, September 1, 1964.

23 Saigon #713, September 2, 1964.

24 Saigon #688, September 1, 1964.

25 "Biographic Data on Nguyen Cao Ky," Saigon Embassy Airgram A-148, August 2, 1973.

26 Saigon #923, September 22, 1964.

27 Khiem later told a senior U.S. embassy official that "he had broken with Khanh in the fall of 1964 because of his refusal to move toward elections and a constitutional govt after Diem was overthrown, and he left the country to become Amb to Washington because he could only see trouble here with a military rule." How much of Khiem's description of events is the truth or revisionism is difficult to determine. Saigon #38135, September 19, 1968.

28 Ahearn, *CIA and the Generals*, 27.

29 *COSVN Chronicle*, 450–451.

30 Ibid, 453.

CHAPTER 7

1 *FRUS*, 1964, vol. 1, #389.

2 "Biodata on RVN Vice President Tran Van Huong," Saigon Embassy Airgram A-243, October 17, 1973.

3 Huong was a founder of the Lien Truong, a group of powerful southern business leaders.

4 Pham Van Minh, *Engaged Buddhism*, 320-321.

5 *Tuoi tre Sai Gon Mau Than 1968* [*Saigon Youth: Tet Mau Than, 1968*] (Ho Chi Minh: Tre Publishing, 2003), 106.

6 *Chung Mot Bong Co (ve Mat Tran Dan Toc Giai Phong Mien Nam Viet Nam)* [*Under One Flag: The National Liberation Front of South Vietnam*] (Ho Chi Minh City: National Political Publishing House, 1993), 157.

7 Nguyen Cao Ky, *Buddha's Child: My Fight to Save Vietnam* (New York: St. Martin's Press, 2001), 110.

8 "Biodata on Tran Quoc Buu," 6.

9 "Deliberations of the AFC on 24 January," CIA IIC, January 25, 1965, Item #F029100040659, TTU.

10 "General Thieu's Assessment of the Situation in Central Vietnam as quite serious," CIA IIC, January 26, 1965.

11 *FRUS*, January–July 1965, vol. II, #9. Some Americans, Lansdale most prominently, would have disputed Taylor's assertion, believing that quiet discussions with the Vietnamese could often produce results.

12 "Khanh Appoints Caretaker Premier," *Chicago Tribune*, January 28, 1865, 2, quoting Khanh.

13 "Discussion with General Thieu, Acting Deputy Prime Minister, on Evening of January 27, 1965," Memcon, Saigon embassy.

14 "Rumors regarding Khanh's approach to French on Question of Neutralization," CIA IIC, December 30, 1964.

15 Ibid.

16 "Denial of Rumors that Khanh is involved in Political Plotting," CIA IIC, December 28, 1964.

17 "Statements of Nguyen Cao Ky concerning lack of support for General Khanh," CIA IIC, January 28, 1965.

18 *FRUS*, January-July 1965, vol. II, #58.

19 Ibid., #41.

20 "Former Saigon Leader Recalls Ouster," *New York Times*, June 17, 1971, 18.

21 "A Vietnamese General on his Role, Exile," *Washington Post*, November 27, 1974.

22 The Americans did eventually confirm the allegations. Shortly after Khanh was exiled, a CIA officer queried Khanh about his supposed contacts with the Communists. Khanh stated he had good connections, and he "claimed he could reestablish these contacts but would do so only if Washington had an 'overall strategic plan'" to end the war." Ahern, *CIA and the Generals*, 35.

23 Tran Van Don, *Vietnam Witness*, 367.

24 Gareth Porter, *Vietnam: The Definitive Documentation of Human Decisions, vol. 2* (Stanfordville, NY: Earl Coleman Productions, 1979), 345–346. Khanh told journalist Arthur Dommen that this was Phat's second letter to him but that he never received Phat's first letter. Dommen interview with Khanh, Bethesda, MD, October 16, 1996.

25 "Plotting to Neutralize Viet," *New York Herald Tribune*, December 20, 1964, 20.

26 Vien was born on November 21, 1919, in Vinh Binh Province in the Delta. His parents were wealthy landowners, and he attended a prestigious French secondary school in Saigon. In 1946, he graduated from the University of Hanoi's Medical School. He joined the Viet Minh and eventually rose to the rank of colonel and chief surgeon of the PAVN 320th Division. He left the Viet Minh in late 1951 after becoming disillusioned with Communist dogma. Moving to Saigon, he became close friends with Tran Van Huong and worked in Diem's government. In April 1960, he was the youngest person to sign the Caravelle Manifesto, which earned him two stints in jail.

27 Phillips, *Why Vietnam Matters*, 245.

28 "Quat Takes Viet Helm, Plans Climate of Unity," *Washington Post*, February 17, 1965, A15.

29 Interview with Bui Diem, June 2, 2016, Rockville, MD.

30 William Westmoreland, *A Soldier Reports* (New York: Doubleday, 1976), 93.

31 Ibid., 97.

32 "Call on General Thieu," Westmoreland Memo, May 31, 1965. Some Vietnamese, like Pham Van Lieu, later accused Thieu of masterminding Thao's arrest and ordering his murder, believing he was covering up his involvement in Thao's various coups. There is no evidence to support that contention.

33 Truong Nhu Tang, *Viet Cong Memoir*, 60.

34 "Personal Relations among Senior RVNAF Officers," Enclosure #2, 13.

35 "Implications of the Saigon Coup Events," CIA Memo, February 20, 1965.

36 Ahern, *CIA and the Generals*, 36.

37 *FRUS*, January-July 1965, vol. II, #63.

38 Ahern, *CIA and the Generals*, 38.

39 Interview with Bui Diem, June 2, 2016, Rockville, MD.

40 Interview with Bui Diem, February 6, 2014, Rockville, MD.

41 "Saigon Rules Out Peace Until Reds Drop Their Role," *New York Times*, March 1, 1965, 6.

42 Bui Diem, *Jaws of History,* 130–131.

43 Truong Nhu Tang, *Viet Cong Memoir*, 92.

44 "Biographic Data on Mrs. Ngo Ba Thanh," Saigon Embassy Airgram A-265, December 10, 1973.

45 "S. Viet Air Force Chief Vows to Back Regime," *Los Angeles Times*, March 18, 1965, 1.

46 *Under One Flag*, 904.

47 Trinh Dinh Thao, *Suy nghi va hanh dong: Hoi ky* [*Thought and Action: A Memoir*] (Ho Chi Minh City: Ho Chi Minh City Publishing House, 1985).

48 Vietnamese Wikipedia entry for Tran Van Do, at https://vi.wikipedia.org/wiki/Trần_Văn_Đỗ. After Geneva, Do became Diem's foreign minister, but he soon resigned in protest over the president's use of force against the sects and over Diem's refusal to delegate authority. Do was another of the famous signatories of the Caravelle Manifesto, but unlike the others, he was not arrested, mainly because he was the uncle of Madame Ngo Dinh Nhu. After 1975, he fled the country and resettled in France. He died in Paris on December 20, 1990.

49 "Negotiations and a Settlement for Vietnam," Saigon Embassy Airgram A-828, May 7, 1965.

50 Ibid.

51 Memcon, May 26, 1965, Personnel Papers of Ambassador Bui Diem. This and subsequent cables are from former ambassador Bui Diem, who graciously allowed me to use his files. Hereafter referred to as Bui Diem papers.

52 Ibid. Taylor reported that he had not discussed peace conditions with Khanh and that he only had this one meeting with Quat, thus confirming the origins of the GVN peace proposals. Saigon #4291, June 19, 1965.

53 According to Cao Van Than, Thieu's future minister for land reform, who was a close friend of the chief medical officer for the Military Security Service, claimed that Thao had died from heart failure caused by the crushing of his testicles.

54 George Carver, "Report on 10 April – 4 May 1965 Visit to Vietnam," May 6, 1965.

55 Saigon #3953, May 30, 1965.

56 "Call on General Thieu," Westmoreland Memo, May 31, 1965.

57 Memcon with Dr. Pham Huy Quat, August 26, 1965.

CHAPTER 8

1 "Biographic Data on Nguyen Cao Ky," Saigon Embassy Airgram A-148, August 2, 1973.

2 "Vietnam's New Leader: Nguyen Van Thieu," *New York Times*, June 15, 1965, 3. Out of the sixty Vietnamese general officers, twenty were either exiled or shunted aside.

3 Pham Van Lieu, *Return Our Land*, vol. II, 307–309.

4 Nguyen Cao Ky, *Twenty Years and Twenty Days* (New York: Stein and Day, 1976), 50–51.

5 Nguyen Xuan Phong, *Hope and Vanquished Reality* (New York: Center for Science of Hope, 2001), 179.

6 Van Van Cua, *Mong Khong Thanh* [*The Unfulfilled Dream*] (Westminster, CA. YTE Distributors, 2000), 100.

7 "Premier Ky's Speech at Military Convention," *Vietnam Press*, September 14, 1965.

8 *FRUS*, June-December 1965, vol. III, #9.

9   Saigon #4282, June 19, 1965.

10 Saigon #4386, June 25, 1965.

11 Pham Van Lieu, *Return Our Land*, vol. II, 319.

12 Saigon #4437, June 30, 1965.

13 Saigon #14, July 1, 1965.

14 Nguyen Cao Ky, *Buddha's Child*, 128–129.

15 Speech by Tran Van Do, June 22, 1965, #2120407033, TTU.

16 *FRUS*, June–December 1965, vol. III, #91.

17 Saigon #961, September 19, 1965.

18 Ibid.

19 Memcon by embassy officer John Burke with Le Van Hoach, June 3, 1965.

20 *FRUS*, June-December 1965, vol. III, #45.

21 The AB series battle plans were an annual plan to guide military strategy. Each was drafted by MACV and then coordinated with the Joint General Staff before issue.

22 *Pentagon Papers*, vol. IV: Evolution of the War, Part 5: The Build-up of U.S. Forces, March–July 1965, 84.

23 *FRUS*, January–June 1965, vol. II, #337.

24 Phan Nhat Nam, *The Stories Must be Told* (Westminster, CA: Nang Moi Publisher, 2002), 38–39.

25 *FRUS*, June-December 1965, vol. III, #1.

26 Ibid.

27 "On the Immediate Situation and Urgent Responsibilities," Resolution of the 11th Plenum of the Central Committee, March 25–27, 1965, in *Collected Party Documents*, 1965, 109.

28 *Quan Khu 5: Thang Loi va Nhung Bai Hoc Trong Khang Chien Chong My, Tap I* [*Military Region 5: Victories and Lessons Learned During the Resistance War Against the Americans, Volume I*] (Hanoi: People's Army Publishing House, 1981), 62.

29 *Su Doan 325, tap II* [*325th Division, vol. II*], 48–49.

30 *FRUS*, June–December 1965, vol. III, #29.

31 "Documents Show Korea's Cool Vietnam Calculations," *Chosun Ilbo* (English language), August 27, 2005. The article cited recently declassified Korean diplomatic records.

32 "Secretary McNamara's Visit: Meeting with the GVN," Saigon Embassy Airgram A-66, July 27, 1965.

33 "Thieu Cites Duties of ROK Troops in Vietnam," *Vietnam Press*, August 7, 1965.

34 "Address by Nguyen Van Thieu before Armed Forces Convention," Saigon Embassy Airgram A-210, September 25, 1965.

35 Westmoreland, *Soldier Reports*, 146.

36 "Saigon Extends Death Penalty," *New York Times*, July 24, 1965, 2.

37 "Vietnam Premier Seen Liberalizing his Views," *New York Times*, September 17, 1965, 2.

38 "Saigon Weighing Plan to Hold Election by 1967," *New York Times*, November 25, 1965, 6.

39 Thang was promoted to brigadier general, a two-star rank in the Vietnamese military, on November 1, 1965. On November 15, the Vietnamese general officer rank structure was realigned to correspond with that of the United States, and Thang automatically became a major general. Thieu became a lieutenant general.

40 Ray Fontaine, *The Dawn of a Free Vietnam: A Biographical Sketch of Dr. Phan Quang Dan* (Brownsville, TX: Pan American Business Services, 1992), 69.

41 Diem had proclaimed October 26 as "National Day" to celebrate the birth of the First Republic after his election victory over Bao Dai.

42 Saigon #2043, December 7, 1965.

CHAPTER 9

1 Lodge to Bundy, January 7, 1966.

2 Saigon #1273, October 13, 1965.

3 *FRUS*, 1966, vol. IV, #23.

4 "Speech by Directorate Chairman Thieu," Saigon Embassy Airgram A-443, January 27, 1966.

5 "Ky Hints Against Foreign Meddling," *South China Morning Post*, January 15, 1966, 30.

6 *Van Kien Dang, Toan Tap, tap 26, 1965* [*Collected Party Documents, vol. 26, 1965*] (Hanoi: National Political Publishing House, 2003), 593–594.

7 "COSVN Report on the Struggle Against FULRO," *COSVN Chronicle*, 2nd edition, 663.

8 Gabriel Kolko, *Anatomy of a War: Vietnam, the United States, and the Modern Historical Experience* (New York: Pantheon Books, 1985), 211. Kolko writes that after Vinh's execution, "the still nervous Chinese elite gave Thieu massive financial backing." Moreover, Mrs. Thieu's sister married one of the wealthiest Chinese businessmen in Saigon. Van Van Cua, the mayor of Saigon and a Ky supporter, agrees that Vinh's death caused the Chinese businessmen to support Thieu. Van Van Cua, *Unfulfilled Dream*, 129.

9 The Chinese labor union was called the General Association of Workers (*Tong Lien Doan Lao Dong*), which was separate from Tran Quoc Buu's union. The association consisted of many small Chinese labor unions in Cho Lon that represented restaurant and hotel employees and factory workers, but the largest number worked in textile factories.

10 "Ky's view that Thi may have lost support of the populace ...," CIA IIC, March 4, 1966.

11 CIA Weekly Report, "The Situation in South Vietnam," March 11, 1966.

12 "Viet Buddhists Threatening 'Rotten' Army Government," *New York Times*, March 16, 1966.

13 James McAllister, 'Only Religions Count in Vietnam:' Thich Tri Quang and the Vietnam War," *Modern Asian Studies*, 42, 4 (2008), 756.

14 Pham Van Minh, *Engaged Buddhism*, 305.

15 The VNQDD was the largest political party in I Corps, with its greatest strength in the provinces of Quang Nam, Quang Tin, and Quang Ngai. The Revolutionary Dai Viets, led by Ha Thuc Ky, were strongest in the two northern provinces of Quang Tri and Thua Thien. The Catholics represented another 10 percent of the local population. Moreover, the 2nd ARVN Division, led by Brigadier General Hoang Xuan Lam, which operated in southern I Corps in Quang Tin and Quang Ngai provinces, remained loyal to the government.

16 Ha Thuc Ky, *Life and Death*, 278.

17 Nguyen Cao Ky, *Buddha's Child*, 199.

18 Saigon #1357, March 19, 1966.

19 "Pro-Regime Buddhists Losing Out," *Los Angeles Times*, April 3, 1966, 4.

20 *FRUS*, 1966, vol. IV, #110.

21 *Quang Nam-Da Nang: 30 Nam Chien Dau va Chien Thang, 1945–1975, Tap II* [*Quang Nam-Da Nang: 30 Years of Fighting and Victory, 1945–1975, Volume II*] (Hanoi: People's Army Publishing House, 1988), 126.

22 Le Duan, *Tho Vao Nam* [*Letters to the South*], 2nd ed. (Hanoi: Su That Publishing House, 1986), 181–182.

23 Dinh was the only general officer arrested during the Khanh coup still on active duty.

He was currently the inspector general of the armed forces and concurrently head of the Military Training department.

24 Westmoreland to Wheeler, MAC #2812, April 13, 1966.

25 "Talk with General Thieu," Lansdale Memo, April 8, 1966.

26 Saigon #3927, April 13, 1966.

27 "Tri Quang Assails both Reds and U.S." *New York Times*, April 20, 1966, 3.

28 "Father Hoang Quynh's Efforts to Prevent Catholics from Demonstrating in Saigon ...," CIA IIC, April 13, 1966.

29 Memcon, "Catholic Attitudes," Saigon embassy, November 15, 1965.

30 Saigon #3927, April 13, 1966.

31 "Directorate Discussions Concerning the Present Government's Policies ...," CIA IIC, April 22, 1966.

32 Saigon #4413, May 6, 1966.

33 Tran Van Don, *Vietnam Witness*, 371.

34 Unlike other political assassinations, postwar Communist publications take no credit for the attempted hit on Minh. Someone on the Nationalist side was probably behind the failed effort.

35 Pham Van Minh, *Engaged Buddhism*, 404. The Buddhist firebrand died in a Communist prison camp in 1978.

36 See Decree Laws No. 21/66 and No. 22/66, June 19, 1966, *PAB* #29, July 1966.

37 *FRUS*, 1966, vol. IV, #162.

38 Nguyen Cao Ky, *Buddha's Child*, 228.

CHAPTER 10

1 Memcon, "Conversation with Bui Diem," September 24, 1965.

2 Pham Van Minh, *Engaged Buddhism*, 376.

3 Decree #22/66, *PAB* #29, July 1966.

4 *PAB* #27, May 1, 1966. In late February 1966, the U.S. embassy began calling the program Rural Development (RD), but the Vietnamese continued to call it Rural Construction.

5 Tran Ngoc Chau, *Vietnam Labyrinth*, 261–269.

6 The Mandarin system was based on Chinese law and language. The French eliminated mandarinate examinations in Chinese in 1916 and replaced them with the French system of academic degrees (Baccalaureate, Licentiate, and Doctorate). In 1933, Bao Dai decreed that Romanized (*quoc ngu*) Vietnamese replace Chinese in official correspondence. Confucian philosophy remained a cultural imprint, but French bureaucracy and language had long replaced Chinese in the Vietnamese Civil Service.

7 Tran Ngoc Chau, *Vietnam Labyrinth*, 261–269.

8 "Economic aid to South Vietnam doubled by the U.S. in two years," *The Globe and Mail*, July 2, 1966, 10.

9 Co was born on February 23, 1925 in Dinh Tuong Province. An ardent southerner, he had a well-deserved reputation for both combat excellence and corruption. In the same decree elevating Thang, Ky removed Co from his post as chief of the JGS and replaced him with Cao Van Vien. To pacify the southerners, Ky promoted Co to major general on November 1 and made him minister of defense. Co then became a lieutenant general in the rank restructuring of November 15.

10 Saigon #6836, September 24, 1966.

11 CIA Weekly, "The Situation in South Vietnam, August 8–14, 1966," August 15, 1966.

12 CIA Weekly, "The Situation in South Vietnam, October 10–16, 1966," October 17, 1966.

13 "Education in Vietnam," USAID Memo, February 1970.

14 CIA Weekly, "The Situation in South Vietnam, July 5–10, 1966," July 11, 1966.

15 "Refugees: The Health Program for 1967," *PAB* #35, February 1967, 93.

16 "Responsibility and Competency of Female Supervisors and Female Camp Workers," December 17, 1966, cited in *PAB* #36, 66.

17 Ibid., 95.

18 "Health in Vietnam," *New York Times*, December 18, 1966, 87. The numerous statistics cited in this wide-ranging article came from USAID.

19 Dr. Nguyen Le Hieu, "Health Care under the Republic of Vietnam, 1955–1975." Paper delivered at the SACEI conference, Arlington, VA.

20 "Memcon between Komer, Bui Diem, and GVN Amb. Vu Van Thai," May 21, 1966.

21 "Monk's Hunger Strike Seen as Dismal Failure," *Los Angeles Times*, September 17, 1966, 8.

22 Saigon #2131, July 28, 1966.

23 "Biodata on Nguyen Luu Vien," Saigon Embassy Airgram A-214, September 26, 1973.

24 Vo Long Trieu, *Hoi Ky, tap I [Memoir, vol. 1]* (Fresno, CA: Nguoi Viet Publishers, 2009), 424.

25 Ibid., 449–450.

26 State #69371, October 19, 1966.

27 Thich Tam Chau, "White Paper on the Split Between An Quang and Viet Nam Quoc Tu," December 31, 1993, 30.

28 Ahern, *CIA and the Generals*, 38. Ahern notes that payments to Quang had stopped in mid-summer 1966.

29 "Political Power of Buddhists Only a Memory in Vietnam," *New York Times*, December 19, 1966, 4.

30 "Joint Communique," October 26, 1966.

31 The Marines, Airborne, and the Rangers were exempt from pacification duties.

32 For the best description of these battles, see Warren Wilkins, *Grab Their Belts to Fight Them: The Viet Cong's Big Unit War Against the U.S., 1965–1966* (Annapolis, MD: Naval Institute Press, 2011).

33 *Pentagon Papers*, vol. 8, "Evolution of the War – Direct Action: the Johnson Commitments," 117.

34 "Conference with General Thieu," Westmoreland Memo, November 16, 1966.

35 "Viet Assemblymen Hit's Regime's Veto Power," *Los Angeles Times*, November 9, 1966, 5.

36 *Cong An Nhan Dan Viet Nam: Lich Su Bien Nien (1954–1975), Quyen II [Vietnam's People's Public Security: Chronology of Events (1954–1975), vol. II]* (Hanoi: People's Public Security Publishing House, 2000), 80.

37 *Cong An Nhan Dan Thanh pho Ho Chi Minh: Bien mien su Kien l ch su (1954–1975) [Ho Chi Minh City People's Public Security: Chronology of Historical Events (1945–1975)]* (National Political Publishing House, Hanoi, 2002), 65. This was the first successful attack against a senior GVN figure. They had tried and failed earlier to kill Ngo Dinh Diem and Phan Huy Quat.

38 Ibid.

CHAPTER II

1 "Red Withdrawal Must Precede Talks, Ky Says," *Los Angeles Times*, August 14, 1966, c9.

2 "Thieu Won't Seek the Presidency," *New York Times*, September 3, 1966, 3.

3 "Conferences with General Vien and General Thieu," Westmoreland Memo, November 22, 1966.

4 "Talk with Ky," Lansdale Memo, November 20, 1966.

5   Saigon #2130, July 28, 1966.

6   Saigon #17618, February 8, 1967.

7   "Talk with Thieu," Lansdale Memo, February 1, 1967.

8   Saigon #15080, January 9, 1967.

9   Interview with Bui Diem, November 13, 2010, Rockville, MD.

10   Bui Diem, *Jaws of History*, 12-21.

11   Bui Diem interview.

12   *Vietnam Bulletin*, Volume 1, #1–2, Jan-Feb 1967, 14.

13   Bui Diem, *Jaws of History*, 180–181.

14   Economic Minister Hanh was a different individual than the ARVN brigadier general of the same name.

15   "Sung's Discussion of the Current Political Situation ...," CIA IIC, April 9, 1967.

16   Huy and Young, *Understanding Vietnam*, 126.

17   Saigon #16547, January 26, 1967.

18   "Saigon Assembly Adopts Charter; Vote Unanimous," *New York Times*, March 19, 1967, 1.

19   Bui Diem, *Jaws of History*, 189.

20   Decree #198-SL/DUHC, "Governing the Reorganization of Village, Hamlet Administration," cited in *PAB* #35. The bulletin includes Decree #199, which outlines election procedures and future training for elected officials.

21   Nguyen Duc Thang, "Report to the Nation," December 27, 1966, cited in *PAB* #35, 26.

22   "Basic Memorandum #23," Ministry of RD, March 2, 1967.

23   CIA Weekly, "The Situation in South Vietnam, February 13–19, 1967," February 20, 1967.

24   Saigon #21428, March 27, 1967.

25   Huy and Young, *Understanding Vietnam*, 126.

26   Saigon #21308, March 25, 1967.

27   "Report on Ambassador Diem's Visit to Saigon," State Department Memcon, June 13, 1967.

28   Nguyen Cao Ky, *Buddha's Child*, 241.

29   "Report on Ambassador Diem's Visit to Saigon," June 13, 1967.

30   Saigon #26779, May 26, 1967.

31   Saigon #23462, April 20, 1967, discusses Lansdale's report on his conversation with Thang.

32   "Comments by Nguyen Van Thieu about possibility of his presidential candidacy," CIA IIC, May 22, 1967.

33   Saigon #26790, May 26, 1967.

34   Truyen was a senior civil servant in the Diem government but left in 1960. In 1959, he was elected vice president of the General Association of Vietnamese Buddhists and helped run the Xa Loi Pagoda, which had been a key seat of Buddhist protests against Diem.

35   Bui Diem interview.

36   "Interview with General Nguyen Van Thieu," *Far Eastern Economic Review*, June 8, 1967, 524–525.

37   Nguyen Cao Ky, *Buddha's Child*, 237–239.

38   *Under One Flag*, 821.

39   Saigon #347, July 5, 1967.

40   CIA Weekly, "The Situation in South Vietnam, July 3–9, 1967," July 10, 1967.

41   "Interview of Nguyen Van Ngan," *Thoi Luan* (Tet Edition 2013), 87. This is only one of two known interviews he gave postwar.

42   All details were separately confirmed by two sources who were present: Lieutenant

General Nguyen Bao Tri, then minister of information and a close Ky supporter, and Lieutenant General Hoang Xuan Lam shortly before he died in 2017. Interview of Nguyen Bao Tri by Lan Cao, January 28, 2017. Interview of Hoang Xuan Lam by Ken Bui, son-in-law, date unspecified, Davis, CA. Separately, two of Thieu's closest aides confirmed the same details. Interview with Hoang Duc Nha, November 27, 2017, Falls Church, VA. Interview of Nguyen Xuan Tam, June 24, 2018, Falls Church, VA.

43 "Journal of Cao Van Vien," August 20, 1995. The author wishes to thank Lan Cao for sharing this extraordinarily private journal.

44 Major Nguyen Xuan Tam, Thieu's chief military aide for many years, confirmed this account. He said Thieu had told him that "he and Ky had no choice. They had to accept the Council's decision." Tam confirmed the intervention of Lam and Loc and Khang's defection, that very few people knew the full details of the decision and that the participants had agreed to keep it to themselves. Interview with Tam, June 23, 2018, Falls Church, VA.

45 Saigon #11967, Jun 26, 70.

46 Saigon #1177, July 16, 1967.

47 "Biographical Data on LTG Hoang Xuan Lam," Saigon Embassy Airgram A-78, April 26, 1974.

48 Nguyen Cao Ky, *Twenty Years*, 106.

49 Nguyen Cao Ky, *Buddha's Child*, 176. One of Ky's closest friends, VNAF Major Hoang Song Liem, agreed that Ky's sister was involved in using VNAF planes to smuggle goods from Laos, but he denies that Ky had any involvement. Interview with Hoang Song Liem, April 25, 2018, Falls Church, VA.

50 "Daily Vietnam Situation Report," July 7, 1967.

51 Nguyen Cao Ky, *Buddha's Child*, 249.

52 "Functioning and Aims of Inner Circle of Generals who Exercise Power of Decision in South Vietnam," CIA IIC, August 10, 1967.

53 "Nature and Form of Agreement signed by Generals on 30 June 1967," CIA IIC, May 21, 1968.

54 Stephen Young, unpublished biography of Ellsworth Bunker, based upon his interviews with Bunker in 1980.

55 Westmoreland, *Soldier Reports*, 218.

56 Bui Diem, *Jaws of History*, 197–198.

CHAPTER 12

1 "Thieu Shuns Anti-Civilian Army Coups," *Baltimore Sun*, August 20, 1967, 1.

2 "Vast Military Reforms Pledged by South Vietnam Ambassador," *Los Angeles Times*, August 11, 1967, A5.

3 Pham Van Lieu, *Return Our Land*, vol. II, 421–422.

4 One scholar disagrees and believes the election was far more tainted than is known. Sean Fear, "A Turning Point for South Vietnam?", *New York Times*, September 1, 2017.

5 Saigon #5038, September 5, 1967. Huy mentions that Dzu had "contacts with leftist politicians in the U.S." but does not elaborate. Huy and Young, *Understanding Vietnam*, 127.

6 Tran Van Don, *Our Endless War*, 174.

7 Allan E. Goodman, *Politics in War: The Bases of Political Community in South Vietnam* (Cambridge, MA: Harvard University Press, 1973), 56.

8 Saigon #5157, September 7, 1967.

9 Ibid. Dzu told Chieu that he had intended to pick Huy as his prime minister if he had won the election.

10 Huy and Young, *Understanding Vietnam*, 127–128.
11 Le Phuoc Sang, unpublished memoir provided to the author.
12 Nguyen Cao Ky, *Buddha's Child*, 248.
13 Saigon #5827, September 13, 1967.
14 *FRUS*, 1967, vol. V, #342.
15 Ibid., #338.
16 *The Bunker Papers, vols. 1–3*, ed. Douglas Pike (Berkeley, CA: Asian Foundation, 1990), 168–169.
17 "Talk with Kieu," Lansdale Memo, October 12, 1967.
18 Saigon #5827, September 13, 1967.
19 "Talk with Ky," Lansdale Memo, October 19, 1967.
20 "Address to the Nation," October 31, 1967.
21 Saigon #14235, December 27, 1967.
22 "Revolutionary Development Policy in 1968," Ministry of RD, September 1, 1967.
23 "1967 Pacification Fact Sheet," January 24, 1968.
24 *FRUS*, 1967, vol. V, #401.
25 *FRUS*, January–August 1968, vol. VI, #16.
26 Ibid.
27 Saigon #16712, January 23, 1968.
28 *Bunker Papers*, vol. 1, 286.
29 Nguyen Anh Tuan, *South Vietnam: Trial and Experience* (Athens, OH: Ohio University, 1987), 130.
30 "Angry Anti-U.S. Mood Appears to Intensify Among Some South Vietnamese," *New York Times*, October 10, 1967.
31 "South Vietnam Army Found Increasingly Ineffective," *Washington Post*, September 17, 1967.
32 Huong Ngoc Lung, *The General Offensives of 1968–1969* (Washington, D.C.: Center for Military History, 1981), 18.
33 The article continued to raise strong emotions years later. In separate interviews, several former RVNAF officers, still angry at how they had been depicted, mentioned this article to the author.
34 "Republic of Vietnam Armed Forces Operations," Joint Chiefs of Staff Memo, January 31, 1968.

CHAPTER 13

1 For two excellent overviews of the Politburo's decision, see Merle Pribbenow, "General Vo Nguyen Giap and the Mysterious Evolution of the Plan for the 1968 Tet Offensive," *Journal of Vietnamese Studies* 3, no. 2 (2008): 1–33, and Nguyen Lien Hang, "The War Politburo: North Vietnam's Diplomatic and Political Road to the Tet Offensive," *Journal of Vietnamese Studies* (2006) vol. 1, numbers 1–2, 4–58.
2 *Lich Su Khang Chien Chong My Cuu Nuoc, 1954–1975, Tap V: Tong Tien Cong Va Noni Day Nam 1968* [*History of the Resistance War Against the Americans to Save the Nation, 1954–1975, Volume V: The 1968 General Offensive and Uprising*] (Hanoi: National Political Publishing House, 2001), 31.
3 For the best description of the offensive, see Erik Villard's *Combat Operations: Staying the Course, October 1967 to September 1968* (Washington, D.C.: Center for Military History, 2017).
4 Interview with Cao Van Vien, November 17, 2011, Alexandria, VA.
5 Hoang Ngoc Lung, *Tet Offensive*, 56–57.
6 *History of the Resistance War*, vol. V, 84.
7 Ibid., 10.

8   Draft Working Paper, "The Probable Strength of the VC Main and Local and North Vietnamese Army Forces in South Vietnam," CIA, January 31, 1968.

9   *Victory in Vietnam*, 211.

10 *History of the Resistance War*, vol. V, 48.

11 *FRUS*, Jan–Aug 1968, vol. VI, #33

12 *Bien nien su kien: Bo tong tham muu trong khang chien chong My, cuu nuoc, tap V (1968)* [*Chronology of Events: General Staff During the Resistance War Against the Americans to Save the Nation, Volume V (1968)*] (Hanoi: People's Army Publishing House, 2005), 274. This report also claims the PAVN killed "205,307 enemy personnel, including 77,760 U.S. troops," which is wildly inaccurate.

13 "Combat Operations Department Report No. 124/Thi," File 1103, February 14, 1969, quoted in *Lich su Nam Bo Khang chin, tap II, 1954–1975* [*History of the Resistance War in Cochin China, Volume II: 1954–1975*] (Hanoi: National Political Publishing House, 2010), 673.

14 Andrew Wiest, *Vietnam's Forgotten Army: Heroism and Betrayal in the ARVN* (New York: New York University Press, 2008), 102–103.

15 Lien Thanh, *Bien Dong Mien Trung: Nhung bi mat lich su ve can giai do n 1966 – 1968 – 1972* [*Upheavals in Central Vietnam: Historical Secrets about 1966, 1968, and 1972*] (Westminster, CA: Self-Published, 2012), 125–127.

16 Erik Villard believes that this was a case of mistaken identity and that the man was simply a courier who had been caught at the wrong place. He believes that Bay Lop was killed the previous day while attacking the Navy Yard. The *History of the Resistance War*, vol. V, does confirm that Lop led the attack on the Navy Yard. While it does not specifically state that Lop was killed there, it implies that he was, noting that all the attackers save two were killed in the assault.

17 Saigon #18269, February 6, 1968.

18 Villard, *Staying the Course*, 442.

19 Martin Loicano, "The Role of Weapons in the Second Indochina War: Republic of Vietnam Perspectives and Perceptions," *Journal of Vietnamese Studies* 8, no. 2 (2013): 37–80.

20 "Assessment of Refugee Program, 1968," CORDS Refugee Division, February 1969.

21 "Summary Report on Enemy Situation During the VC Offensive in the Capital Special Zone," J-2, JGS, File No. 00377/TTM/2/KTB, February 19, 1968.

22 Nguyen Cao Ky, *Buddha's Child*, 271.

23 Phan Quang Dan, "Assessing Viet Cong Attacks," March 9, 1968, reprinted in Saigon Embassy Airgram A-473.

24 Saigon #28958, June 3, 1968.

25 *Huong Tien Cong Saigon-Gia Dinh (Nam 1968)* [*The Offensive in the Saigon-Gia Dinh Sector (1968)*] (Hanoi: Military History Institute of Vietnam, 1988), 85–86.

26 *Bunker Papers*, vol. 2, 372.

27 "Text of Thieu statement on Martial Law," *New York Times*, February 1, 1968, 14.

28 Interview by Nguyen Duc Tu with Thieu's helicopter pilot, who wished to remain anonymous, Huntington Beach, CA, February 4, 2017. The pilot said a grateful Mrs. Thieu gave the crew a cash reward of 200,000 piasters.

29 "Ky tells people of emergency assistance plan," *Foreign Broadcasting Information Service Asia and Pacific*, February 6, 1968. Hereafter *FBIS*.

30 *FRUS*, Jan–Aug 1968, vol. VI, #45.

31 "Thieu, in Tears, Orders Stepped-Up Mobilization," *New York Times*, February 9, 1968, 16.

32 "President Thieu's Concerns over Attempts to Undermine his Position ...," CIA IIC, March 6, 1968.

33 Saigon #21218, March 5, 1968.

34   "Vice President Ky's Belief that Military Dissatisfaction with President Thieu's ...,"
     CIA IIC, March 6, 1968.
35   "President Thieu's Concerns over Attempts to Undermine his Position ...," CIA
     IIC, March 6, 1968.
36   Saigon #17282, January 30, 1968.
37   Saigon #19738, February 18, 1968.
38   "President Thieu's Concern...over Possible American Use of the National Salvation
     Front to Effect a Coalition Government with the Viet Cong," CIA IIC, March 18,
     1968.
39   Tran Van Don, *Vietnam Witness*, 385.
40   Saigon #22386, March 18, 1968.
41   Wellington #1721, April 2, 1968, citing Foreign Minister Do's remarks about Bui
     Diem's meeting.
42   Bui Diem, *Jaws of History*, 226–227.
43   "Korean Officials Caution Humphrey on Dangers of Premature Peace," *Washington
     Post*, January 2, 1966.
44   Nguyen Xuan Phong, *Vanquished Hope*, 195.
45   "Korean President Differs with Johnson on Vietcong Talks," *Washington Post*,
     December 25, 1967, C2.
46   "S. Vietnam Fears U.S. Peace Bid," *Los Angeles Times*, January 21, 1968, 22.
47   "Thieu Firm on Negotiations," *Washington Star*, January 26, 1968.
48   "Thieu Criticizes Attempts by U.S. to Open Talks," *Globe and Mail*, January 16,
     1968, 8.
49   *Bunker Papers*, vol. 2, 305–306.
50   *FRUS*, Jan-Aug 1968, vol. VI, #145.
51   "Foreign Impact of President Johnson's March 31 Speech," CIA Memo, April 11,
     1968, 9.
52   "Koreans Fear Vietnam Settlement Will Bring U.S. Pullout from Asia," *Washington
     Post*, April 5, 1968, A25.
53   "Vietnamese Government Reaction to Impending Peace ...," CIA IIC, April 5, 1968.
54   "Attitudes of Thieu and Ky Toward Peace Negotiations," CIA IIC, April 12, 1968.
55   Thieu's Comments on President Johnson's Speech," CIA IIC, April 4, 1968.
56   Saigon #23912, April 4, 1968.

CHAPTER 14

1   Lansdale, "Nationalist Politics in Vietnam."
2   Saigon #28958, June 3, 1968.
3   *History of the Resistance War*, vol. V, 159–160.
4   Ibid., 177.
5   Ibid., 207–208.
6   "Talk with Thieu," Lansdale memo, May 9, 1968.
7   Vo Long Trieu, *A Memoir*, vol. 2, 86–88.
8   Saigon #33741, July 27, 1968.
9   "President Thieu's Meeting with Ky and the Senior Generals ...," CIA IIC, May 16,
     1968.
10   Ibid.
11   "Senior Generals' Decision not to Oppose Tran Van Huong as Prime Minister ...,"
     CIA IIC, May 21, 1968.
12   Saigon #33741, July 27, 1968.
13   Saigon #34952, August 9, 1968.
14   Xuan Ba, "The Story of a Participant in the Battle of Dien Bien Phu Who Was the
     Son of a President of the Saigon Government, Tran Van Huong," *Tien Phong*, May
     7, 2005.

15 Lan Cao interview with Khiem, September 29, 2018.

16 "Remarks of VP Ky ...," CIA IIC, July 24, 1968.

17 Saigon #28633, May 30, 1968.

18 Saigon #30631, June 15, 1968.

19 Goodman, *Politics in War*, 76.

20 "Talk with Don," Lansdale Memo, May 29, 1968.

21 Saigon #29475, June 8, 1968.

22 "Thieu asks Unity Among Parties," *New York Times*, June 30, 1968, 3.

23 Saigon #32844, July 17, 1968.

24 Saigon #38135, September 11, 1968.

25 "Using Backbiting Words to Cause an Alliance to Collapse," *Events and Witnesses* [*Su Kien & Nhan Chung*] *People's Army* [*Quan Doi Nhan Dan*], September 16, 2011.

26 Saigon #30706, June 23, 1968.

27 Ly Qui Chung, *Hoi Ky Khong Ten* [*Untitled Memoir*] (Saigon: Youth Publishing House, 2004), 140–141.

28 Saigon #37824, September 14, 1968.

29 Richard Hunt, *Pacification: The American Struggle for Vietnam's Hearts and Minds* (San Francisco, CA: Westview Press, 1995), 91.

30 "G.I. Pullout Feasible in '69, Says Thieu," *Washington Post*, July 29, 1968.

31 Nguyen Phu Duc, with Arthur Dommen, *The Viet-Nam Peace Negotiations: Saigon's Side of the Story* (Christiansburg, VA: Dalley Book Service, 2005), 39.

32 Saigon #27140, May 13, 1968.

33 *Bunker Papers*, vol. 2, 470–471.

34 Saigon #28958, June 3, 1968.

35 William Colby, *Lost Victory: A Firsthand Account of America's Sixteen Year Involvement in Vietnam* (Chicago: Contemporary Books, 1989), 242–243.

36 Ngo Quang Truong, *Territorial Forces* (Washington, D.C.: Center for Military History, 1983), 68–71.

37 Saigon #35068, August 11, 1968.

38 "Summary of the National People's Self-Defense Forces Meeting Held 2 April 1969 at the Office of the Prime Minister," Phu Thu Tuong 16633, Vietnam Cong Hoa [Office of the Prime Minister, File 16633, Republic of Vietnam, PTT], National Archives Center II [Trung Tam Luu Tru Quoc Gia II, TTLTQG II].

39 Colby, *Lost Victory*, 254.

40 Hunt, *Pacification*, 181.

41 *Lich Su Khang Chien Chong My Cuu Nuoc, 1954–1975, Tap VI: Thang My Tren Chien Truong Ba Nuoc Dong Duong* [*History of the Resistance War Against the Americans to Save the Nation, 1954–1975, Volume VI: Defeating the Americans in the Three Nations of Indochina*] (Hanoi: National Political Publishing House, 2003), 98–99.

42 "Saigon's Antiwar Voices," *The Washington Star*, April 21, 1968, 3.

43 Saigon #33651, July 26, 1968.

44 State #212078, July 31, 1968.

45 Saigon #36224, August 25, 1968.

46 "The Brighter Side of the Saigon Press," Saigon Embassy Airgram A-902, September 23, 1968.

47 "Law No 10/68, 5/11/1968, issued by the President of the Saigon Government to amend Edict No. 01-UBLDQG of 24 June 1965," PTT 30973, TTLTQG II, in *Cuoc Tong tien Cong cua Quan Giai Phong Mien Nam Viet Nam Nam 1968 (Qua tai lieu luu tru cua chinh quyen Sai Gon)* [*The 1968 General Offensive of the Liberation Army of South Vietnam (Through Documents found in the Archives of the Saigon Government)*] (Hanoi: National Political Publishing House, 2015), 346–347.

48 Saigon #11798, November 24, 1968.

49 "Minh Returns to Saigon From Exile," *Washington Post*, October 6, 1968, A17.

CHAPTER 15

1   *Bunker Papers*, vol. 2, 626.

2   "Secret Politburo Cable," 3 April 1968, *Van Kien Dang, Toan Tap, 29, 1968* [*Collected Party Documents, Volume 29, 1968*] (Hanoi: National Political Publishing House, 2004), 203.

3   "Report Presented to the 15th Plenum of the Party Central Committee, 29 August 1968," *Collected Party Documents, 1968*, 362–364.

4   "Secret Politburo Cable No. 320," 10 October 1968, *Party Documents, 1968*, 470.

5   Saigon #40220, October 14, 1968.

6   Duc was born in North Vietnam on November 13, 1924. He received his Bac II from the Lycee Yersin in Dalat in 1945. He then attended the University of Hanoi, graduating with a law degree. In 1953 he left Vietnam to attend Harvard, where he earned his doctorate. He then spent five years as the first secretary at the GVN embassy in Washington. In 1964 he was appointed chief of the Vietnamese Observer Mission at the U.N., departing a year later. After various assignments, he returned to Saigon in September 1966 and was assigned to Thieu's office. On January 15, 1968, he was appointed Thieu's special assistant for foreign affairs.

7   Nguyen Phu Duc, *Viet-Nam Negotiations*, 96.

8   Cable No. 2164/PTT/VP/M (Phu Tong Thong = Office of the President, Van Phong = Office, Mat = Secret), from Thieu to Bui Diem, October 17, 1968. Translated by Phan Luong Quang. Bui Diem papers.

9   Saigon #41345, October 20, 1968.

10 Nguyen Phu Duc, *Viet-Nam Negotiations*, 107.

11 "Thieu Addresses Nation on Rumored Bombing Halt," *FBIS South Vietnam*, October 21, 1968, L1.

12 Nguyen Phu Duc, *Viet-Nam Negotiations*, 39.

13 Ibid., 116.

14 "HHH Bars Thieu Veto on Bombs," *Washington Post*, October 21, 1968, A8.

15 Cable 2269/M, from Thieu to Diem and Lam, October 26, 1968, Bui Diem papers.

16 Luu Van Loi and Nguyen Anh Vu, *Le Duc Tho-Kissinger Negotiations in Paris* (Hanoi: The Gioi Publishers, 1996), 47.

17 Johnson misinterpreted Hanoi's sudden coolness. He believed that speeches by Humphrey and McGeorge Bundy had directly influenced the Politburo. On September 30, Humphrey announced that he would halt the bombing if Hanoi refrained from attacking across the DMZ, a softening of Johnson's three conditions. When Hanoi immediately rejected any reciprocity, on October 13, McGeorge Bundy, Johnson's former special assistant and brother to State Department official Bill Bundy, went further. He advocated both U.S. troop withdrawals and acceptance of Hanoi's unconditional bombing halt to get peace talks moving. Johnson believed that Bundy's speech and Le Duc Tho's sudden departure were not a coincidence.

18 *FRUS*, Sept. 1968–Jan. 1969, vol. VIII, #143

19 Ibid., 152.

20 Ibid., 102.

21 Saigon #41688, November 1, 1968.

22 "Message of President Nguyen Van Thieu to the Joint Assembly," November 2, 1968.

23 One key proponent of the Nixon conspiracy camp is Ken Hughes, *Chasing Shadows: The Nixon Tapes, the Anna Chennault Affair, and the Origins of Watergate* (Charlottesville, VA: University of Virginia Press, 2014). For a more balanced view, see Luke Nichter, "A Vietnam Myth that Refuses to Die," *Wall Street Journal*, April 19, 2018.

24   Richard Kallina, "Was the 1960 Presidential Election Stolen? The Case of Illinois," *Presidential Studies Quarterly* 15, no. 1, Inaugurating the President (Winter, 1985), 113–118.

25   "Thieu Rejects Report that Candidate Nixon Urged him to Announce that he would Boycott the 1968 Talks," *Radio Bolsa*, August 17, 200.

26   Bui Diem interview.

27   Nguyen Phu Duc, *Viet-Nam Negotiations*, 165.

28   "Request to Chiang Kai-Shek: Anna Chennault has arrived from the U.S. a few days ago and will go to Vietnam for a diplomatic visit - would you appoint a time to meet here?" July 19, 1965, Chiang Ching-kuo collection, file number 005-010306-00010-006, Academia Historica, Taipei, Taiwan. The author thanks Alvin Bui for providing the document and translation.

29   Nguyen Cao Ky, *Twenty Years*, 167.

30   "Nixon Indicates He Seeks Step-Up in War Effort," *New York Times*, April 18, 1967, 2.

31   Memcon of Johnson and Park, April 17, 1968.

32   "Thieu's Views on NLF Participation in Vietnamese Government," October 23, 1968.

33   Nguyen Phu Duc, *Viet-Nam Negotiations*, 160.

34   *FRUS*, vol. VIII, #171.

35   "U.S. Is Reported to Have Bugged Korean President," *New York Times*, June 19, 1977, 1.

36   "The Gimo Fears Chicom Action Toward Offshore Islands and Wants US Reassurances," State INR Report, July 11, 1968.

37   Lan Cao interview of Khiem, October 26, 2017, Irvine, CA.

38   "GRC's Leading Political Warfare Officer Expands View of U.S.," State Airgram A-740, July 3, 1968.

39   "President Thieu's Comments on Peace Talks ...," CIA IIC, November 18, 1968.

40   Report No. 810-PTUTB/R/M (Secret - Most Urgent), 4 May 1968, from the Central Intelligence Organization on "The Agreement Between North Vietnam and the United States on Paris as the Site for their Upcoming Meetings," in *The 1968 General Offensive... in the Archives of the Saigon Government*, 378–383.

41   *FRUS*, Sept 1968–Jan 1969, vol. VIII, #148.

42   Rostow to Johnson, November 2, 1968.

43   Bui Diem interview.

44   Cable #0301/VP/M, November 3, 1968.

45   The NSA intercept can be seen in CAP 82685, Rostow to Johnson. The NSA added two other sentences to his draft. When queried over the differences, Bui Diem did not recall but states that the "situation was changing very rapidly," meaning he may have added those portions before it was sent.

46   *FRUS*, vol. VIII, #192.

47   Ibid., #191.

48   Catherine Mary Forslund, "Woman of Two Worlds: Anna Chennault and Informal Diplomacy in US-Asian Relations, 1950–1990." Dissertation. Washington University, 1997, 194.

49   Nguyen Tien Hung, *Palace File*, 23.

50   Hoang Duc Nha interview, November 27, 2017, Falls Church, VA. Nha mentions this in his prepared remarks given at a conference in Berkeley. Vu and Fear, Republic of Vietnam, 60.

51   Lan Cao interview of Khiem, October 26, 2017.

52   Interview with Doan Huu Dinh, September 28, 2017, Falls Church, MD.

53   Bui Diem interview.

54   "President Thieu's Comments on Peace Talks ...," CIA IIC, November 18, 1968.

55   Anna Chennault, *The Education of Anna* (New York: Times Books, 1980), 186.

56   Lam Le Trinh, "Nguyen Phu Duc, Nguyen Xuan Phong, and Nguyen Tien Hung Write About the Death of the Second Republic," *Thuy Hoa Trang*, August 9, 2005.

57   Hoang Duc Nha interview, June 12, 2012, Rochester, NY.

58   Nguyen Phu Duc, *Viet-Nam Negotiations*, 92.

59   "Conversation with Bui Diem," June 13, 1975, Box 63, Bui Diem Folder, Papers of Neil Sheehan, Library of Congress, Washington, D.C.

60   Thieu and Khiem also maintained contact with her postwar. According to close associates of Thieu, while living in the U.S., he often joined her for dinner when he visited the Washington, D.C.–Virginia area. Khiem had also asked for her help in mid-July 1975 to convince the U.S. government to allow him to quietly emigrate from Taiwan to America.

61   Cable 1506/M from Diem to Nha (in English), April 15, 1971.

62   Harish Mehta, "The Secret Business Diplomacy of Anna Chennault as Nixon's Envoy in South Vietnam, 1967–1974," *The International History Review*, published online on April 22, 2019 at https://doi.org/10.1080/07075332.2019.1592209.

63   "Meeting between the President and Ambassador Kennedy in the President's Oval Office," Memo for the President's File by Alexander Haig, February 25, 1971. There are several instances of Lee meeting Nixon. For example, see Nixon Taped Conversation 505-14, May 16, 1971,

64   White House Tapes, Conversation 140-55, August 21, 1972, 10:26 a.m –10:41 a.m. The author thanks Dr. Luke Nichter for transcribing the tape.

65   The author thanks Dr. Luke Nichter for his insights and our lengthy discussions regarding Chennault, Nixon, and the 1968 election.

CHAPTER 16

1   "Enthusiastic Reaction of Assembly Members to Thieu Speech," CIA IIC, November 4, 1968.

2   CAP #82721, Rostow to Johnson, November 6, 1968.

3   Taipei #0014, January 4, 1969.

4   Taipei #0256, January 27, 1968.

5   CAP 82720, from Rostow to Johnson, November 6, 1968.

6   "Remarks of VP Ky on the Paris Talks Impasse ...," CIA IIC, November 11, 1968.

7   State #269935, November 9, 1968.

8   Nguyen Phu Duc, *Viet-Nam Negotiations*, 161. Italics in the original.

9   "Politburo Directive," *Collected Party Documents, 1968*, 509–521.

10   Lam was born in Vinh Long Province in the Delta in 1918. He received his law degree from the University of Hanoi, then went to work in the Foreign Ministry in 1951. He served as foreign minister in the Minh government, then served as GVN ambassador to the Philippines.

11   Nguyen Xuan Phong, *Vanquished Reality*, 203–205.

12   *FRUS*, Sept 1968–Jan 1969, vol. VIII, #277.

13   *Under One Flag*, 159.

14   "Thieu Stresses Regime Safety," *New York Times*, February 9, 1969, 3.

15   Saigon #2454, February 7, 1969.

16   *History of the Resistance War*, vol. V, 208.

17   "Politburo Directive," *Collected Party Documents, 1968*, 509–521.

18   Tran Trong Trung, *Tong Tu Lenh Vo Nguyen Giap Trong Nhung Nam De Quoc My Leo Thang Chien Tranh (1965–1969)* [*Supreme Commander Vo Nguyen Giap During the Years of American Imperialist Escalation of the War (1965–1969)*] (Hanoi: National Political-Truth Publishing House, 2015), 470.

19   Ibid., 471.
20   Saigon Embassy Airgram A-190, April 1, 1969.
21   Saigon #7830, April 23, 1969.
22   Saigon #6615, April 7, 1969.
23   "Law No 10/68," *PAB* #48, 2.
24   Cable No. 2708/TT/M, Thieu to Bui Diem, January 1, 1969.
25   "A Few Assessments and Recommendations to the President and the Government of the Republic of Vietnam," Cable No. 0400-W/VP/M, Bui Diem to Ky, January 13, 1969.
26   Nguyen Phu Duc, *Viet-Nam Negotiations*, 174.
27   Saigon #845, January 15, 1969.
28   Memcon, "Remarks by President Nguyen Van Thieu on the Paris Peace Talks …," January 18, 1969.
29   Nguyen Phu Duc, *Viet-Nam Negotiations*, 198.
30   Ibid., 176.
31   Memcon, "President Thieu's Overall View of the Situation we Face," March 21, 1969.
32   Nguyen Cao Ky, *Twenty Years*, 172–173.
33   *FRUS*, Jan 69–Jul 70, vol. VI, #28.
34   Saigon #6858, April 3, 1969.
35   Saigon #7461, April 18, 1969.
36   *FRUS*, Jan 69–Jul 70, vol. VI, #58.
37   Bong was often accused of being a secret Dai Viet, but he was not.
38   No cable number, Bui Diem to Thieu, May 7, 1969.
39   "Thieu Vows 'Freedom Fight,'" *Boston Globe*, May 28, 1969, 5.
40   "S. Korea Will Stay Aloof from U.S.-Saigon Talks," *Washington Post*, June 1, 1969, 23.
41   Taipei #1997, June 4, 1969.
42   Nguyen Phu Duc, *Viet-Nam Negotiations*, 213.
43   *FRUS*, Jan 69–Jul 70, vol. VI, #248.
44   Truong Nhu Tang, *Viet Cong Memoir*, 146–147.
45   *Vietnam Press*, June 12, 1969.
46   "Thieu Sees His Country Shifting to 'Political Phase," *Washington Post*, June 19, 1969, A18.
47   *Under One Flag*, 821.
48   Backchannel Kissinger to Bunker, #1071, June 30, 1969.
49   Backchannel Bunker to Kissinger, #489, July 9, 1969.

CHAPTER 17

1   "Reaction to Thieu's Proposal for Elections," *FBIS Asia and Pacific*, July 14, 1969, L1.
2   Backchannel Bunker to Kissinger, #565, July 14, 1969.
3   "Pres. Thieu on Red Rejection of RVN Peace Proposal," *Vietnam Bulletin* III, no. 43 (July 14–20, 1969): 5.
4   *Bunker Papers*, vol. III, 674.
5   Nguyen Phu Duc, *Viet-Nam Negotiations*, 228.
6   *FRUS*, Jan. 69–Jul. 70, vol. VI, #103.
7   *Bunker Papers*, vol. III, 728.
8   Interview with Mai Van Triet, June 15, 2019, Paris, France. Phan Cong Tam, a senior CIO, earlier revealed this exposure of the Kissinger meeting. Phan Cong Tam, "Testimony of a Senior Officer, South Vietnamese Central Intelligence Organization," in *Voices from the Second Republic of South Vietnam (1967–1975)*,

ed. K. W. Taylor (Ithaca, NY: Cornell Southeast Asia Program Publications, 2014), 22.

9   Email from Huong Duc Nha, January 21, 2019.

10 *FRUS*, Jan 69–Jul 70, vol. VI, #103.

11 Nguyen Mau, *N.D.B.: Nganh Dac Biet, Tap I* [S.B.: The Special Branch, Volume I] (San Jose, CA: Self-published, 2007), 121. Mau was head of the Special Branch from 1968 to early 1972.

12 Phan Nhan, "Ong Co Van: Huynh Van Trong La Ai? [Mr. Advisor: Who was Huynh Van Trong?]," *KBC Hai Ngoai*, issue 24, December 2003, 37.

13 For more information on the Trong case, see Ralph McGehee, *Deadly Deceits: My 25 Years in the CIA* (New York: Sheridan Square, 1983), 151–155.

14 Postwar, Nha would be lauded as one of the four "legends" of Communist wartime spies. The other three are Pham Xuan An, Dang Duc Tran, and Pham Ngoc Thao. Tran penetrated the CIO at a high-level. Fearing that the SB was closing in on him, Tran fled Saigon to COSVN headquarters in 1974.

15 "Vietnamese Prison Study Shocks Study Team," *Washington Post*, June 20, 1969, A26.

16 Bui Diem, *Jaws of History*, 268–269, 271.

17 "74 percent in Poll Oppose Immediate Pullout," *New York Times*, November 27, 1969, 20.

18 "On Launching a Broad Political Struggle Movement in South Vietnam," in *Van Kien Dang, Toan Tap 30, 1969* [*Collected Party Documents, Volume 30, 1969*] (Hanoi: National Political Publishing House), 293.

19 Saigon #24034, December 3, 1969.

20 "Senate holds Thieu responsible for massacre," *Times of India*, January 6, 1970, 12.

21 Tran Van Don, *Vietnam Witness*, 392.

22 Tran Van Don, *Endless War*, 180–181.

23 "Ex-Leader Ends Saigon Seclusion," *New York Times*, November 3, 1969, 2.

24 "Big Minh Bars Himself as 'Third Force' Leader," *Los Angeles Times*, November 14, 1969, 20.

25 "The Vietnamese Press: Freedom within Narrower Limits," Saigon Embassy Airgram A-126, July 5, 1973.

26 *Ho Chi Minh City People's Public Security,* 104–105.

27 "Personal Relations among Senior RVNAF Officers," Enclosure #2, 8.

28 "Pacification Attitude Analysis System," Preliminary Survey #1, October 1969. Hereafter *PAAS*. The surveys were conducted by three-person Vietnamese teams trained in interview techniques. They interviewed roughly four thousand people across the country on a monthly basis. The survey asked about a wide variety of topics but usually covered the economy, security, and government efficiency.

29 "New Viet Party Grows Fastest," *Newsday*, October 7, 1969, 6.

30 Saigon #20885, October 17, 1969.

31 Saigon #2449, February 18, 1970.

32 Saigon #22933, November 16, 1969.

33 "Memorandum for President Nixon from President Thieu," August 20, 1969.

34 "President Thieu Addresses National Assembly," *FBIS Asia and Pacific*, October 6, 1969, L6.

35 "AID and PL 480 Programs for Vietnam – FY 1970," Memo from State to Nixon, October 20, 1969.

36 Henry Kissinger, *White House Years* (New York: Little, Brown and Company, 1979), 508.

37 *Tong Ket Cuoc Khang Chien Chong My Cuu Nuoc: Thang Loi va Bai Hoc* [*Review of the Resistance War Against the Americans to Save the Nation: Victory and Lessons*]

(Hanoi: The Guidance Committee for Reviewing the War, Directly Subordinate to the Politburo, 1995), footnote 35, 77.

CHAPTER 18

1   G. E. MaKinen, "Economic Stabilization in Wartime: A Comparative Case Study of Korea and Vietnam," *Journal of Political Economy*, vol. 79, no. 6 (Nov–Dec 1971), 1217.

2   Pham Kim Ngoc, "Economic Independence for Vietnam," *Vietnam Council for Foreign Affairs*, September 12, 1969.

3   Email from Pham Kim Ngoc, April 30, 2013.

4   *Bunker Papers*, vol. III, 733.

5   Nguyen Van Ngan interview, *Thoi Luan*, 87.

6   Saigon #2959, February 27, 1970.

7   Nguyen Ba Can, *Dat Nuoc Toi: Hoi Ky Chanh Tri* [*My Country: A Political Memoir*] (Derwood, MD: Hoa Hao Press, 2003), 190-191.

8   "Thieu Warns S. Vietnamese On Advocates of Third Force," *Atlanta Constitution*, January 9, 1970, 2A.

9   Saigon #1812, February 6, 1970.

10 Nguyen Ba Can, *My Country*, 163.

11 "Thieu and Chau," *New York Times*, March 6, 1970, 2.

12 Saigon #18008, November 11, 1970.

13 Saigon #2915, February 26, 1970.

14 Pierre Brocheux, *The Mekong Delta: Ecology, Economy, and Revolution, 1860–1960* (Madison: University of Wisconsin Press, 2009).

15 The following account comes from several years of interviews with Cao Van Than in Montreal, Canada. The author first spoke to him on August 8, 2012. For his only published account, see Tuong Vu and Sean Fear, eds., *The Republic of Vietnam, 1955–1975: Vietnamese Perspectives on Nation-Building* (Ithaca, NY: Cornell University Press, 2019).

16 Nguyen Dang Hai, *Get Up One More Time: A Personal Odyssey* (Ellicott City, MD: H&T Publishers, 2007), 163.

17 "Ten Year Update of Village Studies," Saigon Embassy Airgram A-90, July 14, 1971.

18 Saigon #8151, April 28, 1969, citing a monitored FBIS report.

19 Saigon #9884, June 23, 1970.

20 Memcon, "Hoang Duc Nha," Saigon embassy, September 1, 1970.

21 The famous quote by the Roman statesman Marcus Tullius *Cicero*.

22 *FRUS*, Jan 69–Jul 70, vol. VI, #187.

23 "The Economic Situation in South Vietnam," CIA Report, May 18, 1970.

24 "Highlights of USIA-Commissioned Public Opinion Survey," May 25, 1970.

25 Pham Kim Ngoc, *Economic Czar or Fire Chief*, unpublished memoir provided to author.

26 Email from Nguyen Duc Cuong, February 26, 2019.

27 "The Question of Stabilizing and Developing the Economy During the Vietnamization Phase of the War," Ngoc Memo to Thieu, April 28, 1970. Translated in Saigon Embassy Airgram A-143, May 4, 1970.

28 Saigon #9571, June 18, 1970.

29 Saigon #8805, June 5, 1970.

30 State #74245, May 14, 1970.

31 "Saigon Sees Need For More U.S. Aid," *New York Times*, June 29, 1970.

32 "An Economic Strategy for Vietnam," Laird Memo to Nixon, July 18, 1970.

33 "Economic Woes Threaten Vietnamization, *Baltimore Sun*, September 28, 1970, A5.

34   Email from Pham Kim Ngoc, April 30, 2013.
35   "A Saigon Minister," *Singapore Herald*, October 17, 1970.
36   Nguyen Anh Tuan, *Trial and Experience*, 167.

CHAPTER 19

1   Allan Goodman, "South Vietnam and the Politics of Self-Support," *Asian Survey* (11), 1, Jan 1971, 1.
2   Nixon speech of April 20, 1970.
3   "A Fighting General: Do Cao Tri," *New York Times*, June 4, 1970, 12.
4   Khoi was born on January 24, 1930, in Kien Hoa Province in the Delta. He served in French armor units in North Vietnam and then in a variety of South Vietnamese armor units in every military region.
5   "Cambodian-South Vietnamese Frictions," CIA Memo, 4–5.
6   Saigon #7986, May 23, 1970.
7   Pham Van Dong, "War Veterans, Invalids, Widows and Orphans in Vietnam," speech to the Saigon Lion's Club, December 8, 1969.
8   Hoang Tuan, "Economic Deprivation, Diminished Manhood, and Anti-Americanism: The Protest Movement of Disabled ARVN Veterans, 1970–1971," paper presented at Texas Tech Vietnam Conference, March 2006.
9   *Vietnam Bulletin*, April 12–18, 1970, 5.
10   *Under One Flag*, 159.
11   Van Nguyen Marshall, "Student Activism in Time of War: Youth in the Republic of Vietnam, 1960–1970s," *Journal of Vietnamese Studies*, vol. 10 (2), 60.
12   Saigon #5003, April 3, 1970.
13   Saigon #5041, April 5, 1970,
14   "Saigon Press, Politicians, Launch Attacks on Thieu," *Washington Post*, April 12, 1970, 19.
15   Don Bordenkircher, *Tiger Cages: An Untold Story* (Cameron, WV: Abby Publishing, 1998), 52.
16   "Viet student tells of 11 months in tiger cage and torture," *Christian Science Monitor*, July 13, 1970, 2.
17   "How we found the cage men," *Guardian*, July 18, 1970, 11.
18   "Meeting One of The Five People Who Denounced the Tiger Cages to the World," *Thanh Tra*, March 1, 2010.
19   "House Panel Urges U.S. to Investigate 'Tiger Cage' Cells," *New York Times*, July 14, 1970, 4.
20   Email from James Nach, February 25, 2012.
21   Saigon #19722, December 16, 1970.
22   Saigon #20218, December 26, 1970.
23   Saigon #10664, July 5, 1970.
24   "Thieu Sees Dim Prospects for Negotiated Peace in Vietnam," *Los Angeles Times*, August 1, 1970, 1.
25   "Plan for Carrying Out the Offensive Approved by the Politburo," in *Dai Su Ky Chuyen De: Dau Tranh Ngoai Giao va Van Dong Quoc Te Trong Khang Chien Chong My Cuu Nuoc, 1954–1975, Tap 4 [Major Events: The Diplomatic Struggle and International Activities During the Resistance War Against the Americans to Save the Nation 1954–1975, Volume 4]* (Hanoi: Ministry of Foreign Affairs, 1987), 264. The author thanks Dr. Nguyen Lien-Hang for sharing the book.
26   *COSVN Chronicle*, 819.
27   *Diplomatic Struggle*, 265–266.
28   Ibid.
29   Thieu speech of October 31 to the National Assembly.

30   "Big Minh raps Thieu," *Newsday*, November 2, 1970, 2.

31   "Minh Hints at Race for the Presidency," *Washington Post*, November 2, 1970, A20.

32   Ngan, the youngest of Thieu's advisors, refused to speak to any U.S. official during the war. Hence despite the enormous power he wielded, he is virtually unknown. Reportedly, he was born in Hue in 1935 and served with the Viet Minh in Quang Ngai. Nhan meet Thieu in 1965 and worked for him as a campaign manager during the 1967 election.

33   Ha Mai Viet, *Steel and Blood: South Vietnamese Armor and the War for Southeast Asia* (Annapolis, MD: Naval Institute Press, 2008), 60–67.

34   Phong was uncertain of the precise date.

35   Interview with Nguyen Xuan Phong, November 30, 2006, and email from Phong, November 22, 2008.

CHAPTER 20

1   "The Intelligence Agent Who Obtained the Plan for the Route 9–Southern Laos Operation," *Kien Thuc*, November 13, 2009.

2   For detailed descriptions of Lam Son 719, see Robert Sander, *Invasion of Laos: Lam Son 719* (Norman: University of Oklahoma Press, 2014), and James Willbanks, *A Raid Too Far: Operation Lam Son 719 and Vietnamization in Laos* (College Station: Texas A&M Press, 2014).

3   Saigon #2422, February 19, 1971.

4   *Chien Dich Phan Cong Duong So 9 – Nam Lao Nam 1971* [*The Route 9-Southern Laos Counteroffensive Campaign, 1971*] (Hanoi: Military History Institute of Vietnam, 1987), 21.

5   *Vietnam: The Ten-Thousand Day War*, Michael Mcclear, producer, Episode 10, "The Village War," Nguyen Van Thieu at 41:35, 1980.

6   *Cong Tac Chien Dich Duong 9 Nam Lao (Tu 28/2 Den 23/3/1971)* [*Route 9–Southern Laos Campaign Rear Services Operations (28 February–23 March 1971)*] (Hanoi: General Rear Services Department, 1987), 31, 35.

7   "608 U.S. Copters Damaged in Laos, S. Viet General Reports," *Los Angeles Times*, April 5, 1971, 1.

8   Nguyen Duy Hinh, *Lam Son 719* (Washington, D.C.: Center for Military History, 1979), 127. For MACV's estimates of enemy casualties, see *FRUS*, Vietnam, vol. VII, July 1970–January 1972, #182.

9   "Lam Son 719 in South Vietnamese Perspective," State Department Research Study, July 7, 1971.

10   Ibid., 149–150.

11   "2 Catholic Priests in Saigon get 9-Month Jail Terms," *New York Times*, February 22, 1971, 11.

12   "Thieu Links Peace Candidates with Communists," *New York Times*, January 27, 1971, 14.

13   "Ky calls for political settlement, viewed as bid to build candidacy," *Globe and Mail*, April 20, 1971, 10.

14   "Information received from the Soviet Ambassador to the DRV," report to the Bulgarian Ambassador to the DRV, May 11, 1971. Translated by Svetlana Shevchenko.

15   Oleg Sarin and Lev Dvoretsky, *Alien Wars: The Soviet Union's Aggression Against the World* (Novato: Presidio Press, 1996), 111.

16   Qiang Zhai, *China and the Vietnam Wars, 1950–1975* (Chapel Hill, NC: University of North Carolina Press, 2000), 195–196. Lorenz Lüthi, "Beyond Betrayal: Beijing, Moscow, and the Paris Negotiations," *Journal of Cold War Studies* 11, no. 1 (Winter 2009): 57–107.

17 *Victory in Vietnam*, 283.

18 *PAAS*, April 1971.

19 "Conversation among Nixon, Bunker, and Kissinger," *FRUS*, vol. VII, #220.

20 *Bunker Papers*, vol. III, 823.

21 Email from Pham Kim Ngoc, September 1, 2018, and November 10, 2018.

22 Nguyen Anh Tuan, *Trial and Experience*, 167.

23 One author believes the GVN did model itself after its Asian allies. Simon Toner, "Imagining Taiwan: The Nixon Administration, the Developmental States, and South Vietnam's Search for Economic Viability, 1969–1975," *Diplomatic History*, 41, no. 4 (September 2017): 772–798.

24 Tran Van Khoi, *Dau Hoa Viet Nam, 1970–1075: Nhung Ngay Con Nho* [*Vietnam's Oil, 1970–1975: I Still Remember Those Days*] (Houston: Self-published, 2002), 62–63.

25 "Critics of U.S. Oil Policies in Vietnam Shift Focus of Their Attacks," *New York Times*, April 2, 1971, 2.

26 Email from Pham Kim Ngoc, April 30, 2013.

27 Saigon #3164, March 4, 1971.

28 Trung married the younger sister of Nguyen Cao Thang's wife, making him a member of the OPV clan.

29 Thieu speech to the National Assembly, November 15, 1971.

30 Given the drain on U.S. gold reserves due to a negative balance of payments, the cost of the war, and the price tag for Johnson's Great Society programs, on August 15, 1971, Nixon implemented wage and price controls and closed the ability to convert dollars directly into gold. This effectively destroyed the Bretton Woods agreement.

31 "Saigon Asking Support for Reforms," *New York Times*, November 16, 1971, 12.

32 "South Vietnam: Problems and Prospects," CIA National Intelligence Estimate, April 29, 1971.

33 "The World Heroin Problem," Report of Special Study Mission, U.S. Congress, June 22, 1971, 18.

34 Memcon, "Secretary Laird's Meeting with Ambassador Bunker," February 4, 1971.

35 Saigon #7007, May 7, 1971.

36 "Thieu, Ky Linked to Drug Trade," *Washington Post*, July 16, 1971, A18.

37 "Thieu had no fear of betrayal," *Guardian*, July 19, 1971, 2.

38 One author portrayed South Vietnam as precisely that. See Alfred McCoy, *The Politics of Heroin: CIA Complicity in the Global Drug Trade* (New York: Harper & Row, 1972).

39 "An Tri Procedures," Prime Minister Decree 1042-TT/Th./PC1/1/M, August 2, 1971, PTTT Files.

40 *FBIS Asia and Pacific*, March 8, 1972, L10.

41 Colby, *Lost Victory*, 295.

42 "President Thieu's Travels to the Countryside," Saigon Embassy Airgram A-43, April 13, 1971.

43 "Text of the Address by President Nixon," *New York Times*, April 8, 1971, 6.

44 "The Political Situation in the U.S., Spring 1971," Memo from Bui Diem to Thieu, May 14, 1971.

45 Bui Diem, *Jaws of History*, 288.

46 Sean Fear, "Saigon Goes Global: South Vietnam's Quest for International Legitimacy in the Age of Détente," *Diplomatic History*, 42, no. 3 (June 2018): 428–455.

47 Sean Fear, "The Ambiguous Legacy of Ngo Dinh Diem in South Vietnam's Second Republic (1967–1975)," *Journal of Vietnamese Studies*, vol. 11, Issue 1, 2016, 1–75.

48 Memcon, "Dinner with Gen. Duong Van Minh," Wesley Fishel, April 2, 1971.

49 Memcon, "Meeting with Don," December 4, 1970.

50   Memcon, "Meeting Between President Thieu, Ambassador Bunker and General Haig," December 17, 1970.

51   "Nguyen Van Ngan, Special Assistant to President Nguyen Van Thieu, Speaks Out in Exclusive Interview," *Dan Chim Viet*, October 2, 2006.

52   Memcon, "July 4 Meeting with Thieu," HAK to White House, July 4, 1971.

53   "Austrian Journalist Interviews President Thieu," Vienna Embassy Airgram A-560, July 15, 1971.

54   "Interview of Nguyen Van Ngan," *Thoi Luan* (Tet Edition 2013), 87

55   Ngan interview. A poll of U.S. provincial advisors agreed with those figures. See "Politics is the Blood Sport of Vietnam," *Los Angeles Times*, August 15, 1971, F2.

56   "Biodata on Tran Van Huong," Saigon Embassy Airgram A-243, October 19, 1973.

57   Ly Qui Chung, *Untitled Memoir*, 223–224.

58   "Guidance Document for the Presidential Election Campaign in the Provinces," no date.

59   Nguyen Cao Ky, *Buddha's Child*, 315.

60   Duong Van Ba, *Nhung Nga Re: Hoi ky* [*Forks in the Road: A Memoir*] (Ho Chi Minh City: Self-published, 2015), 23.

61   "PSDF Support in Encouraging the Village/Hamlet Election in June 1969," Ministry of the Interior 3006/BNV/NDTV/5, May 8, 1969, PTTT Files.

62   "PSDF Support for the Lower House Elections on 29 August 1971," Ministry of the Interior. 459/BNV/NDTV/KH.8, July 21, 1971, PTTT Files. The author thanks Dr. Martin Loicano for sharing both documents.

63   "Antigovernment Protesters, Police Clash in Vietnam," *Austin Statesman*, October 2, 1971.

64   *Under One Flag*, 161.

65   Backchannel Bunker to Kissinger, #198, September 18, 1971.

66   Saigon #15933, October 5, 1971.

67   "The South Vietnamese Political Situation," CIA Memo, August 25, 1971, 1.

68   Ngan interview, *Dan Chim Viet*.

69   Nguyen Ba Can, *My Country*, 212.

70   "Fighting in Vietnam wrong, 65% Feel," *Washington Post*, November 11, 1971, E6.

71   *Ho Chi Minh People's Public Security,* 140.

72   Interview with Hoang Duc Nha, August 4, 2011, New York, NY.

73   Ngan interview, *Thoi Luan*, 90.

74   Nha interview.

75   Ibid.

76   Interview with Jackie Bong-Wright, October 27, 2017, Falls Church, VA.

77   Chau Van Man, *Nhung gay o chien truong, tap II* [*Days on the Battlefield, Volume II*] (Hanoi: People's Public Security Publishing House, 2010), 130.

78   Memcon, "Prof. Nguyen Van Bong," August 30, 1971.

CHAPTER 21

1   Saigon #0694, January 15, 1972.

2   Memcon with Pham Kim Vinh, January 29, 1972.

3   Saigon #3051, March 7, 1972.

4   Saigon #8227, June 3, 1972.

5   "South Vietnam: Thieu Digs in," State INR, February 4, 1972.

6   State #026025, February 15, 1972.

7   Email from Hoang Duc Nha, April 22, 2017.

8   Ngan interview, *Dan Chim Viet*, October 2, 2006.

9   Nguyen Ba Can, *My Country*, 249–251.

10 "Personal loyalty is key to Thieu's new party," *Baltimore Sun*, February 21, 1972, A4.

11 "Thieu is forming a political party," *New York Times*, March 10, 1972, 8.

12 Saigon #18724, November 30, 1971.

13 Tran Van Don, *Vietnam Witness*, 392.

14 *PAAS*, January 1972, Saigon Embassy Airgram A-15, February 8, 1972.

15 "Community Defense and Local Development – 1971," Saigon Embassy Airgram A-20, February 19, 1972.

16 "Transformation of the Rural Development Cadres," Saigon AID Airgram #2924, November 6, 1972.

17 Kevin Boylan, *Losing Binh Dinh: The Failure of Pacification and Vietnamization, 1969–1971* (Lawrence, KS: University of Kansas Press, 2016). Phu Yen Province was also found wanting. See Robert Thompson, "More Sieve than Shield: The U.S. Army and CORDS in the Pacification of Phu Yen Province, Republic of Vietnam, 1965–1972," Dissertation. The University of Southern Mississippi, December 2016.

18 "President Thieu on External Affairs," Saigon Embassy Airgram A-159, September 21, 1971.

19 *FRUS*, Vietnam, vol. VII, #268.

20 Nguyen Phu Duc, *Viet-Nam Negotiations*, 302.

21 Interview with Henry Kissinger, May 29, 2015, New York, NY.

22 Nguyen Tien Hung, *Palace File*, 48.

23 "Memorandum prepared for discussion with Ambassador Bunker," January 15, 1972, File 1231, President Archive, NA II.

24 For a review of the January 1972 discussions, see *FRUS*, Vietnam, vol. VIII, #294.

25 "Thieu, on Radio, Endorses Election Plan," *New York Times*, January 26, 1972, 11.

26 Letter from Thieu to Nixon, January 27, 1972.

27 Cable #1201-VP/M, February 12, 1972, Bui Diem papers.

28 Nha interview, August 4, 2011.

29 "Tran Kim Phuong, new Vietnamese Ambassador to Washington," Saigon Embassy Airgram A-97, May 22, 1972.

30 *Bunker Papers*, vol. III, 851.

31 "On the Politburo Decision to launch a General Offensive on three fronts—military, political, and diplomatic—in order to defeat the enemy's 'Vietnamization' policy," in *Collected Party Documents, 1972*, 207–215.

32 USDEL France #9743, May 19, 1972.

33 For excellent overviews of the 1972 offensive, see Dale Andrade, *America's Last Vietnam Battle: Defeating the Easter Offensive* (Lawrence: University Press of Kansas, 2001); Stephen Randolph, *Powerful and Brutal Weapons: Nixon, Kissinger, and the Easter Offensive* (Cambridge: Harvard University Press, 2007).

34 Saigon #6464, May 4, 1972.

35 Saigon #5732, April 22, 1972.

36 Saigon #6278, May 2, 1972.

37 Interview with Nguyen Xuan Tam, October 15, 2008, Springfield, VA.

38 028-TT/TV/M, April 29, 1972, File 02-394, Prime Minister Archive, NA II.

39 "Interview with Cao Van Vien," June 26, 1972, Neil Sheehan Papers, Manuscript Division, Library of Congress.

40 Saigon #11501, August 5, 1972.

41 Van Nguyen-Marshall, "Appeasing the Spirits Along the 'Highway of Horror': Civic Life in Wartime Republic of Vietnam," *War & Society* 37(3): April 2018, 1–17.

42 For excellent reviews of the battle for An Loc, see James Willbanks, *The Battle of An Loc* (Bloomington, IN: Indiana University Press, 2005); Lam Quang Thi, *Hell in An Loc: The 1972 Easter Invasion and the Battle That Saved South Vietnam* (Denton:

University of North Texas Press, 2009); Tran Van Nhut, *An Loc: The Unfinished War* (Lubbock: Texas Tech University Press, 2009). For Kontum, see Thomas McKenna, *Kontum: The Battle to Save South Vietnam* (Lexington: University Press of Kentucky, 2011); Ly Tong Ba, *Hoi Ky 25 Nam Khoi Lua* [*Memoir of 25 Years of War*] (San Marcos, CA: Self-published, 1999).

43 Stuart Herrington, *Silence was a Weapon: The Vietnam War in the Villages* (San Francisco: Presidio Press, 1982). Eric Bergerud is less sanguine. While he acknowledges that the GVN had made significant strides in Hau Nghia, he states that the GVN could not "claim victory" as the "Front apparatus was still intact, and enemy main force units threatened attack from the safe areas and Cambodia." Eric Bergerud, *The Dynamics of Defeat: The Vietnam War in Hau Nghia Province* (Boulder, CO: Westview Press, 1991), 319.

44 Truong Nhu Tang, *Viet Cong Memoir*, 201.

45 1 Samuel, 20:3. Interview with Pham Duy Tat, October 15, 2008, Burke, VA.

46 "Hanoi Offensive Batters S. Vietnamese Economy," *Washington Post*, June 30, 1973, A3.

47 *FRUS*, Vietnam, vol. VIII, #171.

48 "Biographical Data on Tran Van Don," Saigon Embassy Airgram A-158, July 25, 1974.

49 "South Vietnam: Emergency Program Takes Shape," State INR, July 28, 1972.

50 *FBIS Asia and Pacific*, March 2, 1972, L1.

51 Saigon #4335, March 30, 1972.

52 Prime Minister Decree #120-SL/NV, and Decree #119-TT/NV, August 22, 1972.

53 Saigon #12981, September 4, 1972.

54 Presidential Decree #210/TT/SL, April 12, 1972.

55 Saigon #11417, August 4, 1972.

56 Lien Thanh, *Upheavals in Central Vietnam*, 214–216.

57 "S. Vietnam Seizes Thousands in Roundup by Security Forces," *Los Angeles Times*, June 13, 1972, A1.

58 Saigon #9459, June 26, 1972.

59 "Status of Vietnamese Government Planning for a Cease-Fire," CIA IIC, October 16, 1972.

60 Backchannel Bunker to Kissinger, #187, October 14, 1972.

61 Pham Van Chung, "The Vietnamese Marines and the Battle to Defend Quang Tri," paper presented at the conference "Thirty-Five Years After: The Valiant Struggle of the Armed Forces of The Republic of Vietnam," April 9, 2010, Washington, D.C.

62 *Ngoai Giao Viet Nam: 1945–2000* [*Vietnamese Diplomacy: 1945–2000*] (Hanoi: National Political Publishing House, 2002), 251.

63 "Thieu Assails Colonialists," *New York Times*, September 22, 1972, 3.

64 *FRUS*, Vietnam, vol. VIII, #267.

65 Sophie Quinn-Judge, *The Third Force in the Vietnam War: The Elusive Search for Peace 1954–75* (New York: I. B. Taurus, 2017), 73.

66 "President Thieu's Probable Reaction to the Emerging Package," CIA Memo, October 16, 1972.

67 Doan Huyen, "Defeating the Americans: Fighting and Talking," in *Mat Tran Ngoai Giao Voi Cuoc Dam Phan Paris Ve Viet Nam* [*The Diplomatic Front during the Paris Talks on Vietnam*] (Hanoi: National Political Publishing House, 2004), 138–139.

68 For analysis of the Paris talks, see Henry Kissinger, *Ending the Vietnam War: A History of America's Involvement in and Extraction from the Vietnam War* (New York: Simon and Schuster, 2003); Pierre Asselin, *A Bitter Peace: Washington, Hanoi, and the Making of the Paris Agreement* (Chapel Hill: University of North Carolina Press, 2002); Larry Berman, *No Peace, No Honor: Nixon, Kissinger, and Betrayal in Vietnam* (New York: Free Press, 2001).

69   Nha email, January 28, 2020.
70   Nguyen Phu Duc, *Viet-Nam Negotiations*, 332.
71   Nha email, February 20, 2019.
72   "Thieu's Address to the Nation on the New Proposal for Peace," *New York Times*, October 25, 1972, 17.
73   "South Vietnam: Thieu Rallies Popular Support," State INR, November 10, 1972.
74   "GVN Preparation for Ceasefire: Military Cadets and Civil Service Students Mobilized for PSYOPS," Saigon Airgram A-225, December 2, 1972.
75   Backchannel Bunker to Kissinger, #249, November 4, 1972.
76   Memcon, "Conversation with Prime Minister Tran Thien Khiem," December 21, 1972.
77   Nguyen Tien Hung, *Palace File*, 108.
78   Backchannel White House to Bunker, #2261, November 30, 1972.
79   Ibid.
80   Nguyen Phu Duc, *Viet-Nam Negotiations*, 361–362.
81   *FBIS Asia and Pacific*, January 3, 1973, L5.
82   "Wide Powers for Park after 'democracy fails,'" *Jerusalem Post*, October 29, 1972, 4.
83   "B-52 Vindicates its Role Air Force Aides Assert," *New York Times*, December 24, 1972, 3.
84   Backchannel Bunker to Kissinger, #313, December 30, 1972.
85   Nguyen Xuan Phong, *Vanquished Reality*, 70–72. "Kissinger wants Russia to Control Indochina," *Times of India*, January 15, 1973, 6.

CHAPTER 22

1   Jeffery Clarke, *United States Army in Vietnam: Advice and Support: The Final Years, 1965–1973* (Washington: Center for Military History, 1988), 275.
2   "Democracy Party Development," Saigon Embassy Airgram A-236, December 19, 1972.
3   Saigon #4468, March 19, 1973.
4   "The Economic Situation in South Vietnam," CIA Memo, December 1972.
5   Cable No. 004-TT/CD, January 23, 1973, DIICH, File No. 1299.
6   "National Reconstruction and Development Policy and Program," February 1973, DIICH, File No. 21.
7   Saigon #1145, January 28, 1973.
8   Bangkok #1763, January 30, 1973.
9   Bangkok #1883, January 31, 1973.
10   "Casualty Reporting," USDAO Saigon to JCS, February 21, 1975. Deserters and those missing in action were not listed. RVNAF casualty reporting was criticized in mid-1974, and the DAO and the JGS worked to correct the inaccuracies. This message provided the finalized tally. The author thanks Major General Ira Hunt for providing it.
11   Ira Hunt, *Losing Vietnam: How America Abandoned Southeast Asia* (Lexington: University Press of Kentucky, 2013), 47. Hunt had served in Vietnam as chief of staff of the 9th Division, then returned in 1973 as deputy commander of the United States Support Activities Group in Thailand.
12   Dong Si Nguyen, *The Trans-Truong Son Route* (Hanoi: The Gioi Publishers, 2005), 215. This is the English language version of his memoirs.
13   Phan Khac Hy, "From Down in the Annamite Mountains, Our Hearts Turn to Hanoi," in *Nho lai tran "Ha Noi – Dien Bien Phu tren Khong* [*Remembering the "Hanoi – Dien Bien Phu in the Air" Battle*]. Hanoi: National Political Publishing House, 2012, 199.

14 JGS Message #7130/TTM/P345, cited in Saigon #3849, March 9, 1973.

15 JGS Message #7141/TTM/P370, February 20, 1973.

16 Saigon #3849, March 9, 1973.

17 Saigon #968, January 23, 1973, citing GVN statistics.

18 "The MR-3 Refugee Story," Bien Hoa Consulate Airgram A-46, November 23, 1973.

19 Fontaine, *Dawn of a Free Vietnam*, 106.

20 "Funding of ADDA," Letter from the Prime Minister's Office to the Director General of Budget and Foreign Aid, February 22, 1973. The author thanks Do Huu Ngoc, Deputy to Pham Kim Ngoc, for supplying this document.

21 Email from Pham Kim Ngoc, June 7, 2013.

22 Memorandum, "Danang Area Development Program," January 19, 1973. Document from Do Huu Ngoc.

23 Prime Minister Decree #029-SL/ThT/QTCS, February 20, 1973.

24 Saigon #9445, May 29, 1973.

25 Email from Do Huu Ngoc, April 3, 2017.

26 "Government Initiatives to Alleviate Unemployment ...," Saigon Embassy Airgram A-234, November 15, 1973.

27 Prime Ministerial Circular Directive #193, January 24, 1973.

28 *PAAS,* March 1975, Special Assistant to the Ambassador for Field Operations, Program Briefings, Box 6, NARA II, College Park, MD. SAAFO replaced CORDS after March 1973.

29 Saigon #3515, March 5, 1973.

30 Saigon #5029, March 27, 1973.

31 "Current Status of the Land Reform Program," Bunker Briefing Book, March 5, 1973, Bunker Papers, Box 3, NARA, College Park, MD. The amount distributed during LTTT was in addition to the roughly one and a half million acres of land appropriated and distributed to farmers under Diem's Ordinance 57.

32 Saigon #8581, May 15, 1973.

33 Saigon #5065, March 28, 1973.

34 Email from Cao Van Than, November 2, 2012.

35 Interview with Cao Van Than, August 8, 2012, Montreal, Canada.

36 Saigon #5204, March 29, 1973.

37 Bunker departed on May 11, but Martin did not present his credentials until July 20.

38 Memcon, "The President's Meeting with President Nguyen Van Thieu," April 2, 1973.

39 GVN Aide-Memoire, April 2, 1973.

40 USDEL France #6786, March 19, 1973.

41 The "Freedom in the World" annual survey by Freedom House of freedom and liberties in countries around the globe ranked South Vietnam for the years 1973 to 1975 with a 4 for Political Rights and 5 for Civil Liberties and described it as "Partly Free." One is best the best score, and seven is the worst. North Vietnam received sevens for both categories and was ranked "Not Free."

42 Nguyen Phu Duc, *Viet-Nam Negotiations*, 411.

43 Saigon #7194, April 25, 1973.

44 For a detailed description of the Politburo's decision to return to war, see Chapter 2, George J. Veith, *Black April: The Fall of South Vietnam* (New York: Encounter Books, 2012).

45 Backchannel from Ambassador Whitehouse to Kissinger, #525, June 25, 1973.

46 Saigon #3843, March 9, 1973.

47 "Report of the Special Assistant For Liaison With [Civilian] Organization," March 6, 1973, DIICH, File 190.

48 "Thieu Giving His Bureaucrats Boot-Camp Treatment," *New York Times*, November 28, 1973, 2.
49 Saigon #7622, May 2, 1973.
50 Ibid.
51 Nguyen Anh Tuan, *Trial and Experience*, 191.
52 Interview with Hoang Duc Nha, August 4, 2011, Falls Church, VA.
53 Interview with Dr. Nguyen Hai Binh, deputy finance minister, February 6, 2013, Montreal, Canada.
54 Saigon #226, January 6, 1973.
55 Impact of VAT on Economic Situation," Saigon Embassy Airgram A-144, July 27, 1973.
56 Email from Hoang Duc Nha, May 10, 2017.
57 Saigon #12985, July 18, 1973.
58 "RVNAF Pay at Ceasefire Plus One Year," Saigon Embassy Memo, February 19, 1974.
59 "Saigon Soldiers Openly Abuse Civilians," *New York Times*, June 3, 1973, 1.
60 "Ben Soi: Route to a Bonanza," *Manchester Guardian*, March 26, 1973, 3.
61 Prime Minister Circular #077 TT/Tht/PC2, June 15, 1973.
62 Saigon #13365, July 24, 1973.
63 "Measures to Thwart the Communist Tax Collection and Commodity Purchase," Prime Minister Directive #2040/PThT/TTPT/KH, August 11, 1973.
64 "The Deeping Economic Malaise," Saigon embassy Memo, November 30, 1973.
65 "The Republic of Vietnam in the International Climate of Detente - Reorienting Our National Policy," Hoang Duc Nha to the President, September 28, 1973, DIICH, File No. 1216. In a postwar interview, Nha denies his intent was to centralize economic decision-making or to fire Ngoc. He was simply trying to craft a plan for the president.
66 "South Vietnam Economic Deterioration," CIA Memo, August 3, 1973.
67 Saigon #15453, August 27, 1973.
68 Email from Pham Kim Ngoc, March 24, 2014.
69 Interview with Nguyen Duc Cuong, May 14, 2011, San Jose, CA.
70 Email from Tran Quang Minh, February 20, 2012. Minh was born in 1938 in Chau Doc Province in the Delta. He attended French secondary school in Saigon and received a USAID scholarship, where he received his doctorate in veterinary medicine.
71 Ibid.
72 Saigon #18796, November 1, 1973.

CHAPTER 23

1 Saigon #17946, October 16, 1973.
2 Saigon #530, January 7, 1974
3 Ho Van Ky Thoai, *Can Truong Trong: Chien Bai* [*Valor In Defeat: A Sailor's Journey*] (Virginia: Self-published, 2004). Thoai was the commander of the South Vietnamese Navy's First Coastal Zone in Danang during the battle.
4 Backchannel White House to Martin, #353, undated but probably early January 1974.
5 Backchannel Murray to Guthrie, #1384, August 6, 1974.
6 Backchannel Gayler to O'Keefe, August 19, 1974.
7 Saigon #11475, August 31, 1974.
8 Message #30.243/TTM/P370, JGS to Corps Commanders and VNAF, undated but probably early September 1974.
9 "Open Wounds of an Eternal War," *South China Morning Post*, September 1, 1974, 11.

10 Backchannel Martin to Kissinger, #583, January 14, 1974.

11 Ngan interview, *DCV*, October 2, 2006.

12 Tran Van Don, *Endless War*, 232.

13 "Biodata on Khiem," Saigon Embassy Airgram A-155, August 13, 1974.

14 Nguyen Ba Can, *My Country*, 311–312.

15 Bien Hoa Consulate #587, November 18, 1974.

16 Tran Ngoc Chau, *Vietnam Labyrinth*, 379.

17 Saigon #9835, August 5, 1974.

18 "Biodata for Mrs. Ngo Ba Thanh," Saigon Embassy Airgram A-265, December 10, 1973.

19 Saigon #4897, April 16, 1974.

20 "President Thieu comments," May 11, 1974. This document, provided to the author by Major General Ira Hunt appears to be a transcript from the CIA bug in Thieu's office.

21 Saigon #2968, March 6, 1974.

22 "Assessment of Local Government Services in MR-1," Danang Consulate Memo, June 18, 1974.

23 "GVN Administrative Revolution," Saigon Embassy Airgram A-244, November 27, 1974.

24 Saigon #9452, July 17, 1974.

25 "Government Services at the Local Level," Bien Hoa Consulate Memo, July 3, 1974.

26 "GVN Administration in Military Region II," Nha Trang Consulate Airgram A-007, May 2, 1974.

27 Prime Minister Message #3 – DV/ThT/PC2, January 3, 1974.

28 "The GVN's Economic Blockade in MR-4," Can Tho Consulate Airgram A-007, February 20, 1974.

29 Nha Trang Consulate #774, December 20, 1974.

30 "Rice Policy Implications," Saigon Embassy Memo, December 13, 1974.

31 "Shining, Deathless Examples," *Dan Lam Bao Vietnam*, June 24, 2014.

32 "Enough Self-Burnings, Thieu Tells His Backers," *Washington Post*, September 14, 1974, A19.

33 Saigon #6896, May 25, 1974.

34 Saigon #13261, October 16, 1974.

35 Saigon #1534, February 8, 1975.

36 Nha related that the president "was very strict with his own family" regarding corruption. When he learned about his brother-in-law's activities, "he was pretty pissed off." Nha interview, August 4, 2011.

37 "Thieu: Corruption Must End," *Washington Post*, June 20, 1974, A11.

38 For a deeper review of South Vietnamese Catholic peace efforts, see Tran Thi Linh, "The Challenge for Peace Within South Vietnam's Catholic Community: A History of Peace Activism," *Journal of Peace Research*, vol. 38, no. 4, October 2013, 446–473, and Van Nguyen Marshall, "Tools of Empire?: Vietnamese Catholics and South Vietnam," *Journal of the Canadian Historical Association*, vol. 20, no. 2, 2009, 138–159.

39 "Anti-Red Priest Leads Foes of Thieu," *New York Times*, October 19, 1974, 6.

40 "Seoul's Secret Police Arrest Defiant Bishop," *Washington Post*, July 24, 1974, A30.

41 "Seoul Leaders Draw on Confucian Heritage to Rationalize the Crackdown on Dissidents," *New York Times*, August 5, 1974, 6.

42 Father Tran Huu Thanh, "Indictment No. 1," September 8, 1974.

43 Saigon #12592, September 28, 1974.

44 Saigon #12724, October 1, 1974.

45 Saigon #13059, October 9, 1974.

46 Saigon #15051, December 4, 1974.

47 *Under One Flag*, 812.
48 "President Thieu's Views on his Role as a Leader in the Face of Catholic Opposition," November 29, 1974, in "Catholic Politics In South Vietnam" TTU #2321717015.

CHAPTER 24

1   USDEL JEC Paris #25218, October 24, 1974.
2   Email from Nguyen Xuan Phong, March 29, 2006.
3   Interview with Vuong Van Bac, Paris, France, May 11, 2008.
4   Nha interview, Falls Church, VA, June 4, 2009.
5   Saigon #14657, November 23, 1974.
6   USDEL JEC Paris #28694, November 29, 1974.
7   "Politburo Cable to Pham Hung," December 12, 1968, in *Collected Party Documents, 1968*, 550.
8   Interview with Nguyen Xuan Phong, Orlando, FL, December 3, 2006.
9   "President Pompidou's statement on Vietnam ...," Memo No. 962/BNG/ AUCH/M, November 12, 1971, Folder 1793, NA II. The author thanks Dr. Nguyen Lien-Hang for sharing this document.
10 Paris #24933, September 21, 1973.
11 Paris #22486, October 21, 1974.
12 "From Ba and Sung to Trinh and CP72," November 10, 1974, in *Diplomatic Struggle*, vol. 5, 431.
13 "Le Duan Letter to Pham Hung Describing Conclusions Reached at Politburo Meeting," 10 October 1974, in Le Duan, *Letters to the South*, 374.
14 Saigon #1109, January 29, 1975.
15 Draft letter, "Military Aid for the Armed Forces of the Republic of Vietnam, FY-75," from Cao Van Vien to George Brown, Chairman, JCS, in Tran Mai Hanh, *Bien ban Chien Tranh 1-2-3-4,75* [*War Notes – January, February, March, April 1975*] (Hanoi: National Political Publishing House, Second Edition, with additions, 2016), 448–455.
16 "A Gallup Poll Finds 8 out of 10 Oppose More Aid for Indochina," *New York Times*, March 9, 1975, 18.
17 Memcon, "Codel Farwell Meeting with President Thieu," March 2, 1975.
18 "Notes on 29 March 1975 Delta Swing," CIA memo, date unknown.
19 Saigon #1289, February 2, 1975.
20 Ly Qui Chung, *Untitled Memoir*, 249.
21 "Minh accuses Thieu Regime of 'Tyranny,'" *New York Times*, February 6, 1975, 10.
22 Saigon #1506, February 7, 1975.
23 Saigon #3169, March 20, 1975.
24 For a complete description of the final battles of the war, see George J. Veith, *Black April: The Fall of South Vietnam, 1973–75* (New York: Encounter Books, 2012).
25 "Discussion Between President Thieu and a Group of Moderate Politicians ...," CIA IIC, March 20, 1975.
26 Nguyen Ba Can, *My Country*, 362.
27 Paris #8156, April 2, 1975.
28 Backchannel Martin to Kissinger, #684, April 4, 1975. See also Ky, *Twenty Years*, 213–15.
29 "Comments by Former GVN Prime Minister Khiem," CIA IIC, May 10, 1975.
30 Nha interview, Falls Church, VA, June 4, 2009.
31 There are numerous articles describing Trung's actions that day. For example, "Senior Colonel, Hero Pilot Nguyen Thanh Trung," *Saigon Tiep Thi*, April 26, 2013. His real name was Dinh Khac Trung.
32 Interview with Nguyen Xuan Tam, Springfield, VA., May 10, 2014. Interview with

Tran Thanh Dien, San Jose, CA., May 14, 2011. Interview with Doan Huu Dinh, Falls Church, VA., undated.

33 "Conversation with Thieu," French embassy #733 to MFA, April 17, 1975.

34 Backchannel Martin to Kissinger, #718, April 20, 1975.

35 Interview of Nguyen Van Thieu by Larry Engelmann, San Jose, CA, April 30, 1990.

36 Paris #7276, March 21, 1975.

37 State #84134, April 12, 1975.

38 Nguyen Phuc Luan, *Ngoai Giao Viet Nam Trong Cuoc Dung Dau Lich Su* [*Vietnamese Diplomacy during the Historic Conflict*] (Hanoi: People's Public Security Publishing House, 2005), 325.

39 *Vietnamese Diplomacy: 1945-2000*, 275.

40 Olivier Todd, *Cruel April: The Fall of Saigon*, translated by Stephen Becker (New York: W. W. Norton, 1990), 182. Interview with Olivier Todd, Paris, May 14, 2008.

41 "South Vietnamese Communists Sought Negotiated End," *New York Times*, June 12, 1975, 2. See also "Hanoi's Leaders, as Saigon Tottered Last Year, Were against any Settlement," *New York Times*, May 31, 1975, 2.

42 "PRGRSV 21 March Statement on Situation in South Vietnam," *FBIS Asia and Pacific*, March 21, 75, L3.

43 "Conversation with the Prime Minister of the DRV," French embassy in Hanoi #378 to MFA, March 24, 1975. See also Philippe Richer, *Hanoi 1975: Un diplomate et la réunification du Viêt-Nam* [*Hanoi 1975: A Diplomat and the Reunification of Vietnam*] (Paris: L'Harmattan, 1993).

44 "Vietnam," Memo from the Department of Asia/Oceania, April 8, 1975, Serie: Asie-Oceania, Sous-serie: Viet-Nam conflict, Number de volume: 171.

45 Interview with Pierre Brochand, Paris, France, June 14, 2019.

46 Frank Snepp, *Decent Interval* (New York: Random House, 1977), 326.

47 Backchannel Kissinger to Martin, #50750, April 24, 1975.

48 Nguyen Ba Can, *My Country*, 427.

49 Nguyen Xuan Phong, *Vanquished Hope*, 45

50 Paris #10261, April 22, 1975.

51 Phong interview, November 30, 2006.

52 The author spoke with a former U.S. military officer and noted scholar of the 1979 China-Vietnam War to determine if this was feasible. Based on his analysis of the Chinese airlift capabilities, flight times, etc., he concluded that it would be difficult but possible to accomplish this mission.

53 Kosal Path, "The Sino-Vietnamese Dispute over Territorial Claims, 1974–1978: Vietnamese Nationalism and its Consequences," *International Journal of Asian Studies* 8, no. 2 (2011): 196. Donald Weatherbee, "The USSR-DRV-PRC Triangle in Southeast Asia," *Parameters* 6, no. 1 (1976): 71–86.

54 Alexander Haig, with Charles McGarry, *Inner Circles: How America Changed the World* (New York: Warner Books, 1992), 133–134.

55 Ibid., 261.

56 Nayan Chanda, *Brother Enemy: The War After the War* (New York: Collier Books, 1986), 127.

57 Ibid., 133. Chanda discusses the Chinese efforts to prevent a unified Vietnam comprehensively in Chapter 4.

58 "Why We Lost the War in South Vietnam," transcript of PBS *Firing Line*, October 4, 1975, 8.

59 "China Proposed Coup, Said Ky," *Baltimore Sun*, December 6, 1975, A2.

60 Nguyen Tien Hung, *Palace File*, 313–314.

61 Interview with Jim Eckes, October 11, 2007. French journalist Olivier Todd repeats the same story. Todd, *Cruel April*, 178. Eckes was instrumental in evacuating

the employees of Pan Am Airlines on April 28, 1975. A movie depicting Eckes's
courageous actions called *Last Flight Out* was aired in May 1990.

62   "Peking-Hanoi Wrangling," *Developments in Indochina*, CIA Report, March 4, 1975.

63   Backchannel Martin to Kissinger, #686, April 5, 1975.

64   Hong Kong #3600, April 5, 1975, and other consulate cables discuss China's fear
of a Hanoi victory.

65   Paul Vanuxem, *La Mort du Vietnam* [*The Death of Vietnam*] (Paris: Editions Nouvelle
Aurore, 1975), 22, 61

66   Interview of Nguyen Huu Hanh, March 16, 1981, http://www.youtube.com/
watch?v=HU-eWGEGvL0, from 7:55 to 9:45, accessed May 5, 2016.

67   Ha Binh Nhuong, *Vo b c nhiem mau* [*The Miraculous Cover*] (Hanoi: People's Public
Security Publishing House, 2005).

68   Ly Qui Chung, *Untitled Memoirs*, 403.

69   Nguyen Huu Thai, "Duong Van Minh and I, April 30, 1975," *Sach Hiem* [*Rare
Books*], March 30, 2008.

70   Letter from Trinh Ba Loc, March 22, 2013.

71   Todd, *Cruel April*, 372. Unfortunately, Todd provides no source and he misidentifies
Paul Vanuxem as "Francois."

72   Van Tien Dung, *Our Great Spring Victory: An Account of the Liberation of South
Vietnam*, translated by John Spragens, Jr. (Hanoi: The Gioi Publishers, 2000), 232,
274.

73   "Minutes of Conversation Between Deng Xiaoping and Le Duan," September 29,
1975, https://digitalarchive.wilsoncenter.org/document/111268.

74   *Su That Ve Quan He Viet Nam-Trung Quoc Trong 30 Nam Qua* [*The Truth About
Sino-Vietnamese Relations During the Past 30 Years*] (Hanoi: Su That Publishing
House, 1979), 67.

75   "Comrade B on the Plot of the Reactionary Chinese Clique Against Vietnam,"
1979, translated by Christopher Goscha, https://digitalarchive.wilsoncenter.org/
document/112982. Le Duan, however, did not mention any Chinese effort to
militarily intervene at the end.

76   "History of PRC's 'Hostile Policy' Reviewed," *FBIS Asia and Pacific*, May 8, 1985,
K4.

77   Interview with Catherine Vanuxem and Marcus Durand, Paris, France, November
15, 2016.

78   Brochand interview, Paris, France, June 14, 2019.

79   Interview with Madame Jacqueline Mérillon, Paris, France, November 17, 2016.

80   Snepp, *Decent Interval*, 427.

81   Nha interview, Falls Church, VA, June 4, 2009.

82   Leviticus 26: 17–38.

INDEX